SECOND EDITION

✦

THE HARVEST READER

SECOND EDITION

✦

William A. Heffernan
Saddleback College

Mark Johnston
Quinnipiac College

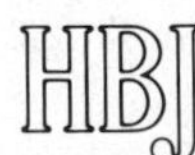

HARCOURT BRACE JOVANOVICH
San Diego New York Chicago Austin Washington, D.C.
London Sydney Tokyo Toronto

Cover: *Ladder to the Moon*, Georgia O'Keeffe. Collection Emily Fisher Landau. Courtesy Georgia O'Keeffe Estate. Photo by Malcolm Varon, N.Y.C. © 1987.

ISBN: 0-15-535252-0

Library of Congress Catalog Number 90-83274

Printed in the United States of America

Copyrights and Acknowledgments begin on page 686 and constitute a continuation of the copyright page.

Preface

In keeping with the metaphor of its title, this second edition of *The Harvest Reader* constitutes a richer, more abundant harvest of readings for freshman writers than its predecessor. We have retained the spirit of the first edition—its clear design, its readable apparatus, and its wide range of contemporary prose—while completely revamping the letter of its contents. Changes in the organization of the book, in its apparatus, and particularly in the selections offered will, we hope, make the new edition of *The Harvest Reader* more varied, more practical, and more engaging for students.

We begin and end on a personal note. Part 1 introduces the student to the various forms of autobiographical writing that instructors often turn to first and that students usually find most immediate to their interests. Part 7 takes up the complex and radically personal matter of prose style. The five central sections of the book offer a diversity of readings in the conventional modes of discourse customarily taught in freshman writing classes: narration, description, exposition, and argumentation, as well as mixed patterns of organization. Within the part on exposition, we offer a variety of readings in all the major subcategories of practical writing, including definition, example, and analogy.

In writing the apparatus of the book, we have striven for clarity, brevity, and usefulness. Students should appreciate the straightforward tone of the apparatus; instructors should appreciate that we have not preempted their function. The headnotes introducing each reading give appropriate biographical and bibliographical information about the authors. Each section of the book—including each subsection on exposition—is introduced by a self-contained essay on the process of writing and on the application of the various modes of discourse to the writing assignments most often faced by freshman composition students. These essays—carefully linked to the selections—take up issues of invention, organization, strategy, and technique that should be helpful to students. The questions and suggestions for writing that follow each selection are designed to provoke students' thinking about aspects of content, rhetoric, and style. We think that the numerous suggestions for writing will engage the students' attention and prove to be an instructive (and moderately pleasurable) means of eliciting thoughtful writing.

The major and perhaps the most welcome changes in this edition lie in the selections we have chosen. Fourteen essays from the first edition have been retained, and the 66 new selections are modern essays, most of them recent. The selections will—because of their quality and timeliness—be eminently enjoyable to students and useful to instructors.

Seven short stories have been added to aid those instructors who teach short fiction in their composition courses. The argumentation section has been greatly expanded, and on three topical issues—the death penalty, liberal education, and bilingual education—paired essays present the opposing sides of arguments. Eight writers are represented by two essays each. We have been particularly conscious of maintaining a balance between male and female writers: forty percent of the selections in the second edition of *The Harvest Reader* are by women.

In general, the changes we have made increase the variety and abundance of the harvest and provide students and instructors with a colorful and usable gathering of fine prose.

As we have edited the book, we have had the pleasure of becoming indebted to a number of people who have authorized and facilitated our work, and who have contributed significantly to its "shape" and quality. Our thanks go to Lenore Beakey, who made valuable suggestions about the selections and who also prepared the Instructor's Manual. The staff at Harcourt Brace Jovanovich has been consistently perceptive, patient, and diligent. Marlane Miriello helped to set the book afloat. Karl Yambert provided incisive and thorough editing of the manuscript. Michael Ferreira skillfully managed the book at the galley and page proof stages. Nancy Simerly and James Hughes handled the art and design aspects of the edition, while Fran Wager oversaw its production. Our special thanks go to Eleanor Garner, who helped ease our way down the tortuous road of gathering permissions, and to Karen Allanson, who guided the book deftly through all its stages of development, and who provided good-humored, intelligent, and unstinting support. All of these people have aided the process of our work and have improved its quality. We are grateful to have had the pleasure of working with them.

William A. Heffernan
Mark Johnston

CONTENTS

THEMATIC TABLE OF CONTENTS

ECONOMICS AND POLITICS

EDUCATION

RELIGION, PHILOSOPHY, AND ETHICS

VIOLENCE AND WAR

Part 1

JOURNALS, DIARIES, AND AUTOBIOGRAPHY

Writing from Personal Experience

Where does writing begin? Does it begin with the thoughts that immediately precede your putting pen to paper, or your touching the keys of your typewriter? Or does it begin further back in the past with something you heard or read that has lain dormant until you begin to write? Rhetoric, the art of finding ideas that will persuade people, has been relatively silent about where these ideas come from, except to say that in persuasive writing we should take into account the knowledge and prejudices of our audience; we need to list those ideas that the audience will accept. But on the actual source of ideas—the starting point of writing—there are few practical hints.

The answer to the question *Where does writing begin?* can be found in the practice of professional writers whose unedited notes, journals, workbooks, diaries, and outlines reveal the gestation of their ideas. This shower of ideas sometimes goes through several stages—more for some writers than for others. Some people hold several conflicting ideas in their minds simultaneously prior to working out their exact relationships, whereas others commit each idea to paper and work out the relationships visually, as it were, before them. For all the variations in the final product—whether a poem, a play, a work of fiction, an essay, or a piece of technical writing—the stages of the process are essentially the same: Some notion begins to interest us; we collect information both consciously and unconsciously over a period of time; broad categories and a "shape" begin to suggest themselves; we start to sort and discard bits of information, all the while extending, restricting, and adjusting our categories.* Even the drafting process involves further gathering in and throwing away.

Because all of this miscellany of activity occurs prior to finally sitting down to begin the first draft of a piece of writing, it is sometimes called prewriting, or brainstorming, sometimes merely note-taking or observing. Listen to John McPhee, a staff writer for *The New Yorker*, describe with fascination the working methods of Henry David Thoreau—methods which, interestingly, McPhee himself duplicates almost exactly in composing his own work.

> He had in his pack some pencils and an oilskin pouch full of scratch paper—actually letters that customers had written to his family's business, ordering plumbago and other printing supplies. On the backs of these discarded letters he made condensed, fragmentary, scarcely legible notes, and weeks later, when he had returned home to Concord, he composed his journal of the trip, slyly using the diary form, and writing at times in the present tense, to gain immediacy, to create the illusion of paragraphs written—as it is generally supposed they were written—virtually in the moments described. With the advantage of retrospect, he constructed the story to reveal a kind of significance that the notes do not reveal. Something new in journalism. With the journals as his principal source, he later crafted still another manuscript, in which he further shaped and rearranged the story, all the while adhering to a structure built on calendar dates. The result, published posthumously in hardcover form, was the book he called *The Maine Woods*.†

As the passage suggests, there is a formal as well as a functional distinction between a diary, a notebook, and a journal. Diaries are meant to be daily records of the events of a day. They may include observations, judgments, and impressions of events, people, and places, but they generally summarize, if kept with constancy, the important events of a single day. Notes, on the other hand, are much

* This is what Donald M. Murray calls the "magnet theory"; bits of information begin to stick to the writer, like metal filings to a magnet. We are indebted to Murray's essay "Write Before Writing," *College Composition and Communication*, 29 (December, 1978), 337–81, for several ideas in this introduction.

† John McPhee, *The Survival of the Bark Canoe* (Farrar, Straus and Giroux, 1975), 36.

more random, and are taken on the spur of the moment, or when that is not practical (as in the case of Thoreau in a canoe), soon afterward. Of the three, journals tend to be the most retrospective; in them, the writer looks back, at not too great a distance in time, and sifts through many impressions for those that seem most important or that form themselves into the most significant patterns. The aim of keeping a journal is not to write a masterpiece but to record facts, impressions, patterns: to have a place where transitory events, random observations, or careful research might safely be stored for possible use when the actual writing begins.

Here is part of a diary kept by a writer who spent a winter in the small isolated town in the Cascade Mountains of central Washington State:

> December 21 Snow is almost three feet deep and still falling. The mail boat has made one of its thrice-weekly winter visits, and most of the village's 40 year-round residents met it—including me.
>
> January 27 We've had a cold spell, with the thermometer shivering around zero. I have to wake up every two hours during the night to stoke the fire in my wood stove to keep the inside water pipes from freezing. Staying warm is almost a full-time job.*

In their most basic form, notebooks, journals, and diaries can be used as a sort of rehearsal, a preliminary or practice for the real thing. They can also be used to overcome the inertia of facing a blank page—as a practical means to get the act of writing going, the "juices flowing." In addition to stimulating the physical momentum of the act of writing, the notebook–journal–diary serves four important purposes:

1. It serves as a *storehouse* from which your observations, descriptions, facts—the whole range of raw material for actual writing—can be retrieved for later use. It takes time not only to think out what you will say—after you have observed, noted, listened, read—but also to allow the facts to come together or jell in your mind. It is here that you can go back to the notebook–journal–diary to read and reread, to see what you can make of the otherwise

* Pat Hutson, "Where Solitude Is in Season," *National Geographic* (April, 1974), 572–74.

fleeting impressions. The notebook–journal–diary, then, is a highly tentative exploration of "facts" that strike you as important at the time they are recorded. It is a good idea to keep a notebook in which you can jot down notes and impressions for any paper you are required to write.

2. It has the effect of *stopping time*, of giving you a chance to study and contemplate what might otherwise be lost or distorted in the welter of events. A notebook–journal–diary places the actions and ideas of the past in perspective. From a train window, nearby objects pass too swiftly to allow either recognition or appreciation, but the rapid movement of the train does not hinder contemplation of more distant objects. The notebook–journal–diary allows you that same kind of distancing—the alchemy of time often renders a clearer meaning to many events. Even though this time gap might not be more than a few days in a writing class, nevertheless, some perspective is gained between note-taking time and drafting time. In an essay entitled "On Keeping a Notebook," Joan Didion talks about rereading earlier entries to recapture the emotional and mental makeup of the person she used to be, a process called "journal feedback" by Ira Progoff.[*]

> It all comes back. Perhaps it is difficult to see the value in having one's self back in that kind of mood, but I do see it; I think we are well advised to keep on nodding terms with the people we used to be, whether we find them attractive company or not. Otherwise they turn up unannounced and surprise us, coming hammering on the mind's door at 4 a.m. of a bad night and demand to know who deserted them, who betrayed them, who is going to make amends. We forget all too soon the things we thought we could never forget. We forget the loves and the betrayals alike, forget what we whispered and what we screamed, forget who we were. . . . It is a good idea, then, to keep in touch, and I suppose that keeping in touch is what notebooks are all about.[†]

3. It *selects* certain events, impressions, and facts out of the mass of details available, thereby investing them with an importance they

[*] Ira Progoff, *At a Journal Workshop* (Dialogue House Library, 1976).
[†] Joan Didion, *Slouching Towards Bethlehem* (Farrar, Straus and Giroux, 1968), 139–40.

lack as part of the whole. Suppose you wish to describe the Arizona desert. Will you tell the truth about the desert if you write down as many facts about it as the pages of a book will hold? Or will you begin by selecting just those facts that will best tell the uninformed what the desert is like? Edward Abbey goes one step further; while insisting he is drawing from the facts recorded in his journals ("journals I kept and filled through the undivided, seamless days of those marvellous summers"), he is equally insistent that the facts are not merely true to the surface of things, but provoke meanings beyond themselves.

> In recording these impressions of the natural scene I have striven above all for accuracy, since I believe that there is a kind of poetry, even a kind of truth, in simple fact. But the desert is a vast world, an oceanic world, as deep in its way and complex and various as the sea. Language makes a mightily loose net with which to go fishing for simple facts, when facts are infinite. . . . What I have tried to do then is something a bit different. . . . Since you cannot get the desert into a book any more than a fisherman can haul up the sea with his nets, I have tried to create a world of words into which the desert figures more as a medium than as material. Not imitation but evocation has been the goal.[*]

Annie Dillard also claims to be setting down more than mere facts, even though most of the time nature seems to present simply more of the same. Receptivity, staying awake to those moments when nature's selection is particularly worth recording, seems to be Dillard's method of sifting through the facts. In *Pilgrim at Tinker Creek*, she writes "I propose to keep here what Thoreau called 'a meteorological journal of the mind,' telling some tales and describing some of the sights of this rather tamed valley, and exploring in fear and trembling, some of the unmapped dim reaches and holy fastnesses to which those tales and sights so dizzyingly lead."

4. It reveals the *patterns* formed by (2) the arresting of time and (3) the selection of facts. By going over and over your notes, invariably some kind of order emerges, as it does for Joan Didion:

[*] Edward Abbey, *Desert Solitaire* (McGraw-Hill, 1968), xii.

> We look for the sermon in the suicide, for the social or moral lesson in the murder of five. We interpret what we see, select the most workable of the multiple choices. We live entirely, especially if we are writers, by the imposition of a narrative line upon disparate images, by the "ideas" with which we have learned to freeze the shifting phantasmagoria which is our actual experience.*

The aim of this chapter, then, is to present the notebook–journal–diary as an aid to your writing, not as an end in itself—as a tool rather than as a finished piece, as a sourcebook rather than as the completed work. Consequently, the four points outlined here have concentrated on the uses of a journal, not the specific techniques of how to keep one.

You will find that the most immediate use for notebook, diary, and journal entries is in autobiographical writing, those forms of self-expression growing directly out of recalled personal experience. Autobiographical writing sorts out diary and journal entries, choosing only those pieces which fit the jigsaw puzzle design of the writer's life. Although it may seem egocentric, the aim of autobiographies is to share those experiences which make us human. In an age which Tom Wolfe has labeled "The Me-Generation," autobiography appears on the best-seller lists more often than any other type of nonfiction, indicating that there is some need to write and read about important moments in our lives. But are popular autobiographies more often embroidery than fact? Is a given autobiography more akin to the "lies" of fiction than to the "facts" as they actually happened? As a writer of autobiographical essays, you should know to what degree artistic license permits you to transform literal facts into an interesting tale, as opposed to a mere documentary recounting that, while literally true and correct, may be dull and lie flat on the page.

A fruitful way to come to grips with autobiography (how truthful it is and what its elements are) is to examine a sampling of passages from several autobiographies. Although the following passages are only fragments, they nevertheless reveal several features characteristic of the autobiographer's art:

* Joan Didion, *The White Album* (Simon and Schuster, 1979), 11.

> You can live a lifetime and, at the end of it, know more about other people than you know about yourself. You learn to watch other people, but you never watch yourself because you strive against loneliness. The abhorrence of loneliness is as natural as wanting to live at all. . . . Being alone in an aeroplane for even so short a time as a night and a day, irrevocably alone, with nothing to observe but your instruments and your own hands in the semi-darkness, nothing to contemplate but the size of your small courage, nothing to wonder about but the beliefs, the faces, and the hopes rooted in your mind—such an experience can be as startling as the first awareness of a stranger walking by your side at night. You are the stranger.*

> Last spring at this time I was coming out of a bout with pneumonia. I went to bed on January first and didn't get up until the end of February. Winter was a cocoon in which my gagging, basso cough shook the dark figures at the end of my bed. Had I read too much Hemingway? Or was I dying? I'd lie on my stomach and look out. Nothing close up interested me. All engagements of mind—the circumlocutions of love interests and internal gossip—appeared false. Only my body was true. And my body was trying to close down, go out the window without me. . . . As I lay in bed, the black room was a screen through which some part of my body travelled, leaving the rest behind. I thought I was a sun flying over a barge whose iron holds soaked me up until I became rust floating on a bright river.†

Even a quick study of these passages shows us some obvious similarities in technique and substance. Notice that writers usually tell their personal history in the *first person*, "I." Using the first person produces a *tone of familiarity*, of intimacy, ease, and informality—as if the reader and writer were in some comfortable room, talking not just about the bare facts of the writer's life, but about those more private thoughts that reveal the inner person, such as Markham's revelation of overwhelming loneliness exposed during her solo transatlantic flight, or Ehrlich's sense of "otherness" about her body as she lay isolated by her illness.

* Beryl Markham, *West with the Night* (Houghton Mifflin, 1942), 283.

† Gretel Ehrlich, "Spring," *Antaeus*, 57 (Autumn, 1986), 173–4.

All autobiographical writers claim to be *telling the truth*, the whole truth, and nothing but the truth. However, this characteristic claim of autobiographies is not as verifiable as it might at first seem. The issue of veracity is complicated by ontological questions (What is reality, and therefore truth?), as well as psychological (How well do we remember?) and artistic questions (Does this detail fit the pattern of the scene I am creating, and if not should I alter or delete it?). Consequently, although the autobiographer may claim to be telling the truth, we must determine which truth and whose version of it is being told before we can judge whether or not an autobiography is an accurate reflection of the facts.

In a lecture published in book form as *Aspects of Biography*, Andre Maurois expressed doubts about the possibility of autobiography accurately representing the truth. "Autobiographical narrative is inaccurate or false," he contended, because we forget; we deliberately falsify on aesthetic grounds; we expurgate the disagreeable; our sense of shame alters things; we rationalize events afterwards; and we wish to protect our friends. Maurois concluded, "It is impossible, then, to retrieve the past; it is impossible not to change it unconsciously, and, further, it is impossible not to change it consciously."

The greatest critic of autobiography, Samuel Johnson, was as aware of the possibility of falsehood as Maurois, but he rejected the notion that it was impossible to tell the truth.

> The writer of his own life has at least the first qualification of an Historian, the knowledge of the truth; and though it may be plausibly objected that his temptations to disguise it are equal to his opportunities of knowing it, yet I cannot but think that impartiality may be expected with equal confidence from him that relates the passages of his own life, as from him that delivers the transactions of another. Certainty of knowledge not only excludes mistakes but fortifies veracity.*

However, *all autobiography is retrospective*—that is, all autobiographers are reviewing past events—and time does affect the way writers perceive events. This is one reason why many of the most accurate and vivid autobiographies have been drawn from

* Samuel Johnson, *Idler*, November 24, 1759.

diaries and journals. Anaïs Nin, for example, began to keep her *Diary* to counteract the distorting power of time.

Each autobiographer justifies writing his or her life story with *some motive, some purpose either personal or societal.* Both Markham and Ehrlich, for example, touch on a purpose common to many autobiographies, namely to reveal the inner person who is at the same time a social creature with friends and with social relationships. Often the autobiography exposes the conflicts inherent in this duality.

Two other important characteristics of autobiography are also suggested in the quoted passages. First, unlike any other kind of writers, *in pure autobiography the author exhibits a curious duality: He or she is both the observer and the subject.* We have already touched on this duality in our discussion of the use of the first person and the nature of truth. If, as many critics believe, all prose is to some extent autobiographical, then the line between factual writing and fictional writing begins to blur. *Time is the other universal subject in autobiography*—both chronological time (from childhood to adulthood, or wherever the autobiography begins and ends) and time in a more ultimate sense, a continuing autobiographical present in which the autobiographer has a sort of second chance, an opportunity to play the game over again. When you write an autobiographical piece, you relive the experience, this time with greater perception gained from hindsight.

A reconstruction of events, dialogues, and travels, a remembrance of the people, places, dangers, and pleasures of our experience—in short, the panorama of a man's or a woman's life—has such cumulative intensity that it can make the past part of the present. Without the past there can be no future. Anthropologist Margaret Mead expressed it this way:

> If I were twenty-one today, I would elect to join the communicating network of those young people, the world over, who recognize the urgency of life—supporting change—as an anthropologist. But even so, I speak out of the experience of my own lifetime of seeing past and future as aspects of the present. Knowledge joined to action—knowledge about what man has been and is—can protect the future. There is hope, I believe, in seeing the human adventure as a whole and in this shared trust

> that knowledge about mankind, sought in reverence for life, can bring life.*

What you can learn from the journal and diary entries that follow is an appreciation for practiced observation—seeing not just shape and color, but transparency and depth; hearing not just sound, but nuance and harmony; feeling texture as well as firmness; tasting sour or tart as well as sweet or bitter; smelling and remembering the smell—in short, the records of minds that can harmoniously blend all these faculties to reveal the normally unobserved connections between objects, ideas, and actions.

Autobiographical writing can teach you that you have something to say that is both interesting and unique. You will discover that it is a pleasure to share a closely felt event or personal thought with a responsive audience. Furthermore, you will develop the confidence that, at least in this area, you are an expert—no one knows more about the subject, which is, after all, *you*.

* Margaret Mead, *Blackberry Winter: My Earlier Years* (William Morrow & Co., 1972), 296.

✦ Wendell Berry ✦
Notes from an Absence and a Return

Wendell Berry combines the best worlds of teaching, writing, and farming. He has written three novels and five volumes of poetry, and is best known for his collections of essays: The Long-Legged House *(1969),* A Continuous Harmony *(1972), and* Essays Cultural and Agricultural *(1982). He teaches English at the University of Kentucky, and lives with his family on a farm on the Kentucky River outside Port Royal, Kentucky. In this journal entry from* A Continuous Harmony, *Berry illustrates his philosophy of "thinking small."*

March 3

IN TEN DAYS WE LEAVE HERE to start back to Kentucky. For half a year now we've lived a life radically unlike the life we've chosen and made there at home. What I get from the experience out here is the awareness that the life we want is not merely the one we have chosen and made; it is the one we must be choosing and making. To keep it alive we must be perpetually choosing it and making its differences from among all contrary and alternative possibilities. We must accept the pain and labor of that, or we lose its satisfactions and its joy. Only by risking it, offering it freely to its possibilities, can we keep it. 1

From Pound, The Great Digest and the Unwobbling Pivot*:*

> " . . . the real man perfects the nation's culture without leaving his fireside." 2
>
> "One humane family can humanize a whole state; one courteous family can lift a whole state into courtesy; one grasping and perverse man can drive a nation to chaos." 3
>
> "Equity is something that springs up from the earth in harmony with earth and with heaven." [Like a plant in a field.] 4

"Thence the man of breed cannot dodge disciplining himself. Thinking of this self-discipline he cannot fail in good acts toward his relatives; thinking of being good to his blood relatives he cannot skimp his understanding of nature and of mankind; wanting to know 5 mankind he must perforce observe the order of nature and of the heavens."

The thinking of professional reformers and revolutionaries usually fails to escape the machine analogy operative in military and other coercive thinking. They want to organize the people into a human machine. And a machine is by definition subservient to the will of only one man. In the formula "Power to the People" I hear "Power to *me,* who am eager to run the show in the name of the People." The People, of course, are those so designated by their benevolent servant-to-be, who knows so well what is good for them. Thus by diseased speech, politics, as usual, dispenses with the facts.

The Confucian mind escapes the machine analogy by placing the emphasis on specific persons and specific acts. It accepts the discipline of details—which is only to say that it accepts a discipline. What produces the sweat and the results of a real encounter with possibility is details, not slogans.

March 12

Farewell supper at Ed's house with Ed's family and Gurney and Chloe. The gathering charged with the sense that in the half year of being together we have made possibilities that did not exist before, the sense of the life of our community that will survive our separation.

Be joyful because it is humanly possible.

March 14

The relief of mountains and deserts after the over-populated, 1
overmechanized regions. The oppression of driving mile after mile under a veil of poison. Now it is only in the wild places that a man can sense the rarity of being a man. In the crowded places he is more and more closed in by the feeling that he is ordinary—and that he is, on the average, expendable.

You can best serve civilization by being against what usually 1
passes for it.

(Kentucky)
March 24

We've been back home since the night of the eighteenth. This is 12
the first rainy day since we got here. I'm at the Camp with a fire going in the heater. Outside it's 50°, some of the maples and elms are starting to bloom, the river shows the dapplings of muddy water. It has been raining steadily all morning.

When we got here the furnace wasn't working, the toilet wasn't 13
working, the other car and the tiller had to be taken to the garage and started. A lot of little tasks of setting things right and getting started and beginning to live here again. I've pruned the trees and vines in the orchard, gone over the garden once with the tiller, clipped the chickens' wings so they can't fly out of the pen, fixed the furnace and the toilet, etc. And this morning I've swept out the Camp and begun to move my work things back into it.

So here I am again. 14

March 28

But to be here again is no simple matter. What is inescapable is 15
the complexity of my being here. Most of my friends seem to have the notion that it must be simply a great relief to me to be back on my home ground. Not so. It *is* a relief, certainly—a deep settling of the spirit; I've slept better since I've been back than in all the time I was gone.

But it is other things too. It is not pure or simple, because I am 16
not a tourist here. I have made this place my life. I am its dependent; it is my dependent. And so in addition to the relief and the joy, the profound steady pleasure, of returning, there is a heavy sense of involvement and responsibility. As never before I'm impressed with the dependence of a human place, such as a farm, on human love. After our seven months' absence our place shows clearly its dependence, not so much on the conscious large acts such as a man might do out of duty, but on the hundreds of trivial acts that a man who loves it does every day, without premeditation, in the course of doing other things. The *duties* have all been done; we have nothing

to complain about on that score. It is the seven months' absence of our own attentiveness and concern that we continue to notice; its marks are everywhere.

The redeeming aspect of the sense of involvement and responsi- 17
bility is that it does not stand alone, but is only part of a process, a way of life that includes joy. Not always or necessarily or even preferably the dramatic joy of surprise—though that is one of its possibilities—but the quiet persistent joy of familiarity.

There is also a peculiar hesitance in returning—as there might 18
be in rejoining a deeply loved woman after a long absence. Have I changed? Has the place? Do I still belong here? And then the joy of finding out that I do. I first began to *live* here again when it rained after having been dry; in the relief I felt then, I re-entered the processes of this place, its time and weather. Day before yesterday there was snow. A heavy frost last night. Today is bright and warming.

March 29

In the woods one of the satisfactions is to return to places that are 19
associated with events in my life, that I am bound to by more than familiarity and affection: places I hunted or wandered in when I was a boy, where I have walked and picnicked with Tanya and the children and with friends, where ideas and words have come to me, where I have sat writing, where I have imagined events in my books taking place, where I know some flower will be blooming later in the year. Tanya says one reason we are happy here is that we are learning where to expect things to happen.

At home the great delight is to see the clover and grass now 20
growing on places that were bare when we came. These small healings of the ground are my model accomplishment—everything else I do must aspire to that. While I was at that work the world gained with every move I made, and I harmed nothing.

Our vision of what we wanted here is fleshing itself out. What we 21
have planted is growing. It becomes clearer what must be planted next.

April 2

The big woods. Late afternoon. Cloudy and warm. Has been 22
raining off and on all day. As I came along the creek the crows were
ganged up over on the hillside, having found a hawk or an owl.

The old oak stump where I often go to sit is covered with a light 23
green patina of moss now. After the work of insects, woodpeckers,
lichens, mosses, fungi, bacteria, by the time a dead tree reaches the
ground it has become earth.

I cross over through the woods to the Woodpecker Hollow and 24
sit down. The peepers are going strong in the little wet-weather
slue. Doves are calling in the distance. There comes once the brief
clear song of a cardinal. Off among the branches I see gray squirrels
playing.

A pair of wood ducks comes in on the slue, thirty or forty feet 25
away. They hit the water like precise knife strokes, in a rush. I didn't
expect them. A great flash in the nerves. As soon as they have
lighted they swim around, the female calling loudly. And then they
catch sight of me, some small movement I make, and fly.

A tall water maple, eighteen inches thick, has fallen across the 26
slue since I was here last, a hump of earth turned up with its roots.

A pair of downy woodpeckers arrives at the hollow, clipping to 27
the tree trunks like little brackets, pecking here and there, flying,
flirting.

A robin sings strongly off in the woods behind me. 28

Way off in the back of the woods I occasionally hear one of the 29
pileated woodpeckers.

5:30. I've been here, I guess, a half hour. The flickers begin to 30
arrive for the night. They drum, call outrageously, bow and wobble
and display themselves.

Heard singly, the peepers' voices are liquid and fluty. Together 31
they make a sound that is utterly surrounding and inundating. It fills
and echoes in the head so that the ears seem to yell back.

I can hear one of the pileateds drumming. A brief roll, building 32
heavily and dwindling.

5:50. A pileated had come to a tree nearby, but I didn't see him 33
until he flew. For all the boldness and grandeur in the presence and
movements of these birds, they have a furtiveness about them.
They are timid and can skulk around like spies. Long before they
finally fly into the hollow for the night, in that swooping, always

breathtaking entrance, one is conscious of them hovering about in the distance, silent and fluttery-seeming as moths at a window.

With the scar of the new road on one side, and on another the 3
huge scrape where they took up dirt for the fill, the life and meaning of this place are more poignant than ever. The little branch now flows over the yellow silt of eroded subsoil. One feels that every natural place now stands under the heavy syllable WHEN?

Something keeps wrinkling the edge of the water. My legs are 3
beginning to go to sleep, so I get up and walk down to see. The peepers all hush at once. Among the dead leaves under the water I see a small salamander. There is a gelatin ball of eggs fastened to a weed stem. Also a few water striders.

I draw back from the edge of the water and squat down in a little 3
patch of cane. About 6:30 a pileated clips itself to a tall slender sycamore and almost at once disappears into a hole. Then two more come, more boldly, the white of their wings flashing in the dusk, and I hear the sounds their wings make, whipping and chuffing as they turn, almost like somebody shaking a throw rug or a pillow slip. I watch one of these go to roost. He stands braced on his tail at the lip of the hole for some time, leaning to look in and then rearing back to look around outside. It is as though they study the difference between the light outside and the dark inside, and will go in for the night only when the difference has grown exactly small enough. I have seen hens behave much the same way going into the hen house to roost. Finally he goes in, and turns and looks out for a few seconds, and then withdraws for the night.

April 13

Phlox, trout lily, poppy, crinkleroot, spring beauty, bloodroot, 3
violets, rue anemone, Dutchman's breeches, bluebell. All those in bloom. And mayapple, hound's tongue, larkspur, columbine, all coming on. The woods floor reminds me now of the foreground of Botticelli's *Spring*. One walks in the crisis of the fear of trampling something exquisitely formed. But also with the sense, joyful if anything is, of time passing beautifully, of time passing *through* beauty, fulfilled in it in degree and detail beyond calculation, and so not wasted or lost. In the woods, as in the place of a skilled and

loving workman, time departs free and unburdened from the past. Walking among all these flowers, I cannot *see* enough. One is aware of the abundance of lovely things—forms, scents, colors—lavished on the earth beyond any human capacity to perceive or number or imitate. And aware of the economy, the modest principle of the building earth under the dead leaves, by which such abundance is assured.

This is the enemy in man's "war against nature." 38

All these places of unforced loveliness, whose details keep touch- 39
ing in my mind the memory of great paintings, now lie within the sound of the approach of an alien army whose bulldozers fly the flag of the American economy (hardly the economy of the topsoil). This country is an unknown place suffering the invasion of a people whose minds have never touched the earth.

As I left the house I saw a yellow-throated warbler in an elm near 40
the barn, and then another at the Three Streams. At the top of the ridge I watched a pair of red-tailed hawks soaring on the rising air currents above the bluffs. They moved in the broad loops of a spiral which slowly advanced above the tilt of the woods. As they turned, the one on the outside veered to the inside, and as they came around again, the one now on the outside veered to the inside. They repeated this over and over. The movement was very dancelike and graceful. It would be impossible, I would guess, to diagram it intelligibly, but free in the sky, leaving no marks, the pattern was clear and simple and coherent. Later I saw one of the pair hunting, circling and screaming, low to the treetops—a very different sort of flight, agitated and urgent. And still later one of them was being bullied by crows on the north slope along Camp Branch.

I come more and more to look on each creature as living and 41
moving always at the center—one of the infinite number of centers—of an arrangement of processes that reaches through the universe. The interlocking lives of the creatures, like a coat of chain mail, by which the creation saves itself from death.

I went across the wooded points above the river and Cane Run 42
and Camp Branch, in and out of the draws, and then down to Camp Branch, and up to the old barn, and up the wagon road, and over the ridge, and down the old landing road, and across the hollow into the pasture behind the house.

This Port Royal, this state of Kentucky, these United States, in which everything is supposedly named and numbered and priced, are unlikely to know what lies out of sight of the paved roads. I walk often through places unknown by any name or fact or event to people who live almost within calling distance of them, yet more worthy of their interest, I think, than the distant places to which they devote so much of their attention. If we were a truly civilized and indigenous people such places would be named for what is characteristic of them, they would be known and talked about, people would visit them as they now visit places of commercial entertainment, as familiarly as they visit their friends. People would walk carefully and attentively and reverently in them. There would be a lore about them that each generation would both inherit and add to. Knowledge of them would pass intimately through families and friendships. The country would be full of such places, each known and visited only by a few. The human value of the land would then come to be what humans *knew* about it, and wealth would no longer prey on it. 4

On my walk I carried a 15× lens. Looked at through it, the bluebells are depthless; you seem to be looking deep in or far out. Like looking down into clear, still, blue water, or off a mountaintop into the sky. 4

After we planted garden last Tuesday Tanya spoke of how much she liked the idea that we had done it, not because of any convention or custom or law, but because it was *time*. 4

April 25

A light frost last night. Mist from the river kept it off the fruit trees. 4

The morning sunny. I left the house after breakfast, and walked up the branch and over the hill. 4

Sitting on a log near the top of the bluebell slope. The woods leafing out. Around me the birds are singing, and in a larger circle I hear the farmers' tractors getting on with spring work. 4

May 21

If you aren't for us you're against us, somebody is always saying. 49
That seems to me a sad little pair of options, insofar as to any kind of intelligence the possibilities ought to be numerous, if not infinite. Intelligence *consists* in being for and against such things as political movements *up to a point*, which it is the task of intelligence to define. In my judgment intelligence never goes whole hog for anything public, especially political movements. Across the whole range of politics now (and I suppose always) you find people willing to act on the assumption that there is some simple abstraction that will explain and solve the problems of the world, and who go direct from the discovery of the abstraction to the forming of an organization to promote it. In my opinion those people are all about equally dangerous, and I don't believe anything they say. What I hold out for is the possibility that a man can live decently *without* knowing all the answers, or believing that he does—can live decently even in the understanding that life is unspeakably complex and unspeakably subtle in its complexity. The decency, I think, would be in acting out of the awareness that personal acts of compassion, love, humility, honesty are better, and more adequate, responses to that complexity than any public abstraction or theory or organization. What is wrong with our cities—and I don't see how you can have a great civilization without great cities—may be that the mode of life in them has become almost inescapably organizational.

It used to be that every time I heard of some public action 50
somewhere to promote some cause I believed in, I would be full of guilt because I wasn't there. If they were marching in Washington to protest the war, and if I deplored the war, then how could my absence from Washington be anything but a sin? That was the organizational protestant conscience: in order to believe in my virtue I needed some organization to pat me on the head and tell me I was virtuous. But if I can't promote what I hope for in Port Royal, Ky., then why go to Washington to promote it?

What succeeds in Port Royal succeeds in the world. 51

June 29

This place has become the form of my work, its discipline, in the same way the sonnet has been the form and discipline of the work of other poets: if it doesn't fit it's not true.

Oct. 25

The work of the growing season is nearly finished. The raspberry bed is mulched. The rye is up in the garden. Last week I cut down a lot of the trees in the big slip in the riverbank. I cut them three or four feet from the ground and only part way through, leaving them attached to the stumps, and letting them fall crisscrossed. They make a kind of loose thatch over the slip. The idea is that they will slow the current when the river is high, and allow the silt to fill the cavity in the bank.

Probably because of the order and rest that this fall work settles into, I've begun to recover a harmony with the seasonal motions and demands of this place. The long stay in California last fall and winter broke this harmony, and I had no way to realize how thoroughly I had lost it until now, when it has begun to come back. That accounts for much of the clumsiness and behindhandedness I felt in the summer's work—work that needed to have been prepared for last fall and winter when I wasn't here. And the connections between times, and between time and work, are so subtle that I apparently have to be here to do the work before I can know what work must be done. I didn't realize what work had been left out last fall until I began to do it *this* fall. In the work is where my relation to this place comes alive. The real knowledge survives in the work, not in the memory. To love this place and hold out for its meanings and keep its memories, without undertaking any of its work, would be to falsify it.

Oct. 26

In the last few months I have had to consider more openly than before that our use of our place is in some ways still far from a success. Out of a history so much ruled by the motto Think Big, we have come to a place and a need that require us to learn to think little. Instead of ostentation we have undertaken modesty; instead of haste, patience; for the discipline of generalizations we have begun to substitute the discipline of details. When we came here, what I knew of farming had been learned on farms of several hundred acres of good land; and we have begun here at a time when the trend is toward ever larger and more specialized operations, and when smaller farmers are giving up or being forced out—when, in short, the skills and the economics of the small holding have been badly weakened. In undertaking to build some sort of integrated family economy on a few acres, mostly steep and mostly neglected, there has been for those reasons and others a good deal of awkwardness and a lot of waste—of effort and time and money. We have invested in the wrong tools and the wrong projects, have become ensnarled in bad plans, have been too slow to recognize the obvious. That is, we often have, not always. But by this awkwardness and this partial success we can see that we have not got to where we are by anything so simple as deciding what we wanted to do and then doing it—as if we had shopped in a display of lives and selected one. We have, instead, in the midst of living, and with time passing, been discovering how we want to live, and inventing the ways.

Oct. 28

When we woke up this morning there was a heavy frost and a 56
thick fog. Before sunup everything was furred with ice, dull gray, and the fog shut off the distances. And then the sun came through—the sudden difference of throwing a bucket of water on sunlit boards. The white frost gleams on everything. Strands of spiderweb looped along tree limbs and fences are thick as trot line, and brilliant. As the day warms it is windless and still, the leaves coming down steady as rain, falling of their own weight. With the sun on it, the tin roof begins to click, warming up.

I haven't been conscious before of how invariably when I have 57
sensed or imagined the life of another creature, a tree or bird or an animal, I have had to begin by imagining my own absence—as though there was a necessary competition between my life and theirs. I looked upon my ability to imagine myself absent as a virtue. It seems to me now that it was an evasion. I began this morning to

feel something truer—the beginning of the knowledge that the other creatures and I are here together.

For years the burden of my work has been the sense of being implicated, by inheritance and by various failures of consciousness of my own, in a phase of history that is malignant. Now what I am suddenly aware of is the possibility—or the hope?—of passing beyond guilt, which is clearly the source of my obsession with the absence metaphor.

The old sycamore down in the corner of the bottom—that survived the ice jam of 1918, that was alive when my grandfathers were boys—*and I* are alive now, this morning, while the spiderwebs are visible with ice and light, and the leaves are falling. We are moving in a relationship, a design, that is definite—though shadowy to me—like people in a dance.

QUESTIONS FOR READING AND WRITING

1. What are some of your reactions to coming home after being away for a while? Do you think it's more fun to be a tourist or to be a resident of a place? Why?
2. How do the following two sentences from the entry for October 26 in Berry's journal help explain how he binds together social observations with descriptions of the beauties of his farm at Port Royal: "Out of a history so much ruled by the motto Think Big, we have come to a place and a need that requires us to think little. Instead of ostentation we have undertaken modesty; instead of haste, patience; for the discipline of generalizations we have begun to substitute the discipline of details"? How does the entry for April 2 illustrate the contrast between big and little thinking?
3. Read Paul Theroux's "Butlin's Holiday Camp" and draw some similarities between his description of commercial tourism and Berry's implications about being a tourist in a place where one has no connection through work.
4. Keep a journal for several weeks of activities in your classes or at work. Apply Berry's statement that in "the midst of living" he and his family discovered "how we want to live." Does your journal bear this out for most people, or do they consciously plan their lives with little reference to their immediate tasks?

✦ Annie Dillard ✦
An American Childhood

Born in Pittsburgh in 1945, Annie Dillard has lived in and written about a wide range of places, for her interests have taken her far beyond the borders of the United States. Poet, naturalist, autobiographer, and critic, Dillard won the Pulitzer Prize for Pilgrim at Tinker Creek *(1974). After moving from Virginia to Washington State, where she wrote* Teaching a Stone to Talk *(1982), Dillard returned to the East, and she now teaches at Wesleyan University in Connecticut. In 1984, she published* Encounters with Chinese Writers, *and she has been a member of the National Commission on U.S.–China Relations. The following excerpt from her autobiographical memoir,* An American Childhood *(1987), is typical of Dillard's style: a concrete incident dissolves to become a shared universal experience.*

NEXT TO ONE OF OUR SIDE YARDS ran a short, dirty dead-end 1
alley. We couldn't see the alley from the house; our parents had planted a row of Lombardy poplars to keep it out of sight. I found an old dime there.

High above the darkest part of the alley, in a teetering set of 2
rooms, lived a terrible old man and a terrible old woman, brother and sister.

Doc Hall appeared only high against the sky, just outside his door 3
at the top of two rickety flights of zigzag stairs. There he stood, grimy with coal dust, in a black suit wrinkled as underwear, and yelled unintelligibly, furiously, down at us children who played on his woodpile. We looked fearfully overhead and saw him stamp his aerial porch, a raven messing up his pile of sticks and littering the ground below. We couldn't understand his curses, but we scattered.

Doc Hall's grim sister went to early Mass at St. Bede's; she passed 4
our house every morning. She was shapeless and sooty, dressed in black; she leaned squeezing a black cane, and walked downcast. No one knew what Mass might be; my parents shuddered to think. She crawled back and down the alley.

The alley ended at an empty, padlocked garage. In summer a few 5
hairs of grass grew down the alley's center. Down the alley's side,

broken glass, old nails, and pellets of foil and candy wrappers spiked the greasy black soil out of which a dirty catalpa and a dirty sycamore grew.

When I found the dime I was crouched in the alley digging dirt with a Popsicle stick under one of the Lombardy poplars. I struck the dime and dug around it; it was buried on edge. I pulled it out, cleaned it between my fingers, and pocketed it. Later I showed it to my father, who had been until then my only imaginable source of income. He read the date—1919—and told me it was an old dime, which might be worth more than ten cents.

He explained that the passage of time had buried the dime; soil tends to pile up around things. In Rome, he went on—looking out the kitchen window as I leaned against a counter looking up at him—in Rome, he had seen old doorways two or three stories underground. When children had once tumbled directly outside from their doors, now visitors had to climb two flights of stairs to meet the light of the street. I stopped listening for a minute. I imagined that if the Roman children had, by awful chance, sat still in their doorways long enough, sat dreaming and forgetting to move, they, too, would have been buried in dirt, up to their chins, over their heads!—only by then, of course, they would be very old. Which was, in fact—the picture swept over me—precisely what had happened to all those Roman children, whether they sat still or not.

I turned the warm dime in my fingers. Father told me that, in general, the older a coin was, the greater its value. The older coins were farther down. I decided to devote my life to unearthing treasure. Beneath my 1919 dime, buried in the little Pittsburgh alley, might be coins older still, coins deeper down, coins from ancient times, from forgotten peoples and times, gold coins, even—pieces of eight, doubloons.

I continually imagined these old, deeply buried coins, and dreamed of them; the alley was thick with them. After I'd unearthed all the layers of wealth I could reach with a Popsicle stick, I would switch to a spade and delve down to the good stuff: to the shining layers of antique Spanish gold, of Roman gold—maybe brass-bound chests of it, maybe diamonds and rubies, maybe dulled gold from days so long past that people didn't manufacture coins at all, but simply carried bags of raw gold or ore in lumps.

That's all. It was the long years of these same few thoughts that 10
wore tracks in my interior life. These things were mine, I figured, because I knew where to look. Because I was willing. Treasure was something you found in the alley. Treasure was something you dug up out of the dirt in a chaotic, half-forbidden, forsaken place far removed from the ordinary comings and goings of people who earned salaries in the light: under some rickety back stairs, near a falling-down pile of discarded lumber, with people yelling at you to get away from there. That I never found another old coin in that particular alley didn't matter at all.

QUESTIONS FOR READING AND WRITING

1. Dillard's autobiographical recollection of finding an old coin in an alley in Pittsburgh is actually a metaphor for searching for the neglected and unconventional. It is perhaps a parable of Dillard's choice of vocation since a writer seeks after the forbidden and the out-of-the-ordinary. Have you had similar experiences, however trivial, which developed your special interests?
2. How does Dillard's father's explanation of the value of the coin add to the romance of discovery? Why does Dillard devote so much attention to the alley and its inhabitants? Compare the inane details here with those of Richard Rhodes' "Cupcake Land."
3. Write an essay showing how a seemingly trivial incident from childhood helped shape your future interests or your personality.

✦ Adam Liptak ✦
Playing Air Guitar

Formerly a staff writer for The New York Times, *Adam Liptak is a student at Yale Law School. His essay on playing air guitar, which first appeared in the "About Men" column in* The New York Times Magazine, *examines his generation's "mode of discourse, which is a mix of the intimate and the ironic."*

WHEN I HEAR A SONG on the radio that I really like, or that used to be a favorite, I sometimes dance around a little bit and pretend to play guitar. I play air guitar. It probably looks dumb to an outsider, but to the man who plays, it is quite serious—a primal and private dance. Men identify with the great rock guitarists the way they do with sports legends, and we mimic their gestures and attitudes in an instinctive quest for grace.

What you do is: extend your left arm sort of crookedly, faking chord changes on the neck of an invisible electric guitar, rhythmically. Your right hand strums. Your head bobs. Your hips twitch. A nearby mirror reflects your grimaces. There is loud music on.

When I was a teen-ager, I used to play all the time. The impulse arose at odd moments. Just walking around, in an empty, late-afternoon school hallway, say, I might be seized by the inner music, drop to a crouch and let loose a devastating solo, the whole thing over in 10 seconds. A favorite song on the car radio, I am embarrassed to recount, could make me take my hands from the wheel and imitate a Stones riff—stopping only to keep my father's car from drifting into the next lane.

Certainly air guitar was handy at parties, where by stiffening and lowering the arms a little it passed for dancing. Countless men still dance this way.

But the true essence of air guitar is intensely personal and a little embarrassing, a strange conflation of fantasy and desire. I remember summer dusks in anticipation of parties—this at a time when a party was a promise of wonder, of a life transformed—climbing out of the shower, the evening's first beer lodged precariously on the soap tray, and hearing the perfect song. Here was pleasure: a long swig, a half-turn on the volume knob, the hallucinatory rush of adrenaline, followed by mindless dancing around in front of the fogged-up mirror.

As with anything, it is possible to play air guitar well or poorly, but it has nothing at all to do with being able to play guitar, which is in fact a drawback. One is after an image, a look; technical proficiency is distracting. The choice of role model is important, but what one copies is stance, attitude and character. Virtuosity is for the most part irrelevant. Only the electric guitar counts; there is no such thing as playing acoustic air guitar. Years of practice help, and so does an appreciation for loud, dumb music. 6

I am certain that the success of the movie "Risky Business" had a great deal to do with the scene in which Tom Cruise bounds about the living room in a shirt, socks and underpants. His parents are out of town, of course. He turns up the stereo and indulges in a whole array of rock-star moves and prancing. 7

Talking with friends afterward, I discovered that our enjoyment of the scene—of its celebratory tone—was tempered by an uneasy feeling of having somehow been found out. A kind of reverse identification had taken place, and we saw ourselves not as guitar heroes but as slightly absurd kids from the suburbs. This shock of recognition was followed by a shudder. 8

In college, I played less often but more openly. Sometimes, at the end of a beery night, my friends and I would put together a whole band—it was always the Stones, and I always wanted to be Keith Richards—and clamber up onto the furniture and play, each of us with his eyes closed, in a way alone. It sounds like a silly and slightly aggressive scene, and it was. 9

At the same time, this was a way men could dance with other men without compromising their version of masculinity. At parties, dancing with women, my best friend and I might step away and take a moment to jam, leaning on each other this way and that, falling over and playing incredible dual solos on our invisible Fenders. The women we abandoned were generally not amused. 10

We joked about it, air guitar being a perfect subject for my generation's mode of discourse, which is a mix of the intimate and the ironic. Here we could say just what we meant, confessing to the odd habit in a deadpan way, so that no listener could be quite sure if we really meant it. Or we could go beyond our own experience— 11 admit to playing naked on city rooftops, say—and then double back and make fun of anyone taken in or, worse, who admitted to doing the same thing.

I have noticed lately the attempt to institutionalize air guitar, in 12
the form of "concerts" at colleges, "lip-sync" contests at certain nightclubs in the boroughs of New York and on television shows. There is something peculiarly American about making the intimate public and competitive, something reassuring at first but in the long run repulsive.

This is not to say that an air guitar contest is without humor. To 13
see four or five people aping the movements of an entire band with the appropriate music in the background can be hilarious. An ensemble called Men Without Instruments, at Princeton University, is funny even to contemplate.

I don't know if teen-agers today find in Prince and Bruce 14
Springsteen adequate idols. I suspect they do. And I suppose they know the moves better than we ever did, thanks to music videos.

These days, I find myself at some emotional distance from most 15
of the popular music I hear, and going to rock concerts has lost its appeal. I still put on loud music first thing in the morning, though, loud enough to hear in the shower, which is down the hall from my stereo. And sometimes, as I start to dress, barefoot, my shirt unbuttoned and my tie loose around my neck, I play a couple of notes if it feels right. And then, refreshed, I finish dressing and go to work.

QUESTIONS FOR READING AND WRITING

1. "Air Guitar" is both an ironic and a serious essay, one that, as Liptak suggests, is "a perfect subject for my generation's mode of discourse, which is a mix of the intimate and the ironic." What other examples of your generation's style contain both the emotional and the "cool"?
2. What does Liptak mean when he says that the gesture of playing air guitar is a way of expressing admiration for the heroes of his generation? Why is it more appropriately a private rather than a public act?
3. Write an essay comparing Liptak's essay with Alice Walker's "Oppressed Hair Puts a Ceiling on the Brain," and Anne Hollander's "Dressed to Thrill." How do each of the generational fads described in the essays reflect the social and political concerns of each generation?

✦ Anaïs Nin ✦
Puerto Vallarta, Mexico

Anaïs Nin (1903–1977) was born in Paris, emigrated to New York as a child, and later returned to Paris, where she joined the bohemian circle of novelist Henry Miller. She became interested in psychoanalysis and studied with Freud's student, Otto Rank. Much of her early fiction was commercially unsuccessful. With the publication of her diaries in the mid-60s, she finally found the audience that had eluded her. Their literary merit and their applicability to the women's movement of the seventies have made Nin's diaries classics. The following selection reveals Nin's zest for the exotic as well as her preoccupation with the dream as a tool for examining the psyche.

FIRST OF ALL THE WARM, CARESSING AIR. It dissolves you into a flower or foliage. It humidifies the sun-opened pores. The body emerges from its swaddling of clothes. Rebirth. Then the colors, the infinite variations of greens, deep, dark or golden. The banana tree the darkest foliage of all, wide, dense, heavy. The fringes and interlacings of palms. Then the birds, vivid, loud, vigorous, talkative, whistles, cries, gossip, clarinets and flutes. Trills, tremolos, vibratos, arabesques. 1

Then the flavor of margaritas, ice cold, with salt on the rim of the glass. 2

Rented a jeep and excursions began, to Los Tres Arcos, three huge rocks with caves and tunnels, delight of snorklers from which they return with descriptions of fish which rival descriptions of fashion shows. Blue stripes and gold tails. Three fan tails of bright red on a silver-gray body, small transparent fish like Lucite. We hike up the mountain, past a little village, along the river, to find a pool. Marianne Greenwood had made a map of what we should see. 3

Nightmares: My mother and I are cleaning up the kitchen, a terribly messy one. We are in our slips. Drudges. My father is coming. Anxiety at what he will think of us, he with his mania for aesthetics and beauty. 4

But the body is healed by the Mexican life. There is a stillness in my head. I am content with warm little pleasures, because of the 5 warm cuddling by the air, the feeling of nervelessness. Passive drinking in of color, the cafés, the shops, people; and the thrill of looking into open homes, open windows, open doors. An old lady in a rocking chair. Photographs on the walls. Palm leaves from last year's ritual Easter. One room reminded me of Barcelona. The whitewashed house. The room painted sky blue. I have known such a room, with potted palms, lace doilies on the table. Pictures of Christ, of course, artificial flowers and bric-a-brac.

I do not understand the nightmares. Again last night I was cleaning the rim of an incredibly dirty bathtub, picking up dirty glasses. My mother was having a sewing party. I went in to consult with her. Why should my spirit be so heavy when my body is at home in Mexico?

Returning on the boat and looking at the lush tropical vegetation, my eyes filled with tears. I do not want to die. I love this earth, the earth of Mexico, the sun.

I sit now on a small beach, facing a huge rock. The snorklers swam through caves, saw bats and darkness. I am surrounded by butterflies, black with gold stripes and pearls at the tip of their wings.

I answer a letter or two a day.

This morning I saw the most beautiful fern in a wild field, feathery, lacy and of a green so light it seemed touched with gold.

I have been reading Arthur Clarke. He envisages a future where our minds are influenced by machines, programmed. People can erase others' memories. Memory banks can distort history. Some practice telepathy. But all this has happened already. TV is the machine which brainwashes us. We do erase others' memories. Our minds are constantly tampered with (distorted, lying history and lying media). We influence each other more than we are aware.

My purple postcards have given stimulus to so many. I drop ten or twenty cards in the letter box each day. I can't answer in many words, but I respond. What they write me is usually gray. It is usually negative. Respond, respond. Turn gray into red, respond, transform gray into gold.

The women washing their laundry in the river. Some have planted umbrellas. They choose a smooth rock. They rub sheets, tablecloths, shirts and underwear. They rinse and fill baskets with clean clothes. The children play at the edge of the river.

The market. Stuffed animals, snakes, iguanas, raccoons. Armadil- 14
los, coatamundis, squirrels. Orange, purple, white shawls. The dress
I found has the tones of Balinese batik, all brown and gold, with
designs of birds and impalas.

✦✦✦✦✦

I am still trying to reach the sun, to immerse myself in the sun, 15
but for several days we have had thunderstorms at night. Drop of
rain fell on the diary yesterday while I sat at the beach. Count them.

Snorklers describe a three-foot sea snake, a fish that is blue, 16
purple, with three light blue electric dots which shine like lights. A
fish with a gray body and a bright yellow stripe running along its
body, and a magenta tail. Another was all black and white, with
three fan tails. Another pure yellow, small, with two black tails.
Another was exactly divided into two colors, front half gray, back jet
black.

River scenes. All the women at work. As the clothes are laid out 17
to dry on the rocks, they form an abstract pattern of red, yellow,
blue, orange, white. Later the women go home with basins filled
with clothes balanced on their heads. One was climbing a hill with
her load. A merry scene because of the children playing around
them, naked, splashing, swimming, teasing each other.

Here comes the sun. 18

In the sun the pelicans sit rigid on the rocks watching for fish. 19
The black-and-red butterflies mate on the sand just barely out of
the reach of the waves. The birds sing with a lust unknown to
Northern birds.

In Los Angeles I became enslaved by my correspondence, such 20
touching, moving, poetic letters. They must be answered. I felt
enmeshed by own responsiveness.

It rains every afternoon, every night. I don't go dancing because 21
the electronic music is too loud. What a difference between the
Latin orchestras of Acapulco, so soft and seductive, and this shriek-
ing ugly rock and roll. It was too loud on the boat too, ruined the
sailing, but I loved watching the dancing. The boat trip took us to a
beach. From there we hiked up a mountain to a pool and a waterfall.

Warm rain. Real steamy jungle. Overloaded mango trees, gliding 22
frigate birds. We sit in a café by the seaside and drink beer.

QUESTIONS FOR READING AND WRITING

1. Nin's *Diary* contrasts the lush, vibrant, life-giving scenes of Mexico with the drab negative spirit of her Los Angeles memories. In your own experience, can you find two such contrasting scenes?
2. Colors serve as a metaphor for the moods which Nin wishes to recreate. How do colors define the nature of experience for Nin? What does she mean by "the body is healed by Mexican life"?
3. Compare Nin's positive picture of travel in Mexico with either Paul Theroux's "Butlin's Holiday Camp," or Gregor von Rezzori's "A Stranger in Lolitaland."

✦ Cynthia Ozick ✦

The First Day of School
Washington Square, 1946

A native New Yorker, Cynthia Ozick earned her bachelor's degree from New York University in 1949 and her masters from Ohio State in the following year. She was a Guggenheim fellow in 1982, and she received an award from the American Academy of Arts and Letters in 1983 for her fiction, poetry, and essays. Among her books of fiction are The Pagan Rabbi and Other Stories *(1971),* Bloodshed and Three Novellas *(1976), and* Levitation: Five Fictions *(1982). Her essays have been collected in* Art and Ardor: Essays *(1983). "The First Day of School: Washington Square, 1946" first appeared in* Harper's, *where it was chosen among the* Best American Essays, 1986. *In this autobiographical reminiscence, Ozick touches the delicate mixture of fear and pain of not fitting into new and strange surroundings.*

This portion of New York appears to many persons the most delectable. It has a kind of established repose which is not of frequent occurrence in other quarters of the long, shrill city; it has a riper, richer, more honorable look than any of the upper ramifications of the great longitudinal thoroughfare—the look of having had something of a social history.

—Henry James, Washington Square

I FIRST CAME DOWN TO WASHINGTON SQUARE on a colorless February morning in 1946. I was seventeen and a half years old and was carrying my lunch in a brown paper bag, just as I had carried it to high school only a month before. It was—I thought it was—the opening day of spring term at Washington Square College, my initiation into my freshman year at New York University. All I knew of NYU then was that my science-minded brother had gone there; he had written from the army that I ought to go there too. With master-of-ceremonies zest he described the Browsing Room on the second floor of the Main Building as a paradisal chamber whose bookish loungers leafed languidly through magazines and exchanged high-principled witticisms between classes. It had the sound of a carpeted Olympian club in Oliver Wendell Holmes's 1

Boston, Hub of the Universe, strewn with leather chairs and delectable old copies of *The Yellow Book*.

On that day I had never heard of Oliver Wendell Holmes or *The Yellow Book*, and Washington Square was a faraway bower where wounded birds fell out of trees. My brother had once brought home from Washington Square Park a baby sparrow with a broken leg, to be nurtured back to flight. It died instead, emitting in its last hours melancholy faint cheeps, and leaving behind a dense recognition of the minute explicitness of mortality. All the same, in the February grayness Washington Square had the allure of the celestial unknown. A sparrow might die, but my own life was luminously new: I felt my youth like a nimbus.

Which dissolves into the dun gauze of a low and sullen city sky. And here I am flying out of the Lexington Avenue subway at Astor Place, just a few yards from Wanamaker's, here I am turning a corner past a secondhand bookstore and a union hall; already late. I begin walking very fast toward the park. The air is smoky with New York winter grit, and on clogged Broadway a mob of trucks shifts squawking gears. But there, just ahead, crisscrossed by paths under high branches, is Washington Square and on a single sidewalk, three clear omens—or call them riddles, intricate and redolent. These I will disclose in a moment, but before that you must push open the heavy brass-and-glass doors of the Main Building and come with me, at a hard and panting pace, into the lobby of Washington Square College on the earliest morning of my freshman year.

On the left, a bank of elevators. Straight ahead, a long burnished corridor, spooky as a lit tunnel. And empty, all empty. I can hear my solitary footsteps reverberate, as in a radio mystery drama: they lead me up a short staircase into a big dark ghost-town cafeteria. My brother's letter, along with his account of the physics and chemistry laboratories (I will never see them), has already explained that this place is called Commons—and here my heart will learn to shake with the merciless newness of life. But not today; today there is nothing. Tables and chairs squat in dead silhouette. I race back through a silent maze of halls and stairways to the brass-and-glass doors—there stands a lonely guard. From the pocket of my coat I retrieve a scrap with a classroom number on it and ask the way. The guard announces in a sly croak that the first day of school is not yet; come back tomorrow, he says.

5 A dumb bad joke: I'm humiliated. I've journeyed the whole way down from the end of the line—Pelham Bay, in the northeast Bronx—to find myself in desolation, all because of a muddle: Tuesday isn't Wednesday. The nimbus of expectation fades. The lunch bag in my fist takes on a greasy sadness. I'm not ready to dive back into the subway—I'll have a look around.

6 Across the street from the Main Building, the three omens. First, a pretzel man with a cart. He's wearing a sweater, a cap that keeps him faceless—he's nothing but the shadows of his creases—and wool gloves with the fingertips cut off. He never moves; he might as well be made of papier-mâché, set up and left out in the open since spring. There are now almost no pretzels for sale, and this gives me a chance to inspect the construction of his bare pretzel-poles. The pretzels are hooked over a column of gray cardboard cylinders, themselves looped around a stick, the way horseshoes drop around a post. The cardboard cylinders are the insides of toilet paper rolls.

7 The pretzel man is rooted between a Chock Full O'Nuts (that's the second omen) and a newsstand (that's the third).

8 The Chock Full: the doors are like fans, whirling remnants of conversation. *She will marry him. She will not marry him.* Fragrance of coffee and hot chocolate. *We can prove that the senses are partial and unreliable vehicles of information, but who is to say that reason is not equally a product of human limitation?* Powdered doughnut sugar on their lips.

9 Attached to a candy store, the newsstand. Copies of *Partisan Review:* the table of the gods. Jean Stafford, Mary McCarthy, Elizabeth Hardwick, Irving Howe, Delmore Schwartz, Alfred Kazin, Clement Greenberg, Stephen Spender, William Phillips, John Berryman, Saul Bellow, Philip Rahv, Richard Chase, Randall Jarrell, Simone de Beauvoir, Karl Shapiro, George Orwell! I don't know a single one of these names, but I feel their small conflagration flaming in the gray street: the succulent hotness of their promise. I mean to penetrate every one of them. Since all the money I have is my subway fare—a nickel—I don't buy a copy (the price of *Partisan* in 1946 is fifty cents); I pass on.

10 I pass on to the row of houses on the north side of the square. Henry James was born in one of these, but I don't know that either. Still, they are plainly old, though no longer aristocratic: haughty

last-century shabbies with shut eyelids, built of rosy-ripe respectable brick, down on their luck. Across the park bulks Judson Church, with its squat squarish bell tower; by the end of the week I will be languishing at the margins of a basketball game in its basement, forlorn in my blue left-over-from-high-school gym suit and mooning over Emily Dickinson:

> There's a certain Slant of light,
> Winter Afternoons—
> That oppresses, like the Heft
> Of Cathedral Tunes—

There is more I don't know. I don't know that W. H. Auden lives just down *there*, and might at any moment be seen striding toward home under his tall rumpled hunch; I don't know that Marianne Moore is only up the block, her doffed tricorn resting on her bedroom dresser. It's Greenwich Village—I know *that*—no more than twenty years after Edna St. Vincent Millay has sent the music of her name (her best, perhaps her only, poem) into these bohemian streets: bohemia, the honeypot of poets. 1

On that first day in the tea-leafed cup of the town I am ignorant, ignorant! But the three riddle-omens are soon to erupt, and all of them together will illumine Washington Square. 1

Begin with the benches in the park. Here, side by side with students and their looseleafs, lean or lie the shadows of the pretzel man, his creased ghosts or doubles: all those pitiables, half-women and half-men, neither awake nor asleep; the discountable, the repudiated, the unseen. No more notice is taken of any of them than of a scudding fragment of newspaper in the path. Even then, even so long ago, the benches of Washington Square are pimpled with this hell-tossed crew, these Mad Margarets and Cokey Joes, these volcanic coughers, shakers, groaners, tremblers, droolers, blasphemers, these public urinators with vomitous breath and rusted teeth stumps, dead-eyed and self-abandoned, dragging their makeshift junkyard shoes, their buttonless layers of raggedy ratfur. The pretzel man with his toilet paper rolls conjures and spews them all—he is a loftier brother to these citizens of the lower pox, he is guardian of the garden of the jettisoned. They rattle along all the seams of Washington Square. They are the pickled city, the true and univer- 1 sal City-Below-Cities, the wolfish vinegar-Babylon that dogs the spittled skirts of bohemia. The toilet paper rolls are the temple columns of this sacred grove.

Next, the whirling doors of Chock Full O' Nuts. Here is the marketplace of Washington Square, its bazaar, its roiling gossip-parlor, its matchmaker's office and arena—the outermost wing, so to speak, evolved from the Commons. On a day like today, when the Commons is closed, the Chock Full is thronged with extra power, a cello making up for a missing viola. Until now, the fire of my vitals has been for the imperious tragedians of the *Aeneid*; I have lived in the narrow throat of poetry. Another year or so of this oblivion, until at last I am hammerstruck with the shock of Europe's skull, the bled planet of death camp and war. Eleanor Roosevelt has not yet written her famous column announcing the discovery of Anne Frank's diary. The term *cold war* is new. The Commons, like the college itself, is overcrowded, veterans in their pragmatic thirties mingling with the reluctant dreamy young. And the Commons is convulsed with politics: a march to the docks is organized, no one knows by whom, to protest the arrival of Walter Gieseking, the German musician who flourished among Nazis. The Communists—two or three readily recognizable cantankerous zealots—stomp through with their daily leaflets and sneers. There is even a Monarchist, a small poker- faced rectangle of a man with secretive tireless eyes who, when approached for his views, always demands, in perfect Bronx tones, the restoration of his king. The engaged girls—how many of them there seem to be!—flash their rings and tangle their ankles in their long New Look skirts. There is no feminism and no feminists: I am, I think, the only one. The Commons is a tide: it washes up the cold war, it washes up the engaged girls' rings, it washes up the several philosophers and the numerous poets. The philosophers are all existentialists; the poets are all influenced by *The Waste Land*. When the Commons overflows, the engaged girls cross the street to show their rings at the Chock Full. 14

Call it density, call it intensity, call it continuity: call it, finally, society. The Commons belongs to the satirists. Here, one afternoon, is Alfred Chester, holding up a hair, a single strand, before a crowd. (He will one day write stories and novels. He will die young.) "What is that hair?" I innocently ask, having come late on the scene. "A 15 pubic hair," he replies, and I feel as Virginia Woolf did when she declared human nature to have "changed on or about December 1910"—soon after her sister Vanessa explained away a spot on her dress as "semen."

In or about February 1946 human nature does not change; it 16
keeps on. On my bedroom wall I tack—cut out from *Life* magazine—the wildest Picasso I can find: a face that is also a belly. Mr. George E. Mutch, a lyrical young English teacher still in his twenties, writes on the blackboard: "When lilacs last in the dooryard bloom'd," and "Bare, ruined choirs, where late the sweet birds sang," and "A green thought in a green shade"; he tells us to burn, like Pater, with a hard, gemlike flame. Another English teacher—older and crustier—compares Walt Whitman to a plumber; the next year he is rumored to have shot himself in a wood. The initial letters of Washington Square College are a device to recall three of the seven deadly sins: Wantonness, Sloth, Covetousness. In the Commons they argue the efficacy of the orgone box. Eda Lou Walton, sprightly as a bird, knows all the Village bards, and is a Village bard herself. Sidney Hook is an intellectual rumble in the logical middle distance. Homer Watt, chairman of the English department, is the very soul who, in a far-off time of bewitchment, hired Thomas Wolfe.

And so, in February 1946, I make my first purchase of a "real" 17
book—which is to say, not for the classroom. It is displayed in the window of the secondhand bookstore between the Astor Place subway station and the union hall, and for weeks I have been coveting it: *Of Time and the River.* I am transfigured; I am pierced through with rapture; skipping gym, I sit among morning mists on a windy bench a foot from the stench of Mad Margaret, sinking into that cascading syrup:

> Man's youth is a wonderful thing: It is so full of anguish and of magic and he never comes to know it as it is, until it is gone from him forever. . . . And what is the essence of that strange and bitter miracle of life which we feel so poignantly, so unutterably, with such a bitter pain and joy, when we are young?

Thomas Wolfe, lost, and by the wind grieved, ghost, come back again! In Washington Square I am appareled in the "numb exultant secrecies of fog, fog-numb air filled with solemn joy of nameless and impending prophecy, an ancient yellow light, the old smoke-ochre of the morning . . ."

The smoke-ochre of the morning. Ah, you who have flung 18
Thomas Wolfe, along with your strange and magical youth, onto the ash-heap of juvenilia and excess, myself among you, isn't this a lovely phrase still? It rises out of the old pavements of Washington Square as delicately colored as an eggshell.

The veterans in their pragmatic thirties are nailed to Need; they 19
have families and futures to attend to. When Mr. George E. Mutch exhorts them to burn with a hard, gemlike flame, and writes across the blackboard the line that reveals his own name,

> The world is too much with us; late and soon,
> Getting and spending, we lay waste our powers,

one of the veterans heckles, "What about getting a Buick, what about spending a buck?" Chester, at sixteen, is a whole year younger than I; he has transparent eyes and a rosebud mouth, and is in love with a poet named Diana. He has already found his way to the Village bars, and keeps in his wallet Truman Capote's secret telephone number. We tie our scarves tight against the cold and walk up and down Fourth Avenue, winding in and out of the rows of secondhand bookshops crammed one against the other. The proprietors sit reading their wares and never look up. The books in all their thousands smell sleepily of cellar. Our envy of them is speckled with longing; our longing is sick with envy. We are the sorrowful literary young.

Every day, month after month, I hang around the newsstand near 20
the candy store, drilling through the enigmatic pages of *Partisan Review*. I still haven't bought a copy; I still can't understand a word. I don't know what cold war means. Who is Trotsky? I haven't read *Ulysses*; my adolescent phantoms are rowing in the ablative absolute with *pius* Aeneas. I'm in my mind's cradle, veiled by the exultant secrecies of fog.

Washington Square will wake me. In a lecture room in the Main 21
Building, Dylan Thomas will cry his webwork syllables. Afterward he'll warm himself at the White Horse Tavern. Across the corridor I will see Sidney Hook plain. I will read the Bhagavad-Gita and Catullus and Lessing, and, in Hebrew, a novel eerily called

Whither? It will be years and years before I am smart enough, worldly enough, to read Alfred Kazin and Mary McCarthy.

In the spring, all of worldly Washington Square will wake up to 22
the luster of little green leaves.

QUESTIONS FOR READING AND WRITING

1. Is Ozick's essay merely a description of New York University in the 1940s, or did you find some of her observations similar to your own experiences at your university during the first week of class?
2. How does Ozick convey the special history of NYU? Point out the places where she reveals how a 17-year-old was unaware of the illustrious names that everyone held in awe. How does Ozick recreate the atmosphere of the times?
3. Write an autobiographical account of your own first week at your university, relating your adjustments to the particular atmosphere of your campus.

✦ Marge Piercy ✦
Rooms Without Walls

One critic has called Marge Piercy "a radical and a writer simultaneously." The poet, essayist, and novelist was born in Detroit, Michigan, in 1936 into a poor white family and grew up in a black neighborhood. She was the first in her family to graduate from college when she earned her A.B. from the University of Michigan in 1957 and then her M.A. from Northwestern in 1958. She has remained throughout her career a radical and an activist, first in civil rights, then in Students for a Democratic Society, and now in the women's movement. While angered at critics who want to "reduce" her poems to "political statements," she does not deny that they are meant to be useful to women who she hopes will put them on their refrigerator doors, read, and recite them. "What I mean by useful is simply that readers will find poems that speak to and for them. . . . To find ourselves spoken for in art gives dignity to our pain, our anger, our lust, our losses." Among her many books of poems are To Be of Use *(1973),* Living in the Open *(1978),* The Moon Is Always Female (1980), *and* Stone, Paper, Knife *(1983). Her fiction includes* Small Changes *(1973),* Woman on the Edge of Time *(1976), and* Fly Away Home *(1984). "Rooms Without Walls" shows another side of Piercy, one of "creative involvement in something outside myself."*

FOR MUCH OF MY ADULT LIFE I lived in city apartments. I traveled light and rarely kept a houseplant. Such plants as I was given died of neglect in a window over a radiator or were passed on to more suitable homes. 1

When I moved to Cape Cod, I did not imagine gardening. I had designed a house built into a hill, oriented for simple solar heat. What I moved into resembled a strip mine. My house was dug into the sand with a great gash sliced out of a hill that was rapidly washing away in the heavy rains of that February. Hardly a shriveled green thing remained where the bulldozer had scraped wide wounds into the land. At once I began to terrace and plant my sandpit, to stop erosion. I gardened with a book in one hand, understanding half of what I read and acting on it with Keystone Cop haste. 2

Some of those early plantings flourished and are still with us— 3
often in awkward placement, crowding each other, the house, or the paths. Some could not survive my rough ministrations or my ignorance. But the habit took. Once I had the hill secured, I began to clear brushy areas and to create outdoor rooms for their beauty and pleasure. Our garden is composed of such rooms—areas created for eating, reading, sunning, sitting, or working—rather than vistas.

Since then I have been a passionate gardener. Although I like to 4
walk at least four miles every day, in fine weather I am more likely to be found among the raspberries than at the beach. In January I go through the seed catalogs with sweaty palms, my lust triggered and my cupidity aroused till I order far more than I can ever plant. Those bulging finely netted melons, those apples glowing in their depths like Japanese lacquerware, those golden peppers sprinkling the page with dew, those roses in their dozens without a blemish of mite or black spot—like pornography they promise impossible consummations.

Yet the reality is pleasant enough. Every gardener wins some and 5
loses some, but the trick is to work with nature and the seasons and the microclimates of your land: the hot spots and the cold spots, the windy heights and the sheltered nooks. I garden organically, which means that I share my garden with a great many other creatures, small and not so small. My garden is also the birds' garden and the garden of moths, bees, toads, and the garter and king snakes. I feed the birds in winter and expect them to work, eating insect eggs and larvae. There are enough strawberries and cherries for all. I enjoy the mockingbird as much as my peonies. It balances.

Living in this new way changed my poems. I came to know the 6
seasons far more sharply. My city friends and my nongardening friends in the country think spring is when it gets warm. Spring starts for me in February when the crocuses bloom along the south wall. It cranks up in March as soon as I can work the soil enough to plant snow peas. By April I am harvesting my first salads, eccentric mélanges of violet leaves and flowers, mints, loose-leaf lettuce, Chinese cabbage, bok choy, turnip and mustard greens, Egyptian multiplying onions. I eat spring, sharp and pungent on my tongue.

Growing fruit and vegetables encourages a preference for eating 7
things in their seasons—tomatoes in August, not in January when

parsnips are fresh—and for eating local produce whenever possible. It leads to a sense of being attuned to the landscape in which I live, of being a part of nature.

My garden is shaggy and rampant. Herbs are mixed with flowers. Marigolds, borage with its starry blue flowers, nasturtiums and cosmos grow among vegetables. I am fond of daylilies and peonies with the capacity to outlive people and continue blooming long after I cease. We have no lawn, except for an informal area where rough grass planted itself. Most sitting areas are brick or flagstone. 8

We have four vegetable plants and three small orchards of dwarf trees, grapevines, and bush fruits (raspberries, blueberries, red currants, and gooseberries) linked by ornamental beds and walks lined with perennials. In our cutting garden, dahlia, canna, and annuals grow. At the front of the house, we use perennials, half sun- and half shade-lovers, under a dogwood and a flowering crab. On the woodside of the house, a rhododendron garden gradually gives way to the natural woods as the rhododendrons go from hybrid to wild. 9

My husband, Ira Wood, and I are both writers. Our work consists of sitting at computers pushing words and images and ideas around in our heads and then on a screen and then on paper. It is detail work, demanding, alone. Gardening takes us outside. It is physical and relaxing. We do it together and feel close. A novel may take anywhere from two to seven or more years to write and is another year in press before it emerges into the world. The changes you make in a garden are visible. You put in a new tree, walk away, turn, and your view is realigned. You create a path or change its surface from pine needles to flagstones. The tone of the landscape alters. 10

You decide to have a blue-and-white garden on the terrace. You put in a hedge of red musk roses. You create a pattern of living knots of thyme. The garden is a form of sculpture in which you work with the plants, cooperating, giving them what they want, and urging them to do what they most want to do. 11

The bed that is purple crocuses and white snowdrops in March is orange emperor tulips and white and orange narcissi in April; in June it is purple and pink irises; in late summer, blue lobelia and bachelor buttons; in fall, bronze and yellow chrysanthemums bloom there. Not only the colors change, but the shapes. The spears of the 12 iris remain, but the spaniel ears of the tulips have shriveled before chrysanthemums begin to rise above their neighbors. Time is one of the elements in the sculpture that is a garden.

Finally, gardening makes me observant of the natural world. I do 1
not have impressions of a month as rainy: I know how much and when it rained. I know which birds eat insects and which eat seeds or fruit. Once there were just bugs. Now assassin bugs are my friends, and squash bugs, my competitors. I know which caterpillar turns into which butterfly. I read the sky, I read the wind. I pay attention, where I used to walk wrapped in myself and my obsessions and my inner dreams. Gardening is an ongoing creative involvement in something outside myself.

QUESTIONS FOR READING AND WRITING

1. Piercy observes that gardening has the effect of being involved with something outside of oneself, of attuning one to seasonal changes, of making one more observant. In your own experience, think of examples of each of these effects, either through gardening or some other pastime.
2. Wendell Berry, William Jordan, and Annie Dillard (in "Sojourner") all write of the different effects of working in and observing nature. What are some of these effects? Do any contradict Piercy's enthusiasm? What similarities and differences are there between Jordan and Piercy?
3. Write an essay about focusing on the minutiae of nature, that is, learning to take the time to look closely at small details.

✦ Sylvia Plath ✦
Notebooks, 1961/2

Sylvia Plath (1932–1963) was born in Boston and graduated from Smith College in 1955. Her autobiographical novel, The Bell Jar *(1963), is about a student editor who attempts suicide (Plath attempted suicide at age 19); it was published several months before her successful suicide attempt at age 30. Her works include* The Colossus *(1960), and the posthumous* Crossing the Water *(1971) and* Johnny Panic and the Bible of Dreams *(1978). The following selection reveals Plath's fascination with the details of death. Her biographer, A. Alvarez, contends that with the poems in* Ariel *(1966) she made "poetry and death inseparable. The one could not exist without the other."*

June 7

WELL, PERCY B IS DYING. That is the verdict. Poor old Perce, 1
says everybody. Rose comes up almost every day. "Te-ed," she calls in her hysterical, throbbing voice. And Ted comes, from the study, the tennis court, the orchard, wherever, to lift the dying man from his armchair to his bed. He is very quiet afterward. He is a bag of bones, says Ted. I saw him in one "turn" or "do," lying back on the bed, toothless, all beakiness of nose and chin, eyes sunken as if they were not, shuddering and blinking in a fearful way. And all about the world is gold and green, dripping with laburnum and buttercups and the sweet stench of June. In the cottage the fire is on and it is dark twilight. The midwife said Percy would go into a coma this weekend and then "anything could happen." The sleeping pills the doctor gives him don't work, says Rose. He is calling all night: Rose, Rose, Rose. It has happened so quickly. First Rose stopped the doctor in January when I had the baby for a look at Percy's running eye and a check on his weight loss. Then he was in hospital for lung X rays. Then in again for a big surgery for "something in his lung." Did they find him so far gone with cancer they sewed him up again? Then home, walking, improving, but oddly quenched in his brightness and his songs. I found a wrinkled white paper bag of dusty jelly babies in the car yesterday from Rose. Then his five strokes. Now his diminishing.

Everybody has so easily given him up. Rose looks younger and younger. Mary G set her hair yesterday. She felt creepy about it, left baby Joyce with me and came over in between rinses in her frilly apron, dark-haired, white-skinned, with her high, sweet child-voice. Percy looked terrible since she had seen him last, she said. She thought cancer went wild if it was exposed to the air. The general sentiment of townsfolk: doctors just experiment on you in hospital. Once you're in, if you're old, you're a goner.

June 9

Met the rector coming out of house-building site across the road. He turned up the lane to the house with me. I could feel his professional gravity coming over him. He read the notice on Rose's door as I went on up, then went round back. "Sylvia!" I heard rose hiss behind me, and turned. She was pantomiming the rector's arrival and making lemon moues and rejecting motions with one hand, very chipper.

July 2

Percy B is dead. He died just at midnight, Monday, June 25th, and was buried Friday, June 29th, at 2:30. I find this difficult to believe. It all began with his eye watering, and Rose calling in the doctor, just after the birth of Nicholas. I have written a long poem, "Berck-Plage," about it. Very moved. Several terrible glimpses.

Ted had for some days stopped lifting Percy in and out of bed. He could not take his sleeping pills, or swallow. The doctor was starting to give him injections. Morphia? He was in pain when he was conscious. The nurse counted forty-five seconds between one breath and another. I decided to see him, I must see him, so went with Ted and Frieda. Rose and the smiling Catholic woman were lying on deck chairs in the yard. Rose's white face crimpled the minute she tried to speak. "The nurse told us to sit out. There's no more we can do. Isn't it awful to see him like this?" See him if you like, she told me. I went in through the quiet kitchen with Ted. The living room was full, still, hot with awful translation taking place. Percy lay back on a heap of white pillows in his striped pajamas, his face already passed from humanity, the nose a spiraling, fleshless beak in thin air, the chin fallen in a point from it, like an opposite pole, and the mouth like an inverted black heart stamped into the yellow flesh between, a great raucous breath coming and going there with great effort like an awful bird, caught, but about to depart. His eyes showed through partly open lids like dissolved soaps or a clotted pus. I was very sick at this and had a bad migraine over my left eye for the rest of the day. The end, even of so marginal a man, a horror.

When Ted and I drove out to Exeter to catch the London train 6
the following morning, the stone house was still, dewy and peaceful, the curtains stirring in the dawn air. He is dead, I said. Or he will be dead when we get back. He had died that night, Mother said over the phone, when I called her up the following evening.

Went down after his death, the next day, the 27th. Ted had been 7
down in the morning, said Percy was still on the bed, very yellow, his jaw bound and a book, a big brown book, propping it till it stiffened properly. When I went down they had just brought the coffin and put him in. The living room where he had lain was in an upheaval—bed rolled from the wall, mattresses on the lawn, sheets and pillows washed and airing. He lay in the sewing room, or parlor, in a long coffin of orangey soap-colored oak with silver handles, the lid propped against the wall at his head with a silver scroll: Percy B, Died June 25th, 1962. The raw date a shock. A sheet covered the coffin. Rose lifted it. A pale white, beaked face, as of paper, rose under the veil that covered the hole cut in the glued white cloth cover. The mouth looked glued, the face powdered. She quickly put down the sheet. I hugged her. She kissed me and burst into tears. The dark, rotund sister from London with purple eye circles deplored: They have no hearse, they have only a cart. Friday, the day of the funeral, hot and blue, with theatrical white clouds passing. Ted and I, dressed in hot blacks, passed the church, saw the bowler-hatted men coming out of the gate with a high spider-wheeled black cart. They are going to call for the corpse, we said; we left a grocery order. The awful feeling of great grins coming onto the face, unstoppable. A relief; this is the hostage for death, we are safe for the time being. We strolled round the church in the bright heat, the pollarded green limes like green balls, the far hills red, just plowed, and one stooked with newly glittering wheat. Debated whether to wait out, or go in. Elsie, with her stump foot, was going in. Then Grace,

Jim's wife. We went in. Heard priest meeting corpse at gate, incanting, coming close. Hair-raising. We stood. The flowery casket, nodding and flirting its petals, led up the aisle. The handsome mourners in black down to gloves and handbag, Rose, three daughters including the marble-beautiful model, one husband, Mrs. G and the Catholic, smiling, only not smiling, the smile in abeyance, suspended. I hardly heard a word of the service, Mr. Lane for once quenched the grandeur of ceremony, a vessel, as it should be.

Then we followed the funeral party after the casket out the side door to the street going up the hill to the cemetery. Behind the high black cart, which had started up, with the priest swaying in black and white, at a decorous pace, the funeral cars—one car, a taxi, then Herbert G, looking green and scared, in his big new red car. We got in with him. "Well, old Perce always wanted to be buried in Devon." You could see he felt he was next. I felt tears come. Ted motioned me to look at the slow, uplifted faces of children in the primary school yard, all seated on rest rugs, utterly without grief, only bland curiosity, turning after us. We got out at the cemetery gate, the day blazing. Followed the black backs of the women. Six bowler hats of the bearers left at the first yew bushes in the grass. The coffin on boards, words said, ashes to ashes—that is what remained, not glory, not heaven. The amazingly narrow coffin lowered into the narrow red earth opening, left. The women led round, in a kind of goodbye circle, Rose rapt and beautiful and frozen, the Catholic dropping a handful of earth, which clattered. A great impulse welled in me to cast earth also, but it seemed as if it might be indecent, hurrying Percy into oblivion. We left the open grave. An unfinished feeling. Is he to be left up there uncovered, all alone? Walked home over the back hill, gathering immense stalks of fuchsia foxgloves and swinging out jackets in the heat.

QUESTIONS FOR READING AND WRITING

1. What is your first recollection of the death of someone? Does Plath's diary seem obsessive about the subject of death?
2. Certain observations recur in different entries. For example, Rose growing younger and more beautiful, the birdlike appearance of

Percy, the combination of indifference and great sorrow. Explain the cumulative effect of these observations.

3. How is the observation about the primary-school children in paragraph 8 appropriate?
4. Write an account of the death or funeral of someone. Include your recollections of your own feelings as well as your observations of others.

✦ May Sarton ✦
Journal of a Solitude

*Born in Belgium in 1912, May Sarton came to the United States as a child. After many years of writing, she settled in a small town in New Hampshire, and later moved to Maine. Her career began in the theater, she has written dozens of novels, and she has won numerous awards for her poetry. Yet it is her journals and autobiographies—*Plant Dreaming Deep *(1968) and* Journal of a Solitude *(1973)—that are her most popular works. As the following selection suggests, there is a bone-baring honesty about Sarton's private meditations and her relationships with friends that touches a nerve in her readers, since her willingness to share even the most intimate details is met by the reader's recognition of similar thoughts and emotions.*

September 15th

BEGIN HERE. IT IS RAINING. I look out on the maple, where a few leaves have turned yellow, and listen to Punch, the parrot, talking to himself and to the rain ticking gently against the windows. I am here alone for the first time in weeks, to take up my "real" life again at last. That is what is strange—that friends, even passionate love, are not my real life unless there is time alone in which to explore and to discover what is happening or has happened. Without the interruptions, nourishing and maddening, this life would become arid. Yet I taste it fully only when I am alone here and "the house and I resume old conversations."

On my desk, small pink roses. Strange how often the autumn roses look sad, fade quickly, frost-browned at the edges! But these are lovely, bright, singing pink. On the mantel, in the Japanese jar, two sprays of white lilies, recurved, maroon pollen on the stamens, and a branch of peony leaves turned a strange pinkish-brown. It is an elegant bouquet; *shibui*, the Japanese would call it. When I am alone the flowers are really seen; I can pay attention to them. They are felt as presences. Without them I would die. Why do I say that? Partly because they change before my eyes. They live and die in a few days; they keep me closely in touch with process, with growth, and also with dying. I am floated on their moments.

3 The ambience here is order and beauty. That is what frightens me when I am first alone again. I feel inadequate. I have made an open place, a place for meditation. What if I cannot find myself inside it?

4 I think of these pages as a way of doing that. For a long time now, every meeting with another human being has been a collision. I feel too much, sense too much, am exhausted by the reverberations after even the simplest conversation. But the deep collision is and has been with my unregenerate, tormenting, and tormented self. I have written every poem, every novel, for the same purpose—to find out what I think, to know where I stand. I am unable to become what I see. I feel like an inadequate machine, a machine that breaks down at crucial moments, grinds to a dreadful halt, "won't go," or, even worse, explodes in some innocent person's face.

5 *Plant Dreaming Deep* has brought me many friends of the work (and also, harder to respond to, people who think they have found in me an intimate friend). But I have begun to realize that, without my own intention, that book gives a false view. The anguish of my life here—its rages—is hardly mentioned. Now I hope to break through into the rough rocky depths, to the matrix itself. There is violence there and anger never resolved. I live alone, perhaps for no good reason, for the reason that I am an impossible creature, set apart by a temperament I have never learned to use as it could be used, thrown off by a word, a glance, a rainy day, or one drink too many. My need to be alone is balanced against my fear of what will happen when suddenly I enter the huge empty silence if I cannot find support there. I go up to Heaven and down to Hell in an hour, and keep alive only by imposing upon myself inexorable routines. I write too many letters and too few poems. It may be outwardly silent here but in the back of my mind is a clamor of human voices, too many needs, hopes, fears. I hardly ever sit still without being haunted by the "undone" and the "unsent." I often feel exhausted, but it is not my work that tires (work is a rest); it is the effort of pushing away the lives and needs of others before I can come to the work with any freshness and zest.

September 17th

6 Cracking open the inner world again, writing even a couple of pages, threw me back into depression, not made easier by the

weather, two gloomy days of darkness and rain. I was attacked by a storm of tears, those tears that appear to be related to frustration, to buried anger, and come upon me without warning. I woke yesterday so depressed that I did not get up till after eight.

I drove to Brattleboro to read poems at the new Unitarian church there in a state of dread and exhaustion. How to summon the vitality needed? I had made an arrangement of religious poems, going back to early books and forward into the new book not yet published. I suppose it went all right—at least it was not a disaster—but I felt (perhaps I am wrong) that the kind, intelligent people gathered in a big room looking out on pine trees did not really want to think about God, His absence (many of the poems speak of that) or His presence. Both are too frightening.

On the way back I stopped to see Perley Cole, my dear old friend, who is dying, separated from his wife, and has just been moved from a Dickensian nursing home into what seems like a far better one. He grows more transparent every day, a skeleton or nearly. Clasping his hand, I fear to break a bone. Yet the only real communication between us now (he is very deaf) is a handclasp. I want to lift him in my arms and hold him like a baby. He is dying a terribly lonely death. Each time I see him he says, "It is rough" or "I did not think it would end like this."

Everywhere I look about this place I see his handiwork: the three small trees by a granite boulder that he pruned and trimmed so they pivot the whole meadow; the new shady border he dug out for me one of the last days he worked here; the pruned-out stone wall between my field and the church. The second field where he cut brush twice a year and cleared out to the stone wall is growing back to wilderness now. What is done here has to be done over and over and needs the dogged strength of a man like Perley. I could have never managed it alone. We cherished this piece of land together, and fought together to bring it to some semblance of order and beauty.

I like to think that this last effort of Perley's had a certain ease 1
about it, a game compared to the hard work of his farming years, and a game where his expert knowledge and skill could be well used. How he enjoyed teasing me about my ignorance!

While he scythed and trimmed, I struggled in somewhat the 1
same way at my desk here, and we were each aware of the compan-

ionship. We each looked forward to noon, when I could stop for the day and he sat on a high stool in the kitchen, drank a glass or two of sherry with me, said, "Court's in session!" and then told me some tall tale he had been cogitating all morning.

It was a strange relationship, for he knew next to nothing about 12
my life, really; yet below all the talk we recognized each other as the same kind. He enjoyed my anger as much as I enjoyed his. Perhaps that was part of it. Deep down there was understanding, not of the facts of our lives so much as of our essential natures. Even now in his hard, lonely end he has immense dignity. But I wish there were some way to make it easier. I leave him with bitter resentment against the circumstances of this death. "I know. But I do not approve. And I am not resigned."

In the mail a letter from a twelve-year-old child, enclosing 13
poems, her mother having pushed her to ask my opinion. This child does really look at things, and I can write something helpful, I think. But it is troubling how many people expect applause, recognition, when they have not even begun to learn an art or a craft. Instant success is the order of the day; "I want it *now*!" I wonder whether this is not part of our corruption by machines. Machines do things very quickly and outside the natural rhythm of life, and we are indignant if a car doesn't start at the first try. So the few things that we still do, such as cooking (though there are TV dinners!), knitting, gardening, anything at all that cannot be hurried, have a very particular value.

September 18th

The value of solitude—one of its values—is, of course, that there 14
is nothing to *cushion* against attacks from within, just as there is nothing to help balance at times of particular stress or depression. A few moments of desultory conversation with dear Arnold Miner, when he comes to take the trash, may calm an inner storm. But the storm, painful as it is, might have had some truth in it. So sometimes one has simply to endure a period of depression for what it may hold of illumination if one can live through it, attentive to what it exposes or demands.

The reasons for depression are not so interesting as the way one 15
handles it, simply to stay alive. This morning I woke at four and lay

awake for an hour or so in a bad state. It is raining again. I got up finally and went about the daily chores, waiting for the sense of doom to lift—and what did it was watering the house plants. Suddenly joy came back because I was fulfilling a simple need, a living one. Dusting never has this effect (and that may be why I am such a poor housekeeper!), but feeding the cats when they are hungry, giving Punch clean water, makes me suddenly feel calm and happy.

Whatever peace I know rests in the natural world, in feeling 1
myself a part of it, even in a small way. Maybe the gaiety of the Warner family, their wisdom, comes from this, that they work close to nature all the time. As simple as that? But it is not simple. Their life requires patient understanding, imagination, the power to endure constant adversity—the weather, for example! To go with, not against the elements, an inexhaustible vitality summoned back each day to do the same tasks, to feed the animals, clean out barns and pens, keep that complex world alive.

September 19th

The sun is out. It rose through the mist, making the raindrops 1
sparkle on the lawn. Now there is blue sky, warm air, and I have just created a wonder—two large autumn crocuses plus a small spray of pink single chrysanthemums and a piece of that silvery leaf (artemisia? arethusa?) whose name I forget in the Venetian glass in the cosy room. May they be benign presences toward this new day!

Neurotic depression is so boring because it is repetitive, literally 1
a wheel that turns and turns. Yesterday I broke off from the wheel when I read a letter from Sister Mary David. She is now manager of a co-op in the small town in South Carolina where she has chosen to work. Always her letters bring me the shock of what is really going on and the recognition of what one single person can do.

✦✦✦✦✦

I felt lifted up on the joy of sending a check and knowing that 1
money would be changed at once into help. We are all fed up, God knows, with institutional charity, with three requests from the same organization in a week and often one to which a check had been mailed two weeks earlier. We are all, receivers and givers alike, computerized. It feels arid compared to the direct human way shown by Sister Mary David; she was not sent down by her order,

but found her own way there on a summer project and then decided that she must stay, and somehow got permission to do so. This must be the tradition of the Sisters of Mercy.

The most hopeful sign, the only one, in these hard times is how 20
much individual initiative manages to make its way up through the asphalt, so many tough shoots of human imagination. And I think at once of Dr. Gatch who started in Beaufort, South Carolina to heal sick blacks on his own. Whatever his tragic end, he did force the situation down there—near starvation—on the attention of Congress and the people of the United States. We have to believe that each person *counts*, counts as a creative force that can move mountains. The great thing Gene McCarthy did, of course, was to prove this on the political scene. While we worked for him we believed that politics might give way to the human voice. It is tragic that the human flaws can then wreck everything—McCarthy's vanity, Gatch's relying on drugs to keep going. We can do anything, or almost, but how balanced, magnanimous, and modest one has to be to do anything! And also how patient. It is as true in the arts as anywhere else.

So . . . to work. It is not a *non sequitur.* I shall never be one of 21
those directly active (except as a teacher, occasionally), but now and then I am made aware that my work, odd though it seems, does help people. But it is only in these last years at Nelson that I have known that for sure.

QUESTIONS FOR READING AND WRITING

1. Sarton writes in her journal that her "need to be alone is balanced against my fear of what will happen when suddenly I enter the huge and empty silence if I cannot find support there. I go up to Heaven and down to hell in an hour" (paragraph 5). How is this a very poignant statement of the human need for solitude and human companionship?
2. Why does Sarton focus on the condition of Perley Cole? How is his condition similar to and different from hers?
3. Write an essay contrasting the solitude with the sociable person. Who is more psychologically healthy? Who is more likely to be creative? Why?

✦ Paul Theroux ✦

Butlin's Holiday Camp

Paul Theroux's interest in travel dates back to his many years as an expatriate living in the Orient and Africa. In addition to his novels, the best known of which was made into the movie Mosquito Coast, *his books on train travel—*The Great Railway Bazaar *(1975),* The Old Patagonian Express *(1979), and* Riding the Iron Rooster *(1988)—are classics of the genre. In this excerpt from* Kingdom by the Sea *(1983), Theroux presents a truly ugly picture of what has been done at the English seacoast in the name of vacation for the masses.*

TO THE EAST, beyond the gray puddly foreshore—the tide was out half a mile—I saw the bright flags of Butlin's, Minehead, and vowed to make a visit. Ever since Bognor I had wanted to snoop inside a coastal holiday camp, but I had passed the fences and gates without going in. It was not possible to make a casual visit. Holiday camps were surrounded by prison fences, with coils of barbed wire at the top. There were dog patrols and BEWARE signs stenciled with skulls. The main entrances were guarded and had turnstiles and a striped barrier that was raised to let certain vehicles through. Butlin's guests had to show passes in order to enter. The whole affair reminded me a little of Jonestown.

And these elaborate security measures fueled my curiosity. What exactly was going on in there? It was no use my peering through the chain-link fence—all I could see at this Butlin's were the Boating Lake and the reception area and some snorers on deck chairs. Clearly, it was very large. Later I discovered that the camp was designed to accommodate fourteen thousand people. That was almost twice the population of Minehead! They called it "Butlinland" and they said it had everything.

I registered as a Day Visitor. I paid a fee. I was given a brochure and a booklet and *Your Holiday Programme*, with a list of the day's events. The security staff seemed wary of me. I had ditched my knapsack in the boardinghouse, but I was still wearing my leather jacket and oily hiking shoes. My knees were muddy. So as not to alarm the gatekeepers, I had pocketed my binoculars. Most of the

Butlin's guests wore sandals and short sleeves, and some wore funny hats—holiday high spirits. The weather was overcast and cold and windy. The flags out front were as big as bedsheets and made a continual cracking. I was the only person at Butlin's dressed for this foul weather. I felt like a commando. It made some people there suspicious.

With its barrackslike buildings and its forbidding fences, it had 4
the prison look of the Butlin's at Bognor. A prison look was also an army-camp look, and just as depressing. This one was the more scary for being brightly painted. It had been tacked together out of plywood and tin panels in primary colors. I had not seen flimsier buildings in England. They were so ugly, they were not pictured anywhere in the Butlin's brochure, but instead shown as simplified floor plans in blue diagrams. They were called "flatlets" and "suites." The acres of barracks were called the Accommodation Area.

It really was like Jonestown! The Accommodation Area with the 5
barracks was divided into camps—Green, Yellow, Blue, and Red Camp. There was a central dining room and a Nursery Center. There was a Camp Chapel. There was also a miniature railway and a chairlift and a monorail—all of them useful: it was a large area to cover on foot. It was just the sort of place the insane preacher must have imagined when he brought his desperate people to Guyana. It was self-contained and self-sufficient. With a fence that high, it had to be.

The Jonestown image was powerful, but Butlin's also had the 6
features of a tinselly New Jerusalem. This, I felt, would be the English coastal town of the future, if most English people had their way. It was already an English town of a sort—glamorized and less substantial than the real thing, but all the same recognizably an English town, with the usual landmarks, a cricket pitch, a football field, a launderette, a supermarket, a bank, a betting shop, and a number of take-away food joints. Of course, it was better organized and had more amenities than most English towns the same size—that was why it was popular. It was also a permanent fun fair. One of Butlin's boasts was "No dirty dishes to wash!" Another was "There is absolutely no need to queue!" No dishwashing, no standing in line—it came near to parody, like a vacation in a Polish joke. But these promises were a sort of timid hype; England was a country of

modest expectations, and no dishes and no lines were part of the English dream.

It was not expensive—£178 ($313) a week for a family of four, and that included two meals a day. It was mostly families—young parents with small children. They slept in a numbered cubicle in the barracks at one of the four camps, and they ate at a numbered table in one of the dining rooms, and they spent the day amusing themselves.

The Windsor Sports Ground (most of the names had regal echoes, an attempt at respectability) and the Angling Lake were not being used by anyone the day I was there. But the two snooker and table tennis rooms were very busy; each room was about half the size of a football field and held scores of tables. No waiting! There was bingo in the Regency Building, in a massive room with a glass wall, which was the bottom half of the indoor swimming pool—fluttering legs and skinny feet in water the color of chicken bouillon. There was no one on the Boating Lake, and no one in the outdoor pool, and the chapel was empty. The Crazy Golf was not popular. So much for the free amusements.

"Yes, it *is* true, nearly everything at Butlin's is free!" the brochure said.

But what most of the people were doing was not free. They were feeding coins into fruit machines and one-armed bandits in the Fun Room. They were playing pinball. They were also shopping for stuffed toys and curios, or buying furs in the Fur Shop, or getting their hair done at the Hairdressing Salon. They were eating. The place had four fish-and-chip shops. There were tea shops, coffee bars, and candy stores. They cost money, but people seemed to be spending fairly briskly. They were also drinking. There were about half a dozen bars. The Embassy Bar (Greek statues, fake chandeliers, red wallpaper) was quite full, although it was the size of a barn. The Exmoor Bar had a hundred and fifty-seven tables and probably held a thousand drinkers. It was the scale of the place that was impressive—the scale and the shabbiness.

It was not Disneyland. Disneyland was a blend of technology and farce. It was mostly fantasy, a tame kind of surrealism, a comfortable cartoon in three dimensions. But the more I saw of Butlin's, the more it resembled English life; it was very close to reality in its narrowness, its privacies, and its pleasures. It was

England without work—leisure had been overtaken by fatigue and dullwittedness: electronic games were easier than sports, and eating junk food had become another recreation. No one seemed to notice how plain the buildings were, how tussocky the grass was, or that everywhere there was a pervasive sizzle and smell of food frying in hot fat.

In that sense, too, it was like a real town. People walked around believing that it was all free; but most pastimes there cost money, and some were very expensive—like a ticket to the cabaret show that night, Freddie and the Dreamers, a group of middle-aged musicians who were a warmed-over version of their sixties' selves. 12

If it had a futuristic feel, it was the deadened imagination and the zombie-like attitude of the strolling people, condemned to a week or two of fun under cloudy skies. And it was also the arrangements for children. The kids were taken care of—they could be turned loose in Butlin's in perfect safety. They couldn't get hurt or lost. There was a high fence around the camp. There was a Nursery Chalet Patrol and a Child Listening Service and a large Children's Playground. In the planned cities of the future, provisions like this would be made for children. 13

Most of the events were for children, apart from whist and bingo. As a Day Visitor, I had my choice of the Corona Junior Fancy Dress Competition, a Kids' Quiz Show, the Trampoline Test, the Donkey Derby, or the Beaver and Junior Talent Contest Auditions. The Donkey Derby was being held in a high wind on Gaiety Green—screaming children and plodding animals. I went to the talent show auditions in the Gaiety Revue Theatre. A girl of eight did a suggestive dance to a lewd pop song; two sisters sang a song about Jesus; Amanda and Kelly sang "Daisy"; and Miranda recited a poem much too fast. Most of the parents were elsewhere—playing the one-armed bandits and drinking beer. 14

I wandered into the Camp Chapel ("A Padre is available in the Centre at all times"). There was a notice stuck to the chapel door: *At all three services prayers are being said for our Forces in the Southern Atlantic.* I scrutinized the Visitors' Book. It asked for nationality, and people had listed "Welsh" or "Cornish" or "English" or "Scottish" next to their names. There was a scattering of Irish. But after the middle of April people had started to put "British" for nationality—that was after the Falklands War had begun. 15

I found three ladies having tea in the Regency Building. Daphne Bunsen, from Bradford, said. "We don't talk about this Falklands business here, 'cause we're on holiday. It's a right depressing soobject."

"Anyway," Mavis Hattery said, "there's only one thing to say."

What was that?

"I say, 'Get it over with! Stop playing cat and mouse!'"

Mrs. Bunsen said they loved Butlin's. They had been here before and would certainly come back. Their sadness was they could not stay longer. "And Mavis' room is right posh!"

"I paid a bit extra," Mrs. Hattery said. "I have a fitted carpet in my shally."

It was easy to mock Butlin's for its dreariness and its brainless pleasures. It was an inadequate answer to leisure, but there were scores of similar camps all around the coast, so there was no denying its popularity. It combined the security and equality of prison with the vulgarity of an amusement park. I asked children what their parents were doing. Usually the father was playing billiards and the mother was shopping, but many said their parents were sleeping—having a kip. Sleeping until noon, not having to cook or mind children, and being a few steps away from the chippy, the bar, and the betting shop—it was a sleazy paradise in which people were treated more or less like animals in a zoo. In time to come, there would be more holiday camps on the British coast— "Cheap and cheerful," Daphne Bunsen said.

Butlin's was staffed by "Redcoats"—young men and women who wore red blazers. It was a Redcoat named Rod Firsby who told me that the camp could accommodate fourteen thousand people ("but nine thousand is about average"). Where did the people come from? I asked. He said they came from all over. It was when I asked him what sorts of jobs they did that he laughed.

"Are you joking, sunshine?" he said.

I said no, I wasn't.

He said, "Half the men here are unemployed. That's the beauty of Butlin's—you can pay for it with your dole money."

QUESTIONS FOR READING AND WRITING

1. Does Butlin's remind you of any place in America? Where? What characteristics do you find in common?
2. Theroux continually compares Butlin's with Jonestown, a settlement in Guiana where a religious sect led by the Reverend Jim Jones committed mass suicide. What is the point of Theroux's comparison? He also focuses on the different activities for the adults and the children. Why?
3. Compare Theroux's account of an English seaside holiday camp with Martin Amis' "In Hefnerland." Why is such organized "fun" insidious?
4. Write an essay on a vacation that was so well organized that it killed any spontaneous pleasure you might have had.

✦ E. B. White ✦

Once More to the Lake

E. B. (Elwyn Brooks) White (1899–1985) is best known to the public as the author of several children's books, among them Charlotte's Web *(1952) and* Stuart Little *(1945). Born in Mount Vernon, New York, he joined the staff of* The New Yorker, *with which his name is now virtually synonymous. The simple direct style of his personal essays transforms the minutiae of daily living into details of much greater significance. "Once More to the Lake," his most famous essay, presents the double vision of the writer, at once both a son and a father, revisiting with his son a Maine lake that was once the scene of summer vacations with his father.*

ONE SUMMER, along about 1904, my father rented a camp on a lake in Maine and took us all there for the month of August. We all got ringworm from some kittens and had to rub Pond's Extract on our arms and legs night and morning, and my father rolled over in a canoe with all his clothes on; but outside of that the vacation was a success and from then on none of us ever thought there was any place in the world like that lake in Maine. We returned summer after summer—always on August 1st for one month. I have since become a salt-water man, but sometimes in summer there are days when the restlessness of the tides and the fearful cold of the sea water and the incessant wind which blows across the afternoon and into the evening make me wish for the placidity of a lake in the woods. A few weeks ago this feeling got so strong I bought myself a couple of bass hooks and a spinner and returned to the lake where we used to go, for a week's fishing and to revisit old haunts.

I took along my son, who had never had any fresh water up his nose and who had seen lily pads only from train windows. On the journey over to the lake I began to wonder what it would be like. I wondered how time would have marred this unique, this holy spot—the coves and streams, the hills that the sun set behind, the camps and the paths behind the camps. I was sure the tarred road would have found it out and I wondered in what other ways it would be desolated. It is strange how much you can remember about places like that once you allow your mind to return into the grooves which lead back. You remember one thing, and that suddenly reminds you of another thing. I guess I remembered clearest of all the early mornings, when the lake was cool and motionless, remembered how the bedroom smelled of the lumber it was made of and of the wet woods whose scent entered through the screen. The partitions in the camp were thin and did not extend clear to the top of the rooms, and as I was always the first up I would dress softly so as not to wake the others, and sneak out into the sweet outdoors and start out in the canoe, keeping close along the shore in the long shadows of the pines. I remembered being very careful never to rub my paddle against the gunwale for fear of disturbing the stillness of the cathedral.

The lake had never been what you would call a wild lake. There 3
were cottages sprinkled around the shores, and it was in farming country although the shores of the lake were quite heavily wooded. Some of the cottages were owned by nearby farmers, and you would live at the shore and eat your meals at the farmhouse. That's what our family did. But although it wasn't wild, it was a fairly large and undisturbed lake and there were places in it which, to a child at least, seemed infinitely remote and primeval.

I was right about the tar: it led to within half a mile of the shore. 4
But when I got back there, with my boy, and we settled into a camp near a farmhouse and into the kind of summertime I had known, I could tell that it was going to be pretty much the same as it had been before—I knew it, lying in bed the first morning, smelling the bedroom, and hearing the boy sneak quietly out and go off along the shore in a boat. I began to sustain the illusion that he was I, and therefore by simple transposition, that I was my father. This sensation persisted, kept cropping up all the time we were there. It was not an entirely new feeling, but in this setting it grew much stronger. I seemed to be living a dual existence. I would be in the middle of some simple act, I would be picking up a bait box or laying down a table fork, or I would be saying something, and suddenly it would be not I but my father who was saying the words or making the gesture. It gave me a creepy sensation.

We went fishing the first morning. I felt the same damp moss 5
covering the worms in the bait can, and saw the dragonfly alight on

the tip of my rod as it hovered a few inches from the surface of the water. It was the arrival of this fly that convinced me beyond any doubt that everything was as it always had been, that the years were a mirage and there had been no years. The small waves were the same, chucking the rowboat under the chin as we fished at anchor, and the boat was the same boat, the same color green and the ribs broken in the same places, and under the floor-boards the same fresh-water leavings and debris—the dead helgramite, the wisps of moss, the rusty discarded fishhook, the dried blood from yesterday's catch. We stared silently at the tips of our rods, at the dragonflies that came and went. I lowered the tip of mine into the water, tentatively, pensively dislodging the fly, which darted two feet away, poised, darted two feet back, and came to a rest again a little farther up the rod. There had been no years between the ducking of this dragonfly and the other one—the one that was part of memory. I looked at the boy, who was silently watching his fly, and it was my hands that held his rod, my eyes watching. I felt dizzy and didn't know which rod I was at the end of.

We caught two bass, hauling them in briskly as though they were mackerel, pulling them over the side of the boat in a businesslike manner without any landing net, and stunning them with a blow on the back of the head. When we got back for a swim before lunch, the lake was exactly where we had left it, the same number of inches from the dock, and there was only the merest suggestion of a breeze. This seemed an utterly enchanted sea, this lake you could leave to its own devices for a few hours and come back to, and find that it had not stirred, this constant and trustworthy body of water. In the shallows, the dark, watersoaked sticks and twigs, smooth and old, were undulating in clusters on the bottom against the clean ribbed sand, and the track of the mussel was plain. A school of minnows swam by, each minnow with its small individual shadow, doubling the attendance, so clear and sharp in the sunlight. Some of the other campers were in swimming, along the shore, one of them with a cake of soap, and the water felt thin and clear and unsubstantial. Over the years there had been this person with the cake of soap, this cultist, and here he was. There had been no years.

Up to the farmhouse to dinner through the teeming, dusty field, the road under our sneakers was only a two-track road. The middle track was missing, the one with the marks of the hooves and the splotches of dried, flaky manure. There had always been three tracks to choose from in choosing which track to walk in; now the choice was narrowed down to two. For a moment I missed terribly the middle alternative. But the way led past the tennis court, and something about the way it lay there in the sun reassured me; the tape had loosened along the backline, the alleys were green with plantains and other weeds, and the net (installed in June and removed in September) sagged in the dry noon, and the whole place steamed with midday heat and hunger and emptiness. There was a choice of pie for dessert, and one was blueberry and one was apple, and the waitresses were the same country girls, there having been no passage of time, only the illusion of it as in a dropped curtain—the waitresses were still fifteen; their hair had been washed, that was the only difference—they had been to the movies and seen the pretty girls with the clean hair.

Summertime, oh summertime, pattern of life indelible, the fade- 8
proof lake, the woods unshatterable, the pasture with the sweetfern and the juniper forever and ever, summer without end; this was the background, and the life along the shore was the design, the cottages with their innocent and tranquil design, their tiny docks with the flagpole and the American flag floating against the white clouds in the blue sky, the little paths over the roots of the trees leading from camp to camp and the paths leading back to the outhouses and the can of lime for sprinkling, and at the souvenir counters at the store the miniature birch-bark canoes and the post cards that showed things looking a little better than they looked. This was the American family at play, escaping the city heat, wondering whether the newcomers in the camp at the head of the cove were "common" or "nice," wondering whether it was true that the people who drove up for Sunday dinner at the farmhouse were turned away because there wasn't enough chicken.

It seemed to me, as I kept remembering all this, that those times 9
and those summers had been infinitely precious and worth saving. There had been jollity and peace and goodness. The arriving (at the beginning of August) had been so big a business in itself, at the railway station the farm wagon drawn up, the first smell of the pine-laden air, the first glimpse of the smiling farmer, and the great importance of the trunks and your father's enormous authority in such matters, and the feel of the wagon under you for the long

ten-mile haul, and at the top of the last long hill catching the first view of the lake after eleven months of not seeing this cherished body of water. The shouts and cries of the other campers when they saw you, and the trunks to be unpacked, to give up their rich burden. (Arriving was less exciting nowadays, when you sneaked up in your car and parked it under a tree near the camp and took out the bags and in five minutes it was all over, no fuss, no loud wonderful fuss about trunks.)

Peace and goodness and jollity. The only thing that was wrong now, really, was the sound of the place, an unfamiliar nervous sound of the outboard motors. This was the note that jarred, the one thing that would sometimes break the illusion and set the years moving. In those other summertimes all motors were inboard; and when they were at a little distance, the noise they made was a sedative, an ingredient of summer sleep. They were one-cylinder and two-cylinder engines, and some were make-and-break and some were jump-spark, but they all made a sleepy sound across the lake. The one-lungers throbbed and fluttered, and the twin-cylinder ones purred and purred, and that was a quiet sound too. But now the campers all had outboards. In the daytime, in the hot mornings, these motors made a petulant, irritable sound; at night, in the still evening when the afterglow lit the water, they whined about one's ears like mosquitoes. My boy loved our rented outboard, and his great desire was to achieve singlehanded mastery over it, and authority, and he soon learned the trick of choking it a little (but not too much), and the adjustment of the needle valve. Watching him I would remember the things you could do with the old one-cylinder engine with the heavy flywheel, how you could have it eating out of your hand if you got really close to it spiritually. Motor boats in those days didn't have clutches, and you would make a landing by shutting off the motor at the proper time and coasting in with a dead rudder. But there was a way of reversing them, if you learned the trick, by cutting the switch and putting it on again exactly on the final dying revolution of the flywheel, so that it would kick back against compression and begin reversing. Approaching a dock in a strong following breeze, it was difficult to slow up sufficiently by the ordinary coasting method, and if a boy felt he had complete mastery over his motor, he was tempted to keep it running beyond its time and then reverse it a few feet from the dock. It took a cool nerve, because if you threw the switch a twentieth of a second too soon you would catch the flywheel when it still had speed enough to go up past center, and the boat would leap ahead, charging bull-fashion at the dock.

We had a good week at the camp. The bass were biting well and the sun shone endlessly, day after day. We would be tired at night and lie down in the accumulated heat of the little bedrooms after the long hot day and the breeze would stir almost imperceptibly outside and the smell of the swamp drift in through the rusty screens. Sleep would come easily and in the morning the red squirrel would be on the roof, tapping out his gay routine. I kept remembering everything, lying in bed in the mornings—the small steamboat that had a long rounded stern like the lip of a Ubangi, and how quietly she ran on the moonlight sails, when the older boys played their mandolins and the girls sang and we ate doughnuts dipped in sugar, and how sweet the music was on the water in the shining night, and what it had felt like to think about girls then. After breakfast we would go up to the store and the things were in the same place—the minnows in a bottle, the plugs and spinners disarranged and pawed over by the youngsters from the boys' camp, the fig newtons and the Beeman's gum. Outside, the road was tarred and cars stood in front of the store. Inside, all was just as it had always been, except there was more Coca-Cola and not so much Moxie and root beer and birch beer and sarsaparilla. We would walk out with a bottle of pop apiece and sometimes the pop would backfire up our noses and hurt. We explored the streams, quietly, where the turtles slid off the sunny logs and dug their way into the soft bottom; and we lay on the town wharf and fed worms to the tame bass. Everywhere we went I had trouble making out which was I, the one walking at my side, the one walking in my pants. 11

One afternoon while we were there at that lake a thunderstorm came up. It was like the revival of an old melodrama that I had seen long ago with childish awe. The second-act climax of the drama of the electrical disturbance over a lake in America had not changed in any important respect. This was the big scene, still the big scene. The whole thing was so familiar, the first feeling of oppression and heat and a general air around camp of not wanting to go very far away. In midafternoon (it was all the same) a curious darkening of 12 the sky, and a lull in everything that had made life tick; and then the way the boats suddenly swung the other way at their moorings with the coming of a breeze out of the new quarter, and the premonitory rumble. Then the kettle drum, then the snare, then the bass drum and cymbals, then crackling light against the dark, and the gods grinning and licking their chops in the hills. Afterward the calm, the rain steadily rustling in the calm lake, the return of light and hope and spirits, and the campers running out in joy and relief to go swimming in the rain, their bright cries perpetuating the deathless joke about how they were getting simply drenched, and the children screaming with delight at the new sensation of bathing in the rain, and the joke about getting drenched linking the generations in a strong indestructible chain. And the comedian who waded in carrying an umbrella.

When the others went swimming my son said he was going in too. 13
He pulled his dripping trunks from the line where they had hung all through the shower, and wrung them out. Languidly, and with no thought of going in, I watched him, his hard little body, skinny and bare, saw him wince slightly as he pulled up around his vitals the small, soggy, icy garment. As he buckled the swollen belt suddenly my groin felt the chill of death.

QUESTIONS FOR READING AND WRITING

1. White's essay is about the connections between generations: how everything is different, yet essentially things never change. For another version of this theme, read N. Scott Momaday's "The Way to Rainy Mountain." Have you experienced a place at two different times and found that place virtually untouched by the passage of time?
2. The more significant theme of White's essay is the shifting identities of father and son. As White puts it, "I began to sustain the illusion that he was I, and therefore by simple transposition, that I was my father" (paragraph 4). This, of course, partly explains the essay's final line. What examples does White provide where he is his father and his son is the younger White?
3. E. B. White is famous for his clear, functional writing style, two hallmarks of which are parallelism and repetition. Cite examples of

these in the essay. Why is the description of the thunderstorm in the second-from-last paragraph particularly effective?

4. What changes have taken place on the lake? Have they substantially changed the quality of the experience? Where does White locate these changes in the essay? Do they stand out there? Why not?
5. Write an essay about a place you visited on two different occasions and focus on whether or not the place had changed.
6. Write an essay on how you have repeated some patterns of your parents' or grandparents' lives.

✦ Roger Wilkins ✦
Confessions of a Blue-Chip Black

Roger Wilkins received his doctorate in law from Central Michigan University in 1974. In Washington, he worked as a special assistant administrator to AID, assistant U.S. Attorney General, program director for the Ford Foundation, and staff writer for the Washington Post. *He was a columnist for* The New York Times *from 1977 to 1979. In this selection, adapted from his autobiography* A Man's Life *(1982), Wilkins explains the disadvantages of being a black raised in white surroundings.*

EARLY IN THE SPRING of 1932—six months after Earl's brother, Roy, left Kansas City to go to New York to join the national staff of the National Association for the Advancement of Colored People, and eight months before Franklin Roosevelt was elected president for the first time—Earl and Helen Wilkins had the first and only child to be born of their union. I was born in a little segregated hospital in Kansas City called Phillis Wheatley. The first time my mother saw me, she cried. My head was too long and my color, she thought, was blue.

My parents never talked about slavery or my ancestors. Images of Africa were images of backwardness and savagery. Once, when I was a little boy, I said to my mother after a friend of my parents left the house: "Mr. Bledsoe is black, isn't he, mama."

"Oh," she exclaimed. "Never say anybody is black. That's a terrible thing to say."

Next time Mr. Bledsoe came to the house, I commented, "Mama, Mr. Bledsoe is navy blue."

When I was two years old and my father was in the tuberculosis sanitarium, he wrote me a letter, which I obviously couldn't read, but which tells a lot about how he planned to raise his Negro son.

Friday, March 22, 1934

Dear Roger—

Let me congratulate you upon having reached your second birthday. Your infancy is now past and it is now that you should begin to turn your thoughts upon those achievements which are expected of a brilliant young gentleman well on his way to manhood.

During the next year, you should learn the alphabet; you should learn certain French and English idioms which are a part of every cultivated person's vocabulary: you should gain complete control of those natural functions which, uncontrolled, are a source of worry and embarrassment to even the best of grandmothers: you should learn how to handle table silver so that you will be able to eat gracefully and conventionally: and you should learn the fundamental rules of social living—politeness, courtesy, consideration for others, and the rest. 7

This should not be difficult for you. You have the best and most patient of mothers in your sterling grandmother and your excellent mother. Great things are expected of you. Never, never forget that. 8

Love,

Your Father

We lived in a neat little stucco house on a hill in a small Negro section called Roundtop. I had no sense of being poor or of any anxiety about money. At our house, not only was there food and furniture and all the rest, there was even a baby grand piano that my mother would play sometimes. And there was a cleaning lady, Mrs. Turner, who came every week. 9

When it was time for me to go to school, the board of education provided us with a big yellow bus, which carried us past four or five perfectly fine schools down to the middle of the large Negro community, to a very old school called Crispus Attucks. I have no memories of those bus rides except for my resentment of the selfishness of the whites who wouldn't let us share those newer-looking schools near to home. 10

My father came home when I was four and died when I was almost nine. He exuded authority. He thought the women hadn't been sufficiently firm with me, so he instituted a spanking program with that same hard hairbrush that my grandmother had used so much to try to insure that I didn't have "nigger-looking" hair. 11

After my father's death, the family moved to New York. Our apartment was in that legendary uptown area called Sugar Hill, where blacks who had it made were said to live the sweet life. I lived 12 with my mother, my grandmother, and my mother's younger sister, Zelma. My Uncle Roy and his wife, Minnie, a New York social worker, lived on the same floor. My Aunt Marvel and her husband, Cecil, lived one floor down.

As life in New York settled into a routine, my life came to be dominated by four women: my mother, her sisters, and her mother. Nobody else had any children, so everybody concentrated on me.

✦✦✦✦✦

Sometime early in 1943 my mother's work with the YMCA took her to Grand Rapids, Michigan, where she made a speech and met a forty-four-year-old bachelor doctor who looked like a white man. He had light skin, green eyes, and "good hair"—that is, hair that was as straight and as flat as white people's hair. He looked so like a white person that he could have passed for white. There was much talk about people who had passed. They were generally deemed to be bad people, for they were not simply selfish, but also cruel to those whom they left behind. On the other hand, people who could pass, but did not, were respected.

My mother remarried in October 1943, and soon I was once more on a train with my grandmother, heading toward Grand Rapids and my new home. This train also took me, at the age of twelve, beyond the last point in my life when I would feel totally at peace with my blackness.

My new home was in the north end of Grand Rapids, a completely white neighborhood. This would be the place I would henceforth think of as home. And it would be the place where I would become more Midwesterner than Harlemite, more American than black, and more complex than was comfortable or necessary for the middle-class conformity that my mother had in mind for me.

Grand Rapids was pretty single-family houses and green spaces. The houses looked like those in *Look* magazine or in *Life*. You could believe, and I did, that there was happiness inside. To me, back then, the people seemed to belong to the houses as the houses belonged to the land, and all of it had to do with being white. They moved and walked and talked as if the place, the country, and the houses were theirs, and I envied them.

I spent the first few weeks exploring Grand Rapids on a new bike my stepfather had bought for me. The people I passed would look back at me with intense and sometimes puzzled looks on their faces as I pedaled by. Nobody waved or even smiled. They just stopped what they were doing to stand and look. As soon as I saw them looking, I would look forward and keep on riding.

One day I rode for miles, down and up and down again. I was past Grand Rapids' squatty little downtown, and farther south until I began to see some Negro people. There were black men and women and some girls, but it was the boys I was looking for. Then I saw a group: four of them. They were about my age, and they were dark. Though their clothes were not as sharp as the boys' in the Harlem Valley, they were old, and I took the look of poverty and the deep darkness of their faces to mean that they were like the hard boys of Harlem. 19

One of them spotted me riding toward them and pointed. "Hey, lookit that bigole skinny bike," he said. Then they all looked at my bike and at me. I couldn't see expressions on their faces; only the blackness and the coarseness of their clothes. Before any of the rest of them had a chance to say anything, I stood up on the pedals and wheeled the bike in a U-turn and headed back on up toward the north end of town. It took miles for the terror to finally subside. 20

Farther on toward home, there was a large athletic field. As I neared the field, I could see some large boys in shorts moving determinedly around a football. When I got to the top of the hill that overlooked the field, I stopped and stood, one foot on the ground and one leg hanging over the crossbar, staring down at them. All the boys were white and big and old—sixteen to eighteen. I had never seen a football workout before, and I was fascinated. I completely forgot everything about color, theirs or mine. 21

Then one of them saw me. He pointed and said, "Look, there's the little coon watchin us." 22

I wanted to be invisible. I was horrified. My heart pounded, and my arms and my legs shook, but I managed to get back on my bike and ride home. 23

The first white friend I made was named Jerry Schild. On the second day of our acquaintance, he took me to his house, above a store run by his parents. I met his three younger siblings, including a very little one toddling around in bare feet and a soiled diaper. 24

While Jerry changed the baby, I looked around the place. It was cheap, all chintz and linoleum. The two soft pieces of furniture, a 25 couch and an overstuffed chair, had gaping holes and were hemorrhaging their fillings. And there were an awful lot of empty brown beer bottles sitting around, both in the kitchen and out on the back porch. While the place was not dirty, it made me very sad. Jerry and his family were poor in a way I had never seen people be poor before, in Kansas City or even in Harlem.

Jerry's father wasn't there that day and Jerry didn't mention him. 26
But later in the week, when I went to call for Jerry, I saw him. I yelled for Jerry from downstairs in the back and his father came to the railing of the porch on the second floor. He was a skinny man in overalls with the bib hanging down crookedly because it was fastened only on the shoulder. His face was narrow and wrinkled and his eyes were set deep in dark hollows. He had a beer bottle in his hand and he looked down at me. "Jerry ain't here," he said. He turned away and went back inside.

One day our front doorbell rang and I could hear my mother's 27
troubled exclamation, "Jerry! What's wrong?" Jerry was crying so hard he could hardly talk. "My father says I can't play with you anymore because you're not good enough for us."

Creston High School, which served all the children from the 28
north end of Grand Rapids, was all white and middle-class. Nobody talked to me that first day, but I was noticed. When I left school at the end of the day I found my bike leaning up against the fence where I had left it, with a huge glob of slimy spit on my shaggy saddle cover. People passed by on their way home and looked at me and spit. I felt a hollowness behind my eyes, but I didn't cry. I just got on the bike, stood up on the pedals, and rode it home without sitting down. And it went that way for about the first two weeks. After the third day, I got rid of the saddle cover because the plain leather was a lot easier to clean.

But the glacier began to thaw. One day in class, the freckle-faced 29
kid with the crewcut sitting next to me was asking everybody for a pencil. And then he looked at me and said, "Maybe you can lend me one." Those were the best words I had heard since I first met Jerry. This kid had included me in the human race in front of everybody. His name was Jack Waltz.

And after a while when the spitters had subsided and I could ride 30
home sitting down, I began to notice that little kids my size were playing pickup games in the end zones of the football field. It

looked interesting, but I didn't know anybody and didn't know how they would respond to me. So I just rode on by for a couple of weeks, slowing down each day, trying to screw up my courage to go in.

But then one day, I saw Jack Waltz there. I stood around the 31
edges of the group watching. It seemed that they played forever without even noticing me, but finally someone had to go home and the sides were unbalanced. Somebody said, "Let's ask him."

As we lined up for our first huddle, I heard somebody on the 32
other side say, "I hope he doesn't have a knife." One of the guys on my side asked me, "Can you run the ball?" I said yes, so they gave me the ball and I ran three quarters of the length of the field for a touchdown. And I made other touchdowns and other long runs before the game was over. When I thought about it later that night, I became certain that part of my success was due to the imaginary knife that was running interference for me. But no matter. By the end of the game, I had a group of friends. Boys named Andy and Don and Bill and Gene and Rich. We left the field together and some of them waved and yelled, "See ya tomorra, Rog."

And Don De Young, a pleasant round-faced boy, even lived quite 33
near me. So, after parting from everybody else, he and I went on together down to the corner of Coit and Knapp. As we parted, he suggested that we meet to go to school together the next day. I had longed for that but I hadn't suggested it for fear of a rebuff for overstepping the limits of my race. I had already learned one of the great tenets of Negro survival in America: to live the reactive life. It was like the old Negro comedian who once said, "When the man asks how the weather is, I know nuff to look keerful at his face 'fore even I look out the window." So, I waited for him to suggest it, and my patience was rewarded. I was overjoyed and grateful.

I didn't spend all my time in the north end. Soon after I moved 34
to Grand Rapids, Pop introduced me to some patients he had with a son my age. The boy's name was Lloyd Brown, and his father was a bellman downtown at the Pantlind Hotel. Lloyd and I often rode bikes and played basketball in his backyard. After a while, my mother asked me why I never had Lloyd come out to visit me. It was a question I dreaded, but she pressed on. "After all," she said, "you've had a lot of meals at his house and it's rude not to invite him back." I knew she was right and I also hated the whole idea of it.

With my friends in the north, race was never mentioned. Ever. I 35 carried my race around with me like an open basket of rotten eggs. I knew I could drop one at any moment and it would explode with a stench over everything. This was in the days when the movies either had no blacks at all or featured rank stereotypes like Stepin Fetchit, and the popular magazines like *Life, Look,* the *Saturday Evening Post,* and *Colliers* carried no stories about Negroes, had no ads depicting Negroes, and generally gave the impression that we did not exist in this society. I knew that my white friends, being well brought up, were just too polite to mention this disability that I had. And I was grateful to them, but terrified, just the same, that maybe someday one of them would have the bad taste to notice what I was.

It seemed to me that my tenuous purchase in this larger white 36 world depended on the maintenance between me and my friends in the north end of our unspoken bargain to ignore my difference, my shame, and their embarrassment. If none of us had to deal with it, I thought, we could all handle it. My white friends behaved as if they perceived the bargain exactly as I did. It was a delicate equation, and I was terrified that Lloyd's presence in the North End would rip apart the balance.

I am so ashamed of that shame now that I cringe when I write it. 37 But I understand that boy now as he could not understand himself then. I was an American boy, though I did not fully comprehend that either. I was fully shaped and formed by America, where white people had all the power in sight, and they owned everything in sight except our house. Their beauty was the real beauty; there wasn't any other beauty. A real human being had straight hair, a white face, and thin lips. Other people, who looked different, were lesser beings.

No wonder, then, that most black men desired the forbidden 38 fruit of white loins. No wonder, too, that we thought that the most beautiful and worthy Negro people were those who looked most white. We blacks used to have a saying: "If you're white, you're all right. If you're brown, stick around. If you're black, stand back." I was brown.

It was not that we in my family were direct victims of racism. On 39 the contrary, my stepfather clearly had a higher income than the parents of most students in my high school. Unlike those of most of my contemporaries, black and white, my parents had college degrees. Within Grand Rapids' tiny Negro community, they were among the elite. The others were the lawyer, the dentist, the undertaker, and the other doctor.

But that is what made race such exquisite agony. I did have a 40
sense that it was unfair for poor Negroes to be relegated to bad jobs—if they had jobs at all—and to bad or miserable housing, but I didn't feel any great sense of identity with them. After all, the poor blacks in New York had also been the hard ones: the ones who tried to take my money, to beat me up, and to keep me perpetually intimidated. Besides, I had heard it intimated around my house that their behavior, sexual or otherwise, left a good deal to be desired.

So I thought that maybe they just weren't ready for this society, 41
but that I was. And it was dreadfully unfair for white people to just look at my face and lips and hair and decide that I was inferior. By being a model student and leader, I thought I was demonstrating how well Negroes could perform if only the handicaps were removed and they were given a chance. But deep down I guess I was also trying to demonstrate that I was not like those other people; that I was different. My message was quite clear: I was *not nigger*. But the world didn't seem quite ready to make such fine distinctions, and it was precisely that fact—though at the time I could scarcely even have admitted it to myself—that was the nub of the race issue for me.

I would sometimes lie on my back and stare up at passing clouds 42
and wonder why God had played a dirty trick by making me a Negro. It all seemed so random. So unfair to me. To *me!* But in school I was gaining more friends, and the teachers respected me. It got so that I could go for days not thinking very much about being Negro, until something made the problem unavoidable.

One day in history class, for instance, the teacher asked each of 43
us to stand and tell in turn where our families had originated. Many of the kids in the class were Dutch with names like Vander Jagt, De Young, and Ripstra. My pal Andy was Scots-Irish. When it came my turn, I stood up and burned with shame and when I would speak, I lied. And then I was even more ashamed because I exposed a deeper shame. "Some of my family was English," I said—Wilkins is an English name—"and the rest of it came from . . . Egypt." Egypt!

One Saturday evening after one of our sandlot games, I went over to Lloyd's. Hearing my stories, Lloyd said mildly that he'd like to come up and play some Saturday. I kept on talking, but all the time my mind was repeating: "Lloyd wants to play. He wants to come up to the North End on Saturday. Next Saturday. Next Saturday." I was trapped.

So, after the final story about the final lunge, when I couldn't put it off any longer, I said, "Sure. Why not?" But, later in the evening, after I had had some time to think, I got Lloyd alone. "Say, look," I said. "Those teams are kinda close, ya know. I mean, we don't switch around. From team to team. Or new guys, ya know?"

Lloyd nodded, but he was getting a funny look on his face . . . part unbelieving and part hurt. So I quickly interjected before he could say anything, "Naw, man. Not like you shouldn't come and play. Just that we gotta have some good reason for you to play on our team, you dig?"

"Yeah," Lloyd said, his face still puzzled, but no longer hurt.

"Hey, I know," I said. "I got it. We'll say you're my cousin. If you're my cousin, see, then you gotta play. Nobody can say you can't be on my team, because you're family, right?"

"Oh, right. Okay," Lloyd said, his face brightening. "Sure, we'll say we're cousins. Solid."

I felt relieved as well. I could have a Negro cousin. It wasn't voluntary. It wouldn't be as if I had gone out and made a Negro friend deliberately. A person couldn't help who his cousins were.

There began to be a cultural difference between me and other blacks my age too. Black street language had evolved since my Harlem days, and I had not kept pace. Customs, attitudes, and the other common social currencies of everyday black life had evolved away from me. I didn't know how to talk, to banter, to move my body. If I was tentative and responsive in the North End, where I lived, I was tense, stiff, and awkward when I was with my black contemporaries. One day I was standing outside the church trying, probably at my mother's urging, to make contact. Conversational sallies flew around me while I stood there stiff and mute, unable to participate. Because the language was so foreign to me, I understood little of what was being said, but I did know that the word used for a white was *paddy*. Then a boy named Nickerson, the one whom my mother particularly wanted me to be friends with, inclined his head slightly toward me and said, to whoops of laughter, "techni-color paddy." My feet felt rooted in stone, and my head was aflame. I never forgot that phrase.

I have rarely felt so alone as I did that day riding home from church. Already partly excluded by my white friends, I was now almost completely alienated from my own people as well. But I felt less uncomfortable and less vulnerable in the white part of town. It was familiar enough to enable me to ward off most unpleasantness. 52

And then there was the problem of girls. They were everywhere, the girls. They all had budding bosoms, they all smelled pink, they all brushed against the boys in the hall, they were all white, and, in 1947–49, they were all inaccessible. 53

There were some things you knew without ever knowing how you knew them. You knew that Mississippi was evil and dangerous, that New York was east, and the Pacific ocean was west. And in the same way you knew that white women were the most desirable and dangerous objects in the world. Blacks were lynched in Mississippi and such places sometimes just for looking with the wrong expression at white women. Blacks of a very young age knew that white women of any quality went with the power and style that went with the governance of America—though, God knows, we had so much self-hate that when a white woman went with a Negro man, we promptly decided she was trash, and we also figured that if she would go with him she would go with any Negro. 54

Nevertheless, as my groin throbbed at fifteen and sixteen and seventeen, *they* were often the only ones there. One of them would be in the hallway opening her locker next to mine. Her blue sweater sleeve would be pushed up to just below the elbow, and as she would reach high on a shelf to stash away a book, I would see the tender dark hair against the white skin of her forearm. And I would ache and want to touch that arm and follow that body hair to its source. 55

Some of my friends, of course, did touch some of those girls. My friends and I would talk about athletics and school and their loves. But they wouldn't say a word about the dances and the hayrides they went to. 56

I perceived they liked me and accepted me as long as I moved aside when life's currents took them to where I wasn't supposed to be. I fit into their ways when they talked about girls, even their 57 personal girls. And, indeed, I fit into the girls' lives when they were talking about boys, most particularly their own personal boys. Because I was a boy, I had insight. But I was also Negro, and therefore a neuter. So a girl who was alive and sensuous night after night in my fantasies would come to me earnestly in the day and talk about Rich or Gene or Andy. She would ask what he thought about her, whether he liked to dance, whether, if she invited him to her house for a party, he would come. She would tell me her fears and her yearnings, never dreaming for an instant that I had yearnings too and that she was their object.

There may be few more powerful obsessions than a teenage boy's 58
fixation on a love object. In my case it came down to a thin brunette named Marge McDowell. She was half a grade behind me, and she lived in a small house on a hill. I found excuses to drive by it all the time. I knew her schedule at school, so I could manage to be in most of the hallways she had to use going from class to class. We knew each other, and she had once confided a strong but fleeting yearning for my friend Rich Kippen. I thought about her constantly.

Finally, late one afternoon after school, I came upon her alone in 59
a hallway. "Marge," I blurted, "can I ask you something?"

She stopped and smiled and said, "Sure, Roger, what?" 60

"Well I was wondering," I said. "I mean. Well, would you go to 61
the hayride next week with me?"

Her jaw dropped and her eyes got huge. Then she uttered a small 62
shriek and turned, hugging her books to her bosom the way girls do, and fled. I writhed with mortification in my bed that night and for many nights after.

In my senior year, I was elected president of the Creston High 63
School student council. It was a breakthrough of sorts.

QUESTIONS FOR READING AND WRITING

1. Wilkins' autobiography is a classic example of tension that can arise between economic success and ethnic identity. While still subject to the racial prejudice of whites, Wilkins is isolated from, and made to feel ashamed of, poor members of his own race. What experience do you have that can help you relate to being either an outsider with

respect to a majority group or a member of a group with which you should feel affinity but to which you are embarrassed to acknowledge your connection?

2. Notice how Wilkins' examples move back and forth between incidents involving white rejection or stereotyping and Wilkins' own shame over his Afro-American heritage. Cite several examples of each of these patterns and illustrate how they make Wilkins' point that he had become a "technicolor paddy."
3. Read the selections by Gloria Naylor, Alice Walker, James Baldwin, Richard Wright, Richard Rodriguez, N. Scott Momaday, and Maxine Hong Kingston, and write an essay on the value of respecting ethnic diversity.

PART 2

NARRATION

Writing to Recreate Events

Narration is often one of the easiest kinds of writing for students to do: it involves telling a story—something that comes naturally to most people—the story often follows a straightforward chronological pattern, the material frequently draws from personal experience, and the story is often told in the first person ("I") by the writer. Sometimes essays written to explain something or to persuade someone will incorporate a narrative segment to help clarify a point. Such essays differ from pure narration in that their primary purpose is explanation rather than entertainment.

Narrative and Plot The best place to begin considering what goes into writing narration is with a time-honored distinction between "narrative" (this happened and then this happened) and "plot" (this happened because this happened). Novelist E.M. Forster illustrates the distinction clearly and succinctly:

> Let us define plot. We have defined a story as a narrative of events arranged in their time sequence. A plot is also a narrative of events, the emphasis falling on causality. "The king died, and then the queen died," is a story. "The king died, and then the queen died of grief" is a plot. The time-sequence is preserved, but the sense of causality overshadows it.*

So, narration focuses on events in their time relationship, which is usually sequential or chronological—that is, events are narrated

* E.M. Forster, *Aspects of the Novel* (Harcourt Brace & Co., 1927), 130.

in the order in which they occurred, whereas a plot adds to this sequence the important element of cause and effect. In plot, events don't merely follow one another like links in a chain, they *cause* one another. Narration merely appeals to the curiosity of the audience—"*What* happens?"—whereas plot appeals to the intelligence of the audience as well—"*Why* did it happen?"

Most assignments in narration require only that you build clear chronological connections between the parts of your narrative, or that you state some overriding purpose or thesis at the outset, to act as a framework for the events narrated, or that your narrative move toward a climax or culminating event (in which the meaning of the narrative is implied). In some ways, plot construction is a more complicated, more difficult order of activity than is constructing this kind of chronological narrative. However, an assignment in chronological narration should not prevent you from attempting to construct a plot in which each event is causatively connected in such a way that the meaning of the piece emerges in stages from each section of the plot, rather than from a preface or epilogue, as it does in chronological narration. George Orwell's classic essay, "A Hanging," has many of the elements of what Forster describes as a plot—that is, one event seems inextricably bound to the next.

Character, or the People of the Story Notice how, although Orwell creates a distinct narrator (perhaps himself) to tell the story and then includes the narrator among the other spectators, ("We"), the narrator and is not a distinct person until the ninth paragraph—that is, until the story is almost half over. The point seems to be that the narrator, a sensitive individual and an accurate observer, is aware that his reactions to the hanging are shared by the others, but that the others are too embarrassed to admit it and too ashamed to closely observe one another. In addition to the narrator, there is Francis, the head jailer, somewhat more calloused by his experience of hangings than the others. The superintendent, who tries to maintain his British source of authority and his nerve, uses anger to hide his own fear and revulsion. Finally, there is the prisoner, who changes from being an object, a source of inconvenience ("The man ought to have been dead by this time"), to a human being ("When I saw the prisoner step aside to avoid the puddle, I saw the mystery, the unspeakable wrongness, of cutting a life short when it is in full tide"), and back again to an object ("The superintendent reached out with his stick and poked the bare body; it oscillated, slightly"). In his book, Forster divides characters into two types: *flat characters*, whose behavior is predictable and typical of the social or occupational category in which the author has placed them, and *round characters* who develop, change, and show qualities unique to them as individuals. The superintendent is, therefore, flat—a typical colonial administrator. The narrator, a colonial functionary, identifies with the prisoner's humanity, and is stunned by the ease and finality with which the line between life and death is crossed; he is clearly a round character.

Setting Remember, in a good piece of narrative writing all the parts fit tightly together. The physical world within which the action and dialogue of the narrative take place is no exception. To select the most obvious example from Orwell's narrative, notice how the opening description of the climatic setting of Burma, as all as the immediate setting of the jail, convey a mood of hopelessness in which humanity seems to have been reduced to its lowest animal common-denominators. Like all good settings, Orwell's description of Burma helps define the characters themselves:

> It was in Burma, a sodden morning of the rains. A sickly light, like yellow tinfoil, was slanting over the high walls into the jail yard. We were waiting outside the condemned cells, a row of sheds fronted with double bars, like small animal cages. Each cell measured about ten feet by ten and was quite bare within except for a plank bed and a pot for drinking water.

Note that Orwell's setting is effective largely because he uses concrete details that appeal to the senses. Figures of speech (comparisons) also aid the reader in recreating the experience ("like yellow tinfoil," "like small animal cages"). Orwell's setting is thus a description, and narrative writing without some description is rare. The primary aim and the primary content of any piece of writing will tell you whether it should properly be called narration or description. We will discuss the mixing of description and narration in a later section.

Symbolism Most of the pieces included in this section, unlike Orwell's essay, are works of fiction. As such, they tend to employ figurative language—and particularly symbolism—with some frequency. Symbols can be defined as objects, events, or even characters that, while actually present in the work, also stand for or *represent* other ideas or themes. Sometimes a symbol has only a transitory, "local" effect, like the mosquitos in J.F. Powers' "The Valiant Woman" or the mother's painted toenails in Gloria Naylor's "Kiswana Browne." At other times, symbolism becomes more elaborate. In "The Astronomer's Wife," Kay Boyle uses the polar symbols of astronomer and plumber to define the extremes of character between which the astronomer's wife seems suspended. In Alice Munro's "Boys and Girls," the way the narrator permits the old mare to escape becomes symbolic of her own desire to escape from her girlhood, even as it leads to her being called "just a girl" by her father. Symbols, then, can be associated with the setting of the story (the mosquitos), with the characters (the toenails), or with the theme (as in the stories by Boyle and Munro). Understanding the resonance and thematic importance of symbols can both enrich your reading and help to make your own narratives more pointed and memorable.

Theme The meaning, significance, or purpose of the narrative is distinct from the moral. Much narrative writing suffers because some explicit moral "tag line" has been attached to an otherwise entertaining story. (The exception to this rule is a type of narrative writing known as a "fable" in which the "moral" is one of the conventions.) Notice how Orwell resists the temptation to turn his narrative into an explicit sermon against capital punishment. Although his ultimate purpose is to show his revulsion for the practice, Orwell lets the details speak for themselves—the incongruous laughter while the Burmese and English share a bottle is juxtaposed with the serious fact that "The dead man was a hundred yards away." Subtle implications should convey the theme; if it is likely that the audience may miss the point, an explicit prologue should contain the meaning and act as a measure of relevance for the incidents that make up the narrative. Often narrative writing is used in other kinds of essays—particularly expository and persuasive essays—to support or develop the writer's main idea. In these cases, narrative writing is used to illustrate a point or provide a dramatic example, and the narrative portion may be only a paragraph or two enclosed within a larger essay.

Point Of View The method by which the story is narrated—that is, who tells the story—determines the point of view. The possibilities are primarily two: you can tell the story in either the first-person point of view ("I") or the third-person point of view ("he," "she," "they," and so forth). Sometimes the narrator of an essay is the author himself, as in Orwell's "A Hanging." Sometimes the first-person narrator is a character made up by the author as in Munro's "Boys and Girls." Note, too, that first-person narrators can be placed as central characters (Munro) or as peripheral ones (Orwell). This will of course affect what the narrators can know about the action, how objective they can be, and how they will be affected by what happens. In third-person narration, which presents an air of greater objectivity, the scope of what we know about the action is usually limited to what one character could perceive, as with Kiswana Browne in the story by Naylor, or as with Mrs. Ames in Boyle's "The Astronomer's Wife."

Conflict A clash between two forces lies at the heart of a good narrative. The audience's interest lies not so much in the passage of time but in the obstacles encountered in getting from one point to another. Out of this tension between two forces—which can be, for example, two people, a person and his or her environment, or two conflicting sets of values within a person—an interesting narrative is built. In Orwell's narrative, for instance, the clash implied between the narrator's professional duty to witness the execution of the prisoner and his humane impulse to identify with the condemned man radiates outward to explain the "strange" behavior of the other characters, including even their otherwise trivial irritation at the presence of the stray dog. Similarly, in Munro's "Boys and Girls," it is the narrator's conflict about her "role"—her desire to remain a person and not become a "girl"—that charges her relationships with her father, her mother, and her brother, thus producing narrative tension.

In a well-constructed narrative, conflict runs through the several parts that make up the *structure of narration*. These parts are (1) *exposition*, in which the background information necessary to understand the nature of the conflict is given; (2) *complications*, or those incidents that actualize and initiate the potential conflict in the exposition; (3) *climax*, or turning point, at which the resolution of the conflict becomes inevitable—that is, from this point forward, although it may not be immediately evident to the reader, one of the forces in the conflict begins to emerge as dominant, while the other is being dominated; (4) *resolution*, where the dominant force clearly emerges as a result of other incidents; and (5) *denouement*, literally the untying or unravelling, in which the nature of the conflict is explained. Modern tastes incline toward a subtle approach, preferring the significance of the narrative to emerge implicitly from the resolution of the conflict rather than from any explicit "unravelling." The structure of narration may be graphically depicted as follows:

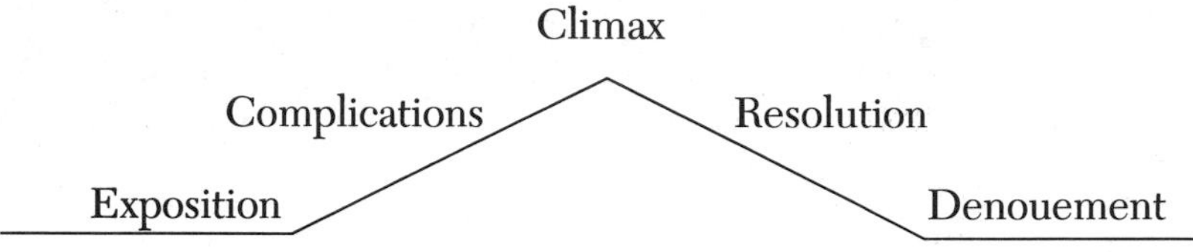

This adaptation of Aristotle's outline of dramatic action from the *Poetics* should be used with caution both as a tool for analysis and as a suggested structure; many narratives do not follow it rigidly or even include all the parts. For example, instead of following a strictly chronological order, many narratives begin with a later event and then, using *reverse chronology*, go back in time to account for it. Almost exactly like this is the device of *flashback*, familiar from the movies, in which a straightforward chronological sequence is interrupted to fill in explanations from earlier events, by going back in time, before the narrative flow into the present is resumed.

If you are like most students, you will find narrative writing enjoyable, relatively easy, and creative, because you can relate your own experiences or those of others in the familiar form of a story.

✦ Kay Boyle ✦
The Astronomer's Wife

Kay Boyle (b. 1903), an American novelist, poet, and short-story writer, lived for many years in Europe, where much of her fiction is set. She has written the novels Plagued by the Nightingale *(1931),* Testament for My Students *(1970), and* The Underground Woman *(1974).* Fifty Stories *appeared in 1980. In the following story she uses the contrasting worldviews of an astronomer and a plumber as a way of revealing the inner life of a married woman.*

THERE IS AN EVIL MOMENT on awakening when all things seem to pause. But for women, they only falter and may be set in action by a single move: a lifted hand and the pendulum will swing, or the voice raised and through every room the pulse takes up its beating. The astronomer's wife felt the interval gaping and at once filled it to the brim. She fetched up her gentle voice and sent it warily down the stairs for coffee, swung her feet out upon the oval mat, and hailed the morning with her bare arms' quivering flesh drawn taut in rhythmic exercise: left, left, left my wife and fourteen children, right, right, right in the middle of the dusty road. 1

The day would proceed from this, beat by beat, without reflection, like every other day. The astronomer was still asleep, or feigning it, and she, once out of bed, had come into her own possession. Although scarcely ever out of sight of the impenetrable silence of his brow, she would be absent from him all the day in being clean, busy, kind. He was a man of other things, a dreamer. At times he lay still for hours, at others he sat upon the roof behind his telescope, or wandered down the pathway to the road and out across the mountains. This day, like any other, would go on from the removal of the spot left there from dinner on the astronomer's vest to the severe thrashing of the mayonnaise for lunch. That man might be each time the new arching wave, and woman the undertow that sucked him back, were things she had been told by his silence were so. 2

In spite of the earliness of the hour, the girl had heard her mistress's voice and was coming up the stairs. At the threshold of the bedroom she paused, and said: "Madame, the plumber is here."

The astronomer's wife put on her white and scarlet smock very quickly and buttoned it at the neck. Then she stepped carefully around the motionless spread of water in the hall.

"Tell him to come right up," she said. She laid her hands on the bannisters and stood looking down the wooden stairway. "Ah, I am Mrs. Ames," she said softly as she saw him mounting. "I am Mrs. Ames," she said softly, softly down the flight of stairs. "I am Mrs. Ames," spoken soft as a willow weeping. "The professor is still sleeping. Just step this way."

The plumber himself looked up and saw Mrs. Ames with her voice hushed, speaking to him. She was a youngish woman, but this she had forgotten. The mystery and silence of her husband's mind lay like a chiding finger on her lips. Her eyes were gray, for the light had been extinguished in them. The strange dim halo of her yellow hair was still uncombed and sideways on her head.

For all of his heavy boots, the plumber quieted the sound of his feet, and together they went down the hall, picking their way around the still lake of water that spread as far as the landing and lay docile there. The plumber was a tough, hardy man; but he took off his hat when he spoke to her and looked her fully, almost insolently in the eye.

"Does it come from the wash-basin," he said, "or from the other . . .?"

"Oh, from the other," said Mrs. Ames without hesitation.

In this place the villas were scattered out few and primitive, and although beauty lay without there was no reflection of her face within. Here all was awkward and unfit; a sense of wrestling with uncouth forces gave everything an austere countenance. Even the plumber, dealing as does a woman with matters under hand, was grave and stately. The mountains round about seemed to have cast them into the shadow of great dignity.

Mrs. Ames began speaking of their arrival that summer in the little villa, mourning each event as it followed on the other.

"Then, just before going to bed last night," she said, "I noticed something was unusual."

The plumber cast down a folded square of sack-cloth on the 13
brimming floor and laid his leather apron on it. Then he stepped boldly onto the heart of the island it shaped and looked long into the overflowing bowl.

"The water should be stopped from the meter in the garden," he 14
said at last.

"Oh, I did that," said Mrs. Ames, "the very first thing last night. I 15
turned it off at once, in my nightgown, as soon as I saw what was happening. But all this had already run in."

The plumber looked for a moment at her red kid slippers. She 16
was standing just at the edge of the clear, pure-seeming tide.

"It's no doubt the soil lines," he said severely. "It may be that 17
something has stopped them, but my opinion is that the water seals aren't working. That's the trouble often enough in such cases. If you had a valve you wouldn't be caught like this."

Mrs. Ames did not know how to meet this rebuke. She stood, 18
swaying a little, looking into the plumber's blue relentless eye.

"I'm sorry—I'm sorry that my husband," she said, "is still—rest- 19
ing and cannot go into this with you. I'm sure it must be very interesting . . ."

"You'll probably have to have the traps sealed," said the plumber 20
grimly, and at the sound of this Mrs. Ames' hand flew in dismay to the side of her face. The plumber made no move, but the set of his mouth as he looked at her seemed to soften. "Anyway, I'll have a look from the garden end," he said.

"Oh, do," said the astronomer's wife in relief. Here was a man 21
who spoke of action and object as simply as women did! But however hushed her voice had been, it carried clearly to Professor Ames who lay, dreaming and solitary, upon his bed. He heard their footsteps come down the hall, pause, and skip across the pool of overflow.

"Katherine!" said the astronomer in a ringing tone. "There's a 22
problem worthy of your mettle!"

Mrs. Ames did not turn her head, but led the plumber swiftly 23
down the stairs. When the sun in the garden struck her face, he saw there was a wave of color in it, but this may have been anything but shame.

"You see how it is," said the plumber, as if leading her mind away. 24
"The drains run from these houses right down the hill, big enough

for a man to stand upright in them, and clean as a whistle too." There they stood in the garden with the vegetation flowering in disorder all about. The plumber looked at the astronomer's wife. "They come out at the torrent on the other side of the forest beyond there," he said.

But the words the astronomer had spoken still sounded in her in despair. The mind of man, she knew, made steep and sprightly flights, pursued illusion, took foothold in the nameless things that cannot pass between the thumb and finger. But whenever the astronomer gave voice to the thoughts that soared within him, she returned in gratitude to the long expanses of his silence. Desert-like they stretched behind and before the articulation of his scorn.

Life, life is an open sea, she sought to explain it in sorrow, and to survive women cling to the floating debris on the tide. But the plumber had suddenly fallen upon his knees in the grass and had crooked his fingers through the ring of the drains' trap-door. When she looked down she saw that he was looking up into her face, and she saw too that his hair was as light as gold.

"Perhaps Mr. Ames," he said rather bitterly, "would like to come down with me and have a look around?"

"Down?" said Mrs. Ames in wonder.

"Into the drains," said the plumber brutally. "They're a study for a man who likes to know what's what."

"Oh, Mr. Ames," said Mrs. Ames in confusion. "He's still—still in bed, you see."

The plumber lifted his strong, weathered face and looked curiously at her. Surely it seemed to him strange for a man to linger in bed, with the sun pouring yellow as wine all over the place. The astronomer's wife saw his lean cheeks, his high, rugged bones, and the deep seams in his brow. His flesh was as firm and clean as wood, stained richly tan with the climate's rigor. His fingers were blunt, but comprehensible to her, gripped in the ring and holding the iron door wide. The backs of his hand were bound round and round with ripe blue veins of blood.

"At any rate," said the astronomer's wife, and the thought of it moved her lips to smile a little, "Mr. Ames would never go down there alive. He likes going up," she said. And she, in her turn, pointed, but impudently, toward the heavens. "On the roof. Or on the mountains. He's been up on the tops of them many times."

"It's a matter of habit," said the plumber, and suddenly he went 33
down the trap. Mrs. Ames saw a bright little piece of his hair still shining, like a star, long after the rest of him had gone. Out of the depths, his voice, hollow and dark with foreboding, returned to her. "I think something has stopped the elbow," was what he said.

This was speech that touched her flesh and bone and made her 34
wonder. When her husband spoke of height, having no sense of it, she could not picture it nor hear. Depth or magic passed her by unless a name were given. But madness in a daily shape, as elbow stopped, she saw clearly and well. She sat down on the grasses, bewildered that it should be a man who had spoken to her so.

She saw the weeds springing up, and she did not move to tear 35
them up from life. She sat powerless, her senses veiled, with no action taking shape beneath her hands. In this way some men sat for hours on end, she knew, tracking, tracking a single thought back to its origin. The mind of man could balance and divide, weed out, destroy. She sat on the full, burdened grasses, seeking to think, and dimly waiting for the plumber to return.

Whereas her husband had always gone up, as the dead go, she 36
knew now that there were others who went down, like the corporeal being of the dead. That men were then divided into two bodies now seemed clear to Mrs. Ames. This knowledge stunned her with its simplicity and took the uneasy motion from her limbs. She could not stir, but sat facing the mountains' rocky flanks, and harking in silence to lucidity. Her husband was the mind, this other man the meat, of all mankind.

After a little, the plumber emerged from the earth: first the light 37
top of his head, then the burnt brow, and then the blue eyes fringed with whitest lash. He braced his thick hands flat on the pavings of the garden-path and swung himself completely from the pit.

"It's the soil lines," he said pleasantly. "The gases," he said as he 38
looked down upon her lifted face, "are backing up the drains."

"What in the world are we going to do?" said the astronomer's 39
wife softly. There was a young and strange delight in putting questions to which true answers would be given. Everything the astronomer had ever said to her was a continuous query to which there could be no response.

"Ah, come, now," said the plumber, looking down and smiling. 40
"There's a remedy for every ill, you know. Sometimes it may be

that," he said as if speaking to a child, "or sometimes the other thing. But there's always a help for everything amiss."

Things come out of herbs and make you young again, he might have been saying to her; or the first good rain will quench any drought; or time of itself will put a broken bone together. 41

"I'm going to follow the ground pipe out right to the torrent," the plumber was saying. "The trouble's between here and there and I'll find it on the way. There's nothing at all that can't be done over for the caring," he was saying, and his eyes were fastened on her face in insolence, or gentleness, or love. 42

The astronomer's wife stood up, fixed a pin in her hair, and turned around towards the kitchen. Even while she was calling the servant's name, the plumber began speaking again. 43

"I once had a cow that lost her cud," the plumber was saying. The girl came out on the kitchen-step and Mrs. Ames stood smiling at her in the sun. 44

"The trouble is very serious, very serious," she said across the garden. "When Mr. Ames gets up, please tell him I've gone down." 45

She pointed briefly to the open door in the pathway, and the plumber hoisted his kit on his arm and put out his hand to help her down. 46

"But I made her another in no time," he was saying, "out of flowers and things and what-not." 47

"Oh," said the astronomer's wife in wonder as she stepped into the heart of the earth. She took his arm, knowing that what he said was true. 48

QUESTIONS FOR READING AND WRITING

1. What two kinds of men (or people) do the astronomer and the plumber represent?
2. What details of the story show how Mrs. Ames feels about the plumber?
3. Explain the following metaphors: (1) "The mystery and silence of her husband's mind lay like a chiding finger on her lips" (paragraph 6); (2) "life is an open sea . . . and to survive women cling to the floating debris on the tide" (paragraph 26); (3) "Her husband was the mind, this other man the meat, of all mankind" (paragraph 36).

4. Using details of the story, evaluate the quality of the Ames' marriage.
5. Describe a couple who seem mismatched (or write a narrative involving such a couple).
6. Drawing both on clichés and on original invention, write a sketch of an "absent-minded professor" you have known.
7. Write a literary analysis that accounts for the "Images of the Body" in "The Astronomer's Wife.'"

✦ Gretel Ehrlich ✦

Wyoming

The Solace of Open Spaces

Gretel Ehrlich (b. 1946) is a native of California but now lives in Wyoming. She has published two collections of essays: The Solace of Open Spaces *(1985), from which the present piece is taken, and* Islands, Universe, and Home *(1988). In the following essay, which mixes some narrative elements into a generally descriptive style, she writes of the spaces, the land, and the people of Wyoming.*

IT'S MAY, and I've just awakened from a nap, curled against sagebrush the way my dog taught me to sleep—sheltered from wind. A front is pulling the huge sky over me, and from the dark a hailstone has hit me on the head. I'm trailing a band of 2000 sheep across a stretch of Wyoming badland, a fifty-mile trip that takes five days because sheep shade up in hot sun and won't budge until it cools. Bunched together now, and excited into a run by the storm, they drift across dry land, tumbling into draws like water and surging out again onto the rugged, choppy plateaus that are the building blocks of this state.

The name Wyoming comes from an Indian word meaning, "at the great plains," but the plains are really valleys, great arid valleys, 1600 square miles, with the horizon bending up on all sides into mountain ranges. This gives the vastness a sheltering look.

Winter lasts six months here. Prevailing winds spill snowdrifts to the east, and new storms from the northwest replenish them. This white bulk is sometimes dizzying, even nauseating, to look at. At twenty, thirty, and forty degrees below zero, not only does your car not work but neither do your mind and body. The landscape hardens into a dungeon of space. During the winter, while I was riding to find a new calf, my legs froze to the saddle, and in the silence that such cold creates I felt like the first person on earth, or the last.

Today the sun is out—only a few clouds billowing. In the east, where the sheep have started off without me, the benchland tilts up in a series of red-earthed, eroded mesas, planed flat on top by a million years of water; behind them, a bold line of muscular scarps rears up 10,000 feet to become the Big Horn Mountains. A tidal pattern is engraved into the ground, as if left by the sea that once covered this state. Canyons curve down like galaxies to meet the oncoming rush of flat land.

To live and work in this kind of open country, with its hundred- 5
mile views, is to lose the distinction between background and foreground. When I asked an older ranch hand to describe Wyoming's openness, he said, "It's all a bunch of nothing—wind and rattlesnakes—and so much of it you can't tell where you're going or where you've been and it don't make much difference." John, a sheepman I know, is tall and handsome and has an explosive temperament. He has a perfect intuition about people and sheep. They call him "Highpockets," because he's so long-legged; his graceful stride matches the distances he has to cover. He says, "Open space hasn't affected me at all. It's all the people moving in on it." The huge ranch he was born on takes up much of one county and spreads into another state; to put 100,000 miles on his pickup in three years and never leave home is not unusual. A friend of mine has an aunt who ranched on Powder River and didn't go off her place for eleven years. When her husband died, she quickly moved to town, bought a car, and drove around the States to see what she'd been missing.

Most people tell me they've simply driven through Wyoming, as 6
if there were nothing to stop for. Or else they've skied in Jackson Hole, a place Wyomingites acknowledge uncomfortably, because its green beauty and chic affluence are mismatched with the rest of the state. Most of Wyoming has a "lean-to" look. Instead of big, roomy barns and Victorian houses, there are dugouts, low sheds, log cabins, sheep camps, and fence lines that look like driftwood blown haphazardly into place. People here still feel pride because they live in such a harsh place, part of the glamorous cowboy past, and they are determined not to be the victims of a mining-dominated future.

Most characteristic of the state's landscape is what a developer 7
euphemistically describes as "indigenous growth right up to your front door"—a reference to waterless stands of salt sage, snakes, jackrabbits, deerflies, red dust, a brief respite of wildflowers, dry washes, and no trees. In the Great Plains, the vistas look like music, like kyries of grass, but Wyoming seems to be the doing of a mad

architect—tumbled and twisted, ribboned with faded, deathbed colors, thrust up and pulled down as if the place had been startled out of a deep sleep and thrown into a pure light.

I came here four years ago. I had not planned to stay, but I couldn't make myself leave. John, the sheepman, put me to work immediately. It was spring, and shearing time. For fourteen days of fourteen hours each, we moved thousands of sheep through sorting corrals to be sheared, branded, and deloused. I suspect that my original motive for coming here was to "lose myself" in new and unpopulated territory. Instead of producing the numbness I thought I wanted, life on the sheep ranch woke me up. The vitality of the people I was working with flushed out what had become a hallucinatory rawness inside me. I threw away my clothes and bought new ones; I cut my hair. The arid country was a clean slate. Its absolute indifference steadied me.

Sagebrush covers 58,000 square miles of Wyoming. The biggest city has a population of 50,000, and there are only five settlements that could be called cities in the whole state. The rest are towns, scattered across the expanse with as much as sixty miles between them, their populations 2000, fifty, or ten. They are fugitive-looking, perched on a barren, windblown bench, or tagged onto a river or a railroad, or laid out straight in a farming valley with implement stores and a block-long Mormon church. In the eastern part of the state, which slides down into the Great Plains, the new mining settlements are boomtowns, trailer cities, metal knots on flat land.

Despite the desolate look, there's a coziness to living in this state. 1
There are so few people (only 470,000) that ranchers who buy and sell cattle know each other statewide; the kids who choose to go to college usually go to the state's one university, in Laramie; hired hands work their way around Wyoming in a lifetime of hirings and firings. And, despite the physical separation, people stay in touch, often driving two or three hours to another ranch for dinner.

Seventy-five years ago, when travel was by buckboard or horse- 1
back, cowboys who were temporarily out of work rode the grub line—drifting from ranch to ranch, mending fences or milking cows, and receiving in exchange a bed and meals. Gossip and messages traveled this slow circuit with them, creating an intimacy between ranchers who were three and four weeks' ride apart. One

old-time couple I know, whose turn-of-the-century homestead was used by an outlaw gang as a relay station for stolen horses, recall that if you were traveling, desperado or not, any lighted ranch house was a welcome sign. Even now, for someone who lives in a remote spot, arriving at a ranch or coming to town for supplies is cause for celebration. To emerge from isolation can be disorienting. Everything looks bright, new, vivid. After I had been herding sheep for only three days, the sound of the camp-tender's pickup flustered me. Longing for human company, I felt a foolish grin take over my face, yet I had to resist an urgent temptation to run and hide.

Things happen suddenly in Wyoming: the change of seasons and 12
weather; for people, the violent swings in and out of isolation. But goodnaturedness is concomitant with severity. Friendliness is a tradition. Strangers passing on the road wave hello. A common sight is two pickups stopped side by side far out on a range, on a dirt track winding through the sage. The drivers will share a cigarette, uncap their thermos bottles, and pass a battered cup, steaming with coffee, between windows. These meetings summon up the details of several generations, because in Wyoming, private histories are largely public knowledge.

Because ranch work is a physical and, these days, economic 13
strain, being "at home on the range" is a matter of vigor, self-reliance, and common sense. A person's life is not a series of dramatic events for which he or she is applauded or exiled but a slow accumulation of days, seasons, years, fleshed out by the generational weight of one's family and anchored by a land-bound sense of place.

In most parts of Wyoming the human population is visibly out- 14
numbered by the animal. Not far from my town of fifty, I rode into a narrow valley and startled a herd of 200 elk. Eagles look like small people as they eat car-killed deer by the road. Antelope, moving in small, graceful bands, travel at 60 miles an hour, their mouths open as if drinking in the space.

The solitude in which westerners live makes them quiet. They 15
telegraph thoughts and feelings by the way they tilt their heads and listen; pulling their Stetsons into a steep dive over their eyes, or pigeon-toeing one boot over the other, they lean against a fence with a fat wedge of snoose beneath their lower lips and take the

whole scene in. These detached looks of quiet amusement are sometimes cynical, but they can also come from a dry-eyed humility as lucid as the air is clear.

Conversation goes on in what sounds like a private code: a few phrases imply a complex of meanings. Asking directions, you get a curious list of details. While trailing sheep, I was told to "ride up to the kinda upturned rock, follow the pink wash, turn left at the dump, and then you'll see the waterhole." One friend told his wife on roundup to "turn at the salt lick and the dead cow," which turned out to be a scattering of bones and no salt lick at all. 16

Sentence structure is shortened to the skin and bones of a thought. Descriptive words are dropped, even verbs; a cowboy looking over a corral full of horses will say to a wrangler, "Which one needs rode?" People hold back their thoughts in what seems to be a dumbfounded silence, then erupt with an excoriating, perceptive remark. Language, so compressed, becomes metaphorical. A rancher ended a relationship with one remark: "You're a bad check," meaning bouncing in and out was intolerable, and even coming back would be no good. 17

What's behind this laconic style is shyness. There is no vocabulary for the subject of feelings. It's not a hangdog shyness, or anything coy—always there's a robust spirit in evidence behind the restraint, as if the earthdredging wind that pulls across Wyoming had carried its people's voices away but everything else in them had shouldered confidently into the breeze. 18

I've spent hours riding to sheep camp at dawn in a pickup when nothing was said; eaten meals in the cookhouse when the only words spoken were a mumbled "Thank you, ma'am" at the end of dinner. The silence is profound. Instead of talking, we seem to share one eye. Keenly observed, the world is transformed. The landscape is engorged with detail, every movement on it chillingly sharp. The air between people is charged. Days unfold, bathed in their own music. Nights become hallucinatory; dreams, prescient. 19

Spring weather is capricious and mean. It snows, then blisters with heat. There have been tornadoes. They lay their elephant trunks out in the sage until they find houses, then slurp everything up and leave. I've noticed that melting snowbanks hiss and rot, viperous, then drip into calm pools where ducklings hatch and livestock, being trailed to summer range, drink. With the ice cover 20 gone, rivers churn a milkshake brown, taking culverts and small bridges with them. Water in such an arid place (the average annual rainfall where I live is less than eight inches) is like blood. It festoons drab land with green veins: a line of cottonwoods following a stream; a strip of alfalfa; and on ditchbanks, wild asparagus growing.

I've moved to a small cattle ranch owned by friends. It's at the foot of the Big Horn Mountains. A few weeks ago, I helped them deliver a calf who was stuck halfway out of his mother's body. By the time he was freed, we could see a heartbeat, but he was straining against a swollen tongue for air. Mary and I held him upside down by his back feet, while Stan, on his hands and knees in the blood, gave the calf mouth-to-mouth resuscitation. I have a vague memory of being pneumonia-choked as a child, my mother giving me her air, which may account for my romance with this windswept state. 21

If anything is endemic to Wyoming, it is wind. This big room of space is swept out daily, leaving a boneyard of fossils, agates, and carcasses in every state of decay. Though it was water that initially shaped the state, wind is the meticulous gardener, raising dust and pruning the sage. 22

I try to imagine a world of uncharted land, in which one could look over an uncompleted map and ride a horse past where all the lines have stopped. There is no wilderness left; wildness, yes, but true wilderness has been gone on this continent since the time of Lewis and Clark's overland journey. 23

Two hundred years ago, the Crow, Shoshone, Arapaho, Cheyenne, and Sioux roamed the intermountains West, orchestrating their movements according to hunger, season, and warfare. Once they acquired horses, they traversed the spines of all the big Wyoming ranges—the Absarokas, the Wind Rivers, the Tetons, the Big Horns—and wintered on the unprotected plains that fan out from them. Space was life. The world was their home. 24

What was life-giving to native Americans was often nightmarish to sodbusters who arrived encumbered with families and ethnic pasts to be transplanted in nearly uninhabitable land. The great distances, the shortage of water and trees, and the loneliness created unexpected hardships for them. In her book *O Pioneers!*, Willa Cather gives a settler's version of the bleak landscape: 25

> The little town behind them had vanished as if it had never been, had fallen behind the swell of the prairie, and the stern

> frozen country received them into its bosom. The homesteads were few and far apart; here and there a windmill gaunt against the sky, a sod house crouching in a hollow.

The emptiness of the West was for others a geography of possibility. Men and women who amassed great chunks of land and struggled to preserve unfenced empires were, despite their self-serving motives, unwitting geographers. They understood the lay of the land. But by the 1850s, the Oregon and Mormon trails sported bumper-to-bumper traffic. Wealthy landowners, many of them aristocratic absentee landlords, known as remittance men because they were paid to come West and get out of their families' hair, overstocked the range with more than a million head of cattle. By 1885, the feed and water were desperately short, and the winter of 1886 laid out the gaunt bodies of dead animals so closely together that when the thaw came, one rancher from Kaycee claimed to have walked on cowhide all the way to Crazy Woman Creek, twenty miles away.

Territorial Wyoming was a boy's world. The land was generous with everything but water. At first there was room enough, food enough, for everyone. And, as with all beginnings, an expansive mood set in. The young cowboys, drifters, shopkeepers, schoolteachers, were heroic, lawless, generous, rowdy, and tenacious. The individualism and optimism generated during those times have endured.

John Tisdale rode north with the trail herds from Texas. He was a college-educated man with enough money to buy a small outfit near the Powder River. While driving home from the town of Buffalo with a buckboard full of Christmas toys for his family and a winter's supply of food, he was shot in the back by an agent of the cattle barons who resented the encroachment of small-time stockmen like him. The wealthy cattlemen tried to control all the public grazing land by restricting membership in the Wyoming Stock Growers Association, as if it were a country club. They ostracized from roundups and brandings cowboys and ranchers who were not members, then denounced them as rustlers. Tisdale's death, the second such cold-blooded murder, kicked off the Johnson County cattle war, which was no simple good-guy-bad-guy shoot-out but a complicated class struggle between landed gentry and less affluent settlers—a shocking reminder that the West was not an egalitarian sanctuary after all.

Fencing ultimately enforced boundaries, but barbed wire abrogated space. It was stretched across the beautiful valleys, into the mountains, over desert badlands, through buffalo grass. The "anything is possible" fever—the lure of any new place—was constricted. The integrity of the land as a geographical body, and the freedom to ride anywhere on it, was lost. 29

I punched cows with a young man named Martin, who is the great-grandson of John Tisdale. His inheritance is not the open land that Tisdale knew and prematurely lost but a rage against restraint. 30

Wyoming tips down as you head northeast; the highest ground—the Laramie Plains—is on the Colorado border. Up where I live, the Big Horn River leaks into difficult, arid terrain. In the basin where it's dammed, sandhill cranes gather and, with delicate leg-work, slice through the stilled water. I was driving by with a rancher one morning when he commented that cranes are "old-fashioned." When I asked why, he said, "Because they mate for life." Then he looked at me with a twinkle in his eyes, as if to say he really did believe in such things but also understood why we break our own rules. 31

In all this open space, values crystallize quickly. People are strong on scruples but tenderhearted about quirky behavior. A friend and I found one ranch hand, who's "not quite right in the head," sitting in front of the badly decayed carcass of a cow, shaking his finger and saying, "Now, I don't want you to do this ever again!" When I asked what was wrong with him, I was told, "He's goofier than hell, just like the rest of us." Perhaps because the West is historically new, conventional morality is still felt to be less important than rock-bottom truths. Though there's always a lot of teasing and sparring around, people are blunt with each other, sometimes even cruel, believing honesty is stronger medicine than sympathy, which may console but often conceals. 32

The formality that goes hand in hand with the rowdiness is known as "the Western Code." It's a list of practical dos and don'ts, faithfully observed. A friend, Cliff, who runs a trapline in the winter, cut off half his foot while axing a hole in the ice. Alone, he dragged himself to his pickup and headed for town, stopping to open the ranch gate as he left, and getting out to close it again, thus losing, in 33 his observance of rules, precious time and blood. Later, he commented, "How would it look, them having to come to the hospital to tell me their cows had gotten out?"

Accustomed to emergencies, my friends doctor each other from the vet's bag with relish. When one old-timer suffered a heart attack in hunting camp, his partner quickly stirred up a brew of red horse liniment and hot water and made the half-conscious victim drink it, then tied him onto a horse and led him twenty miles to town. He regained consciousness and lived.

The roominess of the state has affected political attitudes as well. Ranchers keep up with world politics and the convulsions of the economy but are basically isolationists. Being used to running their own small empires of land and livestock, they're suspicious of big government. It's a "don't fence me in" holdover from a century ago. They still want the elbow room their grandfathers had, so they're strongly conservative, but with a populist twist.

Summer is the season when we get our "cowboy tans"—on the lower parts of our faces and on three fourths of our arms. Excessive heat, in the nineties and higher, sends us outside with the mosquitoes. In winter, we're tucked inside our houses, and the white wasteland outside appears to be expanding, but in summer, all the greenery abridges space. Summer is a go-ahead season. Every living thing is off the block and in the race: battalions of bugs in flight and biting; bats swinging around my log cabin as if the bases were loaded and someone had hit a home run. Some of summer's high-speed growth is ominous: larspur, death camas, and green greasewood can kill sheep—an ironic idea, dying in this desert from eating what is too verdant. With sixteen hours of daylight, farmers and ranchers irrigate feverishly. There are first, second, and third cuttings of hay, some crews averaging only four hours of sleep a night for weeks. And, like the cowboys who in summer ride the night rodeo circuit, nighthawks make daredevil dives at dusk with an eerie whirring that sounds like a plane going down on the shimmering horizon.

In the town where I live, they've had to board up the dance-hall windows because there have been so many fights. There's so little to do except work that people wind up in a state of idle agitation that becomes fatalistic, as if there were nothing to be done about all this untapped energy. So the dark side to the grandeur of these spaces is the small-mindedness that seals people in. Men become hermits; women go mad. Cabin fever explodes into suicides, or into grudges and lifelong family feuds. Two sisters in my area inherited a ranch but found they couldn't get along. They fenced the place in half. When one's cows got out and mixed with the other's the women went at each other with shovels. They ended up in the same hospital room, but never spoke a word to each other for the rest of their lives.

Eccentricity ritualizes behavior. It's a shortcut through unmanageable emotions and strict social conventions. I knew a sheepherder named Fred who, at seventy-eight, still had a handsome face, which he kept smooth by plastering it each day with bag balm and Vaseline. He was curious, well-read, and had a fact-keeping mind to go along with his penchant for hoarding. His reliquary of gunnysacks, fence wire, wood, canned food, unopened Christmas presents, and magazines matched his odd collages of meals: sardines with maple syrup; vegetable soup garnished with Fig Newtons. His wagon was so overloaded that he had to sleep sitting up because there was no room on the bed. Despite his love of up-to-date information, Fred died from gangrene when an old-timer's remedy of fresh sheep manure, applied as a poultice to a bad cut, failed to save him. 38

After the brief lushness of summer, the sun moves south. The range grass is brown. Livestock has been trailed back down from the mountains. Waterholes begin to frost over at night. Last fall Martin asked me to accompany him on a pack trip. With five horses, we followed a river into the mountains behind the tiny Wyoming town of Meeteetse. Groves of aspen, red and orange, gave off a light that made us look toasted. Our hunting camp was so high that clouds skidded across our foreheads, then slowed to sail out across the warm valleys. Except for a bull moose who wandered into our camp and mistook our black gelding for a rival, we shot at nothing. 39

One of our evening entertainments was to watch the night sky. My dog, who also came on the trip, a dingo bred to herd sheep, is so used to the silence and empty skies that when an airplane flies over he always looks up and eyes the distant intruder quizzically. The sky, lately, seems to be much more crowded than it used to be. Satellites make their silent passes in the dark with great regularity. We 40 counted eighteen in one hour's viewing. How odd to think that while they circumnavigated the planet, Martin and I had moved only six miles into our local wilderness, and had seen no other human for the two weeks we stayed there.

At night, by moonlight, the land is whittled to slivers—a ridge, a 4
river, a strip of grassland stretching to the mountains, then the huge sky. One morning a full moon was setting in the west just as the sun was rising. I felt precariously balanced between the two as I loped across a meadow. For a moment, I could believe that the stars, which were still visible, work like cooper's bands, holding everything about Wyoming together.

Space has a spiritual equivalent, and can heal what is divided and 4
burdensome in us. My grandchildren will probably use space shuttles for a honeymoon trip or to recover from heart attacks, but closer to home we might also learn how to carry space inside ourselves in the effortless way we carry our skins. Space represents sanity, not a life purified, dull or "spaced out" but one that might accommodate intelligently any idea or situation.

From the clayey soil of northern Wyoming is mined bentonite, 4
which is used as a filler in candy, gum, and lipstick. We Americans are great on fillers, as if what we have, what we are, is not enough. We have a cultural tendency toward denial, but, being affluent, we strangle ourselves with what we can buy. We have only to look at the houses we build to see how we build against space, the way we drink against pain and loneliness. We fill up space as if it were a pie shell, with things whose opacity further obstructs our ability to see what is already there.

QUESTIONS FOR READING AND WRITING

1. Though Ehrlich's essay consists primarily of description, there are narrative elements in it. Where are they? How do her occasional anecdotes about people help to contribute significantly to her description?
2. What effects did living in Wyoming have upon the narrator? What did she like or dislike about the character of the people of Wyoming?
3. Point out ways in which time—as in most narratives—is used to organize Ehrlich's essay.

4. Ehrlich's last paragraph implies a denial of space on the part of most Americans. What does she mean by this? What are the implied advantages of *open* space?
5. Compare the people of Wyoming as described by Ehrlich with the Texans described by Larry King in "Playing Cowboy."
6. Write an essay that compares Ehrlich's description of life in Wyoming with Tom Wolfe's description of life in New York City in "O Rotten Gotham: Sliding Down into the Behavioral Sink."
7. Write a descriptive essay, with some narrative elements, about your state. Try, as Ehrlich does, to reach toward some valid generalizations about the people of your state: their main traits, their distinguishing qualities, their connection with the land around them.

✦ Liliana Heker ✦
The Stolen Party

Liliana Heker is an Argentinian fiction writer and editor. While still a teenager, she published her first book of short stories, Those Who Beheld the Burning Bush *(1966). In "The Stolen Party," which first appeared in 1982, Heker writes about a girl's experience of class discrimination in a context where she did not expect it—a party at her "friend's" house.*

1 AS SOON AS SHE ARRIVED she went straight to the kitchen to see if the monkey was there. It was: what a relief! She wouldn't have liked to admit that her mother had been right. *Monkeys at a birthday?* her mother had sneered. *Get away with you, believing any nonsense you're told!* She was cross, but not because of the monkey, the girl thought; it's just because of the party.

2 "I don't like you going," she told her. "It's a rich people's party."

3 "Rich people go to Heaven too," said the girl, who studied religion at school.

4 "Get away with Heaven," said the mother. "The problem with you, young lady, is that you like to fart higher than your ass."

5 The girl didn't approve of the way her mother spoke. She was barely nine, and one of the best in her class.

6 "I'm going because I've been invited," she said. "And I've been invited because Luciana is my friend. So there."

7 "Ah yes, your friend," her mother grumbled. She paused. "Listen, Rosaura," she said at last. "That one's not your friend. You know what you are to them? The maid's daughter, that's what."

8 Rosaura blinked hard: she wasn't going to cry. Then she yelled: "Shut up! You know nothing about being friends!"

9 Every afternoon she used to go to Luciana's house and they would both finish their homework while Rosaura's mother did the cleaning. They had their tea in the kitchen and they told each other secrets. Rosaura loved everything in the big house, and she also loved the people who lived there.

10 "I'm going because it will be the most lovely party in the whole world, Luciana told me it would. There will be a magician, and he will bring a monkey and everything."

11 The mother swung around to take a good look at her child, and pompously put her hands on her hips.

12 "Monkeys at a birthday?" she said. "Get away with you, believing any nonsense you're told!"

13 Rosaura was deeply offended. She thought it unfair of her mother to accuse other people of being liars simply because they were rich. Rosaura too wanted to be rich, of course. If one day she managed to live in a beautiful palace, would her mother stop loving her? She felt very sad. She wanted to go to that party more than anything else in the world.

14 "I'll die if I don't go," she whispered, almost without moving her lips.

15 And she wasn't sure whether she had been heard, but on the morning of the party she discovered that her mother had starched her Christmas dress. And in the afternoon, after washing her hair, her mother rinsed it in apple vinegar so that it would be all nice and shiny. Before going out, Rosaura admired herself in the mirror, with her white dress and glossy hair, and thought she looked terribly pretty.

16 Señora Ines also seemed to notice. As soon as she saw her, she said:

17 "How lovely you look today, Rosaura."

18 Rosaura gave her starched skirt a slight toss with her hands and walked into the party with a firm step. She said hello to Luciana and asked about the monkey. Luciana put on a secretive look and whispered into Rosaura's ear: "He's in the kitchen. But don't tell anyone, because it's a surprise."

19 Rosaura wanted to make sure. Carefully she entered the kitchen and there she saw it: deep in thought, inside its cage. It looked so funny that the girl stood there for a while, watching it, and later, every so often, she would slip out of the party unseen and go and admire it. Rosaura was the only one allowed into the kitchen. Señora Ines had said: "You yes, but not the others, they're much too boisterous, they might break something." Rosaura had never broken anything. She even managed the jug of orange juice, carrying it from the kitchen into the dining room. She held it carefully and didn't spill a single drop. And Señora Ines had said: "Are you sure you can manage a jug as big as that?" Of course she could manage. She wasn't a butterfingers, like the others. Like that blonde girl with

the bow in her hair. As soon as she saw Rosaura, the girl with the bow had said:

"And you? Who are you?"

"I'm a friend of Luciana," said Rosaura.

"No," said the girl with the bow, "you are not a friend of Luciana because I'm her cousin and I know all her friends. And I don't know you."

"So what," said Rosaura. "I come here every afternoon with my mother and we do our homework together."

"You and your mother do your homework together?" asked the girl, laughing.

"I and Luciana do our homework together," said Rosaura, very seriously.

The girl with the bow shrugged her shoulders.

"That's not being friends," she said. "Do you go to school together?"

"No."

"So where do you know her from?" said the girl, getting impatient.

Rosaura remembered her mother's words perfectly. She took a deep breath.

"I'm the daughter of the employee," she said.

Her mother had said very clearly: "If someone asks, you say you're the daughter of the employee; that's all." She also told her to add: "And proud of it." But Rosaura thought that never in her life would she dare say something of the sort.

"What employee?" said the girl with the bow. "Employee in a shop?"

"No," said Rosaura angrily. "My mother doesn't sell anything in any shop, so there."

"So how come she's an employee?" said the girl with the bow.

Just then Señora Ines arrived saying *shh shh*, and asked Rosaura if she wouldn't mind helping serve out the hotdogs, as she knew the house so much better than the others.

"See?" said Rosaura to the girl with the bow, and when no one was looking she kicked her in the shin.

Apart from the girl with the bow, all the others were delightful. The one she liked best was Luciana, with her golden birthday crown; and then the boys. Rosaura won the sack race, and nobody managed to catch her when they played tag. When they split into

two teams to play charades, all the boys wanted her for their side.
Rosaura felt she had never been so happy in all her life.

But the best was still to come. The best came after Luciana blew 39
out the candles. First the cake. Señora Ines had asked her to help
pass the cake around, and Rosaura had enjoyed the task immensely,
because everyone called out to her, shouting "Me, me!" Rosaura
remembered a story in which there was a queen who had the power
of life or death over her subjects. She had always loved that, having
the power of life or death. To Luciana and the boys she gave the
largest pieces, and to the girl with the bow she gave a slice so thin
one could see through it.

After the cake came the magician, tall and bony, with a fine red 40
cape. A true magician: he could untie handkerchiefs by blowing on
them and make a chain with links that had no openings. He could
guess what cards were pulled out from a pack, and the monkey was
his assistant. He called the monkey "partner." "Let's see here, partner," he would say, "turn over a card." And, "Don't run away,
partner: time to work now."

The final trick was wonderful. One of the children had to hold 41
the monkey in his arms and the magician said he would make him
disappear.

"What, the boy?" they all shouted. 42

"No, the monkey!" shouted back the magician. 43

Rosaura thought that this was truly the most amusing party in the 44
whole world.

The magician asked a small fat boy to come and help, but the 45
small fat boy got frightened almost at once and dropped the monkey
on the floor. The magician picked him up carefully, whispered
something in his ear, and the monkey nodded almost as if he
understood.

"You mustn't be so unmanly, my friend," the magician said to the 46
fat boy.

"What's unmanly?" said the fat boy. 47

The magician turned around as if to look for spies. 48

"A sissy," said the magician. "Go sit down." 49

Then he stared at all the faces, one by one. Rosaura felt her heart 50
tremble.

"You, with the Spanish eyes," said the magician. And everyone 51
saw that he was pointing at her.

She wasn't afraid. Neither holding the monkey, nor when the magician made him vanish; not even when, at the end, the magician flung his red cape over Rosaura's head and uttered a few magic words . . . and the monkey reappeared, chattering happily, in her arms. The children clapped furiously. And before Rosaura returned to her seat, the magician said:

"Thank you very much, my little countess."

She was so pleased with the compliment that a while later, when her mother came to fetch her, that was the first thing she told her.

"I helped the magician and he said to me, 'Thank you very much, my little countess.'"

It was strange because up to then Rosaura had thought that she was angry with her mother. All along Rosaura had imagined that she would say to her: "See that the monkey wasn't a lie?" But instead she was so thrilled that she told her mother all about the wonderful magician.

Her mother tapped her on the head and said: "So now we're a countess!"

But one could see that she was beaming.

And now they both stood in the entrance, because a moment ago Señora Ines, smiling, had said: "Please wait here a second."

Her mother suddenly seemed worried.

"What is it?" she asked Rosaura.

"What is what?" said Rosaura. "It's nothing; she just wants to get the presents for those who are leaving, see?"

She pointed at the fat boy and at a girl with pigtails who were also waiting there, next to their mothers. And she explained about the presents. She knew, because she had been watching those who left before her. When one of the girls was about to leave, Señora Ines would give her a bracelet. When a boy left, Señora Ines gave him a yo-yo. Rosaura preferred the yo-yo because it sparkled, but she didn't mention that to her mother. Her mother might have said: "So why don't you ask for one, you blockhead?" That's what her mother was like. Rosaura didn't feel like explaining that she'd be horribly ashamed to be the odd one out. Instead she said:

"I was the best-behaved at the party."

And she said no more because Señora Ines came out into the hall with two bags, one pink and one blue.

First she went up to the fat boy, gave him a yo-yo out of the blue bag, and the fat boy left with his mother. Then she went up to the girl and gave her a bracelet out of the pink bag, and the girl with the pigtails left as well. 66

Finally she came up to Rosaura and her mother. She had a big smile on her face and Rosaura liked that. Señora Ines looked down at her, then looked up at her mother, and then said something that made Rosaura proud: 67

"What a marvelous daughter you have, Herminia." 68

For an instant, Rosaura thought that she'd give her two presents: the bracelet and the yo-yo. Señora Ines bent down as if about to look for something. Rosaura also leaned forward, stretching out her arm. But she never completed the movement. 69

Señora Ines didn't look in the pink bag. Nor did she look in the blue bag. Instead she rummaged in her purse. In her hand appeared two bills. 70

"You really and truly earned this," she said handing them over. "Thank you for all your help, my pet." 71

Rosaura felt her arms stiffen, stick close to her body, and then she noticed her mother's hand on her shoulder. Instinctively she pressed herself against her mother's body. That was all. Except her eyes. Rosaura's eyes had a cold, clear look that fixed itself on Señora Ines's face. 72

Señora Ines, motionless, stood there with her hand outstretched. As if she didn't dare draw it back. As if the slightest change might shatter an infinitely delicate balance. 73

QUESTIONS FOR READING AND WRITING

1. Explain the significance of the story's title. In what sense is the party stolen from Rosaura?
2. What part of the story constitutes the exposition? What does this part contribute to the story?
3. How is the conclusion of the story foreshadowed or anticipated? Did you sense that Rosaura ultimately would be disappointed or humiliated?

4. What "infinitely delicate balance" is referred to at the end of the story?
5. Describe a time when you found yourself among rich or "high class" people. Record your perception of what "high class" meant for you and how you felt in the presence of great wealth or social position.
6. Write an essay that recounts a party or other large social gathering through the eyes of a child (yourself or an imagined character).

✦ Bobbie Ann Mason ✦
The Rookers

Bobbie Ann Mason (b. 1940) is a native of Maysfield, Kentucky. She received her Ph.D. in 1972 from the University of Connecticut. Her published work includes Shiloh and Other Stories *(1982),* In Country *(1985),* Spence and Lila *(1988), and* Love Life *(1985). In "The Rookers," she writes about a couple struggling to adjust to their daughter's absence at college. The daughter's visit helps the wife gain insights into her husband's attitudes toward women and toward his life.*

MARY LOU SKAGGS RUNS ERRANDS for her husband. She hauls lumber, delivers bookshelves, even makes a special trip to town just to exchange flathead screws. Mack will occasionally go out to measure people's kitchens for the cabinets and countertops he makes, but he gets uncomfortable if he has to be away long. And the highway makes him nervous. Increasingly, he stays at home, working in his shop in the basement. They live on a main road between two small Kentucky towns, and the shop sign has been torn down by teenagers so many times that Mack has given up trying to keep it repaired. Mary Lou feels that Mack never charges enough for his work, but she has always helped out—keeping the books, canning and sewing, as well as periodically working for H & R Block—and they have managed to send their youngest child to college. The two older daughters are married, with homes nearby, but Judy is a freshman at Murray State. After she left, Mack became so involved with some experimental woodworking projects that Mary Lou thought he had almost failed to notice that the children had all gone. 1

For some neighbors, Mack made a dinette booth out of a church pew salvaged from an abandoned country church. The sanding took days. "I'm sanding off layers of hypocrisy," Mack said. 2

"You sound like that guy that used to stand out on the corner and yell when church let out on Sunday," said Mary Lou. "Here come the hyps,' he'd say." 3

"Who was that?" 4

"Oh, just some guy in town. That was years ago. He led a crusade against fluoride too." 5

"Fluoride's O.K. It hardens the teeth."

For their twenty-fifth anniversary, Mack made Mary Lou a round card table from scrap pine, with an old sprocket from a bulldozer as a base. It was connected to the table with a length of lead pipe. "It didn't cost a thing," Mack said. "Just imagination."

The tabletop, a mosaic of wood scraps, was like a crazy quilt, Mary Lou thought. It was heavily varnished with polyurethane, making a slick surface. Mack had spray-painted the sprocket black.

"Do you like it?" he asked.

"Sure."

"No, you don't. I can tell you don't."

"It's real pretty."

"It's not something you would buy in a store," Mack said apologetically.

Mary Lou had never seen a table like it. Automatically, she counted the oddly shaped pieces Mack had fit together for the top. Twenty-one. It seemed that Mack was trying to put together the years of their marriage into a convincing whole and this was as far as he got. Mary Lou is concerned about Mack. He seems embarrassed that they are alone in the house now for the first time in years. When Judy fails to come home on weekends, he paces around restlessly. He has even started reading books and magazines, as if he can somehow keep up with Judy and her studies. Lately he has become obsessed with the weather. He likes to compare the weather with the predictions in the *Old Farmer's Almanac*. He likes it when the *Almanac* is wrong. Anyone else would be rooting for the *Almanac* to be right.

When the women Mary Lou plays Rook with come over, Mack stays in the den watching TV, hardly emerging to say hello. Thelma Crandall, Clausie Dowdy, and Edda Griffin—the Rookers, Mary Lou calls them—are all much older than Mary Lou, and they are all widows. Mack and Mary Lou married young, and even though they have three grown daughters, they are only in their late forties. Mack says it is unhealthy for her to socialize with senior citizens, but Mary Lou doesn't believe him. It does her good to have some friends.

Mary Lou shows off the new card table when the women arrive one evening. They all come in separate cars, not trusting each other's driving.

"It's set on a bulldozer sprocket," Mary Lou explains. 17

"How did Mack come up with such an idea?" asks Clausie, admiring the table. 18

Thelma, the oldest of the group, is reluctant to sit at the table, for fear she will catch her foot in one of the holes at the base. 19

"Couldn't you cover up the bottom of that table with a rug or something?" asks Edda. "We might catch our feet." 20

Mary Lou finds an old afghan and drapes it around the bulldozer sprocket, tamping it down carefully in the holes. She gets along with old people, and she feels exhilarated when she is playing cards with her friends. "They tickle me," she told Mack once. "Old people are liable to say anything." Mack said old people gave him the creeps, the way they talked about diseases. 21

Mary Lou keeps a list of whose turn it is to deal, because they often lose track. When they deal the cards on the new table, the cards shoot across the slick surface. This evening they discuss curtain material, Edda's granddaughter's ovary infection, a place that appeared on Thelma's arm, and the way the climate has changed. All three of the widows live in nice houses in town. When Mary Lou goes to their houses to play Rook, she is impressed by their shag rugs, their matching sets of furniture, their neat kitchens. Their walls are filled with pictures of grandchildren and great-grandchildren. Mary Lou's pictures are scattered around in drawers, and her kitchen is always a mess. 22

"They're beating the socks off of us," Mary Lou tells Mack when he watches the game for a moment. Mary Lou is teamed up with Thelma. "I had the bird—that was the only trump I had." 23

"I haven't had it a time," says Clausie, a peppy little woman with a trim figure. 24

"I put thirty in the widow and they caught it," Thelma tells Mack. 25

"The rook's a sign of bad luck," Mack says. "A rook ain't nothing but a crow." 26

When he returns to the football game he is watching on TV, Edda says with a laugh, "Did y'all hear what Erma Bombeck said? She said any man who watches more than a hundred and sixty-eight football games in one year ought to be declared legally dead." 27

They all laugh in little bursts and spasms, but Mary Lou says defensively, "Mack doesn't watch that much football. He just watches it because it's on. Usually he has his nose stuck in a book." 28

"I used to read", says Clausie. "But I got out of the habit." 2

Later, Mary Lou complains to Mack about his behavior. "You 3
could at least be friendly," she says.

"I like to see you playing cards," says Mack. 3

"You're changing the subject." 3

"You light up and you look so pretty." 3

"I'll say one thing for those old gals. They get out and *go*. They 3
don't hide under a bushel. Like some people I know."

"I don't hide under a bushel." 3

"You think they're just a bunch of silly old widow women." 3

"You look beautiful when you're having a good time," says Mack, 3
goosing her and making her jump.

"They're not that old, though," says Mary Lou. "They don't act it. 3
Edda's a great-grandmother, but she's just as spry! She goes to Paducah driving that little Bobcat like she owned the road. And Clausie hasn't got a brain in her head. She's just like a kid—"

But now Mack is absorbed in something on TV, a pudding com- 3
mercial. Mary Lou has tried to be patient with Mack, thinking that he will grow out of his current phase. Sooner or later, she and Mack will have to face growing older together. Mack says that having a daughter in college makes him feel he has missed something, but Mary Lou has tried to make him see that they could still enjoy life. Before she began playing regularly with the Rookers, she had several ideas for doing things together, now that they were no longer tied down with a family. She suggested bowling, camping, a trip to Opryland. But Mack said he'd rather improve his mind. He has been reading *Shōgun*. He made excuses about the traffic. They had a chance to go on a free weekend to the Paradise Valley Estates, a resort development in the Ozarks. There was no obligation. All they had to do was hear a talk and watch some slides. But Mack hated the idea and said there was a catch. Mack made Mary Lou feel she was pressuring him, and she decided not to bring up these topics for a while. She would wait for him to come out of his shell. But she was disappointed about the free weekend. The resort had swimming, nature trails, horseback riding, golf, fishing, and pontoon boat rentals. The bathrooms had whirlpools.

When the telephone rings at five o'clock one morning, Mary Lou 4
is certain there must be bad news from Judy. As she runs to the

kitchen to answer the telephone, her mind runs through dope, suicide, dorm fires. The man on the phone has a loud voice that blares out at her. He makes her guess who he is. He turns out to be Ed Williams, her long-lost brother. Mary Lou is speechless, having concluded several years ago that he must be dead. Ed had gone to Texas for his health, traveling with a woman with a dark complexion and pierced ears. Now he tells Mary Lou he is married to that woman, named Linda, and they are living in California with her two children from a former marriage.

"What do you look like?" asks Mary Lou. 41

"I'm a beanpole. I have to bend over to make a shadow." 42

Mary Lou says, "I'm old and fat and ugly. Mack would whip me 43
to hear that. I'm not really, but after nine years, you'd know the difference. It's been nine years, Ed Williams. I could kill you for doing us like that."

"I just finished building me a house, but I don't have a thing I 44
want to put in it except a washer and dryer."

"All the girls are gone. Judy's in college—first one to go. We're 45
proud. She says she's going to make a doctor. Betty and Janie are married, with younguns."

"I've got me a camper and a pickup and a retirement lot," Ed 46
says. "What's Mack up to?"

"Oh, he's so lonesome with all the girls gone that he's acting 47
peculiar."

Disturbed and excited, Mary Lou burns the bacon while she's 48
telling Mack about the call. Mack seems surprised that Ed is still with the same woman.

"How did she get him wrapped around her little finger? Ed 49
would never even stay in one place long enough to get a crop out."

Mary Lou shoves Mack's plate in front of him. "I thought to my 50
soul he was dead. When he went out there, he looked terrible. He thought he had TB. But it was just like him not to write or call or say boo."

"Ed always was wild. I bet he was drunk." 51

Mary Lou sits down to eat. Cautiously, she says, "He wants us to 52
come out and see him."

"Why can't he come here?" 53

"He's got a family now. He's tied down." 54

Mack flips through the *Old Farmer's Almanac* as he eats. 55

Mary Lou says, "We could go out there. We're not tied down."

Mack fastens his finger on a page. "What if Judy wanted to come home? She'd have to stay here by herself."

"You beat all I've ever seen, Mack." Mary Lou smears jelly on her toast and eats a bite. She says, "Ed said he just got to thinking how he wanted to hear from home. He said Christmas was coming up and—you want to know something, Mack? Ed was on my mind all one day last week. An then he calls, just like that. I must have had a premonition. What does the *Farmer's Almanac* say to that?"

Mack points to a weather chart. "It says here we're due for a mild winter—no snow hardly a-tall. But I don't believe it. I believe we're going to have snow before Christmas."

Mack sounds so serious. He sounds like the President delivering a somber message on the economy. Mary Lou doesn't know what to think.

The next evening at Clausie's house, the Rookers are elated over Mary Lou's news, but she doesn't go into details about her brother's bad reputation.

"It sounded just like him," she says. "His voice was just as *clear.*"

Clausie urges Mary Lou to persuade Mack to go to California.

"Oh, we could never afford it," says Mary Lou. "I'm afraid to even bring it up."

"It's awful far," says Thelma. "My oldest girl's daughter went out in May of seventy-three. She left the day school was out."

"Did he say what he was doing?" Edda asks Mary Lou.

"He said he just built him a house and didn't have anything he wanted to put in it but a washer and dryer. Mack's making fun of me for carrying on so, but he never liked Ed anyway. Ed was always a little wild."

For refreshments, Clausie has made lemon chiffon cake and boiled custard. Mary Lou loves being at Clausie's. Her house is like her chiffon cakes, all soft surfaces and pleasant colors, and she has a new factory-waxed Congoleum floor in her kitchen, patterned after a brick wall.

When Clausie clears away the dishes, she pats Mary Lou's hand and says, "Well, maybe your brother will come back home, if you all can't go out. Sounds like his mind's on his family now."

"You and Mack need to go more," says Edda.

"You ought to get Mack out square-dancing!" says Clausie, who belongs to a square-dancing club. 71

Mary Lou has to laugh, that idea is so farfetched. 72

"My fiftieth wedding anniversary would have been day before yesterday," says Thelma, whose husband had died the year before. 73

"It's too bad Otis couldn't have lived just a little longer," says Clausie sympathetically. 74

"He bought us eight grave plots. Otis wanted me and him to have plenty of room." 75

The widows compare prices of caskets. 76

"Law, I wouldn't want to be cremated the way some of them are doing now," says Edda. "To save space." 77

"Me neither," says Clausie with a whoop. "Did y'all see one of them Russians on television while back? At his funeral there was this horse and buggy pulling the body, and instead of a casket there was this little-bitty vase propped up there. It was real odd looking." 78

"The very idea!" cries Edda. "Keeping somebody in a vase on the mantel. Somebody might use it for a ashtray." 79

Clausie and Edda and Thelma are all laughing. Mary Lou shuffles the cards distractedly, the way Mack flips through the *Old Farmer's Almanac*, as if some wisdom might rub off. 80

"Come on, y'all, let's play," she says. 81

But the women cannot settle down and concentrate on the game yet. They are still laughing, overflowing with good humor. Mary Lou shuffles the cards endlessly, as though she can never get them exactly right. 82

Mack hardly watches TV anymore, except when the Rookers are there. He sits in his armchair reading. He belongs to a book club. Since Judy went away to college, he has read *Shōgun*, *Rage of Angels*, *The Clowns of God*, and *The Covenant*. He read parts of *Cosmos*, which Mary Lou brought him from the library. He does not believe anything he has read in *Cosmos*. It was not on TV in their part of the country. Now he is struggling along with *The Encyclopedia of Philosophy*. When he reads that, his face is set in a painful frown. 83

Mary Lou delivers a gun cabinet to a young couple in a trailer park. How they can afford a gun cabinet, she has no idea. She picks up some sandpaper for Mack. Mack will never make a list. He sends 84 her to town for one or two things at a time. At home, he apologizes for not going on the errand himself. He is rubbing a piece of wood with a rag.

"Look at this," he says excitedly, showing Mary Lou a sketch of some shelves. "I decided what I want to make Judy for Christmas, for a surprise."

The sketch is an intricate design with small compartments.

"Judy called while you were gone," Mack says. "After I talked to her, I got an inspiration. I'm making her this for her dorm room. It's going to have a place here for her turntable, and slots for records. It's called a home entertainment center."

"It's pretty. What did Judy call for?"

"She's coming home tomorrow. Her roommate quit school, and Judy's coming home early to study for her exams next week."

"What happened to her roommate?"

"She wouldn't say. She must be in some kind of trouble, though."

"Is Judy all right?"

"Yeah. After she called, I just got to thinking that I wanted to do something nice for her." Mack is fitting sandpaper onto his sander, using a screwdriver to roll it in. Suddenly he says, "You wouldn't go off and leave me, would you?"

"What makes you say that?"

Mack sets down the sander and takes her by the shoulders, then holds her close to him. He smells like turpentine. "You're always wanting to run around," he says. "You might get ideas."

"Don't worry," says Mary Lou. "I wouldn't think of leaving you." She can't help adding sarcastically, "You'd starve."

"You might go off to find Ed."

"Well, not in that pickup anyway," she says. "The brakes are bad."

When he releases her, he looks happy. He turns on the sander and runs it across the piece of wood, moving with the grain. When he turns off the sander and begins rubbing away the fine dust with a tack rag, Mary Lou says, "People were always jealous of Ed. The only reason he ever got in trouble was that people picked on him because he carried so much money around with him. People heard he had money, and when he'd pull into town in that rig he drove, the police would think up some excuse to run him in. People were just jealous. Everything he touched turned to money."

The way Mack is rubbing the board with the tack rag makes Mary 100
Lou think of Aladdin and his lamp. He rubs and rubs, nodding when she speaks.

Judy drives a little Chevette she bought with money she earned 101
working at the Burger Chef. She arrives at suppertime the next day with a pizza and a tote bag of books. Mary Lou serves green beans, corn, and slaw with the pizza. She and Mack hover over their daughter. At their insistence, Judy tries to explain what happened to her roommate.

"Stephanie had a crush on this Western Civ professor and she 102
made it into a big thing. Now her boyfriend is giving her a real hard time. He accused her of running around with the teacher, but she didn't. Now he's mad at her, and she just took off to straighten out her head."

"Did she go back home to her mama and daddy?" Mary Lou asks. 103

Judy shakes her head no, and her hair flies around like a dust mop 104
being shaken. Mary Lou almost expects things to fly out. Judy's hair is curly and flyaway. She had put something on it. Judy is wearing a seashell on a chain around her neck.

"This pizza's cold," says Judy. She won't touch the green beans. 105

Mack says, "I don't see why she won't stay and finish her tests at 106
least. Now she'll have to pay for a whole extra semester."

"Well, I hope she don't go off the deep end like her mama," says 107
Mary Lou. Judy once told them that Stephanie's mother had had several nervous breakdowns.

"Her daddy don't eat meat a-tall?" asks Mack. 108

"No. He's a vegetarian." 109

"And he don't get sick?" 110

Judy shakes her head again. 111

After supper, Judy dumps out the contents of her tote bag on the 112
love seat. She has a math book, a science book, something called *A Rhetoric for the Eighties*, and a heavy psychology book. She sits cross-legged on the love seat, explaining quantum mechanics to Mary Lou and Mack. She calls her teacher Bob.

Judy says, "It's not that weird. It's just the study of elementary 113
particles—the little things in the world, smaller than atoms. There's

some things called photons that disappear if you look for them. Nobody can find them."

"How do they know they're there, then?" asks Mack skeptically. 114

"Where do they go?" Mary Lou asks. 115

The seashell bounces between Judy's breasts as she talks excitedly, moving her arms like a cheerleader. She is wearing a plaid flannel shirt with the cuffs rolled back. She says, "If you try to separate them, they disappear. They don't even *exist* except in a group. Bob says this is one of the most *important* discoveries in the history of the world. He says it just *explodes* all the old ideas about physics." 116

Bob is not the same teacher Stephanie had the crush on. That teacher's name is Tom. Mary Lou has this much straight. Mack is pacing the floor, the way he does sometimes when Judy doesn't come home on the weekend. 117

"I thought it was philosophy you were taking," he says. 118

"No, physics." 119

"Mack's been reading up on philosophy," says Mary Lou. "He thought you were taking philosophy." 120

"It's similar," Judy says. "In quantum mechanics, there's no final answer. Anything you look at might have a dozen different meanings. Bob says the new physics is discovering what the Eastern mystics have known all along." 121

Mary Lou is confused. "If these things don't exist, then how do they know about them?" 122

"They know about them when they're in bunches." Judy begins writing in her notebook. She looks up and says, "Quantum mechanics is like a statistical study of group behavior." 123

Abruptly, Mack goes to the basement. Mary Lou picks up her sewing and begins watching *Real People* on TV. She can hear the signs of her husband's existence: the sound of the drill from the shop, then his saw. A spurt of swearing. 124

The next evening, Judy talks Mary Lou into going to a movie, but Mack says he has work to do. He is busy with the home entertainment center he is building for Judy. Mary Lou is embarrassed to be going to an R-rated movie, but Judy laughs at her. Judy drives her Chevette, and they stop to pick up Clausie, whom Mary Lou has invited. 125

"Clausie changes with the times," Mary Lou tells her daughter apologetically. "You ought to see the way she gets out and goes. She even square-dances." 126

Clausie insists on climbing in the back seat because she is small. "I wore pants 'cause I knew y'all would," she says. "I don't wear them when I come to your house, Mary Lou, because I just don't feel right wearing pants around a man." 127

"I haven't worn a dress since 1980," says Judy. 128

"This show is going to curl our ears," Mary Lou tells Clausie. 129

"Oh, Mom," Judy says. 130

"Is it a dirty movie?" Clausie asks eagerly. 131

"It's R-rated," says Mary Lou. 132

"Well, I say live and learn," says Clausie, laughing. "Thelma and Edda would have a fit if they knew what we was up to." 133

"Mack wouldn't go," says Mary Lou. "He doesn't like to be in the middle of a bunch of women—especially if they're going to say dirty-birds." 134

"Everybody says those words," says Judy. "They don't mean anything." 135

The movie is *Stir Crazy*. Mary Lou has to hold her side, she laughs so hard. When the actors cuss, she sinks in her seat, clutching Judy's arm. Judy doesn't even flinch. As she watches the movie, which drags in places, Mary Lou now and then thinks about how her family has scattered. If you break up a group, the individuals could disappear out of existence. She has the unsettling thought that what is happening with Mack is that he is disappearing like that, disconnected from everybody, the way Ed did. On the screen, Gene Wilder is on a mechanical bull, spinning around and around, raising his arm in triumph. 136

Later, after they drop off Clausie and are driving home, Judy turns on the car radio. Mary Lou is still chuckling over the movie, but Judy seems depressed. She has hardly mentioned her roommate, so Mary Lou asks, "Where'd Stephanie go then, if she didn't go home?" 137

Judy turns the radio down. "She went to her sister's, in Nashville. Her brother-in-law's a record promoter and they've got this big place with a swimming pool and horses and stuff." 138

"Well, maybe she can make up with her boyfriend when she cools off." 139

"I don't think so." Judy turns right at the high school and heads down the highway. She says, "She wants to break up with him, but he won't leave her alone, so she just took off."

Mary Lou sighs. "This day and time, people just do what they please. They just hit the road. Like those guys in the show. And like Ed."

"Stephanie's afraid of Jeff, though, afraid of what he might do."

"What?"

"Oh, I don't know. Just something crazy." Judy turns up the volume of the radio, saying, "Here's a song for you, Mom. It's a dirty song. 'The Horizontal Bop'—get it?"

Mary Lou listens for a moment. "I don't get it," she says, fearing something as abstruse as the photons. In the song, the singer says repeatedly, "Everybody wants to do the Horizontal Bop."

"Oh, I get it," Mary Lou says with a sudden laugh. "I don't dare tell my Rookers about that." A moment later, she says, "But they wouldn't get it. It's the word 'bop.' They probably never heard the word 'bop.'"

Mary Lou feels a little pleased with herself. Bop. Bebop. She's not so old. Her daughter is not so far away. For a brief moment, Mary Lou feels that rush of joy that children experience when they whirl around happily, unconscious of time.

When Mary Lou's friends come to play Rook the following evening, they are curious about Judy's roommate, but Judy won't divulge much. She is curled on the love seat, studying math. Mary Lou explains to the Rookers, "Stephanie comes from a kind of disturbed family. Her mother's had a bunch of nervous breakdowns and her daddy's a vegetarian." Mack has the TV too loud, and it almost seems that the Incredible Hulk is in on the card game. Mary Lou gets Mack to turn down the sound. Later, he turns the TV off and picks up Judy's physics book. As the game goes on, he periodically goes to the telephone and dials the time-and-temperature number. The temperature is dropping, he reports. It is already down to twenty-four. He is hoping for snow, but the Rookers worry about the weather, fearful of driving back in the freezing night air.

When Clausie tells about *Stir Crazy,* Mary Lou tries to describe the scene that cracked her up—Richard Pryor and Gene Wilder dressed up in elaborate feathered costumes. They were supposed to be woodpeckers.

Clausie says, "*I* liked to died when the jailer woke 'em up in the 150
morning, and they was both of 'em trying to use the commode at the same time."

The Rookers keep getting mixed up, missing plays. Thelma plays 151
the wrong color.

"What did you do that for?" asks Edda, her partner tonight. 152
"Trumps is green."

Thelma says, "I'm so bumfuzzled I can't think. I don't know when 153
I've ever listened to such foolishness. Peckerwoods and niggers and a dirty show."

Mary Lou has been thinking of commenting on a new disease she 154
has heard of, in which a person is afflicted by uncontrollable twitching and compulsive swearing, but she realizes that's a bad idea. She jumps up, saying, "Let's stop for refreshments, y'all. I made coconut cake with seven-minute icing."

Mary Lou serves the cake on her good plates, and everyone 155
comments on how moist it is. After finishing her cake and iced tea, Thelma suddenly insists on leaving because of the weather. She says her feet are cold. Mary Lou offers to turn up the heat, but Thelma already has her coat on. She whips out her flashlight and heads for the door. Thelma's Buick sounds like a cement mixer. As they hear it backing out of the driveway, Clausie says, in a confidential tone, "She's mad because we saw that dirty show. The weather, my eye."

"She's real religious," says Edda. 156

"Well, golly-Bill, I'm as Christian as the next one!" cries Mary 157
Lou. "Them words don't mean anything against religion. I bet Mack just got her stirred up about the temperature."

"Thelma's real old-timey," says Clausie. "She don't have any idea 158
some of the things kids do nowadays."

"Times has changed, that's for sure," says Mary Lou. 159

Edda says, "Otis spoiled her. He carried her around on a pillow." 160

Mary Lou takes Mack some cake on a paper plate. He is still 161
reading the physics book.

"We went set," Mary Lou says. "I had the Rook last hand, but it 162
didn't do me any good."

"Thelma fixed your little red wagon, didn't she?" Mack says with 163
a satisfied grin.

"It was your fault, getting her all worked up about the cold. Why don't you play with us—and take Thelma's place?" 1

"I'm busy studying. I think I've found a mistake in this book." He takes a large bite of cake. "Your coconut is my favorite," he says. 1

"I'll give you my recipe," Mary Lou snaps, wheeling away. 1

To Mary Lou's surprise, Judy offers to take Thelma's place and finish the card game. Mary Lou apologizes to her daughter for taking her away from her books, but Judy says she needs a break. Judy wins several hands, trumping with a flourish and grabbing the cards gleefully. Mary Lou is relieved. After Clausie and Edda leave, she feels excited and talkative. She finds herself telling Judy more about Ed, trying to make Judy remember her uncle. Mary Lou finds a box of photographs and shows Judy a picture of him. In the snapshot, he is standing in front of his tractor-trailer truck, holding a can of Hudepohl. 1

Mary Lou says, "He used to drive these long hauls, and when he'd come back through here, the police would try and pick him up. They heard he had money." 1

Mack joins Judy on the love seat. He shuffles silently through the pictures, and Mary Lou talks rapidly. "They'd follow him around, just waiting for him to cross that line, to start something. One time he and his first wife, Pauline, went to the show and when they got out they stuck him with a parking ticket. All because he had a record." 1

Judy and Mack are looking at the pictures together. Mack is studying a picture of himself with Judy, a bald-headed baby clutching a rattle. 1

"How did he get a record?" asks Judy. 1

"Wrecks." 1

"D.W.I.?" asks Judy knowingly. "Driving while intoxicated?" 1

Mary Lou nods. "Wrecks. A man got killed in one." 1

"Did they charge him?" Judy asks with sudden eagerness. 1

"No. It wasn't his fault," Mary Lou says quickly. 1

"You take after Ed," Mack tells Judy. "You kind of favor him around the eyes." 1

"He said he was a beanpole," says Mary Lou. "He said he had to bend over to make a shadow. He never had a ounce of fat on his bones." 1

Judy looks closely at her uncle's picture again, as though trying to 179
memorize it for an exam.

"Wow," she says, "Far out." 180

Mack, shuffling some of the snapshots into a ragged stack, says to 181
Judy in a plaintive tone, "Your mother wants to leave us and go out to California."

"I never said that," says Mary Lou. "When did I say that?" 182

Judy is not listening. She is in the kitchen, searching the refriger- 183
ator. "Don't we have any Cokes?" she asks.

"No. We drunk the last one at supper," says Mary Lou, confused. 184

Judy puts on her jacket. "I'll run out and get some." 185

"It's freezing out there," says Mack anxiously. 186

"They're high at the Convenient," Mary Lou calls as Judy goes 187
out the door. "But I guess that's the only place open this late."

Mary Lou sees Mack looking at her as though he is blaming her 188
for Judy's leaving. "What are you looking at me in that tone of voice for?" she demands. "You're always making fun of me. I feel like an old stringling cat."

"Why, I didn't mean to," says Mack, pretending innocence. 189

"She's gone. Furthermore, she's *grown* and she can go out in the 190
middle of the night if she wants to. She can go to South *America* if she wants to."

Mary Lou puts the cover on the cake stand and runs water in the 191
sink over the cake plates. Before she can say more, Mack has lifted the telephone and is dialing the time-and-temperature number again. He listens, while his mouth drops open, as if in disbelief.

"The temperature's going down a degree every hour," he says in 192
a whisper. "It's down to twenty-one."

Mary Lou suddenly realizes that Mack calls the temperature 193
number because he is afraid to talk on the telephone, and by listening to a recording, he doesn't have to reply. It's his way of pretending that he's involved. He wants it to snow so he won't have to go outside. He is afraid of what might happen. But it occurs to her that what he must really be afraid of is women. Then Mary Lou feels so sick and heavy with her power over him that she wants to cry. She sees the way her husband is standing there, in a frozen pose. Mack looks as though he could stand there all night with the telephone receiver against his ear.

QUESTIONS FOR READING AND WRITING

1. Which character in "The Rookers" do you sympathize with the most? the least? Why? How do you know that Mason is not mocking her characters?
2. What are the principal sources of conflict in the story? How do Mack and Mary Lou differ in their attitudes toward the conflict?
3. What symbolic function is performed by the books mentioned in the story: the *Old Farmer's Almanac*, Mack's novels, and Judy's physics textbook?
4. In what ways do the rookers represent a threat to Mack?
5. What is Mason's apparent purpose in drawing the parallel between Judy and her Uncle Ed?
6. Write an informal narrative that shows how your family was affected when you went off to college (or when you came home from college).
7. Write a narrative whose central conflict occurs within a marriage or another kind of love relationship.

✦ Alice Munro ✦
Boys and Girls

Alice Munro (b. 1931) is a Canadian novelist and short-story writer. Many of her stories, like "Boys and Girls," are set in Jubilee, a fictional town in Ontario. Among her collections of stories are Dance of the Happy Shades *(1968),* Something I've Been Meaning to Tell You *(1974), and* The Moons of Jupiter *(1982). In "Boys and Girls," Munro writes of a girl's conflicts about expectations arising from her gender.*

MY FATHER WAS A FOX FARMER. That is, he raised silver foxes, in pens; and in the fall and early winter, when their fur was prime, he killed them and skinned them and sold their pelts to the Hudson's Bay Company or the Montreal Fur Traders. These companies supplied us with heroic calendars to hang, one on each side of the kitchen door. Against a background of cold blue sky and black pine forests and treacherous northern rivers, plumed adventurers planted the flags of England or of France; magnificent savages bent their backs to the portage. 1

For several weeks before Christmas, my father worked after supper in the cellar of our house. The cellar was whitewashed, and lit by a hundred-watt bulb over the worktable. My brother Laird and I sat on the top step and watched. My father removed the pelt inside-out from the body of the fox, which looked surprisingly small, mean and rat-like, deprived of its arrogant weight of fur. The naked, slippery bodies were collected in a sack and buried at the dump. One time the hired man, Henry Bailey, had taken a swipe at me with this sack, saying, "Christmas present!" My mother thought that was not funny. In fact she disliked the whole pelting operation—that was what the killing, skinning, and preparation of the furs was called—and wished it did not have to take place in the house. There was the smell. After the pelt had been stretched inside-out on a long board my father scraped away delicately, removing the little clotted webs of blood vessels, the bubbles of fat; the smell of blood and animal fat, with the strong primitive odour of the fox itself, penetrated all parts of the house. I found it reassuringly seasonal, like the smell of oranges and pine needles. 2

Henry Bailey suffered from bronchial troubles. He would cough and cough until his narrow face turned scarlet, and his light blue, derisive eyes filled up with tears; then he took the lid off the stove, and, standing well back, shot out a great clot of phlegm—hsss—straight into the heart of the flames. We admired him for this performance and for his ability to make his stomach growl at will, and for his laughter, which was full of high whistlings and gurglings and involved the whole faulty machinery of his chest. It was sometimes hard to tell what he was laughing at, and always possible that it might be us.

After we had been sent to bed we could still smell fox and still hear Henry's laugh, but these things, reminders of the warm, safe, brightly lit downstairs world, seemed lost and diminished, floating on the stale cold air upstairs. We were afraid at night in the winter. We were not afraid of *outside* though this was the time of year when snowdrifts curled around our house like sleeping whales and the wind harassed us all night, coming up from the buried fields, the frozen swamp, with its old bugbear chorus of threats and misery. We were afraid of *inside*, the room where we slept. At this time the upstairs of our house was not finished. A brick chimney went up one wall. In the middle of the floor was a square hole, with a wooden railing around it; that was where the stairs came up. On the other side of the stairwell were the things that nobody had any use for any more—a soldiery roll of linoleum, standing on end, a wicker baby carriage, a fern basket, china jugs and basins with cracks in them, a picture of the Battle of Balaclava, very sad to look at. I had told Laird, as soon as he was old enough to understand such things, that bats and skeletons lived over there; whenever a man escaped from the county jail, twenty miles away, I imagined that he had somehow let himself in the window and was hiding behind the linoleum. But we had rules to keep us safe. When the light was on, we were safe as long as we did not step off the square of worn carpet which defined our bedroom-space; when the light was off no place was safe but the beds themselves. I had to turn out the light kneeling on the end of my bed, and stretching as far as I could to reach the cord.

In the dark we lay on our beds, our narrow life rafts, and fixed our eyes on the faint light coming up the stairwell, and sang songs. Laird sang "Jingle Bells," which he would sing any time, whether it was

Christmas or not, and I sang "Danny Boy." I loved the sound of my own voice, frail and supplicating, rising in the dark. We could make out the tall frosted shapes of the windows now, gloomy and white. When I came to the part, *When I am dead, as dead I well may be*—a fit of shivering caused not by the cold sheets but by pleasurable emotion almost silenced me. *You'll kneel and say, an Ave there above me*—What was an Ave? Every day I forgot to find out.

Laird went straight from singing to sleep. I could hear his long, satisfied, bubbly breaths. Now for the time that remained to me, the most perfectly private and perhaps the best time of the whole day, I arranged myself tightly under the covers and went on with one of the stories I was telling myself from night to night. These stories were about myself, when I had grown a little older; they took place in a world that was recognizably mine, yet one that presented opportunities for courage, boldness and self-sacrifice, as mine never did. I rescued people from a bombed building (it discouraged me that the real war had gone on so far away from Jubilee). I shot two rabid wolves who were menacing the schoolyard (the teachers cowered terrified at my back). I rode a fine horse spiritedly down the main street of Jubilee, acknowledging the townspeople's gratitude for some yet-to-be-worked- out piece of heroism (nobody ever rode a horse there, except King Billy in the Orangemen's Day parade). There was always riding and shooting in these stories, though I had only been on a horse twice—bareback because we did not own a saddle—and the second time I had slid right around and dropped under the horse's feet; it had stepped placidly over me. I really was learning to shoot, but I could not hit anything yet, not even tin cans on fence posts. 6

Alive, the foxes inhabited a world my father made for them. It was surrounded by a high guard fence, like a medieval town, with a gate that was padlocked at night. Along the streets of this town were ranged large, sturdy pens. Each of them had a real door that a man could go through, a wooden ramp along the wire, for the foxes to run up and down on, and a kennel—something like a clothes chest with airholes—where they slept and stayed in winter and had their young. There were feeding and watering dishes attached to the wire in such a way that they could be emptied and cleaned from the 7 outside. The dishes were made of old tin cans, and the ramps and kennels of odds and ends of old lumber. Everything was tidy and ingenious; my father was tirelessly inventive and his favourite book in the world was *Robinson Crusoe*. He had fitted a tin drum on a wheelbarrow, for bringing water down to the pens. This was my job in summer, when the foxes had to have water twice a day. Between nine and ten o'clock in the morning, and again after supper, I filled the drum at the pump and trundled it down through the barnyard to the pens, where I parked it, and filled my watering can and went along the streets. Laird came too, with his little cream and green gardening can, filled too full and knocking against his legs and slopping water on his canvas shoes. I had the real watering can, my father's, though I could only carry it three-quarters full.

The foxes all had names, which were printed on a tin plate and 8
hung beside their doors. They were not named when they were born, but when they survived the first year's pelting and were added to the breeding stock. Those my father had named were called names like Prince, Bob, Wally and Betty. Those I had named were called Star or Turk, or Maureen or Diana. Laird named one Maud after a hired girl we had when he was little, one Harold after a boy at school, and one Mexico, he did not say why.

Naming them did not make pets out of them, or anything like it. 9
Nobody but my father ever went into the pens, and he had twice had blood-poisoning from bites. When I was bringing them their water they prowled up and down on the paths they had made inside their pens, barking seldom—they saved that for nighttime, when they might get up a chorus of community frenzy—but always watching me, their eyes burning, clear gold, in their pointed, malevolent faces. They were beautiful for their delicate legs and heavy, aristocratic tails and the bright fur sprinkled on dark down their backs—which gave them their name—but especially for their faces, drawn exquisitely sharp in pure hostility, and their golden eyes.

Besides carrying water I helped my father when he cut the long 10
grass, and the lamb's quarter and flowering money-musk, that grew between the pens. He cut with the scythe and I raked into piles. Then he took a pitchfork and threw fresh-cut grass all over the top of the pens, to keep the foxes cooler and shade their coats, which were browned by too much sun. My father did not talk to me unless

it was about the job we were doing. In this he was quite different from my mother, who, if she was feeling cheerful, would tell me all sorts of things—the name of a dog she had had when she was a little girl, the names of boys she had gone out with later on when she was grown up, and what certain dresses of hers had looked like—she could not imagine now what had become of them. Whatever thoughts and stories my father had were private, and I was shy of him and would never ask him questions. Nevertheless I worked willingly under his eyes, and with a feeling of pride. One time a feed salesman came down into the pens to talk to him and my father said, "Like to have you meet my new hired man." I turned away and raked furiously, red in the face with pleasure.

"Could of fooled me," said the salesman. "I thought it was only a girl." 11

After the grass was cut, it seemed suddenly much later in the year. I walked on stubble in the earlier evening, aware of the reddening skies, the entering silences, of fall. When I wheeled the tank out of the gate and put the padlock on, it was almost dark. One night at this time I saw my mother and father standing talking on the little rise of ground we called the gangway, in front of the barn. My father had just come from the meathouse; he had his stiff bloody apron on, and a pail of cut-up meat in his hand. 12

It was an odd thing to see my mother down at the barn. She did not often come out of the house unless it was to do something—hang out the wash or dig potatoes in the garden. She looked out of place, with her bare lumpy legs, not touched by the sun, her apron still on and damp across the stomach from the supper dishes. Her hair was tied up in a kerchief, wisps of it falling out. She would tie her hair up like this in the morning, saying she did not have time to do it properly, and it would stay tied up all day. It was true, too; she really did not have time. These days our porch was piled with baskets of peaches and grapes and pears, bought in town, and onions and tomatoes and cucumbers grown at home, all waiting to be made into jelly and jam and preserves, pickles and chili sauce. In the kitchen there was a fire in the stove all day, jars clinked in boiling water, sometimes a cheesecloth bag was strung on a pole between two chairs, straining blue-black grape pulp for jelly. I was given jobs to do and I would sit at the table peeling peaches that had been 13 soaked in the hot water, or cutting up onions, my eyes smarting and streaming. As soon as I was done I ran out of the house, trying to get out of earshot before my mother thought of what she wanted me to do next. I hated the hot dark kitchen in summer, the green blinds and the flypapers, the same old oilcloth table and wavy mirror and bumpy linoleum. My mother was too tired and preoccupied to talk to me, she had no heart to tell about the Normal School Graduation Dance; sweat trickled over her face and she was always counting under her breath, pointing at jars, dumping cups of sugar. It seemed to me that work in the house was endless, dreary and peculiarly depressing; work done out of doors, and in my father's service, was ritualistically important.

I wheeled the tank up to the barn, where it was kept, and I heard 1
my mother saying, "Wait till Laird gets a little bigger, then you'll have a real help."

What my father said I did not hear. I was pleased by the way he 1
stood listening, politely as he would to a salesman or a stranger, but with an air of wanting to get on with his real work. I felt my mother had no business down here and I wanted him to feel the same way. What did she mean about Laird? He was no help to anybody. Where was he now? Swinging himself sick on the swing, going around in circles, or trying to catch caterpillars. He never once stayed with me till I was finished.

"And then I can use her more in the house," I heard my mother 1
say. She had a dead-quiet, regretful way of talking about me that always made me uneasy. "I just get my back turned and she runs off. It's not like I had a girl in the family at all."

I went and sat on a feed bag in the corner of the barn, not wanting 1
to appear when this conversation was going on. My mother, I felt, was not to be trusted. She was kinder than my father and more easily fooled, but you could not depend on her, and the real reasons for the things she said and did were not to be known. She loved me, and she sat up late at night making a dress of the difficult style I wanted, for me to wear when school started, but she was also my enemy. She was always plotting. She was plotting now to get me to stay in the house more, although she knew I hated it (*because* she knew I hated it) and keep me from working for my father. It seemed to me she would do this simply out of perversity, and to try her power. It did not occur to me that she could be lonely, or jealous. No

grown-up could be; they were too fortunate. I sat and kicked my heels monotonously against a feedbag, raising dust, and did not come out till she was gone.

At any rate, I did not expect my father to pay any attention to 18
what she said. Who could imagine Laird doing my work—Laird remembering the padlock and cleaning out the watering-dishes with a leaf on the end of a stick, or even wheeling the tank without it tumbling over? It showed how little my mother knew about the way things really were.

I have forgotten to say what the foxes were fed. My father's 19
bloody apron reminded me. They were fed horsemeat. At this time most farmers still kept horses, and when a horse got too old to work, or broke a leg or got down and would not get up, as they sometimes did, the owner would call my father, and he and Henry went out to the farm in the truck. Usually they shot and butchered the horse there, paying the farmer from five to twelve dollars. If they had already too much meat on hand, they would bring the horse back alive, and keep it for a few days or weeks in our stable, until the meat was needed. After the war the farmers were buying tractors and gradually getting rid of horses altogether, so it sometimes happened that we got a good healthy horse, that there was just no use for any more. If this happened in the winter we might keep the horse in our stable till spring, for we had plenty of hay and if there was a lot of snow—and the plow did not always get our road cleared—it was convenient to be able to go to town with a horse and cutter.

The winter I was eleven years old we had two horses in the stable. 20
We did not know what names they had had before, so we called them Mack and Flora. Mack was an old black workhorse, sooty and indifferent. Flora was a sorrel mare, a driver. We took them both out in the cutter. Mack was slow and easy to handle. Flora was given to fits of violent alarm, veering at cars and even at other horses, but we loved her speed and high-stepping, her general air of gallantry and abandon. On Saturdays we went down to the stable and as soon as we opened the door on its cosy, animal-smelling darkness Flora threw up her head, rolled her eyes, whinnied despairingly and pulled herself through a crisis of nerves on the spot. It was not safe to go into her stall; she would kick.

This winter also I began to hear a great deal more on the theme my mother had sounded when she had been talking in front of the barn. I no longer felt safe. It seemed that in the minds of the people around me there was a steady undercurrent of thought, not to be deflected, on this one subject. The word *girl* had formerly seemed to me innocent and unburdened, like the word *child*; now it appeared that it was no such thing. A girl was not, as I had supposed, simply what I was; it was what I had to become. It was a definition, always touched with emphasis, with reproach and disappointment. Also it was a joke on me. Once Laird and I were fighting, and for the first time ever I had to use all my strength against him; even so, he caught and pinned my arm for a moment, really hurting me. Henry saw this, and laughed, saying, "Oh, that there Laird's gonna show you, one of these days!" Laird was getting a lot bigger. But I was getting bigger too. 2

My grandmother came to stay with us for a few weeks and I heard other things. "Girls don't slam doors like that." "Girls keep their knees together when they sit down." And worse still, when I asked some questions, "That's none of girls' business." I continued to slam the doors and sit as awkwardly as possible, thinking that by such measures I kept myself free. 2

When spring came, the horses were let out in the barnyard. Mack stood against the barn wall trying to scratch his neck and haunches, but Flora trotted up and down and reared at the fences, clattering her hooves against the rails. Snow drifts dwindled quickly, revealing the hard grey and brown earth, the familiar rise and fall of the ground, plain and bare after the fantastic landscape of winter. There was a great feeling of opening-out, of release. We just wore rubbers now, over our shoes; our feet felt ridiculously light. One Saturday we went out to the stable and found all the doors open, letting in the unaccustomed sunlight and fresh air. Henry was there, just idling around looking at his collection of calendars which were tacked up behind the stalls in a part of the stable my mother had probably never seen. 2

"Come to say goodbye to your old friend Mack?" Henry said. "Here, you give him a taste of oats." He poured some oats into Laird's cupped hands and Laird went to feed Mack. Mack's teeth were in bad shape. He ate very slowly, patiently shifting the oats around in his mouth, trying to find a stump of a molar to grind it on. 2

"Poor old Mack," said Henry mournfully. "When a horse's teeth's gone, he's gone. That's about the way."

"Are you going to shoot him today?" I said. Mack and Flora had been in the stable so long I had almost forgotten they were going to be shot. 25

Henry didn't answer me. Instead he started to sing in a high, trembly, mocking-sorrowful voice, *Oh, there's no more work, for poor Uncle Ned, he's gone where the good darkies go*. Mack's thick, blackish, tongue worked diligently at Laird's hand. I went out before the song was ended and sat down on the gangway. 26

I had never seen them shoot a horse, but I knew where it was done. Last summer Laird and I had come upon a horse's entrails before they were buried. We had thought it was a big black snake, coiled up in the sun. That was around in the field that ran up beside the barn. I thought that if we went inside the barn, and found a wide crack or a knothole to look through, we would be able to see them do it. It was not something I wanted to see; just the same, if a thing really happened, it was better to see it, and know. 27

My father came down from the house, carrying the gun. 28

"What are you doing here?" he said. 29

"Nothing." 30

"Go on up and play around the house." 31

He sent Laird out of the stable. I said to Laird, "Do you want to see them shoot Mack?" and without waiting for an answer led him around to the front door of the barn, opened it carefully, and went in. "Be quiet or they'll hear us," I said. We could hear Henry and my father talking in the stable, then the heavy, shuffling steps of Mack being backed out of his stall. 32

In the loft it was cold and dark. Thin, crisscrossed beams of sunlight fell through the cracks. The hay was low. It was a rolling country, hills and hollows, slipping under our feet. About four feet up was a beam going around the walls. We piled hay up in one corner and I boosted Laird up and hoisted myself. The beam was not very wide; we crept along it with our hands flat on the barn walls. There were plenty of knotholes, and I found one that gave me the view I wanted—a corner of the barnyard, the gate, part of the field. Laird did not have a knothole and began to complain. 33

I showed him a widened crack between two boards. "Be quiet and wait. If they hear you you'll get us in trouble." 34

My father came in sight carrying the gun. Henry was leading Mack by the halter. He dropped it and took out his cigarette papers and tobacco; he rolled cigarettes for my father and himself. While this was going on Mack nosed around in the old, dead grass along the fence. Then my father opened the gate and they took Mack through. Henry led Mack way from the path to a patch of ground and they talked together, not loud enough for us to hear. Mack again began searching for a mouthful of fresh grass, which was not to be found. My father walked away in a straight line, and stopped short at a distance which seemed to suit him. Henry was walking away from Mack too, but sideways, still negligently holding on to the halter. My father raised the gun and Mack looked up as if he had noticed something and my father shot him.

Mack did not collapse at once but swayed, lurched sideways and fell, first on his side; then he rolled over on his back and, amazingly, kicked his legs for a few seconds in the air. At this Henry laughed, as if Mack had done a trick for him. Laird, who had drawn a long, groaning breath of surprise when the shot was fired, said out loud, "He's not dead." And it seemed to me it might be true. But his legs stopped, he rolled on his side again, his muscles quivered and sank. The two men walked over and looked at him in a businesslike way; they bent down and examined his forehead where the bullet had gone in, and now I saw his blood on the brown grass.

"Now they just skin him and cut him up," I said. "Let's go." My legs were a little shaky and I jumped gratefully down into the hay. "Now you've seen how they shoot a horse," I said in a congratulatory way, as if I had seen it many times before. "Let's see if any cat's had kittens in the hay." Laird jumped. He seemed young and obedient again. Suddenly I remembered how, when he was little, I had brought him into the barn and told him to climb the ladder to the top beam. That was in the spring, too, when the hay was low. I had done it out of a need for excitement, a desire for something to happen so that I could tell about it. He was wearing a little bulky brown and white checked coat, made down from one of mine. He went all the way up, just as I told him, and sat down on the top beam with the hay far below him on one side, and the barn floor and some old machinery on the other. Then I ran screaming to my father, "Laird's up on the top beam!" My father came, my mother came, my father went up the ladder talking very quietly and brought Laird down under his arm, at which my mother leaned against the ladder and began to cry. They said to me, "Why weren't you watching him?" but nobody ever knew the truth. Laird did not know enough to tell. But whenever I saw the brown and white checked coat hanging in the closet, or at the bottom of the rag bag, which was where it ended up, I felt a weight in my stomach, the sadness of unexorcized guilt.

I looked at Laird who did not even remember this, and I did not like the look on this thin, winter-pale face. His expression was not frightened or upset, but remote, concentrating. "Listen," I said, in an unusually bright and friendly voice, "you aren't going to tell, are you?" 38

"No," he said absently. 39

"Promise." 40

"Promise," he said. I grabbed the hand behind his back to make sure he was not crossing his fingers. Even so, he might have a nightmare; it might come out that way. I decided I had better work hard to get all thoughts of what he had seen out of his mind—which, it seemed to me, could not hold very many things at a time. I got some money I had saved and that afternoon we went into Jubilee and saw a show, with Judy Canova, at which we both laughed a great deal. After that I thought it would be all right. 41

Two weeks later I knew they were going to shoot Flora. I knew from the night before, when I heard my mother ask if the hay was holding out all right, and my father said. "Well, after to-morrow there'll just be the cow, and we should be able to put her out to grass in another week." So I knew it was Flora's turn in the morning. 42

This time I didn't think of watching it. That was something to see just one time. I had not thought about it very often since, but sometimes when I was busy, working at school, or standing in front of the mirror combing my hair and wondering if I would be pretty when I grew up, the whole scene would flash into my mind: I would see the easy, practiced way my father raised the gun, and hear Henry laughing when Mack kicked his legs in the air. I did not have any great feeling of horror and opposition, such as a city child might have had; I was too used to seeing the death of animals as a necessity by which we lived. Yet I felt a little ashamed, and there was a new wariness, a sense of holding-off, in my attitude to my father and his work. 43

It was a fine day, and we were going around the yard picking up 44
tree branches that had been torn off in winter storms. This was something we had been told to do, and also we wanted to use them to make a teepee. We heard Flora whinny, and then my father's voice and Henry's shouting, and we ran down to the barnyard to see what was going on.

The stable door was open. Henry had just brought Flora out, and 45
she had broken away from him. She was running free in the barnyard, from one end to the other. We climbed up on the fence. It was exciting to see her running, whinnying, going up on her hind legs, prancing and threatening like a horse in a Western movie, an unbroken ranch horse, though she was just an old driver, an old sorrel mare. My father and Henry ran after her and tried to grab the dangling halter. They tried to work her into a corner, and they had almost succeeded when she made a run between them, wild-eyed, and disappeared around the corner of the barn. We heard the rails clatter down as she got over the fence, and Henry yelled, "She's into the field now!"

That meant she was in the long L-shaped field that ran up by the 46
house. If she got around the center, heading towards the land, the gate was open; the truck had been driven into the field this morning. My father shouted to me, because I was on the other side of the fence, nearest the lane, "Go shut the gate!"

I could run very fast. I ran across the garden, past the tree where 47
our swing was hung, and jumped across a ditch into the lane. There was the open gate. She had not got out, I could not see her up on the road; she must have run to the other end of the field. The gate was heavy. I lifted it out of the gravel and carried it across the roadway. I had it half-way across when she came in sight, galloping straight towards me. There was just time to get the chain on. Laird came scrambling through the ditch to help me.

Instead of shutting the gate, I opened it as wide as I could. I did 48
not make any decision to do this, it was just what I did. Flora never slowed down; she galloped straight past me, and Laird jumped up and down, yelling, "Shut it, shut it!" even after it was too late. My father and Henry appeared in the field a moment too late to see what I had done. They only saw Flora heading for the township road. They would think I had not got there in time.

They did not waste any time asking about it. They went back to the barn and got the gun and the knives they used, and put these in the truck; then they turned the truck around and came bouncing up the field toward us. Laird called to them, "Let me go too, let me go too!" and Henry stopped the truck and they took him in. I shut the gate after they were all gone. 49

I supposed Laird would tell. I wondered what would happen to me. I had never disobeyed my father before, and I could not understand why I had done it. Flora would not really get away. They would catch up with her in the truck. Or if they did not catch her this morning somebody would see her and telephone us this afternoon or tomorrow. There was no wild country here for her to run to, only farms. What was more, my father had paid for her, we needed the meat to feed the foxes, we needed the foxes to make our living. All I had done was make more work for my father who worked hard enough already. And when my father found out about it he was not going to trust me any more; he would know that I was not entirely on his side. I was on Flora's side, and that made me no use to anybody, not even to her. Just the same, I did not regret it; when she came running at me and I held the gate open, that was the only thing I could do. 50

I went back to the house, and my mother said, "What's all the commotion?" I told her that Flora had kicked down the fence and got away. "Your poor father," she said, "now he'll have to go chasing over the countryside. Well, there isn't any use planning dinner before one." She put up the ironing board. I wanted to tell her, but thought better of it and went upstairs and sat on my bed. 51

Lately I had been trying to make my part of the room fancy, spreading the bed with old lace curtains, and fixing myself a dressing-table with some leftovers of cretonne for a skirt. I planned to put up some kind of barricade between my bed and Laird's, to keep my section separate from his. In the sunlight, the lace curtains were just dusty rags. We did not sing at night any more. One night when I was singing Laird said, "You sound silly," and I went right on but the next night I did not start. There was not so much need to anyway, we were no longer afraid. We knew it was just old furniture over there, old jumble and confusion. We did not keep to the rules. I still stayed awake after Laird was asleep and told myself stories, 52 but even in these stories something different was happening, mysterious alterations took place. A story might start off in the old way, with a spectacular danger, a fire or wild animals, and for a while I might rescue people; then things would change around, and instead, somebody would be rescuing me. It might be a boy from our class at school, or even Mr. Campbell, our teacher, who tickled girls under the arms. And at this point the story concerned itself at great length with what I looked like—how long my hair was, and what kind of dress I had on; by the time I had these details worked out the real excitement of the story was lost.

It was later than one o'clock when the truck came back. The 53
tarpaulin was over the back, which meant there was meat in it. My mother had to heat dinner up all over again. Henry and my father had changed from their bloody overalls into ordinary working overalls in the barn, and they washed their arms and necks and faces at the sink, and splashed water on their hair and combed it. Laird lifted his arm to show off a streak of blood. "We shot old Flora," he said, "and cut her up in fifty pieces."

"Well I don't want to hear about it," my mother said. "And don't 54
come to my table like that."

My father made him go and wash the blood off. 55

We sat down and my father said grace and Henry pasted his 56
chewing-gum on the end of his fork, the way he always did; when he took it off he would have us admire the pattern. We began to pass the bowls of steaming, overcooked vegetables. Laird looked across the table at me and said proudly, distinctly, "Anyway it was her fault Flora got away."

"What?" my father said. 57

"She could of shut the gate and she didn't. She just open' it up 58
and Flora run out."

"Is that right?" my father said. 59

Everybody at the table was looking at me. I nodded, swallowing 60
food with great difficulty. To my shame, tears flooded my eyes.

My father made a curt sound of disgust. "What did you do that 61
for?"

I did not answer. I put down my fork and waited to be sent from 62
the table, still not looking up.

But this did not happen. For some time nobody said anything, 63
then Laird said matter-of-factly, "She's crying."

"Never mind," my father said. He spoke with resignation, even good humour, the words which absolved and dismissed me for good. "She's only a girl," he said. 64

I didn't protest that, even in my heart. Maybe it was true. 65

QUESTIONS FOR READING AND WRITING

1. What advantages and disadvantages arise from Munro's choice of the first-person point of view?
2. In what senses, in the course of the story, does the narrator *become* a girl?
3. Describe the narrator's attitude toward indoor and outdoor work. How do these different attitudes affect the theme of the story?
4. Describe the narrator's ambivalent attitude toward her mother.
5. How does the symbolism of the horses Mack and Flora contribute to, or contrast with, the developmental theme of the story?
6. Write a narrative essay that describes a situation in which, because of your gender, you were expected to act in a particular way. (Remember that how you wanted to act, or how you did act, can be used to counter the expectation and introduce conflict into your story.)
7. Write a first-person biographical essay about a turning point in your development as a girl or as a boy. Concentrate on an incident that helped you to define yourself.

✦ Gloria Naylor ✦
Kiswana Browne

Gloria Naylor (b. 1950) holds a B.A. from Brooklyn College and an M.F.A. in Afro-American Studies from Yale. Her novels are The Women of Brewster Place *(1982)—in which "Kiswana Browne" appeared—*Linden Hills *(1985), and* Mama Day *(1988). In "Kiswana Browne," Naylor writes of a young black activist struggling to uphold her social ideals and to come to terms with her mother, a wise woman who may very well understand her daughter.*

FROM THE WINDOW of her sixth-floor studio apartment, Kiswana could see over the wall at the end of the street to the busy avenue that lay just north of Brewster Place. The late-afternoon shoppers looked like brightly clad marionettes as they moved between the congested traffic, clutching their packages against their bodies to guard them from sudden bursts of the cold autumn wind. A portly mailman had abandoned his cart and was bumping into indignant window-shoppers as he puffed behind the cap that the wind had snatched from his head. Kiswana leaned over to see if he was going to be successful, but the edge of the building cut him off from her view.

A pigeon swept across her window, and she marveled at its liquid movements in the air waves. She placed her dreams on the back of the bird and fantasized that it would glide forever in transparent silver circles until it ascended to the center of the universe and was swallowed up. But the wind died down, and she watched with a sigh as the bird beat its wings in awkward, frantic movements to land on the corroded top of a fire escape on the opposite building. This brought her back to earth.

Humph, it's probably sitting over there crapping on those folks' fire escape, she thought. Now, that's a safety hazard. . . . And her mind was busy again, creating flames and smoke and frustrated tenants whose escape was being hindered because they were slipping and sliding in pigeon shit. She watched their cussing, haphazard descent on the fire escapes until they had all reached the bottom. They were milling around, oblivious to their burning apartments, angrily planning to march on the mayor's office about the pigeons. She materialized placards and banners for them, and they had just reached the corner, boldly sidestepping fire hoses and broken glass, when they all vanished.

A tall copper-skinned woman had met this phantom parade at the corner, and they had dissolved in front of her long, confident strides. She plowed through the remains of their faded mists, unconscious of the lingering wisps of their presence on her leather bag and black fur-trimmed coat. It took a few seconds for this transfer from one realm to another to reach Kiswana, but then suddenly she recognized the woman. 4

"Oh, God, it's Mama!" She looked down guiltily at the forgotten newspaper in her lap and hurriedly circled random job advertisements. 5

By this time Mrs. Browne had reached the front of Kiswana's building and was checking the house number against a piece of paper in her hand. Before she went into the building she stood at the bottom of the stoop and carefully inspected the condition of the street and the adjoining property. Kiswana watched this meticulous inventory with growing annoyance but she involuntarily followed her mother's slowly rotating head, forcing herself to see her new neighborhood through the older woman's eyes. The brightness of the unclouded sky seemed to join forces with her mother as it highlighted every broken stoop railing and missing brick. The afternoon sun glittered and cascaded across even the tiniest fragments of broken bottle, and at that very moment the wind chose to rise up again, sending unswept grime flying into the air, as a stray tin can left by careless garbage collectors went rolling noisily down the center of the street. 6

Kiswana noticed with relief that at least Ben wasn't sitting in his usual place on the old garbage can pushed against the far wall. He was just a harmless old wino, but Kiswana knew her mother only needed one wino or one teenager with a reefer within a twenty-block radius to decide that her daughter was living in a building seething with dope factories and hang-outs for derelicts. If she had seen Ben, nothing would have made her believe that practically every apartment contained a family, a Bible, and a dream that one day enough could be scraped from those meager Friday night paychecks to make Brewster Place a distant memory. 7

As she watched her mother's head disappear into the building, 8
Kiswana gave silent thanks that the elevator was broken. That would give her at least five minutes' grace to straighten up the apartment. She rushed to the sofa bed and hastily closed it without smoothing the rumpled sheets and blanket or removing her nightgown. She felt that somehow the tangled bedcovers would give away the fact that she had not slept alone last night. She silently apologized to Abshu's memory as she heartlessly crushed his spirit between the steel springs of the couch. Lord, that man was sweet. Her toes curled involuntarily at the passing thought of his full lips moving slowly over her instep. Abshu was a foot man, and he always started his lovemaking from the bottom up. For that reason Kiswana changed the color of the polish on her toenails every week. During the course of their relationship she had gone from shades of red to brown and was now into the purples. I'm gonna have to start mixing them soon, she thought aloud as she turned from the couch and raced into the bathroom to remove any traces of Abshu from there. She took up his shaving cream and razor and threw them into the bottom drawer of her dresser beside her diaphragm. Mama wouldn't dare pry into my drawers right in front of me, she thought as she slammed the drawer shut. Well, at least not the *bottom* drawer. She may come up with some sham excuse for opening the top drawer, but never the bottom one.

When she heard the first two short raps on the door, her eyes 9
took a final flight over the small apartment, desperately seeking out any slight misdemeanor that might have to be defended. Well, there was nothing she could do about the crack in the wall over that table. She had been after the landlord to fix it for two months now. And there had been no time to sweep the rug, and everyone knew that off-gray always looked dirtier than it really was. And it was just too damn bad about the kitchen. How was she expected to be out job-hunting every day and still have time to keep a kitchen that looked like her mother's, who didn't even work and still had someone come in twice a month for general cleaning. And besides . . .

Her imaginary argument was abruptly interrupted by a second 10
series of knocks, accompanied by a penetrating, "Melanie, Melanie, are you there?"

Kiswana strode toward the door. She's starting before she even 11
gets in here. She knows that's not my name anymore.

She swung the door open to face her slightly flushed mother. "Oh, hi, Mama. You know, I thought I heard a knock, but I figured it was for the people next door, since no one hardly ever calls me Melanie." Score one for me, she thought. 12

"Well, it's awfully strange you can forget a name you answered to for twenty-three years," Mrs. Browne said, as she moved past Kiswana into the apartment. "My, that was a long climb. How long has your elevator been out? Honey, how do you manage with your laundry and groceries up all those steps? But I guess you're young, and it wouldn't bother you as much as it does me." This long string of questions told Kiswana that her mother had no intentions of beginning her visit with another argument about her new African name. 13

"You know I would have called before I came, but you don't have a phone yet. I didn't want you to feel that I was snooping. As a matter of fact, I didn't expect to find you home at all. I thought you'd be out looking for a job." Mrs. Browne had mentally covered the entire apartment while she was talking and taking off her coat. 14

"Well, I got up late this morning. I thought I'd buy the afternoon paper and start early tomorrow." 15

"That sounds like a good idea." Her mother moved toward the window and picked up the discarded paper and glanced over the hurriedly circled ads. "Since when do you have experience as a fork-lift operator?" 16

Kiswana caught her breath and silently cursed herself for her stupidity. "Oh, my hand slipped—I meant to circle file clerk." She quickly took the paper before her mother could see that she had also marked cutlery salesman and chauffeur. 17

"You're sure you weren't sitting here moping and daydreaming again?" Amber specks of laughter flashed in the corner of Mrs. Browne's eyes. 18

Kiswana threw her shoulders back and unsuccessfully tried to disguise her embarrassment with indignation. 19

"Oh, God, Mama! I haven't done that in years—it's for kids. When are you going to realize that I'm a woman now?" She sought desperately for some womanly thing to do and settled for throwing herself on the couch and crossing her legs in what she hoped looked like a nonchalant arc. 20

"Please, have a seat," she said, attempting the same tones and gestures she'd seen Bette Davis use on the late movies. 21

Mrs. Browne, lowering her eyes to hide her amusement, accepted the invitation and sat at the window, also crossing her legs. Kiswana saw immediately how it should have been done. Her celluloid poise clashed loudly against her mother's quiet dignity, and she quickly uncrossed her legs. Mrs. Browne turned her head toward the window and pretended not to notice.

"At least you have a halfway decent view from here. I was wondering what lay beyond that dreadful wall—it's the boulevard. Honey, did you know that you can see the trees in Linden Hills from here?"

Kiswana knew that very well, because there were many lonely days that she would sit in her gray apartment and stare at those trees and think of home, but she would rather have choked than admit that to her mother.

"Oh, really, I never noticed. So how is Daddy and things at home?"

"Just fine. We're thinking of redoing one of the extra bedrooms since you children have moved out, but Wilson insists that he can manage all that work alone. I told him that he doesn't really have the proper time or energy for all that. As it is, when he gets home from the office, he's so tired he can hardly move. But you know you can't tell your father anything. Whenever he starts complaining about how stubborn you are, I tell him the child came by it honestly. Oh, and your brother was by yesterday," she added, as if it had just occurred to her.

So that's it, thought Kiswana. That's why she's here.

Kiswana's brother, Wilson, had been to visit her two days ago, and she had borrowed twenty dollars from him to get her winter coat out of layaway. That son-of-a-bitch probably ran straight to Mama—and after he swore he wouldn't say anything. I should have known, he was always a snotty-nosed sneak, she thought.

"Was he?" she said aloud. "He came by to see me, too, earlier this week. And I borrowed some money from him because my unemployment checks hadn't cleared in the bank, but now they have and everything's just fine." There, I'll beat you to that one.

"Oh, I didn't know that," Mrs. Browne lied. "He never mentioned you. He had just heard that Beverly was expecting again, and he rushed over to tell us."

31 Damn. Kiswana could have strangled herself.

32 "So she's knocked up again, huh?" she said irritably.

33 Her mother started. "Why do you always have to be so crude?"

34 "Personally, I don't see how she can sleep with Willie. He's such a dishrag."

35 Kiswana still resented the stance her brother had taken in college. When everyone at school was discovering their blackness and protesting on campus, Wilson never took part; he had even refused to wear an Afro. This had outraged Kiswana because, unlike her, he was dark-skinned and had the type of hair that was thick and kinky enough for a good "Fro." Kiswana had still insisted on cutting her own hair, but it was so thin and fine-textured, it refused to thicken even after she washed it. So she had to brush it up and spray it with lacquer to keep it from lying flat. She never forgave Wilson for telling her that she didn't look African, she looked like an electrocuted chicken.

36 "Now that's some way to talk. I don't know why you have an attitude against your brother. He never gave me a restless night's sleep, and now he's settled with a family and a good job."

37 "He's an assistant to an assistant junior partner in a law firm. What's the big deal about that?"

38 "The job has a future, Melanie. And at least he finished school and went on for his law degree."

39 "In other words, not like me, huh?"

40 "Don't put words into my mouth, young lady. I'm perfectly capable of saying what I mean."

41 Amen, thought Kiswana.

42 "And I don't know why you've been trying to start up with me from the moment I walked in. I didn't come here to fight with you. This is your first place away from home, and I just wanted to see how you were living and if you're doing all right. And I must say, you've fixed this apartment up very nicely."

43 "Really, Mama?" She found herself softening in the light of her mother's approval.

44 "Well, considering what you had to work with." This time she scanned the apartment openly.

45 "Look, I know it's not Linden Hills, but a lot can be done with it. As soon as they come and paint, I'm going to hang my Ashanti print

over the couch. And I thought a big Boston Fern would go well in that corner, what do you think?"

"That would be fine, baby. You always had a good eye for balance."

Kiswana was beginning to relax. There was little she did that attracted her mother's approval. It was like a rare bird, and she had to tread carefully around it lest it fly away.

"Are you going to leave that statue out like that?"

"Why, what's wrong with it? Would it look better somewhere else?"

There was a small wooden reproduction of a Yoruba goddess with large protruding breasts on the coffee table.

"Well," Mrs. Browne was beginning to blush, "it's just that it's a bit suggestive, don't you think? Since you live alone now, and I know you'll be having male friends stop by, you wouldn't want to be giving them any ideas. I mean, uh, you know, there's no point in putting yourself in any unpleasant situations because they may get the wrong impressions and uh, you know, I mean, well . . . " Mrs. Browne stammered on miserably.

Kiswana loved it when her mother tried to talk about sex. It was the only time she was at a loss for words.

"Don't worry, Mama." Kiswana smiled. "That wouldn't bother the type of men I date. Now maybe if it had big feet . . . " And she got hysterical, thinking of Abshu.

Her mother looked at her sharply. "What sort of gibberish is that about feet? I'm being serious, Melanie."

"I'm sorry, Mama." She sobered up. "I'll put it away in the closet," she said, knowing that she wouldn't.

"Good," Mrs. Browne said, knowing that she wouldn't either. "I guess you think I'm too picky, but we worry about you over here. And you refuse to put in a phone so we can call and see about you."

"I haven't refused, Mama. They want seventy-five dollars for a deposit, and I can't swing that right now."

"Melanie, I can give you the money."

"I don't want you to be giving me money—I've told you that before. Please, let me make it by myself."

"Well, let me lend it to you, then."

"No!"

"Oh, so you can borrow money from your brother, but not from me."

Kiswana turned her head from the hurt in her mother's eyes. "Mama, when I borrow from Willie, he makes me pay him back. You never let me pay you back," she said into her hands. 63

"I don't care. I still think it's downright selfish of you to be sitting over here with no phone, and sometimes we don't hear from you in two weeks—anything could happen—especially living among these people." 64

Kiswana snapped her head up. "What do you mean, *these* people. They're my people and yours, too, Mama—we're all black. But maybe you've forgotten that over in Linden Hills." 65

"That's not what I'm talking about, and you know it. These streets—this building—it's so shabby and rundown. Honey, you don't have to live like this." 66

"Well, this is how poor people live." 67

"Melanie, you're not poor." 68

"No, Mama, *you're* not poor. And what you have and I have are two totally different things. I don't have a husband in real estate with a five-figure income and a home in Linden Hills—*you* do. What I have is a weekly unemployment check and an overdrawn checking account at United Federal. So this studio on Brewster is all I can afford." 69

"Well, you could afford a lot better," Mrs. Browne snapped, "if you hadn't dropped out of college and had to resort to these dead-end clerical jobs." 70

"Uh-huh, I knew you'd get around to that before long." Kiswana could feel the rings of anger begin to tighten around her lower backbone, and they sent her forward onto the couch. "You'll never understand, will you? Those bourgie schools were counterrevolutionary. My place was in the streets with my people, fighting for equality and a better community." 71

"Counterrevolutionary!" Mrs. Browne was raising her voice. "Where's your revolution now, Melanie? Where are all those black revolutionaries who were shouting and demonstrating and kicking up a lot of dust with you on that campus? Huh? They're sitting in wood-paneled offices with their degrees in mahogany frames, and they won't even drive their cars past this street because the city doesn't fix potholes in this part of town." 72

"Mama," she said, shaking her head slowly in disbelief, "how can you—a black woman—sit there and tell me that what we fought for 73 during the Movement wasn't important just because some people sold out?"

"Melanie, I'm not saying it wasn't important. It was damned important to stand up and say that you were proud of what you were and to get the vote and other social opportunities for every person in this country who had it due. But you kids thought you were going to turn the world upside down, and it just wasn't so. When all the smoke had cleared, you found yourself with a fistful of new federal laws and a country still full of obstacles for black people to fight their way over—just because they're black. There was no revolution, Melanie, and there will be no revolution."

"So what am I supposed to do, huh? Just throw up my hands and not care about what happens to my people? I'm not supposed to keep fighting to make things better?"

"Of course, you can. But you're going to have to fight within the system, because it and these so-called 'bourgie' schools are going to be here for a long time. And that means that you get smart like a lot of your friends and get an important job where you can have some influence. You don't have to sell out, as you say, and work for some corporation, but you could become an assemblywoman or a civil liberties lawyer or open a freedom school in this very neighborhood. That way you could really help the community. But what help are you going to be to these people on Brewster while you're living hand-to-mouth on file-clerk jobs waiting for a revolution? You're wasting your talents, child."

"Well, I don't think they're being wasted. At least I'm here in day-to-day contact with the problems of my people. What good would I be after four or five years of a lot of white brainwashing in some phony, prestige institution, huh? I'd be like you and Daddy and those other educated blacks sitting over there in Linden Hills with a terminal case of middle-class amnesia."

"You don't have to live in a slum to be concerned about social conditions, Melanie. Your father and I have been charter members of the NAACP for the last twenty-five years."

"Oh, God!" Kiswana threw her head back in exaggerated disgust. "That's being concerned? That middle-of-the-road, Uncle Tom dumping ground for black Republicans!"

"You can sneer all you want, young lady, but that organization has been working for black people since the turn of the century, and it's still working for them. Where are all those radical groups of yours that were going to put a Cadillac in every garage and Dick Gregory in the White House? I'll tell you where."

I knew you would, Kiswana thought angrily. 81

"They burned themselves out because they wanted too much too fast. Their goals weren't grounded in reality. And that's always been your problem." 82

"What do you mean, my problem? I know exactly what I'm about." 83

"No, you don't. You constantly live in a fantasy world—always going to extremes—turning butterflies into eagles, and life isn't about that. It's accepting what is and working from that. Lord, I remember how worried you had me, putting all that lacquered hair spray on your head. I thought you were going to get lung cancer—trying to be what you're not." 84

Kiswana jumped up from the couch. "Oh, God, I can't take this anymore. Trying to be something I'm not—trying to be something I'm not, Mama! Trying to be proud of my heritage and the fact that I was of African descent. If that's being what I'm not, then I say fine. But I'd rather be dead than be like you—a white man's nigger who's ashamed of being black!" 85

Kiswana saw streaks of gold and ebony light follow her mother's flying body out of the chair. She was swung around by the shoulders and made to face the deadly stillness in the angry woman's eyes. She was too stunned to cry out from the pain of the long fingernails that dug into her shoulders, and she was brought so close to her mother's face that she saw her reflection, distorted and wavering, in the tears that stood in the older woman's eyes. And she listened in that stillness to a story she had heard from a child. 86

"My grandmother." Mrs. Browne began slowly in a whisper, "was a full-blooded Iroquois, and my grandfather a free black from a long line of journeymen who had lived in Connecticut since the establishment of the colonies. And my father was a Bajan who came to this country as a cabin boy on a merchant mariner." 87

"I know all that," Kiswana said, trying to keep her lips from trembling. 88

"Then, know this." And the nails dug deeper into her flesh. "I am alive because of the blood of proud people who never scraped or begged or apologized for what they were. They lived asking only 89 one thing of this world—to be allowed to be. And I learned through the blood of these people that black isn't beautiful and it isn't ugly—black is! It's not kinky hair and it's not straight hair—it just is.

"It broke my heart when you changed your name. I gave you my grandmother's name, a woman who bore nine children and educated them all, who held off six white men with a shotgun when they tried to drag one of her sons to jail for 'not knowing his place.' Yet you needed to reach into an African dictionary to find a name to make you proud.

"When I brought my babies home from the hospital, my ebony son and my golden daughter, I swore before whatever gods would listen—those of my mother's people or those of my father's people—that I would use everything I had and could ever get to see that my children were prepared to meet this world on its own terms, so that no one could sell them short and make them ashamed of what they were or how they looked—whatever they were or however they looked. And Melanie, that's not being white or red or black—that's being a mother."

Kiswana followed her reflection in the two single tears that moved down her mother's cheeks until it blended with them into the woman's copper skin. There was nothing and then so much that she wanted to say, but her throat kept closing up every time she tried to speak. She kept her head down and her eyes closed, and thought, Oh, God, just let me die. How can I face her now?

Mrs. Browne lifted Kiswana's chin gently. "And the one lesson I wanted you to learn is not to be afraid to face anyone, not even a crafty old lady like me who can outtalk you." And she smiled and winked.

"Oh, Mama, I . . ." and she hugged the woman tightly.

"Yeah, baby." Mrs. Browne patted her back. "I know."

She kissed Kiswana on the forehead and cleared her throat. "Well, now, I better be moving on. It's getting late, there's dinner to be made, and I have to get off my feet—these new shoes are killing me."

Kiswana looked down at the beige leather pumps. "Those are really classy. They're English, aren't they?"

"Yes, but, Lord, do they cut me right across the instep." She removed the shoe and sat on the couch to massage her foot.

Bright red nail polish glared at Kiswana through the stockings. 99
"Since when do you polish your toenails?" she gasped. "You never
did that before."

"Well . . . " Mrs. Browne shrugged her shoulders, "your father 100
sort of talked me into it, and, uh, you know, he likes it and all, so I
thought, uh, you know, why not, so . . . " And she gave Kiswana
an embarrassed smile.

I'll be damned, the young woman thought, feeling her whole face 101
tingle. Daddy's into feet! And she looked at the blushing woman on
her couch and suddenly realized that her mother had trod through
the same universe that she herself was now traveling. Kiswana was
breaking no new trails and would eventually end up just two feet
away on that couch. She stared at the woman she had been and was
to become.

"But I'll never be a Republican," she caught herself saying aloud. 102

"What are you mumbling about, Melanie?" Mrs. Browne slipped 103
on her shoe and got up from the couch.

She went to get her mother's coat. "Nothing, Mama. It's really 104
nice of you to come by. You should do it more often."

"Well, since it's not Sunday, I guess you're allowed at least one 105
lie."

They both laughed. 106

After Kiswana had closed the door and turned around, she spot- 107
ted an envelope sticking between the cushions of her couch. She
went over and opened it up; there was seventy-five dollars in it.

"Oh, Mama, darn it!" She rushed to the window and started to 108
call to the woman, who had just emerged from the building, but she
suddenly changed her mind and sat down in the chair with a long
sigh that caught in the upward draft of the autumn wind and
disappeared over the top of the building.

QUESTIONS FOR READING AND WRITING

1. What key differences can you cite between Kiswana and her mother with respect to their life styles, attitudes toward race, and personal goals?

2. What is the significance of Kiswana's discovery that her mother paints her toenails?
3. Why is Kiswana reluctant to accept money from her mother?
4. Compare Kiswana's relationship with her mother with that between Mary Lou and her daughter Judy in Bobbie Ann Mason's "The Rookers."
5. Write a narrative essay about a time that your parents helped you, in a significant way, with a personal, financial, academic, or legal problem you were facing.
6. Select a significant religious, political, or social question and write an essay that shows how, for the issue you select, your views differ from your parents'.

✦ George Orwell ✦
A Hanging

*George Orwell was the pen name of Eric Blair (1903–1950). Orwell served from 1922 to 1927 in the Indian Imperial Police in Burma, an experience which informed both his fiction (*Burmese Days*, 1934) and his essays (*Shooting an Elephant*, 1950). Many of his books—such as* Animal Farm *(1945) and* 1984 *(1949) speak out against totalitarian forms of government. In the following essay, Orwell narrates how a Burmese prisoner was hanged; the essay has become a classic statement about capital punishment.*

IT WAS IN BURMA, a sodden morning of rains. A sickly light, like yellow tinfoil, was slanting over the walls into the jail yard. We were waiting outside the condemned cells, a row of sheds fronted with double bars, like small animals cages. Each cell measured about ten feet by ten and was quite bare within except for a plank bed and a pot for drinking water. In some of them brown silent men were squatting at the inner bars, with their blankets draped round them. These were the condemned men, due to be hanged within the next week or two. 1

One prisoner had been brought out of his cell. He was a Hindu, a puny wisp of a man, with a shaven head and vague liquid eyes. He had a thick, sprouting moustache, absurdly too big for his body, rather like the moustache of a comic man of the films. Six tall Indian warders were guarding him and getting him ready for the gallows. Two of them stood by with rifles and fixed bayonets, while the others handcuffed him, passed a chain through his handcuffs and fixed it to their belts, and lashed his arms tight to his sides. They crowded very close about him, with their hands always on him in a careful caressing grip, as though all the while feeling him to make sure he was there. It was like men handling a fish which is still alive and may jump back into the water. But he stood quite unresisting, yielding his arms limply to the ropes, as though he hardly noticed what was happening. 2

Eight o'clock struck and a bugle call, desolately thin in the wet air, floated from the distant barracks. The superintendent of the jail, who was standing apart from the rest of us, moodily prodding the 3 gravel with his stick, raised his head at the sound. He was an army doctor, with a grey toothbrush moustache and a gruff voice. "For God's sake hurry up, Francis," he said irritably. "The man ought to have been dead by this time. Aren't you ready yet?"

Francis, the head jailer, a fat Dravidian in a white drill suit and gold spectacles, waved his black hand. "Yes sir, yes sir," he bubbled. "All iss satisfactorily prepared. The hangman iss waiting. We shall proceed."

"Well, quick march, then. The prisoners can't get their breakfast till this job's over."

We set out for the gallows. Two warders marched on either side of the prisoner, with their rifles at the slope; two others marched close against him, gripping him by arm and shoulder, as though at once pushing and supporting him. The rest of us, magistrates and the like, followed behind. Suddenly, when we had gone ten yards, the procession stopped short without any order or warning. A dreadful thing had happened—a dog, come goodness knows whence, had appeared in the yard. It came bounding among us with a loud volley of barks, and leapt round us wagging its whole body, wild with glee at finding so many human beings together. It was a large woolly dog, half Airedale, half pariah. For a moment it pranced round us, and then, before anyone could stop, it had made a dash for the prisoner and, jumping up, tried to lick his face. Everyone stood aghast, too taken aback to even grab at the dog.

"Who let that bloody brute in here?" said the superintendent angrily. "Catch it, someone!"

A warder, detached from the escort, charged clumsily after the dog, but it danced and gambolled just out of his reach, taking everything as part of the game. A young Eurasian jailer picked up a handful of gravel and tried to stone the dog away, but it dodged the stones and came after us again. Its yaps echoed from the jail walls. The prisoner, in the grasp of the two warders, looked on incuriously, as though this was another formality of the hanging. It was several minutes before someone managed to catch the dog. Then we put my handkerchief through its collar and moved off once more, with the dog still straining and whimpering.

It was about forty yards to the gallows. I watched the bare brown back of the prisoner marching in front of me. He walked clumsily with his bound arms, but quite steadily, with that bobbing gait of the

Indian who never straightens his knees. At each step his muscles slid neatly into place, the lock of hair on his scalp danced up and down, his feet printed themselves on the wet gravel. And once, in spite of the men who gripped him by each shoulder, he stepped slightly aside to avoid a puddle on the path.

It is curious, but till that moment I had never realized what it 10
means to destroy a healthy, conscious man. When I saw the prisoner step aside to avoid the puddle I saw the mystery, the unspeakable wrongness, of cutting a life short when it is in full tide. This man was not dying, he was alive just as we are alive. All the organs of his body were working—bowels digesting food, skin renewing itself, nails growing, tissue forming—reasoned all toiling away in solemn foolery. His nails would still be growing when he stood on the drop, when he was falling through the air with a tenth-of-a-second to live. His eyes saw the yellow gravel and the grey walls, and his brain still remembered, foresaw, reasoned—reasoned even about puddles. He and we were a party of men walking together, seeing, hearing, feeling, understanding the same world; and in two minutes, with a sudden snap, one of us would be gone—one mind less, one world less.

The gallows stood in a small yard, separate from the main 11
grounds of the prison, and overgrown with tall prickly weeds. It was a brick erection like three sides of a shed, with planking on top, and above that two beams and a crossbar with the rope dangling. The hangman, a grey-haired convict in the white uniform of the prison, was waiting beside his machine. He greeted us with a servile crouch as we entered. At a word from Francis the two warders, gripping the prisoner more closely than ever, half led half pushed him to the gallows and helped him clumsily up the ladder. Then the hangman climbed up and fixed the rope round the prisoner's neck.

We stood waiting, five yards away. The warders had formed in a 12
rough circle round the gallows. And then, when the noose was fixed, the prisoner began crying out to his god. It was a high, reiterated cry of "Ram! Ram! Ram! Ram!" not urgent and fearful like a prayer or cry for help, but steady, rhythmical, almost like the tolling of a bell. The dog answered the sound with a whine. The hangman, still standing on the gallows, produced a small cotton bag like a flour bag and drew it down over the prisoner's face. But the sound, muffled by the cloth, still persisted, over and over again: "Ram! Ram! Ram! Ram! Ram!"

The hangman climbed down and stood ready, holding the lever. 1
Minutes seemed to pass. The steady, muffled crying from the prisoner went on and on. "Ram! Ram! Ram!" never faltering for an instant. The superintendent, his head on his chest, was slowly poking the ground with his stick; perhaps he was counting the cries, allowing the prisoner a fixed number—fifty, perhaps, or a hundred. Everyone had changed color. The Indians had gone grey like bad coffee, and one or two of the bayonets were wavering. We looked at the lashed, hooded man on the drop, and listened to his cries—each cry another second of life; the same thought was in all our minds: oh, kill him quickly, get it over, stop that abominable noise!

Suddenly the superintendent made up his mind. Throwing up 1
his head he made a swift motion with his stick. "Chalo!" he shouted almost fiercely.

There was a clanking noise, and then dead silence. The prisoner 1
had vanished, and the rope was twisting on itself. I let go of the dog, and it galloped immediately to the back of the gallows; but when it got there it stopped short, barked, and then retreated into a corner of the yard, where it stood among the weeds, looking timorously out at us. We went around the gallows to inspect the prisoner's body. He was dangling with his toes pointed straight downwards, very slowly revolving, as dead as a stone.

The superintendent reached out with his stick and poked the 1
bare brown body; it oscillated slightly. "*He's* all right," said the superintendent. He backed out from under the gallows, and blew out a deep breath. The moody look had gone out of his face quite suddenly. He glanced at his wrist-watch. "Eight minutes past eight. Well, that's all for this morning, thank God."

The warders unfixed bayonets and marched away. The dog, 1
sobered and conscious of having misbehaved itself, slipped after them. We walked out of the gallows yard, past the condemned cells with their waiting prisoners, into the big central yard of the prison. The convicts, under the command of warders armed with lathis, were already receiving their breakfast. They squatted in long rows, each man holding a pannikin, while two warders with buckets marched round ladling out rice; it seemed quite a homely, jolly scene, after the hanging. An enormous relief had come upon us now that the job was done. One felt an impulse to sink, to break into a run, to snigger. All at once every one began chattering gaily.

The Eurasian boy walking beside me nodded towards the way we had come, with a knowing smile: "Do you know, sir, our friend (he meant the dead man) when he heard his appeal had been dismissed, he pissed on the floor of his cell. From fright. Kindly take one of my cigarettes, sir. Do you not admire my new silver case, sir? From the boxwalah, two rupees eight annas. Classy European style." 18

Several people laughed—at what, nobody seemed certain. 19

Francis was walking by the superintendent, talking garrulously: "Well, sir, all hass passed off with the utmost satisfactoriness. It was all finished—flick! like that. It iss not always so—oah, no! I have known cases where the doctor wass obliged to go beneath the gallows and pull the prisoner's legs to ensure decease. Most disagreeable!" 20

"Wriggling about, eh? That's bad," said the superintendent. 21

"Ach, sir, it iss worse when they become refractory! One man, I recall, clung to the bars of hiss cage when we went to take him out. You will scarcely credit, sir, that it took six warders to dislodge him, three pulling each leg. We reasoned with him. 'My dear fellow,' we said, 'think of all the pain and trouble you are causing to us!' But no, he would not listen! Ach, he wass very troublesome!" 22

I found that I was laughing quite loudly. Everyone was laughing. Even the superintendent grinned in a tolerant way. "You'd better all come out and have a drink," he said quite genially. "I've got a bottle of whiskey in the car. We could do with it." 23

We went through the big double gates of the prison into the road. "Pulling at his legs!" exclaimed a Burmese magistrate suddenly; and burst into a loud chuckling. We all began laughing again. At that moment Francis' anecdote seemed extraordinarily funny. We all had a drink together, native and European alike, quite amicably. The dead man was a hundred yards away. 24

QUESTIONS FOR READING AND WRITING

1. How do you feel about the hanged man? Do you see him more as a criminal or as a victim? Has the essay changed any of your ideas about capital punishment?

2. Do the laughter and joking at the end of the essay show the men to be cruel and heartless, or are other emotions being emphasized?
3. What is the mood or atmosphere established by the first two paragraphs of the essay? What words or details help to create this atmosphere?
4. How does the point of view in the essay seem appropriate?
5. What is the symbolic significance of the prisoner's attempt to step around the puddle? How does the presence of the dog contribute to this symbolism?
6. Write a narrative essay in which the narrator unwillingly participates in an unpleasant activity.
7. Write an essay which uses "A Hanging" as the basis for an argument against capital punishment.

✦ J. F. Powers ✦
The Valiant Woman

A native of Illinois, J. F. Powers (b. 1917) has long been known for his portrayals of Catholic clergymen. Many of his stories, like "The Valiant Woman," are set in the rectory. He is the author of Prince of Darkness *(1947),* Morte D'Urban *(1962), which won the National Book Award, and* Wheat That Springeth Green *(1988), which was nominated for the same award. In "The Valiant Woman," Powers focuses on the relationship between a priest and his housekeeper.*

THEY HAD COME TO THE DESSERT in a dinner that was a shambles. "Well, John," Father Nulty said, turning away from Mrs. Stoner and to Father Firman, long gone silent at his own table. "You've got the bishop coming for confirmations next week." 1

"Yes," Mrs. Stoner cut in, "and for dinner. And if he don't eat any more than he did last year—" 2

Father Firman, in a rare moment, faced it. "Mrs. Stoner, the bishop is not well. You know that." 3

"And after I fixed that fine dinner and all." Mrs. Stoner pouted in Father Nulty's direction. 4

"I wouldn't feel bad about it, Mrs. Stoner," Father Nulty said. "He never eats much anywhere." 5

"It's funny. And that new Mrs. Allers said he ate just fine when he was there," Mrs. Stoner argued, and then spit out, "but she's a damned liar!" 6

Father Nulty, unsettled but trying not to show it, said, "Who's Mrs. Allers?" 7

"She's at Holy Cross," Mrs. Stoner said. 8

"She's the housekeeper," Father Firman added, thinking Mrs. Stoner made it sound as though Mrs. Allers were the pastor there. 9

"I swear I don't know what to do about the dinner this year," Mrs. Stoner said. 10

Father Firman moaned. "Just do as you've always done, Mrs. Stoner." 11

"Huh! And have it all to throw out! Is that any way to do?" 12

"Is there any dessert?" Father Firman asked coldly.

Mrs. Stoner leaped up from the table and bolted into the kitchen, mumbling. She came back with a birthday cake. She plunged it in the center of the table. She found a big wooden match in her apron pocket and thrust it at Father Firman.

"I don't like this bishop," she said. "I never did. And the way he went and cut poor Ellen Kennedy out of Father Doolin's will!"

She went back into the kitchen.

"Didn't they talk a lot of filth about Doolin and the housekeeper?" Father Nulty asked.

"I should think they did," Father Firman said. "All because he took her to the movies on Sunday night. After he died and the bishop cut her out of the will, though I hear he gives her a pension privately, they talked about the bishop."

"I don't like this bishop at all," Mrs. Stoner said, appearing with a cake knife. "Bishop Doran—there was the man!"

"We know," Father Firman said. "All man and all priest."

"He did know real estate," Father Nulty said.

Father Firman struck the match.

"Not on the chair!" Mrs. Stoner cried, too late.

Father Firman set the candle burning—it was suspiciously large and yellow, like a blessed one, but he could not be sure. They watched the fluttering flame.

"I'm forgetting the lights!" Mrs. Stoner said, and got up to turn them off. She went into the kitchen again.

The priests had a moment of silence in the candlelight.

"Happy birthday, John," Father Nulty said softly. "Is it fifty-nine you are?"

"As if you didn't know, Frank," Father Firman said, "and you the same but one."

Father Nulty smiled, the old gold of his incisors shining in the flickering light, his collar whiter in the dark, and raised his glass of water, which would have been wine or better in the bygone days, and toasted Father Firman.

"Many of 'em, John."

"Blow it out," Mrs. Stoner said, returning to the room. She waited by the light switch for Father Firman to blow out the candle.

Mrs. Stoner, who ate no desserts, began to clear the dishes into the kitchen, and the priests, finishing their cake and coffee in a hurry, went to sit in the study.

Father Nulty offered a cigar. 33

"John?" 34

"My ulcers, Frank." 35

"Ah, well, you're better off." Father Nulty lit the cigar and 36
crossed his long black legs. "Fish Frawley has got him a Filipino, John. Did you hear?"

Father Firman leaned forward, interested. "He got rid of the 37
woman he had?"

"He did. It seems she snooped." 38

"Snooped, eh?" 39

"She did. And gossiped. Fish introduced two town boys to her, 40
said, 'Would you think these boys were my nephews?' That's all, and the next week the paper had it that his two nephews were visiting him from Erie. After that, he let her believe he was going East to see his parents, though both are dead. The paper carried the story. Fish returned and made a sermon out of it. Then he got the Filipino."

Father Firman squirmed with pleasure in his chair. "That's like 41
Fish, Frank. He can do that." He stared at the tips of his fingers bleakly. "You could never get a Filipino to come to a place like this."

"Probably not," Father Nulty said. "Fish is pretty close to Minne- 42
apolis. Ah, say, do you remember the trick he played on us all in Marmion Hall?"

"That I'll not forget!" Father Firman's eyes remembered. "Get- 43
ting up New Year's morning and finding the toilet seats all painted!"

"*Happy Circumcision*! Hah!" Father Nulty had a coughing fit. 44

When he had got himself together again, a mosquito came and 45
sat on his wrist. He watched it a moment before bringing his heavy hand down. He raised his hand slowly, viewed the dead mosquito, and sent it spinning with a plunk of his middle finger.

"Only the female bites," he said. 46

"I didn't know that," Father Firman said. 47

"Ah, yes . . ." 48

Mrs. Stoner entered the study and sat down with some sewing— 49
Father Firman's black socks.

She smiled pleasantly at Father Nulty. "And what do you think of 50
the atom bomb, Father?"

"Not much," Father Nulty said. 51

Mrs. Stoner had stopped smiling. Father Firman yawned. 52

Mrs. Stoner served up another: "Did you read about this communist convert, Father?"

"He's been in the Church before," Father Nulty said, "and so it's not a conversion, Mrs. Stoner."

"No? Well, I already got him down on my list of Monsignor's converts."

"It's better than a conversion, Mrs. Stoner, for there is more rejoicing in heaven over the return of . . . uh, he that was lost, Mrs. Stoner, is found."

"And that congresswoman, Father?"

"Yes. A convert—she."

"And Henry Ford's grandson, Father. I got him down."

"Yes, to be sure."

Father Firman yawned, this time audibly, and held his jaw.

"But he's one only by marriage, Father," Mrs. Stoner said. "I always say you got to watch those kind."

"Indeed you do, but a convert nonetheless, Mrs. Stoner. Remember, Cardinal Newman himself was one."

Mrs. Stoner was unimpressed. "I see where Henry Ford's making steering wheels out of soybeans, Father."

"I didn't see that."

"I read it in the *Reader's Digest* or some place."

"Yes, well . . ." Father Nulty rose and held his hand out to Father Firman. "John," he said. "It's been good."

"I heard Hirohito's next," Mrs. Stoner said, returning to converts.

"Let's wait and see, Mrs. Stoner," Father Nulty said.

The priests walked to the door.

"You know where I live, John."

"Yes. Come again, Frank. Good night."

Father Firman watched Father Nulty go down the walk to his car at the curb. He hooked the screen door and turned off the porch light. He hesitated at the foot of the stairs, suddenly moved to go to bed. But he went back into the study.

"Phew!" Mrs. Stoner said. "I thought he'd never go. Here it is after eight o'clock."

Father Firman sat down in his rocking chair. "I don't see him often," he said.

"I give up!" Mrs. Stoner exclaimed, flinging the holey socks upon the horsehair sofa. "I'd swear you had a nail in your shoe."

"I told you I looked." 77

"Well, you ought to look again. And cut your toenails, why don't 78
you? Haven't I got enough to do?"

Father Firman scratched in his coat pocket for a pill, found one, 79
swallowed it. He let his head sink back against the chair and closed
his eyes. He could hear her moving about the room, making the
preparations; and how he knew them—the fumbling in the drawer
for a pencil with a point, the rip of the page from his daily calendar,
and finally the leg of the card table sliding up against his leg.

He opened his eyes. She yanked the floor lamp alongside the 80
table, setting the bead fringe tinkling on the shade, and pulled up
her chair on the other side. She sat down and smiled at him for the
first time that day. Now she was happy.

She swept up the cards and began to shuffle with the abandoned 81
virtuosity of an old river-boat gambler, standing them on end, fan-
ning them out, whirling them through her fingers, dancing them
halfway up her arms, cracking the whip over them. At last they lay
before him tamed into a neat deck.

"Cut?" 82

"Go ahead," he said. She liked to go first. 83

She gave him her faint, avenging smile and drew a card, cast it 84
aside for another which he thought must be an ace from the way she
clutched it face down.

She was getting all the cards, as usual, and would have been 85
invincible if she had possessed his restraint and if her cunning had
been of a higher order. He knew a few things about leading and
lying back that she would never learn. Her strategy was attack,
forever attack, with one baffling departure: she might sacrifice
certain tricks as expendable if only she could have the last ones, the
heartbreaking ones, if she could slap them down one after another,
shatteringly.

She played for blood, no bones about it, but for her there was no 86
other way; it was her nature, as it was the lion's and for this reason
he found her ferocity pardonable, more a defect of the flesh, venial,
while his own trouble was all in the will, mortal. He did not sweat
and pray over each card as she must, but he did keep an eye out for
reneging and demanded a cut now and then just to aggravate her,
and he was always secretly hoping for aces.

With one card left in her hand, the telltale trick coming next, she 87
delayed playing it, showing him first the smile, the preview of

defeat. She laid it on the table—so! She held one more trump than he had reasoned possible. Had she palmed it from somewhere? No, she would not go that far; that would not be fair, was worse than reneging, which so easily and often happened accidentally, and she believed in being fair. Besides he had been watching her.

God smote the vines with hail, the sycamore trees with frost, and 8
offered up the flocks to the lightning—but Mrs. Stoner! What a cross Father Firman had from God in Mrs. Stoner! There were other housekeepers as bad, no doubt, walking the rectories of the world, yes, but . . . yes. He could name one and maybe two priests who were worse off. One, maybe two. Cronin. His scraggly blonde of sixty—take her, with her everlasting banging on the grand piano, the gift of the pastor; her proud talk about the goiter operation at the Mayo Brothers', also a gift; her honking the parish Buick at passing strange priests because they were all in the game together. She was worse. She was something to keep the home fires burning. Yes sir. And Cronin said she was not a bad person really, but what was he? He was quite a freak himself.

For that matter, could anyone say that Mrs. Stoner was a bad 8
person? No. He could not say it himself, and he was no freak. She had her points, Mrs. Stoner. She was clean. And though she cooked poorly, could not play the organ, would not take up the collection in an emergency, and went to card parties, and told all—even so, she was clean. She washed everything. Sometimes her underwear hung down beneath her dress like a paratrooper's pants, but it and everything she touched was clean. She washed constantly. She was clean.

She had her other points, to be sure—her faults, you might say. 9
She snooped—no mistake about it—but it was not snooping for snooping's sake; she had a reason. She did other things, always with a reason. She overcharged on rosaries and prayer books, but that was for the sake of the poor. She censored the pamphlet rack, but that was to prevent scandal. She pried into the baptismal and matrimonial records, but there was no other way if Father was out, and in this way she had once uncovered a bastard and flushed him out of the rectory, but that was the perverted decency of the times. She held her nose over bad marriages in the presence of the victims, but that was her sorrow and came from having her husband buried in a mine. And he had caught her telling a bewildered young couple

that there was only one good reason for their wanting to enter into a mixed marriage—the child had to have a name, and that—that was what?

She hid his books, kept him from smoking, picked his friends (usually the pastors of her colleagues), bawled out people for calling after dark, had no humor, except at cards, and then it was grim, very grim, and she sat hatchet-faced every morning at Mass. But she went to Mass, which was all that kept the church from being empty some mornings. She did annoying things all day long. She said annoying things into the night. She said she had given him the best years of her life. Had she? Perhaps—for the miner had her only a year. It was too bad, sinfully bad, when he thought of it like that. But all talk of best years and life was nonsense. He had to consider the heart of the matter, the essence. The essence was that housekeepers were hard to get, harder to get than ushers, than willing workers, than organists, than secretaries—yes, harder to get than assistants or vocations. 91

And she was a *saver*—saved money, saved electricity, saved string, bags, sugar, saved—him. That's what she did. That's what she said she did, and she was right, in a way. In a way, she was usually right. In fact, she was always right—in a way. And you could never get a Filipino to come way out here and live. Not a young one anyway, and he had never seen an old one. Not a Filipino. They liked to dress up and live. 92

Should he let it drop about Fish having one, just to throw a scare into her, let her know he was doing some thinking? No. It would be a perfect cue for the one about a man needing a woman to look after him. He was not up to that again, not tonight. 93

Now she was doing what she liked most of all. She was making a grand slam, playing it out card for card, though it was in the bag, prolonging what would have been cut short out of mercy in gentle company. Father Firman knew the agony of losing. 94

She slashed down the last card, a miserable deuce trump, and did in the hapless king of hearts he had been saving. 95

"Skunked you!" 96

She was awful in victory. Here was the bitter end of their long day together, the final murderous hour in which all they wanted to say—all he wouldn't and all she couldn't—came out in the cards. 97

Whoever won at honeymoon won the day, slept on the other's scalp, and God alone had to help the loser.

"We've been at it long enough, Mrs. Stoner," he said, seeing her assembling the cards for another round.

"Had enough, huh!"

Father Firman grumbled something.

"No?"

"Yes."

She pulled the table away and left it against the wall for the next time. She went out of the study carrying the socks, content and clucking. He closed his eyes after her and began to get under way in the rocking chair, the nightly trip to nowhere. He could hear her brewing a cup of tea in the kitchen and conversing with the cat. She made her way up the stairs, carrying the tea, followed by the cat, purring.

He waited, rocking out to sea, until she would be sure to be through in the bathroom. Then he got up and locked the front door (she looked after the back door) and loosened his collar going upstairs.

In the bathroom he mixed a glass of antiseptic, always afraid of pyorrhea, and gargled to ward off pharyngitis.

When he turned on the light in his room, the moths and beetles began to batter against the screens, the lighter insects humming . . .

Yes, and she had the guest room. How did she come to get that? Why wasn't she in the back room, in her proper place? He knew, if he cared to remember. The screen in the back room—it let in mosquitoes, and if it didn't do that she'd love to sleep back there, Father, looking out at the steeple and the blessed cross on top, Father, if it just weren't for the screen, Father. Very well, Mrs. Stoner. I'll get it fixed or fix it myself. Oh, could you now, Father? I could, Mrs. Stoner, and I will. In the meantime you take the guest room. Yes, Father, and thank you, Father, the house ringing with amenities then. Years ago, all that. She was a pie-faced girl then, not really a girl perhaps, but not too old to marry again. But she never had. In fact, he could not remember that she had even tried for a husband since coming to the rectory, but, of course, he could be wrong, not knowing how they went about it. God! God save us! Had she got her wires crossed and mistaken him all these years for *that*?

That! Him! Suffering God! No. That was going too far. That was getting morbid. No. He must not think of that again, ever. No.

But just the same she had got the guest room and she had it yet. Well, did it matter? Nobody ever came to see him any more, nobody to stay overnight anyway, nobody to stay very long . . . not any more. He knew how they laughed at him. He had heard Frank humming all right—before he saw how serious and sad the situation was and took pity—humming, "Wedding Bells Are Breaking Up That Old Gang of Mine." But then they'd always laughed at him for something—for not being an athlete, for wearing glasses, for having kidney trouble . . . and mail coming addressed to Rev. and Mrs. Stoner. 108

Removing his shirt, he bent over the table to read the volume left open from last night. He read, translating easily, "Eisdem licet cum illis . . . Clerics are allowed to reside only with women about whom there can be no suspicion, either because of a natural bond (as mother, sister, aunt) or of advanced age, combined in both cases with good repute." 109

Last night he had read it, and many nights before, each time as though this time to find what was missing, to find what obviously was not in the paragraph, his problem considered, a way out. She was not mother, not sister, not aunt, and *advanced age* was a relative term (why, she was younger than he was) and so, eureka, she did not meet the letter of the law—but, alas, how she fulfilled the spirit! And besides it would be a slimy way of handling it after all her years of service. He could not afford to pension her off, either. 110

He slammed the book shut. He slapped himself fiercely on the back, missing the wily mosquito, and whirled to find it. He took a magazine and folded it into a swatter. Then he saw it—oh, the preternatural cunning of it!—poised in the beard of St. Joseph on the bookcase. He could not hit it there. He teased it away, wanting it to light on the wall, but it knew his thoughts and flew high away. He swung wildly, hoping to stun it, missed, swung back, catching St. Joseph across the neck. The statue fell to the floor and broke. 111

Mrs. Stoner was panting in the hall outside his door. 112

"What is it?" 113

"Mosquitoes!" 114

"What is it, Father? Are you hurt?" 115

"Mosquitoes—damn it! And only the female bites!" 11

Mrs. Stoner, after a moment, said, "Shame on you, Father. She needs the blood for her eggs." 11

He dropped the magazine and lunged at the mosquito with his bare hand. 11

She went back to her room, saying, "Pshaw, I thought it was burglars murdering you in your bed." 11

He lunged again. 12

QUESTIONS FOR READING AND WRITING

1. How is Mrs. Stoner "valiant"?
2. What purpose is served by the long expository section of the story, where Father Nulty is having dinner with Father Firman?
3. What symbolic role is played by mosquitoes in the story?
4. How does the relationship between Father Firman and Mrs. Stoner resemble that between a husband and a wife? Provide evidence from the text for your judgments.
5. Write a narrative essay in which you portray the "human," everyday side of a priest, pastor, or other religious worker.
6. Write an essay that narrates an incident in which your own religious values played a significant part.

✦ Alice Walker ✦
The Flowers

Alice Walker (b. 1944) was born in Georgia to sharecropper parents. She has written poems, short stories, novels, and essays. Among her works are In Love and Trouble *(1973),* The Color Purple *(1982)—which won the Pulitzer Prize and was later made into a successful film—*In Search of Our Mother's Gardens *(1983), and* The Temple of My Familiar *(1989). In the following symbolic story, she writes of a girl's discovery of the tragic aspects of her heritage.*

IT SEEMED TO MYOP AS SHE SKIPPED lightly from hen house to 1
pigpen to smokehouse that the days had never been as beautiful as these. The air held a keenness that made her nose twitch. The harvesting of the corn and cotton, peanuts and squash, made each day a golden surprise that caused excited little tremors to run up her jaws.

Myop carried a short, knobby stick. She struck out at random at 2
chickens she liked, and worked out the beat of a song on the fence around the pigpen. She felt light and good in the warm sun. She was ten, and nothing existed for her but her song, the stick clutched in her dark brown hand, and the tat-de-ta-ta-ta of accompaniment.

Turning her back on the rusty boards of her family's sharecropper 3
cabin, Myop walked along the fence till it ran into the stream made by the spring. Around the spring, where the family got drinking water, silver ferns and wildflowers grew. Along the shallow banks pigs rooted. Myop watched the tiny white bubbles disrupt the thin black scale of soil and the water that silently rose and slid away down the stream.

She had explored the woods behind the house many times. 4
Often, in late autumn, her mother took her to gather nuts among the fallen leaves. Today she made her own path, bouncing this way and that way, vaguely keeping an eye out for snakes. She found, in addition to various common but pretty ferns and leaves, an armful of strange blue flowers with velvety ridges and a sweetsuds bush full of the brown, fragrant buds.

By twelve o'clock, her arms laden with sprigs of her findings, she 5
was a mile or more from home. She had often been as far before,

but the strangeness of the land made it not as pleasant as her usual haunts. It seemed gloomy in the little cove in which she found herself. The air was damp, the silence close and deep.

Myop began to circle back to the house, back to the peacefulness of the morning. It was then she stepped smack into his eyes. Her heel became lodged in the broken ridge between brow and nose, and she reached down quickly, unafraid, to free herself. It was only when she saw his naked grin that she gave a little yelp of surprise.

He had been a tall man. From feet to neck covered a long space. His head lay beside him. When she pushed back the leaves and layers of earth and debris Myop saw that he'd had large white teeth, all of them cracked or broken, long fingers, and very big bones. All his clothes had rotted away except some threads of blue denim from his overalls. The buckles of the overalls had turned green.

Myop gazed around the spot with interest. Very near where she'd stepped into the head was a wild pink rose. As she picked it to add to her bundle she noticed a raised mound, a ring, around the rose's root. It was the rotted remains of a noose, a bit of shredding plowline, now blending benignly into the soil. Around an overhanging limb of a great spreading oak clung another piece. Frayed, rotted, bleached, and frazzled—barely there—but spinning restlessly in the breeze. Myop laid down her flowers.

And the summer was over.

QUESTIONS FOR READING AND WRITING

1. At the beginning of the story, what is Myop's frame of mind?
2. Suppose "Myop" is an abbreviation of "myopic" or short-sighted. How might this affect your understanding of the story?
3. How is the last sentence of the story symbolic?
4. Compare the image of the flower in the rotted noose with Orwell's image of the dog and the prisoner in "A Hanging." How are the images parallel or related in their meaning?
5. Narrate an incident in which a playful or relatively trivial activity you were engaged in was interrupted by something serious or tragic.
6. Write a narrative paragraph that records your observations of a child at play.

Part 3

DESCRIPTION

Writing To Recreate Persons and Places

When you describe, you are recreating in words the physical characteristics of a person, place, or object, usually in the absence of the thing itself, and for an audience that may be unfamiliar with the thing. For example, New Yorker John McPhee describes the appearance and the working of a farmers' produce market. Although the description is intended for a non–New York audience, even those who have visited that particular market will find new insights through McPhee's powers of observation:

> There is a rhythm in the movement of the crowd, in the stopping, the selecting, the moving on—the time, unconsciously budgeted to assess one farm against another, to convict a tomato, to choose a peach. The seller comes to feel the rate of flow, and—for all the small remarks, the meeting of eyes—to feel as well the seclusion of anonymity that comes with the money aprons and the hanging scales. Rich Hodgson—handing them their blue free plums. They don't know he skis in Utah. Melissa Mousseau—changing a twenty for a bag of pears. They don't know that she goes, too. Hemmingway and Thueson, the athletes, have heard more encouraging sounds from other crowds. "If you charge for three pounds, give me three full pounds and not two pounds and fifteen ounces, boy."*

A description reproduces reality as accurately as possible, but it must also involve both your unique perspective as a writer and your

* John McPhee, *Giving Good Weight* (Farrar, Straus and Giroux, 1979), 67–68.

awareness of how much your audience does or does not know. Description frequently includes the physical characteristics of the thing described, but not all description is limited to the physical. Can you conjure up the essential characteristics or features of a person or a place without reference to outward appearances? Aren't invisible characteristics also part of the essence of a thing? To answer these questions let's examine a pair of descriptions: first John McPhee's physical description of Frank Boyden, the headmaster of Deerfield Academy in Massachusetts, then Adam Smith's description of Baba Ram Dass (Richard Alpert), psychologist and convert to Eastern mysticism.

> His hair is not white but slate-gray, and his demeanor, which hasn't changed in forty years, still suggests a small, grumpy Labrador. He sometimes dresses in gray trousers, a dark-blue jacket, and brown cordovan shoes—choices that are somewhat collegiate and could be taken as a mild sign of age, because for decades he wore dark-blue worsted suits and maroon ties almost exclusively, winter and summer, hanging on to each successive suit until it fell off him in threads. One of his jacket pockets today has a four-inch rip that has been bound with black thread. He doesn't care . . .*

✦✦✦✦✦

> . . . this gentleman is balding, with graying beard and long hair in the back, and the one-stringed instruments have ceased their sound and he just sits there and smiles. And after the longest time, he says, "Well, here we are." And his voice is so warm and he is so relaxed and he smiles and gradually everybody starts to smile, "Here we are," he says again, and here we are, not just in this room but all together on the surface of the planet—"Here we are, and we'll just talk a little, I'll talk some, and then we can get up and walk around and maybe have some cider, and you can talk, or ask questions, and we'll all just hang out for a while."†

Few would quarrel with the notion that both of these are descriptions, but how different they are. Both start with the physical appearance of the person, but McPhee stays on that track except for

* John McPhee, *The Headmaster* (Farrar, Straus and Giroux, 1966), 10.
† Adam Smith, *Powers of Mind* (Random House, 1975), 315.

two brief judgments (". . . could be taken as a mild sign of age," and "He doesn't care"), piling up the physical details: Smith, on the other hand, after relating three brief physical details (balding, graying beard, long hair) shifts to dialogue and narrative except for two later physical characteristics ("his voice is so warm and he is so relaxed"). McPhee concentrates on the external appearance of his subject, whereas Smith is more interested in the aura, the internal characteristics that create the charisma of Baba Ram Dass. Both selections try to capture the distinctive features of their subjects, but the features that account for the individuality of a thing, for its uniqueness, may not all be physical. The defining quality of all descriptions, then, is their ability to *individuate*, to distinguish this thing from all other things that may be like it. In the process, the writer may use expository modes—such as definition, classification, or contrast—or narrative modes, as Smith does in setting a scene and carrying the narrative along with action and dialogue. Because the primary purpose is to reveal the individuating quality of the subject, such a narrative piece would be a description.

Broadly, descriptions are of two kinds:

1. *Realistic*, primarily a documentary approach concentrating mostly on objective externals but verifying as carefully as possible everything that is not purely external. A purely objective description is more of an ideal than a reality because the camera eye of the writer cannot turn to everything and therefore must select some things to be included, others to be left out, and still others to be given special prominence. We have already discussed some problems of selectivity in the introduction to journals. Yet, some highly selective descriptions give the impression of being purely objective. Here is John McPhee's objective description of the Indian Point No. 2 nuclear power plant:

> The containment structure looks vaguely like the Jefferson Memorial—a simple, stunning cylinder under a hemispheric dome, all in white reinforced concrete. Its diameter is a hundred and thirty-five feet. The dome and the side walls are from three and a half to four and a half feet thick and are lined with steel.*

* John McPhee, *The Curve of Binding Energy* (Farrar, Straus and Giroux, 1973), 99.

2. *Impressionistic*, essentially a subjective, personal view of the reality being created. Like an impressionistic painting, an impressionistic description may not tell the literal truth but it nevertheless captures the essential quality of an object in a spot of time, in a certain light. In the sense in which Picasso meant his dictum, "Art is a lie which tells the truth," impressionistic descriptions attempt to capture the essential nature of the thing frequently missed by the more documentary realistic approach. Virginia Woolf's impressionistic description of dusk reflects not only the external scene, its feeling and texture, but also the mind of the viewer. Notice that it recreates not the sights as the light fades, but the diminishing sounds:

> And now as if the cleaning and the scrubbing and the scything and the mowing had drowned it there rose that half-heard melody, that intermittent music which the ear catches but lets fall; a bark, a bleat; irregular, intermittent, yet somehow related; the hum of an insect, the tremor of cut grass, dissevered yet somehow belonging; the jar of a dorbeetle, the squeak of a wheel, loud, low, but mysteriously related; which the ear strains to bring together and is always on the verge of harmonising, but they are never quite heard, never fully harmonised, and at last, in the evening, one after another the sounds die out, and the harmony falters, and silence falls. . . . With the sunset sharpness was lost, and like mist rising, quiet rose, quiet spread, the wind settled; loosely the world shook itself down to sleep, darkly here without a light to it, save what came green suffused through leaves, or pale on the white flowers in the bed by the window.*

A characteristic common to both realistic and impressionistic descriptions—as opposed to narrative writing, in which the subject is changing through time—is that the subject is regarded as static. In this sense, description is similar to painting or photography, which, with a few exceptions, tries to freeze time and capture its subjects at rest, or in a segment of action that does not, itself, change. Narrative can be combined with description, as in the Baba Ram Dass description, but the real subject remains Baba Ram Dass *now*, at the moment in time Smith is describing him.

* Virginia Woolf, *To the Lighthouse* (Harcourt, Brace and World, 1927), 212–13.

With a clearer understanding of what description is, we can now ask a related question: What are some of the elements of successful description?

Details A successful description includes essential details that effectively recreate the subject, making it *perceptible, clear, and consistent for the reader.*

If a description is to be *perceptible*, it must be anchored in one or more sense perceptions. Thomas Wolfe uses such sense perceptions in the following description in which he recreates the main character's childhood memories by evoking a series of smells:

> . . . the exciting smell of chalk and varnished desks; the smell of heavy bread-sandwiches of cold fried meat and butter; the smell of new leather in a saddler's shop, or of a warm leather chair, of honey and of unground coffee; of barrelled sweet-pickles and cheese and all the fragrant compost of the grocer's; the smell of stored apples in the cellar, and of orchard apple smells, of pressed-cider pulp; of pears ripening on a sunny shelf, and of ripe cherries stewing with sugar on hot stoves before preserving; the smell of whittled wood, of all young lumber, of sawdust and shavings; of peaches stuck with cloves and pickled in brandy; of pine sap, and green pine needles; of a horse's pared hoof; of chestnuts roasting, of bowls of nuts and raisins; of hot cracklin, and of young roast pork; of butter and cinnamon melting on hot candied yams.*

This torrent of sense perceptions is fairly unstructured, but that is precisely the point here: It is an accurate description of the way memory presents experience. Wolfe's description is successful because of the accumulated details.

The description of a subjective impression should be anchored in some tangible, sensually *perceptible* phenomenon. Although abstractions, generalizations, and summary statements may occur in descriptions, they should be supported by something the reader can see, taste, smell, hear, or touch. Suppose you wished to describe a highly personal emotion—say, the feeling of nostalgia, as in E. B. White's "Once More to the Lake." You would need to anchor that feeling to something external to communicate it to the reader. White solves the problem by tying his sense of nostalgia to a series

* Thomas Wolfe, *Look Homeward, Angel* (Scribners, 1929), 69.

of sensations, each of which makes the abstract emotion more tangible: the smell of lumber in the camp bedroom, the sight of the dragonfly alighting on the tips of the fishing rods, the orchestrated sounds of a summer thunderstorm on the lake.

There must be some rationale for the selection of details presented to the reader. Often this will follow automatically from the writer's initial conception of the subject; at other times, in order to achieve *clarity* and *consistency*, it is necessary to create a dominant impression, a single overriding and controlling view of the subject. For example, anthropologist Loren Eiseley has described how, awakening just before dawn on the twentieth floor of a midtown hotel in New York, he looked down on the rooftops and saw a strange sight, a bit of wilderness in the city, a reminder of "the downright miraculous nature of the planet."

> I found I was looking down from that great height into a series of curious cupolas or lofts that I could just barely make out in the darkness. As I looked, the outlines of these lofts became more distinct because the light was being reflected from the wings of pigeons who, in utter silence, were beginning to float outward upon the city. In and out through open slits in the cupolas passed the white-winged birds on their mysterious errands. At this hour the city was theirs, and quietly, without the brush of a single wing tip against stone in that high, eerie place, they were taking over the spires of Manhattan. They were pouring upward in a light that was not yet perceptible to human eyes, while far down in the black darkness of the alleys it was still midnight.
>
> As I crouched half asleep across the sill, I had a moment's illusion that the world had changed in the night, as in some immense snowfall, and that if I were to leave, it would have to be as these other inhabitants were doing, by the window. . . . To and fro went the wings, to and fro. There were no sounds from any of them. They knew man was asleep and this light for a while was theirs . . .
>
> Around and around went the wings. It needed only a little courage, only a little shove from the window ledge to enter that city of light.*

* Loren Eiseley, "The Judgement of the Birds," *The Immense Journey* (Random House, 1957), 165–66.

The dominant impression of the scene—whiteness— is repeated seven times in one form or another ("white," "light," "snowfall"); furthermore, the impression is intensified by the contrasting impression of darkness ("dark," "night," "midnight"), and the complementary impression of silence ("no sound," "quietly," "silence.") Eiseley has created an impression of the miraculous in the midst of the ordinary by showing us this whitened scene from "an inverted angle," not just the upside-down view of pigeons seen from above, but something unusual, a coincidence of timing and insight, of man and animal—what Eiseley calls "the border of two worlds." The strange scene is effectively recreated because Eiseley has focused his description on a dominant impression and has effectively screened out any detail that does not contribute to that impression.

Concreteness and Connotations of Words The details of a successful description must be conveyed in language that is concrete and particular, which does not imply that a good description must have long strings of modifiers to be successful. The following sentence was written for humorous effect: "They were a tightly knit, neighborly, backbiting, feuding, forgiving, gracious, vulgar, devout, banal, parochial, charitable, fearful, stalwart community."* Using concrete diction does not mean piling up a series of adjectives before every noun.

The first half of Jonathan Swift's definition of style, "the proper words in the proper place," provides a better clue to writing effective descriptions, namely, finding the right word,—not only the word with the exact connotations or associations, but the more concrete word, the word closest to what S. I. Hayakawa calls extensional reality. Hayakawa's concept of the ladder of abstraction is a graphic way of looking the various synonyms available to describe a subject. The words at the bottom of the ladder are closest to the "real" object; they are most particularized and therefore the most exclusive terms. Those at the top of the ladder, in contrast, are the least concrete, the least particular, and therefore the most inclusive terms. As one goes up the ladder, the terms become increasingly abstract, refer more to mental concepts and less to tangible things. Using the central figure from Truman

* Burton Bernstein, "The Bernstein Family—Part II," *The New Yorker* (March 29, 1982), 68.

Capote's description, and placing her on the ladder, the synonyms available might look like this:

ABSTRACT
writer
fiction writer
chronicler of East Africa
author of Out of Africa
Isak Dinesen
CONCRETE

The point is not to avoid using synonyms, but to recognize that in descriptive writing, barring other considerations such as monotonous repetition of the same word, it is preferable to choose the more concrete words.

In the following description from Ernest Hemingway, notice that the words are all simple and concrete, that the author doesn't shy away from repeating key words for their cumulative effect, that adjectives are used sparingly but precisely, and that the entire description is written in short, crisp sentences appropriate to the subject.

> There was no underbrush in the island pine trees. The trunks of the trees went straight up or slanted toward each other. The trunks were straight and brown without branches. The branches were high above. Some interlocked to make a solid shadow on the brown forest floor. Around the grove of trees was a bare space. It was brown and soft underfoot as Nick walked on it. This was the overlapping of the pine needle floor, extending out beyond the width of the high branches. The trees had grown tall and the branches moved high, leaving in the sun this bare space they had once covered with shadow. Sharp at the edge of this extension of the forest floor commenced the sweet fern.*

Choosing the right word also involves being aware of the connotations of words—that is, all of the suggestions and associations embedded in a word or phrase. Because English offers us so many

* Ernest Hemingway, "Big Two-Hearted River: Part I," *The First Forty-Nine Stories* (Jonathan Cape, 1944), 168–69.

synonyms, the difference between one word and another is often merely the connotations of these words. For example, a small vacation home might be described as a bungalow, a cottage, a cabin, a camp, or a shack. Precise, accurate diction is a matter of choosing both the degree of concreteness and the desired connotations of the various synonyms that mean not the same thing, but only *approximately* the same thing.

Figures of Speech Comparisons or figures of speech help to extend the range of our sensory experience by connecting something being described with something within the reader's experience. Suppose, for example, you were to describe Panama as "an isthmus between the Atlantic and the Pacific Oceans." You would be using literal language, that is, denotative language, which points directly to the thing for which it stands. If, however, you were to say Panama was "like a four-way bridge between North and South America, the Atlantic and the Pacific," you would be using figurative language, in this case a *simile* (a limited comparison using *like* or *as*). Figurative language draws together things not normally associated and coaxes us to see those things in a new light, in a way we have never quite viewed them before. The Chilean poet Pablo Neruda called Panama "the delicate waist of the Americas," employing a *metaphor*, or direct comparison. Metaphors allow you to explore the possibilities of the comparison, in this case the fragility of the link between the two continents. You can extend the comparison by asking, "How many ways is Panama like 'a delicate waist'?" Metaphors are somewhat like *analogies* (see"Analogy" in Part 4), comparisons used to clarify the unfamiliar with the familiar since both can extend the similarities. If you were to say that any United States overseas possession could become another Panama, you would be using Panama as a *symbol*—something that stands in place of something else—and you would have extended your subject to cover an even broader range of implications. Like metaphors, symbols radiate meaning outward; but unlike similes and metaphors, symbols belong to the same conceptual order as the thing symbolized: territories and possessions, not bridges and waists. All three figures of speech make bland abstract descriptions more concrete, more vital and closer to the reader's experience.

Clear and Consistent Organization The details of a description, even if written in concrete and accurate language, still must be arranged in a coherent fashion. This calls for some kind of pattern of organization that will present the material in a clear, consistent, and orderly way. With physical objects, descriptions present fewer problems if a writer follows an appropriate and consistent pattern of *spatial organization*. This means that a place could be described, for example, from top to bottom, from left to right, from near to far, or the reverse of any of these; a person, from head to toe, or the reverse, from prominent features to those less prominent, from clothes or manners to physiological features, or the reverse. A more subjective description would combine spatial organization with some inner judgments; for example, a description could move from important, spatially arranged details to secondary details that fill in the outline, or from outer to inner characteristics, or from first impressions to more lasting ones. The patterns are too numerous to illustrate, but it is important to be consistent in following the pattern chosen.

Climactic order is a pattern that proceeds from the unimportant—often, deliberately, even the trivial—to the important, ending on the most significant detail of the description. Notice how this pattern is adhered to in Flannery O'Connor's chilling description of a family's encounter with three escaped convicts who find the family's car has overturned in a ditch on a lonely country road. The leader, a killer named The Misfit, is described as the family sees him from the bottom of the ditch:

> The driver got out of the car and stood by the side of it, looking down at them. He was an older man than the other two. His hair was just beginning to gray and he wore silver-rimmed spectacles that gave him a scholarly look. He had a long creased face and didn't have on any shirt or undershirt. He had on blue jeans that were too tight for him and was holding a black hat and a gun. The two boys also had guns.*

The description ends on the most important detail, the guns, and it builds to that detail by including successively more important

* Flannery O'Connor, "A Good Man Is Hard To Find," *Complete Stories* (Farrar, Straus and Giroux, 1979), 126.

details such as the ill-fitting jeans of the escaped convict. The clothes (or lack of them) and the guns are a surprise following the opening descriptive details which focus on age and the scholarly look the spectacles lend the killer. *The angle of vision,* from the bottom of the ditch, is consistently maintained throughout with the inclusion of subsequent details one might notice looking up from a ditch: "He had on tan and white shoes and no socks, and his ankles were red and thin." Not only, then, is it important to be consistent in your choice of pattern or organization, but it is equally important to locate yourself with respect to the object being described, and to remain consistent in your *angle of vision*.

A description that effectively captures the uniqueness of a thing—its tangibility or its ineffability—begins when a writer makes a series of strategic choices after answering several questions: What kind of description is this? What details will support the dominant impression? How shall I organize the details? What words and what sentences best express the subject? If the writer is lucky, has answered the questions correctly and chosen the right strategies, then he or she will have created a memorable portrait of the subject and left an eloquent testimony to the recreative power of words.

✦ Harvey Arden ✦
Morocco's Ancient City of Fez

Harvey Arden is a senior writer for National Geographic *magazine. The passage that follows has been excerpted from an essay that deals with the combination of the medieval and the modern in Fez, the latter threatening to destroy the former through overcrowding and pollution. The opening of the essay is a masterful example of the use of dominant impression and sensual detail.*

NIGHT DOESN'T FALL IN FEZ. It *rises.* Hardly has the glaring African sun dipped behind the hills than the darkness wells up from the deep bowl in which the city huddles. The shadows seep quickly upward through claustrophobically narrow streets, pooling inside the thick walls that hug this 1,200-year-old spiritual capital of Morocco in a crumbling stone embrace. 1

For a few moments only the tops of the minarets remain sunstruck. Then they too, like candles on a cake of stone, are snuffed out from below by the rising darkness. 2

Elsewhere it is still afternoon; in Fez it is night. Elsewhere it is still the 20th century; in Fez it is the Middle Ages. 3

The city has many names, many identities: Fez el Bali, or Fez the Old, founded about A.D. 800; Fez the Holy, one of the most renowned religious centers of the Muslim world; Fez the Imperial, one of the four great capitals (along with Marrakech, Rabat, and Meknès) of Morocco's ruling dynasties; Fez the Secret, city of political intrigue and labyrinthine streets whose dizzying turnings seem always to lead to a windowless wall and a locked door with its iron grating rusted shut. 4

Add to these one modern title: Fez the Endangered, a city fighting for its very survival as it threatens to implode from age, disrepair, and staggering population pressures. 5

Night had already risen when I arrived, hot and dusty, after the four-hour taxi ride from Casablanca. It was mid-September, tail end of the hot season that moves up here in summer from the Sahara, some 250 miles south. Temperatures in July and August routinely hit 110°F, and even now hovered in the mid-90s—reminder of the 6 lingering years-long drought that had driven tens of thousands of mountain Arabs and Berbers out of the flanking Rif and Atlas ranges into already desperately overcrowded Fez.

We dipped out of the late afternoon daylight into a deep pool of dark blue shadows at the bottom of which the old walled city—Fez el Bali—lay submerged like some ethereal Atlantis, its few electric lights winking fitfully as if about to sputter out. Our headlights gave dim glimpses of a timeworn stone wall on the right and, on the left, a vast cemetery whose ghost-white tombstones marched up a hill to the skeletal remains of some shattered building. 7

We came at last to a weathered Moorish gateway, and I wondered where in this medieval world my modern hotel could possibly be located. Honking some donkeys out of the way, we drove inside. 8

I blinked my eyes. There, indeed, was the hotel—the Palais Jamai—a gracious pink building rising amid the pleasure gardens of a 19th-century vizier's palace. The taxi door was opened by a tall, fiercely mustachioed man in a white toga-like djellaba. A paradigm of Moroccan traditional dress, he sported a long, curving, silver-sheathed dagger, pointed yellow slip-ons, or babouches, and a black-tasseled fez—the cylindrical Islamic headgear whose distinctive bright red color (today simulated with chemicals) in ancient times derived from natural dyes now lost to memory. 9

Taking one fleeting look at my dusty visage and disheveled clothes, the impeccably attired doorman smiled imperiously, sniffed, and allowed a bellboy to wrestle with my luggage. 10

After dining on French haute cuisine—France, it must be remembered, ruled Morocco from 1912 to 1956—I walked outside for an introductory stroll. It was already past eight, and the little hotel plaza was all shadows. One of these shadows now detached itself from the others. The tall and gangling figure of a man in jeans, T-shirt, and sneakers materialized before me. 11

"A big welcome to you, sir!" came his husky voice. "You are American, yes? May I have the honor of showing you our city?" 12

I mumbled, "No, thank you," and turned down a small dark street. He followed. 13

"Very easy to get lost in Fez," he persisted. "May I walk with you? Please, no money. I am not an official guide. But you can help me with my English, and I can help you with the streets. We can be friends, yes? Is good to have a friend who knows the way." 14

I glanced warily down the long-shadowed street. This fellow's company, I decided, was worth chancing for a few minutes . . . and so I met Abdellatif, the wonderful Fezzi who was to become my constant companion. Together we strode down that dark street, turned a blind corner, and entered the 14th century.

✦✦✦✦✦

We came out on a plaza at the center of the medina, the old city. It was crowded with people—little girls carrying wooden trays of oven-bound bread dough on their heads, veiled women doing the family wash at an exquisitely tiled public fountain, a bearded old man selling caged birds, old Berber ladies with tattooed chins squatting on the curbs with their hands held out in supplication, ragged porters lashing slow-moving donkeys loaded down with ice and sheepskins and Pepsi-Cola cases.

"No cars here, not even motorcycles," Abdellatif said. "The donkey is the taxi of the medina!"

The night air was clangorous with the rhythmic hammerings of the ironworkers at work on their kettles, coppersmiths beating a syncopated tap-da-tap-tap-da-tap on their ornate trays, the rasping voices of the street vendors, the tinselly laughter of schoolgirls in their crisp pastel smocks, and, above it all, the raucous crying of the roosters, which seem to crow all night from the rooftops as if announcing some perpetual dawn of the spirit.

Adding to the sensory assault were a thousand tingling aromas of spices and newly cut cedarwood, of singed oxhorn (used for combs) and sizzling hot cooking oil, of freshly baked bread and ugly-smelling animal hides—all simmering together, as it were, in the warm night air.

✦✦✦✦✦

This is Fez as it has always been—a huge emporium of craftsmen, traders, merchants, and hustlers of every variety, all converging on this great inland crossroads linking the Mediterranean and the Sahara, the Atlantic and Algeria.

Abdellatif led me through a tangled skein of dark alleyways, and suddenly, turning one last blind corner, we were back—somehow—at the Palais Jamai.

That night, a little after 4 a.m., a voice woke me as if in a dream. I stumbled out of bed and out onto the balcony. It was the muezzin of a nearby mosque, calling the faithful to early morning prayer. His voice, a piercing tenor, came right out of the night sky. "*Allahu akba-r-r-r-r,*" it cried—"God is great!"

QUESTIONS FOR READING AND WRITING

1. Some places reveal their essential qualities almost immediately upon first contact. Fez, with its dark shadows, seems quietly forgotten by time, yet also throbs with life. Have you ever been to a place that yielded up its essential character at once, or that was full of paradoxical impressions?
2. Arden's description is built around a series of sense impressions. Until he meets Abdellatif, what is the dominant impression? What sense impressions dominate the description of the medina? Why the difference?
3. Describe a place where you are able to focus on a single dominant impression. Use all the senses in your description, but subordinate all the details to a single impression as Arden does with the image of darkness rising in Fez.

✦ Truman Capote ✦
Isak Dinesen

Truman Capote's first novel, Other Voices, Other Rooms *(1948), met with critical acclaim before he was twenty-five years old. Prior to his death in 1984, the controversial, outspoken author produced novels, short stories, musical plays, television scripts, screenplays, and nonfiction works. The most famous of these may be* Breakfast at Tiffany's *(1958) and* In Cold Blood *(1966), both of which were later adapted as films. His childhood friend, Harper Lee, used her memories of Capote as a child to create the character of Dill in* To Kill a Mockingbird. *In 1954, when he wrote the screenplay for John Huston's cult classic* Beat the Devil, *Truman Capote's reputation as a remarkable stylist with a deep affinity for eccentric characters, both fictional and real, had been well established. By 1980, with the publication of his nonfiction work,* Music for Chameleons, *the controversial author had become as recognizable as the "beautiful people" who were often his subjects. The following portrait, from* The Dogs Bark *(1973), is a delicate description of a frail octogenarian, Isak Dinesen (Karen Blixen), the author of and central figure* in Out of Africa.

RUNGSTED IS A SEA TOWN on the coast road between Copenhagen and Elsinore. Among eighteenth-century travelers the otherwise undistinguished village was well known for the handsomeness of its Inn. The Inn, though it no longer obliges coachmen and their passengers, is still renowned: as the home of Rungsted's first citizen, the Baroness Blixen, alias Isak Dinesen, alias Pierre Andrezel.

The Baroness, weighing a handful of feathers and fragile as a *coquillage* bouquet, entertains callers in a sparse, sparkling parlor sprinkled with sleeping dogs and warmed by a fireplace and a porcelain stove: a room where she, an imposing creation come forward from one of her own Gothic tales, sits bundled in bristling wolfskins and British tweeds, her feet fur-booted, her legs, thin as the thighs of an ortolan, encased in woolen hose, and her neck, round which a ring could fit, looped with frail lilac scarves. Time has refined her, this legend who has lived the adventures of an iron-nerved man: shot charging lions and infuriated buffalo, worked an African farm, flown over Kilimanjaro in the perilous first planes, doctored the Masai; time has reduced her to an essence, as a grape can become a raisin, roses an attar. Quite instantly, even if one were deprived of knowing her dossier, she registers as *la vraie chose*, a true somebody. A face so faceted, its prisms tossing a proud glitter of intelligence and educated compassion, which is to say wisdom, cannot be an accidental occurrence; nor do such eyes, smudges of kohl darkening the lids, deeply set, like velvet animals burrowed in a cave, fall into the possession of ordinary women.

If a visitor is invited to tea, the Baroness serves a very high one: 3
sherry before, afterward a jamboree of toast and varied marmalades, cold pâtés, grilled livers, orange-flavored crêpes. But the hostess cannot partake, she is unwell, she eats nothing, nothing at all, oh, perhaps an oyster, one strawberry, a glass of champagne. Instead, she talks; and like most artists, certainly all old beauties, she is sufficiently self-centered to enjoy herself as conversational subject.

Her lips, just touched with paint, twist in a sideways smile of 4
rather paralytic contour, and speaking an English brushed with British inflections, she might say, "Ah, well, yes, what a lot of stories this old Inn could tell. It belonged to my brother, I bought it from him; *Last Tales* paid the last installment. Now it is mine, absolutely. I have plans for it after I die. It will be an aviary, the grounds, the park, will be a bird sanctuary. All the years in Africa, when I had my highland farm, I never imagined to make my home again in Denmark. When I knew, was certain, the farm was slipping away, saw I'd lost it, that is when I began writing my stories: to forget the unendurable. During the war, too; the house was a way station for Jews escaping to Sweden. Jews in the kitchen and Nazis in the garden. I had to write to save my mind. I wrote *The Angelic Avengers*, which was not a political parable, though it amused me how many decided it to be so. Extraordinary men, the Nazis. I often argued with them, spoke back very sharply. Oh, don't think I mean to seem brave, I risked nothing; they were such a masculine society, they simply didn't care what a woman thought. Another muffin? Please do. I enjoy dining vicariously. I waited for the postman today; I'd hoped he'd bring a new parcel of books. I read so quickly, it's difficult to keep me supplied. What I ask of art is air, an atmosphere. That is very meager on the menu nowadays. I never weary of books that I like, I can read them twenty times—can, and have. *King Lear*. I

always judge a person by what he thinks of *King Lear*. Of course, one does want a new page; a different face. I have a talent for friendship, friends are what I have enjoyed most: to stir, to get about, to meet new people and attach them."

Periodically the Baroness does stir. Leaning on the affectionate arm of forlornly cheerful Miss Clara Svendsen, her long-in-service secretary-companion ("Dear Clara. Originally I hired her as a cook. After three wretched meals I accused her, 'My dear, you are an impostor. Speak the truth!' She wept, and told me she was a schoolteacher from the north of Denmark who loved my books. One day she'd seen an advertisement I'd placed for a kitchen wench. So she came; and she wanted to stay. Since she couldn't cook, we arranged she should be secretary. I regret the decision exceedingly. Clara is an appalling tyrant"), she sets forth for Rome or London, going usually by ship ("One does not travel in a plane; one is merely sent, like a parcel"). Last January, the winter of 1959, she made her initial visit to America, a country to which she is grateful because it provided the first publisher and audience for her work. Her reception was comparable to Jenny Lind; at least out-distanced anything accorded a literary dignitary since Dickens and Shaw. She was televised and *Life*ized, the one public "reading" for which she was scheduled developed into a marathon of ticket-scalper, standing-ovation events, and no one, heaven knows, has ever been guest of honor at so numbing a number of parties ("It was delicious. New York: ah! *That* is where things are happening! Lunches and dinners, champagne, champagne; everyone was too kind. I arrived weighing sixty-five pounds and came home an even fifty-three; the doctors didn't know why I was alive, they insisted I ought to be dead, but oh, I've known that for years, Death is my oldest flirt. No, we *lived*, and Clara—Clara gained a stone").

Her acceptance of immense age and its consequences is not stoically final; notes of healthy hope intrude: "I want to finish a book, I want to see next summer's fruit, and Rome again, Gielgud at Stratford, perhaps America. If only. *Why* am I so weak?" she asks, twitching at her lilac scarves with a brown bony hand; and the question, accompanied by the chimings of a mantel clock and a murmur from Miss Svendsen, invites the guest to depart, permitting the Baroness to doze on a couch next to the fire.

As the visitor goes he may be presented a copy of her favorite of her books ("Because it is about real things"), the beautiful *Out of Africa*. A souvenir inscribed "*Je responderay*—Karen Blixen." 7

"*Je responderay*," she explains, standing at the door and, in farewell, offering her cheek to be kissed, "I answer—a lovely motto. I borrowed it from the Finch-Hatton family. I like it because I believe every one of us has an answer in him." 8

Her own answer has been a yes to life, an affirmation her art echoes with an echo that will echo. 9

QUESTIONS FOR READING AND WRITING

1. Karen Blixen, also known as Isak Dinesen, seems a figure out of another age. It is a quality that she clearly cultivates. Have you ever known someone who was very old and who seemed to step out of another era? What qualities did that person have that seem to have disappeared today? Were these characteristics charming, or hopelessly and annoyingly out-of-date?
2. Capote's descriptions are noted for their effective use of figures of speech. For instance, he notes that Dinesen's legs are as thin "as the thighs of an ortolan [a bobolink]" and that she weighs only "a handful of feathers." What is the effect of these comparisons based on birds?
3. The dominant impression of Capote's description of Isak Dinesen is one of frailty due to age. What details support this impression?
4. Select a person as a subject for a descriptive portrait. Compare the person with something appropriate (as in Capote's essay), and try to sustain the comparison through the details selected as a dominant impression.

✦ William H. Gass ✦
China Still Lifes

An American novelist, philosopher, and critic, William H. Gass (b. 1924) is perhaps best known for the novel Omensetter's Luck *(1966) and for* In the Heart of the Heart of the Country, *a collection of stories published in 1968. He has also written* Fiction and the Figures of Life *(1970) and* The World Within the Word *(1978). His* Habitations of the Word *(1985) won the National Book Critics Circle Award for Criticism in 1985–1986. In the following essay, which originally appeared in* House and Garden *magazine, Gass describes the tumult of modern Chinese life. Drawing on his observations in various cities, Gass emphasizes the paradoxes he encountered: motion and stillness, past and present, centuries-old tradition and rapid change.*

IF YOU ARE A VISITOR in Beijing, a bus will take you to the Great Wall where the people clambering about on it will likely outnumber the stones. However, not everyone in China is standing inside the circle of the buses, breathing his last, or pushing his way up that ancient barrier's many steps and steep slopes, although it may seem so; nor is the Great Wall this incredible country's only dragon-shaped defender, because a billion people require the comfort of at least a million walls: walls concealing houses, safeguarding factories, lending themselves to banks and office buildings, hotels and new construction, defining villages, compounds, parks, and squares, protecting pagodas, temples, shrines, and palaces; and along the top of many of these walls a snakelike creature made of slate and tile and stucco seems to crawl, its odd equine head bearing a dog's teeth, with thin wire flames, like antennae, breathing from its nose. For all their apparent ferocity, the intentions of these monsters are pacific, as are the quiet courses of fired clay they serpentine upon. The city streets themselves appear to pass between walls and beneath trees as if they were enclosed, and the shops open out into them as open doors pour into halls.

In Beijing, alongside even the immediate edge of an avenue, rank after rank of potted flowers have been brought to attention—thousands of salvias, for instance, clearly a favorite—as if a pot had to be put out for every cyclist who might possibly pass. These are protected by low wire loops or sometimes by an iron fence of impeccable design when it is not displaying panda-covered kitsch. Success is hit or miss. For the cyclists, too, collisions are not infrequent. I saw a small truck run over a wheel and a leg as though they were bumps in the road. The wheel bent like soft tin and the cyclist's mouth went "O!" Cyclists *are* the street as water is the river, and you can walk across in safety only if your movements are slow and deliberate and resemble a stone's. The bikes sail down the dark streets at night and show no lights, though the buses like to flare theirs. The Chinese say they do it for safety's sake, but each burst is blinding. In their own much narrower lanes, which in intersections they cannot keep to, trucks and buses honk and growl; you will hear occasionally a hawker's cry; otherwise the city is silent except for the continuous ching-a-ching of the bicycle bells. Serenity is always startling. You take close hold of yourself as if your spirit were about to float away, and you say: "Perhaps it's true, and I have a soul after all, other than the one emitted by the exhaust pipe of the motorcar."

Near the long red line of blooming plants, as if to root them for as many seasons as the trees shall persevere, there is a grand row or two of weeping birch or sycamore, then a handsome wide walk—crowded of course—and finally the rich red or yellow plastered wall of a public garden or royal house, the whitewashed wall of a simple shop, or often, in the poorer quarters, one of loosely stacked brick in both alternating and parallel courses, in chevrons, on edge, at length, sometimes like a pattern book they lie so side by side in every posture, frequently free of mortar too, the builder expressing his mastery of economics, gravity, and tradition in the humblest stretch of work. These are walls against which the spangled shadows of the trees fall like a celebration, and through which the light runs like driven rain. 3

In China, to understand some of its most appealing aspects, Necessity should be the first stop for the mind. The comparative freedom of the streets from cars, the sidewalks from dogs, drunks, and vandals, the gutters from trash: these are a few of the slim benefits of poverty and a socialist state. The brooms of the sweepers pass beneath the feet of shoppers as if the shoppers' shoes were simply leaves. Pets compete for a desperately outstretched food supply, and are therefore only surreptitiously kept. And if an 4 improving economy fills these beautiful streets with automobiles, it will be a calamity. But Necessity is never to be admired; it is, at best, only the stepmother of invention; and in China, as elsewhere, it is the cause (or rather, the excuse) for hurried, cheap, high-rise buildings, which appear to repeat every greedy callous Western gesture.

One should not sentimentalize (at least not overly much) about 5
the rich street-and-alley culture of the slums, yet the cities of China are made of streets made of people—walking, biking, working, hanging out. In the paths between buildings there is a world of narrow outdoor rooms; along the walks of wider streets, goods are set out for display and sale; in the open doorways workers enjoy the air and light and sun while they repair shoes, sew, shave a round of wood for chopsticks, clean chickens, and wash pans. The edges of the street are lined with barrows, the center is filled with pedestrians, and out over everyone, from both sides, waves the household wash, hung from bamboo poles propped out of second-story windows and held firmly by a slammed sash. Hong Kong is a world away, but the poles still bristle from the windows of the high rises there: a bit of wash can flutter away in the wind like a kite ten floors from the street; the sanitation is superior; water rises magically in hidden pipes; there is more than the personal forty square feet of living space which is Shanghai's average; and you can no longer see your neighbor, smell his fires—a situation which many planners and politicians approve. As a visitor, a Westerner, a tourist, unburdened by the local "necessities," I say, "Let the rich rot in their concrete trees like unpicked fruit, and leave the earth to the people."

For the curious passing eye, of course, these open doors and 6
drawn shades, these tiny passageways and little courtyards; including every inadvertent jiggle in the course of the street, afford, literally, a sudden "insight." Chinese gardens, with their doorless doors, round as the eye says the world is, their Gibson girl and keyhole shaped gates, their doors framed like paintings or sometimes like windows, as well as every other kind of intermission in a wall that they delight in—punched, screened, glazed, shuttered, beaded, barred—have established the motif of the maze, that arena for interacting forms which seems endless in its arbitrary variety yet one which does not entirely conceal its underlying plans, as zigzag bridges, covered paths, and pools of multiplying water make a small space large, and negligently wandering walls and their surprising

openings constantly offer charmingly contorted eye lines, while contributing, along with the swooping roofs and undulating levels of the ground, to the ambiguity of every dimension, especially those of out and in, whose mixture is also the experience provided by the city streets.

The big cities now have vast blank squares like Tian Anmen in 7
Beijing—they are people pastures, really—fit mainly for mass meetings, hysteria, and hypnotism, while the new wide and always wounding central avenues are suitable for totalitarian parades and military reviews; although it was no different in the old days, since some of the courtyards in the Imperial Palace can hold a hundred thousand heads together in a state of nodding dunder. This is one reason why it is comforting to find these streets, yards, and squares, filled with running children, strollers, and bicycles, because they are such splendid examples of free movement—of being "under one's own power." Walking, running, swimming, skating, cycling, support the moral realm, as sailing does, inasmuch as each seeks to understand and enjoy energies already present and often self-made, whereas the horse, train, rocket, car and plane require and encourage the skills of domination on the one hand, and passivity on the other. The pedicab, alas, is coming back. And one sees people still pulling heavy loads like beasts. In such cases, the load is truly Lord and Master. But the present regime has lifted many a beastly burden from many a human back. I like to imagine that the warm blue autumn skies I enjoyed during most of my stay in China were the radiant reflection of the faces of the people.

That word, and the familiar image I have called back again into 8
service—"a stream of people"—would not seem farfetched or even hackneyed if you were to look down into Guangzhou's Renmin Road (or"street of the people") where a glut of pedestrians slowly moves, not impatiently, though shoulder to shoulder, but reflectively, as a crowd leaves after a splendid concert. It is not New Year's; it is not an occasion of any kind; it is simply midmorning, and the people twine through the streets, living as closely as fibers in cloth. In this crowded world the wall is like one of those inner skins that keeps organs from intervening in the actions of others; they corner chaos like an unruly dog and command its obedience. I saw in a park a pair of lovers fondling one another while lying perilously in the thick fork of a tree. Couples go to such places to quarrel, too,

or work out their incompatibilities with one another's relatives, to play with the baby by themselves, or simply to have an unobstructed view of their spouse's face. It is that difficult to be alone.

Nor normally is the eye left empty. The tourist will have to look high and low for the fierce stone lion behind the stiff grins and adopted postures of the Chinese, one hundred of whom are having their pictures taken in the lap of a seated Buddha, on the back of a bronze ox, in front of a garden of rock, beside a still and helpless pool: by whatever seems majestical, ancient, and handy. The photographers thrust the camera toward the ground until it hangs from their arms like the seat of a swing. Taking aim from below their knees, they stare down at the viewfinder as though peering into a well. Whatever their reason (perhaps, like me, they are waiting for a clear shot), they take their time, so poses are held like bouquets.

That is, they try to stand as still as the burnished brass bowl or stone lamp or painted door they are leaning against. But their lips quiver and their eyes shift and the heart beats high up in their chest. Bystanders fidget and giggle. Movement, not fixity, neither of photograph or statue, is the essence of life. It is an ancient tenet. These walls that I have made the symbolic center of this piece might be thought to be in opposition to mutability and alteration, but in China this is not so. The Great Wall rolls over the mountain ridges like a coaster.

And within the walls, the walls walk; not slowly, according to some customary means of reckoning, but swiftly, each step of brick marking a year as sand does seconds sliding the sides of its glass; and it is perhaps this paradox we understand least when we try to understand China: how calm, how still, and how steadfastly sustaining change in China is; how quickly, like the expression on a face, even bronze can alter; how smartly the same state can come about like a sailboat in the wind; yet the bronze endures and maintains its vigil; the ship, the water, and the wind remain themselves while disappearing into their actions; so that now, as this great nation opens itself to the West and selects some Western ways to welcome, in nearly every chest, as though it shaped a soft cage for the soul, the revolution still holds its breath, while the breath itself goes in and out of its jar as anciently and as rhythmically, almost, as moods move through a man, and men move from one place to another like vagabonds.

The Great Wall rolls over its ridges, I dared to say, yet the Great Wall stands. The Great Wall draws only tourists now who sometimes steal its stones, not invaders or brigands. Still the Great Wall stands for the past. So it is the past that rolls over the hills here; it is the past which stands, the past which lures the tourist; and the past, when it speaks, speaks obsessively of the present. 12

In China, the long dispute between tradition and revolution, rest and motion, action and contemplation, openness and secrecy, commitment and withdrawal, politics and art, the individual and the mass, the family and the state, the convoluted and the simple continues with voices raised and much at stake. That's why, perhaps, amid the crush and the closeness, the delighted yet frantic building and trading and making, I was struck by slower times and more wall-like movements. 13

On a busy Shanghai street, I am brought face to face, not with faces for a change, but with a weather-beaten wooden box, a bowl, a simple pile of goods, all stacked so as to still life, and my sleeping sensuality is shaken awake as it might be by an appealing nakedness. 14

Or perhaps I notice two women in the act of hanging out a bright banner of wash, arrested for a moment by a thought; or I see on the sidewalk by my feet a display of fruit or school of glistening silver fish or a spread of dried mulberries in the center of which a butterfly has lit and now folds its black-and-white wings. 15

Or it is a set of tools resting against a garden wall in such a way their energies seem harmonized inside them; another time it is a group of whitewash pots, jugs of wine, or sacks of grain, or an alley empty of everything but chickens, or a stretch of silent street with freshly washed honey pots, their lids ajar to breathe, sunning themselves in the doorways. Chairs draped with bedding may be taking the air; a brush has been thrust between a drainpipe and its building to dry, an ooze of color down the wall like a drip of egg. Shadows of trees, wires, wash, the tassels of lanterns: these further animate even the busiest lanes. I fancy I see in them operatic masks, kites, the ghosts of released balloons. Or you discover your own shadow cast across a golden sheet of drying rice, and you realize that you are still at home in Missouri and that this is your shade, loose in the midst of China's life. 16

The sill may rot, the bowl fall, but nothing is more ageless and enduring than the simple act of sitting—simply being here or there. 17

The alleys of every city are creased by ledges, crannies, corners, cracks where a rag is wedged, a pot of paint rests, or a basket hangs, a broom leans, a basin waits; and where a plant, placed out of the way like a locked bike, is not a plant now, but will resume its native movements later.

Down a whitewashed little lane in Suzhou, you may find white bread and flour for sale on a white box beneath a white sheet stretched out like an awning, and casting a shadow so pale it seems white as well. Through an open window with blowing white curtains you will be handed your change in the soiled palm of a white glove.

In the same lane is a teahouse where a Vermeer may be found: benches, table, tray, row of glasses, teapot just so, wall right there—all composed and rendered by the master. On top of the teahouse stove, the tools of the cook's trade lie in a sensuous confusion akin to bedclothes. Even the steam holds its shape and station like a spoon. In front of a few chairs, on a small stage, a lectern for the storyteller has been placed. There is one chair on either side of it, both draped with cloths. I make up an artificial audience, sitting there, looking at the wooden figures where the old tales are spoken, and I am truly overcome by the richness of this world: its care for the small things; this tidiness that transcends need and becomes art; the presence of the past in even the most impoverished places and simplest things, for the act of recitation, too, is as importantly immortal as the lean of a spade or a pot's rest.

China seems today in glorious and healthy tumult, but the visitor, charmed by the plenitude or patient genius of the people, the vast landscape and exotic monuments, should not neglect the corners of quiet—the resting bamboo boats or idle ladders, the humblest honey pot or plastic purse or rouged wall—for these things and spaces are everywhere as well, and they are easily as ancient, fully as lively in their own interior way, and certainly as honestly and openly sensual as any rice-ripe, yellow, autumn landscape or langorous stretch of back or thigh.

So it is not by one of the many Buddhas one may see in China that I am reminded of Rilke's poem about that figure,

> As if he listened. Silence: depth . . .
> And we hold back our breath.

nor is it while I am bemused by the admittedly similar grandeur of the burnished bronze bowl that stands, in company with a carefully regulated tree, in front of a bit of royal wall in the Imperial Palace Garden,

Oh, he is fat Do we suppose
he'll see us? He has need of that

but during another kind of encounter entirely, in a commonplace Shanghai street, with a bunch of baskets hung above a stone sink. There is a lame straw fan nearby, and on the sink a blushing cup from which a watercolor brush has been allowed to stick. What hidden field of force has drawn these objects into their conjunction? A wooden bowl leans at the sink's feet, its rosy basin open to the sun. Beside the sink sits a teapot, while behind it rises a pipe where a washrag, dark still from its own dampness, dangles as though done for. There is also a brazier by the sink's side like a sullen brother, a handled pot perched uneasily on its head where a shiny tin lid similarly slides. On top of the sink, again, an enameled saucer waits on a drainboard of worn wood. It contains another jutting brush—a nice touch. It is by these plain things that the lines about the Buddha were returned to my mind, for I was looking at the altar of a way of life. The simple items of this precise and impertinent collection had been arranged by circumstances so complex, historical, and social, so vagarious and yet determined, that I felt obliged to believe an entire culture—a whole people—had composed it. Vermeer indeed, or some solemn Buddha, could only hold a candle, as though they were another witness, to this peaceful and ardent gathering of things.

For that which lures us to his feet
has circled in him now a million years.
He has forgotten all we must endure,
encloses all we would escape.

QUESTIONS FOR READING AND WRITING

1. How are recent changes in China reflected by some of the descriptive details Gass chooses? Would you agree from what you have seen on TV that Tian Anmen square is "fit mainly for mass meetings, hysteria, and hypnotism" (paragraph 7)?

2. What is the meaning of Gass' title? Give some examples of still lifes from the essay. What meaning does Gass invest these things with? Does the democratic revolution in China reflect these things or run counter to them?
3. What examples of the kinds and functions of walls does Gass include in his essay? What does he mean when he refers to walls as the central symbol of his essay (paragraph 10)? How is the image of the street as a "stream of people" compatible with the privacy afforded by the wall?
4. What new image would you choose to describe the democratic protests in China? What image to describe its repression?
5. Find a dominant image for a city you are familiar with and use it as Gass has used the image of the wall to describe and define Beijing—perhaps skyscrapers in New York, freeways in Los Angeles, or bridges in San Francisco. Use the image to suggest the quality of life. You might find it useful to read first Tom Wolfe's essay on New York.

✦ Gregor von Rezzori ✦
A Stranger in Lolitaland

Well known in Europe, Gregor von Rezzori is a Romanian filmmaker and author who usually writes in German. He has, though, also written several books in English, first attracting attention in the United States with his novel, The Hussar *(1960). His best-known work is* Memoirs of an Anti-Semite *(1981), which he has described as an "ambiguously autobiographical" collection of five stories of Jews who have figured in his life. His most recent work is* The Death of My Brother Abel *(1985). The title of this essay, describing America's sociogeographical landscape, may have been suggested by von Rezzori's earlier translation into English of Vladimir Nabokov's novel, Lolita.*

UP TO THEN WE HAD WALLOWED in the pleasantness of the country. Now it was time that we understood the potential threat in the vast horizons that merged so magnificently with the peach-colored skies at the end of golden days. We could now see that they hatched not only star- filled nights but also blizzards, tornadoes, and droughts. In short, we began to see the land with American eyes. A European sees any landscape as a potential garden. An American sees it as an object of enterprise, a building site for some bold undertaking that might be blown or washed away at any moment. There is a ruthless give-and-take in Americans' relationship with nature. In fact, the few places where nature is regarded for its own sake, as nature—the Grand Canyon, Niagara Falls, Kings Canyon, Yosemite, Yellowstone—are kept in cages, like animals in a zoo. 1

Beatrice was studying the map. I was wondering whether I should do the same in order to be able to give an accurate account of my 13,400-mile trip across the crazy quilt of America. But that would not tell how I saw things, or certainly how I remembered them. Geography is an abstract discipline: our image of the world is not a clear or comprehensible one. Did we emerge originally from the waters? Probably, for in our inner world, things are still floating. In every traveler's mind, his journey is a loose accumulation of impressions, swimming mysteriously between memory gaps. Thinking back, he has to ask himself over and over again the 2 same question: Where was it? Where was it that I saw that beautiful blond girl standing under a maple tree in all its autumnal glory, its leaves showering down on her like the gold on Danaë? Where was that garage sale that told one family's whole history, their likes and dislikes, their whims and ambitions, all laid out in a heap of dishes, frying pans, roller skates, books, pictures, and miscellaneous junk? Where was it that black-bonneted ladies looked out of horse-drawn carriages shaped like European beach chairs, and the men had those archaic short beards under their chins and plowed with oxen, meanwhile keeping their tractors hidden in the barn? Where was that awful joint with the pretty topless dancers who acted sexy to get the country yokels drinking beer and gawking at them to stick ten-dollar bills into their G-strings; who, when they finished their numbers, went and sat in a group in the corner and knitted? And that road that went downhill for a whole day, only downhill, till night fell—where was that? And the big bar with all the saddles and cattle horns and silver dollars nailed to the counter? And the funny graffiti in the men's room: WE AIM TO PLEASE. YOU AIM TOO, PLEASE? And the face of that blind woman with the white hair standing in a wind that rolled the shrubs of the desert like bowling balls? And the unbelievably fresh, clean, rosy gums of those black children playing in the dust and giggling at us, and that frosty morning when it snowed and the rows of orange trees with the ripe fruit hanging on them looked like a Grandma Moses painting—where was all that? The beige, yellow, orange, brown, and lime-green country I, as a child, had dreamily looked at on the globe in my sister's and my nursery in faraway Bukovina had become a jigsaw puzzle of bits and pieces, a patchwork of quick impressions, an album of casual snapshots taken at random in different states of mind. "Do you remember that Diane Arbus photograph of the middle-aged parents looking up helplessly at their giant of a son, who seems ready to grow out of the ceiling of their apartment?" I asked Beatrice. "The more I've seen of the United States, the more it grows out of my comprehension."

It was the end of a long day on the road. We were driving toward 3
the peach-colored brim of one of those infinitely clear skies on which invisible jet planes were drawing white lines. Like blotting paper, it swallowed up the ink of night and soon was drowned by it;

and there ahead, where the last cold fire of the evening had just died, another, even colder gleam arose and slowly grew to a glare. We recognized it as a strip of Lolitaland at the edge of a town. But this was more than just a strip. It was a whole city aflame with multicolored light, and the closer we got to it, the more intensely the cold fire of this hell burned. G.K. Chesterton once said of Times Square at night that a person who couldn't read might think it was Paradise. But this was ten times, a hundred times, Times Square. And it was totally devoid of people. There were thousands of cars, though, but their soft cores had left them and had swarmed into the ephemeral-looking buildings whose outsides glowed so enchantingly in the star-spangled night. Inside those buildings, at hundreds of gambling tables and thousands of slot machines, they were busily trying to make money. We knew that in the morning, these places would be deserted, and that all the splendor before us would have been extinguished, and that there would be nothing left but a tremendous void with a cluster of flimsy buildings on it. And I thought to myself, What a tale Sinbad the Sailor would have to tell about Las Vegas, this splendid place that looked like Paradise at night and a desert during the day, and was populated by rubber-tired steel creatures whose soft cores left them to go and make money. And then I realized that the tremendous dam and power plant we had passed hours earlier existed expressly to re-create, night in, night out, the cold hell of this desert paradise; and that the soft cores of the steel creatures had to destroy nature in order to create their own, artificial nature. Here I had in its essence, the new world of the terrible poetic children: Lolitaland in Disneylandish perfection. The Promised Land's New Jerusalem. Finally I had caught it, *my* butterfly.

QUESTIONS FOR READING AND WRITING

1. One of the stock situations in satire is to place a foreign visitor in a strange land and have him or her comment objectively on the behavior of the inhabitants. Von Rezzori is searching for the essence of

America and he finds it in Las Vegas. Where would you look for the heart of America? What would you find there?

2. How do the examples of von Rezzori's "loose impressions" of America in paragraph 2 characterize the pathos he finds in America?
3. Given the details of paragraph 2, how are the descriptions of Las Vegas and Boulder Dam an appropriate summation? Why does von Rezzori call it Lolitaland? Why are the people "soft cores of the steel creatures" and the neon lights "the cold fire of this hell"?
4. Compare Paul Theroux's description of Butlin's, a British vacation spot, with this American one.
5. Assume the position of a traveller to America for the first time and describe the most American place you can think of from this point of view. You might first read Richard Rhodes' "Cupcake Land," which considers Kansas City as a typically American city.

✦ Richard Rhodes ✦
Cupcake Land

As he indicates in his essay, Richard Rhodes is a native of Kansas City, where he was born in 1937. After taking a bachelor's degree from Yale in 1959, he became a contributing editor for Harper's *and later for* Playboy. *His many nonfiction books on life in the United States include* The Inland Ground *(1970),* The Ungodly *(1973),* The Ozarks *(1974),* Holy Secrets *(1978), and* The Making of the Atomic Bomb, *(1987), for which he won the National Book Award for nonfiction and the Pulitzer Prize in 1988. "Cupcake Land," which originally appeared in* Harper's, *is part of a study of farm life in the Midwest.*

IN ONE CORNER OF A DECORATIVE BRIDGE on the Country Club Plaza, a shopping district in Kansas City, Missouri, a massive bronze sculpture attracts the attention of tourists. They are drawn to the work first of all by the colorful flags of the United States and Great Britain that fly overhead and seem to proclaim for it some undefined official status. Approaching the display, they discover that it depicts a man and a woman seated on or emerging from an undefined bronze mound. The man and the woman turn out to be Winston and Clementine Churchill—Winnie staring moodily ahead, Clemmie with folded hands observing her husband benevolently. *Married Love*, the sculpture is titled. By pushing a button on a sort of wooden jukebox behind it, one can listen to a scratchy recording of Churchill speaking to the British people in the dark days of the Second World War; "blood, toil, tears, and sweat" is sometimes discernible over the noise of traffic—Kansas Citians approaching the Plaza to shop. 1

Married Love originated as a small coffee-table piece by one Oscar Nemon. Nemon was an acquaintance of a Kansas City dentist, Joseph Jacobs; Jacobs saw the Churchill piece in Nemon's Oxford home several years ago. Impressed, Jacobs brought home a photograph. One of his dental patients is Kansas City business leader Miller Nichols, whose father, J.C. Nichols, built the Plaza, and whose realty company operates it today. With Miller Nichols captive in his dentist's chair one day, Jacobs confronted him with the 2 photograph. "It's no wonder that our young people have gotten away from traditional values," the dentist says he told the realtor, "when they don't have symbolism to inspire them." Nichols liked the idea of a Churchill statue on the Plaza; it's been fashionable in Kansas City to celebrate the British wartime leader ever since Joyce Hall, the founder of Hallmark Cards, courted his friendship back in the 1950s by sponsoring a national tour of Churchill's leisure-time paintings. "Get that sculptor over here and let's talk about it," Nichols told Jacobs a few weeks later. Nemon was only too willing to scale the little sculpture up to heroic size.

Nichols, a man who pinches his inherited dollars until the eagles squeal, wasn't about to pay for the work himself. He turned fund-raising over to his wife, Jeannette, who assembled privately the nearly $500,000 that the statue and the endowment for its upkeep required. Jacobs says he suggested the title *Married Love*. What was merely kitsch at coffee-table scale thus found epic realization in bronze; the Country Club Plaza, with statuary already at hand of penguins, Indian braves, and sleeping babes, acquired the world's first Chatty Churchill.

Welcome to Cupcake Land.

I've lived in Kansas City for forty-four of my fifty years. I wasn't responsible for the first eighteen, after which I lit out for the East Coast as fast as my legs would carry me. But I came back here of my own volition, to teach and then to write, and I have to own responsibility for the other twenty-six. Partly I got stuck here—wife, children, then ex-wife with custody of the children. Maybe, as an editor friend once theorized, there's something irredeemably provincial in my soul. I like the country around here, rolling hill, prosperous farms. I even like the weather, which ranges from 20 below zero to 115 in the shade, from blizzards to tornadoes to swampy Bangkok heat, and which prepares you—good preparation for journalism—to be comfortable, even relieved, anywhere in the world.

Kansas City was a paradise once, or so it seemed to me when I was a boy in the years just after World War II. The edges of the rough cow town it once was had been sanded and polished to splinter-free nostalgia by an intelligent, benevolent, remarkably nonpartisan city government: the old arrangement of wide, sweeping boulevards and well-kept parks still functioned, the streets were safe, mass transit by electric streetcars and buses was a dream (miles and miles of clean, quiet travel for a nickel, transfers free—I could and did roam the city unescorted at the age of eight). Neighborhoods abounded: children walked to school; you knew the little girls next door and the old man down the block; ladies hung washboards over the backs of chairs on sunny afternoons and used rainwater and vinegar to wash their waist-length hair; on summer evenings roaring with locusts, lawn chairs came out and people called across front yards.

And then the suburbs arose, Cupcake Land, and sweetened Kansas City's plainspoken urban soul. We were more Elmer Gantry here once than George F. Babbitt. How many cities across the land have been similarly Cupcaked? What the hell happened to my town? 7

Curiously, although the cities of the East and West Coasts regularly forge ahead of the Midwest in many aspects of popular culture, in Cupcaking the Midwest has permanently held the lead. The Holy Grail of Cupcake Land is pleasantness, well-scrubbed and bland, and the Northeast Corridor is too crowded and dirty and ethnic, California too highly coveted, too expensive, and therefore too much on the make, quite to measure up. My hometown is the very heart of Cupcake Land. Not by accident has Kansas City become the best test market for new products in the United States; what we consume (to paraphrase Walt Whitman) you shall consume, for every longing belonging to us as good belongs to you. 8

Cupcake Land is petit point and paisley and white wicker. It's professionally catered deb parties. It's the standing ovation, a tribute audiences here accord almost every performance of classical music or ballet or theater, preferring effusion to critical appreciation and too timid to remain seated when fellow Cupcakes stand. Cupcake Land is Laura Ashley and Buick and Pierre Deux, yellow ribbons on every tree to declare Cupcake solidarity with distant hostages, memorials to Christa McAuliffe a thousand miles from Concord. When the goods at a bake sale staged to raise money for charity cost more to bake than they return in sales, I know I'm in Cupcake Land. I know I'm in Cupcake Land when a thorough search of an expensive, well-furnished house turns up not one serious book. 9

Cupcakes wear Ivy League styles of clothing, sort of: button-down shirts for the men in easy-care Perma-Prest; demure skirts and one-piece bathing suits for the women. Cupcakes usually do not 10 attend Ivy League schools, however; they attend state universities, because they believe that going to school out of state looks pretentious, isolates them from the gang, and excludes them from the network of potential business contacts they will need after graduation. Cupcakes do pledge fraternities and sororities; Cupcake Land itself is a working out in maturity of the values, such as they are, learned so painfully in the crucible of the fraternity or the sorority house.

Cupcake men drink beer in moderation at backyard barbecues; 11
Cupcake women don't drink at all, fearing to misbehave ("I get so silly"), or drink "A glass of white wine, please." If the waiter specifies "Chablis?" they answer "That will be fine." "Chardonnay?" would elicit an identical response. Since to Cupcakes the only point of ordering a glass of wine is not to seem standoffish about drinking, the type of wine isn't an issue; and since Cupcakes in general know little about wine beyond what they've learned from television advertisements, making it an issue would appear snobbish to their friends. So of course they don't.

The suburban home and yard are the sturdy trunk and root of 12
Cupcake Land. The ideal yard in Cupcake Land is a monoculture of bluegrass or zoysia (a hardier Southern hybrid), a carpet of brilliant green maintained unvarying through the vicissitudes of summer with herbicides, pesticides, fertilizer, mowing, trimming, and irrigation. The front yards of Cupcake Land, whatever their extent and however inviting their shaded green swards, aren't used. They're purely decorative, like the pristine curb spaces in front of Cupcake houses, where cars in urban neighborhoods would be parked. Cars in Cupcake Land belong in built-on garages with the garage doors closed. Garages for cars exemplify the Golden Rule of Cupcake Land, which is, *A place for everything and everything in its place*. In the spotless kitchens of Cupcake Land, hoods like the hoods condemned criminals wear to the gallows hide the blender and the food processor, and white-enameled tin lids painted with meadow flowers disguise the plain, functional heating coils on the electric range. In Cupcake bathrooms, a needlepoint cover, slotted on top and bottomless, slips over the Kleenex box.

Cupcakes go to church. They're comforted to find so many 13
similarly dressed and like-minded people gathered together in one place. If the sermons are dull, the setting is peaceful. God's in his

heaven; all's right with the world, except in unimaginable places like Iran.

The Empress of Cupcake Land is Nancy Reagan, whom Kansas City Cupcakes adore—always impeccable, all her deals under the table, devoted to a cause for which she has found a pleasant solution ("Just say no") that is the equivalent of Cupcake Land's pleasant solution to poverty ("Just get a job"), to AIDS and teenage sex ("Just keep your legs crossed"), and to the national debt ("Just quit spending"). Ronald Reagan is the Emperor of Cupcake Land, of course, pleasantness personified, financing the imperial expansion on plastic, resplendent in his new clothes. 14

I've had some luck identifying when Kansas City ceded its south side to Cupcake Land (I grew up on the east side of town, now the black ghetto, where the old urban life persisted a few years longer). It began around the time I was born, not much before. The late Edward Dahlberg remembered a brawnier and more vigorous Kansas City, for example, in his 1964 autobiography, *Because I Was Flesh*. "A vast inland city," he described it, "a wild, concupiscent city." He recalled "a young, seminal town" where "the seed of its men was strong." Clearly this is not yet Cupcake Land; the period Dahlberg is evoking is the decade before the First World War, when he was a small boy. "There was more sporting houses and saloons than churches" in Kansas City then, he says. Remembering those forthcoming days he asks heatedly, "Could the strumpets from the stews of Corinth, Ephesus, or Tarsus fetch a groan or sigh more quickly than the dimpled thighs of lasses from St. Joseph or Topeka?" 15

But by the 1930s, on the evidence of Evan S. Connell's autobiographical 1959 novel, *Mrs. Bridge*, Cupcake Land was up and running, as if it came along one sinister Christmas complete and fully assembled, in a Pandoran box. Mrs. Bridge, a young Kansas City society matron, already shops on the Country Club Plaza, where presumably she bought her guest towels: 16

> She had a supply of Margab, which were the best, at least in the opinion of everyone she knew, and whenever guests were coming to the house she would put the ordinary towels in the laundry and place several of these little pastel towels in each of the bathrooms. They were quite small, not much larger than a handkerchief, and no one ever touched them. After the visitors

> had gone home she would carefully lift them from the rack and replace them in the box till next time. Nobody touched them because they looked too nice; guests always did as she herself did in their homes—she would dry her hands on a piece of Kleenex.

Mrs. Bridge is conversant primarily with just such matters as towels, Connell observes, as well as "the by-laws of certain committees, antique silver, Royal Doulton, Wedgwood, the price of margarine as compared to butter, or what the hemline was expected to do." She knows the bedrock rules of Cupcake Land, which would seem not to have changed much these past sixty years. "Now see here, young lady," she scolds one of her daughters, "in the morning one doesn't wear earrings that dangle."

Edward Dahlberg revisited Kansas City late in life; his cantankerous but perspicacious reaction confirms the area's Cupcaking:

> These cities, which are full of every kind of man and woman dirt, and have the most repulsive sex and movie dives, and prurient penny-arcade nudes, and pornographic postcard streets like Twelfth, have citizens, who are crazy about the word CLEAN. Clean health, clean living, clean politics! Only the corrupt can use this tabu word so easily.

Not many blacks live in Cupcake Land: white flight was a major force behind its founding, and it's nearly impossible to cross the invisible lines that toothless laws tolerate and realtors maintain. Recently I rented an apartment in an old restored building in midtown Kansas City (wonderful Nutbread Land, a slice of the spirited Kansas City I remember from childhood, trucks unloading outside grocery stores and buses going by, people of all sizes and shapes and colors walking real sidewalks, some of them talking to themselves). "Funny thing," the rental agent told me, "the people who rent here are almost always from somewhere else. Kansas Citians all want new." To find the new, however diminished—and to escape the desegregation of the public-school system that began in 1955 and is still not complete—Cupcake recruits moved en masse across the state line into Johnson County, Kansas, last year's cow pasture become this year's pseudo-Colonial or French Provincial suburb. Freight wagons used to follow the Santa Fe Trail from Kansas City out through Johnson County; developers today, putting up houses and shopping malls along that trail, seem bent on moving the city itself to Santa Fe.

20 Not that Kansas City Cupcakes dislike blacks, exactly. They avoid them not necessarily because they think them inferior but because they know them to be different, Cornbread rather than Cupcake, just as the blue-collar whites who live south and east of Kansas City in Pancake Land are different. In that difference Cupcakes measure a strong potential for unpleasant encounter. "What would I *say* to one?"

21 Connell, in *Mrs. Bridge*, reinforces this analysis, depicting discomfort rather than active hostility in black-white relations at the borders of the Country Club District. "The niggers are moving in," Mrs. Bridge's daughter announces provocatively one day:

> Mrs. Bridge slowly put down the tray of cookies. She did not know just what to say. Such situations were awkward. On the one hand, she herself would not care to live next door to a houseful of Negroes; on the other hand, there was no reason not to. She had always liked the colored people she had known. She still thought affectionately of Beulah Mae [a laundress long departed for California] and worried about her, wondering if she was still alive. She had never known any Negroes socially; not that she avoided it, just that there weren't any in the neighborhood, or at the country club, or in the Auxiliary. There just weren't any for her to meet, that was all.

22 The Country Club Plaza is supposed to be a place for strolling, window-shopping, watering at one of its several outdoor cafes. (Alternatively, one may ride in a horse-drawn carriage, à la Central Park: at the height of the season more than a dozen carriages work the Plaza, an area only about ten city blocks in extent. They tour no park but streets of storefronts. They do not want for customers.) A little posse of black children biked into this pleasant setting one afternoon in the heyday of breakdancing. They unrolled their pads of cardboard and linoleum, cranked up their ghetto blasters on a centrally located corner outside a men's clothing store, and got down. They were good; spinning and double-jointing through their repertoire, they drew an appreciative crowd. But the Nichols Company doesn't want vulgar street entertainment within the confines of the Plaza, particularly when the entertainers are unlicensed and black. Security guards elbowed through the crowd, spread-eagled the

children against the wall, handcuffed them (or tried to—the cuffs kept slipping off one small boy's wrists), and dragged them away.

In a subsequent year teenagers began to cruise and promenade the western end of the Plaza, to see and be seen, perhaps drawn by the McDonald's installed in a mall building there without golden arches but with a bronze statue of a seated lad eating a bronze hamburger and reading a bronze book. The Nichols Company reacted to the promenading as if it had been assaulted by Cuban mercenaries. First it tried to barricade the streets. That inconvenienced paying adults as well as conspiring teens. Next it sent in its security guards, gun-toting men paid not much more than minimum wage and trained initially only eight hours in their trade—lawsuits for brutality and false arrest are still pending. Finally the Nichols Company arranged with the Kansas City Police Department to set up a command post on the Plaza, *et in Arcadia ego*, from which police fanned out to arrest anyone committing even the most obscure infraction—shirt unbuttoned, one taillight out, taking a leak in the parking-lot bushes. That draconian measure seems to have cleared the kids away. I walked with them one Saturday night not long before the end. They were, for the most part, clean, wonderfully wide-eyed, and duded up—and black. Their real offense was that they scared Cupcakes away.

To obscure its bawdy history Kansas City lays claim to an ersatz nobility. Its livestock show is the American Royal, its debutantes debut at a Jewel Ball, and the trademark of its best-known local industry, Hallmark Cards, is a crown. An exhaustive Name-the-Team contest that received more than 17,000 entries preceded the establishment in Kansas City of its baseball team; we were asked to believe that team owner Ewing Kauffman, a self-made pharmaceutical tycoon, considered those thousands of alternatives seriously before he came up with his choice, the Kansas City Royals, and with the team logo, a distinctly Hallmark-like crown.

The apotheosis of Kansas City's pretentous Anglophilia was a wedding party in London last June for the twenty-one-year-old stepdaughter of the U.S. Ambassador to the Court of St. James's, Charles Price II, a good-old-boy Kansas City banker whose wife Carol is heiress to Omaha's Swanson TV-dinner fortune. Melissa Price's wedding dominated the pages of *The Kansas City Star*—a headline I particularly cherish read SIX-TIER, 500-EGG CAKE WILL BE SHOWPIECE OF RECEPTION—and nearly one hundred of Kansas City's elect flew to London for the event. "Sensible young people," the *Star's* society editor wrote of the couple thus honored, "who believe in some of life's solid dividends, such as friendships and career." The name of the Berkeley Hotel, the editor noted in a helpful aside, is "pronounced Barkley." There was breathless speculation that Nancy Reagan might attend the wedding, her presence transmuting Cupcake to Pound Cake—the Prices are inevitably canonized in Kansas City social notes as Reagan intimates—but no such imperial benevolence was bestowed.

I've concluded that Kansas Citian Calvin Trillin, writing in the *New Yorker*, declared Arthur Bryant's Kansas City barbecue to be the best in the world to gull such pretensions. Bryant's isn't even the best barbecue in Kansas City (their sauce, which Trillin seems to have confused with Lourdes water, tastes overwhelmingly of cayenne). Bryant's is situated in the heart of Kansas City's black ghetto, a place very few Cupcakes normally, by choice, even remotely approach. Arthur Bryant is gone now, but in his day the tables were rickety, the windows dirty, the neighborhood risky, and the barbecue bad. Back in the 1950s, Bud Trillin's high-school crowd went to Bryant's for barbecue to be daring. Cupcakes traipse down to Seventeenth and Brooklyn now because they think it's sophisticated. Eating greasy cayenne-embittered pork in a ghetto barbecue joint identifies them, mirabile dictu, as *New Yorker* readers. 26

The real humorist in Trillin's family is his daughter, Greenwich Village born, who spotted the change in Kansas City from urban paradise to Cupcake Land on a visit here when she was a little girl. Two days of driving from shopping center to shopping center led her to ask her stolid father, Daddy, is this a city? Dearest daughter, of course it is, Bud informed her. Then how come, she pounced, we never *walk*? 27

Most Kansas City Cupcakes work for large, impersonal corporations which partly explains their enthusiasm for conformity. They commute home from work to Cupcake Land every afternoon fearing for their jobs, and the angst such fear engenders colors all the other hours of their lives. I have heard bright and talented adults, who do not hesitate to speak up on issues of national politics, lower 28 their voices in public places when discussing the doings of their corporations, afraid they might be overheard by someone who might pass on their usually innocuous testimony to the éminences noires of directordom. The Soviet Union can't be any worse in this regard. If you can't say something good about something, as I've been told many times out here, don't say anything at all. Cupcakes don't. They don't dare.

As political institutions, corporations aspire to nationhood; they often do command budgets larger than many of the nations of the world, and expect their employees to die for them. In dispensing raises and advancement they make it clear that they value loyalty more than achievement. Within such institutions even the most talented employees frequently come to believe that they are qualified for no other work (the Man Without a Country syndrome), that only the corporation's benevolence sustains them.

At the bottom of the cup in Cupcake Land is a deep insecurity about the consequences of individual expression. Cupcakes are usually only one generation removed from the urban working class or the farm. They wear their newfound bourgeois respectability awkwardly. Like the maids and nannies of Victorian England, but with no such compelling evidence walking the streets around them, they believe that only their conformity to the narrowest standards of convention protects them from the abyss.

Their fear stales friendship and love; in personal relations Cupcake men and women give off a continual sense of disapproval and unease. They don't mean to be difficult; they're only continually fearful that your actions or theirs might reveal them to be parvenus. "Between you and I" is standard English in Kansas City, Cupcakes working too hard to get their grammar right. When such hypervigilance extends to sex it's deadly; in bed with a Cupcake (to speak in the simplified but useful jargon of transactional analysis), child encounters parents instead of child encountering child. "I don't mind. I enjoy cuddling. Let's try again next time." Cupcakes, I'm afraid, lack spice.

A year ago I moved to the Missouri countryside to find out what rural life had become in the thirty years since I left the farm. (My farm career was an adolescent interlude, six years at a boys' home and farm outside Independence, Missouri—but we bused ourselves to school in Kansas City.) The morning of the first day of my visit I met the farmer I would be following, whom I call Tom Bauer, at the outdoor feeding floor where he finishes hogs for market. One of the hogs had a prolapsed rectum, Tom explained, which he was going to try to fix.

The poor animal wasn't hard to identify. Knee-high, weighing about 100 pounds—half-grown—it was pink, with coarse white hair, and a swollen, bluish tube of tissue protruded from its body behind. Because of attacks by the other hogs the prolapse was bloody. "You cain't always fix 'em," Tom told me. "Sometimes you work them back in and they come back out. Then you've lost the animal for sure. But we're gonna try." 33

Tom's big sixteen-year-old son, Brett, was at hand. He slipped into the pen and skillfully caught the hog by a back leg and dragged it out into the aisle. His father pulled on a sterile plastic glove. "We got to haul it up by its hind legs and hang it over the gate," Tom directed. Brett caught the other leg and worked the animal around as if it was a wheelbarrow until its belly approached the gate, which was framed with smooth iron pipe. But the hog's legs were slippery with brown, pungent hog manure. Strapping kid though he is, a reverse guard in high-school football, Brett struggled to lift the animal into position. 34

I didn't think I was being tested, that first day on the farm, but on the other hand, the boy needed help. I took a deep breath—not, in those redolent surroundings, the wisest decision I ever made—stepped to Brett's side, grabbed one shit-covered leg, timed my effort with the boy's, and heaved the hog over the gate so that it hung down bent at the hip, its butt in the air. Brett and I held on then while Tom carefully worked the poor animal's rectum back into its body, the hog screaming in unavoidable pain. "Gross," Brett said. Then his dad was finished and we let the animal gently down. It didn't prolapse again—it lived, to be trucked at 250 pounds to the slaughterhouse for pork chops to grace the tables of Cupcake Land. 35

I adjusted to the realities of farm work quickly enough, having grown up in the trade. But I realized that first morning as I pushed through my initial cultural shock how far removed Kansas City has become from the countryside that sustains it. Cupcake Land is farther removed yet—too far, I fear, for any straightforward 36 recovery. To make life pleasant seems a worthy enough goal in the abstract, but increasing control and decreasing surprise is finally stifling. Full-blown and pathological, it results in life-threatening sensory deprivation. Cupcake children in their pervasive and much remarked ennui show symptoms of such deprivation. Only last summer a crowd of well-provisioned Johnson County teens raged through their suburban neighborhood smashing cars; Cupcake opinion of the rampage blamed permissive education.

Talk is general these days of a brutal recession on its way, the ugly 3
sequela of the Reagan years. That would be a terrible betrayal of Cupcake trust. Chatty Churchills won't guard the gates to Cupcake Land then, or tea cozies hood the disaster, or cuddling comfort the bewildered, or credit cards pay the bills. If any good might come from such a consequence it would be the lifting of the burden of pretension from Cupcake backs.

Like other Cupcake outposts across the land, this plainspoken 3
river-bluff city I know and still grudgingly love has glazed over its insecurities with pretension. Sooner or later, such artificial barriers always collapse. The Missouri River will still be around then, ready in its brown flood to sweep the stale crumbs away. People I respect who care about this place counsel patience, but it's been a damned long wait.

QUESTIONS FOR READING AND WRITING

1. Cupcakes, the inhabitants of Cupcake Land, are described by Rhodes as pretentious, pleasant, self-righteous, white, middle class, and suburban. Is this list of characteristics limited to just the inhabitants of Kansas City? Where else might you find them? What other term has been used to describe this social class?
2. For each of these characteristics, how does Rhodes make the abstract quality come alive? Find examples of concrete illustrations that make the description live. How do narrative anecdotes help?
3. Why does Rhodes open with the description of the statue of the Churchills? How does it sum up several of the qualities of Cupcake Land?
4. What is the function of the narrative-description of the hog with the prolapsed rectum? How does this description serve to counterpoint

the Churchill anecdote and to indicate the distance Cupcake Land has travelled from its rural surroundings?

5. Read Paul Fussell's "Neckties and Class" and write an essay describing the social pretensions of a group or a region. Following Rhodes' lead, use several concrete examples to support your observations.

Part 4

EXPOSITION

Writing to Explain and Inform

Other than works of literature, most of the material we read or write is expository writing. Exposition is simply the presentation of facts or ideas. In other words, expository writing is explanatory writing. Unsurprisingly, it appears in a multiplicity of forms:

- Cookbooks, automobile repair manuals, directions for assembling a bicycle.
- Newspaper reports, stock-market and weather reports, many government documents.
- Historical texts, explications of literature, science and mathematics textbooks.
- Anthropological case studies, psychological reports, sociological studies.
- Philosophical treatises, informal essays, newspaper editorials.

These varied forms can be condensed into three basic kinds of exposition—scientific, informative, or exploratory—according to the degree of proof, factuality, or speculation they set forth.* For example, a final-examination essay in a chemistry class is likely to be factual and to involve demonstrations in the form of proofs. On the other hand, an essay on a history test would probably be highly informational, though it might also contain speculations that would make it exploratory.

* For this division we are indebted to James L. Kinneavy, *A Theory of Discourse* (Prentice-Hall, 1979).

Scientific Writing Most scientific writing is more objective (that is, more verifiable), uses more concrete language, and is more impersonal than other types of exposition. For example, here is a passage from Barry Commoner's *The Closing Circle:*

> Strontium, a natural, harmless element, and its radioactive isotope, strontium 90, both move through the environment in concert with calcium, a chemically similar element. And calcium is avidly withdrawn from the soil by plants, becoming incorporated into food and then taken up in the human body. Once fallout appeared on earth, inevitably strontium 90 would accompany calcium as it moved through the food chain, ultimately becoming concentrated, along with calcium, in vegetables, in milk, in the bones of people.*

Notice how the language and sentence structure do not call attention to themselves but point dispassionately to Commoner's subject matter. The exposition is straightforward, factual, and makes no appeal to the emotions of the reader. The chain of reasoning here is based on specific, concrete, factual data. The passage begins with a statement describing the presence of the radioactive isotope, strontium 90; moves on to a description of strontium's bonding with calcium; and ends with the logical conclusion that by moving up the food chain, the isotope is inevitably found in the bones of human beings. It does not betray Commoner's strong feelings about the radioactive poisoning of the atmosphere due to nuclear fallout, but relies on the reader to realize that radioactive materials are obviously harmful.

Informative Writing Scientific writing is characterized by a high degree of verifiability—that is, given the facts and the chain of reasoning, the conclusions could be tested. Informative writing, on the other hand, presents information that is "news" in the sense that it is unforeseen, unpredictable, and to some extent unexpected. Since most student writing is informative, this presents several problems. What seems to many students significant information is to many composition instructors trite and obvious. A student who offers the statement, "The Manhattan Telephone Directory is

* Barry Commoner, *The Closing Circle* (Knopf, 1971), 51.

large," as an illustration of the size of New York City is apt to find "So?" written in the margin of the evaluated paper. But Gay Talese, working with the same material writes, "The Manhattan Telephone Directory has 776,300 names, of which 3,316 are Smith, 2,835 are Brown, 2,444 are Williams, 2,070 are Cohen—and one is Mike Krasilovsky."* Talese's article is interesting as well as informative because the facts are so unusual. But how are you to judge whether a detail—or the entire piece of informative writing—is significant, unforeseen, or unusual? The significance of any piece of information depends on the sophistication of the intended audience. Don't overestimate your audience's familiarity with informative material, but don't condescend to your audience either.

Exploratory Writing Exploratory writing is speculation about the implications of the facts explained in informative writing; it investigates significant questions, is less strictly objective or reportorial and perhaps more emotional than either scientific or informative writing. Exploratory writing dissects opinions, hypotheses, and stereotypes to see where they lead. Here is the opening paragraph of an exploratory essay by Joseph Wood Krutch:

> What is "nature"? One standard reference devotes five columns to fifteen different and legitimate definitions of the word. But for the purposes of this article the meaning is simple. Nature is that part of the world which man did not make and which has not been fundamentally changed by him. It is the mountains, the woods, the rivers, the trees, the plants, and the animals, which have continued to be very much what they would have been had he never existed.†

You might say, "This is obvious." Indeed, in one sense, it is. But Krutch's purpose is *not* to present startling new facts about nature but to explore the philosophic and spiritual implications of man's being both part of and distinct from nature. The language is less concrete and the statements more tentative, more speculative, and more open to a variety of explanations than they are in scientific or informative writing.

* Gay Talese, "New York," *Esquire* (July 1960).

† Joseph Wood Krutch, "Man's Ancient, Powerful Link to Nature—A Source of Fear and Joy," *If You Don't Mind My Saying So . . .* (W. Sloan, 1969), 336.

Even though you will seldom consciously set out to produce one of the three types of expository writing, you will always need to determine the level of factuality and objectivity appropriate for what you want to say. To do this, you must determine your primary purpose: Are you writing to prove a scientific hypothesis? Are you presenting "new" information to your audience? Or, are you speculating on a hypothesis to see what its implications are? A clear *purpose*, either stated or implied, is essential to expository prose. A concise statement of your intent, usually in the form of a single sentence, is customarily called a *thesis statement*. The scope of the *topic* (frequently the grammatical subject of the thesis statement) should be sufficiently limited to be handled within the space allotted. Your particular *focus* is spelled out in what is called the *controlling idea* (often the predicate of the sentence). An example of a thesis statement is this sentence from the opening paragraph of an essay by George Orwell, "The English Class System":

Topic	Controlling Idea
The peculiarity of English class distinctions	is . . . that they are *anachronistic.*

With this thesis statement, Orwell limits his discussion to the anachronistic nature of English class distinctions—not everything about them, not their injustice, but the peculiarity of the fact that they are relics of a bygone age.

A thesis statement is clearly useful, but it is often difficult to include the topic and the focus in the same sentence without stretching the language or violating the rule of clarity. The following two thesis statements, the first by George Elliott and the second by George Orwell, are taken from essays with radically different purposes. Notice that the writers take several sentences to fully state their purposes, but use pronouns to link the sentences tightly together in series of connected ideas.

> Culture has another enemy, however, which did not exist to any alarming degree before this century and yet is here to stay. Its ways are so imperfectly understood that many people either do not see it as a threat or else underestimate it. This enemy, which I call pseudoculture, seems to me no less dangerous than the others.*

* George Elliott, "The Enemies of Intimacy," *Harper's* (July 1980), 50.

> When I look through my own recipe for the perfect cup of tea, I find no fewer than eleven outstanding points. On perhaps two of them there would be pretty general agreement, but at least four others are acutely controversial. Here are my own eleven rules, every one of which I regard as golden.*

Clearly, Elliott's topic is pseudoculture and his focus is its destructive effects, but he develops and further qualifies both topic and focus by adding details; he also leads into his topic gradually, taking his reader along with him. Like Elliott, Orwell gradually leads up to his topic (the perfect cup of tea) and focus (how to brew one); in this case, the gradual build-up is almost dictated by the friendly, intimate tone of the piece. In both essays the organization and content are foreshadowed by the thesis.

Sometimes the thesis is called a *generative sentence* because, if properly written, it will generate both the material and the organization to develop the thesis. Suppose, for example, you begin an essay with the sentence, "Most men live in harness." Not only would that sentence provoke a series of examples to substantiate the point—and, perhaps, some narratives to support the examples or even some cause–effect explanations of the example—but it would necessitate exemplification as a pattern of organization.

In fact many instructors insist on an explicit thesis statement at the beginning of an essay to ensure that the essay does not stray from its announced topic and maintains a minimal organization promised by the thesis. However, despite the generative value of a formal statement of purpose, not every piece of writing contains one. The purpose or main idea is frequently diffused throughout the essay in many of the statements that define the subtopics of the essay. Such essays have an implied thesis. (In analyzing these essays it is often good practice to frame a sentence that describes the writer's purpose.)

Just as an entire essay may have an explicit thesis, many supporting paragraphs contain an explicit *topic sentence*. A topic sentence tends to be more general, its language more abstract, and its content more a matter of opinion, inference, or judgment than the sentences that accompany it and develop it. In the following paragraph, the first sentence is a judgment summing up a great many

* George Orwell, "A Nice Cup of Tea," *As I Please* (Harcourt Brace Jovanovich, 1968), 41.

details, whereas the next sentences contain verifiable facts that illustrate and support the opening topic sentence:

> *New York is a city for eccentrics and a center for odd bits of information.* New Yorkers blink twenty-eight times a minute, but forty when tense. Most popcorn chewers at Yankee Stadium stop chewing momentarily just before the pitch. Gum chewers on Macy's escalators stop chewing momentarily just before they get off—to concentrate on the last step. Coins, paper clips, ball-point pens, and little girls' pocketbooks are found by the workmen when they clean the sea lion's pool at the Bronx Zoo.*

The topic sentence assembles what otherwise might seem stray bits of unrelated information. Without the topic sentence, each sentence would be random. With the topic sentence, the other sentences are assembled into a unified paragraph.

The characteristic "shape" of the *standard expository paragraph* is a pyramid:

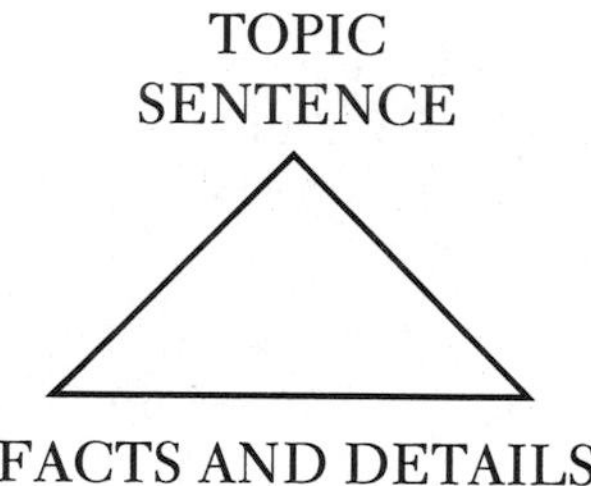

But some expository paragraphs build to a kind of climax, withholding the topic sentence until the end. In the following example, E. B. White gives specific details first, then makes a judgment about them:

> At certain hours on certain days it is almost impossible to find an empty taxi and there is a great deal of chasing around after them. You grab a handle and open the door, and find that some other citizen is entering from the other side. Doormen grow rich blowing their whistles for cabs; and some doormen belong to no door at all—merely wander about through the streets, opening cabs for people as they happen to find them. By com-

* Gay Talese, "New York."

> parison with other less hectic days, the city is uncomfortable and inconvenient; but *New Yorkers temperamentally do not crave comfort and convenience—if they did they would live elsewhere.**

In this sort of paragraph, the most general part, the topic sentence, comes last, linking the many details together, giving them a point, and imparting to the paragraph an inverted pyramid shape:

FACTS AND DETAILS

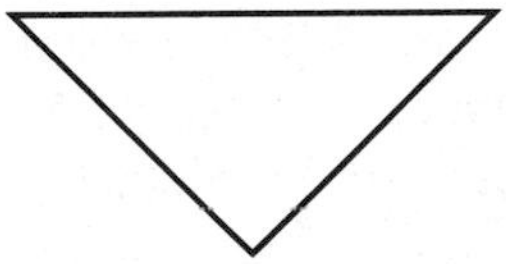

▽

TOPIC
SENTENCE

Bear in mind, however, that these shapes—the inverted triangle and the triangle—are only two of many a writer may employ. In fact, most paragraphs in an essay move back and forth between degrees of generalization and specificity. Notice that the degree of specificity of White's sentences varies. The first is less specific than the two that follow, but more specific than the topic sentence concluding the paragraph. Nonetheless, in a well-constructed essay, the topic sentences are always logical subdivisions of an overall thesis.

The content of the thesis statement dictates the kind of material appropriate for its development and the pattern of organization suitable to that development. In his *Rhetoric,* Aristotle suggested that one way to determine what to say about a subject is to proceed through a list of topics that would apply to any subject in general. Among the many such topics listed by Aristotle are definition, division, consequences, cause and effect, and comparison. If we frame a few of these topics in the form of a series of questions, their ability to generate material for the development of a thesis should become clear.

1. What is it? (definition)
2. Are there examples of it? (exemplification)

* E. B. White, "Here Is New York," *Essays of E. B. White* (Harper & Row, 1977), 132.

3. Can it be divided or classified under a larger category? (division/classification)
4. Is it similar to or different from something else? (comparison/contrast, analogy)
5. What brings it about, or what effects does it have? (cause/effect)
6. How is it made? (process analysis)

By applying these questions to the subject, you can generate a significant amount of information. For example, if your topic involves the subject of inflation, you would, perhaps, begin by telling what constitutes inflation (definition), give some practical examples of items whose price has inflated dramatically over the last few years (exemplification), discuss various kinds of long- and short-term inflation (division), show the differences between inflation and depression (contrast), discuss what factors increase the rate of inflation (cause), and trace the evolution of an inflationary spiral (process analysis).

Each of these questions (and any of the many others we might ask) suggests material that will be arranged in a logical way; consequently, these labels—definition, exemplification, and so on—are often referred to as *patterns of organization.* We will use them in this sense to describe the predominant pattern of organization used in the selections that follow. You will notice immediately that a single pattern rarely dominates an entire piece. An essay often incorporates material generated from answers to several questions about several topics. Therefore, such essays follow several patterns of organization. In this book, the essays are grouped according to the pattern that is the *predominant* pattern of organization used, but that is not the *only* pattern. Because most college writing is expository in nature, you will probably spend most of your time and energy learning to imitate and generate the combinations of organizational patterns that appear in the following essays.

Definition

Definition is a pattern of organization that seeks to answer the question, "What is it?" Through definition a writer reveals the nature of a thing by describing its essential qualities, listing its characteristics, or giving examples of it.

Writers frequently use definition when their subject has more than one acceptable meaning and one of the several meanings must be specified. In technical or scientific writing, terms often must be defined because the audience is unfamiliar with the language of the discipline. For example, through clear definition and example, John McPhee translates the technical term *d-limonene* into laymen's terms as he describes the process by which orange concentrate is made:

> Cutback is mainly fresh orange juice, but it contains additional flavor essences, peel oil and pulp. . . . The chief flavoring element in cutback is d-limonene, which is the main ingredient of peel oil. The oil cells in the skins of all citrus fruit are ninety per cent d-limonene. It is d-limonene that burns the lips of children sucking oranges. . . . D-limonene is what makes the leaves of all orange and grapefruit trees smell like lemons when crushed in the hand.*

Definitions are of several types. A *stipulative definition* in effect says, "Let us agree that for our purposes the word ______ means . . . ." In a *formal definition*, a word is placed in relation to a large category or class (genus) and then is differentiated from all other members of that category according to its specific difference (species). A common dictionary definition of the word *democracy*, for example, follows the pattern of a formal definition: "Democracy is a form of government in which the supreme power is vested in the people and exercised directly by them or their elected agents under a free electoral system."

* John McPhee, *Oranges* (Farrar, Straus and Giroux, 1967), 131.

Word-to-be-defined	=	*Classification*	+	*Differentiation*
"democracy"		"a form of government"		(1) "Supreme power is vested in the people and exercised directly by them" (2) "or by their elected agents under a free electoral system."

An *informal definition* merely lists the characteristics of a thing. Writing of the desert cactus, Edward Abbey lists the characteristics of one species and tells how it got its name:

> The chollas are the prickliest plants in the cactus family, and the prickliest of their kind is the small and shrubby teddy bear cholla. Paradoxically, the teddy bear's fierce armament accounts for its disarming nickname: its straw-colored spines and glochids are so numerous and close-set that the entire plant looks furry, especially when it glistens in a halo of bright sunlight.*

Definition by contrast explains what a thing is by contrasting it with a different item of the same classification. Aldo Leopold opens one of his essays by showing how "land" differs from "country":

> There is much confusion between land and country. Land is the place where corn, gullies and mortgages grow. Country is the personality of land, the collective harmony of its soil life and weather. Country knows no mortgages, no alphabetical agencies, no tobacco road; it is calmly aloof to these petty exigencies of its alleged owners.†

An *etymological definition* reveals what a thing is by going back to the word's origins (its etymology) to show what it originally meant. For example, John McPhee follows the botanical migration of oranges from the East to Europe by tracing the etymology of the word:

> The word "orange" evolved from Sanskrit. The Chinese word for orange, in ancient as well as modern Chinese, is *jyu*, but it did not migrate with the fruit. India was the first major stop in the westward travels of citrus. . . . The Hindus called an

* Edward Abbey, *Cactus Country* (Time-Life, 1973), 88.
† Aldo Leopold, "Country," *A Sand County Almanac* (Oxford University Press, 1981), 165.

> orange a *naranga,* the first syllable of which . . . was a prefix meaning fragrance. This became the Persian *naranj,* a word the Muslims carried through the Mediterranean. In Byzantium, an orange was a *nerantzion.* This, in Neo-Latin, became variously styled as *arangium, arantium,* and *aurantium*—eventually producing *naranja,* in Spain, *laranja* in Portugal, *arancia* in Italy, and *orange* in France.*

Whatever form of definition you use, remember that its purpose is to clarify and explain. A definition should never complicate or obscure a subject; it should add relevant information to the reader's knowledge of the subject.

* John McPhee, *Oranges,* 64.

✦ Dwight Bolinger ✦
Mind in the Grip of Language

Linguist and teacher-author, Dwight Bolinger has been called one of the few academic linguists "who can write well and sees some point in trying to." Born in Topeka, Kansas, in 1907, Bolinger completed his doctorate at the University of Wisconsin in 1936. He has been a professor of Spanish and Romance languages at the University of Southern California and at Colorado and Harvard Universities, and has been a Visiting Professor Emeritus at Stanford. He has published numerous scholarly studies in linguistics; his best-known works are Meaning and Form *(1970),* Aspects of Language *(1968, third edition with D. A. Sears, 1980), and* Language—the Loaded Weapon: The Use and Abuse of Language Today *(1980). Of his writing, Bolinger has said, "My main hope is to make linguistics intelligible and interesting to as wide an audience as possible." The following selection, taken from* Aspects of Language, *discusses the complex relationships between thought, meaning, and the conventions of languages belonging to different language families.*

Language and Thought

NO ONE DENIES that language and thought are related. The question is how and how closely. The ultimate in closeness was claimed by a now outmoded school of psychology which held that thinking is merely talking to oneself, in an implicit sub-vocal way. The opposite view was expressed by W. D. Whitney a century ago: "Language is the spoken means whereby thought is communicated, and it is only that"—thoughts are generated in their own sphere and then formulated in language. A more comfortable position is somewhere between the two extremes: language is a tool in the way an arm with its hand is a tool, something to work with like any other tool and at the same time *part of* the mechanism that drives tools, part of *us*. Language is not only necessary for the formulation of thought but is part of the thinking process itself. Two famous metaphors describe the relationship: "Talking about language is building a fire in a wooden stove"; "Talking about knowledge or science is rebuilding a boat plank by plank while staying afloat in it." We cannot get outside language to reach thought, nor outside thought to reach language.

Thinking is not done in a vacuum, but is always about something. 2
What is the nature of an object of thought? It is rarely the image of a material thing standing before us; most often it is recalled from past experience or transmitted from the experience of others. In the latter case it almost inevitably comes via language. We could imagine of course that when we learn, from what someone tells us or from what we read in a book, that Pluto lies at the outward bounds of the solar system, the linguistic information is translated into some kind of mind-stuff before being filed for future reference. But no one knows what such a recording substance would be like, and it is simpler to assume that what is stored away is a set of appropriate sentences. Memory of our own past experience too is largely possible because we have put that experience into words. Any writer who has ever needed to consult a thesaurus has had the joyless task of trying to pin down an idea which refused to materialize until the word for it came to mind.

Control by Language

The general question of the interdependence of thought and 3
language yields to the particular one of fluidity and rigidity. Mind and spirit have always been conceived (at least in our culture) as a kind of ectoplasm, formless in itself but freely shaped by the act of thinking. Nothing is impervious to it; it penetrates all walls and envelopes all concepts. Language has never had this reputation. It is a structure, warping whatever filters through it. The problem of rigidity was first popularized in the 1930s by a school of philosophy, still active, known as *general semantics*, which saw in our use of *words* a kind of surrender of the flexibility and refinement of thought for the sake of traffic in verbal *things*. Much was made of the uncritical use of generalizations, of the difficulty of pinning a statement like the following down to a set of precise referents: "It is the ability of a community to achieve consensus on the great issues and compromise on the lesser issues which lies at the heart of the democratic process. . . ." The critical reader must ask: Can

communities as a whole have abilities? Can the difference between great and small issues be recognized? Is there ever consensus without compromise? Is democracy a process? And so on.

The Whorf hypothesis

It remained for a linguist, Benjamin Lee Whorf, to turn the question away from individual words and toward the framework of whole languages. He was not the first to take this step—Fritz Mauthner in 1902 declared that "if Aristotle had spoken Chinese or Dakota, his logic and his categories would have been different." Others, including Wilhelm von Humboldt and Whorf's own teacher Edward Sapir, held similar opinions. But Whorf was the most successful in dramatizing it. Since every language has a form and no two forms are the same, it follows that no two cultures having different languages can have identical views of the world. Instead of a perfectly flexible rubber mask that shapes itself to reality, each language is somewhat like a Greek mask, with its own built-in scowl or grin. Whorf's perception of language as a pair of glasses with more or less warped lenses through which we view our surroundings was sharpened by his work with a language about as different from English as any language can be—that of the Hopi, a tribe of Pueblo Indians living in Arizona. Whorf had what Archimedes demanded in order to move the world—a place to stand; and he maintained that French or German or Russian was no good as a platform, since in fundamental structure these languages—in common with others of Indo-European stock—are the same.

One of the chief things that English and its sister languages fasten upon the experience of all their speakers is a prior categorization of the reality outside us into nouns and verbs. The noun pictures things as detached from the processes that surround them, making it possible to say *The wind blows* or *The light flashes,* though wind cannot exist apart from blowing nor flashing apart from light. Not only does it *enable* us to say such things, it *forces* us to: by itself, *snowing*, as our English teacher said, "is not a sentence"; where no subject is handy, we must throw in a plug for one: *It is snowing.* Whorf writes:

> English terms, like *sky, hill, swamp,* persuade us to regard some elusive aspect of nature's endless variety as a distinct *thing,* almost like a table or chair. . . . The real question is:

> What do different languages do, not with . . . artificially isolated objects but with the flowing face of nature in its motion, color, and changing form; with clouds, beaches, and yonder flight of birds? For as goes our segmentation in the face of nature, so goes our physics of the cosmos.

Two examples will suffice to show the arbitrariness of this segmentation, its dependence upon the local interests and transitory needs of the culture that attempts it. The word *vitamin*, coined in 1912 to designate a group of substances supposed at the time to be amines, covers such a strange agglomeration of chemicals that *Webster's Third New International Dictionary* requires fourteen lines to define it, in spite of the fact that it is given only one sense. Yet to the average user of the term it seems to name something as clear and definite as the house next door. 'A thing in nature' becomes 'a thing in commerce,' and the pill-taker is not concerned with what it "really is." Similarly, the term *complex* was applied around 1910 to a combination of psychological factors that, as the name implies, were difficult to separate and simplify; but the existence of the term, and the identification of some particular ailment as a "complex," gave all that was needed for a new entry among our realities. 6

Coupled with a categorization of "thingness" in nouns is a categorization of "substance" in the subgrouping of mass nouns. English and related languages have a special technique of combining these with certain formalized "counters" in order to carve out segments: *a piece of meat, a glass of water, a blade of grass, a grain (bushel) of corn, a stalk of celery.* The resulting picture is one of a universe filled with taffy-like aggregations that can be clipped into pieces by our scheme of numbers: *earth, air, stone, iron, light, shade, fire, disease,* even—and especially—abstractions like *love, honor, dismay, courage, dictatorship,* and *accuracy.* 7

Out of this substance-operated-on-by-numbers, this notion of *jewels* as "contained in" *jewelry* and *guns* as "contained in" *artillery*, our language has evolved an elaborate vocabulary having to do with an all-containing *space*—the term *space* itself is a mass noun that subsumes in an abstract way all other mass nouns. And here is where the world view of our language departs most radically from that of the Hopi: our concepts of space are so pervasive that we are able to transfer them almost totally to *time.* We treat time as a mass, 8 and carve it into units and count them: *five hours.* For it we use the same prepositions: *before, after, in, at;* the same adjectives: *long, short, same, different, right, wrong, hard, nice, more, less;* and many of the same nouns: *stretch* of time, *segment* of time, *amount* of time. And, of course, we capture events in our space-like nouns—the word *event* itself, plus *rain, dance, movement, stir, riot, invasion, courtship,* and countless others. This, Whorf points out, is almost never done in Hopi:

> Our own "time" differs markedly from Hopi "duration." It is conceived as like a space of strictly limited dimensions, or sometimes as like a motion upon such a space. . . . Hopi "duration" seems to be inconceivable in terms of space or motion, being the mode in which life differs from form, and consciousness *in toto* from the spatial elements of consciousness. . . . Our "matter" is the physical sub-type of "substance" or "stuff," which is conceived as the formless extensional item that must be joined with form before there can be any real existence. In Hopi there seems to be nothing corresponding to it; there are no formless extensional items; existence may or may not have form, but what it also has, with or without form, is intensity and duration, these being non-extensional and at bottom the same.

Our custom of quantifying time is illustrated by the sentence *Ten days is greater than nine days,* which contrasts with the Hopi expression of the same idea in terms of duration, *The tenth day is later than the ninth.* Events of brief duration cannot be captured as nouns in Hopi: "lightning, wave, flame, meteor, puff of smoke, pulsation, are verbs."

So where Western philosophers—from Plato and Aristotle with 9
their concepts of matter and form to Kant with his *a priori* space and time—have imagined that they were intuiting general laws that applied to all of nature or at least to all of mankind, what they actually were doing was exteriorizing a way of looking at things that they inherited from their language. Much that is difficult in recent physics as well as in philosophy and logic has been the struggle to climb out of this rut, all the harder to escape because we are in it, unconsciously, from the moment we begin to speak. Whorf surmised that a world view such as that of the Hopi might be more congenial to the concepts of modern physics than the languages of

Western Europe. In a similar vein, Y. R. Chao has argued that Chinese is more congenial than English to certain approaches of symbolic logic. For example, the normal Chinese *Yeou de ren shuo jen huah* 'There are men who tell the truth' is closer to the logical formula than is the normal English *Some men tell the truth.*

Better examples than those in comparisons of structure can be 10
found in comparisons of lexical equivalence; for we do unquestionably "structure" our universe when we apply words to it, sometimes—especially when the phenomena are continuous and do not exhibit seams and sutures—quite arbitrarily.

The example most frequently cited is that of colors. The visual 11
spectrum is a continuum which English parcels out into six segments: *purple, blue, green, yellow, orange* and *red.* Of course painters, interior decorators, and others concerned with finer shades and saturations employ a more elaborate vocabulary; but the additional words are generally defined with those six as reference points: *turquoise* is 'between blue and green'; *reseda* is 'between green and yellow'; *saffron* is 'between yellow and orange'; *crimson* is 'a shade of red'; *emerald* is 'a shade of green.' In Zuni, orange and yellow are combined into a single range named *łupzʔinna* (whose borders are not necessarily the red end of orange and the green end of yellow—all we can say is that *łupzʔinna* roughly coincides with our orange plus our yellow). In Navaho, the two colors *łičííʔ* and *łico* divide somewhere between red and orange-yellow. How these different habits of naming can affect our "thinking"—symptomized by the efficiency with which we communicate—can be shown through recognition tests: the monolingual Zuni, presented with a small set of different colors and then asked after a brief period to pick out the ones he saw from a much larger collection, will have trouble recognizing the ones for which his language does not have convenient names. Young Wolof children can more easily discriminate colors for which their language has names, though adult Wolof monolinguals are not limited in this way. It would seem that whatever initial advantage a concentration on one part of the color spectrum may produce is reduced later as more possibilities of naming and categorizing are opened up. Other continuums present the same problem across languages—temperature, for example, where English *hot–warm–cool–cold* do not coincide lexically or grammaticallly with the corresponding terms in other languages. Even with continuums,

however, linguistic relativism is not absolute. A study of color categories in numerous languages has revealed that they fall into a rather definite evolutionary sequence. *Black* and *white* are basic and always to be found. Next is *red,* followed by *green* and *yellow,* singly or together; after that *blue,* then *brown,* and finally any combination of *pink, purple, orange,* and *gray.*

According to the authors of the Wolof study, more important than mere naming to the influence of language on thinking is how deeply a language organizes concepts into hierarchies:

> In a way quite different from that envisaged by Whorf, we seem to have found an important correspondence between linguistic and conceptual structure. But it relates not to words in isolation but to their depth of hierarchical imbedding both in language and in thought. This correspondence has to do with the presence or absence of higher-order words that can be used to integrate different domains of words and objects into structures.

Schooling supplies some of this hierarchical organization through displacement (talking about things not present) and writing (which frees words from things), thus providing words that elicit other words and concepts that elicit other concepts. This in turn will "push a certain form of cognitive growth better, earlier and longer than others. . . . Less technical societies do not produce so much symbolic imbedding nor so many ways of looking and thinking." As an example, children who had, as part of their language, a concept such as 'color' were able to classify objects (in tests administered to them) at the same conceptual level in terms of 'shape' and 'use' as well as 'color'—for example, the specific colors 'red' and 'blue'—were unable to use the higher, more abstract classifications. By insisting overmuch on *grammatical* relativism and picking only superficial examples of *lexical* relativism, linguists and anthropologists have perhaps missed the most important cognitive manifestation of all, the intricacy of lexical organization. It is an area that is only beginning to be studied.

The "semantic differential"

If the lenses of our language that stand between us and reality are slightly warped, they are also tinted. It is one thing to see a certain kind of fish narrowed down to *eel*; it is something slightly different to see eels as repulsive creatures. Yet our language—plus other associations that we *act out* in connection with eels under the tutelage of fellow members of our culture—decrees both things: the focus and the affect. Every term we use apparently has the power to sway us in one direction or another. Experiments on this semantic differential, as it is called by the psychologist Charles E. Osgood and his co-workers, show that persons presented with pairs of antonyms such as *wise–foolish, good–bad, deep–shallow, light–heavy*, and the like will relate other terms in rather consistent ways to each of these extremes, even when there seems to be no logical connection. The technique is to draw a seven-point scale with the antonyms at either end, for example

light ___ ___ ___ ___ ___ ___ ___ *heavy*

and to give subjects a term such as *skittish* with instructions to locate it at one of the points. While it would not be surprising, in view of associations with other terms such as *lightheaded*, if everyone agreed that *skittish* ought to go well over to the "light" end, what is surprising is that subjects will even agree on where to locate something as apparently outlandish as *wood* on a scale between *severe* and *lenient*.

14 Osgood has found a number of affective dimensions to which concepts can be related in this way, but the most consistent ones in the more than twenty languages tested are three, which he has labeled "evaluation," "potency," and "activity." Evaluation is by all odds the most predictable: virtually every term and its associated concept seems to attract or repel, however slightly. English even formalizes this to some extent in its system of lexical intensifiers, where *well* and *badly* figure as synonyms of *very (well thought out, well out of danger, well ready, well sufficient; badly bungled, badly needed, badly lacking, badly upset)*.

15 Does this mean that, in addition to making us see reality in certain shapes and sizes, our language is also one of the most powerful factors in forcing us to take sides? If all the speakers of a given language share a prejudice, language will transmit it. Take for example the associations of insanity. Most of them are "funny": *crazy, nutty, loony, daffy, half-witted, harebrained, loopy*, and so on. They reflect a culture in which psychopathological states are

not diseases to be treated but deviations to be laughed at. It has required a vigorous reorientation of our attitudes to put mental disease on a footing other than ridicule or shame so that it *could* be treated. We can excuse language by saying that people use words, words don't use people. But this is like saying that people use guns, guns don't use people—the *availability* of guns is one factor in their use.

The evils of word availability have been impressed on us ever since the women's liberation movement first drew attention to them at the beginning of the 1970s. Language consecrates the subordinate role of women in the loss of surnames at marriage, in the labeling of wed or unwed status by *Mrs.* and *Miss* (marital-status labeling is not required of men), in the greater caution expected of women in speech (women are more "polite" than men), in the many opprobrious names for women (*slut, gossip, crone, hoyden, slattern*—the list is endless), in the contempt attached to *spinster* but not to *bachelor*, and in hosts of other ways. Even an epithet for males is an indirect slap at a female: *son of a bitch*. The network of associations among these verbal habits traps us in a set of attitudes from which we can extricate ourselves only by earnest attention to both the attitudes and the words.

We have learned the dangers of acquiescing in defamation in the past decade or two from the upward struggle of minority groups. This has bred an awareness—and conscious avoidance—of the *unintentional* use of the most obvious slurs, such as the noun *nigger* and the verb to *Jew down*. Hardly anyone in an urban community would unthinkingly call a Brazil nut a *niggertoe*. The taboo extends even to unrelated homophonous terms—for example, *niggardly*. But this is a superficial awareness, and we are only beginning to examine other usages that betray—and at the same time help to transmit—uncritical prior judgments. The white (honky?) who would never think of using the word *nigger* may give himself away by venturing opinions on *the negro problem*. The presupposition here of course is that problems are to be identified and defined in white terms—the speaker who uses this phrase is shocked if someone retorts that it is rather *a white problem*. At the same time there are growing signs of a deeper understanding. The very existence of such an expression as *If you're not part of the solution you're part of the problem* shows an awareness of the impertinence of assuming that one has the right to stand outside the process and judge it or manipulate it. The mere presence in the language of the phrase *self-fulfilling prophecy* shows an acceptance of the theory that it is possible, by predicting an event, to influence behavior in a way that will bring the event about. Language to some extent records our intellectual maturity.

QUESTIONS FOR READING AND WRITING

1. Can you think of any examples from your personal experience of what Bolinger calls the "distorting or tinting lens of language"? What prejudices—sexual, religious, ethnic, or geographical—are recorded in the vocabulary we use?
2. Bolinger defines language in two ways: first by contrasting the differing language systems of Indo-European and non-Indo-European languages (chiefly Hopi and Wolof, a language spoken in Senegal); second, by discussing how language works, how it structures our universe. How well were the examples chosen to clarify his definition of language?
3. Read Norman Cousins' "The Mysterious Placebo" and William Safire's "Emphasis on Stress" and comment on whether or not their examples of language and mind control fit Bolinger's thesis.
4. Read James Baldwin's essay on Black (Afro-American) English and comment on Bolinger's definition of language as applied to "Black English."
5. Collect some examples of how our vocabulary or the structure of English distorts our view of reality.

✦ Norman Cousins ✦
The Mysterious Placebo

Norman Cousins (b. 1912) has been associated with The Saturday Review *for over 30 years. His columns have been collected in* Writing for Love or Money *(1949), but since his recovery from a near-fatal illness, Cousins has devoted considerable energy to teaching the value of positive thought in helping patients to recover.* Anatomy of an Illness as Perceived by the Patient: Reflections on Healing and Regeneration *(1979) was a national best seller. "The Mysterious Placebo" typifies Cousins' belief that healing takes place not always as a result of an effective drug, but as a result of the patient's belief in his or her own power to get well.*

OVER LONG CENTURIES, doctors have been educated by their patients to observe the prescription ritual. Most people seem to feel their complaints are not taken seriously unless they are in possession of a little slip of paper with indecipherable but magic markings. To the patient, a prescription is a certificate of assured recovery. It is the doctor's IOU that promises good health. It is the psychological umbilical cord that provides a nourishing and continuing connection between physician and patient. 1

The doctor knows that it is the prescription slip itself, even more than what is written on it, that is often a vital ingredient for enabling a patient to get rid of whatever is ailing him. Drugs are not always necessary. Belief in recovery always is. And so the doctor may prescribe a placebo in cases where reassurance for the patient is far more useful than a famous-name pill three times a day. 2

This strange-sounding word, placebo, is pointing medical science straight in the direction of something akin to a revolution in the theory and practice of medicine. The study of the placebo is opening up vast areas of knowledge about the way the human body heals itself and about the mysterious ability of the brain to order biochemical changes that are essential for combating disease. 3

The word placebo comes from the Latin verb meaning "I shall please." A placebo in the classical sense, then, is an imitation medicine—generally an innocuous milk-sugar tablet dressed up like an 4 authentic pill—given more for the purpose of placating a patient than for meeting a clearly diagnosed organic need. The placebo's most frequent use in recent years, however, has been in the testing of new drugs. Effects achieved by the preparation being tested are measured against those that follow the administration of a "dummy drug" or placebo.

For a long time, placebos were in general disrepute with a large 5
part of the medical profession. The term, for many doctors, had connotations of quack remedies or "pseudomedicaments." There was also a feeling that placebos were largely a shortcut for some practitioners who were unable to take the time and trouble to get at the real source of a patient's malaise.

Today, however, the once lowly placebo is receiving serious at- 6
tention from medical scholars. Medical investigators such as Dr. Arthur K. Shapiro, the late Dr. Henry K. Beecher, Dr. Stewart Wolf, and Dr. Louis Lasagna have found substantial evidence that the placebo not only can be made to look like a powerful medication but can actually act like a medication. They regard it not just as a physician's psychological prop in the treatment of certain patients but as an authentic therapeutic agent for altering body chemistry and for helping to mobilize the body's defenses in combating disorder or disease.

While the way the placebo works inside the body is still not 7
completely understood, some placebo researchers theorize that it activates the cerebral cortex, which in turn switches on the endocrine system in general and the adrenal glands in particular. Whatever the precise pathways through the mind and body, enough evidence already exists to indicate that placebos can be as potent as—and sometimes more potent than—the active drugs they replace.

QUESTIONS FOR READING AND WRITING

1. Have you read about the use of placebos in testing new drugs, for instance those being tested to combat the effects of AIDS? See Stephen Jay Gould's essay, "The Terrifying Normalcy of AIDS." What

is so controversial about their use in these double-blind tests on patients diagnosed as having tested positive for the AIDS virus?

2. In the fourth paragraph, Cousins cites the etymological definition of "placebo." Why does he use this definition to introduce the positive side of prescribing placebos?
3. Why can "placebo" be defined both negatively and positively? What seems to be Cousins' position?
4. Write an essay defining a term around which there is some controversy, for example, abortion, euthanasia or nuclear power. Slant your definition so that, without appearing to do so, you support one definition.

✦ William Safire ✦
Emphasis on Stress

Popular journalist and author, William Safire is known to the public as the author of a series of books on language, for his opinion column, and for a weekly column on language appearing in The New York Times Magazine. *Born in New York City in 1929, Safire attended Syracuse University and began his career as a reporter for the* New York Herald Tribune. *He joined the staff at NBC news and spent nearly two decades in broadcast journalism, culminating in his appointment as a special assistant to President Richard Nixon from 1969 to 1973. He became a columnist with* The New York Times *in 1973. Among his many books on Washington politics are* Safire's Political Dictionary *(1968, rev. 1978),* Before the Fall *(1975), and* Full Disclosure *(1977). He was awarded a Pulitzer Prize in 1978 for Distinguished Commentary. His popular books on language include* On Language *(1980),* What's the Good Word *(1982),* Good Advice *with Leonard Safir (1982),* I Stand Corrected *(1984), and* Take My Word for It *(1986).* Freedom *(1987) is his most recent book. In the following essay from his weekly* Times *column, Safire comments on the uses of that most frequently misused word,* stress.

YOU HAVE TWO MINUTES and 30 seconds to read and fully comprehend this piece. (Snap to it, and better not miss anything because you will be savagely tested and cruelly graded.) 1

"I once had *anxiety*," says a scrawny, straggly haired, self-hugging character in a syndicated strip by the cartoonist Jules Feiffer. "Now I have *stress*." 2

When Mr. Feiffer takes note of language change, lexicographers listen. He was the one, in 1967, who caught the political ring-around-the-rosy in the use of *black:* "As a matter of racial pride we want to be called *blacks*. Which has replaced the term *Afro-American*. Which replaced *Negroes*. Which replaced *colored people*. Which replaced *darkies*. Which replaced *blacks*." 3

Two years before that, The Village Voice cartoonist was the first to grasp the nomenclature of neediness: "I used to think I was *poor*. Then they told me I wasn't *poor*, I was *needy*. They told me it was 4 self-defeating to think of myself as *needy*; I was *deprived*. Then they told me *underprivileged* was overused. I was *disadvantaged*. I still don't have a dime. But I have a great vocabulary."

Accordingly, dictionary makers and language mavens are poring over his analysis of *stress*. "I go to a weekly stress lab . . ." says his character in the wash-and-wear hairdo, her body language shouting out her leaned-on, tugged-at, pushed-around mental state. "And take stress tests and stress-ercise classes. I'm on a stress diet and take stress vitamins. I go out with stress-mates and play stress-games and have stress-sex. *Anxiety* was so isolated," she says, finally smiling. "Thank God for *stress*."

The socialization of stress, and its voguish selection as the root of all modern health evil, has not hitherto been subjected to linguistic examination. (How you doin', reader? Most people your age and social class are about three paragraphs further on. You're sure you grasped the full import of the academese in the sentence before this parenthetical aside? Your peer group is looking over your shoulder.)

Stress, the noun, is a shortening of *distress*, rooted in the Latin *distringere*, "to hinder, molest." *Stress*, the verb, has another root as well: the Latin *stringere*, "to draw tight, press together," which is related to *strain*. Here is a stringent lesson: The result of *stress* is *strain*.

As a generalized noun, *stress* has come to take its meaning from the verb: the pressure—whether through direct force, tension or torsion—exerted on a person or thing. Specialized meanings abound: People in the language dodge use *stress* to mean *accent* (*accent* changes the syllable stressed when it switches from noun to verb). Orators stress certain points ("Let me emphasize, my stressed-out friends . . ."). But those familiar old *stresses* are not the specific *stress* so much in vogue on analysts' couches and in gatherings of the gaseous glitterati.

The stress that is "in"—trendy stress, swank angst—is the mental-physical ailment that psychiatrists call *the stress syndrome* and gastroenterologists, ears cocked to a proliferation of burbling stomachs, call their ticket to a good life. (Lest we treat the problem too lightly, it is good to remember that emotional reactions can cause physiological tensions, which can lead to disease, as ulcer sufferers know.)

10 Dr. George A. Engel, in a 1953 study of ego and stress, wrote that—"*Psychological stress* refers to all processes, whether originating in the external environment or within the person, which impose a demand or requirement upon the organism the resolution or handling of which requires . . . activity of the mental apparatus before any other system is involved or activated." *Stress*, in its psychiatric sense, is what happens when unconscious impulses call for action that conflicts with ordinary behavior. That is somewhat more complex than simple, or layman's, stress, which is how you feel when your boss leans on you to put hospital corners on your spreadsheets, or your spouse makes strange new demands, or your language maven reminds you that you should have finished this piece long ago. (Come on, skim the next graph—you're really holding up your whole cohort.) In either the medical or lay notions of stress, you may suddenly get very tired or break out in a rash or hit the panic button.

11 "*Stress* is now being used as a catchall term for almost any response to anxiety or depression," says Dr. Rex Buxton, a psychiatrist in Potomac, Md. "Most often, it is used by people who feel tired, worn out, and are making an analogy to metallurgy—stressed metal is more brittle, more liable to be fractured." Dr. Howard Bogard, a Manhattan psychologist, does not think of the word as a clinical term, but as a word spread by internists asking patients, "Is there stress in your life, your job, your marriage?" to which the answer is always an enthusiastic yes.

12 Dr. Bruce Dan, senior editor of the Journal of the American Medical Association, recalls a "Life Stress Scale" in the early 1970's that listed hard-to-take conditions like divorce and death of a spouse. "The presence of stress causes physical changes that can be measured," says Dr. Dan. "You can observe increases in pulse, respiration, heartbeat, and this stress can lead to more serious physical problems. It's a very useful word. *Anxiety* is not so much a synonym for *stress* as it is a result of stress."

13 For purists, then, *pressure, tension* and *stress*, which are synonymous in general use, lead to *anxiety* and *strain*, also synonymous. The vogue term, and perhaps that metaphor of metallurgical strain (stressed-out people are sometimes described as *bent*), was presaged by John Locke circa 1698: "Though the faculties of the mind

are improved by exercise, yet they must not be put to a stress beyond their strength."

(You finished last. Now you can relax and enjoy the rest of the paper. But don't feel bad: Did you ever meet a slob who had stress?)

QUESTIONS FOR READING AND WRITING

1. In what contexts are you used to hearing the word *stress*? Is it used as a synonym for *anxiety*, or has it taken on a different meaning? Is being *stressed out* the same thing as *having stress*?
2. Safire employs a number of different kinds of definitions in his essay. Which are effective and which seem repetitive? What is the point of opening with the Feiffer anecdote? Are we meant to take the medical definitions from authorities very seriously?
3. Find some faddish words in current teenage slang. Look up their past meanings and contrast them with the present. Or, take words favored by another generation or group—say terms popular in the 1960s or language favored by yuppies—and write a satiric essay using the terms in the contexts in which they are most often found.

✦ Judy Syfers ✦
I Want A Wife

Born in San Francisco in 1937, Judy Syfers took her degree from the University of Iowa in 1962. She now resides in San Francisco and is a freelance writer. "I Want a Wife," which grew out of the feminist movement of the 1960's and appeared in the inaugural issue of Ms. *magazine in 1971, defines the one-sided nature of a relationship that ensues following society's usual understanding of the term* wife.

I BELONG TO THAT CLASSIFICATION of people known as wives. I am a Wife. And, not altogether incidentally, I am a mother. 1

Not too long ago a male friend of mine appeared on the scene fresh from a recent divorce. He had one child, who is, of course, with his ex-wife. He is obviously looking for another wife. As I thought about him while I was ironing one evening, it suddenly occurred to me that I, too, would like to have a wife. Why do I want a wife? 2

I would like to go back to school so that I can become economically independent, support myself, and, if need be, support those dependent upon me. I want a wife who will work and send me to school. And while I am going to school I want a wife to take care of my children. I want a wife to keep track of the children's doctor and dentist appointments. And to keep track of mine, too. I want a wife to make sure my children eat properly and are kept clean. I want a wife who will wash the children's clothes and keep them mended. I want a wife who is a good nurturant attendant to my children, who arranges for their schooling, makes sure that they have an adequate social life with their peers, takes them to the park, the zoo, etc. I want a wife who takes care of the children when they are sick, a wife who arranges to be around when the children need special care, because, of course, I cannot miss classes at school. My wife must arrange to lose time at work and not lose the job. It may mean a small cut in my wife's income from time to time, but I guess I can tolerate that. Needless to say, my wife will arrange and pay for the care of the children while my wife is working. 3

I want a wife who will take care of *my* physical needs. I want a wife who will keep my house clean. A wife who will pick up after me. I want a wife who will keep my clothes clean, ironed, mended, replaced when need be, and who will see to it that my personal things are kept in their proper place so that I can find what I need the minute I need it. I want a wife who cooks the meals, a wife who is a *good* cook. I want a wife who will plan the menus, do the necessary grocery shopping, prepare the meals, serve them pleasantly, and then do the cleaning up while I do my studying. I want a wife who will care for me when I am sick and sympathize with my pain and loss of time from school. I want a wife to go along when our family takes a vacation so that someone can continue to care for me and my children when I need a rest and change of scene.

I want a wife who will not bother me with rambling complaints about a wife's duties. But I want a wife who will listen to me when I feel the need to explain a rather difficult point I have come across in my course of studies. And I want a wife who will type my papers for me when I have written them.

I want a wife who will take care of the details of my social life. When my wife and I are invited out by my friends, I want a wife who will take care of the babysitting arrangements. When I meet people at school that I like and want to entertain, I want a wife who will have the house clean, will prepare a special meal, serve it to me and my friends, and not interrupt when I talk about the things that interest me and my friends. I want a wife who will have arranged that the children are fed and ready for bed before my guests arrive so that the children do not bother us. I want a wife who takes care of the needs of my guests so that they feel comfortable, who makes sure that they have an ashtray, that they are passed the hors d'oeuvres, that they are offered a second helping of the food, that their wine glasses are replenished when necessary, that their coffee is served to them as they like it. And I want a wife who knows that sometimes I need a night out by myself.

I want a wife who is sensitive to my sexual needs, a wife who makes love passionately and eagerly when I feel like it, a wife who makes sure that I am satisfied. And, of course, I want a wife who will not demand sexual attention when I am not in the mood for it. I want a wife who assumes the complete responsibility for birth control, because I do not want more children. I want a wife who will remain sexually faithful to me so that I do not have to clutter up my intellectual life with jealousies. And I want a wife who understands that *my* sexual needs may entail more than strict adherence to monogamy. I must, after all, be able to relate to people as fully as possible.

If, by chance, I find another person more suitable as a wife than 8
the wife I already have, I want the liberty to replace my present wife with another one. Naturally, I will expect a fresh, new life; my wife will take the children and be solely responsible for them so that I am left free.

When I am through with school and have a job, I want my wife 9
to quit working and remain at home so that my wife can more fully and completely take care of a wife's duties.

My God, who *wouldn't* want a wife? 10

QUESTIONS FOR READING AND WRITING

1. In your experience, is Syfers' definition of a wife still accurate, or has the role of a wife changed? Explain.
2. What is *wife* a synonym for in the essay? Is the tone of the essay angry or satiric? Why does almost every sentence begin with "I want" or "When I"?
3. See the movie *Diary of a Mad Housewife* and write a comparison between the wife depicted by Carrie Snodgrass in the film and Syfers' wife.
4. Read Adrienne Rich's essay, "Claiming an Education," and write a comparison of its view of women with the satiric view presented here.

✦ Alice Walker ✦

Oppressed Hair Puts a Ceiling on the Brain

Alice Walker's essays, like her fiction (see "The Flowers"), deal in an amusing yet perceptive way with Afro-American identity. In the following essay, which was originally delivered as a commencement address at Spelman College, where she was a student, Walker defines the meaning of growth *in an ironic way by referring to how she let her hair outgrow its oppression. The essay first appeared in print in* Ms. *magazine.*

AS SOME OF YOU NO DOUBT KNOW I was a student here myself once, many moons ago. I used to sit in these very seats (sometimes still in pajamas, underneath my coat) and gaze up at the light streaming through these very windows. I listened to dozens of encouraging speakers and sang, and listened to, wonderful music. I believe I sensed I would one day return, to be on this side of the podium. I think that, all those years ago, when I was a student here and still in my teens, I was thinking about what I would say to you now.

It may surprise you that I do not intend (until the question and answer period perhaps) to speak of war and peace, the economy, racism or sexism or the triumphs and tribulations of black people or of women. Or even about movies. Though the discerning ear may hear my concern for some of these things in what I am about to say, I am going to talk about an issue even closer to home. I am going to talk to you about hair. Don't give a thought to the state of yours at the moment. Don't be at all alarmed. This is not an appraisal. I simply want to share with you some of my own experiences with our friend hair and at the most hope to entertain and amuse you.

For a long time, from babyhood through young adulthood mainly, we grow, physically and spiritually (and including the intellectual with the spiritual), without being deeply aware of it. In fact, some periods of our growth are so confusing that we don't even recognize that growth is what is happening. We may feel hostile or angry or weepy and hysterical, or we may feel depressed. It would never occur to us, unless we stumbled on a book or person who explained it to us, that we were in fact in the process of change, of actually becoming larger, spiritually, than we were before. Whenever we grow, we tend to feel it, as a young seed must feel the weight and inertia of the earth as it seeks to break out of its shell on its way to becoming a plant. Often the feeling is anything but pleasant. But what is most unpleasant is the not knowing what is happening. I remember the wave of anxiety that used to engulf me at different periods in my life, always manifesting itself in physical disorders in my body (sleeplessness, for instance), and how frightened I was because I did not even understand how this was possible.

With age and experience, you will be happy to know, growth 4
becomes a conscious, recognized process. Still somewhat frightening, but at least understood for what it is. Those long periods when something inside ourselves seems to be waiting, holding its breath, unsure about what the next step should be, eventually become the periods we wait for, for it is in those periods that we realize we are being prepared for the next phase of our life and that, in all probability, a new level of the personality is about to be revealed.

A few years ago I experienced one such period of restlessness 5
disguised as stillness. That is to say I pretty much withdrew from the larger world in favor of the peace of my personal, smaller one, unplugged myself from television and newspapers (a great relief!), from the more disturbing members of my extended family, and from most of my friends. I seemed to have reached a ceiling in my brain. And under this ceiling my mind was very restless, although all else about me was calm.

As one does in these periods of introspection, I counted the 6
beads of my progress in this world. In my relationship to my family and the ancestors I felt I had behaved respectfully (not all of them would agree, no doubt); in my work I felt I had done to the best of my ability all that was required of me; in my relationship to the persons with whom I daily shared my life I had acted with all the love I could possibly locate within myself. I was also at least beginning to acknowledge my huge responsibility to the earth and my adoration of the universe. What else, then, was required? Why was it that, when I meditated and sought the escape hatch at the top of my brain, which, at an earlier stage of growth I had been fortunate enough to find, I now encountered a ceiling, as if the route to merger with the infinite I had become used to was plastered over?

One day, after I had asked this question earnestly for half a year, it occurred to me that, in my physical self there remained one last barrier to my spiritual liberation, at least in the present phase. My hair.

Not my friend hair itself, for I quickly understood that it was innocent. It was the way I related to it that was the problem. I was always thinking about it. So much so that if my spirit had been a balloon eager to soar away and merge with the infinite, my hair would be the rock that anchored it to earth. I realized that there was no hope of continuing my spiritual development, no hope of future growth of my soul, no hope of really being able to stare at the universe and forget myself entirely in the staring (one of the purest joys!) if I still remained chained to thoughts about my hair. I suddenly understood why nuns and monks shaved their heads!

I looked at myself in the mirror when I understood this mystery, and I laughed with happiness! For I had broken through the seed skin, and was on my way upward through the earth.

Now I began to experiment. For several months I wore long braids (a fashion among black women at the time) made from the hair of Korean women. I loved this. It fulfilled my fantasy of having very long hair and it gave my short, mildly processed (oppressed) hair a chance to grow out. The young woman who braided my hair was someone I grew to love—a struggling young mother, she and her daughter would arrive at my house at seven in the evening and we would talk, listen to music, and eat pizza or burritos while she worked, until one or two o'clock in the morning when she was done. I loved the craft involved in the designs she created for my head. (Basket making! a friend once cried on feeling the intricate weaving atop my head.) I loved sitting between her knees the way I used to sit between my mother's and sister's knees while they braided my hair when I was a child. I loved the fact that my own hair grew out and grew healthy under the "extensions," as the lengths of hair were called. I loved paying a young sister for work that was truly original and very much a part of the black hairstyling tradition. I loved that I did not have to deal with my hair but once every two or three months (for the first time in my life I could wash it every day if I wanted and not have to do anything further). Still, eventually the braids would have to be taken down (a four- to seven-hour job) and redone (another seven to eight hours); nor did I ever quite forget the Korean women, who, according to my young hairdresser, grew their hair expressly to be sold. Naturally this caused me to wonder (and yes, worry) about all other areas of their lives.

When my hair was four inches long I dispensed with the hair of my Korean sisters and braided my own. It was only then that I became reacquainted with its natural character. I found it to be springy, soft, almost sensually responsive to moisture. As the little braids spun off in all directions but the ones I tried to encourage them to go, I discovered my hair's willfulness, so like my own! I saw that my friend hair, given its own life, had a sense of humor. I discovered I liked it. 11

Again I stood in front of the mirror and looked at myself and laughed. My hair was one of those odd, amazing, unbelievable, stop-you-in-your-tracks creations—not unlike a zebra's stripes, an armadillo's ears, or the feet of the electric-blue-footed booby—that the universe makes for no reason other than to express its own limitless imagination. I realized I had never been given the opportunity to appreciate hair for its true self. That it did, in fact, have one. I remembered years of enduring hairdressers—from my mother onward—doing missionary work on my hair. They dominated, suppressed, controlled. Now, more or less free, it stood this way and that. I would call up my friends around the country to report on its antics. It never thought of lying down. Flatness, the missionary position, did not interest it. It grew. Being short, cropped off near the root, another missionary "solution" did not interest it. It sought more and more space, more light, more of itself. It loved to be washed; but that was it. 12

Eventually I knew *precisely* what hair wanted: it wanted to grow, to be itself, to attract lint, if that was its destiny, but to be left alone by anyone, including me, who did not love it as it was. What do you think happened? (Other than that I was now able, as an added bonus, to comprehend Bob Marley as the mystic he always said he was.) The ceiling at the top of my brain lifted; once again my mind (and spirit) could get outside myself. I would not be stuck in restless stillness but continue to grow. The plant was above the ground! 13

This was the gift of my growth during my fortieth year. This and the realization that as long as there is joy in creation there will 14 always be new creations to discover, to rediscover, and that a prime place to look is within and about the self. That even death, being part of life, must offer at least one moment of delight.

QUESTIONS FOR READING AND WRITING

1. Do you agree with the statement in the opening of Walker's essay (paragraph 3) that the feeling of "growth" is often anything but pleasant?
2. Walker is defining growth in a double sense in her essay. Despite the essay's humorous tone, there is an underlying seriousness in Walker's metaphor for growth. While she speaks of the growth of her hair, she is really addressing personal or spiritual growth. Why does she, for instance, refer to her hair as oppressed? How did it put a ceiling on her brain?
3. Why is Walker concerned with the Korean women who sell their hair? What are some of the double entendres in the final three paragraphs which she includes under the term "missionary work" previously done on her hair?
4. Is it just Walker's hair that "regains its natural character," that "has a will of its own," that has "a sense of humor"? What is she really referring to?
5. Define your own growth informally by relating it to some of the external changes that took place in your life during a period of transformation.

Examples

When we want to explain what we mean, we naturally turn to *examples*. Yet we frequently write general statements that need supporting examples—and then forget to supply them. Sometimes we make ambiguous statements that call for illustrations; sometimes we make statements that should be supported with facts; and sometimes our statements need further elaboration or expansion with more particulars and details. The requirements of *clarity*, *proof*, and *sufficient development*, therefore, frequently call for some kind of exemplification.

Clarity The primary function of examples is to clarify. Perhaps the subject is complicated or tends to be abstract. In both cases, give one or more specific examples to illustrate the point and to bring it into contact with the concrete world. Ask yourself who the audience is and whether it is as familiar with the subject as you are. What parts of the subject are likely to need the clarification of an example? As poet Robert Graves has suggested, you need to imagine the reader over your shoulder, looking at the page you've written, asking for explanations and clarifications of points that may not be immediately clear. For example (two words which should appear in nearly every expository essay), when E. B. White tells us that New York "insulates the individual," he follows that statement with several pages of examples of events going on in the city—from murders, accidental deaths, air shows, sporting events, to ocean liner departures, the arrival of the governor, and conventions—none of which White witnessed. The list of examples helps make his point: The events are so numerous and commonplace, they have no direct impact on him.

Proof We make essentially three kinds of statements: reports, inferences, and judgments. "The current air temperature is 80° F" is a *report*, a fact we can verify by checking a thermometer. "It's going to rain" is an *inference*, a conclusion based on an observation of a dark, cloudy sky. "She is the worst governor the state has had in decades" is a *judgment*, simply an opinion regarding relative goodness, badness, and so on. Reports rarely require examples for proof because they are either true or false; their reliability can be easily checked. Inferences and judgments, however, raise questions that demand documentation. "*Why* do you think it will rain?" "*Why* is she the worst governor?" Proper answers to these questions will necessarily be factual and closer to the level of actual experience than the initial statement. That is what writing well involves—making statements on a factual level where the reader can easily understand them. Examples help accomplish this aim.

Development Writers sometimes trap themselves in the belief that their subject involves such general knowledge that readers can fill in the details for themselves. This is almost always a mistake. A subject that is often ripe with opportunity for vivid detail yields a commonplace, stale, vague outline of the potentially perceptive essay. Even if the topic of the essay is generally understood and the thesis widely accepted, through careful development and thoughtful observation of details, the writer can produce a rich, interesting essay.

Expanding your writing through additional detail is not like blowing more hot air into a balloon, but rather is fleshing out for the reader what would otherwise be a skeletal sentence outline. For example, "bad writing confuses the reader and reflects the confusion of the writer's thoughts" is an obvious statement that presents readers with an idea for an essay but not with the details that will convince them that you know what you're talking about. But when George Orwell provides examples of double negatives, tortuous syntax, inflated diction, and mixed metaphors, he brings the concept of confused and confusing writing down to a level of specificity that any reader can apprehend and appreciate.

A final, and seemingly obvious, rule about using examples: They should truly exemplify. An atypical, uncharacteristic example will fail to illustrate, clarify, or prove your point. Orwell's examples, on the other hand, look in two directions—toward the audience that understands them and toward the thesis that the examples support.

✦ Paul Fussell ✦
Neckties and Class

Two words invariably crop up when Paul Fussell is described: curmudgeon and iconoclast. Born in 1924, he earned his doctorate from Harvard, and after 1955 was a professor of eighteenth-century literature, a field in which he has published several scholarly studies. He won the National Book Award in 1976 for his classic study of the literature of World War I, The Great War and Modern Memory. *Presently, he is Donald T. Reagan Professor at the University of Pennsylvania and many of his books deal with the contemporary world in an amusing and satiric manner, most notably:* The Boy Scout Handbook and Other Observations *(1982) and* Class: A Guide Through the American Status System *(1983). "Neckties and Class," taken from the latter book, gives some perceptive illustrations of how to tell a person's class from the kind of tie he or she is wearing.*

THE TOPIC OF THE CLASS IMPLICATIONS of men's neckties deserves a book in itself. Here I can only sketch a few general principles. Skimpy as its contribution of fabric to the total ensemble may be, the tie does add to the effect of layering and for this reason if for no other is identified with high status. But it must be said too that in the right context omitting the tie entirely conveys the message that one is so classy—say, upper-class—as to be above all criticism, and that conventional canons of respectability don't apply. The necktie's association with responsibility, good employeeship, and other presumed attributes of the obedient middle class is well documented by an experiment conducted by Molloy. He had a series of men interviewed for good jobs. Some wore ties, others did not. "Invariably," he found, 1

> those men who wore their ties to interviews were offered jobs; those without them were turned down. And in one almost incredible situation, the interviewer . . . was made so uncomfortable by the applicant's lack of a tie that he gave the man \$6.50, told him to go out and buy a tie, put it on, and then come back to complete the interview. He still didn't get the job.

The same suggestion that the necktie is an important marker of the division between the middle and the prole classes emerges from another of Molloy's experiments, this one performed at the horrible Port Authority Bus Terminal in New York, a traditional locus of every imaginable vice, menace, and outrage. He himself posed as a middle-class man who had left his wallet home and had somehow to get back to the suburbs. At the rush hour, he tried to borrow 75 cents for his bus fare, the first hour wearing a suit but no tie, the second hour properly dressed, tie and all. "In the first hour," he reports, "I made $7.23, but in the second, with my tie on, I made $26, and one man even gave me extra money for a newspaper."

The principle that clothing moves lower in status the more legible it becomes applies to neckties with a vengeance. The ties worn by the top classes eschew the more obvious forms of verbal or even too crudely symbolic statement, relying on stripes, amoeba-like foulard blobs, or small dots to make the point that the wearer possesses too much class to care to specify right out in front what it's based on. (This illustrates the privacy principle, or the principle of mind-your-own-little-disgusting-middle-class-business, a customary element of the aristocratic stance.) Small white dots against a dark background, perhaps the most conservative tie possible, are favored both by uppers and upper-middles and, defensively, by those nervous about being thought low, coarse, drunken, or cynical, like journalists and TV news readers and sportscasters, and by those whose fiduciary honor must be thought beyond question, like the trust officers working for the better metropolitan banks.

Moving down from stripes, blobs, or dots, we come to necktie patterns with a more overt and precise semiotic function. Some, designed to announce that the upper-middle-class wearer is a sport, will display diagonal patterns of little flying pheasants, or small yachts, signal flags, and sextants. ("I hunt and own a yacht. Me rich and sporty!") Just below these are the "milieu" patterns, designed to celebrate the profession of the wearer and to congratulate him on having so fine a profession. These are worn either by insecure members of the upper-middle class (like surgeons) or by members of the middle class aspiring to upper-middle status (like accountants). Thus a tie covered with tiny caduceuses proclaims "Hot damn! I am a physician." (Significantly, there is no milieu tie pattern for dentists.) Little scales signify "I am a lawyer." Musical notes: "I have something to do with music." Dollar signs, or money bags: a stockbroker, banker, perhaps a wildly successful plastic surgeon, or a lottery winner. I've even seen one tie with a pattern of little jeeps, whose meaning I've found baffling, for surely if you were a *driver* in any of our wars you'd not be likely to announce it. Other self-congratulatory patterns like little whales or dolphins or seals can suggest that you love nature and spend a lot of time protecting it and are thus a fine person. And of these milieu ties can be alternated with the "silk rep" model striped with the presumed colors of British (never, *never* German, French, Italian, Spanish, Portuguese, or White Russian) regiments, clubs, or universities.

As we move further down the class hierarchy, actual words begin to appear on ties, and these are meant to be commented on by viewers. One such exhibitionist artifact is the Grandfather's Tie in dark blue with grandchildren's names hand-painted on it, diagonally, in white. Imagine the conversations that ensue when you wear it! Another kind reads "I'd rather be sailing," "skiing," etc., and these can also be effective underminers of privacy—"conversation-starters," and thus useful adjuncts to comfy middle-class status, in the tradition of expecting neighbors to drop in without warning. Some ties down in this stratum affect great cleverness, reading "Thank God It's Friday" or "Oh Hell, It's Monday"; and a way to get a chuckle out of your audience and at the same time raise your class a bit is to have these sentiments abbreviated on your tie with yachting signal flags. At the bottom of the middle class, just before it turns to high prole, we encounter ties depicting large flowers in brilliant colors, or simply bright "artistic" splotches. The message is frequently "I'm a merry dog." These wearers are the ones Molloy is addressing when, discussing neckties, he warns, "Avoid purple under all circumstances." 4

Further down still, where questions of yacht ownership or merry doghood are too preposterous to be claimed even on a necktie, we come upon the high- or mid-prole "bola" tie, a woven or leather thong with a slide (often of turquoise or silver), affected largely by retired persons residing in Sun Belt places like New Mexico. Like any other sort of tie, this one makes a statement, saying: "Despite appearances, I'm really as good as you are, and my 'necktie,' though perhaps unconventional, is really better than your traditional tie, because it suggests the primitive and therefore the unpretentious, pure, and virtuous." Says the bola, "The person wearing me is a child of nature, even though actually eighty years old." Like many 5 things bought by proles, these bola ties can be very expensive, especially when the slide is made of precious metal or displays "artwork." The point again is that money, although important, is not always the most important criterion of class. Below the bola wearers, at the very bottom, stand the low proles, the destitute, and the bottom-out-of-sight, who never wear a tie, or wear one—and one is all they own—so rarely that the day is memorable for that reason. Down here, the tie is an emblem of affection and even effeminacy, and you can earn a reputation for being la-di-da by appearing in one, as if you thought yourself better than other people. One prole wife says of her spouse: "I'm going to bury my husband in his T-shirt if the undertaker will allow it."

QUESTIONS FOR READING AND WRITING

1. Fussell's book, *Class*, contains numerous examples of items of dress proclaiming one's class. What examples of dress among your generation indicate belonging to a particular group?
2. What does Fussell mean when he says that, "clothing moves lower in status the more legible it becomes" (paragraph 2)? Can you think of examples other than clothing where the same principle applies?
3. Why should neckties be so symbolic of status? What other items of dress are almost equally symbolic?
4. Read Anne Hollander's "Dressed to Thrill" and write an essay on how items of dress affect one's statement about his or her sexuality.

✦ Nancy Bazelon Goldstone ✦
A Trader in London

Nancy Bazelon Goldstone is a financial analyst and a stock broker. Her essay, "A Trader in London," which deals with the prejudices a mid-Atlantic woman encounters in the male-dominated world of the New York and London stock exchanges, first appeared in the "Hers" column of The New York Times Magazine.

AT THE AGE OF 27 I became the head foreign-exchange options trader at a major commercial bank in New York. I managed hundreds of millions of dollars' worth of options. I ran offices in New York and London. It was a powerful and demanding position. 1

Few women have had this experience, so I am often asked what it was like to work in a bank trading room on Wall Street. I like to tell the following story: 2

It was a cold day in early February, almost a year to the day since I had started my trading career. We'd had an unusually hectic morning, and I was sitting at my desk, frantically trying to calculate the effect of the morning's trades on the overall position. This had to be done quickly and accurately. 3

I was lost in concentration when suddenly I noticed that there was something wrong. It took me a second or two to realize what was the matter. The room had gone completely quiet. 4

During the entire year I had been trading, I had never experienced so complete a silence. Instinctively, I glanced at the Reuters screen. The currency prices had remained unchanged. Whatever was causing the sudden calm had not yet been acted on in the market. 5

I got to my feet and saw at once that most of the traders in the room were huddled around the spot foreign-exchange desk. This is the place where the latest information comes across a Telerate machine. There is also a television set there so that the traders can listen to important news conferences or bulletins. 6

I swore to myself. What could it be? Something so important that the market hadn't had the time to digest the full implications of the information. I ran over the spot desk, praying silently that it wasn't an assassination. 7

"What is it?" I cried.

Surprised by my intensity, several of the traders turned toward me. Through the opening I saw the cause of the trouble.

The "swimsuit issue" of Sports Illustrated had arrived.

Trading is a profession dominated almost exclusively by men. It's not that I was ever discriminated against. It's just that the atmosphere, outlook and energy of every trading room I've ever been in is distinctly and overtly male. Raunchy jokes are the order of the day—the dirtier, the better. The first half-hour of every morning is spent discussing the previous night's exploits, real or imagined, in vivid detail. I've seen competent, professional traders turned to jelly by the entrance of someone's teen-age daughter. Sometimes this took a little getting used to.

✦✦✦✦✦

For example, in December '85 I proposed to expand my New York operation to London. The bank already had a trading room there dealing in foreign currencies and Eurodollars. It was simply a matter of setting up a desk to trade options and hiring some people locally. Senior management approved my plan, and just before Christmas I flew over to make arrangements for the addition of my group.

By this time I was used to walking into a trading room, so I knew what to expect. A sea of white shirts and blue ties surrounded by a pale gray cloud of cigarette smoke. The only other woman in the room was a secretary whose duties included serving tea in the afternoon.

Although the office had been notified of my visit, it appeared that they were not quite as prepared for me as I was for them. The branch manager's eyes widened slightly when I introduced myself. Surely, I wasn't the woman who was heading up the options unit? I'm afraid I was. He was expecting someone, well, older. I could almost read his thoughts. How could a young woman, wearing lipstick and high heels, possibly be the head of a trading unit that included a staff in New York and the responsibility for a billion-dollar portfolio? It's not that he meant to be rude, you understand. It's just that it was beyond his level of comprehension.

✦✦✦✦✦

My meeting included an inspection of the premises. After the initial shock, the branch manager was exceedingly polite and made a point of introducing me to all of the traders on his staff. They were, to a man, young and friendly, and from their accents I could tell that they were members of the British working class. Just a nice, normal, everyday bunch of guys. The kind who like to drink beer in the pubs after work. Although they were very hospitable, it was clear that they viewed my presence as a kind of joke.

In the spirit of Christmas, the office was decorated with a tree, 16
and there were tinsel and red ribbons scattered about. A bulletin board was overrun with Christmas cards and pictures of naked women.

Pictures of naked women? 17

I'm sure if they'd given the matter any thought, they would have 18
been embarrassed and taken the photographs down prior to my visit. But the pictures had apparently been around for so long that the traders no longer noticed them. Just part of an environment designed to keep them happy and comfortable at their work.

I felt kind of sorry for those guys actually. I knew I was about to 19
do something that would change their lives.

I needed a trader in London. 20

I was going to hire a woman. 21

QUESTIONS FOR READING AND WRITING

1. Goldstone's essay is about sexual stereotyping, about the prejudice that women—especially young, attractive women—don't belong in the world of high finance. What other sexual stereotypes have you encountered in employment?
2. Why does Goldstone begin with the example of the "swimsuit issue" of *Sports Illustrated*? How does it prepare the reader for the two examples she cites from her London experience?
3. Is the tone of the essay deliberately provocative or merely factual? Cite details to support your answer.
4. Is Goldstone herself guilty of stereotyping? Is this deliberate or does it reveal a bias? Support your answer with details.
5. Read Adrienne Rich's essay, "Claiming an Education," and write an essay using examples of stereotyping in education or in employment.

✦ Ellen Goodman ✦

The Maidenform Woman Administers Shock Treatment

Ellen Goodman's column has been syndicated in the nation's newspapers since 1976. Educated at Radcliffe, she became a reporter for Newsweek, then a feature writer for the Detroit Free Press, *and eventually joined the* Boston Globe *as a feature writer, and columnist. In 1980, she was awarded a Pulitzer Prize. Her writing has been collected in* Close to Home *(1979) and* At Large *(1980). "The Maidenform Woman Administers Shock Treatment," and its sequel, "Posing in Your Undies Is Unreal," are characteristic of the concise yet penetrating insights Goodman delivers in her brief essays.*

IT'S NOT THAT I'D NEVER SEEN HER BEFORE.

Years ago, she was photographed outside of her apartment building, dressed in a fur coat and bra and panties. Since then she's been found in similar attire in theater and hotel lobbies. Usually, of course, you get used to this sort of thing if you live in a city long enough.

But it was a shock to see her in a hospital room. There she was, hair tied back primly, medical chart in her left hand, pen in her right hand, long white jacket over her shoulders, exposing her lacy magenta bra and panties.

Was it possible? Why, yes! Stop the presses! The Maidenform Woman Had Become a Doctor! According to the caption under this photograph, she was "making the rounds in her elegant Delectables."

At some point when I wasn't looking, everybody's favorite exhibitionist must have actually gone to medical school. I suppose that I had underestimated her intelligence—this happens so often with attractive women. I always thought she was a candidate for a cold, not a medical degree. I can only imagine the difficulties she had getting accepted, what with her portfolio and all.

By now any number of magazines are featuring her personal success story. On their pages, the Maidenform woman is willingly displaying her new bedside manner in living color. Poised, concerned, even prim, young Dr. Maidenform is photographed looking down compassionately at her bedridden patient. We don't know exactly what the patient thinks of all this. Fortunately for her, his leg is in traction and he can't move. The other doctors in the ad seem quite unconcerned about her outfit. Dr. Maidenform seems to have made it in a world that is entirely non-sexist. They aren't even glancing in the direction of her non-air-brushed belly button!

Quite frankly, I must admit that the Maidenform Woman cured me of a disease. She cured me of creeping complacency. 7

Until I saw her, I had become virtually numb to the advertising image of that handy creature, "The New Woman." We are now out of the era of housewife-as-airhead. We've even come a long way from the year of coming a long way, baby. 8

We are plunging into the "successful woman as sex object" syndrome. The more real women break out of the mold, the more advertisers force them back in. We are now told that, for all the talk, the New Woman is just the Total Woman in updated gear. 9

Under the careful dress-for-success suit of an MBA is a woman buying Office Legs for sex appeal. Around the briefcase of a lawyer is a hand shining with high-color nail gloss. Take away the lab coat, the stethoscope and syringe, and the doctor is just another set of "elegant delectables." The point in all this isn't especially subtle. As Jean Kilbourne, who has long studied media images of women, said, "It's out of the question that they would ever show a male doctor like that. She is aloof but available. Underneath she is still a sex object." Kilbourne's favorite entry in this category is a perfume ad that shows the successful woman mixing business with, uh, pleasure. In the first frame we see the busy executive at a business lunch with three men. In the second frame, we see her under the covers with one. 10

Advertisers have a big investment in this new-old image. I'm not talking about the professional woman market. There are hardly enough women doctors to keep the magenta lace factory in business. But there are now an increasing number of women who see professionals as glamorous and want to identify with them. 11

The advertisers are betting that these women want, as the Maidenform ad puts it, "just what the doctor ordered." So the doctor is ordered to strip, literally, her professional cover. She is revealed in the flesh, to be—yes, indeed—just another woman insecure about her femininity, just another woman in search of sex 12 appeal, just another women who needs "silky satin tricot with antique lace scalloping."

Pretty soon, I suppose, she will need it in the Senate, in the Supreme Court, even in the Oval Office. The Maidenform Woman. You never know where she'll turn up.

QUESTIONS FOR READING AND WRITING

1. In your experience, are some ads even more sexist than the Maidenform ad? Do they have the same double message, that is, do they seem to appeal to the "New Woman" while actually depicting her as a sexual object?
2. In what ways is the Maidenform ad worse than the ads featuring what Goodman calls the "housewife-as-airhead" (paragraph 8)? Are men depicted in similar stereotypical ways? What categories do men fall into in ads?
3. Goodman's essay follows an inductive pattern, beginning with a specific example and then moving toward a general conclusion. Why does Goodman reserve the example of the perfume ad for the section of the essay that deals with general analysis?
4. Are there any similar points in this essay and "A Trader in London" by Nancy Bazelon Goldstone?
5. Select a series of ads that stereotype either men or women and discuss the implications of the stereotype.

✦ Ellen Goodman ✦

Posing in Your Undies Is Unreal

JUST ABOUT THREE YEARS AGO I came upon The Woman in the Maidenform Bra in a hospital room. No, she wasn't sick, although Lord knows, wandering around with nothing under her lab coat but her undies, the lady could catch a terrible cold. 1

What had happened was that a bunch of advertisers had pitched in and sent her to medical school. Faster than you can say stethoscope, a fully accredited Dr. Maidenform reappeared in full color—magenta, I believe—making her rounds in "her elegant delectables." The patient she was tending in the ad, by the way, was in traction, or he might have made a move on her. 2

At the time I marveled at the capacity of advertising to keep updating their image to keep in tune with the times. Only on Madison Avenue, only in a fantasy, would a doctor strip down to her skivvies. 3

Well, circle "False" on my answer sheet. 4

Right in front of me, this very day, I have a portrait of a new underwear medicine woman I might call Dr. Jockey. She is Lynne Pirie, a real-life osteopath and sports-medicine specialist from Arizona. She is standing, smiling for the camera, in front of a scrub sink, surgical mask still tied around her neck, about to remove her blue operating top, baring her beige cotton "Jockey for Her" briefs on her bottom. 5

Dr. Pirie is just one star in a new underwear campaign that boasts "real" women. The merchandisers have also signed up a college graduate, a vice president of a data-processing firm, a mother and a construction worker. 6

The point of this campaign is that real women wear Jockeys. But the subliminal message is that real women with real names and real jobs really pose in their underwear in public. 7

To be fair, some of these women are more "real" than others. Pirie was the 1982 U.S.A. body-building title holder. Rebecca Machan, the designated "mother," was a "top fashion model." Rosalyn Keathley, who poses in her undies with a hard hat on her head and a cast on her leg, is surely the only fire-sprinkler fitter in the 8

Southwest with a red Corvette. But they all come with biographies and rationales.

Consider Jeanie Zadrozny, the executive vice president of a Pittsburgh consulting firm. I met her wearing underwear that matched her royal-blue dress, on the set of the "Today Show." Zadrozny, whose ads are slated for February, happily predicted that posing in her underwear would be good for business because her clients, almost all male, would see her as a whole person, or see more sides of her life. I agreed that they would certainly see more of her.

Zadrozny cast herself as a veritable role model of how to undress for success. No little bow ties and briefcases for Jeanie. Her business portfolio will now include the portrait of her holding the phone with one hand, a rose with another, dressed in nothing but makeup, a camisole and a pair of hipsters.

Mind you, none of these ads are obscene. The underwear in question is more serviceable than sensual. The company nervously points with pride to an award that it got from Women Against Pornography. Unless you count the bare-bottomed baby (a girl, of course) posing with "the mother" in one ad, there is nothing X-rated in the series. But I suspect that our gal Jeanie will find that modeling skivvies is better for the date business than the data-processing business. Similarly, Debbie Erickson, the "young, ambitious trendsetter" with a business degree, will find that this isn't the right sort of exposure to get her career up from under.

It's one thing for men like Jim Palmer to star in a Jockey ad with a tag line that reads: "Take away their uniform and who are they?" But a professional or would-be business woman who poses in her undies is going to find it tough to come in from the cold. Would you buy a used appendectomy from an underwear model?

The message for and about women is a bit too familiar for me to pass over. There are too many who still see a sex object under every success suit. A favorite contemporary fantasy says that once you strip away the medical degree, the vice presidency or the B.A., underneath all that stuff you've got just another girl in pink hipsters. Playboy also features "real women." And Jockey fits the fantasy to a T-shirt.

I'm not longing to retreat to the 1910 era when Jockey's long-undies hit was named the Kenosha Klosed Krotch. But somebody ought to tell these real women about the real world.

QUESTIONS FOR READING AND WRITING

1. In this sequel to her essay on the Maidenform ad, Goodman criticizes the "Jockey for Her" briefs, which employ endorsements by real people. What other examples of endorsements strike you as silly at best, and pernicious at worst?
2. Goodman cites several examples of "real" women who wear Jockey briefs. Why does she find these examples offensive? Do they have the same fantasy element as the Maidenform ads? Why or why not?
3. How does Goodman convey her displeasure with the ads as she describes them, even before the final section where she analyzes them? Why does she emphasize the unusualness of the models despite their seeming ordinariness?
4. Select several ads that employ testimonials from real people, either "average" people or celebrities. How do the ads still appeal to the fantasies that the ad maker wishes to transfer from the celebrity (or ordinary person) to the product? Write an essay on the appeal.

✦ William Jordan ✦
Down to Earth

William Jordan is one of those unusual individuals whose training is in science but whose interests extend to the arts. Educated at the University of California, Riverside, where he received his B.A. in 1966, and at Berkeley, where he received his Ph.D. in biology, Jordan makes his home in Long Beach, California. Combining freelance writing with consulting in biology and filmmaking, Jordan's special interest is insects, as his book Windowsill Ecology *(1977) attests. "Down to Earth," which appeared originally in* the Los Angeles Times Magazine, *reflects his ability to draw connections between the human and the insect worlds.*

SOME OF THE MOST INTELLIGENT PEOPLE I met as a university student were farmers. I was part of an alfalfa-research project, and we worked closely with various farmers who hoped to benefit from what we learned.

The day I met the first of these farmers, I was standing at the edge of an alfalfa field near Salinas, reveling in the beauty of the wind as it washed in ripples across the thick pile of spring growth. The Sierra de Salinas stood west of me across Highway 101, glowering dark and ominous with the legends of the novels that Steinbeck set there, and the white clouds mushroomed above, following a recent storm to the east. In the midst of my reveries, a man of about 35 drove up on an old John Deere tractor and asked if I was "the new guy from the university." He introduced himself as John D'Oro and proceeded to draw me into a conversation that went freewheeling over everything from economics to crime to the price of milk and finally to hippies. D'Oro had seen a bedraggled pair hitchhiking the day before and was perplexed. I asked him what he did when he saw them.

"Why, I gave them a ride," he said. "I wanted to know why they looked that way, unhappy and all. I love my life—these fields, the soil, the air—and I wanted to know."

This was my first inkling that all farmers aren't dull, plodding creatures. The next inkling came when he asked about the research I was planning to do in his fields. That was a serious mistake on his part. Nothing is more insufferable than a graduate student whose whole world is research. I began gushing the facts of the field: That alfalfa out there was not just the source of hay, not just the origin of health food, but an alien world—or, more accurately, a universe. I explained that the alfalfa canopy acted as a kind of natural hothouse where the temperatures were 10 to 15 degrees cooler than ambient on a hot day and 10 to 20 degrees warmer on a cool one. The canopy was also a kind of jungle where at least a thousand different species of insects, mites, spiders and other arthropods lived and fought and hibernated and mated. I named the species, I mentioned how many eggs each laid, how many generations they turned each year, which ones ate which—a flood of book-learned facts—and I noticed that D'Oro still seemed interested. But then he looked at me with what I realized later was a shrewd grin. He said, "Hey, Bill, have you ever *seen* any of this?"

I was caught completely off guard and stuttered back, "Well, no." 5

"What are we waiting for?" he shot back. Turning around, he 6
strode out into the field and lay down flat on his back.

"Come on. Show me!" came drifting up from among the sprouts. 7

So the two of us ended up lying in the alfalfa, learning by direct 8
experience the lessons that no science, no book can teach about this very different world.

And an enchanted world it was. As my head descended, leaves 9
became fronds, stems became trunks, and the air became as still as that of a tropical forest. No more than a few feet above, the wind was blowing a gale, cold and damp, direct from Monterey Bay, but down here it was calm and an amazingly warm 80 degrees.

"What's that?" D'Oro whispered. 10

"That's a damsel bug," I said, flipping through the mental pages 11
of some insect text I had read.

"It looks like it's eating that green thing," he said. 12

"That's a pea aphid it's eating." 13

"What's that beetle with the long nose?" 14

"An alfalfa weevil. That's one of the insects I'll be studying." 15

"No kidding. We had to spray twice for them last year." 16

And so it went. D'Oro's astuteness was almost a bit embarrassing 17
to someone from the university who was supposed to "know" so much.

But together we learned how it was down there in the alfalfa. We 18
discovered brilliant-orange ladybugs feeding on vast flocks of green

aphids that clustered on the tips of the new shoots. We watched cabbage loopers, a kind of inchworm, measuring their way from the main stem out to the tender new leaves they would eat. Little white alfalfa butterflies flitted down into the quiet, still canopy. D'Oro noticed a tiny black wasp with a yellow-green abdomen embracing the lavender vase of an alfalfa blossom. Its head was thrust into the blossom's throat as it literally drank deeply of nectar, with its antennae sticking out above. The wasp finished, wiped its face with the front pair of legs and scurried off.

"That's *Bathyplectes curculionis*," I said, "the one I'm doing my thesis on."

Our friendship grew, and when the day came to move on to research in Northern California, D'Oro stuck out his hand, looked me in the eye and said, "Bill, you'll get along fine with those farmers."

And I did, and over and over again I was struck with how almost mystically perceptive the farmer's awareness of life in the field was. I remember one incident in particular. I was collecting weevils from a field near Adin, a tiny town about 100 miles east of Mt. Shasta, when the owner, a rancher named Russ Meyer, drove up on his tractor pulling a sickle bar to cut the alfalfa. We started talking about the habits of these pests—how they could convert an entire field to useless stubble in less than a week. Then he said, "Funny thing about those little green devils. They pile up on the sickle bar while I'm cutting, and when I swing out into the sage at the end of a run, they fall off into the dust. You know what they do then? They stick their heads up in the air, wave them around a couple of times and start crawling back toward the field. Now, how do they *do* that? I've examined them, and they don't have no eyes, least-wise, none that I can see."

Anyone who has sat on a tractor seat knows that your eyes are at least 12 feet away from where the weevil larvae would fall. The acuteness of vision, the curiosity, to watch and wonder about something as insignificant as a stranded weevil grub—well, it boggles the mind. Excellent scientific research is almost always based on superior observation, but these men of the farms and ranches had a gift for it I've never seen equaled.

The most profound experience of all happened with Kim Brown, an old, crusty rancher who lived about 10 miles down the road at

Lookout, the scattering of shacks in Modoc County where the last lynching in California took place. Brown had come out to see how my work was going and asked if the university had come up with any new weevil predators that would cut down the need for pesticides. I told him I had assumed that all farmers wanted pesticides; they were much easier to use, much faster in their action than predatory insects.

"Heck, no," Brown said. "What's the sense of it? Those pesticides cost money. Bugs don't. Besides, I don't like the *sound* of the field after you spray." 24

I wasn't sure I'd heard right, so I asked him to explain. 25

"You spray with DDT, and the field sounds one way. You spray with malathion, and it sounds different again. Spray with parathion, and there's no sound at all." 26

Standing there in the presence of Mt. Shasta, glacial palace to the Modoc Indian gods, I flashed back to the world of modern, high-tech hospitals where our leaders are born, to the stucco houses and the neat, sterilized lawns where they grow up, to the concrete freeways on which they drive to work, to the glass-and-steel towers from which they run the affairs of our world, and I understood how it is that we mistreat the land and pollute the sea and the air. I wondered if our leaders, even the most liberal and health-conscious, had ever taken communion with the earth, had ever watched alfalfa sprout. 27

QUESTIONS FOR READING AND WRITING

1. Jordan's essay is about the difference between acquired book-learning and direct knowledge through observation. Have you ever met anyone who, while lacking a formal education, was schooled through the ability to observe closely in the world of direct experience?
2. How do the three farmers illustrate Jordan's final point? Why is Jordan surprised by the knowledge and curiosity of the farmers?
3. How is the kind of knowledge of nature in Jordan's essay similar to what Wendell Berry suggests in "Notes from an Absence and a Return"?
4. Write an essay proving that knowledge gained through direct experience is more meaningful than abstract book-learning. Illustrate your point with several examples.

✦ George Orwell ✦

Politics and the English Language

George Orwell is well-known as a novelist, but, as attested by the four volumes of his Collected Essays, Journalism and Letters *(1971), he was also a prolific journalistic reporter and essayist (see, for example, "A Hanging"). Originally appearing in* Shooting an Elephant *(1950), "Politics and the English Language" expresses Orwell's deepest alarm over the relationship between imprecise language and sloppy thinking. It previews by several years Orwell's nightmarish portrait of "newspeak" from* 1984, *and its positive advice on what constitutes "honest" writing is as fresh as if it were given today.*

MOST PEOPLE WHO BOTHER WITH THE MATTER at all would admit that the English language is in a bad way, but it is generally assumed that we cannot by conscious action do anything about it. Our civilization is decadent and our language—so the argument runs—must inevitably share in the general collapse. It follows that any struggle against the abuse of language is a sentimental archaism, like preferring candles to electric light or hansom cabs to aeroplanes. Underneath this lies the half-conscious belief that language is a natural growth and not an instrument which we shape for our own purposes.

Now, it is clear that the decline of a language must ultimately have political and economic causes: it is not due simply to the bad influence of this or that individual writer. But an effect can become a cause, reinforcing the original cause and producing the same effect in an intensified form, and so on indefinitely. A man may take to drink because he feels himself to be a failure, and then fail all the more completely because he drinks. It is rather the same thing that is happening to the English language. It becomes ugly and inaccurate because our thoughts are foolish, but the slovenliness of our language makes it easier for us to have foolish thoughts. The point is that the process is reversible. Modern English, especially written English, is full of bad habits which spread by imitation and which can be avoided if one is willing to take the necessary trouble. If one gets rid of these habits one can think more clearly, and to think clearly is a necessary first step towards political regeneration: so that the fight against bad English is not frivolous and is not the exclusive concern of professional writers. I will come back to this presently, and I hope that by that time the meaning of what I have said here will have become clearer. Meanwhile, here are five specimens of the English language as it is now habitually written.

3 These five passages have not been picked out because they are especially bad—I could have quoted far worse if I had chosen—but because they illustrate various of the mental vices from which we now suffer. They are a little below the average, but are fairly representative samples. I number them so that I can refer back to them when necessary:

1. I am not, indeed, sure whether it is not true to say that the Milton who once seemed not unlike a seventeenth-century Shelley had not become, out of an experience even more bitter in each year, more alien [*sic*] to the founder of that Jesuit sect which nothing could induce him to tolerate.

   Professor Harold Laski
   (Essay in *Freedom of Expression*)

2. Above all, we cannot play ducks and drakes with a native battery of idioms which prescribes such egregious collocations of vocables as the Basic *put up with* for *tolerate* or *put at a loss* for *bewilder*.

   Professor Lancelot Hogben (*Interglossa*)

3. On the one side we have the free personality: by definition it is not neurotic, for it has neither conflict nor dream. Its desires, such as they are, are transparent, for they are just what institutional approval keeps in the forefront of consciousness; another institutional pattern would alter their number and intensity; there is little in them that is natural, irreducible, or culturally dangerous. But *on the other side*, the social bond itself is nothing but the mutual reflection of these self-secure integrities. Recall the definition of love. Is not this the very picture of a small academic? Where is there a place in this hall of mirrors for either personality or fraternity?

   Essay on psychology in *Politics* (New York)

4. All the "best people" from the gentlemen's clubs, and all the frantic fascist captains, united in common hatred of Socialism and bestial horror of the rising tide of the mass revolutionary movement, have

turned to acts of provocation, to foul incendiarism, to medieval legends of poisoned wells, to legalize their own destruction of proletarian organizations, and rouse the agitated petty-bourgeoisie to chauvinistic fervor on behalf of the fight against the revolutionary way out of the crisis.

Communist pamphlet

5. If a new spirit is to be infused into this old country, there is one thorny and contentious reform which must be tackled, and that is the humanization and galvanization of the B.B.C. Timidity here will bespeak canker and atrophy of the soul. The heart of Britain may be sound and of strong beat, for instance, but the British lion's roar at present is like that of Bottom in Shakespeare's *Midsummer Night's Dream*—as gentle as any sucking dove. A virile new Britain cannot continue indefinitely to be traduced in the eyes, or rather ears, of the world by the effete languors of Langham Place, brazenly masquerading as "standard English." When the Voice of Britain is heard at nine o'clock, better far and infinitely less ludicrous to hear aitches honestly dropped than the present priggish, inflated, inhibited, school-ma'amish arch braying of blameless bashful mewing maidens!

Letter in *Tribune*

Each of these passages has faults of its own, but, quite apart from avoidable ugliness, two qualities are common to all of them. The first is staleness of imagery; the other is lack of precision. The writer either has a meaning and cannot express it, or he inadvertently says something else, or he is almost indifferent as to whether his words mean anything or not. This mixture of vagueness and sheer incompetence is the most marked characteristic of modern English prose, and especially of any kind of political writing. As soon as certain topics are raised, the concrete melts into the abstract and no one seems able to think of turns of speech that are not hackneyed: prose consists less and less of *words* chosen for the sake of their meaning, and more and more of *phrases* tacked together like the sections of a prefabricated henhouse. I list below, with notes and examples, various of the tricks by means of which the work of prose-construction is habitually dodged:

Dying metaphors. A newly invented metaphor assists thought by evoking a visual image, while on the other hand a metaphor which is technically "dead" (e.g. *iron resolution*) has in effect reverted to being an ordinary word and can generally be used without loss of vividness. But in between these two classes there is a huge dump of worn-out metaphors which have lost all evocative power and are merely used because they save people the trouble of inventing phrases for themselves. Examples are: *Ring the changes on, take up the cudgels for, toe the line, ride roughshod over, stand shoulder to shoulder with, play into the hands of, no axe to grind, grist to the mill, fishing in troubled waters, on the order of the day, Achilles' heel, swan song, hotbed.* Many of these are used without knowledge of their meaning (what is a "rift," for instance?), and incompatible metaphors are frequently mixed, a sure sign that the writer is not interested in what he is saying. Some metaphors now current have been twisted out of their original meaning without those who use them even being aware of the fact. For example, *toe the line* is sometimes written *tow the line*. Another example is *the hammer and the anvil*, now always used with the implication that the anvil gets the worst of it. In real life it is always the anvil that breaks the hammer, never the other way about: a writer who stopped to think what he was saying would be aware of this, and would avoid perverting the original phrase.

Operators or *verbal false limbs*. These save the trouble of picking out appropriate verbs and nouns, and at the same time pad each sentence with extra syllables which give it an appearance of symmetry. Characteristic phrases are *render inoperative, militate against, make contact with, be subjected to, give rise to, give grounds for, have the effect of, play a leading part (role) in, make itself felt, take effect, exhibit a tendency to, serve the purpose of, etc., etc.* The keynote is the elimination of simple verbs. Instead of being a single word, such as *break, stop, spoil, mend, kill,* a verb becomes a *phrase,* made up of a noun or adjective tacked on to some general-purposes verb such as *prove, serve, form, play, render.* In addition, the passive voice is wherever possible used in preference to the active, and noun constructions are used instead of gerunds (*by examination of* instead of *by examining*). The range of verbs is further cut down by means of the *-ize* and *de-* formations, and the banal statements are given an appearance of profundity by means of the *not un-* formation. Simple conjunctions and prepositions are replaced by such phrases as *with respect to, having regard to, the fact* 6 *that, by dint of, in view of, in the interests of, on the hypothesis that*; and the ends of sentences are saved by anticlimax by such resounding common-places as *greatly to be desired, cannot be left out of account, a development to be expected in the near future, deserving of serious consideration, brought to a satisfactory conclusion,* and so on and so forth.

Pretentious diction. Words like *phenomenon, element, individual* (as noun), *objective, categorical, effective, virtual, basic, primary, promote, constitute, exhibit, exploit, utilize, eliminate, liquidate,* are used to dress up simple statement and give an air of scientific impartiality to biased judgments. Adjectives like *epoch-making, epic, historic, unforgettable, triumphant, age-old, inevitable, inexorable, veritable,* are used to dignify the sordid processes of international politics, while writing that aims at glorifying war usually takes on an archaic color, its characteristic words being: *realm, throne, chariot, mailed fist, trident, sword, shield, buckler, banner, jackboot, clarion.* Foreign words and expressions such as *cul de sac, ancien régime, deus ex machina, mutatis mutandis, status quo, gleichschaltung, weltanschauung,* are used to give an air of culture and elegance. Except for the useful abbreviations *i.e., e.g.,* and *etc.,* there is no real need for any of the hundreds of foreign phrases now current in English. Bad writers, and especially scientific, political and sociological writers, are nearly always haunted by the notion that Latin or Greek words are grander than Saxon ones, and unnecessary words like *expedite, ameliorate, predict, extraneous, deracinated, clandestine, subaqueous* and hundreds of others constantly gain ground from their Anglo-Saxon opposite numbers.[1] The jargon peculiar to Marxist writing (*hyena, hangman, cannibal, petty bourgeois, these gentry, lacquey, flunkey, mad dog, White Guard,* etc.) consists largely of words and phrases translated from Russian, German or French; but the normal way of coining a new word is to use a Latin or Greek root with the appropriate affix and, where necessary, the *-ize* formation. It is often easier to make up words of this kind (*deregionalize, impermissible, extramarital, nonfragmentary*

[1] An interesting illustration of this is the way in which the English flower names which were in use till very recently are being ousted by Greek ones, *snapdragon* becoming *antirrhinum, forget-me-not* becoming *myosotis,* etc. It is hard to see any practical reason for this change of fashion: it is probably due to an instinctive turning-away from the more homely word and a vague feeling that the Greek word is scientific.

and so forth) than to think up the English words that will cover one's meaning. The result, in general, is an increase in slovenliness and vagueness.

Meaningless words. In certain kinds of writing, particularly in art criticism and literary criticism, it is normal to come across long passages which are almost completely lacking in meaning.[2] Words like *romantic, plastic, values, human, dead, sentimental, natural, vitality*, as used in art criticism, are strictly meaningless, in the sense that they not only do not point to any discoverable object, but are hardly ever expected to do so by the reader. When one critic writes, "The outstanding feature of Mr. X's work is its living quality," while another writes, "The immediately striking thing about Mr. X's work is its peculiar deadness," the reader accepts this as a simple difference of opinion. If words like *black* and *white* were involved, instead of the jargon words *dead* and *living*, he would see at once that language was being used in an improper way. Many political words are similarly abused. The word *Fascism* has now no meaning except in so far as it signifies "something not desirable." The words *democracy, socialism, freedom, patriotic, realistic, justice*, have each of them several different meanings which cannot be reconciled with one another. In the case of a word like *democracy*, not only is there no agreed definition, but the attempt to make one is resisted from all sides. It is almost universally felt that when we call a country democratic we are praising it: consequently the defenders of every kind of régime claim that it is a democracy, and fear that they might have to stop using the word if it were tied down to any one meaning. Words of this kind are often used in a consciously dishonest way. That is, the person who uses them has his own private definition, but allows his hearer to think he means something quite different. Statements like *Marshal Pétain was a true patriot, The Soviet Press is the freest in the world, The Catholic Church is opposed to persecution*, are almost always made with intent to deceive. Other words used in variable meanings, in most 8

[2] Example: "Comfort's catholicity of perception and image, strangely Whitmanesque in range, almost the exact opposite in aesthetic compulsion, continues to evoke that trembling atmospheric accumulative hinting at a cruel, an inexorably serene timelessness. . . . Wrey Gardiner scores by aiming at simple bull's-eyes with precision. Only they are not so simple, and through this contented sadness runs more than the surface bitter-sweet of resignation." (*Poetry Quarterly*.)

cases more or less dishonestly, are: *class, totalitarian, science, progressive, reactionary, bourgeois, equality.*

Now that I have made this catalogue of swindles and perversions, let me give another example of the kind of writing that they lead to. This time it must of its nature be an imaginary one. I am going to translate a passage of good English into modern English of the worst sort. Here is a well-known verse from *Ecclesiastes*:

"I returned and saw under the sun, that the race is not to the swift, nor the battle to the strong, neither yet bread to the wise, nor yet riches to men of understanding, nor yet favour to men of skill; but time and chance happeneth to them all."

Here it is in modern English:

"Objective consideration of contemporary phenomena compels the conclusion that success or failure in competitive activities exhibits no tendency to be commensurate with innate capacity, but that a considerable element of the unpredictable must invariably be taken into account."

This is a parody, but not a very gross one. Exhibit (3), above, for instance, contains several patches of the same kind of English. It will be seen that I have not made a full translation. The beginning and ending of the sentence follow the original meaning fairly closely, but in the middle the concrete illustrations—race, battle, bread—dissolve into the vague phrase "success or failure in competitive activities." This had to be so, because no modern writer of the kind I am discussing—no one capable of using phrases like "objective consideration of contemporary phenomena"—would ever tabulate his thoughts in that precise and detailed way. The whole tendency of modern prose is away from concreteness. Now analyse these two sentences a little more closely. The first contains forty-nine words but only sixty syllables, and all its words are those of everyday life. The second contains thirty-eight words of ninety syllables: eighteen of its words are from Latin roots, and one from Greek. The first sentence contains six vivid images, and only one phrase ("time and chance") that could be called vague. The second contains not a single fresh, arresting phrase, and in spite of its ninety syllables it gives only a shortened version of the meaning contained in the first. Yet without a doubt it is the second kind of sentence that is gaining ground in modern English. I do not want to exaggerate. This kind of writing is not yet universal, and outcrops of simplicity will occur here and there in the worst-written page. Still, if you or I were told to write a few lines on the uncertainty of human fortunes, we should probably come much nearer to my imaginary sentence than to the one from *Ecclesiastes*.

As I have tried to show, modern writing at its worst does not consist in picking out words for the sake of their meaning and inventing images in order to make the meaning clearer. It consists in gumming together long strips of words which have already been set in order by someone else, and making the results presentable by sheer humbug. The attraction of this way of writing is that it is easy. It is easier—even quicker, once you have the habit—to say *In my opinion it is not an unjustifiable assumption* than to say *I think*. If you use ready-made phrases, you not only don't have to hunt about for words; you also don't have to bother with the rhythms of your sentences, since these phrases are generally so arranged as to be more or less euphonious. When you are composing in a hurry—when you are dictating to a stenographer, for instance, or making a public speech—it is natural to fall into a pretentious, Latinized style. Tags like *a consideration which we should do well to bear in mind* or *a conclusion to which all of us would readily assent* will save many a sentence from coming down with a bump. By using stale metaphors, similes and idioms, you save much mental effort, at the cost of leaving your meaning vague, not only for your reader but for yourself. This is the significance of mixed metaphors. The sole aim of a metaphor is to call up a visual image. When these images clash—as in *The Fascist octopus has sung its swan song, the jack-boot is thrown into the melting pot*—it can be taken as certain that the writer is not seeing a mental image of the objects he is naming; in other words he is not really thinking. Look again at the examples I gave at the beginning of this essay. Professor Laski (1) uses five negatives in fifty-three words. One of these is superfluous, making nonsense of the whole passage, and in addition there is the slip *alien* for akin, making further nonsense, and several avoidable pieces of clumsiness which increase the general vagueness. Professor Hogben (2) plays ducks and drakes with a battery which is able to write prescriptions, and, while disapproving of the everyday phrase *put up with*, is unwilling to look *egregious* up in the dictionary and see what it means; (3), if one takes an uncharitable attitude towards it, is simply meaningless: probably one could work out its intended 14 meaning by reading the whole of the article in which it occurs. In (4), the writer knows more or less what he wants to say, but an accumulation of stale phrases chokes him like tea leaves blocking a sink. In (5), words and meaning have almost parted company. People who write in this manner usually have a general emotional meaning—they dislike one thing and want to express solidarity with another—but they are not interested in the detail of what they are saying. A scrupulous writer, in every sentence that he writes, will ask himself at least four questions, thus: What am I trying to say? What words will express it? What image or idiom will make it clearer? Is this image fresh enough to have an effect? And he will probably ask himself two more: Could I put it more shortly? Have I said anything that is avoidably ugly? But you are not obliged to go to all this trouble. You can shirk it by simply throwing your mind open and letting the ready-made phrases come crowding in. They will construct your sentences for you—even think your thoughts for you, to a certain extent—and at need they will perform the important service of partially concealing your meaning even from yourself. It is at this point that the special connections between politics and the debasement of language becomes clear.

In our time it is broadly true that political writing is bad writing. 1
Where it is not true, it will generally be found that the writer is some kind of rebel, expressing his private opinions and not a "party line." Orthodoxy, of whatever color, seems to demand a lifeless, imitative style. The political dialects to be found in pamphlets, leading articles, manifestos, White Papers and the speeches of under-secretaries do, of course, vary from party to party, but they are all alike in that one almost never finds in them a fresh, vivid, home-made turn of speech. When one watches some tired hack on the platform mechanically repeating the familiar phrases—*bestial atrocities, iron heel, bloodstained tyranny, free peoples of the world, stand shoulder to shoulder*—one often has a curious feeling that one is not watching a live human being but some kind of dummy: a feeling which suddenly becomes stronger at moments when the light catches the speaker's spectacles and turns them into blank discs which seem to have no eyes behind them. And this is not altogether fanciful. A speaker who uses that kind of phraseology has gone some distance towards turning himself into a machine. The appropriate noises are coming out of his larynx, but his brain is not involved as it would be

if he were choosing his words for himself. If the speech he is making is one that he is accustomed to make over and over again, he may be almost unconscious of what he is saying, as one is when one utters the responses in church. And this reduced state of consciousness, if not indispensable, is at any rate favorable to political conformity.

In our time, political speech and writing are largely the defence 16
of the indefensible. Things like the continuance of British rule in India, the Russian purges and deportations, the dropping of the atom bombs on Japan, can indeed be defended, but only by arguments which are too brutal for most people to face, and which do not square with the professed aims of political parties. Thus political language has to consist largely of euphemism, question-begging and sheer cloudy vagueness. Defenceless villages are bombarded from the air, the inhabitants driven out into the countryside, the cattle machine-gunned, the huts set on fire with incendiary bullets: this is called *pacification*. Millions of peasants are robbed of their farms and sent trudging along the roads with no more than they can carry: this is called *transfer of population* or *rectification of frontiers*. People are imprisoned for years without trial, or shot in the back of the neck or sent to die of scurvy in Arctic lumber camps: this is called *elimination of unreliable elements*. Such phraseology is needed if one wants to name things without calling up mental pictures of them. Consider for instance some comfortable English professor defending Russian totalitarianism. He cannot say outright, "I believe in killing off your opponents when you can get good results by doing so." Probably, therefore, he will say something like this:

"While freely conceding that the Soviet régime exhibits certain 17
features which the humanitarian may be inclined to deplore, we must, I think, agree that a certain curtailment of the right to political opposition is an unavoidable concomitant of transitional periods, and that the rigors which the Russian people have been called upon to undergo have been amply justified in the sphere of concrete achievement."

The inflated style is itself a kind of euphemism. A mass of Latin 18
words falls upon the facts like soft snow, blurring the outlines and covering up all the details. The great enemy of clear language is insincerity. When there is a gap between one's real and one's declared aims, one turns as it were instinctively to long words and

exhausted idioms, like a cuttlefish squirting out ink. In our age there is no such thing as "keeping out of politics." All issues are political issues, and politics itself is a mass of lies, evasions, folly, hatred and schizophrenia. When the general atmosphere is bad, language must suffer. I should expect to find—this is a guess which I have not sufficient knowledge to verify—that the German, Russian and Italian languages have all deteriorated in the last ten or fifteen years, as a result of dictatorship.

But if thought corrupts language, language can also corrupt thought. A bad usage can spread by tradition and imitation, even among people who should and do know better. The debased language that I have been discussing is in some ways very convenient. Phrases like *a not unjustifiable assumption, leaves much to be desired, would serve no good purpose, a consideration which we should do well to bear in mind,* are a continuous temptation, a packet of aspirins always at one's elbow. Look back through this essay, and for certain you will find that I have again and again committed the very faults I am protesting against. By this morning's post I have received a pamphlet dealing with conditions in Germany. The author tells me that he "felt impelled" to write it. I open it at random, and here is almost the first sentence that I see: "[The Allies] have an opportunity not only of achieving a radical transformation of Germany's social and political structure in such a way as to avoid a nationalistic reaction in Germany itself, but at the same time of laying the foundations of a co-operative and unified Europe." You see, he "feels impelled" to write—feels, presumably, that he has something new to say—and yet his words, like cavalry horses answering the bugle, group themselves automatically into the familiar dreary pattern. This invasion of one's mind by ready-made phrases (*lay the foundations, achieve a radical transformation*) can only be prevented if one is constantly on guard against them, and every such phrase anaesthetizes a portion of one's brain.

I said earlier that the decadence of our language is probably curable. Those who deny this would argue, if they produced an argument at all, that language merely reflects existing social conditions, and that we cannot influence its development by any direct tinkering with words and constructions. So far as the general tone or spirit of a language goes, this may be true, but it is not true in detail. Silly words and expressions have often disappeared, not through any evolutionary process but owing to the conscious action of a minority. Two recent examples were *explore every avenue* and *leave no stone unturned*, which were killed by the jeers of a few journalists. There is a long list of flyblown metaphors which could similarly be got rid of if enough people would interest themselves in the job; and it should also be possible to laugh the *not un-* formation out of existence,[3] to reduce the amount of Latin and Greek in the average sentence, to drive out foreign phrases and strayed scientific words, and, in general, to make pretentiousness unfashionable. But all these are minor points. The defence of the English language implies more than this, and perhaps it is best to start by saying what it does *not* imply.

To begin with it has nothing to do with archaism, with the 21
salvaging of obsolete words and turns of speech, or with the setting up of a "standard English" which must never be departed from. On the contrary, it is especially concerned with the scrapping of every word or idiom which has outworn its usefulness. It has nothing to do with correct grammar and syntax, which are of no importance so long as one makes one's meaning clear, or with the avoidance of Americanisms, or with having what is called a "good prose style." On the other hand it is not concerned with fake simplicity and the attempt to make written English colloquial. Nor does it even imply in every case preferring the Saxon word to the Latin one, though it does imply using the fewest and shortest words that will cover one's meaning. What is above all needed is to let the meaning choose the word, and not the other way about. In prose, the worst thing one can do with words is to surrender to them. When you think of a concrete object, you think wordlessly, and then, if you want to describe the thing you have been visualizing you probably hunt about till you find the exact words that seem to fit it. When you think of something abstract you are more inclined to use words from the start, and unless you make a conscious effort to prevent it, the existing dialect will come rushing in and do the job for you, at the expense of blurring or even changing your meaning. Probably it is better to put off using words as long as possible and get one's meaning as clear as one can through pictures or sensations. Afterwards one can choose—not simply *accept*—the phrases that will best cover the

[3] One can cure oneself of the *not un-* formation by memorizing this sentence: *A not unblack dog was chasing a not unsmall rabbit across a not ungreen field.*

meaning, and then switch round and decide what impression one's words are likely to make on another person. This last effort of the mind cuts out all stale or mixed images, all prefabricated phrases, needless repetitions, and humbug and vagueness generally. But one can often be in doubt about the effect of a word or a phrase, and one needs rules that one can rely on when instinct fails. I think the following rules will cover most cases:

(i) Never use a metaphor, simile or other figure of speech which you are used to seeing in print.
(ii) Never use a long word where a short one will do.
(iii) If it is possible to cut a word out, always cut it out.
(iv) Never use the passive where you can use the active.
(v) Never use a foreign phrase, a scientific word or a jargon word if you can think of an everyday English equivalent.
(vi) Break any of these rules sooner than say anything outright barbarous.

These rules sound elementary, and so they are, but they demand a deep change of attitude in anyone who has grown used to writing in the style now fashionable. One could keep all of them and still write bad English, but one could not write the kind of stuff that I quoted in those five specimens at the beginning of this article.

I have not here been considering the literary use of language, but merely language as an instrument for expressing and not for concealing or preventing thought. Stuart Chase and others have come near to claiming that all abstract words are meaningless, and have used this as a pretext for advocating a kind of political quietism. Since you don't know what Fascism is, how can you struggle against Fascism? One need not swallow such absurdities as this, but one ought to recognize that the present political chaos is connected with the decay of language, and that one can probably bring about some improvement by starting at the verbal end. If you simplify your English, you are freed from the worst follies of orthodoxy. You cannot speak any of the necessary dialects, and when you make a stupid remark its stupidity will be obvious, even to yourself. Political language—and with variations this is true of all political parties, from Conservatives to Anarchists—is designed to make lies sound truthful and murder respectable, and to give an appearance of solidity to pure wind. One cannot change this all in a moment, but one can at least change one's own habits, and from time to time one can even, if one jeers loudly enough, send some worn-out and useless phrase—some *jackboot, Achilles' heel, hotbed, melting pot, acid test, veritable inferno* or other lump of verbal refuse—into the dustbin where it belongs.

QUESTIONS FOR READING AND WRITING

1. What examples do you see in politics today of the dishonest use of language, that is, of the deliberately hiding the true meaning of what is said or written?
2. What does Orwell mean when he says a "reduced state of consciousness . . . is . . . favorable to political conformity" (paragraph 15)? If you are familiar with Orwell's novel *1984*, what examples of this statement come to mind?
3. What examples does Orwell give of the four major flaws he finds in contemporary writing? Are these examples still used? What faults does he find when he analyzes the five passages quoted in the opening of the essay?
4. What positive rules does Orwell give? How will following these rules clarify a writer's meaning?
5. Find some of Orwell's metaphors and similes in the essay. How do they illustrate his point about the need for metaphors to evoke a visual image to clarify a point?
6. Do Orwell's theories about how language works fit the theory of language presented in Dwight Bolinger's essay, "Mind in the Grip of Language"? Do they both agree that thought should precede language?
7. Find a political speech, either a "classic" or one given for the moment, and analyze it for examples of either the positive strengths or negative flaws cited by Orwell.

Division and Classification

The pattern of *division* assumes that your subject matter can be broken up into parts. Virtually any subject can be subdivided into types—types of tourists, kinds of sports cars, and so on. An essay that uses this kind of organization is frequently called a "types of" or "kinds of " essay. For example, in her essay "On Being a Woman Writer," Margaret Atwood begins with the general stereotype "woman writer" and then divides it into four sub-stereotypes: the Happy Housewife, Ophelia, Miss Martyr or Movie Mag, and Miss Message.

Classification, in contrast, assumes that the subject is already one smaller part of a larger entity. For instance, to be useful, raw data must be organized around large categories to which specific pieces of data pertain. Such organization is regarded as classification because the movement is from the specific pieces of data to the larger categories (unlike division, which begins with the large categories and proceeds to break them down). Notice that in his essay "Matters of Taste," Alexander Theroux groups specific candies into similar categories according to their primary property—"mumping" candies, trash candies, the coconut category, the peanut group, the licorice group, and so on. In this essay, classification is the organizing principle; Theroux begins with specific candies, then moves toward the more inclusive categories.

Remember, the difference between division and classification is largely in the direction you are moving: down into smaller units (division) or upward toward larger categories (classification). More than one layer of division is possible; the following piece, an interview at a game arcade, illustrates how some divisions can be like Chinese boxes, divisions within divisions:

> "There are three main groups," the first kid said. "There is the 'What-is-this-thing-supposed-to-be?' -they-ask-pointing-to-the-machine-group. Then, there's the average group. And there's the forever-playing group." The same kid, who falls into the would-be-forever-playing-if-he-had-enough-quarters group, proposed a subdivision of dedicated players. "Then, there are three main crowds. The Kong people—Donkey and Crazy—and the Pac people, and the Defender people. The Kong people are the

> people who really just sit and live on the machine, sit and lie on the chairs—plus small people who sit on top of the machine and bug you. About eight people watching and lying and sitting on chairs around one machine. The Defender and Stargate people are sixteen-, seventeen-, eighteen-year-olds who come in two at a time to play doubles and score incredible scores to make the Immortals list. They smoke a lot and say 'damn' a lot—that's the only cuss they ever utter. . . . Ms. Pac-Man players in the Arcade room are mostly four or five minigirls with one older babysitter—an elder person, usually female—sitting on tabletops. . . . In the ice-cream place . . . the Ms. Pac-Man players are twelve-, thirteen-, fourteen-year-old boys, who pound the glass and swear furiously—mostly unmentionables," the first kid said. "I forgot another crowd, the Dig Dug crowd." The second kid disagreed. "That isn't a real crowd. Dig Dug hasn't gotten big enough for that yet."*

Two rules should be followed in using *division* as a principle of organization. First, the subdivisions should be based on a single principle. Following a single principle of division, E. B. White divides New York City into three categories:

> There are roughly three New Yorks. There is, first, the New York of the man or woman who was born here, who takes the city for granted and accepts its size and its turbulence as natural and inevitable.
>
> Second, there is the New York of the commuter—the city that is devoured by locusts each day and spat out each night. Third, there is the New York of the person who was born somewhere else and came to New York in quest of something.†

The principle of division is not violated because the three New Yorks are considered from the perspective of the point of origin of the different people in the city, that is, whether they are from New York itself, the suburbs, or a place out of town. It would not do to introduce, say, a fourth New York, that of the socialite or taxi driver, because class or status is not the operating principle here.

The second rule in division is that the classes should not overlap. In White's scheme, one is either a native resident, a resident by day only, or a resident from elsewhere. The categories are discrete. You

* "The Machines," *The New Yorker* (October 4, 1982), 34.

† E.B. White, *Here Is New York* (Harper & Row, 1949), 17.

couldn't have resident immigrants from the Caribbean as a category because it is not discrete from the other categories—it overlaps with the larger category, residents from elsewhere.

The division/classification pattern of organization should help you to say something significant about your subject; it should not be merely a mechanical way of cutting up a larger topic into parts or of classifying data into meaningless pigeon holes. There should be an operating principle, a purpose, behind the method you choose. This principle will help generate material for the essay and contribute to its organization.

✦ Margaret Atwood ✦
On Being a "A Woman Writer"

Among the foremost Canadian poets and novelists, Margaret Atwood was born in Ottawa, Ontario, in 1939. After taking her bachelor's degree at the University of Toronto and her master's degree at Radcliffe, she joined the faculty at the University of British Columbia in 1964. Although she began publishing poetry in 1961, it wasn't until The Circle Game *(1966) that she received recognition. Since then she has published a total of ten volumes of poetry, including* The Animals of That Country *(1968),* Procedures for Underground *(1970),* Selected Poems *(1976),* True Stories *(1981), and* Interlunar *(1984). Along with her poetry, her fiction and her criticism have gained her wide recognition. Her nine novels include* The Edible Woman *(1969),* Surfacing *(1972),* Life Before Man *(1979),* Bodily Harm *(1981), and* The Handmaid's Tale *(1985). Atwood's essays are collected in* Second Words *(1982), from which "On Being a Woman Writer" is taken. In this essay, Atwood examines the difficulties of being stereotyped a "woman writer" by male reviewers.*

I APPROACH THIS ARTICLE with a good deal of reluctance. Once having promised to do it, in fact, I've been procrastinating to such an extent that my own aversion is probably the first subject I should attempt to deal with. Some of my reservations have to do with the questionable value of writers, male or female, becoming directly involved in political movements of any sort: their involvement may be good for the movement, but it has yet to be demonstrated that it's good for the writer. The rest concern my sense of the enormous complexity not only of the relationships between Man and Woman, but also of those between those other abstract intangibles, Art and Life, Form and Content, Writer and Critic, etcetera. 1

Judging from conversations I've had with many other woman writers in this country, my qualms are not unique. I can think of only one writer I know who has any formal connection with any of the diverse organizations usually lumped together under the titles of Women's Liberation or the Women's Movement. There are several who have gone out of their way to disavow even any fellow-feeling; but the usual attitude is one of grudging admiration, tempered with envy: the younger generation, they feel, has it a hell of a lot better 2 than they did. Most writers old enough to have a career of any length behind them grew up when it was still assumed that a woman's place was in the home and nowhere else, and that anyone who took time off for an individual selfish activity like writing was either neurotic or wicked or both, derelict in her duties to a man, child, aged relatives or whoever else was supposed to justify her existence on earth. I've heard stories of writers so consumed by guilt over what they had been taught to feel was their abnormality that they did their writing at night, secretly, so no one would accuse them of failing as housewives, as "women." These writers accomplished what they did by themselves, often at great personal expense; in order to write at all, they had to defy other women's as well as men's ideas of what was proper, and it's not finally all that comforting to have a phalanx of women—some younger and relatively unscathed, others from their own generation, the bunch that was collecting china, changing diapers and sneering at any female with intellectual pretensions twenty or even ten years ago—come breezing up now to tell them they were right all along. It's like being judged innocent after you've been hanged: the satisfaction, if any, is grim. There's a great temptation to say to Womens' Lib, "Where were you when I really needed you?" or "It's too late for me now." And you can see, too, that it would be fairly galling for these writers, if they have any respect for historical accuracy, which most do, to be hailed as products, spokeswomen, or advocates of the Women's Movement. When they were undergoing their often drastic formative years there *was* no Women's Movement. No matter that a lot of what they say can be taken by the theorists of the Movement as supporting evidence, useful analysis, and so forth: their own inspiration was not theoretical, it came from wherever all writing comes from. Call it experience and imagination. These writers, if they are honest, don't want to be wrongly identified as the children of a movement that did not give birth to them. Being adopted is not the same as being born.

A third area of reservation is undoubtedly a fear of the development of a one-dimensional Feminist Criticism, a way of approaching literature produced by women that would award points according to conformity or non-conformity to an ideological position. A feminist criticism is, in fact, already emerging. I've read at least one review, and I'm sure there have been and will be more, in which a novelist was criticized for not having made her heroine's life different, even though that life was more typical of the average woman's life in this society than the reviewer's "liberated" version would have been. Perhaps Women's Lib reviewers will start demanding that heroines resolve their difficulties with husband, kids, or themselves by stomping out to join a consciousness raising group, which will be no more satisfactory from the point of view of literature than the legendary Socialist Realist romance with one's tractor. However, a feminist criticism need not necessarily be one-dimensional. And—small comfort—no matter how narrow, purblind and stupid such a criticism in its lowest manifestations may be, it cannot possibly be *more* narrow, purblind and stupid than some of the non-feminist critical attitudes and styles that have preceded it.

There's a fourth possible factor, a less noble one: the often observed phenomenon of the member of a despised social group who manages to transcend the limitations imposed on the group, at least enough to become "successful." For such a person the impulse—whether obeyed or not—is to disassociate him/herself from the group and to side with its implicit opponents. Thus the Black millionaire who deplores the Panthers, the rich *Québecois* who is anti-Separatist, the North American immigrant who changes his name to an "English" one; thus, alas, the Canadian writer who makes it, sort of, in New York, and spends many magazine pages decrying provincial dull Canadian writers; and thus the women with successful careers who say "*I've* never had any problems, I don't know what they're talking about." Such a woman tends to regard herself, and to be treated by her male colleagues, as a sort of honorary man. It's the rest of them who are inept, brainless, tearful, self-defeating: not her. "You think like a man," she is told, with admiration and unconscious put-down. For both men and women, it's just too much of a strain to fit together the traditionally incompatible notions of "woman" and "good at something." And if you *are* good at something, why carry with you the stigma attached to that dismal category you've gone to such lengths to escape from? The only reason for rocking the boat is if you're still chained to the oars. Not everyone reacts like this, but this factor may explain some of the more hysterical opposition to Women's Lib on the part of a few woman writers, even though they 4 may have benefitted from the Movement in the form of increased sales and more serious attention.

A couple of ironies remain; perhaps they are even paradoxes. One is that, in the development of modern Western civilization, writing was the first of the arts, before painting, music, composing, and sculpting, which it was possible for women to practice; and it was the fourth of the job categories, after prostitution, domestic service and the stage, and before wide-scale factory work, nursing, secretarial work, telephone operating and school teaching, at which it was possible for them to make any money. The reason for both is the same: writing as a physical activity is private. You do it by yourself, on your own time; no teachers or employers are involved, you don't have to apprentice in a studio or work with musicians. Your only business arrangements are with your publisher, and these can be conducted through the mails; your real "employers" can be deceived, if you choose, by the adoption of an assumed (male) name; witness the Brontës and George Eliot. But the private and individual nature of writing may also account for the low incidence of direct involvement by woman writers in the Movement now. If you are a writer, prejudice against women will affect you *as a writer* not directly but indirectly. You won't suffer from wage discrimination, because you aren't paid any wages; you won't be hired last and fired first, because you aren't hired or fired anyway. You have relatively little to complain of, and, absorbed in your own work as you are likely to be, you will find it quite easy to shut your eyes to what goes on at the spool factory, or even at the university. *Paradox*: reason for involvement then equals reason for non-involvement now.

Another paradox goes like this. As writers, woman writers are like other writers. They have the same professional concerns, they have to deal with the same contracts and publishing procedures, they have the same need for solitude to work and the same concern that their work be accurately evaluated by reviewers. There is nothing "male" or "female" about these conditions; they are just attributes of the activity known as writing. As biological specimens and as citizens, however, women are like other women: subject to the same discriminatory laws, encountering the same demeaning attitudes, burdened with the same good reasons for not walking through the park alone after dark. They too have bodies, the capacity to bear children; they eat, sleep and bleed, just like everyone else. In bookstores and publishers' offices and among groups of other writers, a woman writer may get the impression that she is "special"; but in the eyes of the law, in the loan office or bank, in the hospital and on the street she's just another woman. She doesn't get to wear a sign to the grocery store saying "Respect me, I'm a Woman Writer." No matter how good she may feel about herself, strangers who aren't aware of her shelf-full of nifty volumes with cover blurbs saying how gifted she is will still regard her as a nit.

We all have ways of filtering out aspects of our experience we would rather not think about. Woman writers can keep as much as possible to the "writing" end of their life, avoiding the less desirable aspects of the "woman" end. Or they can divide themselves in two, thinking of themselves as two different people: a "writer" and a "woman." Time after time, I've had interviewers talk to me about my writing for a while, then ask me, "As a woman, what do you think about—for instance—the Women's Movement," as if I could think two sets of thoughts about the same thing, one set as a writer or person, the other as a woman. But no one comes apart this easily; categories like Woman, White, Canadian, Writer are only ways of looking at a thing, and the thing itself is whole, entire and indivisible. *Paradox*: Woman and Writer are separate categories; but in any individual woman writer, they are inseparable. 7

One of the results of the paradox is that there are certain attitudes, some overt, some concealed, which women writers encounter *as* writers, but *because* they are women. I shall try to deal with a few of these, as objectively as I can. After that, I'll attempt a limited personal statement. 8

A. *Reviewing and the Absence of an Adequate Critical Vocabulary*

Cynthia Ozick, in the American magazine *Ms.*, says, "For many years, I had noticed that no book of poetry by a woman was ever reviewed without reference to the poet's sex. The curious thing was that, in the two decades of my scrutiny, there were *no* exceptions whatever. It did not matter whether the reviewer was a man or a woman; in every case, the question of the 'feminine sensibility' of 9 the poet was at the centre of the reviewer's response. The maleness of male poets, on the other hand, hardly ever seemed to matter."

Things aren't this bad in Canada, possibly because we were never 1
fully indoctrinated with the Holy Gospel according to the distorters of Freud. Many reviewers manage to get through a review without displaying the kind of bias Ozick is talking about. But that it does occur was demonstrated to me by a project I was involved with at York University in 1971–72.

One of my groups was attempting to study what we called "sexual 1
bias in reviewing," by which we meant not unfavourable reviews, but points being added or subtracted by the reviewer on the basis of the author's sex and supposedly associated characteristics rather than on the basis of the work itself. Our study fell into two parts: i) a survey of writers, half male, half female, conducted by letter: had they ever experienced sexual bias directed against them in a review? ii) the reading of a large number of reviews from a wide range of periodicals and newspapers.

The results of the writers' survey were perhaps predictable. Of 1
the men, none said Yes, a quarter said Maybe, and three quarters said No. Half of the women said Yes, a quarter said Maybe and a quarter said No. The women replying Yes often wrote long, detailed letters, giving instances and discussing their own attitudes. All the men's letters were short.

This proved only that women were more likely to *feel* they had 1
been discriminated against on the basis of sex. When we got around to the reviews, we discovered that they were sometimes justified. Here are the kinds of things we found.

i) Assignment of reviews

Several of our letter writers mentioned this. Some felt books by 1
women tended to be passed over by book-page editors assigning books for review; others that books by women tended to get assigned to women reviewers. When we started totting up reviews we found that most books in this society are written by men, and so are most reviews. Disproportionately often, books by women were assigned to women reviewers, indicating that books by women fell in the minds of those dishing out the reviews into some kind of "special" category. Likewise, woman reviewers tended to be reviewing books by women rather than by men

(though because of the preponderance of male reviewers, there were quite a few male-written reviews of books by women).

ii) The Quiller-Couch Syndrome

The heading of this one refers to the turn-of-the-century essay by 15
Quiller-Couch, defining "masculine" and "feminine" styles in writing. The "masculine" style is, of course, bold, forceful, clear, vigorous, etc.; the "feminine" style is vague, weak, tremulous, pastel, etc. In the list of pairs you can include "objective" and "subjective," "universal" or "accurate depiction of society" versus "confessional," "personal," or even "narcissistic" and "neurotic." It's roughly seventy years since Quiller-Couch's essay, but the "masculine" group of adjectives is still much more likely to be applied to the work of male writers; female writers are much more likely to get hit with some version of "the feminine style" or "feminine sensibility," whether their work merits it or not.

iii) The Lady Painter, or She Writes Like A Man

This is a pattern in which good equals male, and bad equals fe- 16
male. I call it the Lady Painter Syndrome because of a conversation I had about female painters with a male painter in 1960. "When she's good," he said, "we call her a painter; when she's bad, we call her a lady painter." "She writes like a man" is part of the same pattern; it's usually used by a male reviewer who is impressed by a female writer. It's meant as a compliment. See also "She thinks like a man," which means the author thinks, unlike most women, who are held to be incapable of objective thought (their province is "feeling"). Adjectives which often have similar connotations are ones such as "strong," "gutsy," "hard," "mean," etc. A hard-hitting piece of writing by a man is liable to be thought of as merely realistic; an equivalent piece by a woman is much more likely to be labelled "cruel" or "tough." The assumption is that women are by nature soft, weak and not very good, and that if a woman writer happens to be good, she should be deprived of her identity as a female and provided with higher (male) status. Thus the woman writer has, in the minds of such reviewers, two choices. She can be bad but female, a carrier of the "feminine sensibility" virus; or she can be "good" in male-adjective terms, but sexless. Badness seems to be ascribed then to a surplus of female hor-

mones, whereas badness in a male writer is usually ascribed to nothing but badness (though a "bad" male writer is sometimes held, by adjectives implying sterility or impotence, to be deficient in maleness). "Maleness" is exemplified by the "good" male writer; "femaleness," since it is seen by such reviewers as a handicap or deficiency, is held to be transcended or discarded by the "good" female one. In other words, there is no critical vocabulary for expressing the concept "good/female." Work by a male writer is often spoken of by critics admiring it as having "balls;" ever hear anyone speak admiringly of work by a woman as having "tits?"
Possible antidotes: Development of a "good/female" vocabulary ("Wow, has that ever got Womb . . . "); or, preferably, the development of a vocabulary that can treat structures made of words as though they are exactly that, not biological entities possessed of sexual organs.

iv) Domesticity

One of our writers noted a (usually male) habit of concentrating on domestic themes in the work of a female writer, ignoring any other topic she might have dealt with, then patronizing her for an excessive interest in domestic themes. We found several instances of reviewers identifying an author as a "housewife" and consequently dismissing anything she has produced (since, in our society, a "housewife" is viewed as a relatively brainless and talentless creature). We even found one instance in which the author was called a "housewife" and put down for writing like one when in fact she was no such thing.

For such reviewers, when a man writes about things like doing the dishes, it's realism; when a woman does, it's an unfortunate feminine genetic limitation.

v) Sexual compliment-put-down

This syndrome can be summed up as follows;
She: "How do you like my (design for an airplane/mathematical formula/medical miracle)?"
He: "You sure have a nice ass."
In reviewing it usually takes the form of commenting on the cute picture of the (female) author on the cover, coupled with dismissal of her as a writer.

vi) Panic Reaction

When something the author writes hits too close to home, panic reaction may set in. One of our correspondents noticed this phenomenon in connection with one of her books: she felt that the content of the book threatened male reviewers, who gave it much worse reviews than did any female reviewer. Their reaction seemed to be that if a character such as she'd depicted did exist, they didn't want to know about it. In panic reaction, a reviewer is reacting to content, not to technique or craftsmanship or a book's internal coherence or faithfulness to its own assumptions. (Panic reaction can be touched off in any area, not just male–female relationships.) 21

B. Interviewers and Media Stereotypes

Associated with the reviewing problem, but distinct from it, is the problem of the interview. Reviewers are supposed to concentrate on books, interviewers on the writer as a person, human being, or, in the case of women, woman. This means that an interviewer is ostensibly trying to find out what sort of person you are. In reality, he or she may merely be trying to match you up with a stereotype of "Woman Author" that pre-exists in her/his mind; doing it that way is both easier for the interviewer, since it limits the range and slant of questions, and shorter, since the interview can be practically written in advance. It isn't just women who get this treatment: all writers get it. But the range for male authors is somewhat wider, and usually comes from the literary tradition itself, whereas stereotypes for female authors are often borrowed from other media, since the ones provided by the tradition are limited in number. 22

In a bourgeois, industrial society, so the theory goes, the creative artist is supposed to act out suppressed desires and prohibited activities for the audience; thus we get certain Post-romantic male-author stereotypes, such as Potted Poe, Bleeding Byron, Doomed Dylan, Lustful Layton, Crucified Cohen, etc. Until recently the only personality stereotype of this kind was Elusive Emily, otherwise known as Recluse Rossetti: the woman writer as aberration, neurotically denying herself the delights of sex, kiddies and other fun. The Twentieth Century has added Suicidal Sylvia, a somewhat more dire version of the same thing. The point about these stereotypes is that attention is focused not on the actual achievements of 23 the authors, but on their lives, which are distorted and romanticized; their work is then interpreted in the light of the distorted version. Stereotypes like these, even when the author cooperates in their formation and especially when the author becomes a cult object, do no service to anyone or anything, least of all the author's work. Behind all of them is the notion that authors must be more special, peculiar or weird than other people, and that their lives are more interesting that their work.

The following examples are taken from personal experience 2
(mine, of interviewers); they indicated the range of possibilities. There are a few others, such as Earth Mother, but for those you have to be older.

i) Happy Housewife

This one is almost obsolete: it used to be for Woman's Page or pro- 2
gramme. Questions were about what you liked to fix for dinner; attitude was, "Gosh, all the housework and you're a writer too!" Writing was viewed as a hobby, like knitting, one did in one's spare time.

ii) Ophelia

The writer as crazy freak. Female version of Doomed Dylan, with 2
more than a little hope on the part of the interviewer that you'll turn into Suicidal Sylvia and give them something to *really* write about. Questions like "Do you think you're in danger of going insane?" or "Are writers closer to insanity than other people?" No need to point out that most mental institutions are crammed with people who have never written a word in their life. "Say something interesting," one interviewer said to me. "Say you write all your poems on drugs."

iii) Miss Martyr; or, Movie Mag

Read any movie mag on Liz Taylor and translate it into writing 2
terms and you've got the picture. The writer as someone who *suffers* more than others. Why does the writer suffer more? Because she's successful, and you all know Success Must Be Paid For. In blood and tears, if possible. If you say you're happy and enjoy your life and work, you'll be ignored.

iv) Miss Message

Interviewer incapable of treating your work as what it is, i.e. po- 28
etry and/or fiction. Great attempt to get you to say something about an Issue and then make you into an exponent, spokeswoman or theorist. (The two Messages I'm most frequently saddled with are Women's Lib and Canadian Nationalism, though I belong to no formal organization devoted to either.) Interviewer unable to see that putting, for instance, a nationalist into a novel doesn't make it a nationalistic novel, any more than putting in a preacher makes it a religious novel. Interviewer incapable of handling more than one dimension at a time.

What is Hard to Find is an interviewer who regards writing as a 29
respectable profession, not as some kind of magic, madness, trickery or evasive disguise for a Message; and who regards an author as someone engaged in a professional activity.

C. *Other Writers and Rivalry*

Regarding yourself as an "exception," part of an unspoken quota 30
system, can have interesting results. If there are only so many available slots for your minority in the medical school/law school/literary world, of course you will feel rivalry, not only with members of the majority for whom no quota operates, but especially for members of your minority who are competing with you for the few coveted places. And you will have to be better than the average Majority member to get in at all. But we're familiar with that.

Woman–woman rivalry does occur, though it is surprisingly less 31
severe than you'd expect; it's likely to take the form of *wanting* another woman writer to be better than she is, expecting more of her than you would of a male writer, and being exasperated with certain kinds of traditional "female" writing. One of our correspondents discussed these biases and expectations very thoroughly and with great intelligence: her letter didn't solve any problems but it did emphasize the complexities of the situation. Male–male rivalry is more extreme; we've all been treated to media-exploited examples of it.

What a woman writer is often unprepared for is the unexpected personal attack on her by a jealous male writer. The motivation is envy and competitiveness, but the form is often sexual put-down. "You may be a good writer," one older man said to a young woman writer who had just had a publishing success, "but I wouldn't want to fuck you." Another version goes more like the compliment-put-down noted under Reviewing. In either case, the ploy diverts attention from the woman's achievement as a writer—the area where the man feels threatened—to her sexuality, where either way he can score a verbal point.

Personal Statement

I've been trying to give you a picture of the arena, or that part of 3
it where being a "woman" and "writer," as concepts, overlap. But, of course, the arena I've been talking about has to do largely with externals: reviewing, the media, relationships with other writers. This, for the writer, may affect the tangibles of her career: how she is received, how viewed, how much money she makes. But in relationship to the writing itself, this is a false arena. The real one is in her head, her real struggle the daily battle with words, the language itself. The false arena becomes valid for writing itself only insofar as it becomes part of her material and is transformed into one of the verbal and imaginative structures she is constantly engaged in making. Writers, as writers, are not propagandists or examples of social trends or preachers or politicians. They are makers of books, and unless they can make books well they will be bad writers, no matter what the social validity of their views.

At the beginning of this article, I suggested a few reasons for the 3
infrequent participation in the Movement of woman writers. Maybe these reasons were the wrong ones, and this is the real one: no good writer wants to be merely a transmitter of someone else's ideology, no matter how fine that ideology may be. The aim of propaganda is to convince, and to spur people to action; the aim of writing is to create a plausible and moving imaginative world, and to create it from words. Or, to put it another way, the aim of a political movement is to improve the quality of people's lives on all levels, spiritual and imaginative as well as material (and any political movement that doesn't have this aim is worth nothing). Writing, however, tends to

concentrate more on life, not as it ought to be, but as it is, as the writer feels it, experiences it. Writers are eye-witnesses, I-witnesses. Political movements, once successful, have historically been intolerant of writers, even those writers who initially aided them; in any revolution, writers have been among the first to be lined up against the wall, perhaps for their intransigence, their insistence on saying what they perceive, not what, according to the ideology, ought to exist. Politicians, even revolutionary politicians, have traditionally had no more respect for writing as an activity valuable in itself, quite apart from any message or content, than has the rest of the society. And writers, even revolutionary writers, have traditionally been suspicious of anyone who tells them what they ought to write.

The woman writer, then, exists in a society that, though it may 35
turn certain individual writers into revered cult objects, has little respect for writing as a profession, and not much respect for women either. If there were more of both, articles like this would be obsolete. I hope they become so. In the meantime, it seems to me that the proper path for a woman writer is not an all-out manning (or womaning) of the barricades, however much she may agree with the aims of the Movement. The proper path is to become better as a writer. Insofar as writers are lenses, condensers of their society, her work may include the Movement, since it is so palpably among the things that exist. The picture that she gives of it is altogether another thing, and will depend, at least partly, on the course of the Movement itself.

QUESTIONS FOR READING AND WRITING

1. What are some of the stereotypes that you think of when you think of writers in general? Of women writers?
2. What are some of the reasons why women writers refuse to become identified with the Women's Movement? Do similar reasons exist for women who have risen to positions of authority in the business, academic, or political worlds? Does Atwood acknowledge this is also true of minorities who have "made it"?
3. How accurate are Atwood's divisions of women-author stereotypes held by interviewers? What categories could you create for male authors? Are the categories less flattering for women?

4. Select any profession and stereotype some of the members of that profession, using sex or some other criterion as the basis of your division.
5. Read Adrienne Rich's essay "Claiming an Education" and write an essay on the difficulties women face in choosing a career in the intellectual world.
6. Read Atwood's essay "Pornography" and write a comparison of the social stereotypes held generally about writers and their role in society.

✦ Kai Erikson ✦

Of Accidental Judgments and Casual Slaughters

Austrian-born sociologist, educator, and author, Kai Erikson is the son of Erik Erikson, the famous psychoanalyst. Erikson has taught at Pittsburgh and Emory Universities and has been a professor of sociology at Yale since 1970. He has been the recipient of the MacIver Award and the Sorokin Award from the American Sociological Association. Among his books are Wayward Puritans: A Study of the Sociology of Deviance *(1966) and* Everything in Its Path: Destruction of Community in the Buffalo Creek Flood *(1976) and he has edited his father's book,* In Search of Common Ground *(1973). Erikson's essay, which originally appeared in* The Nation, *examines the kinds of options the American government had after the successful testing of the atomic bomb at Alamogordo, New Mexico, and before dropping the atomic bomb on Hiroshima and Nagasaki. Erikson sees it as a frightening parable for the future.*

THE BOMBINGS of Hiroshima and Nagasaki, which took place forty years ago this month, are among the most thoroughly studied moments on human record. Together they constitute the only occasion in history when atomic weapons were dropped on living populations, and together they constitute the only occasion in history when a decision was made to employ them in that way. 1

I want to reflect here on the second of those points. The "decision to drop"—I will explain in a minute why quotation marks are useful here—is a fascinating historical episode. But it is also an exhibit of the most profound importance as we consider our prospects for the future. It is a case history well worth attending to. A compelling parable. 2

If one were to tell the story of that decision as historians normally do, the details arranged in an ordered narrative, one might begin in 1938 with the discovery of nuclear fission, or perhaps a year later with the delivery of Einstein's famous letter to President Roosevelt. No matter what its opening scene, though, the tale would then proceed along a string of events—a sequence of appointees named, 3 committees formed, reports issued, orders signed, arguments won and lost, minds made up and changed—all of it coming to an end with a pair of tremendous blasts in the soft morning air over Japan.

The difficulty with that way of relating the story, as historians of the period all testify, is that the more closely one examines the record, the harder it is to make out where in the flow of events something that could reasonably be called a decision was reached at all. To be sure, a kind of consensus emerged from the sprawl of ideas and happenings that made up the climate of wartime Washington, but looking back, it is hard to distinguish those pivotal moments in the story when the crucial issues were identified, debated, reasoned through, resolved. The decision, to the extent that one can even speak of such a thing, was shaped and seasoned by a force very like inertia.

Let's say, then, that a wind began to blow, ever so gently at first, down the corridors along which power flows. And as it gradually gathered momentum during the course of the war, the people caught up in it began to assume, without ever checking up on it, that it had a logic and a motive, that it had been set in motion by sure hands acting on the basis of wise counsel.

Harry Truman, in particular, remembered it as a time of tough and lonely choices, and titled his memoir of that period *Year of Decisions*. But the bulk of those choices can in all fairness be said to have involved confirmation of projects already under way or implementation of decisions made at other levels of command. Brig. Gen. Leslie R. Groves, military head of the Manhattan Project, was close to the mark when he described Truman's decision as "one of noninterference—basically, a decision not to upset the existing plans." And J. Robert Oppenheimer spoke equally to the point when he observed some twenty years later: "The decision was implicit in the project. I don't know whether it could have been stopped."

In September of 1944, when it became more and more evident that a bomb would be produced in time for combat use, Franklin Roosevelt and Winston Churchill met at Hyde Park and initialed a brief *aide-mémoire*, noting, among other things, that the new weapon "might, perhaps, after mature consideration, be used against the Japanese." This document does not appear to have had any effect on the conduct of the war, and Truman knew nothing at all about it. But it would not have made a real difference in any case, for neither chief of state did much to initiate the "mature consideration" they spoke of so glancingly, and Truman, in turn, could only suppose that such matters had been considered already. "Truman did not inherit the question," writes Martin J. Sherwin, "he inherited the answer."

What would "mature consideration" have meant in such a setting 8
as that anyway?

First of all, presumably, it would have meant seriously asking 9
whether the weapon should be employed at all. But we have it on the authority of virtually all the principal players that no one in a position to do anything about it ever really considered alternatives to combat use. Henry L. Stimson, Secretary of War:

> At no time, from 1941 to 1945, did I ever hear it suggested by the President, or by any other responsible member of the government, that atomic energy should not be used in the war.

Harry Truman:

> I regarded the bomb as a military weapon and never had any doubt that it should be used.

General Groves:

> Certainly, there was no question in my mind, or, as far as I was ever aware, in the mind of either President Roosevelt or President Truman or any other responsible person, but that we were developing a weapon to be employed against the enemies of the United States.

Winston Churchill:

> There never was a moment's discussion as to whether the atomic bomb should be used or not.

And why should anyone be surprised? We were at war, after all, and with the most resolute of enemies, so the unanimity of that feeling is wholly understandable. But it was not, by any stretch of the imagination, a product of mature consideration.

"Combat use" meant a number of different things, however, and 10
a second question began to be raised with some frequency in the final months of the war, all the more insistently after the defeat of Germany. Might a way be devised to demonstrate the awesome power of the bomb in a convincing enough fashion to induce the surrender of the Japanese without having to destroy huge numbers

of civilians? Roosevelt may have been pondering something of the sort. In September of 1944, for example, three days after initialing the Hyde Park *aide-mémoire*, he asked Vannevar Bush, a trusted science adviser, whether the bomb "should actually be used against the Japanese or whether it should be used only as a threat." While that may have been little more than idle musing, a number of different schemes were explored within both the government and the scientific community in the months following.

One option involved a kind of *benign strike*: the dropping of a bomb on some built-up area, but only after advance notice had been issued so that residents could evacuate the area and leave an empty slate on which the bomb could write its terrifying signature. This plan was full of difficulties. A dud under those dramatic circumstances might do enormous damage to American credibility, and, moreover, to broadcast any warning was to risk the endeavor in other ways. Weak as the Japanese were by this time in the war, it was easy to imagine their finding a way to intercept an incoming airplane if they knew where and when it was expected, and officials in Washington were afraid that it would occur to the Japanese, as it had to them, that the venture would come to an abrupt end if American prisoners of war were brought into the target area.

The second option was a *tactical strike* against a purely military target—an arsenal, railroad yard, depot, factory, harbor—without advance notice. Early in the game, for example, someone had nominated the Japanese fleet concentration at Truk. The problem with this notion, however—and there is more than a passing irony here—was that no known military target had a wide enough compass to contain the whole of the destructive capacity of the weapon and so display its full range and power. The committee inquiring into likely targets wanted one "more than three miles in diameter," because anything smaller would be too inadequate a canvas for the picture it was supposed to hold.

The third option was to stage a kind of *dress rehearsal* by detonating a bomb in some remote corner of the world—a desert or empty island, say—to exhibit to international observers brought in for the purpose what the device could do. The idea had been proposed by a group of scientists in what has since been called the Franck Report, but it commanded no more than a moment's attention. It had the same problems as the benign strike: the risk of being embarrassed by a dud was more than most officials in a position to decide were willing to take, and there was a widespread feeling that any demonstration involving advance notice would give the enemy too much useful information.

The fourth option involved a kind of *warning shot*. The thought here was to drop a bomb without notice over a relatively uninhabited stretch of enemy land so the Japanese high command might see at first hand what was in store for them if they failed to surrender soon. Edward Teller thought that an explosion at night high over Tokyo Bay would serve as a brilliant visual argument, and Adm. Lewis Strauss, soon to become a member (and later chair) of the Atomic Energy Commission, recommended a strike on a local forest, reasoning that the blast would "lay the trees out in windrows from the center of the explosion in all directions as though they were matchsticks," meanwhile igniting a fearsome firestorm at the epicenter. "It seemed to me," he added, "that a demonstration of this sort would prove to the Japanese that we could destroy any of their cities at will." The physicist Ernest O. Lawrence may have been speaking half in jest when he suggested that a bomb might be use to "blow the top off" Mount Fujiyama, but he was quite serious when he assured a friend early in the war: "The bomb will never be dropped on people. As soon as we get it, we'll use it only to dictate peace." 14

Now, hindsight is too easy a talent. But it seems evident on the face of it that the fourth of those options, the warning shot, was much to be preferred over the other three, and even more to be preferred over use on living targets. I do not want to argue the case here. I do want to ask, however, why that possibility was so easily dismissed. 15

The fact of the matter seems to have been that the notion of a demonstration was discussed on only a few occasions once the Manhattan Project neared completion, and most of those discussions were off the record. So a historian trying to reconstruct the drift of those conversations can only flatten an ear against the wall, as it were, and see if any sense can be made of the muffled voices next door. It seems very clear, for example, that the options involving advance notice were brought up so often and so early in official conversations that they came to *mean* demonstration in the minds of several important players. If a James Byrnes, say, soon to be 16 named Secretary of State, were asked why one could not detonate a device in unoccupied territory, he might raise the problem posed by prisoners of war, and if the same question were asked of a James Bryant Conant, another science adviser, he might speak of the embarrassment that would follow a dud—thus, in both cases, joining ideas that had no logical relation to each other. Neither prisoners of war nor fear of failure, of course, posed any argument against a surprise demonstration.

There were two occasions, however, on which persons in a position to affect policy discussed the idea of a nonlethal demonstration. Those two conversations together consumed no more than a matter of minutes, so far as one can tell at this remove, and they, too, were off the record. But they seem to represent virtually the entire investment of the government of the United States in "mature consideration" of the subject.

The first discussion took place at a meeting of what was then called the Interim Committee, a striking gathering of military, scientific and government brass under the chairmanship of Secretary Stimson. This group, which included James Byrnes and Chief of Staff Gen. George C. Marshall, met on a number of occasions in May of 1945 to discuss policy issues raised by the new bomb, and Stimson recalled later that at one of their final meetings the members "carefully considered such alternatives as a detailed advance warning or a demonstration in some uninhabited area." But the minutes of the meeting, as well as the accounts of those present, suggest otherwise. The only exchange on the subject, in fact, took place during a luncheon break, and while we have no way of knowing what was actually said in that conversation, we do know what conclusion emerged from it. One participant, Arthur H. Compton, recalled later:

> Though the possibility of a demonstration that would not destroy human lives was attractive, no one could suggest a way in which it could be made so convincing that it would be likely to stop the war.

And the recording secretary of the meeting later recalled:

> Dr. Oppenheimer . . . said he doubted whether there could be devised any sufficiently startling demonstration that would convince the Japanese they ought to throw in the sponge.

Two weeks later, four physicists who served as advisors to the Interim Committee met in Los Alamos to consider once again the question of demonstration. They were Arthur Compton, Enrico Fermi, Ernest Lawrence and Robert Oppenheimer—as distinguished an assembly of scientific talent as could be imagined—and they concluded, after a discussion of which we have no record: "We can propose no technical demonstration likely to bring an end to the war; we see no acceptable alternative to direct military use." That, so far as anyone can tell, was the end of it.

We cannot be sure that a milder report would have made a difference, for the Manhattan Project was gathering momentum as it moved toward the more steeply pitched inclines of May and June, but we can be sure that the idea of a demonstration was at that point spent. The Los Alamos report ended with something of a disclaimer ("We have, however, no claim to special competence . . ."), but its message was clear enough. When asked about that report nine years later in his security hearings, Oppenheimer said, with what might have been a somewhat defensive edge in his voice, "We did not think exploding one of those things as a firecracker over the desert was likely to be very impressive." 19

Perhaps not. But those fragments are telling for another reason. If you listen to them carefully for a moment or two, you realize that these are the voices of nuclear physicists trying to imagine how a strange and distant people will react to an atomic blast. These are the voices of nuclear physicists dealing with psychological and anthropological questions about Japanese culture, Japanese temperament, Japanese will to resist—topics, we must assume, about which they knew almost nothing. They did not know yet what the bomb could actually do, since its first test was not to take place for another month. But in principle, at least, Oppenheimer and Fermi reflecting on matters relating to the Japanese national character should have had about the same force as Ruth Benedict and Margaret Mead reflecting on matters relating to high-energy physics, the first difference being that Benedict and Mead would not have presumed to do so, and the second being that no one in authority would have listened to them if they had. 20

The first of the two morals I want to draw from the foregoing—this being a parable, after all—is that in moments of critical contemplation, it is often hard to know where the competencies of soldiers 21 and scientists and all the rest of us begin and end. Many an accidental judgment can emerge from such confusions.

But what if the conclusions of the scientists had been correct? What if some kind of demonstration had been staged in a lightly occupied part of Japan and it *had* been greeted as a firecracker in the desert? What then?

Let me shift gears for a moment and discuss the subject in another way. It is standard wisdom for everyone in the United States old enough to remember the war, and for most of those to whom it is ancient history, that the bombings of Hiroshima and Nagasaki were the only alternative to an all-out invasion of the Japanese mainland involving hundreds of thousands and perhaps millions of casualties on both sides. Unless the Japanese came to understand the need to surrender quickly, we would have been drawn by an almost magnetic force toward those dreaded beaches. This has become an almost automatic pairing of ideas, an article of common lore. If you lament that so many civilians were incinerated or blown to bits in Hiroshima and Nagasaki, then somebody will remind you of the American lives thus saved. Truman was the person most frequently asked to account for the bombings, and his views were emphatic on the subject:

> It was a question of saving hundreds of thousands of American lives. I don't mind telling you that you don't feel normal when you have to plan hundreds of thousands of complete, final deaths of American boys who are alive and joking and having fun while you are doing your planning. You break your heart and your head trying to figure out a way to save one life. The name given to our invasion plan was "Olympic," but I saw nothing godly about the killing of all the people that would be necessary to make that invasion. I could not worry about what history would say about my personal morality. I made the only decision I ever knew how to make. I did what I thought was right.*

---

* Merle Miller notes, in *Plain Speaking: An Oral Biography of Harry S. Truman*, that Truman may have had moments of misgiving: "My only insight into Mr. Truman's feeling about the Bomb and its dropping, and it isn't much, came one day in his private library at the Truman Memorial Library. In one corner was every book ever published on the bomb, and at the end of one was Horatio's speech in the last scene of *Hamlet*." Truman had underlined these words:

Veterans of the war, and particularly those who had reason to suppose that they would have been involved in an invasion, have drawn that same connection repeatedly, most recently Paul Fussell in the pages of *The New Republic*. Thank God for the bomb, the argument goes, it saved the lives of countless numbers of us. And so, in a sense, it may have. 24

But the destruction of Hiroshima and Nagasaki had nothing to do with it. It only makes sense to assume, even if few people were well enough positioned in early August to see the situation whole, that there simply was not going to be an invasion. Not ever. 25

For what sane power, with the atomic weapon securely in its arsenal, would hurl a million or more of its sturdiest young men on a heavily fortified mainland? To imagine anyone ordering an invasion when the means were at hand to blast Japan into a sea of gravel at virtually no cost in American lives is to imagine a madness beyond anything even the worst of war can induce. The invasion had not yet been called off, granted. But it surely would have been, and long before the November 1 deadline set for it. 26

The United States did not become a nuclear power on August 6, with the destruction of Hiroshima. It became a nuclear power on July 16, when the first test device was exploded in Alamogordo, New Mexico. Uncertainties remained, of course, many of them. But from that moment on, the United States knew how to produce a bomb, knew how to deliver it and knew it would work. Stimson said shortly after the war that the bombings of Hiroshima and Nagasaki "ended the ghastly specter of a clash of great land armies," but he could have said, with greater justice, that the ghastly specter ended at Alamogordo. Churchill came close to making exactly that point when he first learned of the New Mexico test: 27

> To quell the Japanese resistance man by man and conquer the country yard by yard might well require the loss of a million American lives and half that number of British . . . Now all that nightmare picture had vanished.

And let me speak to the yet unknowing world
How these things came about. So shall you hear
Of carnal, bloody, and unnatural acts,
Of accidental judgments, casual slaughters
Of deaths put on by cunning and forced cause,
And, in this upshot, purposes mistook
Fall'n on the inventors' heads.

It *had* vanished. The age of inch-by-inch crawling over enemy territory, the age of Guadalcanal and Iwo Jima and Okinawa, was just plain over.

The point is that once we had the bomb and were committed to its use, the terrible weight of invasion no longer hung over our heads. The Japanese were incapable of mounting any kind of offensive, as every observer has agreed, and it was our option when to close with the enemy and thus risk casualties. So we could have easily afforded to hold for a moment, to think it over, to introduce what Dwight Eisenhower called "that awful thing" to the world on the basis of something closer to mature consideration. We could have afforded to detonate a bomb over some less lethal target and then pause to see what happened. And do it a second time, maybe a third. And if none of those demonstrations had made a difference, presumably we would have had to strike harder: Hiroshima and Nagasaki would still have been there a few weeks later for that purpose, silent and untouched—"unspoiled" was the term Gen. H. H. Arnold used—for whatever came next. Common lore also has it that there were not bombs enough for such niceties, but that seems not to have been the case. The United States was ready to deliver a third bomb toward the end of August, and Groves had already informed Marshall and Stimson that three or four more bombs would be available in September, a like number in October, at least five in November, and seven in December, with substantial increases to follow in early 1946. Even if we assume that Groves was being too hopeful about the productive machinery he had set in motion, as one expert close to the matter has suggested, a formidable number of bombs would have been available by the date originally set for invasion.

Which brings us back to the matter of momentum. The best way to tell the story of those days is to say that the "decision to drop" had become a force like gravity. It had taken life. The fact that it existed supplied its meaning, its reason for being. Elting E. Morison, Stimson's biographer, put it well:

> Any process started by men toward a special end tends, for reasons logical, biological, aesthetic or whatever they may be, to carry forward, if other things remain equal, to its climax. [This is] the inertia developed in a human system . . . In a process where such a general tendency has been set to work it is diffi-

cult to separate the moment when men were still free to choose from the moment, if such there was, when they were no longer free to choose.

I have said very little about Nagasaki so far because it was not the 31
subject of any thought at all. The orders of the bomber command were to attack Japan as soon as the bombs were ready. One was ready on August 9. Boom. When Groves was later asked why the attack on Nagasaki had come so soon after the attack on Hiroshima, leaving so little time for the Japanese to consider what had happened to them, he simply said: "Once you get your opponent reeling, you keep him reeling and never let him recover." And that is the point, really. There is no law of nature that compels a winning side to press its superiority, but it is hard to slow down, hard to relinquish an advantage, hard to rein the fury. The impulse to charge ahead, to strike at the throat, is so strong a habit of war that it almost ranks as a reflex, and if that thought does not frighten us when we consider our present nuclear predicament, nothing will. Many a casual slaughter can emerge from such moods.

If it is true, as I have suggested, that there were few military or 32
logistic reasons for striking as sharply as we did and that the decision to drop moved in on the crest of an almost irreversible current, then it might be sensible to ask, on the fortieth anniversary of the event, what some of the drifts were that became a part of that larger current. An adequate accounting would have to consider a number of military, political and other matters far beyond the reach of this brief essay, the most important of them by far being the degree to which the huge shadow of the Soviet Union loomed over both official meetings and private thoughts. It is nearly impossible to read the remaining record without assuming that the wish to make a loud announcement to the Russians was a persuasive factor in the minds of many of the principal participants. There were other drifts as well, of course, and I would like to note a few of the sort that sometimes occur to social scientists.

For one thing, an extraordinary amount of money and material 33
had been invested in the Manhattan Project—both of them in short supply in a wartime economy—and many observers thought that so large a public expense would be all the more willingly borne if it were followed by a striking display of what the money had been spent for.

And, too, extraordinary investments had been made in men and talent, both of them in short supply in a wartime economy. The oldest of the people involved in the Manhattan Project—soldiers, engineers and scientists—made sacrifices in the form of separated families, interrupted careers and a variety of other discomforts, and it makes a certain psychological sense that a decisive strike would serve as a kind of vindication for all the trouble. The youngest of them, though, had been held out of combat, thus avoiding the fate of so many men of their generation, by accidents of professional training, personal skill and sheer timing. The project was their theater of war, and it makes even more psychological sense that some of them would want the only shot they fired to be a truly resonant one.

The dropping of such a bomb, moreover, could serve as an ending, something sharp and distinct in a world that had become ever more blurred. The Grand Alliance was breaking up, and with it all hope for a secure postwar world. Roosevelt was dead. The future was full of ambiguity. And, most important, everybody was profoundly tired. In circumstances like that, a resounding strike would serve to clarify things, to give them form, to tidy them up a bit.

There are other matters one might point to, some of them minor, some of them major, all of them strands in the larger weave. There was a feeling, expressed by scientists and government officials alike, that the world needed a rude and decisive shock to awaken it to the realities of the atomic age. There was a feeling, hard to convey in words but easy to sense once one has become immersed in some of the available material, that the bomb had so much power and majesty, was so compelling a force, that one was almost required to give it birth and a chance to mature. There was a feeling, born of war, that for all its ferocity the atomic bomb was nevertheless no more than a minor increment on a scale of horror that already included the firebombings of Tokyo and other Japanese cities. And there was a feeling, also born of war, that living creatures on the other side, even the children, had somehow lost title to the mercies that normally accompany the fact of being human.

The kinds of points I have been making need to be stated either very precisely or in some detail. I have not yet learned to do the former; I do not have space enough here for the latter. So let me just end with the observation that human decisions do not always emerge from reflective counsels where facts are arrayed in order and logic is the prevailing currency of thought. They emerge from complex fields of force, in which the vanities of leaders and the moods of constituencies and the inertias of bureaucracies play a critical part. That is as important a lesson as one can learn from the events of 1945—and as unnerving a one.

The bombings of Hiroshima and Nagasaki supply a rich case 38
study for people who must live in times like ours. It is not important for us to apportion shares of responsibility to persons who played their parts so long ago, and I have not meant to do so here: these were unusually decent and compassionate people for the most part, operating with reflexes that had been tempered by war. We need to attend to such histories as this, however, because they provide the clearest illustrations we have of what human beings can do—this being the final moral to be drawn from our parable—when they find themselves in moments of crisis and literally have more destructive power at their disposal than they know what to do with. That is as good an argument for disarming as any that can be imagined.

QUESTIONS FOR READING AND WRITING

1. Erikson observes that we need to attend to the lessons of Hiroshima and Nagasaki because "they provide the clearest illustrations we have of what human beings can do . . . when they find themselves in moments of crisis and literally have more destructive power at their disposal than they know what to do with" (paragraph 38). Can you think of other examples since World War II of where this same principle is true?
2. Erikson calls his essay a parable. Why a parable? What are its lessons?
3. What were the categories of use to which "mature consideration" was to have been given before the bomb was put to "military use"? What were the reasons for rejecting these alternative uses?
4. Doesn't the fact that a second bomb had to be used on Nagasaki support the contention that nothing short of a civilian target would have broken the resolve of the Japanese? Why does Erikson reject the competence of the key physicists in the Manhattan Project to determine the extent of Japanese resolve? What lesson does he draw from their report?

5. Write an essay in which you demonstrate that the nuclear-arms race is similar to the decision to drop the atomic bomb, in that both emerge from "complex fields of force, in which the vanities of leaders and the moods of constituencies and the inertias of bureaucracies play a critical part" (paragraph 37). Be sure to include a division of the reasons for the arms buildup.
6. Read Jonathan Schell's essay, "Nothing to Report," and write an essay on the ways in which ignorance of the effects of a nuclear exchange make public support of the arms race possible.

✦ Alexander Theroux ✦
Matters of Taste

Alexander Theroux, the older brother of Paul Theroux, is a former Trappist monk, novelist, and author of children's books. His writing has appeared in Esquire *and the* National Review, *and he writes a column for* Boston *magazine. Theroux's style is eccentric and flamboyant, what one critic labelled a "Gothic garden." That style is one reason why his analysis of the various and sundry styles of candy is such fun to read.*

I BELIEVE THERE ARE FEW THINGS that show as much variety—that there is so much of—as American candy. The national profusion of mints and munch, pops and drops, creamfills, cracknels, and chocolate crunch recapitulates the good and plenty of the Higher Who. 1

Candy has its connoisseurs and critics both. To some, for instance, it's a subject of endless fascination—those for whom a root-beer lozenge can taste like a glass of Shakespeare's "brown October" and for whom little pilgrims made of maple sugar can look like Thracian gold—and to others, of course, it's merely a wilderness of abominations. You can sample one piece with a glossoepiglottic gurgle of joy or chew down another empty as shade, thin as fraud. 2

In a matter where tastes touch to such extremes one is compelled to seek through survey what in the inquiry might yield, if not conclusions sociologically diagnostic, then at least a simple truth or two. Which are the best candies? Which are the worst? And why? A sense of fun can feed on queer candy, and there will be no end of argument, needless to say. But, essentially, it's all in the *taste*. 3

The trash candies—a little lobby, all by itself, of the American Dental Association—we can dismiss right away: candy cigarettes, peanut brittle, peppermint lentils, Life Savers (white only), Necco Wafers (black especially), Christmas candy in general, gumballs, and above all that glaucous excuse for tuck called ribbon candy, which little kids, for some reason, pounce on like a duck on a June bug. I would put in this category all rock candy, general Woolworthiana, and all those little nerks, cupcake sparkles, and decorative sugars like silver buckshot that though inedible, are 4 actually eaten by the young and indiscriminate, whose teeth turn eerie almost on contact.

In the category of the most abominable tasting, the winner—on both an aesthetic and a gustatory level—must surely be the inscribed Valentine candy heart ("Be Mine," "Hot Stuff," "Love Ya," et cetera). In high competition, no doubt, are bubble-gum cigars, candy corn, marshmallow chicks (bunnies, pumpkins, et cetera), Wacky Wafers (eight absurd-tasting coins in as many flavors), Blow Pops—an owl's pellet of gum inside a choco-pop!—Canada Mints, which taste like petrified Egyptian lime, and, last but not least, those unmasticable beige near-candy peanuts that, insipid as rubber erasers, not only have no bite—the things just give up—but elicit an indescribable antitaste that is best put somewhere between stale marshmallow and dry wall. Every one of these candies, sweating right now in a glass case at your corner store, is to my mind proof positive of original sin. They can be available, I suggest, only for having become favorites of certain indiscriminate fatties at the Food and Drug Administration who must buy them by the bag. But a bat could see they couldn't be a chum of ours if they chuckled.

Now, there are certain special geniuses who can distinguish candies, like wine, by rare deduction: district, commune, vineyard, growth. They know all the wrappers, can tell twinkle from tartness in an instant, and often from sniffing nothing more than the empty cardboard sled of a good candy bar can summon up the scent of the far Moluccas. It is an art, or a skill at least *tending* to art. I won't boast the ability, but allow me, if you will, to be a professor of the fact of it. The connoisseur, let it be said, has no special advantage. Candy can be found everywhere: the airport lounge, the drugstore, the military PX, the student union, the movie house, the company vending machine—old slugs, staler than natron, bonking down into a tray—but the *locus classicus*, of course, is the corner store.

The old-fashioned candy store, located on a corner in the American consciousness, is almost obsolete. Its proprietor is always named Sam; for some reason he's always Jewish. Wearing a hat and an apron, he shuffles around on spongy shoes, still tweezers down products from the top shelf with one of those antique metal grapplers, and always keeps the lights off. He has the temperament of a black mamba and makes his best customers, little kids with faces like midway balloons, show him their nickels before they order. But he keeps the fullest glass case of penny candy in the city—spiced baby gums, malted milk balls, fruit slices, candy fish, aniseed balls, candy pebbles, jelly beans, raspberry stars, bull's-eyes, boiled sweets, the lot. The hit's pretty basic. You point, he scoops a dollop into a little white bag, weighs it, subtracts two, and then asks, "Wot else?"

A bright rack nearby holds the bars, brickbats, brand names. Your 8
habit's never fixed when you care about candy. You tend to look for new bars, recent mints, old issues. The log genre, you know, is relatively successful: Bolsters, Butterfingers, Clark Bars, Baby Ruths, O. Henrys, and the Zagnut with its sweet razor blades. Although they've dwindled in size, like the dollar that buys fewer and fewer of them, all have a lushness of weight and good nap and nacre, a chewiness, with tastes in suitable *contre coup* to the bite. You pity their distant cousins, the airy and unmemorable Kit-Kats, Choco'lites, Caravels, and Paydays, johnny-come-latelies with shallow souls and Rice Krispie hearts that taste like budgie food. A submember of American candy, the peanut group, is strong—crunch is often the kiss in a candy romance—and you might favorably settle on several: Snickers, Go Aheads, Mr. Goodbars, Reese's Peanut Butter Cups (of negligible crunch however), the Crispy, the Crunch, the Munch—a nice trilogy of onomatopoeia—and even the friendly little Creeper, a peanut-butter-filled tortoise great for one-bite dispatch: Pleep!

Vices, naturally, coexist with virtues. The coconut category, for 9
instance—Mounds, Almond Joys, Waleecos, and their ilk—is toothsome, but can often be tasted in flakes at the folds and rim of your mouth days later. The licorice group, Nibs, Licorice Rolls, Twizzlers, Switzer Twists, and various whips and shoelaces, often smoky to congestion, usually leave a nice smack in the aftertaste. The jawbreaker may last a long time, yes—but who wants it to? Tootsie Pop Drops, Charms, Punch, Starburst Fruit Chews (sic!), base-born products of base beds, are harder than affliction and better used for checker pieces or musket flints or supports to justify a listing bureau.

There are certain candies, however—counter, original, spare 10
strange—that are gems in both the bite and the taste, not the usual grim marriage of magnesium stearate to lactic acid, but rare confections at democratic prices. Like lesser breeds raising pluperfect cain

with the teeth, these are somehow always forgiven; any such list must include: Mary Janes, Tootsie Rolls, Sky Bars, Squirrels, Mint Juleps, the wondrous B-B Bats (a hobbit-sized banana taffy pop still to be had for 3¢), and other unforgettable knops and knurls like turtles, chocolate bark, peanut clusters, burnt peanuts, and those genius-inspired pink pillows with the peanut-butter surprise inside for which we're all so grateful. There's an *intelligence* here that's difficult to explain, a sincerity at the essence of each, where solid line plays against stipple and a truth function is solved always to one's understanding and always—*O altitudo!*—to one's taste.

Candy is sold over the counter, won in raffles, awarded on quiz 1
shows, flogged door to door, shipped wholesale in boxes, thrown out at ethnic festivals, and incessantly hawked on television commercials by magic merrymen—clownish pied-pipers in cap-and-bells—who inspirit thousands of kids to come hopping and hurling after them, singing all the way to Cavityville. Why do we eat it? Who gets us started eating it? What sexual or social or semantic preferences are indicated by which pieces? The human palate—tempted perhaps by Nature *herself* in things like slippery elm, spruce gum, sassafras, and various berries—craves sweetness almost everywhere, so much so, in fact, that the flavor of candy commonly denominates American breath-fresheners, throat discs, mouthwash, lipstick, fluoride treatments, toothpaste, cough syrup, breakfast cereals, and even dental floss, fruit salts, and glazes. It's with candy—whether boxed, bottled, or bowed that we say hello, goodbye, and I'm sorry. There are regional issues, candies that seem at home only in one place and weirdly forbidden in others (you don't eat it at the ballpark, for instance, but on the way there), and of course seasonal candies: Christmas tiffin, Valentine's Day assortments, Thanksgiving mixes, and the diverse quiddities of Easter: spongy chicks, milk-chocolate rabbits, and those monstrositous roclike eggs twilled with piping on the outside and filled with a huge blob of neosaccharine galvaslab! Tastes change, develop, grow fixed. Your aunt likes mints. Old ladies prefer jars of crystallized ginger. Rednecks wolf Bolsters, trollops suck lollipops, college girls opt for berries-in-tins. Truck drivers love to click Gobstoppers around the teeth, pubescents crave sticky sweets, the viler the better, and of course great fat teenage boys, their complexions aflame with pimples and acne, aren't fussy and can gorge down a couple of dollars'

worth of Milky Ways, $100,000 Bars, and forty-eleven liquid cherries at one go!

The novelty factor can't be discounted. The wrapper often memorizes a candy for you; so capitalism, with its Hollywood brain, has devised for us candies in a hundred shapes and shocks—no, I'm not thinking of the comparatively simple Bit-O-Honey, golden lugs on waxed paper, or Little Nips, wax tonic bottles filled with disgustingly sweet liquid, or even the Pez, those little units that, upon being thumbed, dispense one of the most evil-tasting cacochymicals on earth. Buttons-on-paper—a trash candy—is arguably redeemed by inventiveness of vehicle. But here I'm talking about packaging *curiosa*—the real hype! Flying Saucers, for example, a little plasticene capsule with candy twinkles inside! Big Fake Candy Pens, a goofy fountain pen cartridged with tiny pills that taste like canvatex! Razzles ("First It's a Candy, Then It's a Gum")! Bottle Caps ("The Soda Pop Candy")! Candy Rings, a rosary of cement-tasting beads strung to make up a fake watch, the dial of which can be eaten as a final emetic. Rock Candy on a String, blurbed on the box as effective for throat irritation: "Shakespeare in *Henry IV* mentions its therapeutic value." You believe it, right? 12

And then there's the pop group: Astro Pops, an umbrella-shaped sugar candy on a stick: Whistle Pops ("The Lollipop with the Built-in Whistle"); and Ring Pops, cherry- or watermelon-flavored gems on a plastic stick—you suck the jewel. So popular are the fizzing Zotz, the trifling Pixie Stix with its powdered sugar to be lapped out of a straw, the Lik-M-Aid Fun Dip, another do-it-yourself sticklicker, and the explosion candies like Space Dust, Volcano Rocks, and Pop Rocks that candy-store merchants have to keep behind the counter to prevent them from getting nobbled. Still, these pale next to the experience of eating just plain old jimmies (or sprinkles or chocolate shot, depending on where you live), which although generally reserved for, and ancillary to, ice cream, can be deliciously munched by the fistful for a real reward. With jimmies, we enter a new category all its own. M&M's for example: you don't eat them, you mump them. 13

Other mumping candies might be sugar babies, hostia almonds, bridge mixes, burnt peanuts, and pectin jelly beans. (Jelloids in general lend themselves well to the mump.) I don't think Goobers and Raisinets—dull separately—are worth anything unless both are 14 poured into the pocket, commingled, and mumped by the handful at the movies. (The clicking sound they make is surely one of the few pleasures left in life.) This is a family that can also include Pom Poms, Junior Mints, Milk Duds, Boston Baked Beans, Sixlets ("Candy-coated chocolate-flavored candies"—a nice flourish, that), and the disappointingly banal Jujubes—which reminds me. There are certain candies, Jujubes for instance, that one is just too embarrassed to name out loud (forcing one to point through the candy case and simply grunt), and numbered among these must certainly be Nonpareils, Jujufruits, Horehound Drops, and Goldenberg's Peanut Chews. You know what I mean. "Give me a *mrmrglpxph* bar." And you point. Interesting, right?

Interesting. The very word is like a bell that tolls me back to more trenchant observations. Take the Sugar Daddy—it curls up like an elf-shoe after a manly bite and upon being sucked could actually be used for flypaper. (The same might be said for the gummier but more exquisite Bonomo's Turkish Taffy.) The Heath bar—interesting again—a knobby little placket that can be drawn down half-clenched teeth with a slucking sound for an instant chocolate rush, whereupon you're left with a lovely ingot of toffee as a sweet surprise. The flaccid Charleston Chew, warm, paradoxically becomes a proud phallus when cold. (Isn't there a metaphysics in the making here?) Who, until now, has ever given these candies the kind of credit they deserve?

I have my complaints, however, and many of them cross categories. M&M's, for instance, click beautifully but never perspire—it's like eating bits of chrysoprase or sea shingle, you know? Tic Tacs, as well: brittle as gravel and brainless. And while Good 'n' Plenty's are worthy enough mumpers, that little worm of licorice inside somehow puts me off. There is, further, a tactile aspect in candy to be considered. Milk Duds are too nobby and ungeometrical, Junior Mints too relentlessly exact, whereas Reese's Peanut Butter Cups, with their deep-dish delicacy, fascinate me specifically for the strict ribbing around the sides. And then color. The inside of the vapid Three Musketeers bar is the color of wormwood. White bark? Leprosy. Penuche? Death. And then of Hot Tamales, Atom Bombs, cinnamon hearts, and red hots?—swift, slow, sweet, sour, a-dazzle, dim, okay, but personally I think it a matter of breviary that *heat* should have nothing at all to do with candy.

And then Chunkies—tragically, too big for one bite, too little for two. Tootsie Pops are always twiddling off the stick. The damnable tab never works on Hershey Kisses, and it takes a month and two days to open one; even the famous Hershey bar, maddeningly overscored, can never be opened without breaking the bar, and prying is always required to open the ridiculously overglued outer wrapper. (The one with almonds—why?—always slides right out!) And then there are those candies that always promise more than they ever give—the Marathon bar for length, cotton candy for beauty: neither tastes as good as it looks, as no kipper ever tastes as good as it smells; disappointment leads to resentment, and biases form. Jujyfruits—a viscous disaster that is harder than the magnificent British wine-gum (the single greatest candy on earth)—stick in the teeth like tar and have ruined more movies for me than Burt Reynolds, which is frankly going some. And finally Chuckles, father of those respectively descending little clones—spearmint leaves, orange slices, and gum drops—always taste better if dipped in ice water before eating, a want that otherwise keeps sending you to a water fountain for hausts that never seem to end. 17

You may reasonably charge me, in conclusion, with an insensibility for mistreating a particular kind of candy that you, for one reason or another, cherish, or bear me ill will for passing over another without paying it due acknowledgment. But here it's clearly a question of taste, with reasoning generally subjective. Who, after all, can really explain how tastes develop? Where preferences begin? That they exist is sufficient, and fact, I suppose, becomes its own significance. Which leads me to believe that what Dr. Johnson said of Roman Catholics might less stupidly be said of candies: "In every thing in which they differ from us, they are wrong." 18

QUESTIONS FOR READING AND WRITING

1. Theroux's essay is a bit of American nostalgia: the demise of the penny (or nickel, or dime) candy. Has anything else disappeared in your lifetime from the American scene that evokes the same kind of nostalgia?

2. Theroux classifies candies according to several categories: trash, log, peanut, coconut, licorice, pop, mumping. Does he follow any single rule in setting up his categories? Do the allusions to a poem by Gerard Manley Hopkins, "Pied Beauty" (paragraphs 10 and 16), offer any clues as to what seems to be a haphazard system of classification?
3. What is the function of the digression about the candy-store proprietor (paragraph 7)?
4. In the same comic tone as Theroux, subdivide one of the following topics: tourists, elderly drivers, shoppers, audiences at rock concerts, college athletes, nerds, members of health clubs or aerobics classes, boyfriends or girlfriends.

✦ Susan Allen Toth ✦
Cinematypes

Susan Allen Toth teaches English at Macalester College in St. Paul, Minnesota. She has published scholarly articles in The New England Quarterly, Studies in Short Fiction, *and* The American Scholar, *and popular articles in* Harper's, Redbook *and* Ms. *Her first book,* Blooming, *was published in 1981; the sequel,* Ivy Days: Making My Way Out East, *in 1984. "Cinematypes" is a humorous look at how we choose our companions and our entertainment.*

AARON TAKES ME ONLY TO ART FILMS. That's what I call them, anyway: strange movies with vague poetic images I don't always understand, long dreamy movies about a distant Technicolor past, even longer black-and-white movies about the general meaninglessness of life. We do not go unless at least one reputable critic has found the cinematography superb. We went to *The Devil's Eye*, and Aaron turned to me in the middle and said, "My God, this is *funny*." I do not think he was pleased. 1

When Aaron and I go to the movies, we drive our cars separately and meet by the box office. Inside the theater he sits tentatively in his seat, ready to move if he can't see well, poised to leave if the film is disappointing. He leans away from me, careful not to touch the bare flesh of his arm against the bare flesh of mine. Sometimes he leans so far I am afraid he may be touching the woman on his other side. If the movie is very good, he leans forward, too, peering between the heads of the couple in front of us. The light from the screen bounces off his glasses; he gleams with intensity, sitting there on the edge of his seat, watching the screen. Once I tapped him on the arm so I could whisper a comment in his ear. He jumped. 2

After *Belle de Jour* Aaron said he wanted to ask me if he could stay overnight. "But I can't," he shook his head mournfully before I had a chance to answer, "because I know I never sleep well in strange beds." Then he apologized for asking. "It's just that after a film like that," he said, "I feel the need to assert myself." 3

Pete takes me only to movies that he thinks have redeeming social value. He doesn't call them "films." They tend to be about 4 poverty, war, injustice, political corruption, struggling unions in the 1930s, and the military-industrial complex. Pete doesn't like propaganda movies, though, and he doesn't like to be too depressed, either. We stayed away from *The Sorrow and the Pity*; it would be, he said, just too much. Besides, he assured me, things are never that hopeless. So most of the movies we see are made in Hollywood. Because they are always topical, these movies offer what Pete calls "food for thought." When we saw *Coming Home*, Pete's jaw set so firmly with the first half-hour that I knew we would end up at Poppin' Fresh Pies afterward.

When Pete and I go to the movies, we take turns driving so no one owes anyone else anything. We leave the car far from the theater so we don't have to pay for a parking space. If it's raining or snowing, Pete offers to let me off at the door, but I can tell he'll feel better if I go with him while he finds a spot, so we share the walk too. Inside the theater Pete will hold my hand firmly on his knee and cover it completely with his own hand. His knee never twitches. After a while, when the scary part is past, he loosens his hand slightly and I know that is a signal to take mine away. He sits companionably close, letting his jacket just touch my sweater, but he does not infringe. He thinks I ought to know he is there if I need him.

One night, after *The China Syndrome*, I asked Pete if he wouldn't like to stay for a second drink, even though it was past midnight. He thought a while about that, considering my offer from all possible angles, but finally he said no. Relationships today, he said, have a tendency to move too quickly.

Sam likes movies that are entertaining. By that he means movies that Will Jones in the *Minneapolis Tribune* loved and either *Time* or *Newsweek* rather liked; also movies that do not have sappy love stories, are not musicals, do not have subtitles, and will not force him to think. He does not go to movies to think. He liked *California Suite* and *The Seduction of Joe Tynan*, though the plots, he said, could have been zippier. He saw it all coming too far in advance, and that took the fun out. He doesn't like to know what is going to happen. "I just want my brain to be tickled," he says. It is very hard for me to pick out movies for Sam.

When Sam takes me to the movies, he pays for everything. He thinks that's what a man ought to do. But I buy my own popcorn, because he doesn't approve of it; the grease might smear his flannel slacks. Inside the theater, Sam makes himself comfortable. He takes off his jacket, puts one arm around me, and all during the movies he plays with my hand, stroking my palm, beating a small tattoo on my wrist. Although he watches the movie intently, his body operates on instinct. Once I inclined my head and kissed him lightly just behind his ear. He beat a faster tattoo on my wrist, quick and musical, but he didn't look away from the screen.

When Sam takes me home from the movies, he stands outside 9
my door and kisses me long and hard. He would like to come in, he says regretfully, but his steady girlfriend in Duluth wouldn't like it. When the *Tribune* gives a movie four stars, he has to save it to see with her. Otherwise her feelings might be hurt.

I go to some movies by myself. On rainy Sunday afternoons I 10
often sneak into a revival house or a college auditorium for old Technicolor musicals, *Kiss Me Kate, Seven Brides for Seven Brothers, Calamity Jane*, even, once, *The Sound of Music*. Wearing saggy jeans so I can prop my feet on the seat in front, I sit toward the rear where no one will see me. I eat large handfuls of popcorn with double butter. Once the movie starts, I feel completely at home. Howard Keel and I are old friends; I grin back at him on the screen. I know the sound tracks by heart. Sometimes when I get really carried away I hum along with Kathryn Grayson, remembering how I once thought I would fill out a formal like that. I am rather glad now I never did. Skirts whirl, feet tap, acrobatic young men perform impossible feats, and then the camera dissolves into a dream sequence I know I can comfortably follow. It is not, thank God, Bergman.

If I can't find an old musical, I settle for Hepburn and Tracy, 11
vintage Grant or Gable, on adventurous days Claudette Colbert or James Stewart. Before I buy my ticket I make sure it will all end happily. If necessary, I ask the girl at the box office. I have never seen *Stella Dallas* or *Intermezzo*. Over the years I have developed other peccadilloes: I will, for example, see anything that is redeemed by Thelma Ritter. At the end of *Daddy Long Legs* I wait happily for the scene when Fred Clark, no longer angry, at last pours Thelma a convivial drink. They smile at each other, I smile at them, I feel they are smiling at me. In the movies I go to by myself, the men and women always like each other.

QUESTIONS FOR READING AND WRITING

1. Do people's personalities and the movies they enjoy always match? For instance, what kinds of people enjoy horror movies, or escapist adventure movies? Who goes to see fantasy or science-fiction movies?
2. Toth sets up a grid in which her companions are divided by not only the kinds of movies they take her to but also by their behavior before, during, and after the movie. How does their consistency and predictability make the essay funny?
3. A fourth type of moviegoer is represented by Toth herself. How does the final line of the essay make the underlying point? What does she imply has gone wrong with men and women enjoying each other's company? Does the self-centeredness of each companion offer a clue?
4. Take a location that provides a variety of people, such as a concert hall, a sports arena, an airport, a subway car, a bus, a city street, or a beach. Divide the people into types by their appearance, manner, words, and behavior.

Comparison and Contrast

Next to giving examples, *comparison* and *contrast* are two of the most common ways of developing and clarifying a subject. *Comparison* shows the similarities between two or more items in a class or category. For example, you might wish to show how two cars are alike, or two teachers, or two resorts, or two border towns—the list is endless. *Contrast* reveals the differences between selected items of a class or category. In both comparison and contrast, the point is illumination, the attempt to explain a subject by showing how it resembles—or differs from—something else. For example, you might wish to compare the foreign policies of two presidents, or to contrast their domestic policies.

Because the purpose of comparison and contrast is to clarify, to illuminate the subject, both obvious and far-fetched similarities and differences should ordinarily be avoided. It would make little sense, for example, to compare singer Michael Jackson to President George Bush unless you showed that they were both members of some large category—such as "public figures" or "celebrities"—and made some point that linked the two men—such as discussing how they handle threats on their lives.

Once you have your examples in hand, how do you organize a comparison or contrast? Let us return to the earlier hypothetical comparison of the foreign policies of two presidents. Suppose you wish to point out three similarities between the policies of Harry S. Truman and Jimmy Carter: (1) both presidents were confronted with Russian aggression overseas, (2) both contended with a Congress reluctant to assist in implementing their foreign policy, and (3) both were compelled to take unpopular stands on foreign policy issues. No doubt you would want to produce examples to support these similarities, but how should you group this material? The usual methods are called the *unit method* and the *parts method*. In the *unit method*, each item—Truman and Carter—is thought of as a single unit, and all three similarities are discussed in succession, first for one unit, then for the other. Graphically, a unit comparison would look like this:

UNIT METHOD:

Truman	*Carter*
Similarity 1	Similarity 1
Similarity 2	Similarity 2
Similarity 3	Similarity 3

The *parts method* breaks the items into parts (in this case, similarities), discussing first one similarity for each of the units, then another similarity, and so on. A parts comparison would look like this:

PARTS METHOD:

Similarity 1	*Similarity 2*	*Similarity 3*
Truman	Truman	Truman
Carter	Carter	Carter

Neither method is more correct than the other; each has distinct advantages and disadvantages that make it more or less appropriate, depending on your intention. The unit method gives the reader a sense of the complete item in each case, but the comparable or contrasting details may be forgotten unless summary reminders, here and there, recapitulate what went before. The parts method gives a sharper comparison or contrast, but an overall understanding of the items may be lost in its fragmentary approach.

The following selection, which contrasts two different theories about the effectiveness of government monetary and fiscal policies on economic activities, uses the unit method of organizing. Notice how the contrasting characteristics of the Keynesians and the Monetarists are treated in two separate units.

> It's not quite the Montagues and the Capulets, even the Hatfields and the McCoys, again, but a long-time feud has been raging between two prominent "families" of economists.
>
> One clan—the Keynesians, self-styled followers (or disciples) of John Maynard Keynes—argues that money and monetary policy have little or no impact on income and employment, particularly during severe economic downturns; and that government taxation and spending are the most effective remedies for inflation and unemployment, especially the latter.
>
> The other group—the Monetarists, largely rallying around Milton Friedman of the University of Chicago—emphasizes

money's role in the economic process. Spurning the notion that fiscal policy is paramount, they argue that a rule which requires the monetary authorities to cause the stock of money to increase at some constant rate, say 3 percent annually, would effectively reduce fluctuations in prices, output, and employment.*

Many writers mix the two patterns. A writer can present some of the characteristics in unit form and finish up by switching to the parts method. In the short space of this introduction, we can only suggest, how these two patterns can be mixed, but here is a transitional passage from Bruce Catton's essay contrasting the characters of Ulysses S. Grant and Robert E. Lee. The first paragraph sums up the contrasting unit pattern showing the differences between the two Civil War generals; the second paragraph begins the parts pattern that compares the two men.

> So Grant and Lee were in complete contrast, representing two diametrically opposed elements in American life. Grant was the modern man emerging, beyond him, ready to come on the stage, was the great age of steel and machinery, of crowded cities and a restless burgeoning vitality. Lee might have ridden down from the old age of chivalry, lance in hand, silken banner fluttering over his head. Each man the perfect champion of his cause, drawing both his strengths and his weaknesses from the people he led.
>
> Yet it was not all contrast, after all. Different as they were—in background, in personality, in underlying aspiration—these two great soldiers had much in common. Under everything else, they were marvelous fighters. Furthermore, their fighting qualities were really very much alike.†

Like Catton's subjects, many things have *both* similarities and differences; consequently, if it is within your purposes, you can mix comparison with contrast or units with parts.

Successful comparisons and contrasts, then, follow from a clear purpose and a logical plan of organization. Because of their relatively simple design—and perhaps because the human mind delights in noting similarities and differences—comparison and

* J.H. Wood, "Money and Output: Keynes and Friedman in Historical Perspective," *Business Review* (September 1974), 3–4.

† Bruce Catton, "Grant and Lee: A Study in Contrasts," *The American Story*, ed. by Earl Schenck Miers (Channel Press, 1956), 222

contrast essays are particularly versatile and lend themselves to assignments across the curriculum. A science student might want to compare the Ptolemaic and Copernican conceptions of the cosmos. A history student might want to compare the rise of Hitler in Germany with that of Mussolini in Italy. A business student could contrast different methods of motivating workers. A literature student could contrast the tragic downfalls of Macbeth and Othello. Your skill in using comparison and contrast as a developmental technique could prove valuable in a variety of academic contexts.

Two other qualities frequently associated with the comparison and contrast pattern of writing should be noted: it is often linked with other developmental patterns, and it is often used for broadly argumentative purposes. Note that Gloria Steinem uses definition as she contrasts erotica and pornography, and she argues that erotica is intrinsically "healthier" than pornography. Marie Winn analyzes the effects of each activity in contrasting television viewing with reading, and she argues that reading is "better" than watching too much television. This adaptability of comparison and contrast makes it a kind of writing that most writers—student or professional—will often find useful.

✦ Larry L. King ✦

Playing Cowboy

Born and raised in Texas, Larry King (b. 1929) is known primarily as a writer of autobiographical nonfiction. Among his books are Wheeling and Dealing *(1978) and* Of Outlaws, Con Men, Whores, Politicians, and Other Artists *(1980), from which the following essay is taken. In "Playing Cowboy," King attempts to describe his proud but ambivalent attitude toward being a Texan. In doing so, he reveals much about what it means to be a Texan, to be a transplanted Texan, and to live in the gray area between the two.*

WHEN I WAS YOUNG, I didn't know that when you leave a place, it may not be forever. The past, I thought, had served its full uses and could bury its own dead; bridges were for burning; "good-bye" meant exactly what it said. One never looked back except to judge how far one had come. 1

Texas was the place I left behind. And not reluctantly. The leave-taking was so random I trusted the United States Army to relocate me satisfactorily. It did, in 1946, choosing to establish in Queens (then but a five-cent subway ride from the clamorous glamour of Manhattan) a seventeen-year-old former farm boy and small-town sapling green enough to challenge chlorophyll. The assignment would shape my life far more than I then suspected; over the years it would teach me to "play cowboy"—to become, strangely, more "Texas" than I had been. 2

New York offered everything to make an ambitious kid dizzy; I moved through its canyons in a hot walking dream. Looking back, I see myself starring in a bad movie I then accepted as high drama: the Kid, a.k.a. the Bumptious Innocent, discovering the theater, books, a bewildering variety of nightclubs and bars; subways and skyscrapers and respectable wines. There were glancing encounters with Famous Faces: Walter Winchell, the actor Paul Kelly, the ex-heavyweight champion Max Baer, bandleader Stan Kenton. It was easy; spotting them, I simply rushed up, stuck out my hand, sang out my name, and began asking personal questions. 3

Among my discoveries was that I dreaded returning to Texas; where were its excitements, celebrities, promises? As corny as it 4 sounds, one remembers the final scene of that bad movie. Crossing the George Washington Bridge in a Greyhound bus in July 1949—Army discharge papers in my duffel bag—I looked back at Manhattan's spires and actually thought, *I'll be back, New York*. I did not know that scene had been played thousands of times by young men or young women from the provinces, nor did I know that New York cared not a whit whether we might honor the pledge. In time, I got back. On my recent forty-sixth birthday, it dawned that I had spent more than half my life—or twenty-four years—on the eastern seaboard. I guess there's no getting around the fact that this makes me an expatriate Texan.

"Expatriate" remains an exotic word. I think of it as linked to Paris or other European stations in the 1920s: of Sylvia Beach and her famous bookstore; of Hemingway, Fitzgerald, Dos Passos, Ezra Pound, and Gertrude Stein Stein Stein. There is wine in the Paris air, wine and cheese and sunshine, except on rainy days when starving young men in their attics write or paint in contempt of their gut rumbles. Spain. The brave bulls. Dublin's damp fog. Movable feasts. *That's* what "expatriate" means, so how can it apply to one middle-aged grandfather dodging Manhattan's muggers and dog-shit pyramids while grunting a son through boarding school and knocking on the doors of magazine editors? True expatriates, I am certain, do not wait in dental offices, the Port Authority Bus Terminal, or limbo. Neither do they haunt their original root sources three or four times each year, while dreaming of accumulating enough money to return home in style as a gentlemanly rustic combining the best parts of J. Frank Dobie, Lyndon Johnson, Stanley Walker, and the Old Man of the Mountain. Yet that is my story, and that is my plan.

I miss the damned place. Texas is my mind's country, that place I most want to understand and record and preserve. Four generations of my people sleep in its soil; I have children there, and a grandson; the dead past and the living future tie me to it. Not that I always approve it or love it. It vexes and outrages and disappoints me—especially when I am there. It is now the third most urbanized state, behind New York and California, with all the tangles, stench, random violence, architectural rape, historical pillage, neon blight, pollution, and ecological imbalance the term implies. Money and mindless growth remain high on the list of official priorities, breeding a crass boosterism not entirely papered over by an infectious energy. The state legislature—though improving as slowly as an old man's mending bones—still harbors excessive, coon-ass, rural Tory Democrats who fail to understand that 79.7 percent of Texans have flocked to urban areas and may need fewer farm-to-market roads, hide-and-tick inspectors, or outraged oration almost comically declaiming against welfare loafers, creeping socialism, the meddling ol' feds, and sin in the aggregate.

Too much, now, the Texas landscape sings no native notes. The 7
impersonal, standardized superhighways—bending around or by most small towns, and then blatting straightaway toward the urban sprawls—offer homogenized service stations, fast-food-chain outlets, and cluttered shopping centers one might find duplicated in Ohio, Maryland, Illinois, or Anywhere, U.S.A. Yes, there is much to make me protest, as did Mr. Faulkner's Quentin Compson, of the South—"I *don't* hate it. I don't hate it, I *don't* . . ." For all its shrinkages of those country pleasures I once eschewed, and now covet and vainly wish might return, Texas remains in my mind's eye that place to which I shall eventually return to rake the dust for my formative tracks; that place where one hopes to grow introspective and wise as well as old. It is a romantic foolishness, of course; the opiate dream of a nostalgia junkie. When I go back to stay—and I fancy that I will—there doubtless will be opportunities to wonder at my plan's imperfections.

For already I have created in my mind, you see, an improbable 8
corner of paradise: the rustic, rambling ranch house with the clear-singing creek nearby, the clumps of shade trees (under which, possibly, the Sons of the Pioneers will play perpetual string-band concerts), the big cozy library where I will work and read and cogitate between issuing to the Dallas *Times-Herald* or the Houston *Post* those public pronouncements befitting an Elder Statesman of Life and Letters. I will become a late-blooming naturalist and outdoorsman: hiking and camping, and piddling in cattle; never mind that to date I have preferred the sidewalks of New York, and my beef not on the hoof but tricked up with mushroom sauces.

All this will occur about one easy hour out of Austin—my favorite 9
Texas city—and exactly six miles from a tiny, unnamed town looking remarkably like what Walt Disney would have built for a cheery, heart-tugging Texas-based story happening about 1940. The nearest

neighbor will live 3.7 miles away, have absolutely no children or dogs, but will have one beautiful young wife, who adores me; it is she who will permit me, by her periodic attentions, otherwise to live the hermit's uncluttered life. Politicians will come to my door hats in hand, and fledgling Poets and young Philosophers. Basically, they will want to know exactly what is Life's Purpose. Looking out across the gently blowing grasslands, past the grazing blooded cattle, toward a perfect sunset, with even the wind in my favor, and being the physical reincarnation of Hemingway with a dash of Twain in my mood, I shall—of course—be happy to tell them.

Well, we all know that vast gap between fantasy and reality when True Life begins playing the scenario. Likely I will pay twice to thrice the value for a run-down old "farmhouse" where the plumbing hasn't worked since Coolidge, and shall die of a heart attack while digging a cesspool. The nearest neighbor will live directly across the road; he will own seven rambunctious children, five mad dogs, and an ugly harridan with sharp elbows, a shrill voice, and a perverse hatred for dirty old writing men. The nearest town—less than a half mile away and growing by leaps, separated from my digs only by a subdivision of mock Bavarian castles and the new smeltering plant—will be made of plastics, paved parking lots, and puppy-dog tails. The trip to Austin will require three hours if one avoids rush-hour crushes; when I arrive—to preen in Scholz Garten or The Raw Deal or other watering holes where artists congregate—people will say, "Who's that old fart?" Unfortunately I may try to tell them. My books will long have been out of print; probably my secret yearning will be to write a column for the local weekly newspaper. Surrounded by strangers, memories, and galloping growth, I shall sit on my porch—rocking and cackling and talking gibberish to the wind—while watching them build yet another Kwik Stop Kwality Barbecue Pit on the west edge of my crowded acreage. Occasionally I will walk the two dozen yards to the interstate highway to throw stones at passing trucks; my ammunition will peter out long before traffic does. But when I die digging that cesspool, by God, I'll have died at home. That knowledge makes me realize where my heart is.

But the truth, dammit, is that I feel much more the Texan when in the East. New Yorkers, especially, encourage and expect one to perform a social drill I think of as "playing cowboy." Even as a young soldier I discovered a presumption among a high percentage of New Yorkers that my family owned shares in the King Ranch and that my natural equestrian talents were unlimited; all one needed to affirm such groundless suspicions were a drawl and a grin. To this day you may spot me in Manhattan wearing boots and denim jeans with a matching vest and western-cut hat—topped by a furry cattleman's coat straight out of Marlboro Country; if you've seen Dennis Weaver play McCloud, then you've seen me, without my beard.

Never mind that I *like* such garb, grew up wearing it, or that I find it natural, practical, and inexpensive; no, to a shameful degree, I dress for my role. When I learned that Princeton University would pay good money to a working writer for teaching his craft—putting insulated students in touch with the workaday salts and sours of the literary world—do you think I went down there wrapped in an ascot and puffing a briar pipe from Dunhill's? No, good neighbors, I donned my Cowboy Outfit to greet the selection committee and aw-shucksed and consarned 'em half to death; easterners just can't resist a John Wayne quoting Shakespeare; I've got to admit there's satisfaction in it for every good ol' boy who country-slicks the city dudes. 12

New Yorkers tend to think of Mississippians or Georgians or Virginians under the catchall category of "southerners," of Californians as foreigners, and of Texans as the legendary Texan. We are the only outlanders, I think, that they define within a specific state border and assign the burden of an obligatory—i.e., "cowboy"—culture. Perhaps we court such treatment; let it be admitted that Texans are a clannish people. We tend to think of ourselves as Texans no matter how long ago we strayed or how tenuous our home connections. When I enter a New York store and some clerk—alerted by my nasal twang—asks where I am from, I do not answer "East Thirty-second Street," but "Texas," yet my last permanent address there was surrendered when Eisenhower was freshly President and old George Blanda was little more than a rookie quarterback. 13

More than half my close friends—and maybe 20 percent of my overall eastern seaboard acquaintances—are expatriate Texans: writers, musicians, composers, editors, lawyers, athletes, showfolk, a few businessmen, and such would-be politicians or former politi- 14 cians as Bill Moyers and Ramsey Clark. Don Meredith, Liz Smith, Judy Buie, Dan Jenkins, you name 'em, and to one degree or another we play cowboy together. Many of us gather for chili suppers, tell stories with origins in Fort Worth or Odessa or Abilene; sometimes we even play dominoes or listen to country-western records.

There is, God help us, an organization called The New York Texans, and about 2,000 of us actually belong to it. We meet each March 2—Texas Independence Day—to drink beer, hoo-haw at each other in the accents of home, and honor some myth that we can, at best, only ill define. We even have our own newspaper, published quarterly by a lady formerly of Spur, Texas, which largely specializes in stories bragging on how well we've done in the world of the Big Apple. Since people back home are too busy to remind us of our good luck and talents, we remind ourselves.

No matter where you go, other Texans discover you. Sometimes they are themselves expatriates, sometimes tourists, sometimes business-bent travelers. In any case, we whoop a mutual recognition, even though we're strangers or would be unlikely to attract each other if meeting within our native borders. Indeed, one of the puzzling curiosities is why the Dallas banker, or the George Wallace fanatic who owns the little drygoods store in Beeville, and I may drop all prior plans in order to spend an evening together in Monterrey or Oshkosh when—back home—we would consider each other social lepers. Many times I have found myself buddy-buddying with people not all that likable or interesting, sharing Aggie jokes or straight tequila shots or other peculiarities of home.

If you think that sounds pretty dreadful, it often is. Though I am outraged when called a "professional Texan," or when I meet one, certainly I am not always purely innocent. Much of it is a big put-on, of course. We enjoy sharing put-ons against those who expect all Texans to eat with the wrong fork, offer coarse rebel yells, and get all vomity-drunk at the nearest football game. There is this regional defensiveness—LBJ would have known what I mean—leading us to order "a glass of clabber and a mess of chitlins" when faced by the haughty ministrations of the finest French restaurants. (My group does, anyway, though I don't know about the stripe of Texan epitomized, say, by Rex Reed; that bunch has got so smooth you can't see behind the sheen). I hear my Texas friends, expatriates and otherwise, as their accents thicken and their drawls slow down on approaching representatives of other cultures. I observe them as they attempt to come on more lordly and sophisticated than Dean Acheson or more country than Ma and Pa Kettle, depending on what they feel a need to prove.

That they (or I) need to prove anything is weird in itself. It tells 18
you what they—yes, the omnipotent They—put in our young Texas heads. The state's history is required teaching in the public schools, and no student by law may escape the course. They teach Texas history very much fumigated—the Alamo's martyrs, the Indian-killing frontiersmen, the heroic Early Day Pioneers, the Rugged Plainsmen, the Builders and Doers; these had hearts pure where others were soiled—and they teach it and teach it and teach it. I came out of the public schools of Texas knowing naught of Disraeli, Darwin, or Darrow—though well versed in the lore of Sam Houston, Stephen F. Austin, Jim Bowie, the King Ranch, the Goodnight-Loving Trail over which thundered the last of the big herds. No school day was complete but that we sang "The Eyes of Texas," "Texas Our Texas," "Beautiful Texas." I mean, try substituting "Rhode Island" or "North Dakota," and it sounds about half-silly even to a Texan. We were taught again and again that Texas was the biggest state, one of the richest, possibly the toughest, surely the most envied. Most Americans, I guess, grow up convinced that their little corners of the universe are special; Texas, however, takes care to institutionalize the preachment.

To discover a wider world, then, where others fail to hold those 19
views—to learn that Texans are thought ignorant or rich or quite often both, though to the last in number capable of sitting a mean steed—is to begin at once a new education and feel sneaky compulsions toward promoting useless old legends. Long after I knew that the Texas of my youth dealt more with myth than reality, and long past that time when I knew that the vast majority of Texans lived in cities, I continued to play cowboy. This was a social and perhaps a professional advantage in the East; it marked one as unique, permitted one to pose as a son of yesterday, furnished a handy identity among the faceless millions. In time one has a way of becoming in one's head something of the role one has assumed. Often I have actually felt myself the reincarnation or the extension of the old range lords or bedroll cowpokes or buffalo hunters. Such playacting

is harmless so long as one confines it to wearing costumes or to speech patterns—"I'm a-hankerin' for a beefsteak, y'all, and thank I'll mosey on over to P. J. Clarke's"—but becomes counterproductive unless regulated. Nobody has been able to coax me atop a horse since that day a dozen years ago when I proved to be the most comic equestrian ever to visit a given riding stable on Staten Island. Misled by my range garb, accent, and sunlamp tan, the stable manager assigned what surely must have been his most spirited steed. Unhorsed after much graceless grabbing and grappling, I heard my ride described by a laughing fellow with Brooklyn in his voice: "Cheeze, at foist we thought youse was a trick rider. But just before youse fell, we seen youse wasn't nothing but a shoemaker."

Though I wear my Texas garb in Texas, I am more the New Yorker there; not so much in my own mind, perhaps, as in the minds of others. People hold me to account for criticisms I've written of Texas or accuse me of having gone "New York" in my thinking or attitudes. "Nobody's more parochial than a goddamn New Yorker," some of my friends snort—and often they are right. I, too, feel outraged at Manhattan cocktail parties when some clinch-jawed easterner makes it clear he thinks that everything on the wrong side of the George Washington Bridge is quaint, hasn't sense enough to come in from the rain, and maybe lacks toilet training. Yet my Texas friends have their own misconceptions of my adopted home and cause me to defend it. They warn of its violent crime, even though Houston annually vies with Detroit for the title of "Murder Capital of the World." They deride New York's slums and corruptions, even though in South El Paso (and many another Texas city) may be found shameful dirt poverty and felonious social neglect, and Texas erupts in its own political Watergates—banking, insurance, real estate scandals—at least once each decade. So I find myself in the peculiar defense of New York, waving my arms, and my voice growing hotter, saying things like "You goddamn Texans gotta learn that you're not so damned special . . ." *You* goddamn Texans, now.

My friends charge that despite my frequent visits home and my summering on Texas beaches, my view of the place is hopelessly outdated. Fletcher Boone, an Austin artist and entrepreneur—now owner of The Raw Deal—was the latest to straighten out my thinking. "All you goddamn expatriates act like time froze somewhere in the nineteen-fifties or earlier," he said. "You'd think we hadn't discovered television down here, or skin flicks, or dope. Hell, we grew us a *President* down here. We've got tall buildings and long hairs and some of us know how to ski!" Mr. Boone had recently visited New York and now held me to account for its sins: "It's mental masturbation. You go to a party up there, and instead of people making real conversation, they stop the proceedings so somebody can sing opera or play the piano or do a tap dance. It's show biz, man—buncha egomaniacal people using a captive audience to stroke themselves. Whatta they talk about? 'I, I, I. Me, me, me. Mine, mine, mine.'" Well, no, I rebut; they also talk about books, politics, and even *ideas*; only the middle of these, I say, is likely to be remarked in Texas. Boone is offended; he counterattacks that easterners do not live life so much as they attempt to dissect it or, worse, dictate how others should live it by the manipulations of fashion, art, the media. We shout gross generalities, overstatements, "facts" without support. I become the Visiting Smart-ass New Yorker, losing a bit of my drawl.

Well, bless him, there may be something to Fletcher Boone's charge, I found recently when I returned as a quasi sociologist. It was my plan to discover some young, green blue-collar or white-collar, recently removed to the wicked city from upright rural upbringings, and record that unfortunate hick's slippages or shocks. Then I would return to the hick's small place of origin, comparing what he or she had traded for a mess of modern city pottage; family graybeards left behind would be probed for their surrogate shocks and would reveal their fears for their urbanized young. It would be a whiz of a story, having generational gaps and cultural shocks and more disappointments or depletions than the Nixon White House. It would be at once nostalgic, pitiful, and brave; one last angry shout against modernity before Houston sinks beneath the waves, Lubbock dries up and blows away for lack of drinking water, and Dallas-Fort Worth grows together as firmly as Siamese twins. Yes, it would have everything but three tits and, perhaps, originality. 22

Telephone calls to old friends produced no such convenient study. Those recommended turned out to have traveled abroad, attended college in distant places, or otherwise been educated by an urban, mobile society. A young airline hostess in Houston talked mainly of San Francisco or Hawaii; a bank clerk in Dallas sniggered 23 that even in high school days he had spent most of his weekends away from his native village—in city revelry—and thought my idea of "cultural shock" quaint; a petrochemical plant worker failed to qualify when he said, "Shit, life's not all that much different. I live here in Pasadena"—an industrial morass with all the charms and odors of Gary, Indiana—"and I go to my job, watch TV, get drunk with my buddies. Hail, it's not no different from what it was back there in Monahans. Just more traffic and more people and a little less sand." I drove around the state for days, depressed by the urbanization of my former old outback even as I marveled at its energy, before returning to New York, where I might feel, once more, like a Texan: where I might play cowboy; dream again the ancient dreams.

It is somehow easier to conjure up the Texas I once knew from Manhattan. What an expatriate most remembers are not the hard-scrabble times of the 1930s, or the narrow attitudes of a people not then a part of the American mainstream, but a way of life that was passing without one's then realizing it. Quite without knowing it, I witnessed the last of the region's horse culture. Schoolboys tied their mounts to mesquite trees west of the Putnam school and at noon fed them bundled roughage; the pickup truck and the tractor had not yet clearly won out over the horse, though within the decade they would. While the last of the great cattle herds had long ago disappeared up the Chisholm or the Goodnight-Loving Trail, I would see small herds rounded up on my Uncle Raymond's Bar-T-Bar Ranch and loaded from railside corrals for shipment to the stockyards of Fort Worth—or "Cowtown," as it was then called without provoking smiles. (The rough-planked saloons of the brawling North Side of "Cowtown," near the old stockyards, are gone now save for a small stretch lacquered and refurbished in a way so as to make tourists feel they've been where they ain't.) In Abilene, only thirty-two miles to the west, I would hear the chants of cattle auctioneers while smelling feedlot dung, tobacco, saddle leather, and the sweat of men living the outdoor life. Under the watchful eye of my father, I sometimes rode a gentle horse through the shinnery and scrub oaks of the old family farm, helping him bring in the five dehorned milk cows while pretending to be a bad-assed gunslinger herding longhorns on a rank and dangerous trail drive.

But it was all maya, illusion. Even a dreaming little tad knew the buffalo hunters were gone, along with the old frontier forts, the Butterfield stage, the first sodbusters whose barbed wire fenced in the open range and touched off wars continuing to serve Clint Eastwood or James Arness. This was painful knowledge for one succored on myths and legends, on real-life tales of his father's boyhood peregrinations in a covered wagon. Nothing of my original time and place, I felt, would be worth living through or writing about. What I did not then realize (and continue having trouble remembering) is that the past never was as good as it looks from a distance. 25

The expatriate, returning, thus places an unfair burden upon his native habitat: He demands it to have impossibly marked time, to have marched in place, during the decades he has absented himself. He expects it to have preserved itself as his mind recalls it; to furnish evidence that he did not memorize in vain its legends, folk and folklore, mountains and streams and villages. Never mind that he may have removed himself to other places because they offered rapid growth, new excitements, and cultural revolutions not then available at home. 26

We expatriate sons may sometimes be unfair: too critical; fail to give due credit; employ the double standard. Especially do those of us who write flay Texas in the name of our disappointments and melted snows. Perhaps it's good that we do this, the native press being so boosterish and critically timid; but there are times, I suspect, when our critical duty becomes something close to a perverse pleasure. Easterners I have known, visiting my homeplace, come away impressed by its dynamic qualities; they see a New Frontier growing in my native bogs, a continuing spirit of adventure, a bit of trombone and swashbuckle, something fresh and good. Ah, but they did not know Texas when she was young. 27

There is a poignant tale told by the writer John Graves of the last, tamed remnants of a formerly free and proud Indian tribe in Texas: how a small band of them approached an old rancher, begged a scrawny buffalo bull from him, and—spurring their thin ponies—clattered and whooped after it, running it ahead of them, and killed it in the old way—with lances and arrows. They were foolish, I guess, in trying to hold history still for one more hour; 28

probably I'm foolish in the same sentimental way when I sneak off the freeways to snake across the Texas back roads in search of my own past. But there are a couple of familiar stretches making the ride worth it; I most remember one out in the lonely windblown ranch country, between San Angelo and Water Valley, with small rock-dotted hills ahead at the end of a long, flat stretch of road bordered by grasslands, random clumps of trees, wild flowers, grazing cattle, a single distant ranch house whence—one fancies—issues the perfume of baking bread, simmering beans, beef over the flames. There are no billboards, no traffic cloverleafs, no neon, no telephone poles, no Jiffy Tacos or Stuckey's stands, no oil wells, no Big Rich Bastards, no ship channels threatening to ignite because of chemical pollutions, no Howard Johnson flavors. Though old Charley Goodnight lives, Lee Harvey Oswald and Charles Whitman remain unborn.

Never have I rounded the turn leading into that peaceful valley, with the spiny ridge of hills beyond it, that I failed to feel new surges and exhilarations and hope. For a precious few moments I exist in a time warp: I'm back in Old Texas, under a high sky, where all things are again possible and the wind blows free. Invariably, I put the heavy spurs to my trusty Hertz or Avis steed: go flying lickety-split down that lonesome road, whooping a crazy yell and taking deep joyous breaths, sloshing Lone Star beer on my neglected dangling safety belt, and scattering roadside gravel like bursts of buckshot. Ride 'im, cowboy! *Ride* 'im . . .

QUESTIONS FOR READING AND WRITING

1. In what ways—negative and positive—does King's description of the Texan stereotype agree with your own preconceptions about Texans?
2. What principal contrasts does King draw between Texans and New Yorkers?
3. Reexamine paragraph 10 of King's essay. Give examples of how his use of language creates a kind of "down home" flavor.
4. What kinds of values, dreams, and aspirations does King have in mind when, in his last paragraph, he refers to "Old Texas"?
5. Write an essay in which you attempt to describe what it feels like to go "home" after a long absence.
6. Compare or contrast two places where you have lived. Concentrate, for example, on the landscape, the people, or your residences.

✦ Melvin J. Konner ✦
The Aggressors

Melvin J. Konner (b. 1946), biologist, anthropologist, and educator, teaches at Emory University in Georgia. His book The Tangled Wing: Biological Constraints on the Human Spirit *(1982) was nominated for an American Book Award. In "The Aggressors," Konner shows what some recent studies reveal about a major difference between the sexes: testosterone levels.*

DR. DAN OLWEUS KNOWS THE BULLIES in Norway; at least those 8 to 16 years old in a population of 140,000 in 715 public schools. Olweus, a professor of psychology at the University of Bergen, was asked by the Norwegian Government to get a handle on the bullying problem. Concluding his recent study, he estimates that of the 568,000 Norwegian schoolchildren, 41,000 or 7 percent, bully others regularly. The bullies were far more likely to be male: more than 60 percent of the girls and 80 percent of the boys victimized in grades 5 to 7 were bullied by males. The tendency of girls to bully declined with age; in boys, it rose: a twofold difference in the second grade widens to fivefold in the ninth. 1

Many studies, even of remote, primitive societies, show that males predominate overwhelmingly in physical violence. Pick your behavior: grabbing and scratching in toddlers, wrestling and chasing in nursery-school children, contact sports among teen-agers, violent crime in adulthood, tank maneuvers in real, grown-up wars. In 1986, Alice H. Eagly and Valerie J. Steffen, then of Purdue University, published a survey of 63 psychological studies. They emphasized that no category existed in which women were more aggressive than men, and they said the tendency to produce pain or physical injury was far more pronounced in men. Joining a distinguished line of social and psychological researchers, Eagly and Steffen concluded that these differences "are learned as aspects of gender roles and other social roles." 2

That belief, a tenacious modern myth, becomes less justified with every passing year: sex difference in the tendency to do physical harm is intrinsic, fundamental, natural—in a word, biological. 3

Olweus, in a smaller study—one of scores contributing to this new conclusion—selected 58 boys aged 15 through 17 and compared blood levels of testosterone, the male sex hormone, to aggression. He found a strong effect of testosterone on intolerance for frustration and response to provocation. The puzzle of aggression is not yet solved, but it seems increasingly apparent that testosterone is a key. However, it is testosterone circulating not only post-pubertally, as has been commonly thought, but also during early development—specifically, during fetal life, at the stage when the brain is forming. The first clues to this process came from animal studies. In 1973, G. Raisman and P.M. Field reported a significant sex difference in a part of the rat's brain known as the preoptic area—a region that, in females, helps control the reproductive cycle; certain brain-cell connections in this area were more numerous in females. Most interestingly, castration of males at birth, or early treatment of females with testosterone, abolished the adult brain difference.

This was the first of many similar studies showing that the differentiation not only of the brain, but of behavior—especially sexual and aggressive behavior—depends in part on early testosterone exposure. This has proved to be true of rats, mice, hamsters, rabbits and monkeys, among other species. Clear anatomical differences have been found in the hypothalmus and amygdala regions of the brain as well as the preoptic area.

One ingenious study showed that the tendency to fight in adult mice, although greater by far in males, differs among females, depending on whether they spent their fetal life near males or other females in the womb. Females with males on each side in utero grew up to be fighters, but those with only one adjacent male were less pugnacious as adults. Those flanked by two other females in the womb became the least aggressive adults. Separate evidence indicated that the three groups of females also differed in their degree of exposure to intrauterine testosterone—which had evidently come from the blood of the nearby males.

No experimental evidence is available for humans, of course, but some clinical studies are suggestive. Sometimes human fetuses are exposed to hormones that have effects similar to those of testosterone—for example, synthetic progestins, used to maintain pregnancy. June M. Reinisch, now director of the Kinsey Institute, studied 25 girls and boys with a history of such exposure and found them more aggressive than their same-sex siblings, as indicated by a paper-and-pencil test. This finding was in line with studies of monkeys and other animals exposed to male sex hormones in utero. Females with such exposure engaged in more rough-and-tumble play during development than other females. As in the human study, the differences became apparent before puberty.

Some years ago, there was a bitter controversy over whether men with an extra male-determining Y chromosome—the XYZ syndrome—were hypermasculine. One not-so-subtle humorist wrote in to Science that it was silly to get so excited over the extremely rare XYZ syndrome, when 49 percent of the species was already afflicted with the XY syndrome—an uncontroversial disorder known to cause hyperactivity and learning disabilities in childhood, premature mortality in adulthood and an egregious tendency to irrational violence throughout life. "Testosterone poisoning," a colleague of mine calls it. 8

Is there no contribution of culture, then, to the consistent male excess in violence? Of course there is; but it acts on an organism already primed for the sex difference. Cultures can dampen it or exaggerate it. The role of modeling in encouraging aggression is well proved. Give a girl a steady diet of Wonder Woman and lady wrestlers while her brother gets Mr. Rogers, and you may well push them past each other on the continuum. But we now have a pretty good answer to Margaret Mead's famous question: What if an average boy and an average girl were raised in exactly similar environments? We don't know, she said. Now we do. The boy would hit, kick, wrestle, scratch, grab, shove and bite more than the girl and be more likely to commit a violent crime later in life. 9

Mead became famous for her elegant demonstrations of cultural variation in sex roles. Among the Tchambuli, a New Guinea fishing society, the women, "brisk, unadorned, managing and industrious, fish and go to market; the men, decorative and adorned, carve and paint the practice dance steps." Among the Mundugumor, river-dwelling cannibals, also in New Guinea, "the women are as assertive and vigorous as the men; they detest bearing and rearing children, and provide most of the food. . . . " These quotations from her 1949 book "Male and Female" helped provide the basis for the modern conception of the tremendous flexibility of sex roles—as well they should have. But the Tchambuli men, when they finished 10 their dance steps, went headhunting. And note that Mead's own words following her often-cited quote on the Mundugumor are: "*leaving the men free to plot and fight.*" In every known society, homicidal violence, whether spontaneous and outlawed or organized and sanctioned for military purposes, is committed overwhelmingly by men.

The conclusion would seem to be that women should run the world. If we can agree that the greatest threat to human survival over the long haul is posed by human violence itself, then the facts of human violence—the sex difference, and its biological basis—can lead nowhere else. But what of Margaret Thatcher, Indira Gandhi, Golda Meir; what of Catherine the Great and Elizabeth I, in earlier eras? They are no use as test cases. All were women who had clambered to the tops of relentlessly male political and military hierarchies. They could scarcely restrain the surges of all those millions of gallons of testosterone continually in flux under their scepters. And again: the categories overlap; the consistent differences are in averages. The gauntlets those five women ran to get to the top and stay there can scarcely be said to have been at the least-aggressive end of the female spectrum. And women in a male world often find themselves outmachoing the men—to gain credibility, to consolidate power, to survive.

Those negative examples notwithstanding, a steady, massive infusion of women into positions of power, in a balanced way, throughout the world, should in fact reduce the risk that irrational factors—"Come on, make my day" sorts of factors—will bring about an end to life on earth. Political scientists and historians often argue as if there were no resemblance between fistfights and war. Anthropologists and biologists know better.

Interestingly, that same Norway that sent Dan Olweus off to study—and try to diminish—bullying, appears to be in the vanguard. Not only the Prime Minister, but 8 of the 18 members of the Cabinet, are currently free of testosterone poisoning. In an almost-all-male, consistently violent world of national governments, this little boat of the Norwegian Cabinet may run into some high seas. But it is a far cry from the Viking ships of yore, and I, for one, am keeping a hopeful eye on its prow.

QUESTIONS FOR READING AND WRITING

1. In Konner's essay, what two things are being compared?
2. Konner's essay cites biological differences based on differing levels of testosterone. What other physical differences distinguish the sexes? What are the practical consequences, in our culture, of these differences?
3. How valid is Konner's conclusion that, because of men's greater aggressiveness, women should ideally have more power in government?
4. In paragraph 9, Konner states that "cultures can dampen [the male excess in violence] or exaggerate it." What does he mean by this? Can you think of ways in which our society dampens or exaggerates the male tendency to violence?
5. Write a character sketch or anecdote about a notable bully, male or female, that you have known.
6. Write an essay that distinguishes between aggressiveness and assertiveness.
7. Write an essay detailing some of the predictable problems a male nurse or a female police officer might have. Try to use some of the ideas expressed in Konner's essay.

✦ Phyllis Rose ✦

Tools of Torture

An Essay on Beauty and Pain

Since 1969, Phyllis Rose (b. 1942) has been a member of the English Department at Wesleyan University in Middletown, Connecticut. Her most famous book, Parallel Lives: Five Victorian Marriages, *appeared in 1983. She is also the author of* Writing of Women *(1985). In the following essay, she comments on the disturbing "institution" of human torture, which she calls "the dark side of sensuality."*

IN A GALLERY off the rue Dauphine, near the *parfumerie* where I get my massage, I happened upon an exhibit of medieval torture instruments. It made me think that pain must be as great a challenge to the human imagination as pleasure. Otherwise there's no accounting for the number of torture instruments. One would be quite enough. The simple pincer, let's say, which rips out flesh. Or the head crusher, which breaks first your tooth sockets, then your skull. But in addition I saw tongs, thumbscrews, a rack, a ladder, ropes and pulleys, a grill, a garrote, a Spanish horse, a Judas cradle, an iron maiden, a cage, a gag, a strappado, a stretching table, a saw, a wheel, a twisting stork, an inquisitor's chair, a breast breaker, and a scourge. You don't need complicated machinery to cause incredible pain. If you want to saw your victim down the middle, for example, all you need is a slightly bigger than usual saw. If you hold the victim upside down so the blood stays in his head, hold his legs apart, and start sawing at the groin, you can get as far as the navel before he loses consciousness.

Even in the Middle Ages, before electricity, there were many things you could do to torment a person. You could tie him up in an iron belt that held the arms and legs up to the chest and left no point of rest, so that all his muscles went into spasm within minutes and he was driven mad within hours. This was the twisting stork, a benign-looking object. You could stretch him out backward over a thin piece of wood so that his whole body weight rested on his spine, which pressed against the sharp wood. Then you could stop up his nostrils and force water into his stomach through his mouth. Then, if you wanted to finish him off, you and your helper could jump on his stomach, causing internal hemorrhage. This torture was called the rack. If you wanted to burn someone to death without hearing him scream, you could use a tongue lock, a metal rod between the jaw and collarbone that prevented him from opening his mouth. You could put a person in a chair with spikes on the seat and arms, tie him down against the spikes, and beat him, so that every time he flinched from the beating he drove his own flesh deeper onto the spikes. This was the inquisitor's chair. If you wanted to make it worse, you could heat the spikes. You could suspend a person over a pointed wooden pyramid and whenever he started to fall asleep, you could drop him onto the point. If you were Ippolito Marsili, the inventor of this torture, known as the Judas cradle, you could tell yourself you had invented something humane, a torture that worked without burning flesh or breaking bones. For the torture here was supposed to be sleep deprivation.

The secret of torture, like the secret of French cuisine, is that nothing is unthinkable. The human body is like a foodstuff, to be grilled, pounded, filleted. Every opening exists to be stuffed, all flesh to be carved off the bone. You take an ordinary wheel, a heavy wooden wheel with spokes. You lay the victim on the ground with blocks of wood at strategic points under his shoulders, legs, and arms. You use the wheel to break every bone in his body. Next you tie his body onto the wheel. With all its bones broken, it will be pliable. However, the victim will not be dead. If you want to kill him, you hoist the wheel aloft on the end of a pole and leave him to starve. Who would have thought to do this with a man and a wheel? But, then, who would have thought to take the disgusting snail, force it to render its ooze, stuff it in its own shell with garlic butter, bake it, and eat it? 3

Not long ago I had a facial—only in part because I thought I needed one. It was research into the nature and function of pleasure. In a dark booth at the back of the beauty salon, the aesthetician put me on a table and applied a series of ointments to my face, some cool, some warmed. After a while she put something into my hand, cold and metallic. "Don't be afraid, madame," she said. "It is an electrode. It will not hurt you. The other end is attached to two metal cylinders, which I roll over your face. They break down the 4 electricity barrier on your skin and allow the moisturizers to penetrate deeply." I didn't believe this hocus-pocus. I didn't believe in the electricity barrier or in the ability of these rollers to break it down. But it all felt very good. The cold metal on my face was a pleasant change from the soft warmth of the aesthetician's fingers. Still, since Algeria it's hard to hear the word "electrode" without fear. So when she left me for a few minutes with a moist, refreshing cheesecloth over my face, I thought, What if the goal of her expertise had been pain, not moisture? What if the electrodes had been electrodes in the Algerian sense? What if the cheesecloth mask were dipped in acid?

In Paris, where the body is so pampered, torture seems particularly sinister, not because it's hard to understand but because—as the dark side of sensuality—it seems so easy. Beauty care is among the glories of Paris. *Soins esthétiques* include makeup, facials, massages (both relaxing and reducing), depilations (partial and complete), manicures, pedicures, and tanning, in addition to the usual run of *soins* for the hair: cutting, brushing, setting, waving, styling, blowing, coloring, and streaking. In Paris the state of your skin, hair, and nerves is taken seriously, and there is little of the puritanical thinking that tries to persuade us that beauty comes from within. Nor do the French think, as Americans do, that beauty should be offhand and low-maintenance. Spending time and money on *soins esthétiques* is appropriate and necessary, not self-indulgent. Should that loving attention to the body turn malevolent, you have torture. You have the procedure—the aesthetic, as it were—of torture, the explanation for the rich diversity of torture instruments, but you do not have the cause.

Historically torture has been a tool of legal systems, used to get information needed for a trial or, more directly, to determine guilt or innocence. In the Middle Ages confession was considered the best of all proofs, and torture was the way to produce a confession. In other words, torture didn't come into existence to give vent to human sadism. It is not always private and perverse but sometimes social and institutional, vetted by the government and, of course, the Church. (There have been few bigger fans of torture than Christianity and Islam.) Righteousness, as much as viciousness, produces torture. There aren't squads of sadists beating down the doors to the torture chambers begging for jobs. Rather, as a recent book on torture by Edward Peters says, the institution of torture creates sadists; the weight of a culture, Peters suggests, is necessary to recruit torturers. You have to convince people that they are working for a great goal in order to get them to overcome their repugnance to the task of causing physical pain to another person. Usually the great goal is the preservation of society, and the victim is presented to the torturer as being in some way out to destroy it.

From another point of view, what's horrifying is how easily you can persuade someone that he is working for the common good. Perhaps the most appalling psychological experiment of modern times, by Stanley Milgram, showed that ordinary, decent people in New Haven, Connecticut, could be brought to the point of inflicting (as they thought) severe electric shocks on other people in obedience to an authority and in pursuit of a goal, the advancement of knowledge, of which they approved. Milgram used—some would say abused—the prestige of science and the university to make his point, but his point is chilling nonetheless. We can cluck over torture, but the evidence at least suggests that with intelligent handling most of us could be brought to do it ourselves. 7

In the Middle Ages, Milgram's experiment would have had no point. It would have shocked no one that people were capable of cruelty in the interest of something they believed in. That was as it should be. Only recently in the history of human thought has the avoidance of cruelty moved to the forefront of ethics. "Putting cruelty first," as Judith Shklar says in *Ordinary Vices*, is comparatively new. The belief that the "pursuit of happiness" is one of man's inalienable rights, the idea that "cruel and unusual punishment" is an evil in itself, the Benthamite notion that behavior should be guided by what will produce the greatest happiness for the greatest number—all these principles are only two centuries old. They were born with the eighteenth-century democratic revolutions. And in two hundred years they have not been universally accepted. Wherever people believe strongly in some cause, they will justify torture—not just the Nazis, but the French in Algeria. 8

Many people who wouldn't hurt a fly have annexed to fashion the imagery of torture—the thongs and spikes and metal studs—hence reducing it to the frivolous and transitory. Because torture has been in the mainstream and not on the margins of history, nothing could be healthier. For torture to be merely kinky would be a big advance. 9

Exhibitions like the one I saw in Paris, which presented itself as educational, may be guilty of pandering to the tastes they deplore. Solemnity may be the wrong tone. If taking one's goals too seriously is the danger, the best discouragement of torture may be a radical hedonism that denies that any goal is worth the means, that refuses to allow the nobly abstract to seduce us from the sweetness of the concrete. Give people a good croissant and a good cup of coffee in the morning. Give them an occasional facial and a plate of escargots. Marie Antoinette picked a bad moment to say "Let them eat cake," but I've often thought she was on the right track.

All of which brings me back to Paris, for Paris exists in the imagination of much of the world as the capital of pleasure—of fun, food, art, folly, seduction, gallantry, and beauty. Paris is civilization's reminder to itself that nothing leads you less wrong than your awareness of your own pleasure and genial desire to spread it around. In that sense the myth of Paris constitutes a moral touchstone, standing for the selfish frivolity that helps keep priorities straight.

QUESTIONS FOR READING AND WRITING

1. What does Rose say or imply about the relationship between torture and a human tendency toward sadistic behavior?
2. What effect is created by the long list of devices of torture that Rose gives in paragraph 1?
3. What essential contrasts between beauty and torture does Rose cite? How does Paris function in her essay?
4. The United States Constitution forbids what its writers called "cruel and unusual punishment." Write an essay in which you define what is, or is not, cruel and unusual punishment.
5. Turning Rose's essay upside down, write an essay about how attempts to enhance beauty involve torture, or at least high levels of discomfort. Consider eyebrow curlers and tweezers, hair removers, facial masks, pierced ears, high heels, and so forth.

✦ Gloria Steinem ✦
Erotica and Pornography

A founding editor of Ms. *magazine (1971), Gloria Steinem has long been an activist and spokesperson in the women's movement. In the following essay, which appeared in her collection of essays and articles entitled* Outrageous Acts and Everyday Rebellions *(1983), Steinem examines the crucial differences between erotica and pornography to show the violence and the degradation of women that pornography both encourages and reflects.*

HUMAN BEINGS ARE THE ONLY ANIMALS that experience the same sex drive at times when we can—and cannot—conceive. 1

Just as we developed uniquely human capacities for language, planning, memory, and invention along our evolutionary path, we also developed sexuality as a form of expression; a way of communicating that is separable from our need for sex as a way of perpetuating ourselves. For humans alone, sexuality can be and often is primarily a way of bonding, of giving and receiving pleasure, bridging differentness, discovering sameness, and communicating emotion. 2

We developed this and other human gifts through our ability to change our environment, adapt physically, and in the long run, to affect our own evolution. But as an emotional result of this spiraling path away from other animals, we seem to alternate between periods of exploring our unique abilities to change new boundaries, and feelings of loneliness in the unknown that we ourselves have created; a fear that sometimes sends us back to the comfort of the animal world by encouraging us to exaggerate our sameness. 3

The separation of "play" from "work," for instance, is a problem only in the human world. So is the difference between art and nature, or an intellectual accomplishment and a physical one. As a result, we celebrate play, art, and invention as leaps into the unknown; but any imbalance can send us back to nostalgia for our primate past and the conviction that the basics of work, nature, and physical labor are somehow more worthwhile or even moral. 4

In the same way, we have explored our sexuality as separable from conception: a pleasurable, empathetic bridge to strangers of the same species. We have even invented contraception—a skill that has probably existed in some form since our ancestors figured out the process of birth—in order to extend this uniquely human difference. Yet we also have times of atavistic suspicion that sex is not complete—or even legal or intended-by-god—if it cannot end in conception.

No wonder the concepts of "erotica" and "pornography" can be so crucially different, and yet so confused. Both assume that sexuality can be separated from conception, and therefore can be used to carry a personal message. That's a major reason why, even in our current culture, both may be called equally "shocking" or legally "obscene," a word whose Latin derivative means "dirty, containing filth." This gross condemnation of all sexuality that isn't harnessed to childbirth and marriage has been increased by the current backlash against women's progress. Out of fear that the whole patriarchal structure might be upset if women really had the autonomous power to decide our reproductive futures (that is, if we controlled the most basic means of production), right-wing groups are not only denouncing prochoice abortion literature as "pornographic," but are trying to stop the sending of all contraceptive information through the mails by invoking obscenity laws. In fact, Phyllis Schlafly recently denounced the entire Women's Movement as "obscene."

Not surprisingly, this religious, visceral backlash has a secular, intellectual counterpart that relies heavily on applying the "natural" behavior of the animal world to humans. That is questionable in itself, but these Lionel Tiger-ish studies make their political purpose even more clear in the particular animals they select and the habits they choose to emphasize. The message is that females should accept their "destiny" of being sexually dependent and devote themselves to bearing and rearing their young.

Defending against such reaction in turn leads to another temptation: to merely reverse the terms, and declare that *all* nonprocreative sex is good. In fact, however, this human activity can be as constructive as destructive, moral or immoral, as any other. Sex as communication can send messages as different as life and death; even the origins of "erotica" and "pornography" reflect that fact.

After all, "erotica" is rooted in *eros* or passionate love, and thus in the idea of positive choice, free will, the yearning for a particular person. (Interestingly, the definition of erotica leaves open the question of gender.) "Pornography" begins with a root meaning "prostitution" or "female captives," thus letting us know that the subject is not mutual love, or love at all, but domination and violence against women. (Though, of course, homosexual pornography may imitate this violence by putting a man in the "feminine" role of victim.) It ends with a root meaning "writing about" or "description of" which puts still more distance between subject and object, and replaces a spontaneous yearning for closeness with objectification and a voyeur.

The difference is clear in the words. It becomes even more so by example. 9

Look at any photo or film of people making love; really making love. The images may be diverse, but there is usually a sensuality and touch and warmth, an acceptance of bodies and nerve endings. There is always a spontaneous sense of people who are there because they *want* to be, out of shared pleasure. 10

Now look at any depiction of sex in which there is clear force, or an unequal power that spells coercion. It may be very blatant, with weapons or torture or bondage, wounds and bruises, some clear humiliation, or an adult's sexual power being used over a child. It may be much more subtle: a physical attitude of conqueror and victim, the use of race or class difference to imply the same thing, perhaps a very unequal nudity, with one person exposed and vulnerable while the other is clothed. In either case, there is no sense of equal choice or equal power. 11

The first is erotic: a mutually pleasurable, sexual expression between people who have enough power to be there by positive choice. It may or may not strike a sense-memory in the viewer, or be creative enough to make the unknown seem real; but it doesn't require us to identify with a conqueror or a victim. It is truly sensuous, and may give us a contagion of pleasure. 12

The second is pornographic: its message is violence, dominance, and conquest. It is sex being used to reinforce some inequality, or to create one, or to tell us the lie that pain and humiliation (ours or someone else's) are really the same as pleasure. If we are to feel anything, we must identify with conqueror or victim. That means 13 we can only experience pleasure through the adoption of some degree of sadism or masochism. It also means that we may feel diminished by the role of conqueror, or enraged, humiliated, and vengeful by sharing identity with the victim.

Perhaps one could simply say that erotica is about sexuality, but pornography is about power and sex-as-weapon—in the same way we have come to understand that rape is about violence, and not really about sexuality at all.

Yes, it's true that there are women who have been forced by violent families and dominating men to confuse love with pain; so much so that they have become masochists. (A fact that in no way excuses those who administer such pain.) But the truth is that, for most women—and for men with enough humanity to imagine themselves into the predicament of women—true pornography could serve as aversion therapy for sex.

Of course, there will always be personal differences about what is and is not erotic, and there may be cultural differences for a long time to come. Many women feel that sex makes them vulnerable and therefore may continue to need more sense of personal connection and safety before allowing any erotic feelings. We now find competence and expertise erotic in men, but that may pass as we develop those qualities in ourselves. Men, on the other hand, may continue to feel less vulnerable, and therefore more open to such potential danger as sex with strangers. As some men replace the need for submission from childlike women with the pleasure of cooperation from equals, they may find a partner's competence to be erotic, too.

Such group changes plus individual differences will continue to be reflected in sexual love between people of the same gender, as well as between women and men. The point is not to dictate sameness, but to discover ourselves and each other through sexuality that is an exploring, pleasurable, empathetic part of our lives; a human sexuality that is unchained both from unwanted pregnancies and from violence.

But that is a hope, not a reality. At the moment, fear of change is increasing both the indiscriminate repression of all nonprocreative sex in the religious and "conservative" male world, and the pornographic vengeance against women's sexuality in the secular world of "liberal" and "radical" men. It's almost futuristic to debate what is and is not truly erotic, when many women are again being forced into compulsory motherhood, and the number of pornographic murders, tortures, and woman-hating images are on the increase in both popular culture and real life.

It's a familiar division: wife or whore, "good" woman who is constantly vulnerable to pregnancy or "bad" woman who is unprotected from violence. *Both* roles would be upset if we were to control our own sexuality. And that's exactly what we must do. 19

In spite of all our atavistic suspicions and training for the "natural" role of motherhood, we took up the complicated battle for reproductive freedom. Our bodies had borne the health burden of endless births and poor abortions, and we had a greater motive for separating sexuality and conception. 20

Now we have to take up the equally complex burden of explaining that all nonprocreative sex is *not* alike. We have a motive: our right to a uniquely human sexuality, and sometimes even to survival. As it is, our bodies have too rarely been enough our own to develop erotica in our own lives, much less in art and literature. And our bodies have too often been the objects of pornography and the woman-hating, violent practice that it preaches. Consider also our spirits that break a little each time we see ourselves in chains or full labial display for the conquering male viewer, bruised or on our knees, screaming a real or pretended pain to delight the sadist, pretending to enjoy what we don't enjoy, to be blind to the images of our sisters that really haunt us—humiliated often enough ourselves by the truly obscene idea that sex and the domination of women must be combined. 21

Sexuality *is* human, free, separate—and so are we. 22

But until we untangle the lethal confusion of sex with violence, there will be more pornography and less erotica. There will be little murders in our beds—and very little love. 23

QUESTIONS FOR READING AND WRITING

1. Outline the key distinctions Steinem makes between erotica and pornography.

2. Steinem's contrasting of erotica and pornography serves as a springboard for a broader consideration of attitudes toward women and toward sexuality in general. What are these attitudes?
3. What does Steinem mean when, in her last paragraph, she refers to "little murders in our beds"?
4. Write an essay that details the key differences between play and work (note that comparison or contrast usually involves definition to some degree.) In your essay, try to find examples where the distinctions between play and work become blurred.
5. Write an essay that shows how reproductive freedom (the "pro-choice" attitude underlies Steinem's ideas about erotica and pornography.

✦ Marie Winn ✦
Television and Reading

Born in Czechoslovakia, Marie Winn (b. 1937) is known primarily for her books about the effects of television viewing: The Plug-in Drug: Television, Children, and the Family *(1977) and* Unplugging the Plug-in Drug *(1987). In the following excerpt from the first of these books, Winn describes the fundamental differences between reading and watching television. She stresses the addictive and ultimately damaging effects of watching too much television.*

UNTIL THE TELEVISION ERA a young child's access to symbolic representations of reality was limited. Unable to read, he entered the world of fantasy primarily by way of stories told to him or read to him from a book. But rarely did such "literary" experiences take up a significant proportion of a child's waking time; even when a willing reader or storyteller was available, an hour or so a day was more time than most children spent ensconced in the imagination of others. And when the pre-television child *did* enter those imaginary worlds, he always had a grown-up escort along to interpret, explain, and comfort, if need be. Before he learned to read, it was difficult for the child to enter the fantasy world alone. 1

For this reason the impact of television was undoubtedly greater on preschoolers and pre-readers than on any other group. By means of television, very young children were able to enter and spend sizable portions of their waking time in a secondary world of incorporeal people and intangible things, unaccompanied, in too many cases, by an adult guide or comforter. School-age children fell into a different category. Because they could read, they had other opportunities to leave reality behind. For these children television was merely *another* imaginary world. 2

But since reading, once the school child's major imaginative experience, has now been virtually eclipsed by television, the television experience must be compared with the reading experience to try to discover whether they are, indeed, similar activities fulfilling similar needs in a child's life. 3

What Happens When You Read

It is not enough to compare television watching and reading from the viewpoint of quality. Although the quality of the material available in each medium varies enormously, from junky books and shoddy programs to literary masterpieces and fine, thoughtful television shows, the *nature* of the two experiences is different and that difference significantly affects the impact of the material taken in.

Few people besides linguistics students and teachers of reading are aware of the complex mental manipulations involved in the reading process. Shortly after learning to read, a person assimilates the process into his life so completely that the words in books seem to acquire an existence almost equal to the objects or acts they represent. It requires a fresh look at a printed page to recognize that those symbols that we call letters of the alphabet are completely abstract shapes bearing no inherent "meaning" of their own. Look at an "o," for instance, or a "k." The "o" is a curved figure; the "k" is an intersection of three straight lines. Yet it is hard to divorce their familiar figures from their sounds, though there is nothing "o-ish" about an "o" or "k-ish" about a "k." A reader unfamiliar with the Russian alphabet will find it easy to look at the symbol"Щ" and see it as an abstract shape; a Russian reader will find it harder to detach that symbol from its sound, *shch*. And even when trying to consider "k" as an abstract symbol, we cannot see it without the feeling of a "k" sound somewhere between the throat and the ears, a silent pronunciation of "k" that occurs the instant we see the letter.

That is the beginning of reading: we learn to transform abstract figures into sounds, and groups of symbols into the combined sounds that make up the words of our language. As the mind transforms the abstract symbols into sounds and the sounds into words, it "hears" the words, as it were, and thereby invests them with meanings previously learned in the spoken language. Invariably, as the skill of reading develops, the meaning of each word begins to seem to dwell within those symbols that make up the word. The word "dog," for instance, comes to bear some relationship with the real animal. Indeed, the word "dog" seems to *be* a dog in a certain sense, to possess some of the qualities of a dog. But it is only as a result of a swift and complex series of mental activities that the word "dog" is transformed from a series of meaningless squiggles into an idea of something real. This process goes on smoothly and continuously as we read, and yet it becomes no less complex. The brain must carry out all the steps of decoding and investing with meaning each time we read; but it becomes more adept at it as the skill develops, so that we lose the sense of struggling with symbols and meanings that children have when they first learn to read.

But not merely does the mind *hear* words in the process of 7
reading; it is important to remember that reading involves images as well. For when the reader sees the word "dog" and understands the idea of "dog," an image representing a dog is conjured up as well. The precise nature of this "reading image" is little understood, nor is there agreement about what relation it bears to visual images taken in directly by the eyes. Nevertheless images necessarily color our reading, else we would perceive no meaning, merely empty words. The great difference between these "reading images" and the images we take in when viewing television is this: we *create* our own images when reading, based upon our own life experiences and reflecting our own individual needs, while we must accept what we receive when watching television images. This aspect of reading, which might be called "creative" in the narrow sense of the word, is present during all reading experiences, regardless of *what* is being read. The reader "creates" his own images as he reads, almost as if he were creating his own, small, inner television program. The result is a nourishing experience for the imagination. As Bruno Bettelheim notes, "Television captures the imagination but does not liberate it. A good book at once stimulates and frees the mind."

Television images do not go through a complex symbolic trans- 8
formation. The mind does not have to decode and manipulate during the television experience. Perhaps this is a reason why the visual images received directly from a television set are strong, stronger, it appears, than the images conjured up mentally while reading. But ultimately they satisfy less. A ten-year-old child reports on the effects of seeing television dramatizations of books he has previously read: "The TV people leave a stronger impression. Once you've seen a character on TV, he'll always look like that in your mind, even if you made a different picture of him in your mind

before, when you read the book yourself." And yet, as the same child reports, "The thing about a book is that you have so much freedom. You can make each character look exactly the way you want him to look. You're more in control of things when you read a book than when you see something on TV."

It may be that television-bred children's reduced opportunities to indulge in this "inner picture-making" accounts for the curious inability of so many children today to adjust to nonvisual experiences. This is commonly reported by experienced teachers who bridge the gap between the pretelevision and the television eras.

"When I read them a story without showing them pictures, the children always complain—'I can't see.' Their attention flags," reports a first-grade teacher. "They'll begin to talk or wander off. I have to really work to develop their visualizing skills. I tell them that there's nothing to see, that the story is coming out of my mouth, and that they can make their own pictures in their 'mind's eye.' They get better at visualizing, with practice. But children never needed to learn how to visualize before television, it seems to me."

Viewing vs. Reading: Concentration

Because reading demands complex mental manipulations, a reader is required to concentrate far more than a television viewer. An audio expert notes that "with the electronic media it is openness [that counts]. Openness permits auditory and visual stimuli more direct access to the brain . . . someone who is taught to concentrate will fail to perceive many patterns of information conveyed by the electronic stimuli."

It may be that a predisposition toward concentration, acquired, perhaps, through one's reading experiences, makes one an inadequate television watcher. But it seems far more likely that the reverse situation obtains: that a predisposition toward "openness" (which may be understood to mean the opposite of focal concentration), acquired through years and years of television viewing, has influenced adversely viewers' ability to concentrate, to read, to write clearly—in short, to demonstrate any of the verbal skills a literate society requires.

Pace

A comparison between reading and viewing may be made in respect to the pace of each experience, and the relative control a person has over that pace, for the pace may influence the ways one uses the material received in each experience. In addition, the pace of each experience may determine how much it intrudes upon other aspects of one's life. 13

The pace of reading, clearly, depends entirely upon the reader. He may read as slowly or as rapidly as he can or wishes to read. If he does not understand something, he may stop and reread it, or go in search of elucidation before continuing. The reader can accelerate his pace when the material is easy or less than interesting, and slow down when it is difficult or enthralling. If what he reads is moving, he can put down the book for a few moments and cope with his emotions without fear of losing anything. 14

The pace of the television experience cannot be controlled by the viewer; only its beginning and end are within his control as he clicks the knob on and off. He cannot slow down a delightful program or speed up a dreary one. He cannot "turn back" if a word or phrase is not understood. The program moves inexorably forward, and what is lost or misunderstood remains so. 15

Nor can the television viewer readily transform the material he receives into a form that might suit his particular emotional needs, as he invariably does with material he reads. The images move too quickly. He cannot use his own imagination to invest the people and events portrayed on television with the personal meanings that would help him understand and resolve relationships and conflicts in his own life; he is under the power of the imagination of the show's creators. In the television experience the eyes and ears are overwhelmed with the immediacy of sights and sounds. They flash from the television set just fast enough for the eyes and ears to take them in before moving on quickly to the new pictures and sounds . . . so as *not to lose the thread.* 16

Not to lose the thread . . . it is this need, occasioned by the irreversible direction and relentless velocity of the television experience, that not only limits the workings of the viewer's imagination, but also causes television to intrude into human affairs far more 17 than reading experiences can ever do. If someone enters the room while one is watching television—a friend, a relative, a child, someone, perhaps, one has not seen for some time—one must continue to watch or one will lose the thread. The greetings must wait, for the television program will not. A book, of course, can be set aside, with a pang of regret, perhaps, but with no sense of permanent loss.

A grandparent describes a situation that is, by all reports, not uncommon:

"Sometimes when I come to visit the girls, I'll walk into their room and they're watching a TV program. Well, I know they love me, but it makes me feel *bad* when I tell them hello, and they say, without even looking up, 'Wait a minute . . . we have to see the end of this program.' It hurts me to have them care more about that machine and those little pictures than about being glad to see me. I know that they probably can't help it, but still. . . . "

Can they help it? Ultimately the power of a television viewer to release himself from his viewing in order to attend to human demands arising in the course of his viewing is not altogether a function of the pace of the program. After all, the viewer might *choose* to operate according to human priorities rather than electronic dictatorship. He might quickly decide "to hell with this program" and simply stop watching when a friend entered the room or a child needed attention.

He might . . . but the hypnotic power of television makes it difficult to shift one's attention away, makes one desperate not to lose the thread of the program. . . .

The Basic Building Blocks

There is another difference between reading and television viewing that must affect the response to each experience. This is the relative acquaintance of readers and viewers with the fundamental elements of each medium. While the reader is familiar with the basic building blocks of the reading medium, the television viewer has little acquaintance with those of the television medium.

As a person reads, he has his own writing experience to fall back upon. His understanding of what he reads, and his feelings about it, are necessarily affected, and deepened, by his possession of writing as a means of communicating. As a child begins to learn reading, he begins to acquire the rudiments of writing. That these two skills are always acquired together is important and not coincidental. As the child learns to read words, he needs to understand that a word is something he can write himself, though his muscle control may temporarily prevent him from writing it clearly. That he wields such power over the words he is struggling to decipher makes the reading experience a satisfying one right from the start.

A young child watching television enters a realm of materials completely beyond his control—and understanding. Though the images that appear on the screen may be reflections of familiar people and things, they appear as if by magic. The child cannot create similar images, nor even begin to understand how those flickering, electronic shapes and forms come into being. He takes on a far more powerless and ignorant role in front of the television set than in front of a book. 24

There is no doubt that many young children have a confused relationship to the television medium. When a group of preschool children were asked, "How do kids get to be on your TV ?"only 22 percent of them showed any real comprehension of the nature of the television images. When asked "Where do the people and kids and things go when your TV is turned off?" only 20 percent of the three-year-olds showed the smallest glimmer of understanding. Although there was an increase in comprehension among the four-year-olds, the authors of the study note that "even among the older children the vast majority still did not grasp the nature of television pictures." 25

The child's feelings of power and competence are nourished by another feature of the reading experience that does not obtain for television: the nonmechanical, easily accessible, and easily transportable nature of reading matter. The child can always count on a book for pleasure, though the television set may break down at a crucial moment. The child may take a book with him wherever he goes, to his room, to the park, to his friend's house, to school to read under his desk: he can *control* his use of books and reading materials. The television set is stuck in a certain place; it cannot be moved easily. It certainly cannot be casually transported from place to place by a child. The child must not only watch television wherever 26 the set is located, but he must watch certain programs at certain times, and is powerless to change what comes out of the set and when it comes out.

In this comparison of reading and television experiences a picture begins to emerge that quite confirms the commonly held notion that reading is somehow "better" than television viewing. Reading involves a complex form of mental activity, trains the mind in concentration skills, develops the powers of imagination and inner visualization; the flexibility of its pace lends itself to a better and deeper comprehension of the material communicated. Reading engrosses, but does not hypnotize or seduce the reader from his human responsibilities. Reading is a two-way process: the reader can also write; television viewing is a one-way street: the viewer cannot create television images. And books are ever available, ever controllable. Television controls.

QUESTIONS FOR READING AND WRITING

1. Show how Winn's conclusion—that reading is somehow a "better" activity than watching television—follows from her contrast of the two activities. If you watch television more than you read, describe your reasons for doing so.
2. What Winn says about the "pace" of a television show could almost equally apply to the "pace" of a dramatic production; it cannot be turned back, it cannot be stopped, and so forth. How, then, do plays differ from television shows, *as media*?
3. Unlike television programs, material recorded on videocassettes can be stopped, rewound, and advanced. Does this capability undercut Winn's arguments against television? Or, on the contrary, do VCRs merely add to the problems Winn cites? If so, how?
4. Look up the derivation of the word *program*. Compare its usage in television and in computer jargon.
5. Winn emphasizes the hypnotic, seductive power of television. Write an essay in which you analyze a popular television program or cable channel (such as *MTV*) to show how it manages to create its seductive effect—the effect that might keep a viewer watching it even when Grandmother enters the room!
6. Interview a child about his or her viewing and reading habits. Base your questions on Winn's essay. Write up the results and comment on the implications of what you find out.

Analogy

We use *analogy* to compare two things that belong to different classes or categories. An analogy stipulates limited likenesses between two things that are essentially dissimilar. For example, if you wished to explain how the heart works, you might decide to compare it to a pump. Like a pump, the heart circulates material in a closed system by keeping it at a constant pressure; like a pump, the heart has valves that open and close; and like a pump, the heart's operation can be interrupted if one of the tubes leading to it becomes blocked. The introduction of mechanical hearts may have made this analogy seem more like a comparison, but the living heart and the mechanical pump still belong to different orders of being; consequently, they form an analogy. Often, an analogy involves a familiar term and an unfamiliar one, the objective being to explain the unfamiliar term by comparing it with the familiar one. In the previous example, you would be assuming your audience was familiar with how a pump works but less familiar with how the heart works.

Analogy differs from direct comparison in that in comparison the two items *do* belong to the same class; moreover, to point out similarities in a comparison is to insist that they are, in fact, alike. Analogy serves to clarify the unfamiliar, whereas comparison specifies the actual features that two things have in common. To compare Protestantism and Catholicism—two forms of Christianity—for instance would be a straightforward comparison because the items obviously belong to the same class, and the purpose would be to illuminate both. But to compare government with religion is to draw an analogy, since the two are essentially unalike. In the following analogy by Richard Reeves, notice how government and religion are brought together to comment on Americans' attitudes toward government; notice, too, that the items are juxtaposed only temporarily to clarify a point. Reeves actually does not believe that government and religion are similar institutions, except in the limited ways he points out in the analogy.

> The government, trusted and feared, obeyed and avoided, revered and disdained, had become very much like a religion. Its

> role was to confront evil for the rest of us. Somehow, it had to make us better than we knew we were, because the ideas that were being enforced, the ideas of America, were bigger and better than Americans. Most Americans supported the reinforcement of the national rhetoric, even while protesting the growth of the secular church to meet evils old or new, growing or being redefined. The support, the basic trust in the public solution, existed even as the American congregation sought out private solutions—and new ways to evade the multiplying laws and the bureaus, rules, and enforcers. It was, of course, the way people have always believed in and dealt with religions. No one can play by all those rules, all those commandments. But they can say they do, and they can try—and trying makes them, often, hypocrites and fools. And often decent. And democrats. Americans.*

In framing an analogy to clarify a difficult subject, it is often useful to put it in the form of a question. For example: "How is Congress like a circus?" "How is inflation like a parasite?" "How is getting a college education like running a race (or participating in any sport)?" "How is writing a paper like cooking a meal?" "How is travelling in a foreign country like being blindfolded?" Because creating analogies is like creating figures of speech, everyone has his or her own ideas about where to find similarities; however, audience receptivity must be kept in mind if the analogy is to succeed in clarifying the subject.

Finally, because an analogy is a partial comparison of two things, it is clear that the differences will outweigh the similarities. Should you explore the differences as well? The only answer to the question is equivocal: "It depends." It depends on whether pointing out the differences would undermine the similarities the analogy has already constructed or would further clarify the unfamiliar item you are attempting to explain. Notice in the following quotation how Jonathan Schell begins by rejecting someone else's analogy of the earth as a biological cell before going ahead to offer his own analogy of the earth as an individual person:

> Dr. [Lewis] Thomas, for one, has likened the earth to a cell. The analogy is compelling, but in one noteworthy respect, at least, there is a difference between the earth and a cell:

* Richard Reeves, "Along Tocqueville's Path," *The New Yorker* (April 12, 1982), 104–106.

> whereas each cell is one among billions struck from the same genetic mold, the earth, as the mother of all life, has no living parent. If the behavior of the cells is often predictable, it is because they exist en masse, and what a billion of them, programmed by their genetic material, do a billion times the billion and first is likely to do again. But the earth is a member of no class as yet open to our observation which would permit the drawing of such inferences by generalization. When it comes to predict its tolerance to perturbances, we are in the position of someone asked to deduce the whole of medicine by observing one human being. With respect to its individuality, then, the earth is not so much like a cell as like an individual person. Like a person, the earth is unique; like a person, it is sacred; and like a person, it is unpredictable by the generalizing laws of science.*

If extended too far, analogies can lapse into absurdity. Lewis Thomas' analogy between an attic and the human brain would break down if he attempted to show that our brains are filled with nothing but discarded junk and items that we use during particular seasons. Also, analogies are not logical evidence—they clarify, yes, but they do not *prove* anything. Annie Dillard's analogy between a mangrove island and the planet earth gives us an unusual perspective on the human condition. But her essay does not prove—and is not *meant* to prove—that the physical and biological processes at work in a mangrove island are also those that drive human culture. Analogies, finally, are effective if they are handled judiciously to explain a difficult idea or event by likening it to something that the reader knows well, as James Rettie does by drawing the analogy between the sweep of geological time and a common clock. Poorly done, an analogy will seem forced, illogical, and limiting; if well managed, however, an analogy can spark a clear, vivid, ingenious, and memorable explanation.

* Jonathan Schell, "The Fate of the Earth—Part I," *The New Yorker* (February 1, 1982), 100.

✦ Annie Dillard ✦
Sojourner

An American essayist and poet, Annie Dillard (b. 1945) won the Pulitzer Prize for her best-selling first book, Pilgrim at Tinker Creek *(1974). Her most recent book is the autobiographical* An American Childhood *(1987). "Sojourner" first appeared in* Teaching a Stone to Talk *(1982). In this essay, she uses the apparently far-fetched analogy between a mangrove island and the planet earth to express her perceptions about the beauty of accumulated human culture.*

IF SURVIVAL IS AN ART, then mangroves are artists of the beautiful: not only that they exist at all—smooth-barked, glossy-leaved, thickets of lapped mystery—but that they can and do exist as floating islands, as trees upright and loose, alive and homeless on the water.

I have seen mangroves, always on tropical ocean shores, in Florida and in the Galápagos. There is the red mangrove, the yellow, the button, and the black. They are all short, messy trees, waxy-leaved, laced all over with aerial roots, woody arching buttresses, and weird leathery berry pods. All this tangles from a black muck soil, a black muck matted like a mud-sopped rag, a muck without any other plants, shaded, cold to the touch, tracked at the water's edge by herons and nosed by sharks.

It is these shoreline trees which, by a fairly common accident, can become floating islands. A hurricane flood or a riptide can wrest a tree from the shore, or from the mouth of a tidal river, and hurl it into the ocean. It floats. It is a mangrove island, blown.

There are floating islands on the planet; it amazes me. Credulous Pliny described some islands thought to be mangrove islands floating on a river. The people called these river islands *the dancers*, "because in any consort of musicians singing, they stir and move at the stroke of the feet, keeping time and measure."

Trees floating on rivers are less amazing than trees floating on the poisonous sea. A tree cannot live in salt. Mangrove trees exude salt from their leaves; you can see it, even on shoreline black mangroves, as a thin white crust. Lick a leaf and your tongue curls and coils; your mouth's a heap of salt.

Nor can a tree live without soil. A hurricane-born mangrove island may bring its own soil to the sea. But other mangrove trees make their own soil—and their own islands—from scratch. These are the ones which interest me. The seeds germinate in the fruit on the tree. The germinated embryo can drop anywhere—say, onto a dab of floating muck. The heavy root end sinks; a leafy plumule unfurls. The tiny seedling, afloat, is on its way. Soon aerial roots shooting out in all directions trap debris. The sapling's networks twine, the interstices narrow, and water calms in the lee. Bacteria thrive on organic broth; amphipods swarm. These creatures grow and die at the trees' wet feet. The soil thickens, accumulating rainwater, leaf rot, seashells, and guano; the island spreads. 6

More seeds and more muck yield more trees on the new island. A society grows, interlocked in a tangle of dependencies. The island rocks less in the swells. Fish throng to the backwaters stilled in snarled roots. Soon, Asian mudskippers—little four-inch fish—clamber up the mangrove roots into the air and peer about from periscope eyes on stalks, like snails. Oysters clamp to submersed roots, as do starfish, dog whelk, and the creatures that live among tangled kelp. Shrimp seek shelter there, limpets a holdfast, pelagic birds a rest. 7

And the mangrove island wanders on, afloat and adrift. It walks teetering and wanton before the wind. Its fate and direction are random. It may bob across an ocean and catch on another mainland's shores. It may starve or dry while it is still a sapling. It may topple in a storm, or pitchpole. By the rarest of chances, it may stave into another mangrove island in a crash of clacking roots, and mesh. What it is most likely to do is drift anywhere in the alien ocean, feeding on death and growing, netting a makeshift soil as it goes, shrimp in its toes and terns in its hair. 8

We could do worse. 9

I alternate between thinking of the planet as home—dear and familiar stone hearth and garden—and as a hard land of exile in which we are all sojourners. Today I favor the latter view. The word "sojourner" occurs often in the English Old Testament. It invokes a nomadic people's sense of vagrancy, a praying people's knowledge of estrangement, a thinking people's intuition of sharp loss: "For we are strangers before thee, and sojourners, as were all our fathers: our days on the earth are as a shadow, and there is none abiding." 10

We don't know where we belong, but in times of sorrow it doesn't seem to be here, here with these silly pansies and witless mountains, here with sponges and hard-eyed birds. In times of sorrow the innocence of the other creatures—from whom and with whom we evolved—seems a mockery. Their ways are not our ways. We seem set among them as among lifelike props for a tragedy—or a broad lampoon—on a thrust rock stage.

It doesn't seem to be here that we belong, here where space is curved, the earth is round, we're all going to die, and it seems as wise to stay in bed as budge. It is strange here, not quite warm enough, or too warm, too leafy, or inedible, or windy, or dead. It is not, frankly, the sort of home for people one would have thought of—although I lack the fancy to imagine another.

The planet itself is a sojourner in airless space, a wet ball flung across nowhere. The few objects in the universe scatter. The coherence of matter dwindles and crumbles toward stillness. I have read, and repeated, that our solar system as a whole is careering through space toward a point east of Hercules. Now I wonder: what could that possibly mean, east of Hercules? Isn't space curved? When we get "there," how will our course change, and why? Will we slide down the universe's inside arc like mud slung at a wall? Or what sort of welcoming shore is this east of Hercules? Surely we don't anchor there, and disembark, and sweep into dinner with our host. Does someone cry, "Last stop, last stop"? At any rate, east of Hercules, like east of Eden, isn't a place to call home. It is a course without direction; it is "out." And we are cast.

These are enervating thoughts, the thoughts of despair. They crowd back, unbidden, when human life as it unrolls goes ill, when we lose control of our lives or the illusion of control, and it seems that we are not moving toward any end but merely blown. Our life seems cursed to be a wiggle merely, and a wandering without end. Even nature is hostile and poisonous, as though it were impossible for our vulnerability to survive on these acrid stones.

Whether these thoughts are true or not I find less interesting than the possibilities for beauty they may hold. We are down here in time, where beauty grows. Even if things are as bad as they could possibly be, and as meaningless, then matters of truth are themselves indifferent; we may as well please our sensibilities and, with as much spirit as we can muster, go out with a buck and wing.

The planet is less like an enclosed spaceship—spaceship earth—than it is like an exposed mangrove island beautiful and loose. We the people started small and have since accumulated a great and solacing muck of soil, of human culture. We are rooted in it; we are bearing it with us across nowhere. The word "nowhere"is our cue: the consort of musicians strikes up, and we in the chorus stir and move and start twirling our hats. A mangrove island turns drift to dance. It creates its own soil as it goes, rocking over the salt sea at random, rocking day and night and round the sun, rocking round the sun and out toward east of Hercules. 16

QUESTIONS FOR READING AND WRITING

1. What vision of human life or "destiny" is implied by Dillard's essay? In what way is this vision similar to or different from that implied by James Rettie in "But a Watch in the Night"?
2. Compare the "pace" with which Dillard delivers her analogy with that used by Lewis Thomas in "The Attic of the Brain." What effects are created by these different paces?
3. In her first eight paragraphs, Dillard describes mangrove islands. Only at the end of her essay does she compare earth to a mangrove island. What are the points of contact between the two?
4. Write an analogy that compares "life in the world" (or memory, or experience) to a drama, a carnival, a garden, a museum, or a race. (Feel free to replace any of these suggestions with your own.)

✦ James C. Rettie ✦

But a Watch in the Night

A Scientific Fable

James C. Rettie (1904–1969), an American conservationist and economist, worked for the federal government in both the Department of Agriculture and the Department of the Interior. "But a Watch in the Night" first appeared in 1950 in a collection of essays entitled Forever the Land, *edited by Russell and Kate Lord. In this essay, Rettie compresses the time of the earth's history into one 24-hour period. The results are both surprising and disturbing.*

OUT BEYOND OUR SOLAR SYSTEM there is a planet called Copernicus. It came into existence some four or five billion years before the birth of our Earth. In due course of time it became inhabited by a race of intelligent men.

About 750 million years ago the Copernicans had developed the motion picture machine to a point well in advance of the stage that we have reached. Most of the cameras that we now use in motion picture work are geared to take twenty-four pictures per second on a continuous strip of film. When such film is run through a projector, it throws a series of images on the screen and these change with a rapidity that gives the visual impression of normal movement. If a motion is too swift for the human eye to see it in detail, it can be captured and artificially slowed down by means of the slow-motion camera. This one is geared to take many more shots per second—ninety-six or even more than that. When the slow-motion film is projected at the normal speed of twenty-four pictures per second, we can see just how the jumping horse goes over a hurdle.

What about motion that is too slow to be seen by the human eye? That problem has been solved by the use of the time-lapse camera. In this one, the shutter is geared to take only one shot per second, or one per minute or even one per hour—depending upon the kind of movement that is being photographed. When the time-lapse film is projected at the normal speed of twenty-four pictures per second, it is possible to see a bean sprout growing up out of the ground.

Time-lapse films are useful in the study of many types of motion too slow to be observed by the unaided human eye.

The Copernicans, it seems, had time-lapse cameras some 757 million years ago and they also had superpowered telescopes that gave them a clear view of what was happening upon this Earth. They decided to make a film record of the life history of Earth and to make it on the scale of one picture per year. The photography has been in progress during the last 757 million years. 4

In the near future, a Copernican interstellar expedition will arrive upon our Earth and bring with it a copy of the time-lapse film. Arrangements will be made for showing the entire film in one continuous run. This will begin at midnight on New Year's eve and continue day and night without a single stop until midnight of December 31. The rate of projection will be twenty-four pictures per second. Time on the screen will thus seem to move at the rate of twenty-four years per second; 1,440 years per minute; 86,400 years per hour; approximately two million years per day; and 62 million years per month. The normal life-span of individual man will occupy about three seconds. The full period of Earth history that will be unfolded on the screen (some 757 million years) will extend from what the geologists call Pre-Cambrian times up to the present. This will, by no means, cover the full time-span of the Earth's geological history but it will embrace the period since the advent of living organisms. 5

During the months of January, February and March the picture will be desolate and dreary. The shape of the land masses and the oceans will bear little or no resemblance to those that we know. The violence of geological erosion will be much in evidence. Rains will pour down on the land and promptly go booming down to the seas. There will be no clear streams anywhere except where the rains fall upon hard rock. Everywhere on the steeper ground the stream channels will be filled with boulders hurled down by rushing waters. Raging torrents and dry stream beds will keep alternating in quick succession. High mountains will seem to melt like so much butter in the sun. The shifting of land into the seas, later to be thrust up as new mountains, will be going on a grand scale. 6

Early in April there will be some indication of the presence of single-celled living organisms in some of the warmer and sheltered 7 coastal waters. By the end of the month it will be noticed that some of these organisms have become multicellular. A few of them, including the Trilobites, will be encased in hard shells.

Toward the end of May, the first vertebrates will appear, but they will still be aquatic creatures. In June about 60 percent of the land area that we know as North America will be under water. One broad channel will occupy the space where the Rocky Mountains now stand. Great deposits of limestone will be forming under some of the shallower seas. Oil and gas deposits will be in process of formation—also under shallow seas. On land there will be no sign of vegetation. Erosion will be rampant, tearing loose particles and chunks of rock and grinding them into sand and silt to be spewed out by the streams into bays and estuaries.

About the middle of July the first land plants will appear and take up the tremendous job of soil building. Slowly, very slowly, the mat of vegetation will spread, always battling for its life against the power of erosion. Almost foot by foot, the plant life will advance, lacing down with its root structures whatever pulverized rock material it can find. Leaves and stems will be giving added protection against the loss of the soil foothold. The increasing vegetation will pave the way for the land animals that will live upon it.

Early in August the seas will be teeming with fish. This will be what geologists call the Devonian period. Some of the races of these fish will be breathing by means of lung tissue instead of through gill tissues. Before the month is over, some of the lung fish will go ashore and take on a crude lizard-like appearance. Here are the first amphibians.

In early September the insects will put in their appearance. Some will look like huge dragon flies and will have a wingspread of 24 inches. Large portions of the land masses will now be covered with heavy vegetation that will include the primitive spore-propagating trees. Layer upon layer of this plant growth will build up, later to appear as the coal deposits. About the middle of this month, there will be evidence of the first seed-bearing plants and the first reptiles. Heretofore, the land animals will have been amphibians that could reproduce their kind only by depositing a soft egg mass in quiet waters. The reptiles will be shown to be freed from the aquatic bond because they can reproduce by means of a shelled egg in which the embryo and its nurturing liquids are sealed in and thus protected from destructive evaporation. Before September is over, the first dinosaurs will be seen—creatures destined to dominate the animal realm for about 140 million years and then to disappear.

In October there will be a series of mountain uplifts along what 12
is now the eastern coast of the United States. A creature with feathered limbs—half bird and half reptile in appearance—will take itself into the air. Some small and rather unpretentious animals will be seen to bring forth their young in a form that is a miniature replica of the parents and to feed these young on milk secreted by mammary glands in the female parent. The emergence of this mammalian form of animal life will be recognized as one of the great events in geologic time. October will also witness the high water mark of the dinosaurs—creatures ranging in size from that of the modern goat to monsters like Brontosaurus that weighed some 40 tons. Most of them will be placid vegetarians, but a few will be hideous-looking carnivores, like Allosaurus and Tyrannosaurus. Some of the herbivorous dinosaurs will be clad in body armor for protection against their flesh-eating comrades.

November will bring pictures of a sea extending from the Gulf of 13
Mexico to the Arctic in space now occupied by the Rocky Mountains. A few of the reptiles will take to the air on bat-like wings. One of these, called Pteranodon, will have a wingspread of 15 feet. There will be a rapid development of the modern flowering plants, modern trees, and modern insects. The dinosaurs will disappear. Toward the end of the month there will be a tremendous land disturbance in which the Rocky Mountains will rise out of the sea to assume a dominating place in the North American landscape.

As the picture runs on into December it will show the mammals 14
in command of the animal life. Seed-bearing trees and grasses will have covered most of the land with a heavy mantle of vegetation. Only the areas newly thrust up from the sea will be barren. Most of the streams will be crystal clear. The turmoil of geologic erosion will be confined to localized areas. About December 25 will begin the cutting of the Grand Canyon of the Colorado River. Grinding down through layer after layer of sedimentary strata, this stream will finally expose deposits laid down in Pre-Cambrian times. Thus in the walls of that canyon will appear geological formations dating from recent times to the period when the earth had no living organisms upon it.

The picture will run on through the latter days of December and even up to its final day with still no sign of mankind. The spectators will become alarmed in the fear that man has somehow been left out. But not so; sometime about noon on December 31 (one million years ago) will appear a stooped, massive creature of man-like proportions. This will be Pithecanthropus, the Java ape man. For tools and weapons he will have nothing but crude stone and wooden clubs. His children will live a precarious existence threatened on the one side by hostile animals and on the other by tremendous climatic changes. Ice sheets—in places 4000 feet deep—will form in the northern parts of North America and Eurasia. Four times this glacial ice will push southward to cover half the continents. With each advance the plant and animal life will be swept under or pushed southward. With each recession of the ice, life will struggle to reestablish itself in the wake of the retreating glaciers. The wooly mammoth, the musk ox, and the caribou all will fight to maintain themselves near the ice line. Sometimes they will be caught and put into cold storage—skin, flesh, blood, bones and all.

The picture will run on through supper time with still very little evidence of man's presence on the Earth. It will be about 11 o'clock when Neanderthal man appears. Another half hour will go by before the appearance of Cro-Magnon man living in caves and painting crude animal pictures on the walls of his dwelling. Fifteen minutes more will bring Neolithic man, knowing how to chip stone and thus produce sharp cutting edges for spears and tools. In a few minutes more it will appear that man has domesticated the dog, the sheep and, possibly, other animals. He will then begin the use of milk. He will also learn the arts of basket weaving and the making of pottery and dugout canoes.

The dawn of civilization will not come until about five or six minutes before the end of the picture. The story of the Egyptians, the Babylonians, the Greeks, and the Romans will unroll during the fourth, the third and the second minute before the end. At 58 minutes and 43 seconds past 11:00 P.M. (just 1 minute and 17 seconds before the end) will come the beginning of the Christian era. Columbus will discover the new world 20 seconds before the end. The Declaration of Independence will be signed just 17 seconds before the final curtain comes down.

In those few moments of geologic time will be the story of all that has happened since we became a nation. And what a story it will be! A human swarm will sweep across the face of the continent and take it away from the . . . red men. They will change it far more radically than it has ever been changed before in a comparable time. The great virgin forests will be seen going down before ax and fire. The soil, covered for aeons by its protective mantle of trees and grasses, will be laid bare to the ravages of water and wind erosion. Streams that had been flowing clear will, once again, take up a load of silt and push it toward the seas. Humus and mineral salts, both vital elements of productive soil, will be seen to vanish at a terrifying rate. The railroads and highways and cities that will spring up may divert attention, but they cannot cover up the blight of man's recent activities. In great sections of Asia, it will be seen that man must utilize cow dung and every scrap of available straw or grass for fuel to cook his food. The forests that once provided wood for this purpose will be gone without a trace. The use of these agricultural wastes for fuel, in place of returning them to the land, will be leading to increasing soil impoverishment. Here and there will be seen a dust storm darkening the landscape over an area a thousand miles across. Man-creatures will be shown counting their wealth in terms of bits of printed paper representing other bits of a scarce but comparatively useless yellow metal that is kept buried in strong vaults. Meanwhile, the soil, the only real wealth that can keep mankind alive on the face of this Earth is savagely being cut loose from its ancient moorings and washed into the seven seas. 18

We have just arrived upon this Earth. How long will we stay? 19

QUESTIONS FOR READING AND WRITING

1. What does Rettie's essay imply about the relative significance of humankind's role in the earth's history?
2. Why does Rettie devote so much space (paragraphs 2–5) to the Copernicans and to the techniques of motion-picture photography?
3. Which words in the next-to-last paragraph help to convey Rettie's concern for ecology, for the way humans treat their planet?

4. How does Rettie's analogy between all of geological time and the time of one year help us to realize the worth of the earth's "gifts" to us?
5. Write an essay in which, using Rettie's techniques, you "condense" your life into a 24-hour period. (Note: if you are eighteen, one year of your life would pass in one hour and twenty minutes.)
6. Write an essay in which you compare the major historical events of a given year of your life with the corresponding year in your parents' lives. (For example, if you were born in 1972, you were 8 years old when Ronald Reagan was elected President; if your mother was born in 1944, she was 8 years old when Dwight Eisenhower was elected President.)

✦ Lewis Thomas ✦
The Attic of the Brain

An American physician, teacher, and essayist, Lewis Thomas (b. 1913) is Emeritus President at the Sloan Kettering Cancer Center in New York City. Among his books of essays are The Lives of a Cell *(1974),* The Medusa and the Snail *(1979), and* Late Night Thoughts on Listening to Mahler's Ninth Symphony *(1983). In the following essay, in which he draws an analogy between the human brain and an attic, he speculates that we might be better off if all of our thoughts were not open for public inspection.*

MY PARENTS' HOUSE HAD AN ATTIC, the darkest and strangest part of the building, reachable only by placing a stepladder beneath the trapdoor and filled with unidentifiable articles too important to be thrown out with the trash but no longer suitable to have at hand. This mysterious space was the memory of the place. After many years all the things deposited in it became, one by one, lost to consciousness. But they were still there, we knew, safely and comfortably stored in the tissues of the house. 1

These days most of us live in smaller, more modern houses or in apartments, and attics have vanished. Even the deep closets in which we used to pile things up for temporary forgetting are rarely designed into new homes. 2

Everything now is out in the open, openly acknowledged and displayed, and whenever we grow tired of a memory, an old chair, a trunkful of old letters, they are carted off to the dump for burning. 3

This has seemed a healthier way to live, except maybe for the smoke—everything out to be looked at, nothing strange hidden under the roof, nothing forgotten because of no place left in impenetrable darkness to forget. Openness is the new life-style, no undisclosed belongings, no private secrets. Candor is the rule in architecture. The house is a machine for living, and what kind of a machine would hide away its worn-out, obsolescent parts? 4

But it is in our nature as human beings to clutter, and we hanker for places set aside, reserved for storage. We tend to accumulate and outgrow possessions at the same time, and it is an endlessly 5 discomforting mental task to keep sorting out the ones to get rid of. We might, we think, remember them later and find a use for them, and if they are gone for good, off to the dump, this is a source of nervousness. I think it may be one of the reasons we drum our fingers so much these days.

We might take a lesson here from what has been learned about our brains in this century. We thought we discovered, first off, the attic, although its existence has been mentioned from time to time by all the people we used to call great writers. What we really found was the trapdoor and a stepladder, and off we clambered, shining flashlights into the corners, vacuuming the dust out of bureau drawers, puzzling over the names of objects, tossing them down to the floor below, and finally paying around fifty dollars an hour to have them carted off for burning.

After several generations of this new way of doing things we took up openness and candor with the febrile intensity of a new religion, everything laid out in full view, and as in the design of our new houses it seemed a healthier way to live, except maybe again for smoke.

And now, I think, we have a new kind of worry. There is no place for functionless, untidy, inexplicable notions, no dark comfortable parts of the mind to hide away the things we'd like to keep but at the same time forget. The attic is still there, but with the trapdoor always open and the stepladder in place we are always in and out of it, flashing lights around, naming everything, unmystified.

I have an earnest proposal for psychiatry, a novel set of therapeutic rules, although I know it means waiting in line.

Bring back the old attic. Give new instructions to the patients who are made nervous by our times, including me, to make a conscious effort to hide a reasonable proportion of thought. It would have to be a gradual process, considering how far we have come in the other direction talking, talking all the way. Perhaps only one or two thoughts should be repressed each day, at the outset. The easiest, gentlest way might be to start with dreams, first by forbidding the patient to mention any dream, much less to recount its details, then encouraging the outright forgetting that there was a dream at all, remembering nothing beyond the vague sense that during sleep there had been the familiar sound of something shifting and sliding, up under the roof.

We might, in this way, regain the kind of spontaneity and zest for ideas, things popping into the mind, uncontrollable and ungovernable thoughts, the feel that this notion is somehow connected unaccountably with that one. We could come again into possession of real memory, the kind of memory that can come only from jumbled forgotten furniture, old photographs, fragments of music. 11

It has been one of the great errors of our time to think that by thinking about thinking, and then talking about it, we could possibly straighten out and tidy up our minds. There is no delusion more damaging than to get the idea in your head that you understand the functioning of your own brain. Once you acquire such a notion, you run the danger of moving in to take charge, guiding your thoughts, shepherding your mind from place to place, *controlling* it, making lists of regulations. The human mind is not meant to be governed, certainly not by any book of rules yet written; it is supposed to run itself, and we are obliged to follow it along, trying to keep up with it as best we can. It is all very well to be aware of your awareness, even proud of it, but never try to operate it. You are not up to the job. 12

I leave it to the analysts to work out the techniques for doing what now needs doing. They are presumably the professionals most familiar with the route, and all they have to do is turn back and go the other way, session by session, step by step. It takes a certain amount of hard swallowing and a lot of revised jargon, and I have great sympathy for their plight, but it is time to reverse course. 13

If after all, as seems to be true, we are endowed with unconscious minds in our brains, these should be regarded as normal structures, installed wherever they are for a purpose. I am not sure what they are built to contain, but as a biologist, impressed by the usefulness of everything alive, I would take it for granted that they are useful, probably indispensable organs of thought. It cannot be a bad thing to own one, but I would no more think of meddling with it than trying to exorcise my liver, an equally mysterious apparatus. Until we know a lot more, it would be wise, as we have learned from other fields in medicine, to let them be, above all not to interfere. Maybe, even—and this is the notion I wish to suggest to my psychiatric friends—to stock them up, put more things into them, make *use* of them. Forget whatever you feel like forgetting. From time to time, practice *not* being open, discover new things *not* to talk about, learn reserve, hold the tongue. But above all, develop the human talent 14 for forgetting words, phrases, whole unwelcome sentences, all experiences involving wincing. If we should ever lose the loss of memory, we might lose as well that most attractive of signals ever flashed from the human face, the blush. If we should give away the capacity for embarrassment, the touch of fingertips might be the next to go, and then the suddenness of laughter, the unaccountable sure sense of something gone wrong, and, finally, the marvelous conviction that being human is the best thing to be.

Attempting to operate one's own mind, powered by such a magical instrument as the human brain, strikes me as rather like using the world's biggest computer to add columns of figures, or towing a Rolls-Royce with a nylon rope.

I have tried to think of a name for the new professional activity, but each time I think of a good one I forget it before I can get it written down. Psychorepression is the only one I've hung on to, but I can't guess at the fee schedule.

QUESTIONS FOR READING AND WRITING

1. Construct a chart that lists the points of comparison Thomas draws between an attic and the human brain.
2. What dangers does Thomas see in our modern tendency to be too open, to reveal too much of ourselves to each other or to professional analysts?
3. What, according to Thomas, is the connection between memory and spontaneity?
4. In a paragraph, describe what Thomas means by "psychorepression" (paragraph 16).
5. Reexamine your own attic (a closet or a "junk" drawer may work as well) and write an essay based on the memories it evokes.

✦ Tom Wolfe ✦

O Rotten Gotham

Sliding Down into the Behavioral Sink

Tom Wolfe (b. 1931), known as the creator of the New Journalism, developed his idiosyncratic style as a means of getting the reader's attention. The titles of his meticulously researched books reflect his flamboyance: The Kandy-Kolored Tangerine-Flake Streamline Baby *(1965),* The Electric Kool-Aid Acid Test *(1968), and* From Bauhaus to Our House *(1981). Wolfe's comments about American society are incisive, witty, and irreverent, but few critics would quarrel with his ability to recreate accurately the essentials of a scene. In the following selection from* The Pump House Gang *(1968), Wolfe uses an analogy between humans and rats to comment upon the behavior of humans in pressurized urban environments.*

I JUST SPENT TWO DAYS with Edward T. Hall, an anthropologist, 1
watching thousands of my fellow New Yorkers short-circuiting themselves into hot little twitching death balls with jolts of their own adrenalin. Dr. Hall says it is overcrowding that does it. Overcrowding gets the adrenalin going, and the adrenalin gets them queer, autistic, sadistic, barren, batty, sloppy, hot-in-the-pants, chancred-on-the-flankers, leering, puling, numb—the usual in New York, in other words, and God knows what else. Dr. Hall has the theory that overcrowding has already thrown New York into a state of behavioral sink. Behavioral sink is a term from ethology, which is the study of how animals relate to their environment. Among animals, the sink winds up with a "population collapse" or "massive die-off." O rotten Gotham.

It got to be easy to look at New Yorkers as animals, especially 2
looking down from some place like a balcony at Grand Central at the rush hour Friday afternoon. The floor was filled with the poor white humans, running around, dodging, blinking their eyes, making a sound like a pen full of starlings or rats or something.

"Listen to them skid," says Dr. Hall. 3

He was right. The poor old etiolate animals were out there 4
skidding on their rubber soles. You could hear it once he pointed it out. They stop short to keep from hitting somebody or because they

are disoriented and they suddenly stop and look around, and they skid on their rubber-soled shoes, and a screech goes up. They pour out onto the floor down the escalators from the Pan-Am Building, from 42nd Street, from Lexington Avenue, up out of subways, down into subways, railroad trains, up into helicopters—

"You can also hear the helicopters all the way down here," says Dr. Hall. The sound of the helicopters using the roof of the Pan-Am Building nearly fifty stories up beats right through. "If it weren't for this ceiling"—he is referring to the very high ceiling in Grand Central—"this place would be unbearable with this kind of crowding. And yet they'll probably never 'waste' space like this again."

They screech! And the adrenal glands in all those poor white animals enlarge, micrometer by micrometer, to the size of cantaloupes. Dr. Hall pulls a Minox camera out of a holster he has on his belt and starts shooting away at the human scurry. The Sink!

Dr. Hall has the Minox up to his eye—he is a slender man, calm, 52 years old, young-looking, an anthropologist who has worked with Navajos, Hopis, Spanish-Americans, Negroes, Trukese. He was the most important anthropologist in the government during the crucial years of the foreign aid program, the 1950s. He directed both the Point Four training program and the Human Relations Area Files. He wrote *The Silent Language* and *The Hidden Dimension,* two books that are picking up the kind of "underground" following his friend Marshall McLuhan started picking up about five years ago. He teaches at the Illinois Institute of Technology, lives with his wife, Mildred, in a high-ceilinged town house on one of the last great residential streets in downtown Chicago, Astor Street; he has a grown son and daughter, loves good food, good wine, the relaxed, civilized life—but comes to New York with a Minox at his eye to record!—perfect—The Sink.

We really got down in there by walking down into the Lexington Avenue line subway stop under Grand Central. We inhaled those nice big fluffy fumes of human sweat, urine, effluvia, and sebaceous secretions. One old female human was already stroked out on the upper level, on a stretcher, with two policemen standing by. The other humans barely looked at her. They rushed into line. They bellied each other, haunch to paunch, down the stairs. Human heads shone through the gratings. The species North European tried to create bubbles of space around themselves, about a foot and a half in diameter—

"See, he's reacting against the line," says Dr. Hall. 9

—but the species Mediterranean presses on in. The hell with bubbles of space. The species North European resents that, this male human behind him presses forward toward the booth . . . *breathing* on him, he's disgusted, he pulls out of the line entirely, the species Mediterranean resents him for resenting it, and neither of them realizes what the hell they are getting irritable about exactly. And in all of them the old adrenals grow another micrometer. 10

Dr. Hall whips out the Minox. Too perfect! The bottom of The Sink. 11

It is the sheer overcrowding, such as occurs in the business sections of Manhattan five days a week and in Harlem, Bedford-Stuyvesant, southeast Bronx every day—sheer overcrowding is converting New Yorkers into animals in a sink pen. Dr. Hall's argument runs as follows: all animals, including birds, seem to have a built-in inherited requirement to have a certain amount of territory, space, to lead their lives in. Even if they have all the food they need, and there are no predatory animals threatening them, they cannot tolerate crowding beyond a certain point. No more than two hundred wild Norway rats can survive on a quarter acre of ground, for example, even when they are given all the food they can eat. They just die off. 12

But why? To find out, ethologists have run experiments on all sorts of animals, from stickleback crabs to Sika deer. In one major experiment, an ethologist named John Calhoun put some domesticated white Norway rats in a pen with four sections to it, connected by ramps. Calhoun knew from previous experiments that the rats tend to split up into groups of ten to twelve and that the pen, therefore, would hold forty to forty-eight rats comfortably, assuming they formed four equal groups. He allowed them to reproduce until there were eighty rats, balanced between male and female, but did not let it get any more crowded. He kept them supplied with plenty of food, water, and nesting materials. In other words, all their more obvious needs were taken care of. A less obvious need—space—was not. To the human eye, the pen did not even 13 look especially crowded. But to the rats, it was crowded beyond endurance.

The entire colony was soon plunged into a profound behavioral sink. "The sink," said Calhoun, "is the outcome of any behavioral process that collects animals together in unusually great numbers. The unhealthy connotations of the term are not accidental: a behavioral sink does act to aggravate all forms of pathology that can be found within a group."

For a start, long before the rat population reached eighty, a status hierarchy had developed in the pen. Two dominant male rats took over the two end sections, acquired harems of eight to ten females each, and forced the rest of the rats into the two middle pens. All the overcrowding took place in the middle pens. That was where the "sink" hit. The aristocrat rats at the end grew bigger, sleeker, healthier, and more secure the whole time.

In The Sink, meanwhile, nest building, courting, sex behavior, reproduction, social organization, health—all of it went to pieces. Normally, Norway rats have a mating ritual in which the male chases the female, the female ducks down into a burrow and sticks her head up to watch the male. He performs a little dance outside the burrow, then she comes out, and he mounts her, usually for a few seconds. When The Sink set in, however, no more than three males—the dominant males in the middle sections—kept up the old customs. The rest tried everything from satyrism to homosexuality or else gave up on sex altogether. Some of the subordinate males spent all their time chasing females. Three or four might chase one female at the same time, and instead of stopping at the burrow entrance for the ritual, they would charge right in. Once mounted, they would hold on for minutes instead of the usual seconds.

Homosexuality rose sharply. So did bisexuality. Some males would mount anything—males, females, babies, senescent rats, anything. Still other males dropped sexual activity altogether, wouldn't fight and, in fact, would hardly move except when the other rats slept. Occasionally, a female from the aristocrat rats' harems would come over the ramps and into the middle sections to sample life in The Sink. When she had had enough, she would run back up the ramp. Sink males would give chase up to the top of the ramp, which is to say, to the very edge of the aristocratic preserve.

But one glance from one of the king rats would stop them cold and they would return to The Sink.

The slumming females from the harems had their adventures and then returned to a placid, healthy life. Females in The Sink, however, were ravaged, physically and psychologically. Pregnant rats had trouble continuing pregnancy. The rate of miscarriages increased significantly, and females started dying from tumors and other disorders of the mammary glands, sex organs, uterus, ovaries, and Fallopian tubes. Typically, their kidneys, livers, and adrenals were also enlarged or diseased or showed other signs associated with stress. 18

Child-rearing became totally disorganized. The females lost the interest or the stamina to build nests and did not keep them up if they did build them. In the general filth and confusion, they would not put themselves out to save offspring they were momentarily separated from. Frantic, even sadistic competition among the males was going on all around them and rendering their lives chaotic. The males began unprovoked and senseless assaults upon one another, often in the form of tail-biting. Ordinarily, rats will suppress this kind of behavior when it crops up. In The Sink, male rats gave up all policing and just looked out for themselves. The "pecking order" among males in The Sink was never stable. Normally, male rats set up a three-class structure. Under the pressure of overcrowding, however, they broke up into all sorts of unstable subclasses, cliques, packs—and constantly pushed, probed, explored, tested one another's power. Anyone was fair game, except for the aristocrats in the end pens. 19

Calhoun kept the population down to eighty, so that the next stage, "population collapse" or "massive die-off," did not occur. But the autopsies showed that the pattern—as in the diseases among the female rats—was already there. 20

The classic study of die-off was John J. Christian's study of Sika deer on James Island in the Chesapeake Bay, west of Cambridge, Maryland. Four or five of the deer had been released on the island, which was 280 acres and uninhabited, in 1916. By 1955 they had bred freely into a herd of 280 to 300. The population density was only about one deer per acre at this point, but Christian knew that this was already too high for the Sikas' inborn space requirements, and something would give before long. For two years the number 21 of deer remained 280 to 300. But suddenly, in 1958, over half the deer died; 161 carcasses were recovered. In 1959 more deer died and the population steadied at about 80.

In two years, two-thirds of the herd had died. Why? It was not starvation. In fact, all the deer collected were in excellent condition, with well-developed muscles, shining coats, and fat deposits between the muscles. In practically all the deer, however, the adrenal glands had enlarged by 50 percent. Christian concluded that the die-off was due to "shock following severe metabolic disturbance, probably as a result of prolonged adrenocortical hyperactivity. . . . There was no evidence of infection, starvation, or other obvious cause to explain the mass mortality." In other words, the constant stress of overpopulation, plus the normal stress of the cold of the winter, had kept the adrenalin flowing so constantly in the deer that their systems were depleted of blood sugar and they died of shock.

Well, the white humans are still skidding and darting across the floor of Grand Central. Dr. Hall listens a moment longer to the skidding and the darting noises, and then says, "You know, I've been on commuter trains here after everyone has been through one of these rushes, and I'll tell you, there is enough acid flowing in the stomachs in every car to dissolve the rails underneath."

Just a little invisible acid bath for the linings to round off the day. The ulcers the acids cause, of course, are the one disease people have already been taught to associate with the stress of city life. But overcrowding, as Dr. Hall sees it, raises a lot more hell with the body than just ulcers. In everyday life in New York—just the usual, getting to work, working in massively congested areas like 42nd Street between Fifth Avenue and Lexington, especially now that the Pan-Am Building is set in there, working in cubicles such as those in the editorial offices at Time-Life, Inc., which Dr. Hall cites as typical of New York's poor handling of space, working in cubicles with low ceilings and, often, no access to a window, while construction crews all over Manhattan drive everybody up the Masonite wall with air-pressure generators with noises up to the boil-a-brain decibel level, then rushing to get home, piling into subways and trains, fighting for time and for space, the usual day in New York—the whole now-normal thing keeps shooting jolts of adrenalin into the body, breaking down the body's defenses and winding up with the work-a-daddy human animal stroked out at the breakfast table with his head apoplexed like a cauliflower out of his $6.95 semi-spread Pima-cotton shirt, and nosed over into a plate of No-Kloresto egg substitute, signing off with the black thrombosis, cancer, kidney, liver, or stomach failure, and the adrenals ooze to a halt, the size of eggplants in July.

One of the people whose work Dr. Hall is interested in on this 25
score is Rene Dubos at the Rockefeller Institute. Dubos's work indicates that specific organisms, such as the tuberculosis bacillus or a pneumonia virus, can seldom be considered "the cause" of a disease. The germ or virus, apparently, has to work in combination with other things that have already broken the body down in some way—such as the old adrenal hyperactivity. Dr. Hall would like to see some autopsy studies made to record the size of adrenal glands in New York, especially of people crowded into slums and people who go through the full rush-hour-work-rush-hour cycle every day. He is afraid that until there is some clinical, statistical data on how overcrowding actually ravages the human body, no one will be willing to do anything about it. Even in so obvious a thing as air pollution, the pattern is familiar. Until people can actually see the smoke or smell the sulphur or feel the sting in their eyes, politicians will not get excited about it, even though it is well known that many of the lethal substances polluting the air are invisible and odorless. For one thing, most politicians are like the aristocrat rats. They are insulated from The Sink by practically sultanic buffers—limousines, chauffeurs, secretaries, aides-de-camp, doormen, shuttered houses, high-floor apartments. They almost never ride subways, fight rush hours, much less live in the slums or work in the Pan-Am Building.

QUESTIONS FOR READING AND WRITING

1. What rhetorical advantage does Wolfe gain by referring frequently to the anthropologist Edward T. Hall and his work?
2. Reread paragraph 24. How do the rhythm and pace of Wolfe's sentences support what he is saying about life in the big city?
3. What qualities of urban life does Wolfe most clearly emphasize by employing his analogy between animals—particularly rats—and humans?

4. Write an essay that describes some of the irritations that are part of life in a crowded dormitory or apartment building.
5. Observe the behavior of the human species in a lunchroom, bar, bus terminal, subway, or grocery store. Report what you observe.
6. Create a fable in which you use animals and their behavior to make a statement about the behavior of human beings.

Cause and Effect

Many thesis statements suffer from a lack of significance. Often, the remedy for these trite and commonplace statements is simply to add the word *because* or *since* and complete the sentence. Such an addition can transform an obvious thesis into an insightful and interesting *cause and effect* essay. If you begin an essay with a thesis that contends, "The Watts Riot was destructive," you have reached a virtual dead end, leaving you nothing to say except to document what you have already asserted. But if you add "because" and complete the sentence—"the Watts Riot was destructive, not because of the physical damage done, although that was great, but because it destroyed much of the economic and community base, the leadership segment, on which that section of Los Angeles had formerly depended"—you have a thesis that is potentially perceptive and informative.

One way to view cause and effect productively is to visualize it in terms of a temporal sequence. Consider your subject as an *effect* taking place now, or having taken place, and go back in time to trace the causes that produced it. Or, think first of your subject as a *cause*, then move ahead in time toward the present or into the future to account for, or predict, what effects will follow:

Past	Present	Future
CAUSE(S)←———	EFFECT(S)	
	CAUSE(S)———	→EFFECT(S)

In our Watts Riot example, if you regard the subject as an effect, you would retrace the time line to cite the causes of the riot—high unemployment, police violence, a long hot summer, substandard housing, poor educational facilities, outside-owned businesses. If, on the other hand, you regard the Watts Riot as a cause, moving ahead on the time line would yield such potential effects as massive physical destruction to property, disruption of the community social structure, bitterness toward the establishment, and the establishing of community action programs, a police review board, local control of the school board, and locally owned businesses. Notice that some of the effects are past and some are still happening, but the thrust of the cause-to-effect essay is toward the future, just as the thrust of the effect-to-cause essay is toward the past.

Quite often, especially in science and social-science essays, causes and effects will be mixed in a chain in which one effect will, in turn, become a cause of a subsequent effect, and so on until the end of the chain is reached. Here is an example describing the chain of interrelated effects that would follow the explosion of a nuclear device over an American city:

> Whereas most conventional bombs produce only one destructive effect—the shock wave—nuclear weapons produce many destructive effects. At the moment of explosion, when the temperature of the weapon material, instantly gasified, is at the superstellar level, the pressure is millions of times the normal atmospheric pressure. Immediately, radiation, consisting mainly of gamma rays, which are a very high-energy form of electromagnetic radiation, begins to stream outward into the environment. This is called the "initial nuclear radiation," and is the first of the destructive effects of a nuclear explosion. In an air burst of a one-megaton bomb—a bomb with the explosive yield of a million tons of TNT, which is a medium-sized weapon in present-day nuclear arsenals—the initial nuclear radiation can kill unprotected human beings in an area of some six square miles. Virtually simultaneously with the initial nuclear radiation, in a second destructive effect of the explosion, an electromagnetic pulse is generated by the intense gamma radiation acting on the air. In a high-altitude detonation, the pulse can knock out electrical equipment over a wide area by inducing a powerful surge of voltage through various conductors, such as antennas, overhead power lines, pipes, and railroad tracks. The Defense Department's Civil Preparedness Agency reported in 1977 that a single multi-kiloton nuclear weapon detonated one hundred and twenty-five miles over Omaha, Nebraska, could generate an electromagnetic pulse strong enough to damage solid-state electrical circuits throughout the entire continental United States and in parts of Canada and Mexico, and thus threaten to bring the economies of these countries to a halt. When the fusion and fission reactions have blown themselves out, a fireball takes shape. As it expands, energy is absorbed in the form of Xrays by the surrounding air, and then the air re-radiates a portion of that energy into the environment in the form of the thermal pulse—a wave of

> blinding light and intense heat—which is the third of the destructive effects of a nuclear explosion.*

In diagrammatic form, the chain of cause and effect looks something like this:

Principal Cause	Chain of Effects (numbered sequentially)
Detonation of a nuclear device	1. initial nuclear radiation gamma rays death of unprotected humans
	2. electromagnetic pulse surge of voltage damage to solid-state circuits disruption of economy
	3. fireball absorption of X rays thermal pulse

In a chain of cause and effect such as the one used by Schell, the problem of organization is largely solved by the chronology of the chain, so effects are described in the time sequence in which they occur. In some essays, such as in the hypothetical paper on Watts, some further strategy is called for, such as dividing the effects into favorable and unfavorable effects; which would come first would depend on the point you wanted to convey. It is good advice to end the essay with the effects that you feel are most important to making your point, and to bury in the middle of the essay the effect that is the weakest, the one you wish to deemphasize.

Of all the patterns of development that we have been discussing, cause and effect demands the highest kind of reasoned discourse between you and the reader. It demands not only that you prove the logic of the cause and effect relationship, but that you offer examples to support it. In no other pattern is the demand for logic so great or is its absence so clearly obvious to the reader. Despite these demands, cause and effect remains one of the most potent patterns for arousing high reader interest in your essay.

* Jonathan Schell, "The Fate of the Earth," *The New Yorker* (February 1, 1982), 55–56.

Moreover, the analysis of cause and effect is one of the most versatile patterns of writing you have at your disposal. It can be applied to any discipline. With it, you can analyze the causes of the Great Depression; you can trace the effects of Hamlet's delay in killing his Uncle Claudius; you can show the effects of overcrowding in large cities; or you can describe the causes of a nuclear reaction. Perhaps more than any other mode, cause and effect writing symbolizes the need for, and the possibility of, coherent, logical, and thoughtful expression in any context. It is well worth the time you'll take in mastering it.

✦ Anne Hollander ✦
Dressed to Thrill

Anne Hollander, who once described herself as "a formal student of art history and a private student of costume history," has published a book, Seeing Through Clothes *(1978), about dress and its social and esthetic implications. She was a Guggenheim Fellow in 1975–6. In the following essay, Hollander writes about the causes and consequences of our androgynous—unisex—style of clothing and what this style reveals about our preoccupations and desires.*

WHEN QUENTIN BELL applied Veblen's principles of Conspicuous Consumption and Conspicuous Waste to fashion, he added another—Conspicuous Outrage. This one now clearly leads the other two. In this decade we want the latest trends in appearance to strain our sense of the suitable and give us a real jolt. The old social systems that generated a need for conspicuous display have modified enough to dull the chic of straight extravagance: the chic of shock has continuous vitality. Dramatically perverse sexual signals are always powerful elements in the modern fashionable vocabulary; and the most sensational component among present trends is something referred to as androgyny. Many modish women's clothes imitate what Robert Taylor wore in 1940 publicity stills, and Michael Jackson's startling feminine beauty challenges public responses from every store window, as well as in many living replicas. 1

The mode in appearance mirrors collective fantasy, not fundamental aims and beliefs. We are not all really longing for two sexes in a single body, and the true hermaphrodite still counts as a monster. We are not seeing a complete and free interchange of physical characteristics across the sexual divide. There are no silky false moustaches or dashing fake goatees finely crafted of imported sable for the discriminating woman, or luxuriant jaw-length sideburns of the softest bristle sold with moisturizing glue and a designer applicator. Although the new ideal feminine torso has strong square shoulders, flat hips, and no belly at all, the corresponding ideal male body is certainly not displaying the beauties of 2 a soft round stomach, flaring hips, full thighs, and delicately sloping shoulders. On the new woman's ideally athletic shape, breasts may be large or not—a flat chest is not required; and below the belt in back, the buttocks may sharply protrude. But no space remains in front to house a safely cushioned uterus and ovaries, or even well-upholstered labia: under the lower half of the new, high-cut minimal swimsuits, there is room only for a clitoris. Meanwhile the thrilling style of male beauty embodied by Michael Jackson runs chiefly to unprecedented surface adornment—cosmetics and sequins, jewels and elaborate hair, all the old privileges once granted to women, to give them every erotic advantage in the sex wars of the past.

The point about all this is clearly not androgyny at all, but the idea of detachable pleasure. Each sex is not trying to take up the fundamental qualities of the other sex, but rather of the other sexuality—the erotic dimension, which can transcend biology and its attendant social assumptions and institutions. Eroticism is being shown to float free of sexual function. Virility is displayed as a capacity for feeling and generating excitement, not for felling trees or enemies and generating children. Femininity has abandoned the old gestures of passivity to take on main force: ravishing female models now stare purposefully into the viewer's eyes instead of flashing provocative glances or gazing remotely away. Erotic attractiveness appears ready to exert its strength in unforeseeable and formerly forbidden ways and places. Recognition is now being given to sexual desire for objects of all kinds once considered unsuitable—some of them inanimate, judging from the seductiveness of most advertising photography.

Homosexual desire is now an acknowledged aspect of common life, deserving of truthful representation in popular culture, not just in coterie vehicles of expression. The aging parents of youthful characters in movie and television dramas are no longer rendered as mentally stuffy and physically withered, but as stunningly attractive sexual beings—legitimate and nonridiculous rivals for the lustful attentions of the young. The curved flanks of travel irons and food processors in Bloomingdale's catalogue make as strong an appeal to erotic desire as the satiny behinds and moist lips of the makeup and underwear models. So do the unfolding petals of lettuces and the rosy flesh of cut tomatoes on TV food commercials. In this general eroticization of the material world, visual culture is openly acknowledging that lust is by nature wayward.

To register as attractive under current assumptions, a female body may now show its affinities not only with delicious objects but with attractive male bodies, without having to relinquish any feminine erotic resources. Male beauty may be enhanced by feminine usages that increase rather than diminish its masculine effect. Men and women may both wear clothes loosely fashioned by designers like Gianni Versace or Issey Miyake to render all bodies attractive whatever their structure, like the drapery of antiquity. In such clothes, sexuality is expressed obliquely in a fluid fabric envelope that follows bodily movement and also forms a graceful counterpoint to the nonchalant postures of modern repose. The aim of such dress is to emphasize the sexiness of a rather generalized sensuality, not of male or female characteristics; and our present sense of personal appearance, like our sense of all material display, shows that we are more interested in generalized sensuality than in anything else. In our multiform culture, it seems to serve as an equalizer. 5

In fashion, however, pervasive eroticism is still frequently being represented as the perpetual overthrow of all the restrictive categories left over from the last century, a sort of ongoing revolution. We are still pretending to congratulate ourselves on what a long way we have come. The lush men and strong girls now on view in the media may be continuing a long-range trend that began between the World Wars; but there have been significant interruptions and an important shift of tone. Then, too, men had smooth faces, thick, wavy hair and full, pouting lips, and women often wore pants, had shingled hair, and athletic torsos. But the important point in those days was to be as anti-Victorian as possible. The rigid and bearded Victorian male was being eased out of his tight carapace and distancing whiskers; the whole ladylike panoply was being simplified so that the actual woman became apparent to the eye and touch. Much of our present female mannishness and feminized manhood is a nostalgic reference to the effects fashionable for men and women in those pioneering days, rather than a new revolutionary expression of the same authentic kind. 6

There is obviously more to it all now than there was between the wars. We have already gone through some fake Victorian revivals, 7 both unself-conscious in the 1950s and self-conscious in the sixties and seventies, and lately our sense of all style has become slightly corrupt. Apart from the sexiness of sex, we have discovered the stylishness of style and the fashionableness of fashion. Evolving conventions of dress and sudden revolts from them have both become stylistically forced; there have been heavy quotation marks around almost all conspicuous modes of clothing in the last fifteen or twenty years, as there were not in more hopeful days. Life is now recognized to have a grotesque and inflated media dimension by which ordinary experience is measured, and all fashion has taken to looking over its own shoulder. Our contemporary revolutionary modes are mostly theatrical costumes, since we have now learned to assume that appearances are detachable and interchangeable and only have provisional meanings.

Many of the more extreme new sartorial phenomena display such uncooked incoherence that they fail to represent any main trend in twentieth-century taste except a certain perverse taste for garbage—which is similarly fragmented and inexpressive, even though it can always be sifted and categorized. We have become obsessed with picking over the past instead of plowing it under, where it can do some good. Perversity has moreover been fostered in fashion by its relentless presentation as a form of ongoing public entertainment. The need for constant impact naturally causes originality to get confused with the capacity to cause a sensation; and sensations can always be created, just as in all show business, by the crudest of allusions.

In the twenties, the revolutionary new fashions were much more important but much less brutally intrusive. Photos from the twenties, thirties, and even the very early forties, show the young Tyrone Power and Robert Taylor smiling with scintillating confidence, caressed by soft focus and glittering highlights, and wearing the full-cut, casual topcoats with the collar up that we see in today's ads for women, then as now opened to show the fully-draped trousers, loose sweaters, and long, broad jackets of that time. Then it was an alluringly modern and feminized version of male beauty, freshly suggesting pleasure without violence or loss of decorum, a high level of civilization without any forbidding and tyrannical stiffness or antiquated formality. At the same time, women's fashions were stressing an articulated female shape that sought to be perceived as clearly as the male. Both were the first modern styles to take up the flavor of general physical ease, in timely and pertinent defiance of the social restrictions and symbolic sexual distinctions made by dress in the preceding time. Now, however, those same easy men's clothes are being worn by women; and the honest old figure of freedom seems to be dressed up in the spirit of pastiche. We did come a long way for a while, but then we stopped and went on the stage.

10 Strong and separate sexual definition in the old Victorian manner tried to forbid the generally erotic and foster the romantic. Against such a background even slightly blurring the definition automatically did the opposite; and so when Victorian women dared adopt any partial assortment of male dress they were always extremely disturbing. They called attention to those aspects of female sexuality that develop in sharp contrast to both female biology and romantic rhetoric. Consequently, when female fashion underwent its great changes early in this century, such aspects were deliberately and vehemently emphasized by a new mobility and quasi-masculine leanness. Women with no plump extensions at all but with obvious and movable legs suddenly made their appearance, occasionally even in trousers. They indicated a mettlesome eagerness for action, even unencumbered amorous action, and great lack of interest in sitting still receiving homage or rocking the cradle. Meanwhile when men adopted the casual suits of modern leisure, they began to suggest a certain new readiness to sit and talk, to listen and laugh at themselves, to dally and tarry rather than couple briskly and straightway depart for work or battle. Men and women visibly desired to rewrite the rules about how the two sexes should express their interest in sex; and the liberated modern ideal was crystallized.

11 But a sexual ideal of maturity and enlightened savoir faire also informed that period of our imaginative history. In the fantasy of the thirties, manifested in the films of Claudette Colbert, for example, or Gable and Lombard, adult men and women ideally pursued pleasure without sacrificing reason, humor, or courtesy—even in those dramas devoted to the ridiculous. The sexes were still regarded as fundamentally different kinds of being, although the style of their sexuality was reconceived. The aim of amorous life was still

to take on the challenging dialectic of the sexes, which alone could yield the fullest kind of sexual pleasure. Erotic feeling was inseparable from dramatic situation.

By those same thirties, modern adult clothing was also a fully developed stylistic achievement. It duly continued to refine, until it finally became unbearably mannered in the first half of the sixties. The famous ensuing sartorial revolution, though perfectly authentic, was also the first to occur in front of the camera—always in the mirror, as it were. And somehow the subsequent two decades have seen a great fragmentation both of fashion and of sexuality.

Extreme imagery, much of it androgynous like Boy George's looks, or the many punk styles and all the raunchier fashion photos, has become quite commonplace; but it has also become progressively remote from most common practice. It offers appearances that we may label "fashion," but that we really know to be media inventions created especially to stun, provoke, and dismay us. At the same time, some very conventional outrageous effects have been revived in the realm of accessible fashion, where there is always room for them. Ordinary outrageousness and perverse daring in dress are the signs of licensed play, never the signal of serious action. They are licitly engaged in by the basically powerless, including clowns and children and other innocuous performers, who are always allowed to make extreme emotional claims that may stir up strong personal responses but have no serious public importance. Women's fashion constantly made use of outrage in this way during the centuries of female powerlessness, and selective borrowing from men was one of its most effective motifs.

After the sixties and before the present menswear mode, the masculine components in women's fashions still made girls look either excitingly shocking or touchingly pathetic. The various neat tuxedos made famous by Yves St. Laurent, for example, were intended to give a woman the look of a depraved youth, a sort of tempting Dorian Gray. The *Annie Hall* clothes swamped the woman in oversized male garments, so that she looked at first like a small child being funny in adult gear, and then like a fragile girl wrapped in a strong man's coat, a combined emblem of bruised innocence and clownishness. These are both familiar "outrageous" devices culled particularly from the theatrical past.

Long before modern fashion took it up, the conventionally outrageous theme of an attractive feminine woman in breeches proved an invariably stimulating refinement in the long history of racy popular art, both for the stage and in print. The most important erotic aim of this theme was never to make a woman actually seem to be a man—looking butch has never been generally attractive—but to make a girl assume the unsettling beauty that dwells in the sexual uncertainty of an adolescent boy. It is an obvious clever move for modern fashionable women to combine the old show-business-like excitement of the suggestive trousered female with the cultivated self-possession of early twentieth-century menswear—itself already a feminized male style. It suits, especially in the present disintegrated erotic climate that has rendered the purer forms of outrageousness somewhat passé. 15

Such uses of men's clothes have nothing to do with an impulse toward androgyny. They instead invoke all the old tension between the sexes; and complete drag, whichever sex wears it, also insists on sexual polarity. Most drag for men veers toward the exaggerated accoutrements of the standard siren; and on the current screen, *Tootsie* and *Yentl* are both demonstrating how different and how divided the sexes are. 16

While the extreme phenomena are getting all the attention, however, we are acting out quite another forbidden fantasy in our ordinary lives. The really androgynous realm in personal appearance is that of active sports clothing. The unprecedented appeal of running gear and gym clothes and all the other garb associated with strenuous physical effort seems to be offering an alternative in sexual expression. Beyond the simple pleasures of physical fitness, and the right-minded satisfactions of banishing class difference that were first expressed in the blue-jeans revolution of the sixties, this version of pastoral suggests a new erotic appeal in the perceived androgyny of childhood. The short shorts and other ingenuous bright play clothes in primary colors that now clothe bodies of all sizes and sexes are giving a startling kindergarten cast to everybody's public looks, especially in summer. 17

The real excitement of androgynous appearance is again revealed as associated only with extreme youth—apparently the more extreme the better. The natural androgyny of old age has acquired no 18 appeal. The tendency of male and female bodies to resemble each other in late maturity is still conventionally ridiculous and deplorable; sportswear on old women looks crisp and convenient, not sexually attractive. But the fresh, unfinished androgyny of the nursery is evidently a newly expanded arena for sexual fantasy.

In the unisex look of the ordinary clothing that has become increasingly common in the past two decades, there has been a submerged but unmistakable element of child-worship. This note has been struck at a great distance from the slick and expensive ambiguities of high fashion that include couture children's clothes aping the vagaries of current adult chic. It resonates instead in the everyday sexual ambiguity of rough duck or corduroy pants, flannel shirts, T-shirts, sweaters, and sneakers. Any subway car or supermarket is full of people dressed this way. The guises for this fantasy have extended past play clothes to children's underwear, the little knitted shirts and briefs that everyone wears at the age of five. One ubiquitous ad for these even showed a shirtee sliding up to expose an adult breast, to emphasize the sexiness of the fashion; but the breast has been prudently canceled in publicly displayed versions.

Our erotic obsession with children has overt and easily deplored expressions in the media, where steamy twelve-year-old fashion models star in ads and twelve-year-old prostitutes figure in dramas and news stories. The high-fashion modes for children also have the flavor of forced eroticism. Child abuse and kiddy porn are now publicly discussed concerns, ventilated in the righteous spirit of reform; and yet unconscious custom reflects the same preoccupation with the sexual condition of childhood. The androgynous sportswear that was formerly the acceptable everyday dress only of children is now everyone's leisure clothing; its new currency must have more than one meaning.

On the surface, of course, it invokes the straight appeal of the physical life, the rural life, and perhaps even especially the taxing life of the dedicated athlete, which used to include sexual abstinence along with the chance of glory. The world may wish to look as if it were constantly in training to win, or equipped to explore; but there is another condition it is also less obviously longing for—freedom from the strain of fully adult sexuality. These styles of clothing signal a retreat into the unfinished, undefined sexuality of childhood that we are now finding so erotic, and that carries no difficult social or personal responsibilities.

From 1925 to 1965, four-year-old girls and boys could tumble in the sandbox in identical cotton overalls or knitted suits, innocently aping the clothes of skiers, railroadmen, or miners, while their mom wore a dress, hat, and stockings, and their dad a suit, hat, and tie—the modern dress of sexual maturity, also worn by Gable, Lombard, and all the young and glittering Hollywood company. Now the whole family wears sweat suits and overalls and goes bareheaded. Such gear is also designed to encourage the game of dressing up like all the non-amorous and ultraphysical heroes of modern folklore—forest rangers and cowboys, spacemen and frogmen, pilots and motorcyclists, migrant workers and terrorists—that is constantly urged on children. The great masquerade party of the late sixties ostensibly came to an end; but it had irreversibly given to ordinary grownups the right to wear fancy costumes for fun that was formerly a child's privilege. The traditional dress of the separate adult sexes is reserved for public appearances, and in general it is now socially correct to express impatience with it. "Informal" is the only proper style in middle-class social life; and for private leisure, when impulse governs choices, kids' clothes are the leading one. Apparently the erotic androgynous child is the new forbidden creature of unconscious fantasy, not only the infantile fashion model or rock star but the ordinary kid, who has exciting sexual potential hidden under its unsexed dress-up play clothes. 22

Fashions of the remote past dealt straightforwardly with the sexuality of children by dressing them just like ordinary adults, suitably different according to sex. But in Romantic times, children were perceived to exist in a special condition much purer and closer to beneficent nature than their elders, requiring clothes that kept them visibly separate from the complex corruptions of adult society, including full-scale erotic awareness. The habit of putting children in fancy dress began then, too, especially boys. They were dressed as wee, chubby, and harmless soldiers and sailors, or Turks and Romans, to emphasize their innocence by contrast. Children's clothes still differed according to sex—girls had sweet little chemises and sashes instead of fancy costumes—but their overriding common flavor was one of artlessness. 23

Later on the Victorians overdid it, and loaded their children with clothing, but it was still two-sexed and distinctively designed for them. Finally the enlightened twentieth century invented the use of mock sportswear for the wiggly little bodies of both boys and girls. Nevertheless, the costumes now suitable for children on display still tend toward the Victorian, with a good deal of nostalgic velvet and lace. In line with Romantic views of women, some feminine styles also used to feature infantine suggestions drawn from little girls' costumes: the last was the tiny baby dress worn with big shoes and big hair in the later sixties, just before the eruption of the women's movement. But only since then has a whole generation of adults felt like dressing up in mock rough gear, like androgynous children at play, to form a race of apparently presexual but unmistakably erotic beings.

Once again, very pointedly, the clothes for the role are male. Our modern sense of artlessness seems to prefer the masculine brand; and when we dress our little boys and girls alike to blur their sexuality—or ourselves in imitation of them—that means we dress the girls like the boys, in the manifold costumes celebrating nonsexual physical prowess. At leisure, both men and women prefer to suggest versions of Adam alone in Eden before he knew he had a sex, innocently wearing his primal sweat suit made only of native worth and honor.

The Romantic sense of the child as naturally privileged and instinctively good like Adam seems to stay with us. But we have lately added the belief in a child's potential depravity, which may go unpaid for and unpunished just because of all children's categorical innocence. Perhaps this society abuses its children, and also aggressively dresses them in lipstick and sequins, for the same reason it imitates them—from a helpless envy of what they get away with. The everyday androgynous costume is the suit of diminished erotic responsibility and exemption from adult sexual risk. What it clothes is the child's license to make demands and receive gratification with no risk of dishonor—to be erotic, but to pose as unsexual and therefore unaccountable.

Even more forbidden and outrageous than the sexual child is its near relation, the erotic angel. While the ordinary world is routinely dressing itself and its kids in unisex jeans, it is simultaneously conjuring up mercurial apparitions who offer an enchanting counterpoint of life's mundane transactions. In the rock star form, they embody the opposing fantasy face of the troublesome domestic child or adolescent: the angelic visitor who needs to obey no earthly rules. Funny little E.T. was only one version. The type includes all those supremely compelling creatures who may shine while they stomp and whirl and scream and hum and never suffer the slightest humiliation.

A child, however ideologized, is always real and problematic, but 28
an angel has a fine mythic remoteness however palpable he seems. The opposing kind of androgyny invests him: he exists not before but beyond human sexual life, and he comes as a powerful messenger from spheres where there is no taking or giving in marriage, but where extreme kinds of joy are said to be infinite. Our rock-video beings cultivate the unhuman look of ultimate synthesis: they aim to transcend sexual conflict by becoming fearsome angels, universally stimulating creatures fit for real existence only out of this world. Like all angels, they profoundly excite; but they don't excite desire, even though they do make the air crackle with promise and menace. Their job is to bring the message and then leave, having somehow transformed the world. Michael Jackson reportedly leads a life both angelic and artificially childlike, and he makes his appearances in epiphanic style. David Bowie still appears to be the man who fell to earth, not someone born here. Grace Jones also seems to come from altogether elsewhere. Such idols only function in the sphere of unattainability. While they flourish they remain sojourners, leading lives of vivid otherness in what seems a sexual no man's land.

Angels were in fact once firmly male and uncompromisingly 29
austere. The disturbing sensuality they acquired in the art of later centuries, like that of the luscious angel in Leonardo's *Virgin of the Rocks*, always reads as a feminization—and from this one must conclude that adding feminine elements to the male is what produces androgyny's most intense effects. Almost all our androgynous stars are in fact males in feminized trim; their muscular and crop-haired female counterparts, such as Annie Lennox, are less numerous and have a more limited appeal. The meaning in all our androgyny, both modish and ordinary, still seems to be the same: the male is the primary sex, straightforward, simple, and active. He can

be improved and embellished, however, and have and give a better time if he allows himself to be modified by the complexities of female influence.

The process does not work the other way. Elegant women in fashionable menswear expound the same thought, not its opposite: traditional jackets and trousers are austerely beautiful, but they are patently enhanced by high heels, flowing scarves, cosmetics, and earrings. Lisa Lyon, the body builder, has been photographed by Robert Mapplethorpe to show that her excessively developed muscles do not make her mannish but instead have been feminized to go with, not against, her flowered hats and lipstick. Ordinary women wearing men's active gear while wheeling strollers on the street or carrying bags across the parking lot are subduing and adapting harsh male dress to flexible female life and giving it some new scope. Common androgynous costume is always some kind of suit or jumpsuit, or pants, shirt and jacket, not some kind of dress, bodice and skirt, or gown. A hat may go with it, or perhaps a hood or scarf, but not a coif or veil. A few real female skirts (not kilts or Greek evzone skirts) are now being very occasionally and sensationally tried out by some highly visible men—daring designers, media performers and their imitators, fashion models and theirs—but all kinds of pants are being worn by all kinds of women all the time. We can read the message: the male is the first sex, now at last prepared to consider the other one anew, with much fanfare. It is still a case of female sexuality enlightening the straight male world—still the arrival of Eve and all her subsequent business in and beyond the garden—that is being celebrated. The "androgynous" mode for both sexes suggests that the female has come on the scene to educate the male about the imaginative pleasures of sex, signified chiefly by the pleasures of adornment. About its difficulties, summed up by that glaringly absent round belly, she is naturally keeping quiet.

Meanwhile the more glittering versions of modish androgyny continue to reflect what we adore in fantasy. Many of us seem to feel that the most erotic condition of all could not be that of any man or woman, or of any child, or of a human being with two sexes, but that of a very young and effeminate male angel—a new version of art history's lascivious *putto*. Such a being may give and take a guiltless delight, wield limitless sexual power without sexual politics, feel all the pleasures of sex with none of the personal risks, can never grow up, never get wise, and never be old. It is a futureless vision, undoubtedly appropriate to a nuclear age; but if any of us manages to survive, the soft round belly will surely again have its day.

In the meantime, as we approach the end of the century and the 32
millennium, the impulse toward a certain fusion in the habits of the sexes may have a more hopeful meaning. After a hundred years of underground struggle, trousers are no longer male dress sometimes worn by women. They have been successfully feminized so as to become authentic costume for both sexes, and to regain the authoritative bisexual status the gown once had in the early Middle Ages. This development is clearly not a quick trend but a true change, generations in the making. Male skirts have yet to prove themselves; but men have in fact succeeded in making long-term capital out of the short-lived and now forgotten Peacock Revolution of the late sixties. Whole new ranges of rich color, interesting pattern, texture, and unusual cut have become generally acceptable in male dress since then, and so has a variety of jewelry. The sort of fashionable experiment once associated only with women has become a standard male option. Some new agreement between the sexes may actually be forming, signaled by all these persistent visual projections; but just what that accord will turn out to be it is not safe to predict, nor whether it will continue to civilize us further or only perplex us more.

QUESTIONS FOR READING AND WRITING

1. Look up the etymology of *androgyny*. Give examples of an androgynous "look" in recent men's and women's fashions.
2. Examine the covers of ten recent magazines designed primarily for women (*Elle, Vogue, Glamour, Mademoiselle*, and so forth). Do the clothes worn by the models on the covers of these magazines confirm or contradict what Hollander says about recent fashion trends?
3. What does Hollander mean in paragraph 7 when she says that "appearances are detachable and interchangeable"?
4. In what ways does the last paragraph of this essay qualify and temper what has come before?

5. Hollander's essay implies that clothes make statements of various kinds: social, economic, political, and sexual. Write a description or classification essay about types of "looks" created by contemporary clothing.
6. Write an essay about the clothes worn by contemporary rock stars. What images or messages do they convey? Are they shocking? Do they confirm Hollander's ideas? What will the rock star of the future look like?

✦ Mark Jacobson ✦
On Rediscovering Evil

A staff writer for Esquire *magazine, Mark Jacobson regularly contributes articles on ethical issues. In the following essay, he grapples with the concept of evil as it presents itself to us in contemporary dress, that is, in a secularized world where the idea of fighting Satan is perhaps outmoded, but where—in the persons of such as Hitler, Stalin, and Pol Pot—evil is still very much a force to be fought at all costs.*

ONE MOMENT I WAS IN A COFFEE SHOP idly thumbing through a newspaper article about the fugitive Nazi doctor, Josef Mengele. Then, as if triggered by a primordial posthypnotic suggestion, my mission came clear. I was to secure proper weaponry, get on a plane, fly to Paraguay, go upriver, locate Mengele, and blow his head off. Then I would return in time for dinner, and when my wife asked me if anything interesting had happened that day, I'd shrug, say no, that I had just run a few necessary errands. 1

Now, after Mengele's supposed death, when I think of this instant, I still get shivers. This was because I believe that I was in touch with something in me (or possibly outside me) that was very powerful. Maybe I went crazy there for a moment, and the only thing that kept me from becoming a *New York Post* headline was that my commanding hallucination ordered me to kill a Nazi doctor in a remote, inaccessible land, rather than my wife and children right beside me. But more than that, there is an inescapable sense of regret. Part of me laments the lost opportunity, not trying to kill Mengele during that wild crease when my psyche somehow made that act a viable choice. For Mengele was, from all accounts, a man who deserved no better. He was an evil man. 2

For someone who has always taken his status as a Freudian-based garden-variety rationalist for granted, it was a shock imagining that there was a man on earth possessed by so medieval a concept as evil. It was never in my program to believe in "bad seeds," to think that not every Ted Bundy has a terrible childhood to account for his serial murders, or that it isn't simple political mendacity that motivates people like Henry Kissinger to instigate bombing raids and 3 population destabilizations. Yet here I was, not only entertaining the possibility that evil existed as a palpable force, but also that it was *my obligation* to oppose it.

Beyond this, I've come to the conclusion that I am not alone in this contractual responsibility. I think it's everyone's duty to grapple with these issues, to examine their personal cosmology and make an individual declaration on the topic. Evil, if it truly exists, is everyone's business.

I hear myself saying these things and feel like a sandwich-board Forty-second Street shouter. Nevertheless, my Manchurian Candidate summons to murder Mengele wasn't the first of these strange impulses. Once, twenty years ago, I was walking down Dwight Way in Berkeley on a bright, sunny day when I heard someone whistling at me. I looked around but didn't see anyone. The whistle continued, refusing to let me be. Then I saw a youngish guy in a T-shirt and jeans sitting on a lawn across the street. I was certain I'd looked at that lawn a moment before and no one was there. "Yeah, you," the teenager said, motioning me over. He had an alarming aspect to him, with his slicked- back DA and exceedingly aquiline nose. "Give me twenty-five dollars to get the bus," he said. When I told him I didn't have it, he grasped his hands together like Robert Mitchum in *The Night of the Hunter* and said I should get the money and come with him. "Because it's great, where I'm going." I didn't like the feel of his gaze on my skin, so I said no thanks and pushed on. When I looked back, the guy was beckoning another hippie.

For years I've been skeptical of the meaning of this encounter, regarding it as an everyday item I'd for some reason chosen to infuse with a malignant supernaturalness because I found it racy to collect images of metaphysical danger. But I'll tell you: ten people a day ask me for money, and I don't remember them. That kid stays with me. I'm on the subway, riding in a car, and he's inside my head, sitting on that lawn, telling me to come along. And when I think of him I feel anxious, endangered. I sense the presence of evil.

Thinking this way hurls me into the dreadful otherworld of myth. I imagine myself a secret sharer, along for Conrad's *Heart of Darkness* cruise, on my personal Congo, ravaged with fear, yet inexorably drawn to "face the abomination." Talk about adventure travel! Booking passage in the twentieth century, that regular devil's workshop, genocide's stomping ground, is to be issued an exploding ticket. The head spins. The spiel of the newscaster nooses around your neck, every tabloid headline crimps the tourniquet. There are, of course, remedies. Mention "evil" and people's ears perk up. They push on you their gris-gris, their system, their exorcism. Their religion. "It works for me," they say, and not all of them are the kind who ask you to place your hand on the TV to be healed, electronically. Some are quite admirable; when they say the invocation of Christ chases evil, you have no choice but to respect them. But for the modern ironist, these stratagems smack of throwing last millennium's playbook into the onrush of barbarism. Evil has retooled, made an end run around the three-thousand-year-old spiritual Maginot Line.

That's the crux of the modern disease, isn't it? We face many of the same dilemmas we always have, yet the weapons we are handed to fight these malaises seem insufficient, hopelessly outmoded. The evil I sense is a distinctly up-to-date variety. It's the evil of how some guy in Arkansas wakes up one morning and decides to kill his whole family. It's the evil of a man who asks what the health benefits are before he accepts his position as the state torturer. The evil of today is beyond what we can conceive. By this I mean: you read about a man who went crazy and emptied his pistol into his child's body. As hideous as this is, it can be envisioned. However, the other day there was an item about a man who shot his child thirty-two times with a 9mm pistol. This particular 9mm model carries fourteen rounds in the magazine and one in the chamber. That means the killer would have had to reload, maybe twice. That's the inconceivable part, the reloading. To my mind that's where that act leaves the realm of human aberration and enters the preserve of evil. 8

Faced with a century of the inconceivable, a time when almost everyone can name at least ten mass murderers off the top of his head (go ahead, do it), the potential spiritual warrior stands clueless. Where to start this lonely crusade? As anyone who ever looked, darkly, through a bulletproof glass booth knows, evil can take a less than fire-breathing form. Who's to say I wouldn't get down to Paraguay and find Mengele to have been hit on the head with a coconut, an amnesia victim, not remembering for a moment why he once preferred blue eyes to brown. What would I say then, "Oh, 9 never mind"? Once there was a consensus on the form of evil. It was a snake. A serpent. A dragon. A reddish-toned man with horns. A mysterious stranger. Those were the icons, and when inveighing against the inconceivable, icons can be of great help; they at least give the illusion that the enemy can be crowded into a single frame, that he can be recognized. In today's small world, chockfull of mysterious strangers, including, very likely, some potential Travis Bickle who just that day was laid off from his job at the post office, we have lost the ability to picture evil, to encapsulate it.

The popular iconography has broken down. Last month, indulging dim passion for movies about devil cars and devil dogs, I saw *Prince of Darkness*. The director, the half-bright John Carpenter, was actually groping toward some updating of the formula, having the Unnameable speaking through computer terminals. Yet when it came time to bring out the bad guy, all he could offer was the Bad Guy, that ole scaly-wag, Lucifer. There he was, horns and all, this face from the hot-sauce bottle, a bitter anachronism.

Clearly, we need to redefine evil and its manifestations. To this end, I've been conducting a small, exceedingly informal poll. At first I feared my findings would not meet Gallupian muster, as only fifteen of the twenty-six respondents allowed that there was "such a thing as evil." However, when they were asked to fill in their ballots as if evil *did* exist, the results were interesting in their uniformity. While one person jocularly defined wickedness as the "subversion of art through the profusion and championing of mediocre ideas," almost everyone else thought that in order to be "evil or possessed of evil," an individual had to "cause unwarranted and *wholesale* suffering and death." In line with this, when I requested that the group write a list of the "ten potentially most evil people of this century, in order of their evilness," the returns were again surprisingly similar. While the bottom slots were filled with idiosyncratic, near-capricious selections (Walter O'Malley, the man who moved the Dodgers from Brooklyn, was mentioned three times), first on every ballot, outdistancing top contenders Joseph Stalin, Pol Pot, and Richard Nixon, was Adolf Hitler. Der Führer was the unanimous choice. When I asked people to draw a "face of evil," many added a brush moustache, even when the face they made bore no other resemblance to Hitler. It was weird, but a few days later when my five-year-old daughter drew a picture of "a bad man," she came up with Adolf's signature hairline. I interrogated her. She said she thought she'd heard of Hitler, but didn't know what he looked like or had done.

Is it possible that a large segment of the population has already internalized the Nazi as the new paradigm of evil? Could that have been the reason for my urge to kill Mengele? (When asked if, given the chance, they would have killed Hitler in his cradle, everyone said yes.) But does this help us to identify evil? Can we tell a Nazi without his insignias, his salute? When evil recasts itself in a more subtle form than that of the South African policeman, will we always be able to comprehend it? 12

It is an unsettling idea, that Adolf Hitler and his mutant crew are simply a milk stop in the seemingly uncontrollable bloom of modern-day evil. Worse yet is trying to guess what the new, more functional imagery of evil will turn out to be, now that Satan has become such a picked-over concept as to be the rallying cry of thuggish Long Island teenagers and Iranian zealots both. You wonder, what sort of Big Picture is needed to finally banish the snake from our subconscious? I can only hope that, should we turn the clocks ahead a century or so and peer into the blitzed minds of our survivors, searching for the new internalized image of evil, we do not find a roiling, billowing mushroom cloud. 13

For someone who senses himself reflexing toward the combat of evil, thoughts of the upcoming rumble can induce a despairing paranoia so virulent as to short-circuit every synapse. Still, there is a cure, the same cure every traditional wisdom system offers: knowledge that however strong Evil may be, Good must be stronger, or else we would not be here. It does not matter if this idea is true or not, only that we believe it; not believing it forfeits all sanity, plummets us into a fouler Hell than Dante could ever conjure. 14

So, accepting that I know almost nothing, armed with the knowledge that Good covers Evil like rock smashes scissors, a weighty stack of near-impenetrable books by French philosophers under my arm, I venture forth, on my inevitable journey upriver to face whatever abomination awaits me. It's a trip no one can afford to miss. 15

QUESTIONS FOR READING AND WRITING

1. Who was Josef Mengele? Using the resources of your library, find out what he did that brings Jacobson to call him evil and to fantasize about killing him.
2. Locate examples of how Jacobson refers to himself and to his personal life to make his essay more accessible and familiar. Do any of these examples run the risk of trivializing his subject?
3. Why is evil "everyone's business"?
4. Why have "evil" and "evilness" become difficult concepts to grasp?
5. According to Jacobson, what effects should our recognition of the presence of evil have upon us?
6. After conducting some appropriate research, write an essay about the causes of evil as it is manifested in such men as Hitler, Pol Pot, and Stalin.
7. Write a definition essay that attempts to clarify your meaning of evil. Attempt to distinguish evil from that which is "merely" bad, immoral, or illegal.

✦ Jonathan Schell ✦
Nothing to Report

An American writer and editor, Jonathan Schell (b. 1943) has written two books about the Vietnam War, one about the presidency of Richard Nixon, and two about the perils of a nuclear holocaust: The Fate of the Earth *(1982) and* The Abolition *(1984). In the following excerpt from* The Fate of the Earth, *Schell attempts to explain the unfathomable: the effects of a nuclear attack. After a chilling description of the immediate effects, Schell introduces the far more troubling notion that most of the people who could possibly describe the effects of an actual attack would be dead.*

WHEREAS MOST CONVENTIONAL BOMBS produce only one destructive effect—the shock wave—nuclear weapons produce many destructive effects. At the moment of the explosion, when the temperature of the weapon material, instantly gasified, is at the superstellar level, the pressure is millions of times the normal atmospheric pressure. Immediately, radiation, consisting mainly of gamma rays, which are a very high-energy form of electromagnetic radiation, begins to stream outward into the environment. This is called the "initial nuclear radiation," and is the first of the destructive effects of a nuclear explosion. In an air burst of a one-megaton bomb—a bomb with the explosive yield of a million tons of TNT, which is a medium- sized weapon in present-day nuclear arsenals—the initial nuclear radiation can kill unprotected human beings in an area of some six square miles. Virtually simultaneously with the initial nuclear radiation, in a second destructive effect of the explosion, an electromagnetic pulse is generated by the intense gamma radiation acting on the air. In a high-altitude detonation, the pulse can knock out electrical equipment over a wide area by inducing a powerful surge of voltage through various conductors, such as antennas, overhead power lines, pipes, and railroad tracks. The Defense Department's Civil Preparedness Agency reported in 1977 that a single multi-kiloton nuclear weapon detonated one hundred and twenty-five miles over Omaha, Nebraska, could generate an electromagnetic pulse strong enough to damage solid-state 1 electrical circuits throughout the entire continental United States and in part of Canada and Mexico, and thus threaten to bring the economies of these countries to a halt. When the fusion and fission reactions have blown themselves out, a fireball takes shape. As it expands, energy is absorbed in the form of Xrays by the surrounding air, and then the air re-radiates a portion of that energy into the environment in the form of the thermal pulse—a wave of blinding light and intense heat—which is the third of the destructive effects of a nuclear explosion. (If the burst is low enough, the fireball touches the ground, vaporizing or incinerating almost everything within it.) The thermal pulse of a one-megaton bomb lasts for about ten seconds and can cause second-degree burns in exposed human beings at a distance of nine and a half miles, or in an area of more than two hundred and eighty square miles, and that of a twenty-megaton bomb (a large weapon by modern standards) lasts for about twenty seconds and can produce the same consequences at a distance of twenty-eight miles, or in an area of two thousand four hundred and sixty square miles. As the fireball expands, it also sends out a blast wave in all directions, and this is the fourth destructive effect of the explosion. The blast wave of an air-burst one-megaton bomb can flatten or severely damage all but the strongest buildings within a radius of four and a half miles, and that of a twenty-megaton bomb can do the same within a radius of twelve miles. As the fireball burns, it rises, condensing water from the surrounding atmosphere to form the characteristic mushroom cloud. If the bomb has been set off on the ground or close enough to it so that the fireball touches the surface, in a so-called ground burst, a crater will be formed, and tons of dust and debris will be fused with the intensely radioactive fission products and sucked up into the mushroom cloud. This mixture will return to earth as radioactive fallout, most of it in the form of fine ash, in the fifth destructive effect of the explosion. Depending upon the composition of the surface, from forty to seventy per cent of this fallout—often called the "early" or "local" fallout—descends to earth within about a day of the explosion, in the vicinity of the blast and downwind from it, exposing human beings to radiation disease, an illness that is fatal when exposure is intense. Air bursts may also produce local fallout, but in much small quantities. The lethal range of the local fallout depends on a number of circumstances, including the weather, but under average conditions a one-megaton ground burst would, according to the report by the Office of Technology Assessment, lethally contaminate over a thousand square miles. (A lethal dose, by convention, is considered to be the amount of radiation that, if delivered over a short period of time, would kill half the able-bodied young adult population.)

The initial nuclear radiation, the electromagnetic pulse, the ther- 2
mal pulse, the blast wave, and the local fallout may be described as the local primary effects of nuclear weapons. Naturally, when many bombs are exploded the scope of these effects is increased accordingly. But in addition these primary effects produce innumerable secondary effects on societies and natural environments, some of which may be even more harmful than the primary ones. To give just one example, nuclear weapons, by flattening and setting fire to huge, heavily built-up areas, generate mass fires, and in some cases these may kill more people than the original thermal pulses and blast waves. Moreover, there are—quite distinct from both the local primary effects of individual bombs and their secondary effects—global primary effects, which do not become significant unless thousands of bombs are detonated all around the earth. And these global primary effects produce innumerable secondary effects of their own throughout the ecosystem of the earth as a whole. For a full-scale holocaust is more than the sum of its local parts; it is also a powerful direct blow to the ecosphere. In that sense, a holocaust is to the earth what a single bomb is to a city. Three grave direct global effects have been discovered so far. The first is the "delayed," or "worldwide," fallout. In detonations greater than one hundred kilotons, part of the fallout does not fall to the ground in the vicinity of the explosion but rises high into the troposphere and into the stratosphere, circulates around the earth, and then, over months or years, descends, contaminating the whole surface of the globe—although with doses of radiation far weaker than those delivered by the local fallout. Nuclear-fission products comprise some three hundred radioactive isotopes, and though some of them decay to relatively harmless levels of radioactivity within a few hours, minutes, or even seconds, others persist to emit radiation for up to millions of years. The short-lived isotopes are the ones most responsible for the lethal effects of the local fallout, and the long-lived ones are responsible for the contamination of the earth by stratospheric

fallout. The energy released by all fallout from a thermonuclear explosion is about five per cent of the total. By convention, this energy is not calculated in the stated yield of a weapon, yet in a ten-thousand-megaton attack the equivalent of five hundred megatons of explosive energy, or forty thousand times the yield of the Hiroshima bomb, would be released in the form of radioactivity. This release may be considered a protracted afterburst, which is dispersed into the land, air, and sea, and into the tissues, bones, roots, stems, and leaves of living things, and goes on detonating there almost indefinitely after the explosion. The second of the global effects that have been discovered so far is the lofting, from ground bursts, of millions of tons of dust into the stratosphere; this is likely to produce general cooling of the earth's surface. The third of the global effects is a predicted partial destruction of the layer of ozone that surrounds the entire earth in the stratosphere. A nuclear fireball, by burning nitrogen in the air, produces large quantities of oxides of nitrogen. These are carried by the heat of the blast into the stratosphere, where, through a series of chemical reactions, they bring about a depletion of the ozone layer. Such a depletion may persist for years. The 1975 N.A.S. report has estimated that in a holocaust in which ten thousand megatons were detonated in the Northern Hemisphere the reduction of ozone in this hemisphere could be as high as seventy per cent and in the Southern Hemisphere as high as forty per cent, and that it could take as long as thirty years for the ozone level to return to normal. The ozone layer is crucial to life on earth, because it shields the surface of the earth from lethal levels of ultraviolet radiation, which is present in sunlight. Glasstone remarks simply, "If it were not for the absorption of much of the solar ultraviolet radiation by the ozone, life as currently known could not exist except possibly in the ocean." Without the ozone shield, sunlight, the life-giver, would become a life-extinguisher. In judging the global effects of a holocaust, therefore, the primary question is not how many people would be irradiated, burned, or crushed to death by the immediate effects of the bombs but how well the ecosphere, regarded as a single living entity, on which all forms of life depend for their continued existence, would hold up. The issue is the habitability of the earth, and it is in this context, not in the context of the direct slaughter of hundreds of millions of people by the local effects, that the question of human survival arises.

Usually, people wait for things to occur before trying to describe them. (Futurology has never been a very respectable field of inquiry.) But since we cannot afford under any circumstances to let a holocaust occur, we are forced in this one case to become the historians of the future—to chronicle and commit to memory an event that we have never experienced and must never experience. This unique endeavor, in which foresight is asked to perform a task usually reserved for hindsight, raises a host of special difficulties. There is a categorical difference, often overlooked, between trying to describe an event that has already happened (whether it is Napoleon's invasion of Russia or the pollution of the environment by acid rain) and trying to describe one that has yet to happen—and one, in addition, for which there is no precedent, or even near-precedent, in history. Lacking experience to guide our thoughts and impress itself on our feelings, we resort to speculation. But speculation, however brilliantly it may be carried out, is at best only a poor substitute for experience. Experience gives us facts, whereas in pure speculation we are thrown back on theory, which has never been a very reliable guide to future events. Moreover, experience engraves its lessons in our hearts through suffering and the other consequences that it has for our lives; but speculation leaves our lives untouched, and so gives us leeway to reject its conclusions, no matter how well argued they may be. (In the world of strategic theory, in particular, where strategists labor to simulate actual situations on the far side of the nuclear abyss, so that generals and statesmen can prepare to make their decisions in case the worst happens, there is sometimes an unfortunate tendency to mistake pure ratiocination for reality, and to pretend to a knowledge of the future that is not given to human beings to have.) Our knowledge of the local primary effects of the bombs, which is based both on the physical principles that made their construction possible and on experience gathered from the bombings of Hiroshima and Nagasaki and from testing, is quite solid. And our knowledge of the extent of the local primary effects of many weapons used together, which is obtained simply by using the multiplication table, is also solid: knowing that the thermal pulse of 3 a twenty-megaton bomb can give people at least second-degree burns in an area of two thousand four hundred and sixty square miles, we can easily figure out that the pulses of a hundred twenty-megaton bombs can give people at least second-degree burns in an area of two hundred and forty-six thousand square miles. Nevertheless, it may be that our knowledge even of the primary effects is still incomplete, for during our test program new ones kept being discovered. One example is the electromagnetic pulse, whose importance was not recognized until around 1960, when, after more than a decade of tests, scientists realized that this effect accounted for unexpected electrical failures that had been occurring all along in equipment around the test sites. And it is only in recent years that the Defense Department has been trying to take account strategically of this startling capacity of just one bomb to put the technical equipment of a whole continent out of action.

When we proceed from the local effects of single explosions to the effects of thousands of them on societies and environments, the picture clouds considerably, because then we go beyond both the certainties of physics and our slender base of experience, and speculatively encounter the full complexity of human affairs and of the biosphere. Looked at in its entirety, a nuclear holocaust can be said to assail human life at three levels: the level of individual life, the level of human society, and the level of the natural environment—including the environment of the earth as a whole. At none of these levels can the destructiveness of nuclear weapons be measured in terms of firepower alone. At each level, life has both considerable recuperative powers, which might restore it even after devastating injury, and points of exceptional vulnerability, which leave it open to sudden, wholesale, and permanent collapse, even when comparatively little violence has been applied. Just as a machine may break down if one small part is removed, and a person may die if a single artery or vein is blocked, a modern technological society may come to a standstill if its fuel supply is cut off, and an ecosystem may collapse if its ozone shield is depleted. Nuclear weapons thus do not only kill directly, with their tremendous violence, but also kill indirectly, by breaking down the man-made and the natural systems on which individual lives collectively depend. Human beings require constant provision and care, supplied both by their societies and by the natural environment, and if these are suddenly removed people will die just as surely as if they had been struck by a bullet. Nuclear weapons are unique in that they attack the support systems of life at every level. And these systems, of course, are not isolated from each other but are parts of a single whole: ecological collapse, if it goes far enough, will bring about social collapse, and social collapse will bring about individual deaths. Furthermore, the destructive consequences of a nuclear attack are immeasurably compounded by the likelihood that all or most of the bombs will be detonated within the space of a few hours, in a single huge concussion. Normally, a locality devastated by a catastrophe, whether natural or man-made, will sooner or later receive help from untouched outside areas, as Hiroshima and Nagasaki did after they were bombed; but a nuclear holocaust would devastate the "outside" areas as well, leaving the victims to fend for themselves in a shattered society and natural environment. And what is true for each city is also true for the earth as a whole: a devastated earth can hardly expect "outside" help. The earth is the largest of the support systems for life, and the impairment of the earth is the largest of the perils posed by nuclear weapons.

The incredible complexity of all these effects, acting, interacting, 5
and interacting again, precludes confident detailed representation of the events in a holocaust. We deal inevitably with approximations, probabilities, even guesses. However, it is important to point out that our uncertainty pertains not to *whether* the effects will interact, multiplying their destructive power as they do so, but only to *how*. It follows that our almost built-in bias, determined by the limitations of the human mind in judging future events, is to underestimate the harm. The fear interactive consequences that we cannot predict, or even imagine, may not be impossible, but it is very difficult. Let us consider, for example, some of the possible ways in which a person in a targeted country might die. He might be incinerated by the fireball or the thermal pulse. He might be lethally irradiated by the initial nuclear radiation. He might be crushed to death or hurled to his death by the blast wave or its debris. He might be lethally irradiated by the local fallout. He might be burned to death in a firestorm. He might be injured by one or another of these effects and then die of his wounds before he was able to make his way out of the devastated zone in which he found himself. He might die of starvation, because the economy had

collapsed and no food was being grown or delivered, or because existing local crops had been killed by radiation, or because the local ecosystem had been ruined, or because the ecosphere of the earth as a whole was collapsing. He might die of cold, for lack of heat and clothing, or of exposure, for lack of shelter. He might be killed by people seeking food or shelter that he had obtained. He might die of an illness spread in an epidemic. He might be killed by exposure to the sun if he stayed outside too long following serious ozone depletion. Or he might be killed by any combination of these perils. But while there is almost no end to the ways to die in and after a holocaust, each person has only one life to lose: someone who has been killed by the thermal pulse can't be killed again in an epidemic. Therefore, anyone who wishes to describe a holocaust is always at risk of depicting scenes of devastation that in reality would never take place, because the people in them would already have been killed off in some earlier scene of devastation. The task is made all the more confusing by the fact that causes of death and destruction do not exist side by side in the world but often encompass one another, in widening rings. Thus, if it turned out that a holocaust rendered the earth uninhabitable by human beings, then all the more immediate forms of death would be nothing more than redundant preliminaries, leading up to the extinction of the whole species by a hostile environment. Or if a continental ecosystem was so thoroughly destroyed by a direct attack that it could no longer sustain a significant human population, the more immediate causes of death would again decline in importance. In much the same way, if an airplane is hit by gunfire, and thereby caused to crash, dooming all the passengers, it makes little difference whether the shots also killed a few of the passengers in advance of the crash. On the other hand, if the larger consequences, which are less predictable than the local ones, failed to occur, then the local ones would have their full importance again.

Faced with uncertainties of this kind, some analysts of nuclear destruction have resorted to fiction, assigning to the imagination the work that investigation is unable to do. But then the results are just what one would expect: fiction. An approach more appropriate to our intellectual circumstances would be to acknowledge a high degree of uncertainty as an intrinsic and extremely important part of dealing with a possible holocaust. A nuclear holocaust is an event that is obscure because it is future, and uncertainty, while it has to be recognized in all calculations of future events, has a special place in calculations of a nuclear holocaust, because a holocaust is something that we aspire to keep in the future forever, and never to permit into the present. You might say that uncertainty, like the thermal pulses or the blast waves, is one of the features of a holocaust. Our procedure, then, should be not to insist on a precision that is beyond our grasp but to inquire into the rough probabilities of various results insofar as we can judge them, and then to ask ourselves what our political responsibilities are in the light of these probabilities. This embrace of investigative modesty—this acceptance of our limited ability to predict the consequences of a holocaust—would itself be a token of our reluctance to extinguish ourselves.

There are two further aspects of a holocaust which, though they do not further obscure the factual picture, nevertheless vex our understanding of this event. The first is that although in imagination we can try to survey the whole prospective scene of destruction, inquiring into how many would live and how many would die and how far the collapse of the environment would go under attacks of different sizes, and piling up statistics on how many square miles would be lethally contaminated, or what percentage of the population would receive first-, second-, or third-degree burns, or be trapped in the rubble of its burning houses, or be irradiated to death, no one actually experiencing a holocaust would have any such overview. The news of other parts necessary to put together that picture would be one of the things that were immediately lost, and each surviving person, his vision drastically foreshortened by the collapse of his world, and his impressions clouded by his pain, shock, bewilderment, and grief, would see only as far as whatever scene of chaos and agony happened to lie at hand. For it would not be only such abstractions as "industry" and "society" and "the environment" that would be destroyed in a nuclear holocaust; it would also be, over and over again, the small collections of cherished things, known landscapes, and beloved people that made up the immediate contents of individual lives. 7

The other obstacle to our understanding is that when we strain to picture what the scene would be like after a holocaust we tend to forget that for most people, and perhaps for all, it wouldn't be *like* 8 anything, because they would be dead. To depict the scene as it would appear to the living is to that extent a falsification, and the greater the number killed, the greater the falsification. The right vantage point from which to view a holocaust is that of a corpse, but from that vantage point, of course, there is nothing to report.

QUESTIONS FOR READING AND WRITING

1. What is the derivation of the word *holocaust*? What does Schell mean by the phrase "historians of the future" (paragraph 3)?
2. How, if at all, has this essay changed your attitude toward nuclear weaponry and toward the people who speak out against it?
3. How is Schell's cause and effect essay organized?
4. How do the last two paragraphs of the essay change your perspective on what precedes them?
5. Adopting the role of a "historian of the future," and to bring Schell's remarks "closer to home," write an essay that analyzes the effects of detonating a 20-megaton nuclear device on your community. In other words, try to conceive of the holocaust as your community's *immediate problem.*
6. Write an essay that examines what the average citizen can do to protect all of us from the grim possibilities Schell considers.

✦ Barbara Tuchman ✦
The Decline of Quality

One of America's most popular historians, Barbara Tuchman (1912–1988) won two Pulitzer Prizes, one for The Guns of August *(1962) and one for* Stillwell and the American Experience in China, 1911–1945 *(1971). Her other books include* A Distant Mirror *(1978),* Practicing History *(1981), and* The March of Folly *(1984). In the following essay, Tuchman attempts to distinguish between quality and nonquality; she laments the incompetence, trashiness, and vulgarity to be found at so many levels of American culture.*

A QUESTION RAISED BY OUR CULTURE of the last two or three decades is whether quality in product and effort has become a vanishing element of current civilization. The word "quality" has, of course, two meanings: first, the nature or essential characteristic of something, as in "His voice has the quality of command"; second, a condition of excellence implying fine quality as distinct from poor quality. The second, obviously, is my subject. 1

The discussion that follows is not, except for a few samples, based on documentary or other hard evidence according to usual historical method; rather it represents the personal reflections of an observer with half a century's awareness of and occasional participation in public affairs, supported by the study and writing of history. It offers opinion on a pervasive problem and, as opinion, should and, I hope, may be supplemented by factual studies on special areas of the problem, such as education, labor and merchandising. 2

In the hope of possibly reducing the hail of censure which is certain to greet this essay (I am thinking of going to Alaska or possibly Patagonia in the week it is published), let me say that quality, as I understand it, means investment of the best skill and effort possible to produce the finest and most admirable result possible. Its presence or absence in some degree characterizes every man-made object, service, skilled or unskilled labor—laying bricks, painting a picture, ironing shirts, practicing medicine, shoemaking, scholarship, writing a book. You do it well or you do it half-well. Materials are sound and durable or they are sleazy; 3

method is painstaking or whatever is easiest. Quality is achieving or reaching for the highest standard as against being satisfied with the sloppy or fraudulent. It is honesty of purpose as against catering to cheap or sensational sentiment. It does not allow compromise with the second-rate.

When Michelangelo started work on the Sistine Chapel ceiling, five friends who were painters came to assist him and advise him in the techniques of fresco, in which they were practiced and he was not. Finding their work not what he desired, he resolved to accomplish the whole task by himself, locked the doors of the chapel until his friends gave up and went home, and through four painful years on a scaffold carried the work to completion, as Vasari tells us, "with the utmost solicitude, labor and study." That is what makes for quality—and its cost—and what helped to make Michelangelo one of the greatest artists, if not, as some think, the greatest, of all time. Creating quality is self-nourishing. Michelangelo, Vasari goes on to say, "became more and more kindled every day by his fervor in the work and encouraged by his growing proficiency and improvement." Genius and effort go together, or if they do not, the genius will be wasted.

Quality, however, can be attained without genius. Art, in any case, is a slippery area for discussion of the problem, because values in the perception of art change radically from one generation to another. Everyone knows how the French Impressionists were scorned when they first exhibited, only in recent decades to reach the peak of repute and honor and what seems to be permanent popularity. Now, in our time, we are confronted by new schools of challenging, not to say puzzling, expression. In some individuals among the moderns, quality is emphatic *because* it is individual: in Louise Nevelson's impressive and innovative work, for example; in the intensity of loneliness in Hopper's mature paintings. With regard to the schools—as distinct from individuals—of Pop Art, Abstract Expressionism, Minimalism, hard-edge, scrawny-edge and whatnot, the two criteria of quality—intensive effort and honesty of purpose—often seem missing. The paintings seem thin, if not empty; one feels nothing behind the surface of the canvas. By contrast, behind the glow and mystery of a Turner, for instance, a whole world of ships and storms and eerie seas and men laboring over mountain passes stretches the imagination far beyond the canvas. It occurs to me to wonder whether museums hang the modern abstracts, and the public crowds to see them, in some vast pretense of seeing something where there is nothing; that in the present state of our culture, many do not know the difference.

Here we must confront the contentious question whether quality is something inherent in a given work or something socially induced—as the ultra-feminists say of sex—in the eye and period-consciousness of the beholder. I unhesitatingly opt for the inherent (as I do for sense of gender in the individual). In architecture there is something inherently right in certain proportions of windows to wall space, or for example in the Double Cube Room at Wilton House in England. One may be an architectural illiterate and still recognize, indeed *feel,* the perfection. Any kind of illiterate will recognize a difference in quality between, let us say, Matisse's exhilarating interiors and hotel art of little waifs with big black eyes, or between Michelangelo's marble Moses or David and that school of sculpture which consists of jigsaw puzzles lying on a museum floor, or, alternatively, the ceramic Snow Whites and Bambis advertised at such fancy prices in *The New Yorker.* 6

The difference is not only a matter of artistic skill, but of intent. Although the Moses and David are period pieces, they are timeless, universal, noble. They were intended to be—and they are—supreme. The others fall considerably short of that measure because they are designed for lesser reasons: the ceramic princesses and companions for commercial appeal to cheap sentiment, the floor puzzles for appeal to false sentiment—that is, worship of the avant-garde for its own sake as chic. 7

These examples represent the posing of extremes in which quality versus nonquality is unmistakable. If I come closer, however, and suggest that quality is inherent in, let us say, the stark, exquisite fiction of Jean Rhys but not in "Princess Daisy," in New England's white-steepled churches but not in Howard Johnson's orange-roofed eateries, in the film "Ninotchka" but not in "Star Wars," in Fred Astaire but not in Johnny Carson, I shall be pelted with accusations of failure to understand that what was once considered quality has given way under a change of social values to appreciation of new qualities and new values; that the admirers of the ceramic dolls and trash fiction and plastic furniture and television talk and entertainment shows with their idiotic laughter find something in 8 these objects and diversions that means quality to *them*—in short, that quality is subjective. Yes, indeed, just as there are men who believe and loudly insist they are sober and who stumble and weave and pass out five minutes later. The judgment is subjective but the condition is not.

Contemporary life undeniably marks many improvements over the past, in freedom and nonconformity and most strikingly in material welfare. Such fine devices as the microchips that govern computer systems, a lifesaving mechanism like the cardiac pacemaker, drip-water techniques that permit arid-zone agriculture and a thousand other developments that have added to human efficiency and well-being may be cited as evidence of modern quality. Nevertheless, these are technological and seem to me to belong to a different scheme of things from the creative components of civilized life.

In two other areas, morals and politics, loss of quality is widely felt, but as I am not sure that the present level in these areas is much lower than at many other periods in history, I shall leave them out of the discussion.

In labor and culture, standards are certainly lower. Everyone is conscious of the prevalence of slipshod performance in clerical, manual and bureaucratic work. Much of it is slow, late, inaccurate, inefficient, either from lack of training or lack of caring or both. Secretaries still exist who care and who produce a perfectly typed letter, but more and more letters appear like one I recently received which contained—whether owed to writer or typist—"parred" for "pared," "deline," for "decline," "in tact" for "intact," and the information that removal of portions of an author's text "eschews his political intentions."

The writer in this case was certainly ignorant of the meaning of the word "eschews," while it is impossible to say whether the other errors represent ignorance or simple slackness. Either way, though only a sample, no more manifest evidence could be had of what has become prevalent in many fields. Even more striking is recognition that no such letter could have been written from a reasonably literate office 10 or 15 years ago. The decline has been precipitate, perhaps as one result of the student movements of the 1960's, when learning skills are renounced in favor of "doing your own thing" or consciousness-raising and other exercises in self-fulfillment. It is good for the self to be fulfilled but better if coping skills are acquired first.

In culture the tides of trash rise a little higher by the week: in fast foods and junky clothes and cute greeting cards; in films devoted nowadays either to sadism or teen-agers and consequently either nasty or boring; in the frantic razzle-dazzle of Bloomingdale's and its proliferating imitators; in endless paperbacks of sex and slaughter, Gothics and westerns; in the advertising of sensation-fiction which presents each book as the ultimate in horror, catastrophe, political plot or world crime, each by an unknown author who is never heard from again—fortunately. 13

Examining the evidence, one could apply a system of Q and non-Q for quality, on the model of the famous system of U (for upper-class) and non-U in language sponsored by Nancy Mitford. Her categories were devised to distinguish social class, which brings us to the dangerous problem of the relationship of quality to class. 14

Quality is undeniably, though not necessarily, related to class, not in its nature but in circumstances. In former times, the princely patron had the resources in wealth and power to commission the finest workmanship, materials and design. Since his motive was generally self-glorification, the result was as beautiful and magnificent as he could command: in crystal and gold and tapestry, in exquisite silks and brocades, in the jeweled and enameled masterpieces of Cellini, the carved staircases of Grinling Gibbons. It is also true that cities and states caused works of equal value to be created not for individual glory but for the good of the whole, as in the Greek temples and theaters, the Colosseum of Rome, the Gothic cathedrals, the public parks of London. 15

The decline that has since set in has a good historical reason: The age of privilege is over and civilization has passed into the age of the masses. The many exceptions that can be made to this statement do not invalidate it. No change takes place wholly or all at once and many components of privilege and of capitalist control remain functioning parts of society and will, I expect, continue as such for some time. Nevertheless, the turn has taken place, with the result that our culture has been taken over by commercialism directed to the mass market and necessarily to mass taste. De Tocqueville stated the problem, already appearing in his time, succinctly when he wrote, "When only the wealthy had watches they were very good 16 ones; few are now made that are worth much but everyone has one in his pocket."

In the absence of the princely patron, the public is now the consumer, or if government is the patron, it is answerable to the public. The criterion for the goods and services and arts that society produces is the pleasure and purchasing power of the greatest number, not of the most discerning. Therein lies the history of non-Q. Arts and luxuries may still be directed to the few and most discerning, but when the dominant culture is mass-directed and the rewards in money and celebrity go with it, we have to consider whether popular appeal will become the governing criterion and gradually submerge all but isolated rocks of quality.

Will the tides of trash obey Gresham's law to the effect that bad money drives out good? This means, I am told, that as between two coinages of equal denomination but different intrinsic value in gold or silver content, the one of lesser will drive out the one of higher value. I do not know whether, according to our ever-flexible economists, Gresham's law remains valid, but as regards quality in culture, it has gloomy implications.

Quality cannot be put down altogether. As the would-be philosopher said of cheerfulness, it keeps breaking in, and I suspect always will. It appears in the crafts movement that, in a reaction to floods of the tawdry, has been expanding in the last decade, producing fine hand-woven fabrics and handmade utensils and ornaments of pottery, glass and wood. There are art and design in these and individual skills that make for Q. We come across Q here and there in every field of endeavor, from a symphony orchestra to a well-run grocery and on the covers of the Audubon bimonthly magazine. For all its appearances we are grateful and by them encouraged, yet we have to recognize that the prevailing tendency is non-Q.

This is not confined to the taste of the masses. It reaches into the richer ranks, where purchasing power has outdistanced cultivated judgment. Persons in this difficulty tend to buy purses and scarfs and various garments—even sheets—adorned with the designer's or manufacturer's initials in the illusion that, without risking individual judgment, they are thus acquiring the stamp of Q. In fact, they are merely proclaiming that they lack reliable taste of their own. If I were to adopt the Mitford tone, I would have to say that wearing anything bearing commercial initials is definitely non-Q.

Most of the products of non-Q have the economic excuse that they supply needs to pocketbooks that can afford them. An entire level of society has arisen that can now afford to obtain goods, services and entertainment formerly beyond its means. Consequently these are now produced at a price level attractive to the greatest number of consumers and likewise at a cultural level, or level of taste, that presumably the greatest number wants or will respond to. Whether the merchandiser or advertiser is invariably a good judge of what the public wants is open to doubt. Whereas one used naively to believe that, under the infallible test of profit, business knew what it was doing, we have now witnessed the most monumental goof in business history committed by the very kind of American enterprise, the auto industry. If Detroit with all its resources errs, can the rest be far behind? 21

A question that puzzles me is why inexpensive things must be ugly; why walking through the aisles in a discount chain store causes acute discomfort in the esthetic nerve cells. I have heard it suggested that raucous colors and hideous decoration are meant to distract the purchaser's eye from shoddy workmanship, but since that only results in a remedy worse than the disease, it cannot be the whole explanation. One had supposed that ugly, oversize packaging obeyed some mysterious law of merchandising, the merchandisers having proved that if the package were neat, discreet and elegant, it would not sell. I wonder if they really know this, based on careful tests, with controls, of consumer response, or whether gratuitous ugliness is not just a presumption of what the public is supposed to like. The automobile companies thought they knew too and they were so wrong that the taxpayer is now bailing them out in survival loans and unemployment insurance to the workers they had to let go. 22

I do not see why the presumption cannot be made the other way: that the consumer would respond to good design rather than bad, and to quality insofar as it can be mass-produced, rather than junk. The answer will doubtless be that when this experiment has been tried the mass of consumers fails to respond. For this failure, I believe, two institutions of our culture are largely to blame: education and advertising. 23

We have some superb schools, public and private, in this country but the dominant tendency, once again, is non-Q. Education for the 24 majority has slipped to a level undemanding of effort, satisfied with the least, lacking respect for its own values, and actually teaching very little. We read in the press that, despite the anxious concern and experiments of educators, college-entrance scores are sinking and the national rate of schoolchildren reading at below-grade levels hovers at 50 percent. The common tendency is to blame television, and while I suppose that the two-minute attention span it fosters, and the passive involvement of the viewer, must negatively affect the learning process, I suspect something more basic is at fault.

That something, I believe, lies in new attitudes toward both teaching and learning. Schoolchildren are not taught to work. Homework is frivolous or absent. The idea has grown that learning must be fun; students must study what they like, therefore courses have largely become elective. Work is left to the highly motivated, and failure for the others does not matter because, owing to certain socially concerned but ill-conceived rules, students in many school systems cannot be flunked. Except by the few who learn because they cannot be stopped, the coping skills society needs are not acquired by the promoted failures, and the gulf between the few and the mass will widen.

Further, one becomes aware through occasional glimpses into curriculums, that subject matter makes increasing concessions to junk. Where are the summer reading lists and book reports of former years? A high-school student of my acquaintance in affluent suburbia was recently assigned by his English teacher, no less, to watch television for a week and keep a record on 3-by-5 index cards of what he had seen. This in the literature of Shakespeare to Mark Twain, Jane Austen to J. D. Salinger! How will the young become acquainted with quality if they are not exposed to it?

The effect appears at the next level. A professor of classics at a major Eastern university told me recently that, in a discussion with his students of the heroes of Greek legend, he tried to elicit their concept of the hero without success, and resorted to asking if anyone could name a hero. Only one student, a girl, raised her hand, and replied "Dustin Hoffman."

I feel sure that Mr. Hoffman, whose real persona is not at stake, will forgive his name being used to illustrate a case of modern know-nothingism. The girl neither knew what a hero was, nor apparently that an actor represents a character without being it. If she could not distinguish between make-believe and real, her school is unlikely to have equipped her to distinguish between quality and vulgarity or fraud, between Q and non-Q. She does not know the difference. Consequently, when the market offers her junk, she and her contemporaries buy it and listen to it and wear it because that is all they know.

Advertising augments the condition. From infancy to adulthood, 29
advertising is the air Americans breathe, the information we absorb, almost without knowing it. It floods our minds with pictures of perfection and goals of happiness easy to attain. Face cream will banish age, decaffeinated coffee will banish nerves, floor wax will bring in neighbors for a cheery bridge game or gossip, grandchildren will love you if your disposition improves with the right laxative, storekeepers and pharmacists overflow with sound avuncular advice, the right beer endows you with hearty masculine identity, and almost anything from deodorants to cigarettes; toothpaste, hair shampoo and lately even antacids will bring love affairs, usually on horseback or on a beach. Moreover, all the people engaged in these delights are beautiful. Dare I suggest that this is not the true world? We are feeding on foolery, of which a steady diet, for those who feed on little else, cannot help but leave a certain fuzziness of perceptions.

When it comes to standards of labor, the uncomfortable fact must 30
be faced that decline in quality of work is connected with the rise in the security of the worker. No one likes to admit this, because it is depressing and because it does not fit into the sentimental conviction that all's well that is meant well, that good things have only good results. The unhappy fact is that they have mixed results. Work may be a satisfaction to those who can choose their own line of endeavor and who enjoy what they do, but for the majority work is a more or less disagreeable necessity. Therefore, when holding a job no longer depends upon quality of performance but on union rules and bureaucratic protections, the incentive to excellent work is reduced. Like the failing student who cannot be flunked, the inadequate worker cannot be fired, short of some extreme dereliction. If he is laid off or quits for reasons of his own, unemployment insurance provides a temporary substitute for the pay envelope and, in the long run, the various supports of social welfare preclude destitution.

No one this side of the lunatic fringe suggests that these rights and protections of labor should be abandoned or weakened because loss of quality has been part of their price. Gain in one aspect of society generally means loss in another, and social gain in the well-being of the masses has been the major development of the last two centuries. We have put a floor under misery in the West and few would wish it removed because its measures have been abused. The privileged abuse their opportunities too, by monopolies, trusts, graft, bribery, tax evasion, pollution—and with far higher returns. At whatever cost, the working class has obtained access to comforts and pleasures, possessions and vacations that have changed immeasurably not only their lives but the whole of our economy and culture. On balance, this is social progress, but let us not suppose it has been unalloyed.

Other factors have played a part: The alienating nature of the assembly line and mass production is one, but this has been present since the Industrial Revolution. The great change has come with the complacency of—on the whole, in America—a comfortable society (previous to present inflation and recession). As in education, the change has been in attitude. The pressures and needs that once drove us have relaxed. Today's watchword is "Why knock yourself out?" The Asians in our midst—Koreans who put a whole family to work in a grocery of neat, washed, fresh produce, and stay open for 24 hours—exemplify the difference.

What of prognosis? The new egalitarians would like to make the whole question of quality vanish by adopting a flat philosophy of the equality of everything. No fact or event is of greater or less value than any other; no person or thing is superior or inferior to any other. Any reference to quality is instantly castigated as elitism, which seems to inspire in users of the word the sentiments of Jacobins denouncing aristos to the guillotine.

In fact, elitism is the equivalent of quality. Without it, management of everything would be on a par with the United States Postal Service, which, mercifully, is not yet quite the case. Difference in capacity does exist and superiority makes itself felt. It wins the ski race and promotion on the job and admission to the college of its choice. There are A students and D students, and their lives and fortunes will be different. I do not know if egalitarianism applies to horses, but if so how does it account for Seattle Slew and Affirmed sweeping the triple crown; and if all are equal, why do we hold horse races? Given the evidence of daily life, the egalitarian credo must be difficult to maintain and succeeds, I imagine, in deceiving chiefly its advocates.

However, because egalitarianism obviously appeals to those least 35
likely to excel—and they are many—its appeal is wide, and not altogether harmless. It sponsors mediocrity, which, as we learned a few years ago on the occasion of President Nixon's nomination of Judge G. Harrold Carswell to the Supreme Court, has an important constituency in this country. The general criticism of Carswell as mediocre prompted from Senator Roman L. Hruska of Nebraska one of the historic remarks of the century. He did not think Carswell should be disqualified on the grounds of an undistinguished judicial career, because, he said, "Even if he were mediocre, there are a lot of mediocre judges and people and lawyers and they are entitled to a little representation, aren't they?"

The more I ponder this idea of a seat for mediocrity on the 36
Supreme Court, the more it haunts me. The Hruska Principle is only a logical extension, after all, of majority rule, and if carried to its logical conclusion must mean that the mediocre shall inherit the earth. (Carswell was rejected, of course, but for alleged racism, not for mediocrity.)

In the 18th century, Montesquieu saw political egalitarianism as 37
a "dangerous fallacy" that could lead only to incompetence—and, he added, mob control, by which he meant democracy. We are less afraid of democracy than he was because we already have it, but growing incompetence is undoubtedly a feature of contemporary life, although it is not necessarily an attribute of democracy. There never was greater incompetence than in the Bourbon monarchy in the last decade before the French Revolution. It brought the old regime down in ruins, but we need not take that precedent too closely to heart for, despite present appearances, I think our society has built itself more safeguards and a firmer foundation.

I cannot believe we shall founder under the rising tide of 38
incompetence and trash. Perhaps that is merely a matter of temperament; it is difficult to believe in fatality. Although I know we have already grown accustomed to less beauty, less elegance, less excellence—and less hypocrisy, too—yet perversely I have confidence in the opposite of egalitarianism: in the competence and

excellence of the best among us. I meet this often enough, if not quite as often as the reverse, to believe that the urge for the best is an element of humankind as inherent as the heartbeat. It does not command society, and it may be crushed temporarily in a period of heavy non-Q, but it cannot be eliminated. If incompetence does not kill us first, Q will continue the combat against numbers. It will not win, but it will provide a refuge for the trash-beleaguered. It will supply scattered beauty, pride in accomplishment, the charm of fine things—and it will win horse races. As long as people exist, some will always strive for the best; some will attain it.

QUESTIONS FOR READING AND WRITING

1. Given the fact that she was a professional historian, why might Tuchman choose to describe and qualify her methods in paragraph 2?
2. What characteristics, according to Tuchman, distinguish quality from nonquality?
3. What political, social, or economic causes does Tuchman cite in accounting for the decline of quality in our culture?
4. What are elitism and egalitarianism? How does Tuchman defend herself against charges of elitism? How does egalitarianism support the decline of quality?
5. Visit a grocery store, a department store, or a toy store, and write a descriptive essay about what you see. Concentrate on flashy, garish, "tacky" details that, Tuchman might say, signal a lack of quality in our goods.
6. Watch television for two hours, then write an essay about the advertisements you have observed. What "worldview," what values and ideals, do the ads imply?
7. Write a narrative essay that describes your own experience with the frustrations of confronting shoddy goods or services (the car that proves to be a lemon, the radio that won't work, the teacher who never returns your papers, and so forth).

Process Analysis

Process analysis, like narration, involves telling a story—in this case the story of how something is made, how it works, how it is done, or even, how it came into being. A process analysis essay is often called a "how to" paper, and it includes such diverse types of writing as recipes in a cookbook, an account of how a bill becomes a law in a political science text, an explanation of how to change a tire in an automobile owner's manual, directions in a chemistry lab manual about how to make hydrogen sulfide, and a description of how a baleen whale feeds. All of these different kinds of writing have one thing in common—they explain "how."

The best examples of a process essay's pattern of organization are cookbook recipes because they describe all four of the essential elements of a process: what's needed, the time involved, the process itself, and the end product.

Scrambled Omelette

This is best in a French omelette pan, but a skillet can be used. For 1 omelette, 1 to 2 servings. Time: Less than 30 seconds of cooking.

2 or 3 eggs
Big pinch of salt
Pinch of pepper
A mixing bowl
A table fork
1 Tablespoon butter
An omelette pan 7 inches in diameter at the bottom

Step 1
Beat the eggs and seasonings in the mixing bowl for 20 to 30 seconds until the white and yolks are just blended.

Step 2
Place the butter in the pan and set over very high heat. If you have an electric heat element, it should be red hot. As the butter melts, tilt the pan in all directions to film the sides. When you see that the foam has almost subsided in the pan and the butter is on the point of coloring, it is an indication that it is hot enough to pour in the eggs.

Step 3
Hold the panhandle with your left hand, thumb on top, and immediately start sliding the pan back and forth rapidly over the heat. At the same time, fork in right hand, its flat side against the bottom of the pan, stir the eggs quickly to spread them continuously all over the bottom of the pan as they thicken. In 3 or 4 seconds they will become a light, broken custard. (A filling would go in at this point.)

Step 4
Then lift the handle of the pan to tilt it at a 45-degree angle over the heat, and rapidly gather the eggs at the far lip of the pan with the back of your fork. Still holding the pan tilted over the heat, run your fork around the lip of the pan under the far edge of the omelette to be sure it has not adhered to the pan.

Step 5
Give 4 or 5 short, sharp blows on the handle of the pan with your right fist to loosen the omelette and make the far edge curl over onto itself.

Hold the pan tilted over the heat for 1 or 2 seconds, very lightly, but not too long or the egg will overcook. The center of the omelette should remain soft and creamy.

Turn the omelette onto the plate . . . , rub the top with a bit of butter, and serve as soon as possible.*

Keeping this recipe in mind, let's examine the four elements of a process.

1. *What's needed* Most processes—the mechanical ones and scientific ones, anyway—involve some raw materials or ingredients that are about to undergo some kind of change. There is often some sort of machinery needed to cause the change. The cookbook recipe begins with the list of ingredients—eggs, butter, spices—and any equipment necessary to make the recipe: a 7" pan, a blender.
2. *The element of time* A cookbook recipe indicates how long each stage should take, and the stages themselves are presented in a chronological order: "Beat the eggs and seasonings . . . for 20 to 30 seconds."

* Julia Child, Louisette Bertholle, Simone Beck, *Mastering the Art of French Cooking* (Alfred A. Knopf, 1971), Vol. 1, 129–31.

3. *The process itself* The process involves a narration of the step-by-step procedure in the order that makes the most logical sense. The steps are numbered or are signalled by words like *next, then,* or *when,* which mark the transitions between the steps. The changes brought about in the product are indicated as it goes through temporary transformations; in our omelette recipe, for example, "when you see that the foam has almost subsided in the pan . . ."
4. *The end product* The cookbook recipe tells you at the outset what process you are up to, whether it's making brownies or a soup. The quantity or physical appearance of the final product is also indicated at the conclusion of the process; thus a cookbook indicates how many the recipe serves, and perhaps something of the dish's color, shape, or texture.

Because there are several types of processes, it is wise to determine which type you are dealing with: Some emphasize change more than others; some involve tools, machinery, or apparatus while others do not; and some involve as much description as narration and explanation.

Mechanical Process We encounter mechanical processes every day when we read instructions about how to put something together. The many do-it-yourself books, which teach everything from how to build your own patio to how to change the sparkplugs in your car, are all examples of mechanical processes.

The following is a simple mechanical process explaining how to replace spark plugs in three easy steps:

1. Unfasten the spark-plug cables by pulling on the boot, not on the cable itself.
2. Unscrew and remove the old spark plugs with their metal gaskets.
3. Set the gap on the new plugs to the correct clearance, and install them. Reconnect the spark-plug cables in the correct order.

Notice that the process simply involves performing the necessary steps; the writer is unconcerned with the scientific principles that lie behind the functioning of the spark plug.

Scientific Process Any process that involves the demonstration of scientific principles—or an explanation of a natural process that is not purely mechanical—is a scientific process. There may seem little difference between the mechanical process (which explains how to replace spark plugs) and the following paragraph (which explains how an accumulator battery works), but this second example is a scientific process because it emphasizes the scientific principles, the chemistry involved in the process:

> By far the most common batteries are accumulators of the lead acid type. These have interleaved lead grids, alternately connected to the positive and negative terminal posts, immersed in dilute sulphuric acid. The positive plate of a charged accumulator has its grids filled with lead peroxide and the negative plate with spongy lead.
>
> As the battery discharges, the peroxide changes to lead sulphate, having taken some of the sulphur from the acid, and the same change affects the spongy lead plate. When both plates are the same and all the sulphur has gone from the acid, leaving only water, the battery cannot produce any more current. By applying a charging current across the terminals the chemical action can be reversed.*

As this example shows, the explanation of a scientific process and the analysis of cause and effect often overlap, offering an excellent example of how rhetorical modes are sometimes combined. A species of narration is used to tell the story of the process; exposition is used to detail the causal sequences of the events.

Historical Process All processes involve time and change of some kind, but when you chronicle the stages of change, you are involved in documenting historical process. (This activity differs from the historian's search for the meaning of historic events, an activity involving causal analysis). The chronological account of how the Federal Constitution was adopted, state by state, or the many historical accounts of how the frontier was settled are accounts of historical processes. Peter Matthiessen's book *Wildlife in America* (1959) contains many historical accounts of how a number of once plentiful species became extinct or endangered. His account of the

* John Day, *The Bosch Book of the Motor Car* (St. Martin's Press, 1976), 207.

destruction of the passenger pigeon, a historical process, doesn't dwell so much on the biology of the species (or on the causal factors of its extinction), but on the historical stages which, in Matthiessen's words, "whirled into the vortex of extinction . . . the most numerous bird ever to exist on earth."

Process analysis may not seem the most elegant or intellectual pattern of organization. However, in an increasingly specialized world where one person's knowledge of a process is another person's ignorance, process analysis becomes increasingly necessary to both readers and writers. Without process analysis to provide explanations in fields outside our own range of expertise, it would be virtually impossible to follow or give many explanations intended for a nonspecialized audience.

✦ Tracy Kidder ✦
The Future of the Photovoltaic Cell

A veteran of the war in Vietnam, Tracy Kidder received the 1982 Pulitzer Prize for The Soul of a New Machine *(1981). His earlier book* The Road to Yuba City *(1974) deals with the Juan Corona mass-murder case. Although he has also written prize-winning fiction, Kidder is best known for his lucid approach to complicated technical aspects. For example, when Kidder explains it, the transformation of sunlight to electrical energy in a silicon wafer seems a simple process.*

IN SOLID STATE PHYSICS lies a fundamental surprise, like the rabbit inside a magician's top hat. This is the recognition that the apparently quiescent, lumpish things of nature may be veritable carnivals of change and motion on the inside. Most solar cells on the market today are made of silicon, which along with oxygen is found in ordinary sand and is the second most abundant element on earth. A few complex, expensive processes tear the silicon away from the oxygen and convert it into a very thin wafer of crystal. Sunlight penetrating such a crystalline wafer will transfer some of its energy to some of the atomic particles inside—specifically, to the little bits of matter called electrons. (As high school courses in physics teach, electrons are what make electricity; a flow of electrons *is* an electrical current.) In effect, the light that enters the wafer of silicon will knock some electrons away from their atoms and set them free.

But to manage this small internal ferment, to make the electrons move in an orderly, useful fashion, the manufacturer must turn the silicon wafer into a sandwich. Imagine two slightly different slices of material fused together face to face. In a sense, a very rough and incomplete one, this sandwich is a battery, one slice representing the positive pole, the other the negative; an external wire connects the two open faces. Put this contraption out in the sun. The light passes through one slice of the sandwich and, reaching the area where the two slices meet, breaks chemical bonds, releasing electrons. If the wafer were not a sandwich but all of a piece, the freed electrons would quickly return where they came from, and that would be the end of it. But by giving the wafer two sides, imbued with opposite electrical properties, the manufacturer has created an internal pressure which forces the loosened electrons to one side of the sandwich and the broken bonds to the other. The broken bonds and electrons are of opposite charges. They are attracted to each other. But they cannot flow back the way they came: the pressure is one-way. So the electrons take the path of least resistance, and flow outward to the open face on their side of the wafer and into the external wire. Attach to this wire a small bulb and it should light up.

QUESTIONS FOR READING AND WRITING

1. Why does Kidder's first paragraph concentrate on the chemistry and physics of the process? Why does he use the analogy of the sandwich in the second paragraph to explain the process?
2. Are all the stages of a scientific process contained in this brief process analysis? What is the end product?
3. Kidder has written on a variety of topics from supercomputers to building a house. No matter how complicated the subject, Kidder breaks it down into easily comprehensible stages. Choose a process which you are familiar with, and assuming no knowledge on your audience's part, trace the stages of the process from materials to final product.

✦ John McPhee ✦
How to Make a Nuclear Bomb

John McPhee (b. 1931) has written about everything from the New York Knicks (A Sense of Where You Are, *1969) to Alaska* (Coming into the Country, *1977) to nuclear fission* (The Curve of Binding Energy, *1974) to the Loch Ness monster* (Pieces of the Frame, *1975). In this excerpt from* The Curve of Binding Energy, *he narrates, through physicist Ted Taylor, how a simple nuclear device could be made by someone familiar with nuclear physics.*

LUNCHTIME ON A BRIGHT FALL DAY at the Maryland cabin, Taylor opened a can of beer, took a bite of a ham sandwich, and began to consider what might be done with plutonium. Some people thought plutonium was too difficult to handle and would only frustrate an amateur bombmaker, but he did not agree. Seaborg, a co-discoverer of plutonium, had said, "It would take sophisticated, scientifically literate gangsterism to cope with it," and Taylor had no quarrel with that. True, uranium would be easier to deal with, but, for various reasons, he felt that plutonium was the material more likely to be used in a clandestine bomb. In the first place, a designer of nuclear weapons would select plutonium over uranium in the same way that a cabinet-maker would choose mahogany over yellow pine. The mass of plutonium needed for a sustained chain reaction is a third that of uranium. Plutonium's efficiency in an explosion could be expected to be far greater. A bad bomb made with plutonium might produce more yield than a fair one made with uranium. Moreover, with the coming of breeder reactors, and with plutonium recycle, plutonium will be, for thievery, by far the more available material.

The process might begin with plutonium nitrate in solution, because that is the form in which plutonium has generally been shipped and stored. In each four-foot flask, which is like a long thermos bottle, is about two and a half kilograms of plutonium, and, even if the bombmaker were not very skilled, only three or four flasks would be enough. Shipments include twenty to thirty flasks. Taylor guessed that a relative amateur, proceeding cautiously, would probably refer to the *Plutonium Handbook* (Gordon & Breach, New York, 1967, two volumes; $81.50), a guide to plutonium technology, and to the *Reactor Handbook* (Wiley, New York, 1960–64, four volumes; $123), which he called a how-to book that contains details of plutonium processing. Plutonium would require equipment on a scale more complicated and expensive than would uranium. The most expensive item needed might be a fifteen-hundred-dollar induction furnace, a device that produces a magnetic field and can heat up to high temperatures anything within it that is resistant to electricity—for example, plutonium. Such furnaces are sold by metallurgical-equipment-and-supply companies. They are also available at Fisher Scientific. A crucible in the ten-dollar range would be needed, too—and, of course, a glove box. The Stainless Equipment Company, in Denver, sells glove boxes for a few hundred dollars apiece, but a wooden one, made at home, would do well enough.

In one particular sense, Taylor said, a person trying to make a 3
plutonium bomb at home today would indeed be imitating the Manhattan Project. Carpentered wooden glove boxes were used at Los Alamos in 1945. The first bomb, the one exploded near Alamogordo, was a plutonium bomb, and it was made at Los Alamos in an old icehouse. The making of the bomb itself was only the last and least onerous of the many tasks of Project Y. Chemists and metallurgists scavenged the country for supportive equipment. Eventually, they got the bomb together in circumstances not importantly different from what someone might do in a private way these days. Taylor said he remembered his friend Dick Baker, a metallurgist, telling him that he had worked weekends fashioning ceramic crucibles with his own hands in preparation for the making of the Alamogordo bomb. (Baker, amplifying the story himself, would tell us at Los Alamos, "Frankly, the only unique thing to the production of an atomic weapon is the fissile material. We developed no great special equipment for the bomb during the war. We just put fissile material with commercial materials. It's not that complicated, if you see what I mean. The early bomb work was something like what might happen in a garage now. For the reflector and so forth, all you need, frankly, is a good machine shop." A slight and gentle person, around sixty, in rimless bifocal glasses, Baker went on to say, "Trained people could work plutonium without getting into a serious health

problem. But in order to perform a clandestine operation you don't need to be as conscious of safety as we are at Los Alamos. People are sort of expendable, you know. You could have a bomb that didn't have to be near as refined as the first ones we made here and you'd still have a bomb.")

Taylor mused on, ignoring his beer and his sandwich. This was October in Maryland, not wartime in Los Alamos, but what might happen in a secluded place like this was pretty much what had happened there. The typical way to get metal out of a solution is to add something that makes an insoluble compound with metal. When the compound precipitates, filter it. Add, say, oxalic acid to plutonium nitrate. The precipitate is plutonium oxalate in crystals that hold water. Remove the water with heat. Now you have a cake of anhydrous plutonium oxalate. Now further dry it by running a stream of hydrogen-fluoride gas through a sealed crucible.

"How?"

"Oh, simply enough. Buy some hydrofluoric acid and heat it in a quartz container—ten dollars. Hydrogen-fluoride gas comes off and goes into the crucible through a quartz tube. Anhydrous plutonium oxalate cooked at five hundred degrees centigrade in hydrogen fluoride becomes plutonium fluoride. Do it in batches of a few hundred grams—small enough to avoid going critical. Build up a stockpile of plutonium fluoride. Now line a crucible with magnesium oxide. You mix it with water and make a paste. Form it. Work it. Dry it. It's like clay. This is what Dick Baker did at Los Alamos in 1945. Now get some metallic calcium and crystalline iodine from a chemical-supply house. Put five hundred grams of plutonium fluoride in the crucible. Add a hundred and seventy grams of calcium and fifty grams of iodine. Cover with argon, which is a heavy inert gas. Close the lid. Now heat up the crucible inside an induction furnace to seven hundred and fifty degrees centigrade. At that point, the mixture in the crucible reacts and, in one minute, heats *itself* up to sixteen hundred degrees. The pressure is considerable. In the next ten minutes, the whole thing cools itself to eight hundred degrees. Remember, this is just what they did to make the first bomb. Now remove the crucible from the induction furnace. Let it stand until it comes to room temperature. Open the lid. Metallic plutonium is in there with some calcium-iodine junk. Use nitric acid to wash off the iodine flakes and the calcium-fluoride salt. What you have left is a small lump of plutonium. You can hold it in your hand. It won't hurt you. It feels a little warm, from alpha decay."

Taylor fell silent for a while, and there was no sound but some 7
wind in the turning leaves. Finally, he said, "Of course, you could just boil away the water, get plutonium-nitrate crystals, and make a bomb out of the crystals. It would not be much of a bomb—only a tenth of a kiloton, say—but that's enough to knock down the World Trade Center. When recycle comes in, the reactor-fuel rods will probably contain mixed uranium and plutonium oxides. The uranium would be only slightly enriched and not usable in a bomb, but the plutonium would be. There is good, better, and worse, but there is no nonweapons-grade plutonium involved in the nuclear industry. Mixed uranium and plutonium oxides can be separated chemically. It's not a difficult thing to do, but you'd better be pretty careful, because plutonium is so poisonous. You would add nitric acid to put the pellets into solution. Then add oxalic acid. The plutonium forms plutonium oxalate. The uranium remains in solution, because it does not combine with oxalic acid. So you filter out the plutonium oxalate with filter paper. Now you are where you were when you had plutonium oxalate before—and you proceed to make metal. Or you can heat up the plutonium oxalate in a furnace to a thousand degrees centigrade, and you get plutonium oxide, which is weapons material in itself, although less efficient. When plutonium recycle really gets going, incidentally, this stuff—plutonium oxide, out of which bombs can be made directly, without any chemical processing—will exist in huge quantities all over the country, both in transit and in storage." The afternoon by now was well along. Taylor's beer remained open but untouched. He had taken two bites out of his sandwich.

QUESTIONS FOR READING AND WRITING

1. Ted Taylor, one of the Alamogordo physicists who developed the atomic bomb and whose specialization is the miniaturization of atomic weapons, is elsewhere quoted by John McPhee as saying he could develop a nuclear weapon that could fit in a suitcase and topple the twin towers of the World Trade Center. How do his musings here,

which read like a cookbook, present a frightening omen for the future?

2. How does McPhee's occasional breaking away to details of the setting ("there was no sound but some wind in the turning leaves") affect the dire tone of the account? Do some reactors (breeder reactors) still produce plutonium?
3. Compare McPhee's account of how to make a nuclear device with Jonathan Schell's account of the effects of one in "Nothing to Report."
4. Write a process analysis of a common biological or chemical process, such as mitosis, photosynthesis, the molting of an animal's skin, or the Bessemer process for converting iron to steel. Show, at various stages, the importance of the process.

✦ Jessica Mitford ✦
Parting the Formaldehyde Curtain

Born into an aristocratic English family in 1917, Jessica Mitford hardly seems to have had the beginnings for an investigative reporter. Yet her exposé of the practices of the American funeral industry, The American Way of Death *(1963), may have been the single most influential cause for reform of what were then common practices. Her* Trial of Dr. Spock *(1969), written at the height of the protest movement against the war in Vietnam, and* Kind and Unusual Punishment: The Prison Business *(1973) helped establish her as one of the grittiest of muckraking reporters. In the following excerpt from* The American Way of Death, *Mitford doesn't flinch from the most gruesome details of the embalming process in which a corpse is prepared for viewing.*

THE DRAMA BEGINS TO UNFOLD with the arrival of the corpse at the mortuary. 1

Alas, poor Yorick! How surprised he would be to see how his counterpart of today is whisked off to a funeral parlor and is in short order sprayed, sliced, pierced, pickled, trussed, trimmed, creamed, waxed, painted, rouged and neatly dressed—transformed from a common corpse into a Beautiful Memory Picture. This process is known in the trade as embalming and restorative art, and is so universally employed in the United States and Canada that the funeral director does it routinely, without consulting corpse or kin. He regards as eccentric those few who are hardy enough to suggest that it might be dispensed with. Yet no law requires embalming, no religious doctrine commends it, nor is it dictated by considerations of health, sanitation, or even of personal daintiness. In no part of the world but in Northern America is it widely used. The purpose of embalming is to make the corpse presentable for viewing in a suitably costly container; and here too the funeral director routinely, without first consulting the family, prepares the body for public display. 2

Is all this legal? The processes to which a dead body may be subjected are after all to some extent circumscribed by law. In most states, for instance, the signature of next of kin must be obtained before an autopsy may be performed, before the deceased may be 3 cremated, before the body may be turned over to a medical school for research purposes; or such provision must be made in the decedent's will. In the case of embalming, no such permission is required nor is it ever sought. A textbook, *The Principles and Practices of Embalming*, comments on this: "There is some question regarding the legality of much that is done within the preparation room." The author points out that it would be most unusual for a responsible member of a bereaved family to instruct the mortician, in so many words, to "embalm" the body of a deceased relative. The very term "embalming" is so seldom used that the mortician must rely upon custom in the matter. The author concludes that unless the family specifies otherwise, the act of entrusting the body to the care of a funeral establishment carries with it an implied permission to go ahead and embalm.

Embalming is indeed a most extraordinary procedure, and one must wonder at the docility of Americans who each year pay hundreds of millions of dollars for its perpetuation, blissfully ignorant of what it is all about, what is done, how it is done. Not one in ten thousand has any idea of what actually takes place. Books on the subject are extremely hard to come by. They are not to be found in most libraries or bookshops.

In an era when huge television audiences watch surgical operations in the comfort of their living rooms, when, thanks to the animated cartoon, the geography of the digestive system has become familiar territory even to the nursery school set, in a land where the satisfaction of curiosity about almost all matters is a national pastime, the secrecy surrounding embalming can, surely, hardly be attributed to the inherent gruesomeness of the subject. Custom in this regard has within this century suffered a complete reversal. In the early days of American embalming, when it was performed in the home of the deceased, it was almost mandatory for some relative to stay by the embalmer's side and witness the procedure. Today, family members who might wish to be in attendance would certainly be dissuaded by the funeral director. All others, except apprentices, are excluded by law from the preparation room.

A close look at what does actually take place may explain in large measure the undertaker's intractable reticence concerning a procedure that has become his major *raison d'être*. Is it possible he fears that public information about embalming might lead patrons to wonder if they really want this service? If the funeral men are loath to discuss the subject outside the trade, the reader may, understandably, be equally loath to go on reading at this point. For those who have the stomach for it, let us part the formaldehyde curtain. . . .

The body is first laid out in the undertaker's morgue—or rather, Mr. Jones is reposing in the preparation room—to be readied to bid the world farewell. 7

The preparation room in any of the better funeral establishments has the tiled and sterile look of a surgery, and indeed the embalmer-restorative artist who does his chores there is beginning to adopt the term "dermasurgeon" (appropriately corrupted by some mortician-writers as "demi-surgeon") to describe his calling. His equipment, consisting of scalpels, scissors, augers, forceps, clamps, needles, pumps, tubes, bowls and basins, is crudely imitative of the surgeon's, as is his technique, acquired in a nine- or twelve-month post-high-school course in an embalming school. He is supplied by an advanced chemical industry with a bewildering array of fluids, sprays, pastes, oils, powders, creams, to fix or soften tissue, shrink or distend it as needed, dry it here, restore the moisture there. There are cosmetics, waxes and paints to fill and cover features, even plaster of Paris to replace entire limbs. There are ingenious aids to prop and stabilize the cadaver: a Vari-Pose Head Rest, the Edwards Arm and Hand Positioner, the Repose Block (to support the shoulders during the embalming), and the Throop Foot Positioner, which resembles an old-fashioned stocks. 8

Mr. John H. Eckels, president of the Eckels College of Mortuary Science, thus describes the first part of the embalming procedure: "In the hands of a skilled practitioner, this work may be done in a comparatively short time and without mutilating the body other than by slight incision—so slight that it scarcely would cause serious inconvenience if made upon a living person. It is necessary to remove the blood, and doing this not only helps in the disinfecting, but removes the principal cause of disfigurements due to discoloration." 9

Another textbook discusses the all-important time element: "The earlier this is done, the better, for every hour that elapses between death and embalming will add to the problems and complications encountered. . . ." Just how soon should one get going on the 10 embalming? The author tells us, "On the basis of such scanty information made available to this profession through its rudimentary and haphazard system of technical research, we must conclude that the best results are to be obtained if the subject is embalmed before life is completely extinct—that is, before cellular death has occurred. In the average case, this would mean within an hour after somatic death." For those who feel that there is something a little rudimentary, not to say haphazard, about this advice, a comforting thought is offered by another writer. Speaking of fears entertained in early days of premature burial, he points out, "One of the effects of embalming by chemical injection, however, has been to dispel fears of live burial." How true; once the blood is removed, chances of live burial are indeed remote.

To return to Mr. Jones, the blood is drained out through the veins and replaced by embalming fluid pumped in through the arteries. As noted in *The Principles and Practices of Embalming*, "every operator has a favorite injection and drainage point—a fact which becomes a handicap only if he fails or refuses to forsake his favorites when conditions demand it." Typical favorites are the carotid artery, femoral artery, jugular vein, subclavian vein. There are various choices of embalming fluid. If Flextone is used, it will produce a "mild, flexible rigidity. The skin retains a velvety softness, the tissues are rubbery and pliable. Ideal for women and children." It may be blended with B. and G. Products Company's Lyf-Lyk tint, which is guaranteed to reproduce "nature's own skin texture . . . the velvety appearance of living tissue." Suntone comes in three separate tints: Suntan; Special Cosmetic Tint, a pink shade "especially indicated for young female subjects"; and Regular Cosmetic Tint, moderately pink.

About three to six gallons of a dyed and perfumed solution of formaldehyde, glycerin, borax, phenol, alcohol and water is soon circulating through Mr. Jones, whose mouth has been sewn together with a "needle directed upward between the upper lip and gum and brought out through the left nostril," with the corners raised slightly "for a more pleasant expression." If he should be bucktoothed, his teeth are cleaned with Bon Ami and coated with colorless nail polish. His eyes, meanwhile, are closed with flesh-tinted eye caps and eye cement.

The next step is to have at Mr. Jones with a thing called a trocar. 13
This is a long, hollow needle attached to a tube. It is jabbed into the abdomen, poked around the entrails and chest cavity, the contents of which are pumped out and replaced with "cavity fluid." This done, and the hole in the abdomen sewn up, Mr. Jones's face is heavily creamed (to protect the skin from burns which may be caused by leakage of the chemicals), and he is covered with a sheet and left unmolested for a while. But not for long—there is more, much more, in store for him. He has been embalmed, but not yet restored, and the best time to start the restorative work is eight to ten hours after embalming, when the tissues have become firm and dry.

The object of all this attention to the corpse, it must be remem- 14
bered, is to make it presentable for viewing in an attitude of healthy repose. "Our customs require the presentation of our dead in the semblance of normality . . . unmarred by the ravages of illness, disease or mutilation," says Mr. J. Sheridan Mayer in his *Restorative Art.* This is rather a large order since few people die in the full bloom of health, unravaged by illness and unmarked by some disfigurement. The funeral industry is equal to the challenge: "In some cases the gruesome appearance of a mutilated or disease-ridden subject may be quite discouraging. The task of restoration may seem impossible and shake the confidence of the embalmer. This is the time for intestinal fortitude and determination. Once the formative work is begun and affected tissues are cleaned or removed, all doubts of success vanish. It is surprising and gratifying to discover the results which may be obtained."

The embalmer, having allowed an appropriate interval to elapse, 15
returns to the attack, but now he brings into play the skill and equipment of sculptor and cosmetician. Is a hand missing? Casting one in plaster of Paris is a simple matter. "For replacement purposes, only a cast of the back of the hand is necessary; this is within the ability of the average operator and is quite adequate." If a lip or two, a nose or an ear should be missing, the embalmer has at hand a variety of restorative waxes with which to model replacements. Pores and skin texture are simulated by stippling with a little brush, and over this cosmetics are laid on. Head off? Decapitation cases are rather routinely handled. Ragged edges are trimmed, and head

joined to torso with a series of splints, wires and sutures. It is a good idea to have a little something at the neck—a scarf or a high collar—when time for viewing comes. Swollen mouth? Cut out tissue as needed from inside the lips. If too much is removed, the surface contour can easily be restored by padding with cotton. Swollen necks and cheeks are reduced by removing tissue through vertical incisions made down each side of the neck. "When the deceased is casketed, the pillow will hide the suture incisions . . . as an extra precaution against leakage, the suture may be painted with liquid sealer."

The opposite condition is more likely to present itself—that of emaciation. His hypodermic syringe now loaded with massage cream, the embalmer seeks out and fills the hollowed and sunken areas by injection. In this procedure the backs of the hands and fingers and the under-chin area should not be neglected.

Positioning the lips is a problem that recurrently challenges the ingenuity of the embalmer. Closed too tightly, they tend to give a stern, even disapproving expression. Ideally, embalmers feel, the lips should give the impression of being ever so slightly parted, the upper lip protruding slightly for a more youthful appearance. This takes some engineering, however, as the lips tend to drift apart. Lip drift can sometimes be remedied by pushing one or two straight pins through the inner margin of the lower lip and then inserting them between the two front upper teeth. If Mr. Jones happens to have no teeth, the pins can just as easily be anchored in his Armstrong Face Former and Denture Replacer. Another method to maintain lip closure is to dislocate the lower jaw, which is then held in its new position by a wire run through holes which have been drilled through the upper and lower jaws at the midline. As the French are fond of saying, *il faut souffrir pour être belle.*

If Mr. Jones has died of jaundice, the embalming fluid will very likely turn him green. Does this deter the embalmer? Not if he has intestinal fortitude. Masking pastes and cosmetics are heavily laid on, burial garments and casket interiors are color-correlated with particular care, and Jones is displayed beneath rose-colored lights. Friends will say "How *well* he looks." Death by carbon monoxide, on the other hand, can be rather a good thing from the embalmer's viewpoint: "One advantage is the fact that this type of discoloration is an exaggerated form of a natural pink coloration." This is nice because the healthy glow is already present and needs but little attention.

The patching and filling completed, Mr. Jones is now shaved, washed and dressed. Cream-based cosmetic, available in pink, flesh, suntan, brunette and blond, is applied to his hands and face, his hair is shampooed and combed (and, in the case of Mrs. Jones, set), his hands manicured. For the horny-handed son of toil special care must be taken; cream should be applied to remove ingrained grime, and the nails cleaned. "If he were not in the habit of having them manicured in life, trimming and shaping is advised for better appearance—never questioned by kin." 19

Jones is now ready for casketing (this is the present participle of the verb "to casket"). In this operation his right shoulder should be depressed slightly "to turn the body a bit to the right and soften the appearance of lying flat on the back." Positioning the hands is a matter of importance, and special rubber positioning blocks may be used. The hands should be cupped slightly for a more lifelike, relaxed appearance. Proper placement of the body requires a delicate sense of balance. It should lie as high as possible in the casket, yet not so high that the lid, when lowered, will hit the nose. On the other hand, we are cautioned, placing the body too low "creates the impression that the body is in a box." 20

Jones is next wheeled into the appointed slumber room where a few last touches may be added—his favorite pipe placed in his hand or, if he was a great reader, a book propped into position. (In the case of little Master Jones a Teddy bear may be clutched.) Here he will hold open house for a few days, visiting hours 10 A.M. to 9 P.M. 21

All now being in readiness, the funeral director calls a staff conference to make sure that each assistant knows his precise duties. Mr. Wilber Kriege writes: "This makes your staff feel that they are a part of the team, with a definite assignment that must be properly carried out if the whole plan is to succeed. You never heard of a football coach who failed to talk to his entire team before they go on the field. They have drilled on the plays they are to execute for hours and days, and yet the successful coach knows the importance of making even the bench-warming third-string substitute feel that he is important if the game is to be won." The winning of *this* game is predicated upon glass-smooth handling of the logistics. The funeral director has notified the pallbearers whose names were 22 furnished by the family, has arranged for the presence of clergyman, organist, and soloist, has provided transportation for everybody, has organized and listed the flowers sent by friends. In *Psychology of Funeral Service* Mr. Edward A. Martin points out: "He may not always do as much as the family thinks he is doing, but it is his helpful guidance that they appreciate in knowing they are proceeding as they should. . . . The important thing is how well his services can be used to make the family believe they are giving unlimited expression to their own sentiment."

The religious service may be held in a church or in the chapel of the funeral home; the funeral director vastly prefers the latter arrangement, for not only is it more convenient for him but it affords him the opportunity to show off his beautiful facilities to the gathered mourners. After the clergyman has had his say, the mourners queue up to file past the casket for a last look at the deceased. The family is *never* asked whether they want an open-casket ceremony; in the absence of their instruction to the contrary, this is taken for granted. Consequently well over 90 per cent of all American funerals feature the open casket—a custom unknown in other parts of the world. Foreigners are astonished by it. An English woman living in San Francisco described her reaction in a letter to the writer:

> I myself have attended only one funeral here—that of an elderly fellow worker of mine. After the service I could not understand why everyone was walking towards the coffin (sorry, I mean casket), but thought I had better follow the crowd. It shook me rigid to get there and find the casket open and poor old Oscar lying there in his brown tweed suit, wearing a suntan makeup and just the wrong shade of lipstick. If I had not been extremely fond of the old boy, I have a horrible feeling that I might have giggled. Then and there I decided that I could never face another American funeral—even dead.

The casket (which has been resting throughout the service on a Classic Beauty Ultra Metal Casket Bier) is now transferred by a hydraulically operated device called Porto-Lift to a balloon-tired, Glide Easy casket carriage which will wheel it to yet another conveyance, the Cadillac Funeral Coach. This may be lavender, cream, light green—anything but black. Interiors, of course, are color-correlated, "for the man who cannot stop short of perfection."

At graveside, the casket is lowered into the earth. This office, once the prerogative of friends of the deceased, is now performed by a patented mechanical lowering device. A "Lifetime Green" artificial grass mat is at the ready to conceal the sere earth, and overhead, to conceal the sky, is a portable Steril Chapel Tent ("resists the intense heat and humidity of summer and the terrific storms of winter . . . available in Silver Grey, Rose or Evergreen"). Now is the time for the ritual scattering of earth over the coffin, as the solemn words "earth to earth, ashes to ashes, dust to dust" are pronounced by the officiating cleric. This can today be accomplished "with a mere flick of the wrist with the Gordon Leak-Proof Earth Dispenser. No grasping of a handful of dirt, no soiled fingers. Simple, dignified, beautiful, reverent! The modern way!" The Gordon Earth Dispenser (at $5) is of nickel-plated brass construction. It is not only "attractive to the eye and long wearing"; it is also "one of the 'tools' for building better public relations" if presented as "an appropriate non-commercial gift" to the clergyman. It is shaped something like a salt-shaker. 25

Untouched by human hand, the coffin and the earth are now united. 26

It is in the function of directing the participants through this maze of gadgetry that the funeral director has assigned to himself his relatively new role of "grief therapist." He has relieved the family of every detail, he has revamped the corpse to look like a living doll, he has arranged for it to nap for a few days in a slumber room, he has put on a well-oiled performance in which the concept of *death* has played no part whatsoever—unless it was inconsiderately mentioned by the clergyman who conducted the religious service. He has done everything in his power to make the funeral a real pleasure for everybody concerned. He and his team have given their all to score an upset victory over death. 27

QUESTIONS FOR READING AND WRITING

1. Are people still as obsessed with the details of funeral arrangements as in the past, or have Mitford's book *The American Way of Death* and other exposés of the funeral industry changed that?

2. The ironic tone with which Mitford describes the embalming process creates much of the gallows humor of the piece. Cite some examples of Mitford's word choice responsible for the irreverence of the essay. How does she gain humor by quoting textbooks from the funeral industry? How does she use the industry's jargon for humorous effect?
3. Read Phyllis Rose's "Tools of Torture" and comment on the similarities of cosmetic science in life and after death.
4. Read Sylvia Plath's "Notebooks, 1961/2" and discuss the fascination with the details of death here and in Mitford's account of embalming.
5. Write an essay comparing the account by Mitford with the process of cosmetology in the opening scenes of Evelyn Waugh's *The Loved One*.

✦ Sara B. Stein ✦

Let's Get Botanical

The Lowdown on the Sex Life of a Flower

Sara B. Stein is best known for her numerous nonfiction books for children. Her Open Family *series is designed to involve parents and children in explaining various problems of day-to-day living by providing opposite page texts for parents and children on such subjects as handicaps, conception, adoption, divorce and dying. She has received numerous awards for her arts-and-crafts and science books for children, including* A Piece of Red Paper *(1973) and* The Science Book *(1979). "Let's Get Botanical" appears in* My Weeds: A Gardener's Botany *(1988). In this essay, Stein questions the old Victorian idea of teaching reproduction to children through the illustration of the birds and the bees, since the actual process of reproduction only incidentally uses these pollinators.*

THE SEXUALITY OF FLOWERS IS A GIVEN in the human psyche. 1
The coyness of a daisy's practiced daintiness, the suggestive fullness of a lady's slipper's belly, the summoning odor of a rose speak of sex without translation. I suppose that is why Victorians, shy on directness, hoped bees and flowers would guide them through the maze of 19th-century sex education. But I am glad my mother neglected to tell me about the birds and the bees. The facts of life as she taught them to me were simple; I found incredible only that anyone would wish to do what had to be done to grow a baby. Birds and bees are poor exemplars of human sexuality. Most birds lack a penis, the reproductive organ most interesting to children. The bees one sees fertilize flowers, not one another. And flowers, despite their allure, belong to asexual plants.

The facts of life as they pertain to plants escaped either my notice 2
or my comprehension for half a century. During all those years I thought watermelon vines and pomegranate trees were sexy plants that made eggs and fertilized them, and I know of no gardener who knows better. My mother never told me about spores. A spore is the kind of reproductive cell made by every flowering plant. All on their own without fertilization, spores grow into sexual plants reduced

almost to invisibility and hidden within flowers that are not of their making. This botanical revelation stunned me.

I tried out my new knowledge at a dinner party once, where it was not well received, and on an arborist, the manager of a tree-repair company, who disbelieved me. I can now see that the sex education of the public at large is woefully deficient, and that even my mother's straightforward presentation failed to convey the fundamentals of reproduction, without which the doings of plants are not to be believed.

Reproduction doesn't require the coupling of sperm and egg. Virgin birth is common in the insect world. Observe the aphid on the rose. Those you see in the full flush of summer are wingless wonders born of a virgin parent, their mother. Only as food becomes scarce do some females grow wings and fly to find a mate. The differences between an aphid conceived in innocence and one conceived in sex are not grossly apparent. The benefit of having two parents is the store of information available from two sets of genes, information that may come in handy to aphids who will emerge the following spring into an unknown future. But either set by itself contains all the information necessary to make the complete organism, and an aphid with only its mother's know-how is perfectly normal.

Eggs in general do not always recognize sperm as crucial to their fulfillment. Frogs and rabbits have been raised to adulthood from eggs pricked by a needle dipped in blood. The prick is the only stimulus needed to urge the egg to begin dividing; some substance in blood, presumably similar to a substance contained in sperm, is necessary to keep the egg dividing past the first few divisions, but reproduction proceeds normally without a double dose of genes.

At least a frog's reproductive cell grows up to be a frog. A rose's reproductive cell does not. Why should it? It need not read the genes its parent reads, but may instead peruse some volume hidden from the mother rose and containing another sort of wisdom. This is what a rose spore does: it reads a book on sex its asexual parent never found, and so grows up to be a sexual plant that makes not spores but sperm or eggs.

One clings to the hope that this sexual generation of a flower will accord with one's lush presumptions. That is so of moist and sexy mosses whose sperm swims through the dew to fertilize eggs waiting in the moss plants' furry tips, but it's not true of blossomers. The spores of flowering plants remain inside the parent's bloom. Spores made in the ovary at the base of a flower's pistil grow into female sexual plants that produce eggs. Spores made in the anther—the tip of each stamen—grow into male sexual plants that produce sperm. At maturity, each female sexual plant hidden in the ovary is usually all of seven cells big. One of the cells is the egg. The grown-up male has only two cells, one of which will ultimately divide into two sperm. It is a pollen grain.

I imagine my Victorian great-grandmother dressed in black taffeta with a bonnet on her head, ensconced in a wicker chair beside a trellis of roses and leaving it to the bees to demonstrate to her five children how they had come to be. Pollination is a breezy act, unembarrassing to watch. But it is not a sex act. The pollen manages fertilization by itself in a way my great-grandmother would not have approved. 8

Having been dropped off by the pollinator on the sticky stigma that tips the pistil, the pollen grain secretes an enzyme that digests the stigma surface. One of its two cells elongates into a tube that digests its way into the pistil and burrows down through its flesh into the ovary at its base. Meanwhile the other cell divides into two tailless sperm that ride the tube to their target, an ovule in which lies the egg. The two sperm enter through a pore; the first to reach the egg fuses with it,and inoculates it with its genetic material. The fertilized egg then begins its division into an embryo rosebush. 9

In view of the truth about plants' private lives, I wonder about the wisdom of teaching children anything at all about the reproductive goings-on of plants lest the young draw the wrong conclusions, or worry about their own reproductive competence, or develop unhealthy fantasies. Wouldn't it be dangerous to tell a toddler that a rose's baby boy is a pollen grain? Should a kindergartner know that flowers have sperm in their stamens *and* eggs in their ovaries? I'm sure youngsters ought not to hear what is going on in their dandelions. 10

But maybe if the Victorians had understood flowers adequately, they might have served as a parable through which to hint at the facts of life while disguising how, exactly, reproduction is achieved. The true story of a blossom and a bee is of courtship between two chaste individuals met, by chance, on a byway of evolution. Fertil- 11 ization of parties unknown to either is achieved unwittingly by two innocents who are unaware of the significance of their graceful blooming and sweet sipping, and I think my great-grandmother would have approved of that.

QUESTIONS FOR READING AND WRITING

1. Stein's wry essay discusses the reproductive processes of various plants while couching the particulars within comments on Victorian sex education. What information in the essay surprised you?
2. Does Stein explain the use of such terms as *spore, sexual,* and *asexual plants*? Why does she use the example of the aphid from the insect world before returning to the reproductive process of plants?
3. How is the transition from frogs to roses managed?
4. How does the description of the process by which the pollen grain fertilizes the egg surprise the reader? What is the function of the bee (pollinator)? Why does Stein end the essay with the observation about the "innocence" of the flower and the bee? Why would her great-grandmother have approved?
5. Choose a simple process in nature—biological, chemical, physical, geological—and explain in simple terms how it works.

Part 5

MIXED PATTERNS OF EXPOSITION

You have already learned that patterns of organizing expository writing—definition, examples, division and classification, and so on—actually derive from ways of finding ideas, a procedure that dates back to Aristotle. So if, like Norman Cousins, you wished to write about "placebos," you might logically begin with the question, "What is a placebo?" The answer to this question would lead you inevitably to use definition as your pattern of organization. Or if, like Edward Abbey, you were writing about the Great American Desert, you might begin with the question, "What kinds of desert are there?" You would then use division as your method of organizing the answer. Or if, again like Cousins, you wanted to know what were the effects of placebos on patients, you would organize your material in one of the patterns appropriate to cause and effect.

You have also seen at the end of the sections on narration and description that it is rare for a piece of writing to use exclusively one organizational pattern or another; in fact, it is more common for a writer to employ several techniques of organization within the same piece. Carefully examine the following selection. Notice that each section addresses a different question about the subject, and that each section *of the same essay* uses a different pattern of organization.

Definition ***What is it?***	Inflation, in the simplest of words, is an unhealthily rapid rise in prices over a relatively short span of time.

Its results, expressed in one way: a sharp erosion in the buying power of the currency you use to conduct all your transactions at home and in your business or profession; plus a dwindling in the future buying power of the funds you put away in cash savings or the equivalent (life insurance, U.S. savings bonds, and the like); an undermining in the value of most other investments.

Its results, expressed in another way: an upsurge in your living costs, which few can offset successfully and which, therefore, puts you in a budget squeeze, reduces your standard of living despite pay hikes you may win, all but destroys your confidence and peace of mind.

Division
What kinds are there?

But that's not the whole tale, for there are two types of inflation—drastically different from each other.

The first type is called "demand-pull," which means that demands for goods and services during a specified period are exceeding the available supplies of those goods and services and this excess of demand (fueled by more than adequate cash or credit in the hands of buyers) is "pulling up" prices.

A classic illustration of demand-pull inflation occurred in food prices—especially meat prices—during the early post-World War II period. Millions of newly prosperous U.S. workers and their families sharply hiked their demands for meat, more millions steadily increased their purchases of higher quality meats, shoppers the nation over loaded their supermarket carts with roasts, steaks, lamb, veal.

The continued buying of a limited supply of meats rapidly pulled up meat prices, until the spiral culminated in the blowoff in meat prices in the wild inflation of 1974—and (at least temporarily) interrupted the long-term upsurge in our consumption of meats.

The second type is called "cost-push," which means that mounting costs of producing goods and services during a specified period are "pushing up" prices. For many, many years—possibly the longest span in modern times—we have been in the clutch of this cost-push inflation in the United States. And no end to this form of inflation is yet in sight. The leapfrogging of prices over wages, then wages over prices, then prices over wages, and on and on continues.

Cause–effect What are its effects? Perhaps the most insidious evil in the overall evil of pernicious inflation is the spreading expectation that inflation will become permanent—a "psychology of inflation" that is dangerously self-fulfilling.

As millions of Americans become resigned to the prospect that the price spiral is a fact of life to be accepted for the indefinite future, these unhealthy developments follow:

More and more workers demand wage hikes to keep up with past price increases and to get a jump ahead of future price increases—thereby adding to the current inflation rate.

More and more union leaders insist on cost of living adjustment clauses in their union contracts to give them automatic pay raises as the Consumer Price Index climbs. As the 1980s approached, an estimated half of our total population—Social Security and welfare recipients as well as workers—already were converted by "COLAs."

More and more businesses boost prices in anticipation of the wage demands and of the eventual imposition of mandatory wage-price controls.

More and more consumers try to buy big- and small-ticket items "ahead" to beat the price increases they are sure will come.

The whole sick pyramid collapses into a business slump, which leads to "reflation" policies and a new round of inflation*

This example—and the other examples in this section—show that real writing grows out of the writer's search for material about the subject. The appropriate pattern of organization follows this search. This is no less true of utilitarian writing explaining how

* Sylvia Porter, *Sylvia Porter's New Money Book for the 80's* (Avon, 1980), 4–6.

something works than of more profound writing about social and economic issues. Most professional writing is the end product of a complicated series of choices that lead to the pattern of organization the essay finally employs.

But how does this process of choices work in practice? How conscious are writers about the choices they make when they select certain patterns to organize their material? Do they think of these forms as they write or do these emerge spontaneously? In one of his letters, E. B. White wrote, "I always write a thing first and think about it afterward, which is not a bad procedure, because the easiest way to have consecutive thoughts is to start putting them down." Edward Hoagland has written about the dissolving of forms in contemporary prose, where all types of writing mix: "Prose has no partitions now . . . No forms exist anymore, except that to work as a single observer, using the resources of only one mind, and to work with words—this is being a writer." If these remarks seem to indicate that forms are ignored by writers, let's listen to descriptions of how two writers work: John McPhee (a deliberate writer searching for the underlying organic form hidden somewhere in the voluminous notes he has transcribed) and Tom Wolfe (also wondering in what shape to cast several month's worth of research, but more impatient than McPhee to get it down on paper).

McPhee's painstaking analysis of his material, his search for the right form or pattern of organization, typifies the logical approach favored by many writers. The plan grows out of the material; the form that emerges serves both to eliminate material and to shape the remaining contents. Here is how McPhee works:

> These are his topics, the formal segments of narrative, which he then writes on a series of index cards. After assembling the stack, he fans them out and begins to play a sort of writer's solitaire, studying the possibilities of order. Decisions don't come easily; a story has many potential sequences, and each chain produces a calculus of desired and undesired effects, depending on factors like character and theme. When he has the cards in a satisfactory arrangement, he thumbtacks them to a large bulletin board . . .
>
> [H]e next codes the duplicate set of notes and then scissors its sheets apart, cutting large blocks of paragraphs and two or three line ribbons. In a few hours he has reduced the sheets to

> thousands of scraps, which he sorts into file folders, one folder for each topical index card on the bulletin board. These folders are precompositional skeletons of the narrative segments he will refine when writing a first draft. With the folders squared away in a vertical file, he is ready to write. A large steel dart on the bulletin board marks his progress. He stabs the dart under an index card, opens a folder, further sorts scraps and ribbons until this segment also has a "logical" structure. Then, without invoking the muse, he begins to type his first draft, picking up where the lead ends. When he finishes a folder, he moves the dart, gets the next folder, sorts it out, and continues to type.*

If this seems too deliberate, too mechanical a procedure, compare McPhee's approach with this account by Tom Wolfe which explains that he has just about given up trying to find any form that will fit his miscellaneous rough notes, so he simply begins to type out those notes in a narrative explaining where he got his information.

> At first I couldn't even write the story. . . . I had a lot of trouble analyzing exactly what I had on my hands. . . . I started typing the notes out in the form of a memorandum that began, "Dear Byron." I started typing away, starting right with the first time I saw any custom cars in California. I started recording it all, and inside of a couple of hours, typing along like a madman, I could tell that something was beginning to happen. . . . I wrapped up the memorandum about 6:15 a.m., and by this time it was 49 pages long. I took it over to *Esquire* as soon as they opened up, about 9:30 a.m. About 4 p.m. I got a call from Byron Dobell [the managing editor at *Esquire*]. He told me they were striking out the "Dear Byron" at the top of the memorandum and running the rest of it in the magazine. That was the story, "The Kandy-Kolored Tangerine-Flake Streamline Baby."†

What these two accounts say, finally, is that really good writing reduces itself not only to the search for interesting and original ideas and an effective style, but also to the right organizational pattern or form—what Aristotle called "disposition." To find the right order of ideas, you must first know the patterns available to

* John McPhee, *The John McPhee Reader*, edited and with an introduction by William L. Howarth (Farrar, Straus & Giroux, 1976), *xv*.

† Tom Wolfe, *The Kandy-Kolored Tangerine-Flake Streamline Baby* (Farrar, Straus & Giroux, 1965), *xii–xiii*.

you and then use them—any or all of them—not mechanically, but with discretion, searching for that effective combination of patterns that will most completely develop your ideas and express the corrections between them. Rarely will one of these patterns alone sufficiently contain all your ideas; more likely, as in the selections that follow, your essays will employ several patterns. As essayist/novelist Herb Gold has observed, "Not all organizing and structuring are rational." It may help to know that a famous sports writer, A. J. Liebling, once called one of his essays that used a variety of patterns, "a mixed pickles story." The essential criterion is: "Does it work?" Regardless of which patterns, or how many of them, you use to communicate your thoughts, if the form and content match, your essay is at least well organized. If good organization is coupled with effective style and interesting ideas, you may, like the writers who follow, produce a memorable piece of prose writing.

✦ Stephen Jay Gould ✦
Evolution as Fact and Theory

Stephen Jay Gould was born in New York City in 1941 and received his Ph.D. from Columbia in 1967, the year he joined the faculty at Harvard. Controversial and outspoken, Gould has made a career out of uncompromisingly explaining the concepts of geology and biology in terms the average person can understand. His regular columns in Natural History *have been collected in* Ever Since Darwin *(1977),* The Panda's Thumb *(1980),* Hen's Teeth and Horse's Toes *(1983), and* The Flamingo's Smile *(1985). Reprinted from* Hen's Teeth and Horse's Toes, *"Evolution as Fact and Theory" typifies Gould's essential qualities: addressing the issues of a controversy squarely, clearly defining the terms of the disagreement, and bringing the scientific method to bear when the issue demands it. Gould's writing is a model of clear writing for the nonspecialist interested in the implications of recent scientific theory.*

KIRTLEY MATHER, who died last year at age ninety, was a pillar of both science and Christian religion in America and one of my dearest friends. The difference of a half-century in our ages evaporated before our common interests. The most curious thing we shared was a battle we each fought at the same age. For Kirtley had gone to Tennessee with Clarence Darrow to testify for evolution at the Scopes trial of 1925. When I think that we are enmeshed again in the same struggle for one of the best documented, most compelling and exciting concepts in all of science, I don't know whether to laugh or cry. 1

According to idealized principles of scientific discourse, the arousal of dormant issues should reflect fresh data that give renewed life to abandoned notions. Those outside the current debate may therefore be excused for suspecting that creationists have come up with something new, or that evolutionists have generated some serious internal trouble. But nothing has changed; the creationists have presented not a single new fact or argument. Darrow and Bryan were at least more entertaining than we lesser antagonists today. The rise of creationism is politics, pure and simple; it represents one issue (and by no means the major concern) 2 of the resurgent evangelical right. Arguments that seemed kooky just a decade ago have reentered the mainstream.

The basic attack of modern creationists falls apart on two general counts before we even reach the supposed factual details of their assault against evolution. First, they play upon a vernacular misunderstanding of the word "theory" to convey the false impression that we evolutionists are covering up the rotten core of our edifice. Second, they misuse a popular philosophy of science to argue that they are behaving scientifically in attacking evolution. Yet the same philosophy demonstrates that their own belief is not science, and that "scientific creationism" is a meaningless and self-contradictory phrase, an example of what Orwell called "newspeak."

In the American vernacular, "theory" often means "imperfect fact"—part of a hierarchy of confidence running downhill from fact to theory to hypothesis to guess. Thus, creationists can (and do) argue: evolution is "only" a theory, and intense debate now rages about many aspects of the theory. If evolution is less than a fact, and scientists can't even make up their minds about the theory, then what confidence can we have in it? Indeed, President Reagan echoed this argument before an evangelical group in Dallas when he said (in what I devoutly hope was campaign rhetoric): "Well, it is a theory. It is a scientific theory only, and it has in recent years been challenged in the world of science—that is, not believed in the scientific community to be as infallible as it once was."

Well, evolution *is* a theory. It is also a fact. And facts and theories are different things, not rungs in a hierarchy of increasing certainty. Facts are the world's data. Theories are structures of ideas that explain and interpret facts. Facts do not go away while scientists debate rival theories for explaining them. Einstein's theory of gravitation replaced Newton's, but apples did not suspend themselves in mid-air pending the outcome. And human beings evolved from apelike ancestors whether they did so by Darwin's proposed mechanism or by some other, yet to be discovered.

Moreover, "fact" does not mean "absolute certainty." The final proofs of logic and mathematics flow deductively from stated premises and achieve certainty only because they are *not* about the empirical world. Evolutionists make no claim for perpetual truth, though creationists often do (and then attack us for a style of argument that they themselves favor). In science, "fact" can only mean "confirmed to such a degree that it would be perverse to withhold provisional assent." I suppose that apples might start to rise tomorrow, but the possibility does not merit equal time in physics classrooms.

Evolutionists have been clear about this distinction between fact and theory from the very beginning, if only because we have always acknowledged how far we are from completely understanding the mechanisms (theory) by which evolution (fact) occurred. Darwin continually emphasized the difference between his two great and separate accomplishments: establishing the fact of evolution, and proposing a theory—natural selection—to explain the mechanism of evolution. He wrote in *The Descent of Man*: "I had two distinct objects in view; firstly, to show that species had not been separately created, and secondly, that natural selection had been the chief agent of change . . . Hence if I have erred in . . . having exaggerated its [natural selection's] power . . . I have at least, as I hope, done good service in aiding to overthrow the dogma of separate creations." 7

Thus Darwin acknowledged the provisional nature of natural selection while affirming the fact of evolution. The fruitful theoretical debate that Darwin initiated has never ceased. From the 1940s through the 1960s, Darwin's own theory of natural selection did achieve a temporary hegemony that it never enjoyed in his lifetime. But renewed debate characterizes our decade, and, while no biologist questions the importance of natural selection, many now doubt its ubiquity. In particular, many evolutionists argue that substantial amounts of genetic change may not be subject to natural selection and may spread through populations at random. Others are challenging Darwin's linking of natural selection with gradual, imperceptible change through all intermediary degrees; they are arguing that most evolutionary events may occur far more rapidly than Darwin envisioned. 8

Scientists regard debates on fundamental issues of theory as a sign of intellectual health and a source of excitement. Science is—and how else can I say it?—most fun when it plays with interesting ideas, examines their implications, and recognizes that old information may be explained in surprisingly new ways. Evolutionary theory is now enjoying this uncommon vigor. Yet amidst all this turmoil no biologist has been led to doubt the fact that evolution 9 occurred; we are debating *how* it happened. We are all trying to explain the same thing: the tree of evolutionary descent linking all organisms by ties of genealogy. Creationists pervert and caricature this debate by conveniently neglecting the common conviction that underlies it, and by falsely suggesting that we now doubt the very phenomenon we are struggling to understand.

Secondly, creationists claim that "the dogma of separate creations," as Darwin characterized it a century ago, is a scientific theory meriting equal time with evolution in high school biology curricula. But a popular viewpoint among philosophers of science belies this creationist argument. Philosopher Karl Popper has argued for decades that the primary criterion of science is the falsifiability of its theories. We can never prove absolutely, but we can falsify. A set of ideas that cannot, in principle, be falsified is not science.

The entire creationist program includes little more than a rhetorical attempt to falsify evolution by presenting supposed contradictions among its supporters. Their brand of creationism, they claim, is "scientific" because it follows the Popperian model in trying to demolish evolution. Yet Popper's argument must apply in both directions. One does not become a scientist by the simple act of trying to falsify a rival and truly scientific system; one has to present an alternative system that also meets Popper's criterion—it too must be falsifiable in principle.

"Scientific creationism" is a self-contradictory, nonsense phrase precisely because it cannot be falsified. I can envision observations and experiments that would disprove any evolutionary theory I know, but I cannot imagine what potential data could lead creationists to abandon their beliefs. Unbeatable systems are dogma, not science. Lest I seem harsh or rhetorical, I quote creationism's leading intellectual, Duane Gish, Ph.D., from his recent (1978) book, *Evolution? The Fossils Say No!* "By creation we mean the bringing into being by a supernatural Creator of the basic kinds of plants and animals by the process of sudden, or fiat, creation. We do not know how the Creator created, what processes He used, *for He used processes which are not now operating anywhere in the natural universe* [Gish's italics]. This is why we refer to creation as special creation. We cannot discover by scientific investigations anything about the creative processes used by the Creator." Pray tell, Dr. Gish, in the light of your last sentence, what then is "scientific" creationism?

Our confidence that evolution occurred centers upon three general arguments. First, we have abundant, direct, observational evidence of evolution in action, from both field and laboratory. This evidence ranges from countless experiments on change in nearly everything about fruit flies subjected to artificial selection in the laboratory to the famous populations of British moths that became black when industrial soot darkened the trees upon which the moths rest. (Moths gain protection from sharp-sighted bird predators by blending into the background.) Creationists do not deny these observations; how could they? Creationists have tightened their act. They now argue that God only created "basic kinds," and allowed for limited evolutionary meandering within them. Thus toy poodles and Great Danes come from the dog kind and moths can change color, but nature cannot convert a dog to a cat or a monkey to a man. 13

The second and third arguments for evolution—the case for major changes—do not involve direct observation of evolution in action. They rest upon inference, but are no less secure for that reason. Major evolutionary change requires too much time for direct observation on the scale of recorded human history. All historical sciences rest upon inference, and evolution is no different from geology, cosmology, or human history in this respect. In principle, we cannot observe processes that operated in the past. We must infer them from results that still surround us: living and fossil organisms for evolution, documents and artifacts for human history, strata and topography for geology. 14

The second argument—that the imperfection of nature reveals evolution—strikes many people as ironic, for they feel that evolution should be most elegantly displayed in the nearly perfect adaptation expressed by some organisms—the camber of a gull's wing, or butterflies that cannot be seen in ground litter because they mimic leaves so precisely. But perfection could be imposed by a wise creator or evolved by natural selection. Perfection covers the tracks of past history. And past history—the evidence of descent—is the mark of evolution. 15

Evolution lies exposed in the *imperfections* that record a history of descent. Why should a rat run, a bat fly, a porpoise swim, and I 16 type this essay with structures built of the same bones unless we all inherited them from a common ancestor? An engineer, starting from scratch, could design better limbs in each case. Why should all the large native mammals of Australia be marsupials, unless they descended from a common ancestor isolated on this island continent? Marsupials are not "better," or ideally suited for Australia; many have been wiped out by placental mammals imported by man from other continents. This principle of imperfection extends to all historical sciences. When we recognize the etymology of September, October, November, and December (seventh, eighth, ninth, and tenth), we know that the year once started in March, or that two additional months must have been added to an original calendar of ten months.

The third argument is more direct: transitions are often found in 17
the fossil record. Preserved transitions are not common—and should not be, according to our understanding of evolution (see next section)—but they are not entirely wanting, as creationists often claim. The lower jaw of reptiles contains several bones, that of mammals only one. The non-mammalian jawbones are reduced, step by step, in mammalian ancestors until they become tiny nubbins located at the back of the jaw. The "hammer" and "anvil" bones of the mammalian ear are descendants of these nubbins. How could such a transition be accomplished? the creationists ask. Surely a bone is either entirely in the jaw or in the ear. Yet paleontologists have discovered two transitional lineages of therapsids (the so-called mammal-like reptiles) with a double jaw joint—one composed of the old quadrate and articular bones (soon to become the hammer and anvil), the other of the squamosal and dentary bones (as in modern mammals). For that matter, what better transitional form could we expect to find than the oldest human, *Australopithecus afarensis*, with its apelike palate, its human upright stance, and a cranial capacity larger than any ape's of the same body size but a full 1,000 cubic centimeters below ours? If God made each of the half-dozen human species discovered in ancient rocks, why did he create in an unbroken temporal sequence of progressively more modern features—increasing cranial capacity, reduced face and teeth, larger body size? Did he create to mimic evolution and test our faith thereby?

Faced with these facts of evolution and the philosophical bankruptcy of their own position, creationists rely upon distortion and innuendo to buttress their rhetorical claim. If I sound sharp or bitter, indeed I am—for I have become a major target of these practices. 18

I count myself among the evolutionists who argue for a jerky, or episodic, rather than a smoothly gradual, pace of change. In 1972 my colleague Niles Eldredge and I developed the theory of punctuated equilibrium. We argued that two outstanding facts of the fossil record—geologically "sudden" origin of new species and failure to change thereafter (stasis)—reflect the predictions of evolutionary theory, not the imperfections of the fossil record. In most theories, small isolated populations are the source of new species, and the process of speciation takes thousands or tens of thousands of years. This amount of time, so long when measured against our lives, is a geological microsecond. It represents much less than 1 per cent of the average lifespan for a fossil invertebrate species—more than ten million years. Large, widespread, and well established species, on the other hand, are not expected to change very much. We believe that the inertia of large populations explains the stasis of most fossil species over millions of years. 19

We proposed the theory of punctuated equilibrium largely to provide a different explanation for pervasive trends in the fossil record. Trends, we argued, cannot be attributed to gradual transformation within lineages, but must arise from the differential success of certain kinds of species. A trend, we argued, is more like climbing a flight of stairs (punctuations and stasis) than rolling up an inclined plane. 20

Since we proposed punctuated equilibria to explain trends, it is infuriating to be quoted again and again by creationists—whether through design or stupidity, I do not know—as admitting that the fossil record includes no transitional forms. Transitional forms are generally lacking at the species level, but they are abundant between larger groups. Yet a pamphlet entitled "Harvard Scientists Agree Evolution Is a Hoax" states: "The facts of punctuated equilibrium which Gould and Eldredge . . . are forcing Darwinists to swallow fit the picture that Bryan insisted on, and which God has revealed to us in the Bible." 21

Continuing the distortion, several creationists have equated the theory of punctuated equilibrium with a caricature of the beliefs of Richard Goldschmidt, a great early geneticist. Goldschmidt argued, in a famous book published in 1940, that new groups can arise all at once through major mutations. He referred to these suddenly transformed creatures as "hopeful monsters." (I am attracted to some aspects of the non-caricatured version, but Goldschmidt's theory still has nothing to do with punctuated equilibrium. . . .) Creationist Luther Sunderland talks of the "punctuated equilibrium hopeful monster theory" and tells his hopeful readers that "it amounts to tacit admission that anti-evolutionists are correct in asserting there is no fossil evidence supporting the theory that all life is connected to a common ancestor." Duane Gish writes, "According to Goldschmidt, and now apparently according to Gould, a reptile laid an egg from which the first bird, feathers and all, was produced." Any evolutionist who believed such nonsense would rightly be laughed off the intellectual stage; yet the only theory that could ever envision such a scenario for the origin of birds is creationism—with God acting in the egg.

I am both angry at and amused by the creationists; but mostly I am deeply sad. Sad for many reasons. Sad because so many people who respond to creationists appeals are troubled for the right reason, but venting their anger at the wrong target. It is true that scientists have often been dogmatic and elitist. It is true that we have often allowed the white-coated, advertising image to represent us—"Scientists say that Brand X cures bunions ten times faster than . . . " We have not fought it adequately because we derive benefits from appearing as a new priesthood. It is also true that faceless and bureaucratic state power intrudes more and more into our lives and removes choices that should belong to individuals and communities. I can understand that school curricula, imposed from above and without local input, might be seen as one more insult on all these grounds. But the culprit is not, and cannot be, evolution or any other fact of the natural world. Identify and fight your legitimate enemies by all means, but we are not among them.

I am sad because the practical result of this brouhaha will not be expanded coverage to include creationism (that would also make me sad), but the reduction or excision of evolution from high school curricula. Evolution is one of the half dozen "great ideas" developed by science. It speaks to the profound issues of genealogy that fascinate all of us—the "roots" phenomenon writ large. Where did we come from? Where did life arise? How did it develop? How are organisms related? It forces us to think, ponder, and wonder. Shall we deprive millions of this knowledge and once again teach biology as a set of dull and unconnected facts, without the thread that weaves diverse material into a supple unity?

But most of all I am saddened by a trend I am just beginning to discern among my colleagues. I sense that some now wish to mute the healthy debate about theory that has brought new life to evolutionary biology. It provides grist for creationist mills, they say, even if only by distortion. Perhaps we should lie low and rally round the flag of strict Darwinism, at least for the moment—a kind of old-time religion on our part. 25

But we should borrow another metaphor and recognize that we too have to tread a straight and narrow path, surrounded by roads to perdition. For if we ever begin to suppress our search to understand nature, to quench our own intellectual excitement in a misguided effort to present a united front where it does not and should not exist, then we are truly lost. 26

QUESTIONS FOR READING AND WRITING

1. What experiences have you had with the renewed attack on evolution by the evangelical right? Has teaching evolution come under attack in schools in your community?
2. Gould draws a distinction between "theory" and "fact" by defining the two terms. What is that distinction? How does the blurring of that difference make it seem that there are new doubts about evolution among scientists? How did Darwin himself acknowledge this difference in proposing natural selection?
3. What are some of the differences in the approaches between evolutionists and creationists? Why does Gould contend that the term "scientific creationism" is a "self-contradictory, nonsense phrase" (paragraph 11)?
4. What are some of the reasons offered by scientists to support the idea that evolution actually occurred? How does Gould explain how evolution works even when we don't directly observe it at work?

5. Read some of the creationist literature mentioned by Gould to see whether or not it distorts his theory of "punctuated equilibria." Or, locate some of the attacks on evolution that have appeared in the popular media—for example, letters to the editor—and see whether they violate the distinction Gould makes between theory and fact.

✦ Barry Lopez ✦
The Stone Horse

Naturalist, essayist, and fiction writer, Barry Lopez was born in New York in 1945 and educated at Notre Dame University and the University of Oregon. Best known for his perceptive, unsentimental nature writing, Lopez was awarded the John Burroughs Medal for Of Wolves and Men *in 1979 and the National Book Award in 1986 for* Arctic Dreams. *A contributing editor to* Harper's *and* North American Review, *Lopez' most recent book is* Crossing Open Ground. *"The Stone Horse," which originally appeared in* Antaeus, *expresses an interest in native American culture by connecting the present with the past in an intensely personal way.*

1

THE DESERTS OF SOUTHERN CALIFORNIA, the high, relatively cooler and wetter Mojave and the hotter, dryer Sonoran to the south of it, carry the signatures of many cultures. Prehistoric rock drawings in the Mojave's Coso Range, probably the greatest concentration of petroglyphs in North America, are at least three thousand years old. Big-game-hunting cultures that flourished six or seven thousand years before that are known from broken spear tips, choppers, and burins left scattered along the shores of great Pleistocene lakes, long since evaporated. Weapons and tools discovered at China Lake may be thirty thousand years old; and worked stone from a quarry in the Calico Mountains is, some argue, evidence that human beings were here more than 200,000 years ago. 1

Because of the long-term stability of such arid environments, much of this prehistoric stone evidence still lies exposed on the ground, accessible to anyone who passes by—the studious, the acquisitive, the indifferent, the merely curious. Archaeologists do not agree on the sequence of cultural history beyond about twelve thousand years ago, but it is clear that these broken bits of chalcedony, chert, and obsidian, like the animal drawings and geometric 2 designs etched on walls of basalt throughout the desert, anchor the earliest threads of human history, the first record of human endeavor here.

Western man did not enter the California desert until the end of the eighteenth century, 250 years after Coronado brought his soldiers into the Zuni pueblos in a bewildered search for the cities of Cibola. The earliest appraisals of the land were cursory, hurried. People traveled *through* it, en route to Santa Fe or the California coastal settlements. Only miners tarried. In 1823 what had been Spain's became Mexico's, and in 1848 what had been Mexico's became America's; but the bare, jagged mountains and dry lake beds, the vast and uniform plains of creosote bush and yucca plants, remained as obscure as the northern Sudan until the end of the nineteenth century.

Before 1940 the tangible evidence of twentieth-century man's passage here consisted of very little—the hard tracery of travel corridors; the widely scattered, relatively insignificant evidence of mining operations; and the fair expanse of irrigated fields at the desert's periphery. In the space of a hundred years or so the wagon roads were paved, railroads were laid down, and canals and high-tension lines were built to bring water and electricity across the desert to Los Angeles from the Colorado River. The dark mouths of gold, talc, and tin mines yawned from the bony flanks of desert ranges. Dust-encrusted chemical plants stood at work on the lonely edges of dry lake beds. And crops of grapes, lettuce, dates, alfalfa, and cotton covered the Coachella and Imperial valleys, north and south of the Salton Sea, and the Palo Verde Valley along the Colorado.

These developments proceeded with little or no awareness of earlier human occupations by cultures that preceded those of the historic Indians—the Mojave, the Chemehuevi, the Quechan. (Extensive irrigation began actually to change the climate of the Sonoran Desert, and human settlements, the railroads, and farming introduced many new, successful plants into the region.)

During World War II, the American military moved into the desert in great force, to train troops and to test equipment. They found the clear weather conducive to year-round flying, the dry air and isolation very attractive. After the war, a complex of training grounds, storage facilities, and gunnery and test ranges was permanently settled on more than three million acres of military reservations. Few perceived the extent or significance of the destruction of the aboriginal sites that took place during tank maneuvers and bombing runs or in the laying out of highways, railroads, mining districts, and irrigated fields. The few who intuited that something like an American Dordogne Valley lay exposed here were (only) amateur archaeologists; even they reasoned that the desert was too vast for any of this to matter.

After World War II, people began moving out of the crowded Los Angeles basin into homes in Lucerne, Apple, and Antelope valleys in the western Mojave. They emigrated as well to a stretch of resort land at the foot of the San Jacinto Mountains that included Palm Springs, and farther out to old railroad and military towns like Twentynine Palms and Barstow. People also began exploring the desert, at first in military-surplus jeeps and then with a variety of all-terrain and off-road vehicles that became available in the 1960s. By the mid-1970s, the number of people using such vehicles for desert recreation had increased exponentially. Most came and went in innocent curiosity; the few who didn't wreaked a havoc all out of proportion to their numbers. The disturbance of previously isolated archaeological sites increased by an order of magnitude. Many sites were vandalized before archaeologists, themselves late to the desert, had any firm grasp of the bounds of human history in the desert. It was as though in the same moment an Aztec library had been discovered intact various lacunae had begun to appear. 7

The vandalism was of three sorts: the general disturbance usually caused by souvenir hunters and by the curious and the oblivious; the wholesale stripping of a place by professional thieves for black-market sale and trade; and outright destruction, in which vehicles were actually used to ram and trench an area. By 1980, the Bureau of Land Management estimated that probably 35 percent of the archaeological sites in the desert had been vandalized. The destruction at some places by rifles and shotguns, or by power winches mounted on vehicles, was, if one cared for history, demoralizing to behold. 8

In spite of public education, land closures, and stricter law enforcement in recent years, the BLM estimates that, annually, about 1 percent of the archaeological record in the desert continues to be destroyed or stolen. 9

2

A BLM archaeologist told me, with understandable reluctance, 10
where to find the intaglio. I spread my Automobile Club of Southern California map of Imperial County out on his desk, and he traced the route with a pink felt-tip pen. The line crossed Interstate 8 and then turned west along the Mexican border.

"You can't drive any farther than about here," he said, marking a 11
small X. "There's boulders in the wash. You walk up past them."

On a separate piece of paper he drew a route in a smaller scale 12
that would take me up the arroyo to a certain point where I was to cross back east, to another arroyo. At its head, on higher ground just to the north, I would find the horse.

"It's tough to spot unless you know it's there. Once you pick it up 13
. . . " He shook his head slowly, in a gesture of wonder at its existence.

I waited until I held his eye. I assured him I would not tell anyone 14
else how to get there. He looked at me with stoical despair, like a man who had been robbed twice, whose belief in human beings was offered without conviction.

I did not go until the following day because I wanted to see it at 15
dawn. I ate breakfast at four A.M. in El Centro and then drove south. The route was easy to follow, though the last section of road proved difficult, broken and drifted over with sand in some spots. I came to the barricade of boulders and parked. It was light enough by then to find my way over the ground with little trouble. The contours of the landscape were stark, without any masking vegetation. I worried only about rattlesnakes.

I traversed the stone plain as directed, but, in spite of the frank- 16
ness of the land, I came on the horse unawares. In the first moment of recognition I was without feeling. I recalled later being startled, and that I held my breath. It was laid out on the ground with its head to the east, three times life size. As I took in its outline I felt a growing concentration of all my senses, as though my attentiveness to the pale rose color of the morning sky and other peripheral images had now ceased to be important. I was aware that I was straining for sound in the windless air, and I felt the uneven pressure of the earth hard against my feet. The horse, outlined in a standing profile on the dark ground, was as vivid before me as a bed of tulips.

I've come upon animals suddenly before, and felt a similar tension, a precipitate heightening of the senses. And I have felt the inexplicable but sharply boosted intensity of a wild moment in the bush, where it is not until some minutes later that you discover the source of electricity—the warm remains of a grizzly bear kill, or the still moist tracks of a wolverine. 17

But this was slightly different. I felt I had stepped into an unoccupied corridor. I had no familiar sense of history, the temporal structure in which to think: this horse was made by Quechan people three hundred years ago. I felt instead a headlong rush of images: people hunting wild horses with spears on the Pleistocene veld of southern California; Cortés riding across the causeway into Montezuma's Tenochtitlán; a short-legged Comanche, astride his horse like some sort of ferret, slashing through cavalry lines of young men who rode like farmers; a hoof exploding past my face one morning in a corral in Wyoming. These images had the weight and silence of stone. 18

When I released my breath, the images softened. My initial feeling, of facing a wild animal in a remote region, was replaced with a calm sense of antiquity. It was then that I became conscious, like an ordinary tourist, of what was before me, and thought: this horse was probably laid out by Quechan people. But when? I wondered. The first horses they saw, I knew, might have been those that came north from Mexico in 1692 with Father Eusebio Kino. But Cocopa people, I recalled, also came this far north on occasion, to fight with their neighbors, the Quechan. And *they* could have seen horses with Melchior Díaz, at the mouth of the Colorado River in the fall of 1540. So, it could be four hundred years old. (No one in fact knows.) 19

I still had not moved. I took my eyes off the horse for a moment to look south over the desert plain into Mexico, to look east past its head at the brightening sunrise, to situate myself. Then, finally, I brought my trailing foot slowly forward and stood erect. Sunlight was running like a thin sheet of water over the stony ground and it threw the horse into relief. It looked as though no hand had ever disturbed the stones that gave it its form. 20

The horse had been brought to life on ground called desert pavement, a tight, flat matrix of small cobbles blasted smooth by sand-laden winds. The uniform, monochromatic blackness of the 21 stones, a patina of iron and magnesium oxides called desert varnish, is caused by long-term exposure to the sun. To make this type of low-relief ground glyph, or intaglio, the artist either selectively turns individual stones over to their lighter side or removes areas of stone to expose the lighter soil underneath, creating a negative image. This horse, about eighteen feet from brow to rump and eight feet from withers to hoof, had been made in the latter way, and its outline was bermed at certain points with low ridges of stone a few inches high to enhance its three-dimensional qualities. (The left side of the horse was in full profile; each leg was extended at 90 degrees to the body and fully visible, as though seen in three-quarter profile.)

I was not eager to move. The moment I did I would be back in the flow of time, the horse no longer quivering in the same way before me. I did not want to feel again the sequence of quotidian events—to be drawn off into deliberation and analysis. A human being, a four-footed animal, the open land. That was all that was present—and a "thoughtless" understanding of the very old desires bearing on this particular animal: to hunt it, to render it, to fathom it, to subjugate it, to honor it, to take it as a companion.

What finally made me move was the light. The sun now filled the shallow basin of the horse's body. The weighted line of the stone berm created the illusion of a mane and the distinctive roundness of an equine belly. The change in definition impelled me. I moved to the left, circling past its rump, to see how the light might flesh the horse out from various points of view. I circled it completely before squatting on my haunches. Ten or fifteen minutes later I chose another view. The third time I moved, to a point near the rear hooves, I spotted a stone tool at my feet. I stared at it a long while, more in awe than disbelief, before reaching out to pick it up. I turned it over in my left palm and took it between my fingers to feel its cutting edge. It is always difficult, especially with something so portable, to rechannel the desire to steal.

I spent several hours with the horse. As I changed positions and as the angle of the light continued to change I noticed a number of things. The angle at which the pastern carried the hoof away from the ankle was perfect. Also, stones had been placed within the image to suggest at precisely the right spot the left shoulder above the foreleg. The line that joined thigh and hock was similarly accurate. The muzzle alone seemed distorted—but perhaps these stones had been moved by a later hand. It was an admirably accurate representation, but not what a breeder would call perfect conformation. There was the suggestion of a bowed neck and an undershot jaw, and the tail, as full as a winter coyote's, did not appear to be precisely to scale.

The more I thought about it, the more I felt I was looking at an individual horse, a unique combination of generic and specific detail. It was easy to imagine one of Kino's horses as a model, or a horse that ran off from one of Coronado's columns. What kind of horses would these have been? I wondered. In the sixteenth century the most sought-after horses in Europe were Spanish, the offspring of Arabian stock and Barbary horses that the Moors brought to Iberia and bred to the older, eastern European strains brought in by the Romans. The model for this horse, I speculated, could easily have been a palomino, or a descendant of horses trained for lion hunting in North Africa. 25

A few generations ago, cowboys, cavalry quartermasters, and draymen would have taken this horse before me under consideration and not let up their scrutiny until they had its heritage fixed to their satisfaction. Today, the distinction between draft and harness horses is arcane knowledge, and no image may come to mind for a blue roan or a claybank horse. The loss of such refinement in everyday conversation leaves me unsettled. People praise the Eskimo's ability to distinguish among forty types of snow but forget the skill of others who routinely differentiate between overo and tobiano pintos. Such distinctions are made for the same reason. You have to do it to be able to talk clearly about the world. 26

For parts of two years I worked as a horse wrangler and packer in Wyoming. It is dim knowledge now; I would have to think to remember if a buckskin was a kind of dun horse. And I couldn't throw a double-diamond hitch over a set of panniers—the packer's basic tie-down—without guidance. As I squatted there in the desert, however, these more personal memories seemed tenuous in comparison with the sweep of this animal in human time. My memories had no depth. I thought of the Hittite cavalry riding against the Syrians 3,500 years ago. And the first of the Chinese emperors, Ch'in Shih Huang, buried in Shensi Province in 210 B.C. with thousands of life-size horses and soldiers, a terra-cotta 27 guardian army. What could I know of what was in the mind of whoever made this horse? Was there some racial memory of it as an animal that had once fed the artist's ancestors and then disappeared from North America? And then returned in this strange alliance with another race of men?

Certainly, whoever it was, the artist had observed the animal very closely. Certainly the animal's speed had impressed him. Among the first things the Quechan would have learned from an encounter with Kino's horses was that their own long-distance runners—men who could run down mule deer—were no match for this animal.

From where I squatted I could look far out over the Mexican plain. Juan Bautista de Anza passed this way in 1774, extending El Camino Real into Alta California from Sinaloa. He was followed by others, all of them astride the magical horse; *gente de razón*, the people of reason, coming into the country of *los primitivos*. The horse, like the stone animals of Egypt, urged these memories upon me. And as I drew them up from some forgotten corner of my mind—huge horses carved in the white chalk downs of southern England by an Iron Age people; Spanish horses rearing and wheeling in fear before alligators in Florida—the images seemed tethered before me. With this sense of proportion, a memory of my own—the morning I almost lost my face to a horse's hoof—now had somewhere to fit.

I rose up and began to walk slowly around the horse again. I had taken the first long measure of it and was now looking for a way to depart, a new angle of light, a fading of the image itself before the rising sun, that would break its hold on me. As I circled, feeling both heady and serene at the encounter, I realized again how strangely vivid it was. It had been created on a barren bajada between two arroyos, as nondescript a place as one could imagine. The only plant life here was a few wands of ocotillo cactus. The ground beneath my shoes was so hard it wouldn't take the print of a heavy animal even after a rain. The only sounds I heard here were the voices of quail.

The archaeologist had been correct. For all its forcefulness, the horse is inconspicuous. If you don't care to see it you can walk right past it. That pleases him, I think. Unmarked on this bleak shoulder of the plain, the site signals to no one; so he wants no protective fences here, no informative plaque, to act as beacons. He would rather take a chance that no motorcyclist, no aimless wanderer with a flair for violence and a depth of ignorance, will ever find his way here.

The archaeologist had given me something before I left his office that now seemed peculiar—an aerial photograph of the horse. It is widely believed that an aerial view of an intaglio provides a fair and accurate depiction. It does not. In the photograph the horse looks somewhat crudely constructed; from the ground it appears far more deftly rendered. The photograph is of a single moment, and in that split second the horse seems vaguely impotent. I watched light pool in the intaglio at dawn; I imagine you could watch it withdraw at dusk and sense the same animation I did. In those prolonged moments its shape and so, too, its general character changed—noticeably. The living quality of the image, its immediacy to the eye, was brought out by the light-in-time, not, at least here, in the camera's frozen instant. 32

Intaglios, I thought, were never meant to be seen by gods in the sky above. They were meant to be seen by people on the ground, over a long period of shifting light. This could even be true of the huge figures on the Plain of Nazca in Peru, where people could walk for the length of a day beside them. It is our own impatience that leads us to think otherwise. 33

This process of abstraction, almost unintentional, drew me gradually away from the horse. I came to a position of attention at the edge of the sphere of its influence. With a slight bow I paid my respects to the horse, its maker, and the history of us all, and departed. 34

3

A short distance away I stopped the car in the middle of the road to make a few notes. I could not write down what I was thinking when I was with the horse. It would have seemed disrespectful, and it would have required another kind of attention. So now I patiently drained my memory of the details it had fastened itself upon. The road I'd stopped on was adjacent to the All American Canal, the major source of water for the Imperial and Coachella valleys. The water flowed west placidly. A disjointed flock of coots, small, dark birds with white bills, was paddling against the current, foraging in the rushes. 35

I was peripherally aware of the birds as I wrote, the only movement in the desert, and of a series of sounds from a village a half-mile away. The first sounds from this collection of ramshackle houses in a grove of cottonwoods where the distracted dawn voices of dogs. I heard them intermingled with the cries of a rooster. Later, the high-pitched voices of children calling out to each other came disembodied through the dry desert air. Now, a little after seven, I could hear someone practicing on the trumpet, the same rough phrases played over and over. I suddenly remembered how as children we had tried to get the rhythm of a galloping horse with hands against our thighs, or by fluttering our tongues against the roofs of our mouths.

After the trumpet, the impatient calls of adults summoning children. Sunday morning. Wood smoke hung like a lens in the trees. The first car starts—a cold eight-cylinder engine, of Chrysler extraction perhaps, goosed to life, then throttled back to murmur through dual mufflers, the obbligato music of a shade-tree mechanic. The rote bark of mongrel dogs at dawn, the jagged outcries of men and women, an engine coming to life. Like a thousand villages from West Virginia to Guadalajara.

I finished my notes—where was I going to find a description of the horses that came north with the conquistadors? Did their manes come forward prominently over the brow, like this one's, like the forelocks of Blackfeet and Assiniboin men in nineteenth-century paintings? I set the notes on the seat beside me.

The road followed the canal for a while and then arced north, toward Interstate 8. It was slow driving and I fell to thinking how the desert had changed since Anza had come through. New plants and animals—the MacDougall cottonwood, the English house sparrow, the chukar from India—have about them now the air of the native born. Of the native species, some—no one knows how many—are extinct. The populations of many others, especially the animals, have been sharply reduced. The idea of a desert impoverished by agricultural poisons and varmint hunters, by off-road vehicles and military operations, did not seem as disturbing to me, however, as this other horror, now that I had been those hours with the horse. The vandals, the few who crowbar rock art off the desert's wall, who dig up graves, who punish the ground that holds intaglios, are people who devour history. Their self-centered scorn, their disrespect for ideas and images beyond their ken, create the awful atmosphere of loose ends in which totalitarianism thrives, in which the past is merely curious or wrong.

I thought about the horse sitting out there on the unprotected plain. I enumerated its qualities in my mind until a sense of its vulnerability receded and it became an anchor for something else. I remembered that history, a history like this one, which ran deeper than Mexico, deeper than the Spanish, was a kind of medicine. It permitted the great breadth of human expression to reverberate, and it did not urge you to locate its apotheosis in the present. 40

Each of us, individuals and civilizations, has been held upside down like Achilles in the River Styx. The artist mixing his colors in the dim light of Altamira; an Egyptian ruler lying still now, wrapped in his byssus, stored against time in a pyramid; the faded Dorset culture of the Arctic; the Hmong and Samburu and Walbiri of historic time; the modern nations. This great, imperfect stretch of human expression is the clarification and encouragement, the urging and the reminder, we call history. And it is inscribed everywhere in the face of the land, from the mountain passes of the Himalayas to a nameless bajada in the California desert. 41

Small birds rose up in the road ahead, startled, and flew off. I prayed no infidel would ever find that horse. 42

QUESTIONS FOR READING AND WRITING

1. Lopez begins and ends his essay with the concern that the intaglio of the horse might be vandalized. What examples have you encountered of vandalism of some previously unspoiled bit of nature or some human artifact?
2. Lopez uses narrative to describe the history of the California Mojave and Sonoran deserts and to recount the history of the horse's introduction to this region, as well as its probable impact on the artist who made the horse. How effective are these narrative sections? Are the narratives of Lopez' drive to and from the area of the intaglio strictly relevant? What do they add? Why does Lopez include the final description of the village awakening?
3. Why does Lopez give such extensive space to the description of the actual features of the horse? Why does he contrast it with the

photograph given him by the archaeologist? What lesson does he draw from the differences?

4. What have been some of the effects of human contacts with the desert over the last century? Does Lopez simply fear the coming of the vandal to destroy the horse, or does this lead him to a larger view of history?
5. Visit some monument or historic site that has captured the emotions of an era—for example, a California mission, a pueblo, a restored historic section of a city, one of the monuments in Washington, D.C., or the site of a Revolutionary or Civil War battle—and describe the emotions that the details of the monument evoke.

✦ John McPhee ✦
Pieces of the Frame

John McPhee (see "How to Make a Nuclear Bomb") often uses a spell-binding narrative to join different kinds of material. "Pieces of the Frame" starts out with the story of a family picnic in Scotland, weaves in material about Scotland's geology, and works its way toward considering the mystery of the Loch Ness Monster.

ON THE EDGE OF INVERMORISTON FOREST, I was trying to explain raised beaches, the fifty-foot beaches of Scotland, so called because they are about that far above the sea. Waves never touch them. Tides don't come near reaching them. Shell and shingle, whitened like bones, they are aftereffects of the ice, two miles thick, that once rested on Scotland and actually shoved Scotland down into the earth. When the ice melted, the sea slowly came up, but so did the land, sluggishly recovering its buoyancy over the molten center of things. After the sea had increased as much as it was going to, the land kept rising, and beaches were lifted into the air, some as much as fifty feet. 1

That was how I understood the story, and I was doing what I could to say it in a way that would make it intelligible to an audience of four children (mine—all girls, and all quite young), but the distractions were so numerous that I never really had a chance. My family and I were having a lakeside lunch—milk, potato sticks, lambs' tongues, shortbread, white chocolate, Mini-Dunlop cheese—beside a stream in a grove of birches that was backed by dense reforested pines. The pines covered steep slopes toward summits two thousand feet above us. It was late spring, but there were snowfields up there nonetheless, and the water we drank had been snow in the mountains that morning. 2

Near us, another family, also with small children, was having what was evidently a birthday picnic. They had arrived after we were already settled, and they had chosen—I don't know why, with acre upon acre of unpeopled and essentially similar terrain to move about in—to unpack all their special effects (a glistening white cake, noisemakers, conical cardboard orange hats) only forty or fifty yards 3 away. I tried to ignore them and go on with my ruminations on the raised beaches. There were no raised beaches in that place, at least not in the usual form, but the children had seen them and had played on them elsewhere in the Highlands, and I thought that if they could understand how such phenomena had come to be, they might in turn be able to imagine the great, long lake now before them—Loch Ness—as the sea lock, the arm of the Atlantic, that it once was, and how marine creatures in exceptional variety had once freely moved in and out of it, some inevitably remaining.

Losing interest in the birthday party, my youngest daughter said, "I want to see the monster."

This had already become another distraction. In much the way that, in the United States, NO HUNTING signs are posted every other tree along blacktop country roads, cardboard signs of about the same size had been tacked to trees and poles along the lake. There were several in the birch grove. Printed in royal blue on a white background, they said "Any members of the general public who genuinely believe they have seen an unusual creature or object in or on the shores of Loch Ness are requested to report the occurrence to Expedition Headquarters at Achnahannet, two miles south of Urquhart Castle. If unable to report in person, they may telephone the Expedition (No. Drumnadrochit 358). Reports will only be of interest from people willing to give their full name and address and fill in a Sighting Report Form, which will be sent on request. Thank you for your cooperation. Published by the Loch Ness Phenomena Investigation Bureau, 23 Ashley Place, London, S.W.1, and printed at the Courier Office, Inverness."

"What makes you think the monster wants to see *you*?" I said to my youngest one. "There won't be any sightings today, anyway. There's too much wind out there."

The wind on the lake was quite strong. It was blowing from the north. There were whitecaps, and the ranks of the waves were uniform in our perspective, which was high. Watching the waves, I remembered canoe trips when I was ten or eleven years old, trying to achieve some sort of momentum against white-capping headwinds between Rogers Rock and Sabbath Day Point on Lake George. Lake George was for beginners who could learn in its unwild basin the essentials they would need to know on longer trips in later years in wildernesses they would seek out. But now, watching the north wind go down the lake in Scotland, I could not remember headwinds anywhere as powerful and savage as they had been in that so-styled lake for beginners, and I could feel again the skin rubbed off my hands. The likeness was in more than the wind, however. It was in appearance, the shape, and the scale—about a mile from side to side—of Loch Ness, which, like the American lake, is at least twenty times longer than it is wide, a long deep cleft, positioned like some great geophysical ax-cut between its lateral hills. I remember being told, around the fire at night, stories of the first white man who saw Lake George. He was a travelling French priest, intent on converting the Mohawks and other nations of the Iroquois. He had come from Orléans. He said that the lake was the most beautiful he had ever seen, and he named it the Lake of the Blessed Sacrament. The Indians, observing that the priest blessed them with his right hand, held him down and chewed away his fingers until the fingers were stumps and the hand was pulp. Later, when the priest did not stop his work, the Indians axed the top of his skull, and then cut off his head.

Lake George is so clear that objects far below the surface, such 8
as white stones or hovering bass, can be seen in total definition. The water of Loch Ness is so dark with the tints of peat that on a flat-calm day it looks like black glass. Three or four feet below the surface is an obscurity so complete that experienced divers have retreated from it in frustration, and in some cases in fear. A swimmer looking up toward a bright sky from a distance of inches beneath the surface has the impression that he is afloat in very dark tea. Lake George is nearly two hundred feet deep in places, has numerous islands, and with its bays and points, is prototypal of beautiful mountain lakes of grand dimension in every part of the world. Loch Ness is like almost no other lake anywhere. Its shores are formidably and somewhat unnaturally parallel. It has no islands. Its riparian walls go straight down. It's bottom is flat, and in most places is seven hundred feet deep, a mean depth far greater than the mean depth of the North Sea. Loch Ness holds a fantastic volume of water, the entire runoff of any number of northern glens—Glen Affric, Glen Cannich, Glen Moriston, Glen Farrar, Glen Urquhart. All these valleys, impressive in themselves, are

petals to Glen More, the Great Glen. Loch Ness is the principal basin of the Great Glen, and the Great Glen is the epicenter of the Highlands. A few miles of silt, carried into the lake by rivers, long ago dammed the seaward end, changing the original sea loch into a freshwater lake, but so slowly that marine creatures trapped within it had a chance to adapt themselves. Meanwhile the land kept rising, and with it the new lake. The surface of Loch Ness is fifty-two feet above sea level.

My wife listened with some interest when, repeating all this, I made an expanded attempt to enrich everyone's experience, but nothing was going through to the children. "I want to see the monster," the youngest one said again, speaking for all. They didn't want to know how or why the so-called monster might have come into that particular lake. They just wanted to see it. But the wind was not slowing up out there on the lake.

All of us looked now at the family that was having the birthday picnic, for the father had stood up shouting and had flung a large piece of the birthday cake at his wife. It missed her and spattered in bits in the branches of a tree. She shouted back at him something to the effect that he was depraved and cruel, and he in turn bellowed that she was a carbon of her bloody mother and that he was fed up. She said she had had all she could ever take, and was going home—to England, apparently. With that, she ran up the hillside and soon was out of sight in the pines. At first, he did not follow, but he suddenly was on his feet and shouting serial threats as he too went out of range in the pines. Meanwhile, their children, all but one, were crying. The one that wasn't crying was the girl whose birthday it was, and she just sat without moving, under a conical orange hat, staring emptily in the direction of the lake.

We went to our car and sat in it for some time, trying not to be keeping too obvious an eye on the children in the birch grove, who eventually began to play at being bailiffs of the birthday picnic and made such a mess that finally the girl whose birthday it was began to cry, and she was still crying when her father came out of the pines. I then drove north.

The road—the A-82—stayed close to the lake, often on ledges that had been blasted into the mountainsides. The steep forests continued, broken now and again, on one shore or the other, by fields of fern, clumps of bright-yellow whin, and isolated stands of cedar. Along the far shore were widely separated houses and farms, which to the eyes of a traveller appeared almost unbelievably luxuriant after the spare desolation of some higher glens. We came to the top of the rise and suddenly saw, on the right-hand side of the road, on the edge of a high meadow that sloped sharply a considerable distance to the lake, a cluster of caravans and other vehicles, arranged in the shape of a C, with an opening toward the road—much like a circle of prairie schooners, formed for protection against savage attack. All but one or two of the vehicles were painted bright lily-pad green. The compound, in its compact half acre, was surrounded by a fence, to keep out, among other things, sheep, which were grazing all over the slope in deep-green turf among buttercups, daisies, and thistles. Gulls above beat hard into the wind, then turned and planed toward the south. Gulls are inland birds in Scotland, there being so little distance from anywhere to the sea. A big fireplace had been made from rocks of the sort that were scattered all over the meadow. And on the lakeward side a platform had been built, its level eminence emphasizing the declivity of the hill, which dropped away below it. Mounted on the platform was a thirty-five millimeter motion-picture camera with an enormous telephoto lens. From its point of view, two hundred feet above the lake and protruding like a gargoyle, the camera could take in a bedazzling panorama that covered thousands of acres of water.

This was Expedition Headquarters, the principal field station of 13
the Loch Ness Phenomena Investigation Bureau—dues five pounds per annum, life membership one hundred pounds, tax on donations recoverable under covenant. Those who join the bureau receive newsletters and annual reports, and are eligible to participate in the fieldwork if they so desire. I turned into the compound and parked between two bright-green reconditioned old London taxis. The central area had long since been worn grassless, and was covered at this moment with fine-grain dust. People were coming and going. The place seemed rather public, as if it were a depot. No one even halfway interested in the natural history of the Great Glen would think of driving up the A-82 without stopping in there. Since the A-82 is the principal route between Glasgow and Inverness, it is not surprising that the apparently amphibious creature as yet unnamed, the so-called Loch Ness Monster, has been seen not only from the highway but on it.

The atmosphere around the headquarters suggested a scientific frontier and also a boom town, much as Cape Canaveral and Cocoa Beach do. There were, as well, cirrus wisps of show business and fine arts. Probably the one word that might have been applied to everyone present was adventurer. There was, at any rate, nothing emphatically laboratorial about the place, although the prevailing mood seemed to be one not of holiday but of matter-of-fact application and patient dedication. A telephone call came in that day, to the caravan that served as an office, from a woman who owned an inn south of Inverarigaig, on the other side of the lake. She said that she had seen the creature that morning just forty yards offshore—three humps, nothing else to report, and being very busy just now, thank you very much, good day. This was recorded, with no particular display of excitement, by an extremely attractive young woman who appeared to be in her late twenties, an artist from London who had missed but one summer at Loch Ness in seven years. She wore sandals, dungarees, a firmly stretched black pullover, and gold earrings. Her name was Mary Piercy, and her toes were painted pink. The bulletin board where she recorded the sighting resembled the kind used in railway stations for the listing of incoming trains.

The office walls were decorated with photographs of the monster in various postures—basking, cruising, diving, splashing, looking up inquisitively. A counter was covered with some of the essential bibliography: the bureau's annual report (twenty-nine sightings the previous year), J. A. Carruth's *Loch Ness and Its Monster* (The Abbey Press, Fort Augustus), Tim Dinsdale's *Loch Ness Monster* (Routledge and Kegan Paul, London), and a report by the Joint Air Reconnaissance Center of the Royal Air Force on a motion picture of the monster swimming about half a mile on the lake's surface. These books and documents could, in turn, lead the interested reader to less available but nonetheless highly relevant works such as R. T. Gould's *Loch Ness Monster and Others* and Constance Whytes's *More Than a Legend*.

My children looked over the photographs with absorption but not a great deal of awe, and they bought about a dozen postcards with glossy prints of a picture of the monster—three humps showing, much the same sight that the innkeeper had described—that had been taken by a man named Stuart, directly across the lake from Urquhart Castle. The three younger girls then ran out into the meadow and began to pick daisies and buttercups. Their mother and sister sat down in the sun to read about the creature in the lake, and to write postcards. We were on our way to Inverness, but with no need to hurry. "Dear Grammy, we came to see the monster today."

From the office to the camera-observation platform to the caravan that served as a pocket mess hall, I wandered around among the crew, was offered and accepted tea, and squinted with imaginary experience up and down the lake, where the whitecaps had, if anything, increased. Among the crew at the time were two Canadians, a Swede, an Australian, three Americans, two Englishmen, a Welshman, and one Scot. Two were women. When I asked one of the crew members if he knew what some of the others did, vocationally, when they were not at Loch Ness, he said, "I'm not sure what they are. We don't go into that." This was obviously a place where now was all that mattered, and in such a milieu it is distinctly pleasant to accept that approach to things. Nonetheless, I found that I couldn't adhere completely to this principle, and I did find out that one man was a medical doctor, another a farmer, another a retired naval officer, and that several, inevitably, were students. The daily watch begins at four in the morning and goes on, as one fellow put it, "as long as we can stand up." It has been the pattern among the hundred of sightings reported that the early-morning hours are the most promising ones. Camera stations are manned until ten at night, dawn and sunset being so close to midnight at that latitude in summer, but the sentries tend to thin out with the lengthening of the day. During the autumn, the size of the crew reduces precipitously toward one. 17

One man lives at the headquarters all year long. His name is Clem Lister Skelton. "I've been staring at that bloody piece of water since five o'clock," he said, while he drank tea in the mess caravan. 18

"Is there a technique?" I asked him. 19

"Just look," he said. "Look. Run your eye over the water in one quick skim. What we're looking for is not hard to see. You just sit and sort of gaze at the loch, that's all. Mutter a few incantations. That's all there is to do. In wintertime, very often, it's just myself. And of course one keeps a very much more perfunctory watch in 20 the winter. I saw it once in a snowstorm, though, and that was the only time I've had a clear view of the head and neck. The neck is obviously very mobile. The creature was quite big, but it wasn't as big as a seventy-foot MFV. Motor fishing vessel. I'd been closer to it, but I hadn't seen as much of it before. I've seen it eight times. The last time was in September. Only the back. Just the sort of upturned boat, which is the classic view of it."

Skelton drank some more tea, and refilled a cup he had given me. "I must know what it is," he went on. "I shall never rest peacefully until I know what it is. Some of the largest creatures in the world are out there, and we can't name them. It may take ten years, but we're going to identify the genus. Most people are not as fanatical as I, but I would like to see this through to the end, if I don't get too broke first."

Skelton is a tall, offhand man, English, with reddish hair that is disheveled in long strings from the thinning crown of his head. In outline, Skelton's life there in the caravan on the edge of the high meadow over the lake, in a place that must be uncorrectably gloomy during the wet rains of winter, seemed cagelike and hopeless to me—unacceptably lonely. The impression he gave was of a man who had drawn a circle around himself many hundreds of miles from the rest of his life. But how could I know? He was saying that he had flown Super-marine Spitfires for the R.A.F. during the Second World War. His father had been a soldier, and when Skelton was a boy, he lived, as he put it, "all over the place." As an adult, he became first an actor, later a writer and director of films. He acted in London in plays like *March Hare* and *Saraband for Dead Lovers*. One film he directed was, in his words, "a dreadful thing called *Saul and David*." These appearances on the surface apparently did not occur so frequently that he needed to do nothing else for a livelihood. He also directed, in the course of many years, several hundred educational films. The publisher who distributed some of these films was David James, a friend of Skelton's, and at that time a Member of Parliament. James happened to be, as well, the founder of the Loch Ness Phenomena Investigation Bureau—phenomena, because, for breeding purposes, there would have to be at least two monsters living in the lake at any one time, probably more, and in fact two had on occasion been sighted simultaneously. James asked Skelton if he would go up to the lake and give the bureau the benefit of his technical knowledge of movie cameras. "Anything for a laugh," Skelton had said to James. This was in the early nineteen-sixties. "I came for a fortnight," Skelton said now, in the caravan. "And I saw it. I wanted to know what it was, and I've wanted to know what it was ever since. I thought I'd have time to write up here, but I haven't. I don't do anything now except hunt this beast."

Skelton talked on about what the monster might be—a magnified newt, a long-necked variety of giant seal, an unextinct *Elasmosaurus*. Visitors wandered by in groups outside the caravan, and unexplained strangers kept coming in for tea. In the air was a feeling, utterly belied by the relative permanence of the place, of a country carnival on a two-night stand. The caravans themselves, in their alignment, suggested a section of a midway. I remembered a woman shouting to attract people to a big caravan on a carnival midway one night in May in New Jersey. That was some time ago. I must have been nineteen. The woman, who was standing on a small platform, was fifty or sixty, and she was trying to get people to go into the caravan to see big jungle cats, I suppose, and brown bears—"Ferocious Beasts," at any rate, according to block lettering on the side of the caravan. A steel cage containing a small black bear had been set up on two sawhorses outside the caravan—a fragment to imply what might be found on a larger scale inside. 23

So young that it was no more than two feet from nose to tail, the bear was engaged in desperate motion, racing along one side of the cage from corner to corner, striking the steel bars bluntly with its nose. Whirling then, tossing its head over its shoulder like a racing swimmer, it turned and bolted crazily for the opposite end. Its eyes were deep red, and shining in a kind of full-sighted blindness. It had gone mad there in the cage, and its motion, rhythmic and tortured, never ceased, back and forth, back and forth, the head tossing with each jarring turn. The animal abraded its flanks on the steel bars as it ran. Hair and skin had scraped from its sides so that pink flesh showed in the downpour of the carnival arc lights. Blood drained freely through the thinned hair of its belly and dropped onto the floor of the cage. What had a paralyzing effect on me was the animal's almost perfect and now involuntary rhythm—the wild toss of the head after the crash into the corner, the turn, the scraping run, the crash again at the other end, never stopping, metronomic—the exposed interior of some brutal and organic timepiece. 24

Beside the cage, the plump, impervious woman, red-faced, red-nosed, kept shouting to the crowds, but she said to me, leaning down, her own eyes bloodshot, "Why don't you move on, sonny, if you ain't going to buy a ticket? Beat it. Come on, now. Move on."

"We argue about what it is," Skelton said. "I'm inclined to think it's a giant slug, but there is an amazingly impressive theory for its being a worm. You can't rule out that it's one of the big dinosaurs, but I think this is more wishful thinking than anything else." In the late nineteen-thirties, a large and exotic footprint was found along the shore of Loch Ness. It was meticulously studied by various people and was assumed, for a time, to be an impression from a foot or flipper of the monster. Eventually, the print was identified. Someone who owned the preserved foot of a hippopotamus had successfully brought off a hoax that put layers of mockery and incredibility over the creature in the lake for many years. The Second World War further diverted any serious interest that amateurs or naturalists might have taken. Sightings continued, however, in a consistent pattern, and finally, in the early nineteen-sixties, the Loch Ness Phenomena Investigation Bureau was established. "I have no plans whatever for leaving," Skelton said. "I am prepared to stay here ad infinitum. All my worldly goods are here."

A dark-haired young woman had stepped into the caravan and poured herself a cup of tea. Skelton, introducing her to me, said, "If the beast has done nothing else, it has brought me a wife. She was studying Gaelic and Scottish history at Edinburgh University, and she walked into the glen one day, and I said, 'That is the girl I am going to marry.'" He gestured toward a window of the caravan, which framed a view of the hills and the lake. "The Great Glen is one of the most beautiful places in the world," he continued. "It is peaceful here. I'd be happy here all my life, even if there were nothing in the loch. I've even committed the unforgivable sin of going to sleep in the sun during a flat calm. With enough time, we could shoot the beast with a crossbow and a line, and get a bit of skin. We could also shoot a small transmitter into its hide and learn more than we know now about its habits and characteristics."

The creature swims with remarkable speed, as much as ten or fifteen knots when it is really moving. It makes no noise other than seismic splashes, but it is apparently responsive in a highly sensitive way to sound. A shout, an approaching engine, any loud report, will send it into an immediate dive,and this shyness is in large part the cause of its inaccessibility, and therefore of its mystery. Curiously, though, reverberate sound was what apparently brought the creature widespread attention, for the first sequence of frequent sightings occurred in 1933, when the A-82 was blasted into the cliffsides of the western shore of the lake. Immense boulders kept falling into the depths, and shock waves from dynamite repeatedly ran through the water, causing the creature to lose confidence in its environment and to alter, at least temporarily, its shy and preferentially nocturnal life. In that year it was first observed on land, perhaps attempting to seek a way out forever from the detonations that had alarmed it. A couple named Spicer saw it, near Inverarigaig, and later described its long, serpentine neck, followed by an ungainly hulk of body, lurching toward the lake and disappearing into high undergrowth as they approached.

With the exception of one report recorder in the sixth century, 29
which said that a monster (fitting the description of the contemporary creatures of the lake) had killed a man with a single bite, there have been no other examples of savagery on its part. To the contrary, its sensitivity to people seems to be acute, and it keeps a wide margin between itself and mankind. In all likelihood, it feeds on fish and particularly on eels, of which there are millions in the lake. Loch Ness is unparalleled in eel-fishing circles, and had drawn commercial eel fishermen from all over the United Kingdom. The monster has been observed with its neck bent down in the water, like a swan feeding. When the creatures die, they apparently settle into the seven-hundred-foot floor of the lake, where the temperature is always forty-two degrees Fahrenheit—so cold that the lake is known for never giving up its dead. Loch Ness never freezes, despite its high latitude, so if the creature breathes air, as has seemed apparent from the reports of observers who have watched its mouth rhythmically opening and closing, it does not lose access to the surface in winter. It clearly prefers the smooth, unbaked waterscapes of summer, however, for it seems to love to bask in the sun, like an upturned boat, slowly rolling, plunging, squirming around with what can only be taken as pleasure. By observers' reports, the creature has two pairs of lateral flippers, and when it swims off, tail thrashing, it leaves behind it a wake as impressive as

the wake of a small warship. When it dives from a still position, it inexplicably goes down without leaving a bubble. When it dives as it swims, it leaves on the surface a churning signature of foam.

Skelton leaned back against the wall of the caravan in a slouched and nonchalant posture. He was wearing a dark blue tie that was monogrammed in small block letters sewn with white thread—L.N.I. (Loch Ness Investigation). Above the monogram and embroidered also in white thread was a small depiction of the monster—humps undulant, head high, tail extending astern. Skelton gave the tie a flick with one hand. "You get this with a five-pound membership," he said.

The sea-serpent effect given by the white thread on the tie was less a stylization than an attempt toward a naturalistic sketch. As I studied it there, framed on Skelton's chest, the thought occurred to me that there was something inconvenient about the monster's actual appearance. In every sense except possibly the sense that involves cruelty, the creature in Loch Ness is indeed a monster. An average taken from many films and sightings gives its mature length at about forty feet. Its general appearance is repulsive, in the instant and radical sense in which reptiles are repulsive to many human beings, and any number of people might find difficulty in accepting a creature that looks like the one that was slain by St. George. Its neck, about six feet long, columnar, powerfully muscled, is the neck of a serpent. Its head, scarcely broader than the neck, is a serpent's head, with uncompromising, lenticular eyes. Sometimes as it swims it holds its head and neck erect. The creature's mouth is at least a foot wide. Its body undulates. Its skin glistens when wet and appears coarse, mottled, gray, and elephantine when exposed to the air long enough to become dry. The tail, long and columnar, stretches back to something of a point. It seemed to me, sitting there at Headquarters, that the classical, mythical, dragon likeness of this animate thing—the modified dinosaur, the fantastically exaggerated newt—was an impediment to the work of the investigation bureau, which has no pertinent interest in what the monster resembles or calls to mind but a great deal in what it actually is, the goal being a final and positive identification of the genus.

"What we need is a good, lengthy, basking sighting," Skelton said. "We've had one long surfacing—twenty-five minutes. I saw it. Opposite Urquhart Castle. We only had a twelve-inch lens then, at four and a half miles. We have thirty-six inch lenses now. We need a long, clear, close-up—in color."

33 My children had watched, some months earlier, the killing of a small snake on a lawn in Maryland. About eighteen inches long, it came out from a basement-window well, through a covering lattice of redwood, and was noticed with shouts and shrieks by the children and a young retriever that barked at the snake and leaped about it in a circle. We were the weekend guests of another family, and eight children in all crowded around the snake, which had been gliding slowly across the lawn during the moments after it had been seen, but had now stopped and was turning its head from side to side in apparent indecision. Our host hurried into his garage and came running back to the lawn with a long shovel. Before he killed the snake, his wife urged him not to. She said the snake could not possibly be poisonous. He said, "How do you know?" The children, mine and theirs, looked back and forth from him to her. The dog began to bark more rapidly and at a higher pitch.

34 "It has none of the markings. There is nothing triangular about its head," she told him.

35 "That may very well be," he said. "But you can't be sure."

36 "It is *not* poisonous. Leave it alone. Look at all these children."

37 "I can't help that."

38 "It is *not* poisonous."

39 "How do you know?"

40 "I know."

41 He hit the snake with the flat of the shovel, and it writhed. He hit it again. It kept moving. He hit it a third time, and it stopped. Its underside, whitish green, segmental, turned up. The children moved in for a closer look.

QUESTIONS FOR READING AND WRITING

1. The Loch Ness Monster has fascinated people because of its connection with ancient legends of sea monsters. What seems to be McPhee's attitude toward the desire to solve the mystery of the monster? Would he rather live in a world with or without mysteries? How do you know?

2. What is the conflict in McPhee's narrative? Explain how the following quotations illustrate the two forces in conflict: "I must know what it is. I shall never rest peacefully until I know what it is." "Its general appearance is repulsive, in the instant and radical sense in which reptiles are repulsive to many human beings."
3. Characterize Clem Lister Skelton. Is he a stereotyped character, one whose traits are commonly recognized? In what ways? In what ways is he not?
4. McPhee's essays are notable for their unusual organization. Frequently, he interrupts the flow of a story with what seems extraneous material. Examine several of these "digressions" to see how they function to build the conflict or resolve it.
5. What is the function of the description of Scotland's fifty-foot-high beaches? Why does McPhee open his narrative with the violent ending of picnicking family's birthday outing and close with another violent act?
6. Why does McPhee include a comparison between Loch Ness and Lake George (paragraphs 7–8) in his narrative? What is the function of the flashback to McPhee's childhood recollection of a carnival and caged bear (paragraphs 23–25)? Why is the snake-killing incident (paragraphs 33–41) placed as a resolution?
7. Write an essay about a place or a person around whom some local legend has developed. In the essay, draw some general conclusions about the human hunger for legends.

✦ N. Scott Momaday ✦
The Way to Rainy Mountain

N. Scott Momaday, one of America's foremost Native American writers, was born in Oklahoma in 1934, graduated from the University of New Mexico, and received a Ph.D. from Stanford University. His Kiowa ancestry is a significant feature of his fiction and his nonfiction. In 1969, he won the Pulitzer Prize for his novel House Made of Dawn. *In this excerpt from the autobiographical* The Way to Rainy Mountain *(1969), Momaday traces his roots to the migration of the Kiowas to Oklahoma and describes the last of the old people, his grandmother, who remembered the old ways.*

A SINGLE KNOLL RISES OUT OF THE PLAIN in Oklahoma, north and west of the Wichita Range. For my people, the Kiowas, it is an old landmark, and they gave it the name Rainy Mountain. The hardest weather in the world is there. Winter brings blizzards, hot tornadic winds arise in the spring, and in summer the prairie is an anvil's edge. The grass turns brittle and brown, and it cracks beneath your feet. There are green belts along the rivers and creeks, linear groves of hickory and pecan, willow and witch hazel. At a distance in July or August the steaming foilage seems almost to writhe in fire. Great green-and-yellow grasshoppers are everywhere in the tall grass, popping up like corn to sting the flesh, and tortoises crawl about on the red earth, going nowhere in the plenty of time. Loneliness is an aspect of the land. All things in the plain are isolate; there is no confusion of objects in the eye, but *one* hill or *one* tree or *one* man. To look upon that landscape in the early morning, with the sun at your back, is to lose the sense of proportion. Your imagination comes to life, and this, you think, is where Creation was begun. 1

I returned to Rainy Mountain in July. My grandmother had died in the spring, and I wanted to be at her grave. She had lived to be very old and at last infirm. Her only living daughter was with her when she died, and I was told that in death her face was that of a child. 2

I like to think of her as a child. When she was born, the Kiowas were living that last great moment of their history. For more than a hundred years they had controlled the open range from the Smoky Hill River to the Red, from the headwaters of the Canadian to the fork of the Arkansas and Cimarron. In alliance with the Comanches, they had ruled the whole of the southern Plains. War was their sacred business, and they were among the finest horsemen the world has ever known. But warfare for the Kiowas was preeminently a matter of disposition rather than of survival, and they never understood the grim, unrelenting advance of the U.S. Cavalry. When at last, divided and ill-provisioned, they were driven onto the Staked Plains in the cold rains of autumn, they fell into panic. In Palo Duro Canyon they abandoned their crucial stores to pillage and had nothing then but their lives. In order to save themselves, they surrendered to the soldiers at Fort Sill and were imprisoned in the old stone corral that now stands as a military museum. My grandmother was spared the humiliation of those high gray walls by eight or ten years, but she must have known from birth the affliction of defeat, the dark brooding of old warriors.

Her name was Aho, and she belonged to the last culture to evolve in North America. Her forebears came down from the high country in western Montana nearly three centuries ago. They were a mountain people, a mysterious tribe of hunters whose language has never been positively classified in any major group. In the late seventeenth century they began a long migration to the south and east. It was a long journey toward the dawn, and it led to a golden age. Along the way the Kiowas were befriended by the Crows, who gave them the culture and religion of the Plains. They acquired horses, and their ancient nomadic spirit was suddenly free of the ground. They acquired Tai-me, the sacred Sun Dance doll, from that moment the object and symbol of their worship, and so shared in the divinity of the sun. Not least, they acquired the sense of destiny, therefore courage and pride. When they entered upon the southern Plains, they had been transformed. No longer were they slaves to the simple necessity of survival; they were a lordly and dangerous society of fighters and thieves, hunters and priests of the sun. According to their origin myth, they entered the world through a hollow log. From one point of view, their migration was the fruit of an old prophecy, for indeed they emerged from a sunless world.

Although my grandmother lived out her long life in the shadow of Rainy Mountain, the immense landscape of the continental interior lay like memory in her blood. She could tell of the Crows, whom she had never seen, and of the Black Hills, where she had never been. I wanted to see in reality what she had seen more perfectly in the mind's eye, and traveled fifteen hundred miles to begin my pilgrimage. 5

Yellowstone, it seemed to me, was the top of the world, a region of deep lakes and dark timber, canyons and waterfalls. But, beautiful as it is, one might have the sense of confinement there. The skyline in all directions is close at hand, the high wall of the woods and deep cleavages of shade. There is a perfect freedom in the mountains, but it belongs to the eagle and the elk, the badger and the bear. The Kiowas reckoned their stature by the distance they could see, and they were bent and blind in the wilderness. 6

Descending eastward, the highland meadows are a stairway to the plain. In July the inland slope of the Rockies is luxuriant with flax and buckwheat, stonecrop and larkspur. The earth unfolds and the limit of the land recedes. Clusters of trees and animals grazing far in the distance cause the vision to reach away and wonder to build upon the mind. The sun follows a longer course in the day, and the sky is immense beyond all comparison. The great billowing clouds that sail upon it are shadows that move upon the grain like water, dividing light. Farther down, in the land of the Crows and Blackfeet, the plain is yellow. Sweet clover takes hold of the hills and bends upon itself to cover and seal the soil. There the Kiowas paused on their way; they had come to the place where they must change their lives. The sun is at home on the plains. Precisely there does it have the certain character of a god. When the Kiowas came to the land of the Crows, they could see the dark lees of the hills at dawn across the Bighorn River, the profusion of light on the grain shelves, the oldest deity ranging after the solstices. Not yet would they veer southward to the caldron of the land that lay below; they must wean their blood from the northern winter and hold the mountains a while longer in their view. They bore Tai-me in procession to the east. 7

A dark mist lay over the Black Hills, and the land was like iron. At the top of a ridge I caught sight of Devil's Tower upthrust against the gray sky as if in the birth of time the core of the earth had broken 8 through its crust and the motion of the world was begun. There are things in nature that engender an awful quiet in the heart of man; Devil's Tower is one of them. Two centuries ago, because they could not do otherwise, the Kiowas made a legend at the base of the rock. My grandmother said:

> "Eight children were there at play, seven sisters and their brother. Suddenly the boy was struck dumb; he trembled and began to run upon his hands and feet. His fingers became claws, and his body was covered with fur. Directly there was a bear where the boy had been. The sisters were terrified; they ran, and the bear after them. They came to the stump of a great tree, and the tree spoke to them. It bade them climb upon it, and as they did so, it began to rise into the air. The bear came to kill them, but they were just beyond its reach. It reared against the tree and scored the bark all around with its claws. The seven sisters were borne into the sky, and they became the stars of the Big Dipper."

From that moment, and so long as the legend lives, the Kiowas have kinsmen in the night sky. Whatever they were in the mountains, they could be no more. However tenuous their well-being, however much they had suffered and would suffer again, they had found a way out of the wilderness.

My grandmother had a reverence for the sun, a holy regard that now is all but gone out of mankind. There was a wariness in her, and an ancient awe. She was a Christian in her later years, but she had come a long way about, and she never forgot her birthright. As a child she had been to the Sun Dances; she had taken part in those annual rites, and by them she had learned the restoration of her people in the presence of Tai-me. She was about seven when the last Kiowa Sun Dance was held in 1887 on the Washita River above Rainy Mountain Creek. The buffalo were gone. In order to consummate the ancient sacrifice—to impale the head of a buffalo bull upon the medicine tree—a delegation of old men journeyed into Texas, there to beg and barter for an animal from the Goodnight herd. She was ten when the Kiowas came together for the last time as a living Sun Dance culture. They could find no buffalo; they had to hand an old hide from the sacred tree. Before the dance could begin, a company of soldiers rode out from Fort Sill under orders to disperse the tribe. Forbidden without cause the essential act of their faith, having seen the wild herds slaughtered and left to rot upon the ground, the Kiowas backed away forever from the medicine tree. That was July 20, 1890, at the great bend of the Washita. My grandmother was there. Without bitterness, and for as long as she lived, she bore a vision of deicide.

Now that I can have her only in memory, I see my grandmother 10
in the several postures that were peculiar to her: standing at the wood stove on a winter morning and turning meat in a great iron skillet; sitting at the south window, bent above her beadwork, and afterwards, when her vision had failed, looking down for a long time into the fold of her hands; going out upon a cane, very slowly as she did when the weight of age came upon her; praying. I remember her most often at prayer. She made long, rambling prayers out of suffering and hope, having seen many things. I was never sure that I had the right to hear, so exclusive were they of all mere custom and company. The last time I saw her she prayed standing by the side of her bed at night, naked to the waist, the light of a kerosene lamp moving upon her dark skin. Her long, black hair, always drawn and braided in the day, lay upon her shoulders and against her breasts like a shawl. I do not speak Kiowa, and I never understood her prayers, but there was something inherently sad in the sound, some merest hesitation upon the syllables of sorrow. She began in a high and descending pitch, exhausting her breath to silence; then again and again—and always the same intensity of effort, of something that is, and is not, like urgency in the human voice. Transported so in the dancing light among the shadows of her room, she seemed beyond the reach of time. But that was illusion; I think I knew then that I should not see her again.

Houses are like sentinels in the plain, old keepers of the weather 11
watch. There, in a very little while, wood takes on the appearance of great age. All colors wear soon away in the wind and rain, and then the wood is burned gray and the grain appears and the nails turn red with rust. The windowpanes are black and opaque; you imagine there is nothing within, and indeed there are many ghosts, bones given up to the land. They stand here and there against the sky, and you approach them for a longer time than you expect. They belong in the distance; it is their domain.

Once there was a lot of sound in my grandmother's house, a lot 12
of coming and going, feasting and talk. The summers there were full

of excitement and reunion. The Kiowas are a summer people; they abide the cold and keep to themselves; but when the season turns and the land becomes warm and vital, they cannot hold still; an old love of going returns upon them. The aged visitors who came to my grandmother's house when I was a child were made of lean and leather, and they bore themselves upright. They wore great black hats and bright ample shirts that shook in the wind. They rubbed fat upon their hair and wound their braids with strips of colored cloth. Some of them painted their faces and carried the scars of old and cherished enmities. They were an old council of warlords, come to remind and be reminded of who they were. Their wives and daughters served them well. The women might indulge themselves; gossip was at once the mark and compensation of their servitude. They made loud and elaborate talk among themselves, full of jest and gesture, fright and false alarm. They went abroad in fringed and flowered shawls, bright beadwork and German silver. They were at home in the kitchen, and they prepared meals that were banquets.

There were frequent prayer meetings, and great nocturnal feasts. When I was a child, I played with my cousins outside, where the lamplight fell upon the ground and the singing of the old people rose up around us and carried away into the darkness. There were a lot of good things to eat, a lot of laughter and surprise. And afterwards, when the quiet returned, I lay down with my grandmother and could hear the frogs away by the river and feel the motion of the air.

Now there is a funeral silence in the rooms, the endless wake of some final word. The walls have closed in upon my grandmother's house. When I returned to it in mourning, I saw for the first time in my life how small it was. It was late at night, and there was a white moon, nearly full. I sat for a long time on the stone steps by the kitchen door. From there I could see out across the land; I could see the long row of trees by the creek, the low light upon the rolling plains, and the stars of the Big Dipper. Once I looked at the moon and caught sight of a strange thing. A cricket had perched upon the handrail, only a few inches away from me. My line of vision was such that the creature filled the moon like a fossil. It had gone there, I thought, to live and die, for there of all places, was its small definition made whole and eternal. A warm wind rose up and purled like the longing within me.

The next morning I awoke at dawn and went out on the dirt road 15
to Rainy Mountain. It was already hot, and the grasshoppers began to fill the air. Still, it was early in the morning, and the birds sang out of the shadows. The long yellow grass on the mountain shone in the bright light, and a scissortail hied above the land. There, where it ought to be, at the end of a long and legendary way, was my grandmother's grave. Here and there on the dark stones were ancestral names. Looking back once, I saw the mountain and came away.

QUESTIONS FOR READING AND WRITING

1. One writer has observed that we are often influenced more by our grandparents than by our parents. While this seems to be true for Momaday, do you find it equally true for you?
2. Why does Rainy Mountain stir in Momaday memories of his grandmother and the great migration of the Kiowas from the northern mountains?
3. How does the adoption of the sun god define Kiowa life after the tribe reached the Great Plains? How does Momaday's opening description reflect this new emphasis in Kiowa life?
4. Examine the legends Momaday has embodied in his narrative. What does he mean when he says, in paragraph 8, "the Kiowas have kinsmen in the night sky"?
5. Momaday has combined a description of his grandmother with a narrative of the Kiowa people. Where does one clearly break off and the other begin?
6. In paragraphs 14–15, when Momaday brings us back to the period after his grandmother's death, he resumes the descriptive mode with which he began the piece. Is there any difference in the mood and substance of the final descriptive paragraphs and those of the opening paragraphs?
7. Read the essays by E.B. White, Alice Munro, Donald Hall, and Maxine Hong Kingston and compare the influence of parents and grandparents each records with that of Momaday.
8. Write an essay on the memories of a parent or grandparent that have influenced you in your choice of values or career.
9. Write an essay about returning for a visit to a place connected with your family history and the effects the visit had on you.

Part 6

PERSUASION: Writing to Convince

One of the most forceful public demonstrations of the power of persuasion occurred on August 28, 1963, when Dr. Martin Luther King delivered his famous "I Have a Dream" speech to a crowd of 250,000 gathered for the March on Washington. Here are the final words of that speech.

> I say to you today even though we face the difficulties of today and tomorrow, I still have a dream. It is a dream that is deeply rooted in the American dream. I have a dream that one day this nation will rise up, live out the true meaning of its creed: We hold these truths to be self-evident, that all men are created equal.
>
> I have a dream that one day on the red hills of Georgia the sons of former slaves and the sons of former slaveowners will be able to sit down together at the table of brotherhood. I have a dream that one day even the state of Mississippi, a state sweltering with the heat of oppression, will be transformed into an oasis of freedom and justice.
>
> I have a dream that my four little children one day will live in a nation where they will not be judged by the color of their skin, but by the content of their character.
>
> I have a dream that one day every valley shall be exalted, every hill and mountain shall be made low. The rough places will be made plain and the crooked places will be made straight. This is the faith that I go back to the South with. With this faith we will be able to hew out of the mountains of despair

> the stone of hope. With this faith we will be able to work together, to pray together, to struggle together, to go to jail together, to stand up for freedom together, knowing we will be free one day.
>
> This will be the day when all of God's children will be able to sing with new meaning, 'Let freedom ring.' So let freedom ring from the prodigious hilltops of New Hampshire; let freedom ring from the mighty mountains of New York. But not only that. Let freedom ring from Stone Mountain of Georgia. Let freedom ring from every hill and molehill of Mississippi, from every mountainside.
>
> When we allow freedom to ring from every town and every hamlet, from every state and every city, we will be able to speed up that day when all of God's children, black men and white men, Jews and Gentiles, Protestants and Catholics, will be able to join hands and sing in the words of the old Negro spiritual, "Free at last! Free at last! Great God A- mighty, we are free at last!"

What makes this speech so powerful is the sweep of emotion that carried the audience along on the tide of the repeated refrains: "I have a dream . . . . ," "With this faith . . . ," "Let freedom ring. . . ." The audience was also moved by the echoes from the Declaration of Independence ("We hold these truths to be self-evident . . .") and the Bible ("Every valley shall be exalted . . ."), and by the figurative language ("an oasis of freedom and justice," "hew out of the mountain of despair the stone of hope"). What finally makes the speech so persuasive is Dr. King's obvious sincerity.

All three of these things—emotions and ideas, style, and the character of the speaker—constitute what we call rhetoric. Aristotle defined rhetoric as "the faculty of discovering . . . what are the available means of persuasion." In fact, until well into the nineteenth century, *rhetoric* and *persuasion* were synonymous. Originally rhetoric involved the means by which speakers could move people to action, stir their emotions, or gain their conviction. As such, rhetoric dealt with three things: first, the character of the speaker (since we are concerned with writing, we will use the term *writer*); second, the seeming or plausible proofs for the writer's position—that is, finding the arguments that would emotionally or intellectually persuade the audience; third, the verbal act or message—that is, the rhetorical style that would accomplish the first two ends.

In persuasion, the primary focus is on what works with the audience—that is, how convincing the writer is personally, intellectually, and stylistically in gaining the audience's confidence, agreement, and admiration. Persuasion is not concerned with whether the speech or essay is true—whether or not it mirrors reality—but with whether or not it will effectively move the audience. The *rhetor* is in search of those arguments that are already "in" the audience, those convictions, positions, ideas that they already accept as true. As a result of this pragmatic approach, today the word *rhetoric* is sometimes used to refer to an insincere statement, something with more form than substance. Perhaps some of our distrust of rhetoric stems from our fear of being manipulated. Often the word is preceded by an adjective such as *empty* or *political,* but you need not take this cynical viewpoint to justify the use of persuasion for a desirable social or political end. Some of the persuasive essays that follow, for example, argue for a more critical view of pornography (Atwood), for or against bilingual education (Gonsalez and Rodriguez), and for equality of educational opportunities for women (Rich). After reading any of these persuasive essays, it would be difficult to take a cynical view of the art of persuasion. So rhetoric can be used for society's benefit or its detriment, depending on how the audience and the persuader interact. The means of persuasion are available to everyone—not only to Tom Paines, Abraham Lincolns, and John Kennedys, but to Stalins and Hitlers as well. Effective rhetoric consists of four kinds of arguments: ethical, pathetic, logical, and rhetorical.

Ethical argument deals with the character of the writer—that is, in the modern sense, the writer's "image." According to Aristotle, the writer should have practical knowledge of the subject, should not appear to represent special interests but should have the welfare of the audience at heart, and should appear unlikely to deceive the audience. Some of these qualities are conveyed by the style of the writer (which reflects his or her personality and potential objectivity or bias) and some are a result of the material (the facts, and the author's familiarity with them).

Another kind of argument, instead of emphasizing the character of the speaker or writer, emphasizes the emotions of the audience being addressed. The Greek word for emotions is *pathos*; therefore *pathetic argument* consists of appeals to those emotions that are likely to sway the particular audience. For example, President Kennedy's "Inaugural Address" appealed to Americans' sense of patriotism, their generosity to poorer nations, their desire for peace, their determination to remain militarily strong, and their sense of excitement at the wonders of science and space exploration:

> To those people in the huts and villages of half the globe struggling to break the bonds of mass misery, we pledge our best efforts to help them help themselves, for whatever period is required—not because the communists may be doing it, not because we seek their votes, but because it is right. If a free society cannot help the many who are poor, it cannot save the few who are rich. . . .
>
> Finally, to those nations who would make themselves our adversary, we offer not a pledge but a request: that both sides begin anew the quest for peace, before the dark powers of destruction unleashed by science engulf all humanity in planned or accidental self-destruction.
>
> We dare not tempt them with weakness. For only when our arms are sufficient beyond doubt can we be certain beyond doubt that they will never be employed.
>
> But neither can two great and powerful groups of nations take comfort from our present course—both sides overburdened by the cost of modern weapons, both rightly alarmed by the steady spread of the deadly atom, yet both racing to alter that uncertain balance of terror that stays the hand of mankind's final war. . . .
>
> Let both sides seek to invoke the wonders of science instead of its terrors. Together let us explore the stars, conquer the deserts, eradicate disease, tap the ocean depths and encourage the arts and commerce.
>
> Let both sides unite to heed in all corners of the earth the command of Isaiah—to "undo the heavy burdens . . . (and) let the oppressed go free."
>
> And if a beach-head of cooperation may push back the jungle of suspicion, let both sides join in creating a new endeavor, not a new balance of power, but a new world of law, where the strong are just and the weak secure and the peace preserved.

A study of the emotional appeals of even this brief excerpt reveals that the speech maintains a balance between appealing to the conflicting fear of change and to the desire for change under the leadership of the New Frontier, thereby meeting the various emotional needs of its audience. Notice, for example, that Kennedy speaks of "the dark powers of destruction unleashed by science," of "the deadly atom," and of "the uncertain balance of terror" before he "invokes the wonders of science." Clearly, Kennedy has manipulated his audience's fears before appealing to their idealism.

Logical argument consists in finding the most effective arguments to support the writer's thesis. Aristotle presents several lists of *topoi*—literally "places" where one can go to find an appropriate argument. One of the exercises in the schools of rhetoric was to take a subject through each of the topics to see what information it would yield. For example, under the *topoi* of "definition" you might place the subject of "mercy killing," thereby asking, "What is mercy killing?" The possible answers would then lead to several distinctions such as between pulling the plug on life-support systems, discontinuing medication, or terminating the life of a patient by more direct means. By placing the subject or any of the answers under other *topoi*—such as induction, time, division, consequences—you then systematically examine what you, or more importantly (since it is the audience that needs to be convinced), what the audience already knows. Not surprisingly, some of the *topoi* later become methods of paragraph development.

Aristotle also advocated the use of *enthymemes*, shortened deductive syllogisms in which one or more of the steps have been omitted because it has already been accepted as true by the audience. For example, here is a deductive syllogism:

MAJOR PREMISE Mercy killing is a direct act.
MINOR PREMISE Withholding drugs is not a direct act.
CONCLUSION Therefore, withholding drugs is not mercy killing.

Were it to appear as an enthymeme, it might take this form:

MAJOR PREMISE Mercy killing is a direct act.
CONCLUSION Therefore, withholding drugs is not mercy killing.

(The MINOR PREMISE, "Withholding drugs is not a direct act," is understood and accepted as true.)

or:

MINOR PREMISE Withholding drugs is not a direct act.
CONCLUSION Therefore, withholding drugs is not mercy killing.
(The MAJOR PREMISE, "Mercy killing is a direct act," is understood and accepted as true.)

Persuasive writing rarely contains a complete syllogism. Instead, one of the premises or the conclusion itself will be left unstated, largely because that is the part the writer has determined the audience has already accepted.

Before we leave logical proof, let's examine the distinction between the previously introduced terms *deduction,* and *induction.* As we have seen, *deductive reasoning* follows the formal pattern of reasoning (syllogism) from already-established premises (major and minor) to a conclusion. The premises must be true if the conclusion that follows them is to be true. *Inductive reasoning* is often identified with the scientific method. Induction reasons from a series of specific, verifiable observations to a general conclusion that incorporates the observations. For example, if for three successive years you saw cherry trees blooming in April in Washington, D.C., you would arrive at the inductive conclusion, "Cherry trees bloom in April in Washington, D.C." Your inductive conclusion would, however, be only as strong as your evidence (an early spring might force you to change the generalization). These forms of reasoning, plus facts and examples to support them, make up what is called logical argument.

Rhetorical argument is, strictly speaking, not an argument in the same sense as the others, but is the style of a persuasive essay that lends support to the other arguments. Aristotle describes effective rhetorical style as having the following characteristics:

1. Clarity—the subject matter is presented in a manner that the audience can follow.
2. Dignity—the style leaves a good impression on the audience.

3. Propriety—the style has been adapted to the audience's levels of sophistication and knowledge.
4. Correctness—the style follows the rules of the language.

Although many rhetoricians disagree about how many parts a persuasive essay should have, the ancient rhetorical tradition listed seven. It is interesting to analyze modern practice to see how many of these parts are still to be found in a work, and in what order they occur. The traditional parts of a persuasive speech (essay) are:

1. Entrance—in which the writer introduces the topic.
2. Exposition—in which the writer gives the background or circumstances necessary to understand the points at issue.
3. Proposition—in which the writer explicitly states his or her position.
4. Division—in which the writer outlines the points he or she will prove.
5. Confirmation—in which the writer gives the body of the proofs.
6. Confutation—in which the writer refutes the opposition's arguments.
7. Conclusion—in which the writer summarizes key points, reviews the issues, and finally appeals to the emotions of the audience.

Although a writer who adhered rigidly to this outline would produce a highly artificial essay, the outline does provide a useful working model that anyone can use to structure the parts of a persuasive essay.

✦ Margaret Atwood ✦
Pornography

A native of Canada, Margaret Atwood (b. 1939) has written novels, poetry, and criticism (see "On Being a 'Woman Writer'"). Among her many books are The Circle Game *(poetry, 1966),* True Stories *(poetry, 1981), and the novels* Surfacing *(1972),* The Handmaid's Tale *(1985), and* Cat's Eye *(1989). In the following essay, Atwood attempts to attack pornography—which she sees as hateful, often violent, and degrading of women—without advocating rampant censorship of all sexually explicit material. Her ideas remind us of the difficulties (which we all must face) of achieving sexual health and dignity.*

WHEN I WAS IN FINLAND a few years ago for an international writers' conference, I had occasion to say a few paragraphs in public on the subject of pornography. The context was a discussion of political repression, and I was suggesting the possibility of a link between the two. The immediate result was that a male journalist took several large bites out of me. Prudery and pornography are two halves of the same coin, said he, and I was clearly a prude. What could you expect from an Anglo-Canadian? Afterward, a couple of pleasant Scandinavian men asked me what I had been so worked up about. All "pornography" means, they said, is graphic depictions of whores, and what was the harm in that?

Not until then did it strike me that the male journalist and I had two entirely different things in mind. By "pornography," he meant naked bodies and sex. I, on the other hand, had recently been doing the research for my novel *Bodily Harm*, and was still in a state of shock from some of the material I had seen, including the Ontario Board of Film Censors' "outtakes." By "pornography," I meant women getting their nipples snipped off with garden shears, having meat hooks stuck into their vaginas, being disemboweled; little girls being raped; men (yes, there are some men) being smashed to a pulp and forcibly sodomized. The cutting edge of pornography, as far as I could see, was no longer simple old copulation, hanging from the chandelier or otherwise: it was death, messy, explicit and highly sadistic. I explained this to the nice Scandinavian men. "Oh, but that's just the United States," they said. "Everyone knows they're sick." In their country, they said, violent "pornography" of that kind was not permitted on television or in movies; indeed, excessive violence of any kind was not permitted. They had drawn a clear line between erotica, which earlier studies had shown did not incite men to more aggressive and brutal behavior toward women, and violence, which later studies indicated did.

Some time after that I was in Saskatchewan, where, because of the scenes in *Bodily Harm,* I found myself on an open-line radio show answering questions about "pornography." Almost no one who phoned in was in favor of it, but again they weren't talking about the same stuff I was, because they hadn't seen it. Some of them were all set to stamp out bathing suits and negligees, and, if possible, any depictions of the female body whatsoever. God, it was implied, did not approve of female bodies, and sex of any kind, including that practised by bumblebees, should be shoved back into the dark, where it belonged. I had more than a suspicion that *Lady Chatterley's Lover,* Margaret Laurence's *The Diviners,* and indeed most books by most serious modern authors would have ended up as confetti if left in the hands of these callers. 3

For me, these two experiences illustrate the two poles of the emotionally heated debate that is now thundering around this issue. They also underline the desirability and even the necessity of defining the terms. "Pornography" is now one of those catchalls, like "Marxism" and "feminism," that have become so broad they can mean almost anything, ranging from certain verses in the Bible, ads for skin lotion and sex texts for children to the contents of Penthouse, Naughty '90s postcards and films with titles containing the word *Nazi* that show vicious scenes of torture and killing. It's easy to say that sensible people can tell the difference. Unfortunately, opinions on what constitutes a sensible person vary. 4

But even sensible people tend to lose their cool when they start talking about this subject. They soon stop talking and start yelling, and the name-calling begins. Those in favor of censorship (which may include groups not noticeably in agreement on other issues, such as some feminists and religious fundamentalists) accuse the others of exploiting women through the use of degrading images, contributing to the corruption of children, and adding to the general climate of violence and threat in which both women and 5 children live in this society; or, though they may not give much of a hoot about actual women and children, they invoke moral standards and God's supposed aversion to "filth," "smut" and deviated *perversion*, which may mean ankles.

The camp in favor of total "freedom of expression" often comes out howling as loud as the Romans would have if told they could no longer have innocent fun watching the lions eat up Christians. It too may include segments of the population who are not natural bedfellows: those who proclaim their God-given right to freedom, including the freedom to tote guns, drive when drunk, drool over chicken porn and get off on videotapes of women being raped and beaten, may be waving the same anticensorship banner as responsible liberals who fear the return of Mrs. Grundy, or gay groups for whom sexual emancipation involves the concept of "sexual theatre." *Whatever turns you on* is a handy motto, as is *A man's home is his castle* (and if it includes a dungeon with beautiful maidens strung up in chains and bleeding from every pore, that's his business).

Meanwhile, theoreticians theorize and speculators speculate. Is today's pornography yet another indication of the hatred of the body, the deep mind-body split, which is supposed to pervade Western Christian society? Is it a backlash against the women's movement by men who are threatened by uppity female behavior in real life, so like to fantasize about women done up like outsize parcels, being turned into hamburger, kneeling at their feet in slavelike adoration or sucking off guns? Is it a sign of collective impotence, of a generation of men who can't relate to real women at all but have to make do with bits of celluloid and paper? Is the current flood just a result of smart marketing and aggressive promotion by the money men in what has now become a multibillion-dollar industry? If they were selling movies about men getting their testicles stuck full of knitting needles by women with swastikas on their sleeves, would they do as well, or is this penchant somehow peculiarly male? If so, why? Is pornography a power trip rather than a sex one? Some say that those ropes, chains, muzzles and other restraining devices are an argument for the immense power female sexuality still wields in the male imagination: you don't put these things on dogs unless you're afraid of them. Others, more literary, wonder about the shift from the 19th-century Magic Woman or Femme Fatale image to the lollipop-licker, airhead or turkey-carcass treatment of women in porn today. The proporners don't care much about theory: they merely demand product. The anti-porners don't care about it in the final analysis either: there's dirt on the street, and they want it cleaned up, now.

It seems to me that this conversation, with its *You're-a-prude/You're-a-pervert* dialectic, will never get anywhere as long as we continue to think of this material as just "entertainment." Possibly we're deluded by the packaging, the format: magazine, book, movie, theatrical presentation. We're used to thinking of these things as part of the "entertainment industry," and we're used to thinking of ourselves as free adult people who ought to be able to see any kind of "entertainment" we want to. That was what the First Choice pay-TV debate was all about. After all, it's only entertainment, right? Entertainment means fun, and only a killjoy would be antifun. What's the harm? 8

This is obviously the central question: *What's the harm?* If there isn't any real harm to any real people, then the antiporners can tsk-tsk and/or throw up as much as they like, but they can't rightfully expect more legal controls or sanctions. However, the no-harm position is far from being proven. 9

(For instance, there's a clear-cut case for banning—as the federal government has proposed—movies, photos and videos that depict children engaging in sex with adults: real children are used to make the movies, and hardly anybody thinks this is ethical. The possibilities for coercion are too great.) 10

To shift the viewpoint, I'd like to suggest three other models for looking at "pornography"—and here I mean the violent kind. 11

Those who find the idea of regulating pornographic materials repugnant because they think it's Fascist or Communist or otherwise not in accordance with the principles of an open democratic society should consider that Canada has made it illegal to disseminate material that may lead to hatred toward any group because of race or religion. I suggest that if pornography of the violent kind depicted these acts being done predominantly to Chinese, to blacks, to Catholics, it would be off the market immediately, under the present laws. Why is hate literature illegal? Because whoever made the law thought that such material might incite real people to do real awful things to other real people. The human brain is to a certain extent a computer: garbage in, garbage out. We only hear 12 about the extreme cases (like that of American multimurderer Ted Bundy) in which pornography has contributed to the death and/or mutilation of women and/or men. Although pornography is not the only factor involved in the creation of such deviance, it certainly has upped the ante by suggesting both a variety of techniques and the social acceptability of such actions. Nobody knows yet what effect this stuff is having on the less psychotic.

Studies have shown that a large part of the market for all kinds of porn, soft and hard, is drawn from the 16-to-21-year-old population of young men. Boys used to learn about sex on the street, or (in Italy, according to Fellini movies) from friendly whores, or, in more genteel surroundings, from girls, their parents, or, once upon a time, in school, more or less. Now porn has been added, and sex education in the schools is rapidly being phased out. The buck has been passed, and boys are being taught that all women secretly like to be raped and that real men get high on scooping out women's digestive tracts.

Boys learn their concept of masculinity from other men: is this what most men want them to be learning? If word gets around that rapists are "normal" and even admirable men, will boys feel that in order to be normal, admirable and masculine they will have to be rapists? Human beings are enormously flexible, and how they turn out depends a lot on how they're educated, by the society in which they're immersed as well as by their teachers. In a society that advertises and glorifies rape or even implicitly condones it, more women get raped. It becomes socially acceptable. And at a time when men and the traditional male role have taken a lot of flak and men are confused and casting around for an acceptable way of being male (and, in some cases, not getting much comfort from women on that score), this must be at times a pleasing thought.

It would be naïve to think of violent pornography as just harmless entertainment. It's also an educational tool and a powerful propaganda device. What happens when boy educated on porn meets girl brought up on Harlequin romances? The clash of expectations can be heard around the block. She wants him to get down on his knees with a ring, he wants her to get down on all fours with a ring in her nose. Can this marriage be saved?

Pornography has certain things in common with such addictive substances as alcohol and drugs: for some, though by no means for all, it induces chemical changes in the body, which the user finds exciting and pleasurable. It also appears to attract a "hard core" of habitual users and a penumbra of those who use it occasionally but aren't dependent on it in any way. There are also significant numbers of men who aren't much interested in it, not because they're undersexed but because real life is satisfying their needs, which may not require as many appliances as those of users.

For the "hard core," pornography may function as alcohol does for the alcoholic: tolerance develops, and a little is no longer enough. This may account for the short viewing time and fast turnover in porn theatres. Mary Brown, chairwoman of the Ontario Board of Film Censors, estimates that for every one mainstream movie requesting entrance to Ontario, there is one porno flick. Not only the quantity consumed but the quality of explicitness must escalate, which may account for the growing violence: once the big deal was breasts, then it was genitals, then copulation, then that was no longer enough and the hard users had to have more. The ultimate kick is death, and after that, as the Marquis de Sade so boringly demonstrated, multiple death. 17

The existence of alcoholism has not led us to ban social drinking. On the other hand, we do have laws about drinking and driving, excessive drunkenness and other abuses of alcohol that may result in injury or death to others. 18

This leads us back to the key question: what's the harm? Nobody knows, but this society should find out fast, before the saturation point is reached. The Scandinavian studies that showed a connection between depictions of sexual violence and increased impulse toward it on the part of male viewers would be a starting point, but many more questions remain to be raised as well as answered. What, for instance, is the crucial difference between men who are users and men who are not? Does using affect a man's relationship with actual women, and, if so, adversely? Is there a clear line between erotica and violent pornography, or are they on an escalating continuum? Is this a "men versus women" issue, with all men secretly siding with the proporners and all women secretly siding against? (I think not; there *are* lots of men who don't think that running their true love through the Cuisinart is the best way they can think of to spend a Saturday night, and they're just as nauseated by films of someone else doing it as women are.) Is pornography 19 merely an expression of the sexual confusion of this age or an active contributor to it?

Nobody wants to go back to the age of official repression, when even piano legs were referred to as "limbs" and had to wear pantaloons to be decent. Neither do we want to end up in George Orwell's *1984*, in which pornography is turned out by the State to keep the proles in a state of torpor, sex itself is considered dirty and the approved practise it only for reproduction. But Rome under the emperors isn't such a good model either.

If all men and women respected each other, if sex were considered joyful and life-enhancing instead of a wallow in germ-filled glop, if everyone were in love all the time, if, in other words, many people's lives were more satisfactory for them than they appear to be now, pornography might just go away on its own. But since this is obviously not happening, we as a society are going to have to make some informed and responsible decisions about how to deal with it.

QUESTIONS FOR READING AND WRITING

1. How does Atwood use comparison and definition in constructing her argument against pornography?
2. What are the two extreme positions that Atwood's argument mediates between?
3. What are the origins of the following words: *pornography, prostitution, censorship, sadism, masochism, prude,* and *pervert*?
4. Is pornography essentially a male/female issue, that is, a male *versus* female issue?
5. What effects upon her argument are produced by Atwood's references to Canadian and Scandanavian studies and laws?
6. In paragraph 18, Atwood cites an analogy between laws against pornography and laws against drunk driving or other excessive forms of alcohol-related behavior. Taking off from this analogy, argue in favor of a set of restrictions upon pornography that are similar to arguments used to restrict or punish the harmful use of alcohol.
7. Write an essay that compares Atwood's views on pornography with those of Gloria Steinem in her essay "Erotica and Pornography."
8. Pick up any Harlequin Romance (or a similar romance novel). Read any group of four pages upon which no dialogue is recorded. Write an analysis of the sexual implications of those four pages. Focus your essay on the issues of sexual stereotyping and "sex and power."

✦ James Baldwin ✦

If Black English Isn't a Language, Then Tell Me, What Is?

Born in Harlem, James Baldwin (1924–1987) began his writing career when he moved to France in 1948. He is best known for his novels, which include Go Tell It On the Mountain *(1953) and* Another Country *(1962), and for his collections of essays on social and racial issues, including* Notes of a Native Son *(1955) and* Nobody Knows My Name *(1961). Though his later work did not bring him as much fame, Baldwin is still widely regarded as one of the great black writers of the twentieth century. In the following essay, Baldwin argues for the integrity of black English as a vehicle for expressing the complex social and political conditions under which blacks have lived in the United States.*

THE ARGUMENT CONCERNING THE USE, or the status, or the reality, of black English is rooted in American history and has absolutely nothing to do with the question the argument supposes itself to be posing. The argument has nothing to do with language itself but with the *role* of language. Language, incontestably, reveals the speaker. Language, also, far more dubiously, is meant to define the other—and, in this case, the other is refusing to be defined by a language that has never been able to recognize him. 1

People evoke a language in order to describe and thus control their circumstances, or in order not to be submerged by a reality that they cannot articulate. (And, if they cannot articulate it, they *are* submerged.) A Frenchman living in Paris speaks a subtly and crucially different language from that of the man living in Marseilles; neither sounds very much like a man living in Quebec; and they would all have great difficulty in apprehending what the man from Guadeloupe, or Martinique, is saying, to say nothing of the man from Senegal—although the "common" language of all these areas is French. But each has paid, and is paying, a different price for this "common" language, in which, as it turns out, they are not saying, and cannot be saying, the same things: They each have very different realities to articulate, or control. 2

What joins all languages, and all men, is the necessity to confront life, in order, not inconceivably, to outwit death: The price for this is the acceptance, and achievement, of one's temporal identity. So that, for example, though it is not taught in the schools (and this has the potential of becoming a political issue) the south of France still clings to its ancient and musical Provençal, which resists being described as a "dialect." And much of the tension in the Basque countries, and in Wales, is due to the Basque and Welsh determination not to allow their languages to be destroyed. This determination also feeds the flames in Ireland for among the many indignities the Irish have been forced to undergo at English hands is the English contempt for their language.

It goes without saying, then, that language is also a political instrument, means, and proof of power. It is the most vivid and crucial key to identity: it reveals the private identity, and connects one with, or divorces one from, the larger, public, or communal identity. There have been, and are, times, and places, when to speak a certain language could be dangerous, even fatal. Or, one may speak the same language, but in such a way that one's antecedents are revealed, or (one hopes) hidden. This is true in France, and is absolutely true in England: The range (and reign) of accents on that damp little island make England coherent for the English and totally incomprehensible for everyone else. To open your mouth in England is (if I may use black English) to "put your business in the street": You have confessed your parents, your youth, your school, your salary, your self-esteem, and alas, your future.

Now, I do not know what white Americans would sound like if there had never been any black people in the United States, but they would not sound the way they sound. *Jazz,* for example, is a very specific sexual term, as in *jazz me, baby,* but white people purified it into the Jazz Age. *Sock it to me*, which means, roughly, the same thing, has been adopted by Nathaniel Hawthorne's descendants with no qualms or hesitations at all, along with *let it all hang out* and *right on! Beat to his socks,* which was once the black's most total and despairing image of poverty, was transformed into a thing called the Beat Generation, which phenomenon was, largely, composed of *uptight,* middle-class white people, imitating poverty, trying to *get down*, to get *with it,* doing their *thing,* doing their despairing best to be *funky,* which we, the blacks, never dreamed of doing—we *were* funky, baby, like *funk* was going out of style.

Now, no one can eat his cake, and have it, too, and it is late in the day to attempt to penalize black people for having created a language that permits the nation its only glimpse of reality, a language without which the nation would be even more *whipped* than it is. 6

I say that this present skirmish is rooted in American history, and it is. Black English is the creation of the black diaspora. Blacks came to the United States chained to each other, but from different tribes: Neither could speak the other's language. If two black people, at that bitter hour of the world's history, had been able to speak to each other, the institution of chattel slavery could never have lasted as long as it did. Subsequently, the slave was given, under the eye, and the gun, of his master, Congo Square, and the Bible—or, in other words, and under these conditions, the slave began the formation of the black church, and it is within this unprecedented tabernacle that black English began to be formed. This was not, merely, as in the European example, the adoption of a foreign tongue, but an alchemy that transformed ancient elements into a new language: *A language comes into existence by means of brutal necessity, and the rules of the language are dictated by what the language must convey.* 7

There was a moment, in time, and in this place, when my brother, or my mother, or my father, or my sister, had to convey to me, for example, the danger in which I was standing from the white man standing just behind me, and to convey this with a speed, and in a language, that the white man could not possibly understand, and that, indeed, he cannot understand, until today. He cannot afford to understand it. This understanding would reveal to him too much about himself, and smash that mirror before which he has been frozen for so long. 8

Now, if this passion, this skill, this (to quote Toni Morrison) "sheer intelligence," this incredible music, the mighty achievement of having brought a people utterly unknown to, or despised by "history"—to have brought this people to their present, troubled, troubling, and unassailable and unanswerable place—if this absolutely unprecedented journey does not indicate that black English is a language, I am curious to know what definition of language is to be trusted. 9

A people at the center of the Western world, and in the midst of so hostile a population, has not endured and transcended by means of what is patronizingly called a "dialect." We, the blacks, are in 10 trouble, certainly, but we are not doomed, and we are not inarticulate because we are not compelled to defend a morality that we know to be a lie.

The brutal truth is that the bulk of the white people in America never had any interest in educating black people, except as this could serve white purposes. It is not the black child's language that is in question, it is not his language that is despised: It is his experience. A child cannot be taught by anyone who despises him, and a child cannot afford to be fooled. A child cannot be taught by anyone whose demand, essentially, is that the child repudiate his experience, and all that gives him sustenance, and enter a limbo in which he will no longer be black, and in which he knows that he can never become white. Black people have lost too many black children that way.

And, after all, finally, in a country with standards so untrustworthy, a country that makes heroes of so many criminal mediocrities, a country unable to face why so many of the nonwhite are in prison, or on the needle, or standing, futureless, in the streets—it may very well be that both the child, and his elder, have concluded that they have nothing whatever to learn from the people of a country that has managed to learn so little.

QUESTIONS FOR READING AND WRITING

1. Define *diaspora* and *chattel* (paragraph 7).
2. What is the tone of Baldwin's essay? How is this tone created?
3. Why, according to Baldwin, did blacks in the United States have to develop a language that was, at some points, incomprehensible to whites?
4. What is the function of the references, in paragraph 2, to the varieties of the French language?
5. In what ways can someone's use of language lead to assumptions about them (their education, where they come from, their socioeconomic background, their interests, their attitudes toward women or ethnic groups, and so forth)?
6. Listen to several black rap songs. Write an essay about the values and attitudes their language expresses.
7. Write an essay about an occasion upon which you were intimidated by someone else's use of language.

✦ Allan Bloom ✦

The Poverty of an Open Mind

Allan Bloom (b. 1930) earned his Ph.D. at the University of Chicago. He now teaches there, as well as serving as the co-director of the John M. Olin Center for Inquiry into the Theory and Practice of Democracy. His best-selling book, The Closing of the American Mind *(1987), offers a trenchant critique of contemporary American education. In the following excerpt from the introduction to that book, Bloom attempts to show how our passion for open-mindedness in fact creates conformism and closed-mindedness.*

THERE IS ONE THING A PROFESSOR can be absolutely certain of: almost every student entering the university believes, or says he believes, that truth is relative. If this belief is put to the test, one can count on the students' reaction: they will be uncomprehending. That anyone should regard the proposition as not self-evident astonishes them, as though he were calling into question 2+2=4. These are things you don't think about. The students' backgrounds are as various as America can provide. Some are religious, some atheists; some are to the Left, some to the Right; some intend to be scientists, some humanists or professionals or businessmen; some are poor, some rich. They are unified only in their relativism and in their allegiance to equality. And the two are related in a moral intention. The relativity of truth is not a theoretical insight but a moral postulate, the condition of a free society, or so they see it. They have all been equipped with this framework early on, and it is the modern replacement for the inalienable natural rights that used to be the traditional American grounds for a free society. That it is a moral issue for students is revealed by the character of their response when challenged—a combination of disbelief and indignation: "Are you an absolutist?," the only alternative they know, uttered in the same tone as "Are you a monarchist?" or "Do you really believe in witches?" This latter leads into the indignation, for someone who believes in witches might well be a witchhunter or a Salem judge. The danger they have been taught to fear from absolutism is not error but intolerance. Relativism is necessary to 1 openness; and this is the virtue, the only virtue, which all primary education for more than fifty years has dedicated itself to inculcating. Openness—and the relativism that makes it the only plausible stance in the face of various claims to truth and various ways of life and kinds of human beings—is the great insight of our times. The true believer is the real danger. The study of history and of culture teaches that all the world was mad in the past; men always thought they were right, and that led to wars, persecutions, slavery, xenophobia, racism, and chauvinism. The point is not to correct the mistakes and really be right; rather it is not to think you are right at all.

The students, of course, cannot defend their opinion. It is something with which they have been indoctrinated. The best they can do is point out all the opinions and cultures there are and have been. What right, they ask, do I or anyone else have to say one is better than the others? If I pose the routine questions designed to confute them and make them think, such as, "If you had been a British administrator in India, would you have let the natives under your governance burn the widow at the funeral of a man who had died?," they either remain silent or reply that the British should never have been there in the first place. It is not that they know very much about other nations, or about their own. The purpose of their education is not to make them scholars but to provide them with a moral virtue—openness.

Every educational system has a moral goal that it tries to attain and that informs its curriculum. It wants to produce a certain kind of human being. This intention is more or less explicit, more or less a result of reflection; but even the neutral subjects, like reading and writing and arithmetic, take their place in a vision of the educated person. In some nations the goal was the pious person, in others the warlike, in others the industrious. Always important is the political regime, which needs citizens who are in accord with its fundamental principle. Aristocracies want gentlemen, oligarchies men who respect and pursue money, and democracies lovers of equality. Democratic education, whether it admits it or not, wants and needs to produce men and women who have the tastes, knowledge, and character supportive of a democratic regime. Over the history of our republic, there have obviously been changes of opinion as to what kind of man is best for our regime. We began with the model of the rational and industrious man, who was honest, respected the laws, and was dedicated to the family (his own family—what has in its decay been dubbed the nuclear family). Above all he was to know the rights doctrine; the Constitution, which embodied it; and American history, which presented and celebrated the founding of a nation "conceived in liberty and dedicated to the proposition that all men are created equal." A powerful attachment to the letter and the spirit of the Declaration of Independence gently conveyed, appealing to each man's reason, was the goal of the education of democratic man. This called for something very different from the kinds of attachment required for traditional communities where myth and passion as well as severe discipline, authority, and the extended family produced an instinctive, unqualified, even fanatic patriotism, unlike the reflected, rational, calm, even self-interested loyalty—not so much to the country but to the form of government and its rational principles—required in the United States. This was an entirely new experiment in politics, and with it came a new education. This education has evolved in the last half-century from the education of democratic man to the education of the democratic personality.

The palpable difference between these two can easily be found 4
in the changed understanding of what it means to be an American. The old view was that, by recognizing and accepting man's natural rights, men found a fundamental basis of unity and sameness. Class, race, religion, national origin or culture all disappear or become dim when bathed in the light of natural rights, which give men common interests and make them truly brothers. The immigrant had to put behind him the claims of the Old World in favor of a new and easily acquired education. This did not necessarily mean abandoning old daily habits or religions, but it did mean subordinating them to new principles. There was a tendency, if not a necessity, to homogenize nature itself.

The recent education of openness has rejected all that. It pays 5
no attention to natural rights or the historical origins of our regime, which are now thought to have been essentially flawed and regressive. It is progressive and forward-looking. It does not demand fundamental agreement or the abandonment of old or new beliefs in favor of the natural ones. It is open to all kinds of men, all kinds of life-styles, all ideologies. There is no enemy other than the man

who is not open to everything. But when there are no shared goals or vision of the public good, is the social contract any longer possible? . . .

The upshot of all this for the education of young Americans is that they know much less about American history and those who were held to be its heroes. This was one of the few things that they used to come to college with that had something to do with their lives. Nothing has taken its place except a smattering of facts learned about other nations or cultures and a few social science formulas. None of this means much, partly because little attention has been paid to what is required in order truly to convey the spirit of other places and other times to young people, or for that matter to anyone, partly because the students see no relevance in any of it to the lives they are going to lead or to their prevailing passions. It is the rarest of occurrences to find a youngster who has been infused by this education with a longing to know all about China or the Romans or the Jews.

All to the contrary. There is an indifference to such things, for relativism has extinguished the real motive of education, the search for a good life. Young Americans have less and less knowledge of and interest in foreign places. In the past there were many students who actually knew something about and loved England, France, Germany, or Italy, for they dreamed of living there or thought their lives would be made more interesting by assimilating their languages and literatures. Such students have almost disappeared, replaced at most by students who are interested in the political problems of Third World countries and in helping them to modernize, with due respect to their old cultures, of course. This is not learning from others but condescension and a disguised form of a new imperialism. It is the Peace Corps mentality, which is not a spur to learning but to a secularized version of doing good works.

Actually openness results in American conformism—out there in the rest of the world is a drab diversity that teaches only that values are relative, whereas here we can create all the life-styles we want. Our openness means we do not need others. Thus what is advertised as a great opening is a great closing. No longer is there a hope that there are great wise men in other places and times who can reveal the truth about life—except for the few remaining young people who look for a quick fix from a guru. Gone is the real historical sense of a Machiavelli who wrested a few hours from each busy day in which "to don regal and courtly garments, enter the courts of the ancients and speak with them."

None of this concerns those who promote the new curriculum. 9
The point is to propagandize acceptance of different ways, and indifference to their real content is as good a means as any. It was not necessarily the best of times in America when Catholics and Protestants were suspicious of and hated one another, but at least they were taking their beliefs seriously, and the more or less satisfactory accommodations they worked out were not simply the result of apathy about the state of their souls. Practically all that young Americans have today is an insubstantial awareness that there are many cultures, accompanied by a saccharine moral drawn from that awareness: We should all get along. Why fight? In 1980, during the crisis with Iran, the mother of one of the hostages expressed our current educational principles very well. She went to Iran to beg for her son's release, against the express wishes of the government of her country, the very week a rescue of the hostages was attempted. She justified her conduct by explaining that a mother has a right to try to save her son and also to learn a new culture. These are two basic rights, and her trip enabled her to kill two birds with one stone. . . .

One of the techniques of opening young people up is to require 10
a college course in a non-Western culture. Although many of the persons teaching such courses are real scholars and lovers of the areas they study, in every case I have seen this requirement—when there are so many other things that can and should be learned but are not required, when philosophy and religion are no longer required—has a demagogic intention. The point is to force students to recognize that there are other ways of thinking and that Western ways are not better. It is again not the content that counts but the lesson to be drawn. Such requirements are part of the effort to establish a world community and train its member—the person devoid of prejudice. But if the students were really to learn something of the minds of any of these non-Western cultures—which they do not—they would find that each and every one of these cultures is ethnocentric. All of them think their way is the best way, and all others are inferior. Herodotus tells us that the Persians thought that they were the best, that those nations bordering on

them were next best, that those nations bordering on the nations bordering on them were third best, and so on, their worth declining as the concentric circles were farther from the Persian center. This is the very definition of ethnocentrism. Something like this is as ubiquitous as the prohibition against incest between mother and son.

Only in the Western nations, i.e., those influenced by Greek philosophy, is there some willingness to doubt the identification of the good with one's own way. One should conclude from the study of non-Western cultures that not only to prefer one's own way but to believe it best, superior to all others, is primary and even natural—exactly the opposite of what is intended by requiring students to study these cultures. What we are really doing is applying a Western prejudice—which we covertly take to indicate the superiority of our culture—and deforming the evidence of those other cultures to attest to its validity. The scientific study of other cultures is almost exclusively a Western phenomenon, and in its origin was obviously connected with the search for new and better ways, or at least for validation of the hope that our own culture really is the better way, a validation for which there is no felt need in other cultures. If we are to learn from those cultures, we must wonder whether such scientific study is a good idea. Consistency would seem to require professors of openness to respect the ethnocentrism or closedness they find everywhere else. However, in attacking ethnocentrism, what they actually do is assert unawares the superiority of their scientific understanding and the inferiority of the other cultures which do not recognize it at the same time that they reject all such claims to superiority. They both affirm and deny the goodness of their science. They face a problem akin to that faced by Pascal in the conflict between reason and revelation, without the intellectual intransigence that forced him to abandon science in favor of faith.

The reason for the non-Western closedness, or ethnocentrism, is clear. Men must love and be loyal to their families and their peoples in order to preserve them. Only if they think their own things are good can they rest content with them. A father must prefer his child to other children, a citizen his country to others. That is why there are myths—to justify these attachments. And a man needs a place and opinions by which to orient himself. This is strongly asserted by those who talk about the importance of roots. The problem of getting along with outsiders is secondary to, and sometimes in conflict with, having an inside, a people, a culture, a way of life. A very great narrowness is not incompatible with the health of an individual or a people, whereas with great openness it is hard to avoid decomposition. The firm binding of the good with one's own, the refusal to see a distinction between the two, a vision of the cosmos that has a special place for one's people, seem to be conditions of culture. This is what really follows from the study of non-Western cultures proposed for undergraduates. It points them back to passionate attachment to their own and away from the science which liberates them from it. Science now appears as a threat to culture and a dangerous uprooting charm. In short, they are lost in a non-man's-land between the goodness of knowing and goodness of culture, where they have been placed by their teachers who no longer have the resources to guide them. Help must be sought elsewhere.

Greek philosophers were the first men we know to address the problems of ethnocentrism. Distinctions between the good and one's own, between nature and convention, between the just and the legal are the signs of this movement of thought. They related the good to the fulfillment of the whole natural human potential and were aware that few, if any, of the nations of men had ways that allowed such fulfillment. They were open to the good. They had to use the good, which was not their own, to judge their own. This was a dangerous business because it tended to weaken wholehearted attachment to their own, hence weaken their peoples as well as to expose themselves to the anger of family, friends, and countrymen. Loyalty versus quest for the good introduced an unresolvable tension into life. But the awareness of the good as such and the desire to possess it are priceless humanizing acquisitions. 13

This is the sound motive contained, along with many other less sound ones, in openness as we understand it. Men cannot remain content with what is given them by their culture if they are to be fully human. This is what Plato meant to show by the image of the cave in the *Republic* and by representing us as prisoners in it. A culture is a cave. He did not suggest going around to other cultures as a solution to the limitations of the cave. Nature should be the standard by which we judge our own lives and the lives of peoples. 14

That is why philosophy, not history or anthropology, is the most important human science. Only dogmatic assurance that thought is culture-bound, that there is no nature, is what makes our educators so certain that the only way to escape the limitations of our time and place is to study other cultures. History and anthropology were understood by the Greeks to be useful only in discovering what the past and other peoples had to contribute to the discovery of nature. Historians and anthropologists were to put peoples and their conventions to the test, as Socrates did individuals, and go beyond them. These scientists were superior to their subjects because they saw a problem where others refused to see one, and they were engaged in the quest to solve it. They wanted to be able to evaluate themselves and others.

This point of view, particularly the need to know nature in order to have a standard, is uncomfortably buried beneath our human sciences, whether they like it or not, and accounts for the ambiguities and contradictions I have been pointing out. They want to make us culture-beings with the instruments that were invented to liberate us from culture. Openness used to be the virtue that permitted us to seek the good by using reason. It now means accepting everything and denying reason's power. The unrestrained and thoughtless pursuit of openness, without recognizing the inherent political, social, or cultural problem of openness as the goal of nature, has rendered openness meaningless. Cultural relativism destroys both one's own and the good. What is most characteristic of the West is science, particularly understood as the quest to know nature and the consequent denigration of convention—i.e., culture or the West understood as a culture—in favor of what is accessible to all men as men through their common and distinctive faculty, reason. Science's latest attempts to grasp the human situation—cultural relativism, historicism, the fact-value distinction—are the suicide of science. Culture, hence closedness, reigns supreme. Openness to closedness is what we teach.

Cultural relativism succeeds in destroying the West's universal or 1
intellectually imperialistic claims, leaving it to be just another culture. So there is equality in the republic of cultures. Unfortunately the West is defined by its need for justification of its ways or values, by its need for discovery of nature, by its need for philosophy and science. This is its cultural imperative. Deprived of that, it will

collapse. The United States is one of the highest and most extreme achievements of the rational quest for the good life according to nature. What makes its political structure possible is the use of the rational principles of natural right to found a people, thus uniting the good with one's own. Or, to put it otherwise, the regime established here promised untrammeled freedom to reason—not to everything indiscriminately, but to reason, the essential freedom that justifies the other freedoms, and on the basis of which, and for the sake of which, much deviance is also tolerated. An openness that denies the special claim of reason bursts the mainspring keeping the mechanism of this regime in motion. And this regime, contrary to all claims to the contrary, was founded to overcome ethnocentrism, which is in no sense a discovery of social science.

It is important to emphasize that the lesson the students are 17
drawing from their studies is simply untrue. History and study of cultures do not teach or prove that values or cultures are relative. All to the contrary, that is a philosophical premise that we now bring to our study of them. This premise is unproven and dogmatically asserted for what are largely political reasons. History and culture are interpreted in the light of it, and then are said to prove the premise. Yet the fact that there have been different opinions about good and bad in different times and places in no way proves that none is true or superior to others. To say that it does so prove is as absurd as to say that the diversity of points of view expressed in a college bull session proves there is no truth. On the face of it, the difference of opinion would seem to raise the question as to which is true or right rather than to banish it. The natural reaction is to try to resolve the difference, to examine the claims and reasons for each opinion.

Only the unhistorical and inhuman belief that opinions are held 18
for no reason would prevent the undertaking of such an exciting activity. Men and nations always think they have reasons, and it could be understood to be historians' and social scientists' most important responsibility to make explicit and test those reasons. It was always known that there were many and conflicting opinions about the good, and nations embodying each of them. Herodotus was at least as aware as we are of the rich diversity of cultures. But he took that observation to be an invitation to investigate all of them to see what was good and bad about each and find out what he could

learn about good and bad from them. Modern relativists take that same observation as proof that such investigation is impossible and that we must be respectful of them all. Thus students, and the rest of us, are deprived of the primary excitement derived from the discovery of diversity, the impulse of Odysseus, who, according to Dante, traveled the world to see the virtues and vices of men. History and anthropology cannot provide the answers, but they can provide the material on which judgment can work.

I know that men are likely to bring what are only their prejudices to the judgment of alien peoples. Avoiding that is one of the main purposes of education. But trying to prevent it by removing the authority of men's reason is to render ineffective the instrument that can correct their prejudices. True openness is the accompaniment of the desire to know, hence of the awareness of ignorance. To deny the possibility of knowing good and bad is to suppress true openness. A proper historical attitude would lead one to doubt the truth of historicism (the view that all thought is essentially related to and cannot transcend its own time) and treat it as a peculiarity of contemporary history. Historicism and cultural relativism actually are a means to avoid testing our own prejudices and asking, for example, whether men are really equal or whether that opinion is merely a democratic prejudice. . . .

Thus there are two kinds of openness, the openness of indifference—promoted with the twin purposes of humbling our intellectual pride and letting us be whatever we want to be, just as long as we don't want to be knowers—and the openness that invites us to the quest for knowledge and certitude, for which history and the various cultures provide a brilliant array of examples of examination. This second kind of openness encourages the desire that animates and makes interesting every serious student—"I want to know what is good for me, what will make me happy"—while the former stunts that desire.

Openness, as currently conceived, is a way of making surrender to whatever is most powerful, or worship of vulgar success, look principled. It is historicism's ruse to remove all resistance to history, which in our day means public opinion, a day when public opinion already rules. How often I have heard the abandonment of requirements to learn languages or philosophy or science lauded as a progress of openness. Here is where the two kinds of openness clash. To be open to knowing, there are certain kinds of things one must know which most people don't want to bother to learn and which appear boring and irrelevant. Even the life of reason is often unappealing; and useless knowledge, i.e., knowledge that is not obviously useful for a career, has no place in the student's vision of the curriculum. So the university that stands intransigently for humane learning must necessarily look closed and rigid. If openness means to "go with the flow," it is necessarily an accommodation to the present. That present is so closed to doubt about so many things impeding the progress of its principles that unqualified openness to it would mean forgetting the despised alternatives to it, knowledge of which makes us aware of what is doubtful in it. True openness means closedness to all the charms that make us comfortable with the present.

When I was a young teacher at Cornell, I once had a debate 22
about education with a professor of psychology. He said that it was his function to get rid of prejudices in his students. He knocked them down like tenpins. I began to wonder what he replaced those prejudices with. He did not seem to have much of an idea of what the opposite of a prejudice might be. He reminded me of the little boy who gravely informed me when I was four that there is no Santa Claus, who wanted me to bathe in the brilliant light of truth. Did this professor know what those prejudices meant for the students and what effect being deprived of them would have? Did he believe that there are truths that could guide their lives as did their prejudices? Had he considered how to give students the love of the truth necessary to seek unprejudiced beliefs, or would he render them passive, disconsolate, indifferent, and subject to authorities like himself, or the best of contemporary thought? My informant about Santa Claus was just showing off, proving his superiority to me. He had not created the Santa Claus that had to be there in order to be refuted. Think of all we learn about the world from men's belief in Santa Clauses, and all that we learn about the soul from those who believe in them. By contrast, merely methodological excision from the soul of the imagination that projects Gods and heroes onto the wall of the cave does not promote knowledge of the soul; it only lobotomizes it, cripples its powers.

I found myself responding to the professor of psychology that I 23
personally tried to teach my students prejudices, since nowadays—

with the general success of his method—they had learned to doubt beliefs even before they believed in anything. Without people like me, he would be out of business. Descartes had a whole wonderful world of old beliefs, of prescientific experience and articulations of the order of things, beliefs firmly and even fanatically held, before he even began his systematic and radical doubt. One has to have the experience of really believing before one can have the thrill of liberation. So I proposed a division of labor in which I would help to grow the flowers in the field and he could mow them down.

Prejudices, strong prejudices, are visions about the way things are. They are divinations of the order of the whole of things, and hence the road to a knowledge of that whole is by the way of erroneous opinions about it. Error is indeed our enemy, but it alone points to the truth and therefore deserves our respectful treatment. The mind that has no prejudices at the outset is empty. It can only have been constituted by a method that is unaware of how difficult it is to recognize that a prejudice is a prejudice. Only Socrates knew, after a lifetime of unceasing labor, that he was ignorant. Now every high-school student knows that. How did it become so easy? What accounts for our amazing progress? Could it be that our experience has been so impoverished by our various methods, of which openness is only the latest, that there is nothing substantial enough left there to resist criticism, and we therefore have no world left of which to be really ignorant? Have we so simplified the soul that it is no longer difficult to explain? To an eye of dogmatic skepticism, nature herself, in all her lush profusion of expressions, might appear to be a prejudice. In her place we put a gray network of critical concepts, which were invented to interpret nature's phenomena but which strangled them and therewith destroyed their own *raison d'être*. Perhaps it is our first task to resuscitate those phenomena so that we may again have a world to which we can put our questions and be able to philosophize. This seems to me to be our educational challenge.

QUESTIONS FOR READING AND WRITING

1. In paragraph 5, Bloom describes a central tendency of recent education. What faults lie in its apparent virtues?

2. In paragraph 7, Bloom says that "the real motive of education" is the "search for a good life." How, from your present perspective, would you define a good life? In what ways might your definition differ from what Bloom might say?
3. Explain the paradox Bloom describes in paragraph 8.
4. In paragraphs 10–14, Bloom offers a critique of the wisdom of making students take courses in non-Western civilization. What is the logic of his critique? Why does he object to such courses as they are currently taught?
5. Write an essay that compares Bloom's main ideas with those of Norman Cousins in "How to Make People Smaller Than They Are."
6. Write an essay in which you propose an ideal curriculum for accomplishing what Bloom finds desirable. Or, review the requirements of your own school or major and write an essay that defends or attacks those requirements. In doing so, you should imply or state where your own educational values lie.

✦ Norman Cousins ✦

How to Make People Smaller Than They Are

An American journalist and editor, Norman Cousins (b. 1915) was the editor of the Saturday Review *from 1942 to 1971 and again from 1975 to 1978. His most famous book,* Anatomy of an Illness *(1979), concerns the means by which he overcame a near-fatal disease. He is now a Professor of Medical Humanities at UCLA. In the following essay, first published in the* Saturday Review *in 1978, Cousins surveys the damage that occurs when liberal education is deemphasized for the sake of greater vocational training.*

THREE MONTHS AGO in this space we wrote about the costly retreat from the humanities on all the levels of American education. Since that time, we have had occasion to visit a number of campuses and have been troubled to find that the general situation is even more serious than we had thought. It has become apparent to us that one of the biggest problems confronting American education today is the increasing vocationalization of our colleges and universities. Throughout the country, schools are under pressure to become job-training centers and employment agencies.

The pressure comes mainly from two sources. One is the growing determination of many citizens to reduce taxes—understandable and even commendable in itself, but irrational and irresponsible when connected to the reduction or dismantling of vital public services. The second source of pressure comes from parents and students who tend to scorn courses of study that do not teach people how to become attractive to employers in a rapidly tightening job market.

It is absurd to believe that the development of skills does not also require the systematic development of the human mind. Education is being measured more by the size of the benefits the individual can extract from society than by the extent to which the individual can come into possession of his or her full powers. The result is that the life-giving juices are in danger of being drained out of education.

Emphasis on "practicalities" is being characterized by the subordination of words to numbers. History is seen not as essential experience to be transmitted to new generations, but as abstractions that carry dank odors. Art is regarded as something that calls for indulgence or patronage and that has no place among the practical realities. Political science is viewed more as a specialized subject for people who want to go into politics than as an opportunity for citizens to develop a knowledgeable relationship with the systems by which human societies are governed. Finally, literature and philosophy are assigned the role of add-ons—intellectual adornments that have nothing to do with "genuine" education. 4

Instead of trying to shrink the liberal arts, the American people ought to be putting pressure on colleges and universities to increase the ratio of the humanities to the sciences. Most serious studies of medical-school curricula in recent years have called attention to the stark gaps in the liberal education of medical students. The experts agree that the schools shouldn't leave it up to students to close those gaps. 5

The irony of the emphasis being placed on careers is that nothing is more valuable for anyone who has had a professional or vocational education than to be able to deal with abstractions or complexities, or to feel comfortable with subtleties of thought or language, or to think sequentially. The doctor who knows only disease is at a disadvantage alongside the doctor who knows at least as much about people as he does about pathological organisms. The lawyer who argues in court from a narrow legal base is no match for the lawyer who can connect legal precedents to historical experience and who employs wide-ranging intellectual resources. The business executive whose competence in general management is bolstered by an artistic ability to deal with people is of prime value to his company. For the technologist, the engineering of consent can be just as important as the engineering of moving parts. In all these respects, the liberal arts have much to offer. Just in terms of career preparation, therefore, a student is shortchanging himself by shortcutting the humanities. 6

But even if it could be demonstrated that the humanities contribute nothing directly to a job, they would still be an essential part of the educational equipment of any person who wants to come to terms with life. The humanities would be expendable only if human 7 beings didn't have to make decisions that affect their lives and the lives of others; if the human past never existed or had nothing to tell us about the present; if thought processes were irrelevant to the achievement of purpose; if creativity was beyond the human mind and had nothing to do with the joy of living; if human relationships were random aspects of life; if human beings never had to cope with panic or pain, or if they never had to anticipate the connection between cause and effect; if all the mysteries of mind and nature were fully plumbed; and if no special demands arose from the accident of being born a human being instead of a hen or a hog.

Finally, there would be good reason to eliminate the humanities if a free society were not absolutely dependent on a functioning citizenry. If the main purpose of a university is job training, then the underlying philosophy of our government has little meaning. The debates that went into the making of American society concerned not just institutions or governing principles but the capacity of humans to sustain those institutions. Whatever the disagreements were over other issues at the American Constitutional Convention, the fundamental question sensed by everyone, a question that lay over the entire assembly, was whether the people themselves would understand what it meant to hold the ultimate power of society, and whether they had enough of a sense of history and destiny to know where they had been and where they ought to be going.

Jefferson was prouder of having been the founder of the University of Virginia than of having been President of the United States. He knew that the educated and developed mind was the best assurance that a political system could be made to work—a system based on the informed consent of the governed. If this idea fails, then all the saved tax dollars in the world will not be enough to prevent the nation from turning on itself.

QUESTIONS FOR READING AND WRITING

1. What does Cousins mean by the "increasing vocationalization"of American colleges (paragraph 1)? Is he implying that colleges should not ensure that their graduates can be gainfully employed?
2. In what ways can you justify taking courses that are not directly related to your major or to your career plans?

3. In what ways, according to Cousins, are liberal arts courses, in fact, quite "relevant" to most vocations?
4. What does Cousins mean by "the subordination of words to numbers" (paragraph 4)? What numbers is he referring to? What are "word-oriented" courses? If such "word-oriented" courses are not directed toward vocational ends, what value do they have?
5. Write an essay in which you record the results of an interview you conduct with one of your humanities professors. Question him or her about the importance and "relevance" of the discipline he or she teaches.
6. Interview several working adults, including some recent college graduates. Ask them about the appropriateness of any "vocational" training they received in college. Also ask them if they feel any different about liberal-arts courses now that they are in the work force than they did when they were in college. Write up your results in an essay assessing the importance of liberal-arts education.

✦ Clarence Darrow ✦
The Futility of the Death Penalty

Clarence Darrow (1857–1938) is one of America's most famous lawyers. In 1924, he defended two confessed killers, Nathan Leopold and Richard Loeb, and, despite public "demand" for the death penalty, was able to obtain a prison sentence (rather than death) for the criminals. In the following essay, first published in 1928, Darrow attempts to show that the death penalty does not, itself, deter crime, and should therefore be abolished.

LITTLE MORE THAN A CENTURY AGO, in England, there were over two hundred offenses that were punishable with death. The death sentence was passed upon children under ten years old. And every time the sentimentalist sought to lessen the number of crimes punishable by death, the self-righteous said no, that it would be the destruction of the state; that it would be better to kill for more transgressions rather than for less.

Today, both in England and America, the number of capital offenses has been reduced to a very few, and capital punishment would doubtless be abolished altogether were it not for the self-righteous, who still defend it with the same old arguments. Their major claim is that capital punishment decreases the number of murders, and hence, that the state must retain the institution as its last defense against the criminal.

It is my purpose in this article to prove, first, that capital punishment is no deterrent to crime; and second, that the state continues to kill its victims, not so much to defend society against them—for it could do that equally well by imprisonment—but to appease the mob's emotions of hatred and revenge.

Behind the idea of capital punishment lie false training and crude views of human conduct. People do evil things, say the judges, lawyers, and preachers, because of depraved hearts. Human conduct is not determined by the causes which determine the conduct of other animal and plant life in the universe. For some mysterious reason human beings act as they please; and if they do not please to act in a certain way, it is because, having the power of choice, they deliberately choose to act wrongly. The world once applied this doctrine to disease and insanity in men. It was also applied to animals, and even inanimate things were once tried and condemned to destruction. The world knows better now, but the rule has not yet been extended to human beings.

5 The simple fact is that every person starts life with a certain physical structure, more or less sensitive, stronger or weaker. He is played upon by everything that reaches him from without, and in this he is like everything else in the universe, inorganic matter as well as organic. How a man will act depends upon the character of his human machine, and the strength of the various stimuli that affect it. Everyone knows that this is so in disease and insanity. Most investigators know that it applies to crime. But the great mass of people still sit in judgment, robed with self-righteousness, and determine the fate of their less fortunate fellows. When this question is studied like any other, we shall then know how to get rid of most of the conduct that we call "criminal," just as we are now getting rid of much of the disease that once afflicted mankind.

6 If crime were really the result of wilful depravity, we should be ready to concede that capital punishment may serve as a deterrent to the criminally inclined. But it is hardly probable that the great majority of people refrain from killing their neighbors because they are afraid; they refrain because they never had the inclination. Human beings are creatures of habit; and, as a rule, they are not in the habit of killing. The circumstances that lead to killings are manifold, but in a particular individual the inducing cause is not easily found. In one case, homicide may have been induced by indigestion in the killer; in another, it may be traceable to some weakness inherited from a remote ancestor; but that it results from *something* tangible and understandable, if all the facts were known, must be plain to everyone who believes in cause and effect.

7 Of course, no one will be converted to this point of view by statistics of crime. In the first place, it is impossible to obtain reliable ones; and in the second place, the conditions to which they apply are never the same. But if one cares to analyze the figures, such as we have, it is easy to trace the more frequent causes of homicide. The greatest number of killings occur during attempted burglaries and robberies. The robber knows that penalties for

burglary do not average more than five years in prison. He also knows that the penalty for murder is death or life imprisonment. Faced with this alternative, what does the burglar do when he is detected and threatened with arrest? He shoots to kill. He deliberately takes the chance of death to save himself from a five-year term in prison. It is therefore as obvious as anything can be that fear of death has no effect in diminishing homicides of this kind, which are more numerous than any other type.

The next largest number of homicides may be classed as "sex murders." Quarrels between husbands and wives, disappointed love, or love too much requited cause many killings. They are the result of primal emotions so deep that the fear of death has not the slightest effect in preventing them. Spontaneous feelings overflow in criminal acts, and consequences do not count.

Then there are cases of sudden anger, uncontrollable rage. The fear of death never enters into such cases; if the anger is strong enough, consequences are not considered until too late. The old-fashioned stories of men deliberately plotting and committing murder in cold blood have little foundation in real life. Such killings are so rare that they need not concern us here. The point to be emphasized is that practically all homicides are manifestations of well-recognized human emotions, and it is perfectly plain that the fear of excessive punishment does not enter into them.

In addition to these personal forces which overwhelm weak men and lead them to commit murder, there are also many social and economic forces which must be listed among the causes of homicides, and human beings have even less control over these than over their own emotions. It is often said that in America there are more homicides in proportion to population than in England. This is true. There are likewise more in the United States than in Canada. But such comparisons are meaningless until one takes into consideration the social and economic differences in the countries compared. Then it becomes apparent why the homicide rate in the United States is higher. Canada's population is largely rural; that of the United States is crowded into cities whose slums are the natural breeding places of crime. Moreover, the population of England and Canada is homogeneous, while the United States has gathered together people of every color from every nation in the world.

Racial differences intensify social, religious, and industrial problems, and the confusion which attends this indiscriminate mixing of races and nationalities is one of the most fertile sources of crime.

Will capital punishment remedy these conditions? Of course it won't; but its advocates argue that the fear of this extreme penalty will hold the victims of adverse conditions in check. To this piece of sophistry the continuance and increase of crime in our large cities is a sufficient answer. No, the plea that capital punishment acts as a deterrent to crime will not stand. The real reason why this barbarous practice persists in a so-called civilized world is that people still hold the primitive belief that the taking of one human life can be atoned for by taking another. It is the age-old obsession with punishment that keeps the official headsman busy plying his trade. 11

And it is precisely upon this point that I would build my case against capital punishment. Even if one grants that the idea of punishment is sound, crime calls for something more—for careful study, for an understanding of causes, for proper remedies. To attempt to abolish crime by killing the criminal is the easy and foolish way out of a serious situation. Unless a remedy deals with the conditions which foster crime, criminals will breed faster than the hangman can spring his trap. Capital punishment ignores the causes of crime just as completely as the primitive witch doctor ignored the causes of disease; and, like the methods of the witch doctor, it is not only ineffective as a remedy, but is positively vicious in at least two ways. In the first place, the spectacle of state executions feeds the basest passions of the mob. And in the second place, so long as the state rests content to deal with crime in this barbaric and futile manner, society will be lulled by a false sense of security, and effective methods of dealing with crime will be discouraged. 12

It seems to be a general impression that there are fewer homicides in Great Britain than in America because in England punishment is more certain, more prompt, and more severe. As a matter of fact, the reverse is true. In England the average term for burglary is eighteen months; with us it is probably four or five years. In England, imprisonment for life means twenty years. Prison sentences in the United States are harder than in any country in the world that could be classed as civilized. This is true largely because, with us, practically no official dares to act on his own judgment. The mob 13 is all-powerful and demands blood for blood. That intangible body of people called "the public" vents its hatred upon the criminal and enjoys the sensation of having him put to death by the state—this without any definite idea that it is really necessary.

For the last five or six years, in England and Wales, the homicides reported by the police range from sixty-five to seventy a year. Death sentences meted out by jurors have averaged about thirty-five, and hangings, fifteen. More than half of those convicted by juries were saved by appeals to the Home Office. But in America there is no such percentage of lives saved after conviction. Governors are afraid to grant clemency. If they did, the newspapers and the populace would refuse to re-elect them.

It is true that trials are somewhat prompter in England than America, but there no newspaper dares publish the details of any case until after the trial. In America the accused is often convicted by the public within twenty-four hours of the time a homicide occurs. The courts sidetrack all other business so that a homicide that is widely discussed may receive prompt attention. The road to the gallows is not only opened but greased for the opportunity of killing another victim.

Thus, while capital punishment panders to the passions of the mob, no one takes the pains to understand the meaning of crime. People speak of crime or criminals as if the world were divided into the good and the bad. This is not true. All of us have the same emotions, but since the balance of emotions is never the same, nor the inducing causes identical, human conduct presents a wide range of differences, shading by almost imperceptible degrees from that of the saint to that of the murderer. Of those kinds of conduct which are classed as dangerous, by no means all are made criminal offenses. Who can clearly define the difference between certain legal offenses and many kinds of dangerous conduct not singled out by criminal statute? Why are many cases of cheating entirely omitted from the criminal code, such as false and misleading advertisements, selling watered stock, forestalling the market, and all the different ways in which great fortunes are accumulated to the envy and despair of those who would like to have money but do not know how to get it? Why do we kill people for the crime of homicide and administer a lesser penalty for burglary, robbery, and cheating? Can anyone tell which is the greater crime and which is the lesser?

Human conduct is by no means so simple as our moralists have 17
led us to believe. There is no sharp line separating good actions from bad. The greed for money, the display of wealth, the despair of those who witness the display, the poverty, oppression, and hopelessness of the unfortunate—all these are factors which enter into human conduct and of which the world takes no account. Many people have learned no other profession but robbery and burglary. The processions moving steadily through our prisons to the gallows are in the main made up of these unfortunates. And how do we dare to consider ourselves civilized creatures when, ignoring the causes of crime, we rest content to mete out harsh punishments to the victims of conditions over which they have no control?

Even now, are not all imaginative and humane people shocked at 18
the spectacle of a killing by the state? How many men and women would be willing to act as executioners? How many fathers and mothers would want their children to witness an official killing? What kind of people read the sensational reports of an execution? If all right-thinking men and women were not ashamed of it, why would it be needful that judges and lawyers and preachers apologize for the barbarity? How can the state censure the cruelty of the man who—moved by strong passions, or acting to save his freedom, or influenced by weakness or fear—takes human life, when everyone knows that the state itself, after long premeditation and settled hatred, not only kills, but first tortures and bedevils its victims for weeks with the impending doom?

For the last hundred years the world has shown a gradual ten- 19
dency to mitigate punishment. We are slowly learning that this way of controlling human beings is both cruel and ineffective. In England the criminal code has consistently grown more humane, until now the offenses punishable by death are reduced to practically one. There is no doubt whatever that the world is growing more humane and more sensitive and more understanding. The time will come when all people will view with horror the light way in which society and its courts of law now take human life; and when that time comes, the way will be clear to devise some better method of dealing with poverty and ignorance and their frequent byproducts, which we call crime.

QUESTIONS FOR READING AND WRITING

1. Do you think that potential criminals are deterred from committing crimes because they think of the death penalty?
2. Would you advocate capital punishment if you knew that its use would cause the death of even one completely innocent person?
3. According to Darrow, what part do social conditions play in causing crime? What specifically American social conditions contribute to the large number of murders in the United States?
4. Do you agree with Darrow's implication, in paragraph 15, that the media help the public to prejudge criminal cases?
5. Reread the first and last paragraphs of Darrow's essay. What is his point in referring to capital punishment in Great Britain?
6. We can probably assume that today there are more murders committed in the United States than in Darrow's day, and we can safely assume that fewer criminals are executed now than in his day. Why does this not necessarily disprove his contention that capital punishment deters murder?
7. Write an essay that compares Darrow's views of capital punishment with those of Edward Koch in "Death and Justice."

✦ Angelo Gonsalez ✦

Bilingualism, Pro

The Key to Basic Skills

In the following essay, Angelo Gonsalez, a Hispanic educator, argues in favor of bilingual education for Hispanic children. Without such education, Gonsalez contends, the chances will increase that these children will fall behind their non-Hispanic counterparts.

IF WE ACCEPT THAT A CHILD CANNOT LEARN unless taught through the language he speaks and understands; that a child who does not speak or understand English must fall behind when English is the dominant medium of instruction; that one needs to learn English so as to be able to participate in an English-speaking society; that self-esteem and motivation are necessary for effective learning; that rejection of a child's native language and culture is detrimental to the learning process: then any necessary effective educational program for limited or no English-speaking ability must incorporate the following: 1

- Language arts and comprehensive reading programs taught in the child's native language.
- Curriculum content areas taught in the native language to further comprehension and academic achievement.
- Intensive instruction in English.
- Use of materials sensitive to and reflecting the culture of children within the program.

Most Important Goal

The mastery of basic reading skills is the most important goal in primary education since reading is the basis for much of all subsequent learning. Ordinarily these skills are learned at home. But where beginning reading is taught in English, only the English-speaking child profits from these early acquired skills that are prerequisites to successful reading development. Reading pro- 2 grams taught in English to children with Spanish as a first language wastes their acquired linguistic attributes and also impedes learning by forcing them to absorb skills of reading simultaneously with a new language.

Both local and national research data provide ample evidence for the efficacy of well-implemented programs. The New York City Board of Education Report on Bilingual Pupil Services for 1982–83 indicated that in all areas of the curriculum—English, Spanish and mathematics—and at all grade levels, students demonstrated statistically significant gains in tests of reading in English and Spanish and in math. In all but two of the programs reviewed, the attendance rates of students in the program, ranging from 86 to 94 percent, were higher than those of the general school population. Similar higher attendance rates were found among students in high school bilingual programs.

At Yale University, Kenji Hakuta, a linguist, reported recently on a study of working-class Hispanic students in the New Haven bilingual program. He found that children who were the most bilingual, that is, who developed English without the loss of Spanish, were brighter in both verbal and nonverbal tests. Over time, there was an increasing correlation between English and Spanish—a finding that clearly contradicts the charge that teaching in the home language is detrimental to English. Rather the two languages are interdependent within the bilingual child, reinforcing each other.

Essential Contribution

As Jim Cummins of the Ontario Institute for Studies in Education has argued, the use and development of the native language makes an essential contribution to the development of minority children's subject-matter knowledge and academic learning potential. In fact, at least three national data bases— the National Assessment of Educational Progress, National Center for Educational Statistics–High School and Beyond Studies, and the Survey of Income and Education—suggest that there are long-term positive effects among high school students who have participated in bilingual-education programs. These students are achieving higher scores on tests of verbal and mathematics skills.

These and similar findings buttress the argument stated persuasively in the recent joint recommendation of the Academy for Educational Development and the Hazen Foundation, namely, that America needs to become a more multilingual nation and children who speak a non-English language are a national resource to be nurtured in school. 6

Unfortunately, the present Administration's educational policies would seem to be leading us in the opposite direction. Under the guise of protecting the common language of public life in the United States, William J. Bennett, the Secretary of Education, unleashed a frontal attack on bilingual education. In a major policy address, he engaged in rhetorical distortions about the nature and effectiveness of bilingual programs, pointing only to unnamed negative research findings to justify the Administration's retrenchment efforts. 7

Arguing for the need to give local school districts greater flexibility in determining appropriate methodologies in serving limited-English-proficient students, Mr. Bennett fails to realize that, in fact, districts serving large numbers of language-minority students, as is the case in New York City, do have that flexibility. Left to their own devices in implementing legal mandates, many school districts have performed poorly at providing services to all entitled language-minority students. 8

A Harsh Reality

The harsh reality in New York City for language-minority students was documented comprehensively last month by the Educational Priorities Panel. The panel's findings revealed that of the 113,831 students identified as being limited in English proficiency, as many as 44,000 entitled students are not receiving any bilingual services. The issue at hand is, therefore, not one of choice but rather violation of the rights of almost 40 percent of language-minority children to equal educational opportunity. In light of these findings the Reagan Administration's recent statements only serve to exacerbate existing inequities in the American educational system for linguistic-minority children. Rather than adding fuel to a misguided debate, the Administration would serve these children best by 9 insuring the full funding of the 1984 Bilingual Education Reauthorization Act as passed by the Congress.

QUESTIONS FOR READING AND WRITING

1. What advantages—in school or in public life—does a bilingual child or adult possess?
2. Should bilingual education be a national or a local issue? What advantages or disadvantages for bilingual education occur when city or state governments, as opposed to the federal government, are allowed to establish the guidelines?
3. Explain the different implications of a national religion (Christianity, for instance) and a national, "official" language (English).
4. Drawing upon your own experience, write an essay that shows how your family has retained or lost customs particular to your ethnic or national background. Cite, where possible, what has been gained or lost by assimilation and/or separateness.
5. Compare Gonsalez' essay with Richard Rodriguez' "Bilingualism, Con: Outdated and Unrealistic." Write an essay that argues in favor of a middle ground between the two viewpoints.

✦ Stephen Jay Gould ✦
The Terrifying Normalcy of AIDS

Stephen Jay Gould (b. 1941) received his Ph.D. from Columbia in 1967. He is now a professor of geology and zoology at Harvard University. A prolific writer, he has done much to bring the recent discoveries of geological and zoological science to an audience of lay readers. His several books include Ever Since Darwin *(1977),* The Panda's Thumb *(1980), and* Time's Arrow, Time's Cycle: Myth and Metaphor in the Discovery of Geological Time *(1987). The following essay appeared in* The New York Times Magazine *in 1987. In it, Gould argues against our tendency to be complacent about the inevitability of scientific progress. AIDS will not disappear automatically as medical science progresses; it is, rather, a disease that we must "fight like hell" to rid ourselves of.*

DISNEY'S EPCOT CENTER IN ORLANDO, FLA., is a technological tour de force and a conceptual desert. In this permanent World's Fair, American industrial giants have built their versions of an unblemished future. These masterful entertainments convey but one message, brilliantly packaged and relentlessly expressed: progress through technology is the solution to all human problems. G.E. proclaims from Horizons: "If we can dream it, we can do it." A.T.&.T. speaks from on high within its giant golf ball: We are now "unbounded by space and time." United Technologies bubbles from the depths of Living Seas: "With the help of modern technology, we feel there's really no limit to what can be accomplished." 1

Yet several of these exhibits at the Experimental Prototype Community of Tomorrow, all predating last year's space disaster, belie their stated message from within by using the launch of the shuttle as a visual metaphor for technological triumph. The Challenger disaster may represent a general malaise, but it remains an incident. The AIDS pandemic, an issue that may rank with nuclear weaponry as the greatest danger of our era, provides a more striking proof that mind and technology are not omnipotent and that we have not canceled our bond to nature. 2

In 1984, John Platt, a biophysicist who taught at the University of Chicago for many years, wrote a short paper for private circulation. 3

At a time when most of us were either ignoring AIDS, or viewing it as a contained and peculiar affliction of homosexual men, Platt recognized that the limited data on the origin of AIDS and its spread in America suggested a more frightening prospect: we are all susceptible to AIDS, and the disease has been spreading in a simple exponential manner.

Exponential growth is a geometric increase. Remember the old kiddy problem: if you place a penny on square one of a checkerboard and double the number of coins on each subsequent square—2, 4, 8, 16, 32 . . . —how big is the stack by the 64th square? The answer: about as high as the universe is wide. Nothing in the external environment inhibits this increase, thus giving to exponential processes their relentless character. In the real, non-infinite world, of course, some limit will eventually arise, and the process slows down, reaches a steady state, or destroys the entire system: the stack of pennies falls over, the bacterial cells exhaust their supply of nutrients.

Platt noticed that data for the initial spread of AIDS fell right on an exponential curve. He then followed the simplest possible procedure of extrapolating the curve unabated into the 1990's. Most of us were incredulous, accusing Platt of the mathematical gamesmanship that scientist call "curve fitting." After all, aren't exponential models unrealistic? Surely we are not all susceptible to AIDS. Is it not spread only by odd practices to odd people? Will it not, therefore, quickly run its short course within a confined group?

Well, hello 1987—worldwide data still match Platt's extrapolated curve. This will not, of course, go on forever. AIDS has probably already saturated the African areas where it probably originated, and where the sex ratio of afflicted people is 1-to-1, male-female. But AIDS still has far to spread, and may be moving exponentially, through the rest of the world. We have learned enough about the cause of AIDS to slow its spread, if we can make rapid and fundamental changes in our handling of that most powerful part of human biology—our own sexuality. But medicine, as yet, has nothing to offer as a cure and precious little even for palliation.

This exponential spread of AIDS not only illuminates its, and our, biology, but also underscores the tragedy of our moralistic misperception. Exponential processes have a definite time and place of origin, an initial point of "inoculation"—in this case, Africa. We didn't notice the spread at first. In a population of billions, we pay little attention when 1 increases to 2, or 8 to 16, but when 1 million becomes 2 million, we panic, even though the *rate* of doubling has not increased.

The infection has to start somewhere, and its initial locus may be little more than an accident of circumstance. For a while, it remains confined to those in close contact with the primary source, but only by accident of proximity, not by intrinsic susceptibility. Eventually, given the power and liability of human sexuality, it spreads outside the initial group and into the general population. And now AIDS has begun its march through our own heterosexual community. 8

What a tragedy that our moral stupidity caused us to lose precious time, the greatest enemy in fighting an exponential spread, by downplaying the danger because we thought that AIDS was a disease of three irregular groups of minorities: minorities of life style (needle users), of sexual preference (homosexuals) and of color (Haitians). If AIDS had first been imported from Africa into a Park Avenue apartment, we would not have dithered as the exponential march began. 9

The message of Orlando—the inevitability of technological solutions—is wrong, and we need to understand why. 10

Our species has not won its independence from nature, and we cannot do all that we can dream. Or at least we cannot do it at the rate required to avoid tragedy, for we are not unbounded from time. Viral diseases are preventable in principle, and I suspect that an AIDS vaccine will one day be produced. But how will this discovery avail us if it takes until the millenium, and by then AIDS has fully run its exponential course and saturated our population, killing a substantial percentage of the human race? A fight against an exponential enemy is primarily a race against time. 11

We must also grasp the perspective of ecology and evolutionary biology and recognize, once we reinsert ourselves properly into nature, that AIDS represents the ordinary workings of biology, not an irrational or diabolical plague with a moral meaning. Disease, including epidemic spread, is a natural phenomenon, part of human history from the beginning. An entire subdiscipline of my profession, paleopathology, studies the evidence of ancient diseases 12 preserved in the fossil remains of organisms. Human history has been marked by episodic plagues. More native peoples died of imported disease than ever fell before the gun during the era of colonial expansion. Our memories are short, and we have had a respite, really, only since the influenza pandemic at the end of World War I, but AIDS must be viewed as a virulent expression of an ordinary natural phenomenon.

I do not say this to foster either comfort or complacency. The evolutionary perspective is correct, but utterly inappropriate for our human scale. Yes, AIDS is a natural phenomenon, one of a recurring class of pandemic diseases. Yes, AIDS may run through the entire population, and may carry off a quarter or more of us. Yes, it may make no *biological* difference to Homo sapiens in the long run: there will still be plenty of us left and we can start again. Evolution cares as little for its agents—organisms struggling for reproductive success—as physics cares for individual atoms of hydrogen in the sun. But we care. These atoms are our neighbors, our lovers, our children and ourselves. AIDS is both a natural phenomenon and, potentially, the greatest natural tragedy in human history.

The cardboard message of Epcot fosters the wrong attitudes; we must both reinsert ourselves into nature and view AIDS as a natural phenomenon in order to fight properly. If we stand above nature and if technology is all-powerful, then AIDS is a horrifying anomaly that must be trying to tell us something. If so, we can adopt one of two attitudes, each potentially fatal. We can either become complacent, because we believe the message of Epcot and assume that medicine will soon generate a cure, or we can panic in confusion and seek a scapegoat for something so irregular that it must have been visited upon us to teach us a moral lesson.

But AIDS is not irregular. It is part of nature. So are we. This should galvanize us and give us hope, not prompt the worst of all responses: a kind of "new-age" negativisim that equates natural with what we must accept and cannot, or even should not, change. When we view AIDS as natural, and when we recognize both the exponential property of its spread and the accidental character of its point of entry into America, we can break through our destructive tendencies to blame others and to free ourselves of concern.

If AIDS is natural, then there is no *message* in its spread. But by all that science has learned and all that rationality proclaims, AIDS works by a *mechanism*—and we can discover it. Victory is not ordained by any principle of progress, or any slogan of technology, so we shall have to fight like hell, and be watchful. There is no message, but there is a mechanism.

QUESTIONS FOR READING AND WRITING

1. What point is Gould making by referring to the optimistic tone of "Epcot technology" in paragraph 1?
2. Is Gould optimistic or pessimistic about our ability to control or to eradicate AIDS?
3. Why is it that AIDS somehow seems more of a problem—in the eyes of the general public—now that the public realizes that the spread of AIDS is not confined to the "minority groups" Gould mentions in paragraph 9? What does he mean by the phrase "our moral stupidity" in paragraph 9?
4. Conduct informal research among your classmates about how the fear of AIDS has affected their sexual behavior. Write an essay that records what you find out.

✦ Martin Luther King ✦
Letter from Birmingham Jail

An American clergyman, writer, and civil-rights leader, Martin Luther King, Jr., (1929–1968) was one of the main forces behind black social activism in the 1960s. He received his Ph.D. in religion from Boston University. In 1963 King, along with some 2400 other protesters, was arrested in Birmingham, Alabama, during racial confrontation there. In jail, King wrote this now-classic essay about the righteousness of defying unjust laws.

April 16, 1963

My Dear Fellow Clergymen:

While confined here in the Birmingham city jail, I came across your recent statement calling my present activities "unwise and untimely." Seldom do I pause to answer criticism of my work and ideas. If I sought to answer all the criticisms that cross my desk, my secretaries would have little time for anything other than such correspondence in the course of the day, and I would have no time for constructive work. But since I feel that you are men of genuine good will and that your criticisms are sincerely set forth, I want to try to answer your statement in what I hope will be patient and reasonable terms.

I think I should indicate why I am here in Birmingham, since you have been influenced by the view which argues against "outsiders coming in." I have the honor of serving as president of the Southern Christian Leadership Conference, an organization operating in every southern state, with headquarters in Atlanta, Georgia. We have some eighty-five affiliated organizations across the South, and

AUTHOR'S NOTE: This response to a published statement by eight fellow clergymen from Alabama (Bishop C. C. J. Carpenter, Bishop Joseph A. Durick, Rabbi Hilton L. Grafman, Bishop Paul Hardin, Bishop Holan B. Harmon, the Reverend George M. Murray, the Reverend Edward V. Ramage and the Reverend Earl Stallings) was composed under somewhat constricting circumstances. Begun on the margins of the newspaper in which the statement appeared while I was in jail, the letter was continued on scraps of writing paper supplied by a friendly Negro trusty, and concluded on a pad my attorneys were eventually permitted to leave me. Although the text remains in substance unaltered, I have indulged in the author's prerogative of polishing it for publication.

one of them is the Alabama Christian Movement for Human Rights. Frequently we share staff, educational and financial resources with our affiliates. Several months ago the affiliate here in Birmingham asked us to be on call to engage in a nonviolent direct-action program if such were deemed necessary. We readily consented, and when the hour came we lived up to our promise. So I, along with several members of my staff, am here because I was invited here. I am here because I have organizational ties here.

But more basically, I am in Birmingham because injustice is here. 3
Just as the prophets of the eighth century B.C. left their villages and carried their "thus saith the Lord" far beyond the boundaries of their home towns, and, just as the Apostle Paul left his village of Tarsus and carried the gospel of Jesus Christ to the far corners of the Greco-Roman world, so am I compelled to carry the gospel of freedom beyond my own home town. Like Paul, I must constantly respond to the Macedonian call for aid.

Moreover, I am cognizant of the interrelatedness of all commu- 4
nities and states. I cannot sit idly by in Atlanta and not be concerned about what happens in Birmingham. Injustice anywhere is a threat to justice everywhere. We are caught in an inescapable network of mutuality, tied in a single garment of destiny. Whatever affects one directly, affects all indirectly. Never again can we afford to live with the narrow, provincial "outside agitator" idea. Anyone who lives inside the United States can never be considered an outsider anywhere within its bounds.

You deplore the demonstrations taking place in Birmingham. But 5
your statement, I am sorry to say, fails to express a similar concern for the conditions that brought about the demonstrations. I am sure that none of you would want to rest content with the superficial kind of social analysis that deals merely with effects and does not grapple with underlying causes. It is unfortunate that demonstrations are taking place in Birmingham, but it is even more unfortunate that the city's white power structure left the Negro community with no alternative.

In any nonviolent campaign there are four basic steps: collection 6
of the facts to determine whether injustices exist; negotiation; self-purification; and direct action. We have gone through all these steps in Birmingham. There can be no gainsaying the fact that racial injustice engulfs this community. Birmingham is probably the most

thoroughly segregated city in the United States. An ugly record of brutality is widely known. Negroes have experienced grossly unjust treatment in the courts. There have been more unsolved bombings of Negro homes and churches in Birmingham than in any other city in the nation. These are the hard brutal facts of the case. On the basis of these conditions, Negro leaders sought to negotiate with the city fathers. But the latter consistently refused to engage in good-faith negotiation.

Then, last September, came the opportunity to talk with leaders of Birmingham's economic community. In the course of the negotiations, certain promises were made by the merchants—for example, to remove the stores' humiliating racial signs. On the basis of these promises, the Reverend Fred Shuttlesworth and the leaders of the Alabama Christian Movement for Human Rights agreed to a moratorium on all demonstrations. As the weeks and months went by, we realized that we were the victims of a broken promise. A few signs, briefly removed, returned; the others remained.

As in so many past experiences, our hopes had been blasted, and the shadow of deep disappointment settled upon us. We had no alternative except to prepare for direct action, whereby we would present our very bodies as a means of laying our case before the conscience of the local and the national community. Mindful of the difficulties involved, we decided to undertake a process of self-purification. We began a series of workshops on nonviolence, and we repeatedly asked ourselves: "Are you able to accept blows without retaliating?" "Are you able to endure the ordeal of jail?" We decided to schedule our direct-action program for the Easter season, realizing that except for Christmas, this is the main shopping period of the year. Knowing that a strong economic-withdrawal program would be the by-product of direct action, we felt that this would be the best time to bring pressure to bear on the merchants for the needed change.

Then it occurred to us that Birmingham's mayoralty election was coming up in March, and we speedily decided to postpone action until after election day. When we discovered that the Commissioner of Public Safety, Eugene "Bull" Connor, had piled up enough votes to be in the run-off, we decided again to postpone action until the day after the run-off so that the demonstrations could not be used to cloud the issues. Like many others, we waited to see Mr. Connor defeated, and to this end we endured postponement after postponement. Having aided in this community need, we felt that our direct-action program could be delayed no longer.

You may well ask: "Why direct action? Why sit-ins, marches and so forth? Isn't negotiation a better path?" You are quite right in calling for negotiation. Indeed, this is the very purpose of direct action. Nonviolent direct action seeks to create such a crisis and foster such a tension that a community which has constantly refused to negotiate is forced to confront the issue. It seeks so to dramatize the issue that it can no longer be ignored. My citing the creation of tension as part of the work of the nonviolent-resister may sound rather shocking. But I must confess that I am not afraid of the word "tension." I have earnestly opposed violent tension, but there is a type of constructive nonviolent tension which is necessary for growth. Just as Socrates felt that it was necessary to create a tension in the mind so that individuals could rise from the bondage of myths and half-truths to the unfettered realm of creative analysis, and objective appraisal, so must we see the need for nonviolent gadflies to create the kind of tension in society that will help men rise from the dark depths of prejudice and racism to the majestic heights of understanding and brotherhood. 10

The purpose of our direct-action program is to create a situation so crisis-packed that it will inevitably open the door to negotiation. I therefore concur with you in your call for negotiation. Too long has our beloved Southland been bogged down in a tragic effort to live in monologue rather than dialogue. 11

One of the basic points in your statement is that the action that I and my associates have taken in Birmingham is untimely. Some have asked: "Why didn't you give the new city administration time to act?" The only answer that I can give to this query is that the new Birmingham administration must be prodded about as much as the outgoing one, before it will act. We are sadly mistaken if we feel that the election of Albert Boutwell as mayor will bring the millennium to Birmingham. While Mr. Boutwell is a much more gentle person than Mr. Connor, they are both segregationists, dedicated to maintenance of the status quo. I have hope that Mr. Boutwell will be reasonable enough to see the futility of massive resistance to desegregation. But he will not see this without pressure from devotees of civil rights. My friends, I must say to you that we have not made a 12 single gain in civil rights without determined legal and nonviolent pressure. Lamentably, it is an historical fact that privileged groups seldom give up their privileges voluntarily. Individuals may see the moral light and voluntarily give up their unjust posture; but, as Reinhold Niebuhr has reminded us, groups tend to be more immoral than individuals.

We know through painful experience that freedom is never voluntarily given by the oppressor; it must be demanded by the oppressed. Frankly, I have yet to engage in a direct-action campaign that was "well timed" in the view of those who have not suffered unduly from the disease of segregation. For years now I have heard the word "Wait!" It rings in the ear of every Negro with piercing familiarity. This "Wait" has almost always meant "Never." We must come to see, with one of our distinguished jurists, that "justice too long delayed is justice denied."

We have waited for more than 340 years for our constitutional and Godgiven rights. The nations of Asia and Africa are moving with jetlike speed toward gaining political independence, but we still creep at horse-and-buggy pace toward gaining a cup of coffee at a lunch counter. Perhaps it is easy for those who have never felt the stinging darts of segregation to say, "Wait." But when you have seen vicious mobs lynch your mothers and fathers at will and drown your sisters and brothers at whim; when you have seen hate-filled policemen curse, kick and even kill your black brothers and sisters; when you see the vast majority of your twenty million Negro brothers smothering in an airtight cage of poverty in the midst of an affluent society; when you suddenly find your tongue twisted and your speech stammering as you seek to explain to your six-year-old daughter why she can't go to the public amusement park that has just been advertised on television, and see tears welling up in her eyes when she is told that Funtown is closed to colored children, and see ominous clouds of inferiority beginning to form in her little mental sky, and see her beginning to distort her personality by developing an unconscious bitterness toward white people; when you have to concoct an answer for a five-year-old son who is asking: "Daddy, why do white people treat colored people so mean?"; when you take a cross-country drive and find it necessary to sleep night after night in the uncomfortable corners of your automobile because no motel will accept you; when you are humiliated day in and day out by nagging signs reading "white" and "colored"; when your first name becomes "nigger," your middle name becomes "boy" (however old you are) and your last name becomes "John," and your wife and mother are never given the respected title "Mrs."; when you are harried by day and haunted by night by the fact that you are a Negro, living constantly at tiptoe stance, never quite knowing what to expect next, and are plagued with inner fears and outer resentments; when you are forever fighting a degenerating sense of "nobodiness"—then you will understand why we find it difficult to wait. There comes a time when the cup of endurance runs over, and men are no longer willing to be plunged into the abyss of despair. I hope, sirs, you can understand our legitimate and unavoidable impatience.

You express a great deal of anxiety over our willingness to break 15
laws. This is certainly a legitimate concern. Since we so diligently urge people to obey the Supreme Court's decision of 1954 outlawing segregation in the public schools, at first glance it may seem rather paradoxical for us consciously to break laws. One may well ask: "How can you advocate breaking some laws and obeying others?" The answer lies in the fact that there are two types of laws: just and unjust. I would be the first to advocate obeying just laws. One has not only a legal but a moral responsibility to obey just laws. Conversely, one has a moral responsibility to disobey unjust laws. I would agree with St. Augustine that "an unjust law is no law at all."

Now, what is the difference between the two? How does one 16
determine whether a law is just or unjust? A just law is a man-made code that squares with the moral law or the law of God. An unjust law is a code that is out of harmony with the moral law. To put it in the terms of St. Thomas Aquinas: An unjust law is a human law that is not rooted in eternal law and natural law. Any law that uplifts human personality is just. Any law that degrades human personality is unjust. All segregation statutes are unjust because segregation distorts the soul and damages the personality. It gives the segregator a false sense of superiority and the segregated a false sense of inferiority. Segregation, to use the terminology of the Jewish philosopher Martin Buber, substitutes an "I-it" relationship for an "I-thou" relationship and ends up relegating persons to the status of things. Hence segregation is not only politically, economically and sociologically unsound, it is morally wrong and sinful. Paul Tillich

has said that sin is separation. Is not segregation an existential expression of man's tragic separation, his awful estrangement, his terrible sinfulness? Thus it is that I can urge men to obey the 1954 decision of the Supreme Court, for it is morally right; and I can urge them to disobey segregation ordinances, for they are morally wrong.

Let us consider a more concrete example of just and unjust laws. An unjust law is a code that a numerical or power majority group compels a minority group to obey but does not make binding on itself. This is *difference* made legal. By the same token, a just law is a code that a majority compels a minority to follow and that it is willing to follow itself. This is *sameness* made legal.

Let me give another explanation. A law is unjust if it is inflicted on a minority that, as a result of being denied the right to vote, had no part in enacting or devising the law. Who can say that the legislature of Alabama which set up that state's segregation laws was democratically elected? Throughout Alabama all sorts of devious methods are used to prevent Negroes from becoming registered voters, and there are some counties in which even though Negroes constitute a majority of the population, not a single Negro is registered. Can any law enacted under such circumstances be considered democratically structured?

Sometimes a law is just on its face and unjust in its application. For instance, I have been arrested on a charge of parading without a permit. Now, there is nothing wrong in having an ordinance which requires a permit for a parade. But such an ordinance becomes unjust when it is used to maintain segregation and to deny citizens the First-Amendment privilege of peaceful assembly and protest.

I hope you are able to see the distinction I am trying to point out. In no sense do I advocate evading or defying the law, as would the rabid segregationist. That would lead to anarchy. One who breaks an unjust law must do so openly, lovingly, and with a willingness to accept the penalty. I submit that an individual who breaks a law that conscience tells him is unjust, and who willingly accepts the penalty of imprisonment in order to arouse the conscience of the community over its injustice, is in reality expressing the highest respect for law.

Of course, there is nothing new about this kind of civil disobedience. It was evidenced sublimely in the refusal of Shadrach, Meshach and Abednego to obey the laws of Nebuchadnezzar, on the ground that a higher moral law was at stake. It was practiced superbly by the early Christians, who were willing to face hungry lions and the excruciating pain of chopping blocks rather than submit to certain unjust laws of the Roman Empire. To a degree, academic freedom is a reality today because Socrates practiced civil disobedience. In our own nation, the Boston Tea Party represented a massive act of civil disobedience.

We should never forget that everything Adolf Hitler did in Germany was "legal" and everything the Hungarian freedom fighters did in Hungary was "illegal." It was "illegal" to aid and comfort a Jew in Hitler's Germany. Even so, I am sure that, had I lived in Germany at the time, I would have aided and comforted my Jewish brothers. If today I lived in a Communist country where certain principles dear to the Christian faith are suppressed, I would openly advocate disobeying that country's antireligious laws. 22

I must make two honest confessions to you, my Christian and Jewish brothers. First, I must confess that over the past few years I have been gravely disappointed with the white moderate. I have almost reached the regrettable conclusion that the Negro's great stumbling block in his stride toward freedom is not the White Citizen's Counciler or the Ku Klux Klanner, but the white moderate, who is more devoted to "order" than to justice; who prefers a negative peace which is the absence of tension to a positive peace which is the presence of justice; who constantly says: "I agree with you in the goal you seek, but I cannot agree with your methods of direct action"; who paternalistically believes he can set the timetable for another man's freedom; who lives by a mythical concept of time and who constantly advises the Negro to wait for a "more convenient season." Shallow understanding from people of good will is more frustrating than absolute misunderstanding from people of ill will. Lukewarm acceptance is much more bewildering than outright rejection. 23

I had hoped that the white moderate would understand that law and order exist for the purpose of establishing justice and that when they fail in this purpose they become the dangerously structured dams that block the flow of social progress. I had hoped that the white moderate would understand that the present tension in the South is a necessary phase of the transition from an obnoxious negative peace, in which the Negro passively accepted his unjust plight, to a substantive and positive peace, in which all men will 24 respect the dignity and worth of human personality. Actually, we who engage in nonviolent direct action are not the creators of tension. We merely bring to the surface the hidden tension that is already alive. We bring it out in the open, where it can be seen and dealt with. Like a boil that can never be cured so long as it is covered up but must be opened with all its ugliness to the natural medicines of air and light, injustice must be exposed, with all the tension its exposure creates, to the light of human conscience and the air of national opinion before it can be cured.

In your statement you assert that our actions, even though peaceful, must be condemned because they precipitate violence. But is this a logical assertion? Isn't this like condemning a robbed man because his possession of money precipitated the evil act of robbery? Isn't this like condemning Socrates because his unswerving commitment to truth and his philosophical inquiries precipitated the act by the misguided populace in which they made him drink hemlock? Isn't this like condemning Jesus because his unique God-consciousness and never-ceasing devotion to God's will precipitated the evil act of crucifixion? We must come to see that, as the federal courts have consistently affirmed, it is wrong to urge an individual to cease his efforts to gain his basic constitutional rights because the quest may precipitate violence. Society must protect the robbed and punish the robber.

I had also hoped that the white moderate would reject the myth concerning time in relation to the struggle for freedom. I have just received a letter from a white brother in Texas. He writes: "All Christians know that the colored people will receive equal rights eventually, but it is possible that you are in too great a religious hurry. It has taken Christianity almost two thousand years to accomplish what it has. The teachings of Christ take time to come to earth." Such an attitude stems from a tragic misconception of time, from the strangely irrational notion that there is something in the very flow of time that will inevitably cure all ills. Actually, time itself is neutral; it can be used either destructively or constructively. More and more I feel that the people of ill will have used time much more effectively than have the people of good will. We will have to repent in this generation not merely for the hateful words and actions of the bad people but for the appalling silence of the good people. Human progress never rolls in on wheels of inevitability; it comes through the tireless efforts of men willing to be co-workers with God, and without his hard work, time itself becomes an ally of the forces of social stagnation. We must use time creatively, in the knowledge that the time is always ripe to do right. Now is the time to make real the promise of democracy and transform our pending national elegy into a creative psalm of brotherhood. Now is the time to lift our national policy from the quicksand of racial injustice to the solid rock of human dignity.

You speak of our activity in Birmingham as extreme. At first I was 27
rather disappointed that fellow clergymen would see my nonviolent efforts as those of an extremist. I began thinking about the fact that I stand in the middle of two opposing forces in the Negro community. One is a force of complacency, made up in part of Negroes who, as a result of long years of oppression, are so drained of self-respect and a sense of "somebodiness" that they have adjusted to segregation; and in part of a few middle-class Negroes who, because of a degree of academic and economic security and because in some ways they profit by segregation, have become insensitive to the problems of the masses. The other force is one of bitterness and hatred, and it comes perilously close to advocating violence. It is expressed in the various black nationalist groups that are springing up across the nation, the largest and best-known being Elijah Muhammad's Muslim movement. Nourished by the Negro's frustration over the continued existence of racial discrimination, this movement is made up of people who have lost faith in America, who have absolutely repudiated Christianity, and who have concluded that the white man is an incorrigible "devil."

I have tried to stand between these two forces, saying that we 28
need emulate neither the "do-nothingism" of the complacent nor the hatred and despair of the black nationalist. For there is the more excellent way of love and nonviolent protest. I am grateful to God that, through the influence of the Negro church, the way of nonviolence became an integral part of our struggle.

If this philosophy had not emerged, by now many streets of the 29
South would, I am convinced, be flowing with blood. And I am further convinced that if our white brothers dismiss as "rabble-rousers" and "outside agitators" those of us who employ nonviolent direct action, and if they refuse to support our nonviolent efforts, millions of Negroes will, out of frustration and despair, seek solace

and security in black-nationalist ideologies—a development that would inevitably lead to a frightening racial nightmare.

Oppressed people cannot remain oppressed forever. The yearning for freedom eventually manifests itself, and that is what has happened to the American Negro. Something within has reminded him of his birthright of freedom, and something without has reminded him that it can be gained. Consciously or unconsciously, he has been caught up by the *Zeitgeist*, and with his black brothers of Africa and his brown and yellow brothers of Asia, South America and the Caribbean, the United States Negro is moving with a sense of great urgency toward the promised land of racial justice. If one recognizes this vital urge that has engulfed the Negro community, one should readily understand why public demonstrations are taking place. The Negro has many pent-up resentments and latent frustrations, and he must release them. So let him march; let him make prayer pilgrimages to the city hall; let him go on freedom rides—and try to understand why he must do so. If his repressed emotions are not released in nonviolent ways, they will seek expression through violence; this is not a threat but a fact of history. So I have not said to my people: "Get rid of your discontent." Rather, I have tried to say that this normal and healthy discontent can be channeled into the creative outlet of nonviolent direct action. And now this approach is being termed extremist.

But though I was initially disappointed at being categorized as an extremist, as I continued to think about the matter I gradually gained a measure of satisfaction from the label. Was not Jesus an extremist for love: "Love your enemies, bless them that curse you, do good to them that hate you, and pray for them which despitefully use you, and persecute you." Was not Amos an extremist for justice: "Let justice roll down like waters and righteousness like an ever-flowing stream." Was not Paul an extremist for the Christian gospel: "I bear in my body the marks of the Lord Jesus." Was not Martin Luther an extremist: "Here I stand; I cannot do otherwise, so help me God." And John Bunyan: "I will stay in jail to the end of my days before I make a butchery of my conscience." And Abraham Lincoln: "This nation cannot survive half slave and half free." And Thomas Jefferson: "We hold these truths to be self-evident, that all men are created equal. . . . " So the question is not whether we will be extremists, but what kind of extremists we will be. Will we be extremists for hate or for love? Will we be extremists for the preservation of injustice or for the extension of justice? In that dramatic scene on Calvary's hill three men were crucified. We must never forget that all three were crucified for the same crime—the crime of extremism. Two were extremists for immorality, and thus fell below their environment. The other, Jesus Christ, was an extremist for love, truth and goodness, and thereby rose above his environment. Perhaps the South, the nation and the world are in dire need of creative extremists.

I had hoped that the white moderate would see this need. Per- 32
haps I was too optimistic; perhaps I expected too much. I suppose I should have realized that few members of the oppressor race can understand the deep groans and passionate yearnings of the oppressed race, and still fewer have the vision to see that injustice must be rooted out by strong, persistent and determined action. I am thankful, however, that some of our white brothers in the South have grasped the meaning of this social revolution and committed themselves to it. They are still all too few in quantity, but they are big in quality. Some—such as Ralph McGill, Lillian Smith, Harry Golden, James McBride Dabbs, Ann Braden and Sarah Patton Boyle—have written about our struggle in eloquent and prophetic terms. Others have marched with us down nameless streets of the South. They have languished in filthy, roach- infested jails, suffering the abuse and brutality of policemen who view them as "dirty nigger-lovers." Unlike so many of their moderate brothers and sisters, they have recognized the urgency of the moment and sensed the need for powerful "action" antidotes to combat the disease of segregation.

Let me take note of my other major disappointment. I have been 33
so greatly disappointed with the white church and its leadership. Of course, there are some notable exceptions. I am not unmindful of the fact that each of you has taken some significant stands on this issue. I commend you, Reverend Stallings, for your Christian stand on this past Sunday, in welcoming Negroes to your worship service on a nonsegregated basis. I commend the Catholic leaders of this state for integrating Spring Hill College several years ago.

But despite these notable exceptions, I must honestly reiterate 34
that I have been disappointed with the church. I do not say this as one of those negative critics who can always find something wrong

with the church. I say this as a minister of the gospel, who loves the church; who was nurtured in its bosom; who has been sustained by its spiritual blessings and who will remain true to it as long as the cord of life shall lengthen.

When I was suddenly catapulted into the leadership of the bus protest in Montgomery, Alabama, a few years ago, I felt we would be supported by the white church. I felt that the white ministers, priests and rabbis of the South would be among our strongest allies. Instead, some have been outright opponents, refusing to understand the freedom movement and misrepresenting its leaders; all too many others have been more cautious than courageous and have remained silent behind the anesthetizing security of stained-glass windows.

In spite of my shattered dreams, I came to Birmingham with the hope that the white religious leadership of this community would see the justice of our cause and, with deep moral concern, would serve as the channel through which our just grievances could reach the power structure. I had hoped that each of you would understand. But again I have been disappointed.

I have heard numerous southern religious leaders admonish their worshipers to comply with a desegregation decision because it is the law, but I have longed to hear white ministers declare: "Follow this decree because integration is morally right and because the Negro is your brother." In the midst of blatant injustices inflicted upon the Negro, I have watched white churchmen stand on the sideline and mouth pious irrelevancies and sanctimonious trivialities. In the midst of a mighty struggle to rid our nation of racial and economic injustice, I have heard many ministers say: "Those are social issues, with which the gospel has no real concern." And I have watched many churches commit themselves to a completely other-worldly religion which makes a strange, un-Biblical distinction between body and soul, between the sacred and the secular.

I have traveled the length and breadth of Alabama, Mississippi and all the other southern states. On sweltering summer days and crisp autumn mornings I have looked at the South's beautiful churches with their lofty spires pointing heavenward. I have beheld the impressive outlines of her massive religious-education buildings. Over and over I have found myself asking: "What kind of people worship here? Who is their God? Where were their voices when the lips of Governor Barnett dripped with words of interposition and nullification? Where were they when Governor Wallace gave a clarion call for defiance and hatred? Where were their voices of support when bruised and weary Negro men and women decided to rise from the dark dungeons of complacency to the bright hills of creative protest?"

Yes, these questions are still in my mind. In deep disappointment 39
I have wept over the laxity of the church. But be assured that my tears have been tears of love. There can be no deep disappointment where there is not deep love. Yes, I love the church. How could I do otherwise? I am in the rather unique position of being the son, the grandson and the great-grandson of preachers. Yes, I see the church as the body of Christ. But, oh! How we have blemished and scarred that body through social neglect and through fear of being nonconformists.

There was a time when the church was very powerful—in the 40
time when the early Christians rejoiced at being deemed worthy to suffer for what they believed. In those days the church was not merely a thermometer that recorded the ideas and principles of popular opinion; it was a thermostat that transformed the mores of society. Whenever the early Christians entered a town, the people in power became disturbed and immediately sought to convict the Christians for being "disturbers of the peace" and "outside agitators." But the Christians pressed on, in the conviction that they were "a colony of heaven," called to obey God rather than man. Small in number, they were big in commitment. They were too God-intoxicated to be "astronomically intimidated." By their effort and example they brought an end to such ancient evils as infanticide and gladiatorial contests.

Things are different now. So often the contemporary church is a 41
weak, ineffectual voice with an uncertain sound. So often it is an archdefender of the status quo. Far from being disturbed by the presence of the church, the power structure of the average community is consoled by the church's silent—and often even vocal—sanction of things as they are.

But the judgment of God is upon the church as never before. If 42
today's church does not recapture the sacrificial spirit of the early church, it will lose its authenticity, forfeit the loyalty of millions, and

be dismissed as an irrelevant social club with no meaning for the twentieth century. Every day I meet young people whose disappointment with the church has turned into outright disgust.

Perhaps I have once again been too optimistic. Is organized religion too inextricably bound to the status quo to save our nation and the world? Perhaps I must turn my faith to the inner spiritual church, the church within the church, as the true *ekklesia* and the hope of the world. But again I am thankful to God that some noble souls from the ranks of organized religion have broken loose from the paralyzing chains of conformity and joined us as active partners in the struggle for freedom. They have left their secure congregations and walked the streets of Albany, Georgia, with us. They have gone down the highways of the South on tortuous rides for freedom. Yes, they have gone to jail with us. Some have been dismissed from their churches, have lost the support of their bishops and fellow ministers. But they have acted in the faith that right defeated is stronger than evil triumphant. Their witness has been the spiritual salt that has preserved the true meaning of the gospel in these troubled times. They have carved a tunnel of hope through the dark mountain of disappointment.

I hope the church as a whole will meet the challenge of this decisive hour. But even if the church does not come to the aid of justice, I have no despair about the future. I have no fear about the outcome of our struggle in Birmingham, even if our motives are at present misunderstood. We will reach the goal of freedom in Birmingham and all over the nation, because the goal of America is freedom. Abused and scorned though we may be, our destiny is tied up with America's destiny. Before the pilgrims landed at Plymouth, we were here. Before the pen of Jefferson etched the majestic words of the Declaration of Independence across the pages of history, we were here. For more than two centuries our forebears labored in this country without wages; they made cotton king; they built the homes of their masters while suffering gross injustice and shameful humiliation—and yet out of a bottomless vitality they continued to thrive and develop. If the inexpressible cruelties of slavery could not stop us, the opposition we now face will surely fail. We will win our freedom because the sacred heritage of our nation and the eternal will of God are embodied in our echoing demands.

Before closing I feel impelled to mention one other point in your 45
statement that has troubled me profoundly. You warmly commended the Birmingham police force for keeping "order" and "preventing violence." I doubt that you would have so warmly commended the police force if you had seen its dogs sinking their teeth into unarmed, nonviolent Negroes. I doubt that you would so quickly commend the policemen if you were to observe their ugly and inhumane treatment of Negroes here in the city jail; if you were to watch them push and curse old Negro women and young Negro girls; if you were to see them slap and kick old Negro men and young boys; if you were to observe them as they did on two occasions, refuse to give us food because we wanted to sing our grace together. I cannot join you in your praise of the Birmingham police department.

It is true that the police have exercised a degree of discipline in 46
handling the demonstrators. In this sense they have conducted themselves rather "nonviolently" in public. But for what purpose? To preserve the evil system of segregation. Over the past few years I have consistently preached that nonviolence demands that the means we use must be as a pure as the ends we seek. I have tried to make clear that it is wrong to use immoral means to attain moral ends. But now I must affirm that it is just as wrong, or perhaps even more so, to use moral means to preserve immoral ends. Perhaps Mr. Connor and his policemen have been rather nonviolent in public, as was Chief Pritchett in Albany, Georgia, but they have used the moral means of nonviolence to maintain the immoral end of racial injustice. As T. S. Eliot has said: "The last temptation is the greatest treason: To do the right deed for the wrong reason."

I wish you had commended the Negro sit-inners and demonstra- 47
tors of Birmingham for their sublime courage, their willingness to suffer and their amazing discipline in the midst of great provocation. One day the South will recognize its real heroes. They will be the James Merediths, with the noble sense of purpose that enables them to face jeering and hostile mobs, and with the agonizing loneliness that characterizes the life of the pioneer. They will be old, oppressed, battered Negro women, symbolized in a seventy-two-year-old woman in Montgomery, Alabama, who rose up with a sense of dignity and with her people decided not to ride segregated buses,

and who responded with ungrammatical profundity to one who inquired about her weariness: "My feet is tired, but my soul is at rest." They will be the young high school and college students, the young ministers of the gospel and a host of their elders, courageously and nonviolently sitting in at lunch counters and willingly going to jail for conscience' sake. One day the South will know that when these disinherited children of God sat down at lunch counters, they were in reality standing up for what is best in the American dream and for the most sacred values in our Judaeo-Christian heritage, thereby bringing our nation back to those great wells of democracy which were dug deep by the founding fathers in their formulation of the Constitution and the Declaration of Independence.

Never before have I written so long a letter. I'm afraid it is much too long to take your precious time. I can assure you that it would have been much shorter if I had been writing from a comfortable desk, but what else can one do when he is alone in a narrow jail cell, other than write long letters, think long thoughts and pray long prayers?

If I have said anything in this letter that overstates the truth and indicates an unreasonable impatience, I beg you to forgive me. If I have said anything that understates the truth and indicates my having a patience that allows me to settle for anything less than brotherhood, I beg God to forgive me.

I hope this letter finds you strong in the faith. I also hope that circumstances will soon make it possible for me to meet each of you, not as an integrationist or a civil-rights leader but as a fellow clergyman and a Christian brother. Let us all hope that the dark clouds of racial prejudice will soon pass away and the deep fog of misunderstanding will be lifted from our fear-drenched communities, and in some not too distant tomorrow the radiant stars of love and brotherhood will shine over our great nation with all their scintillating beauty.

Yours for the cause of Peace and Brotherhood,
Martin Luther King, Jr.

QUESTIONS FOR READING AND WRITING

1. Many of the specific laws that King objected to in this essay have long been overturned. In what ways, though, has the essay retained its relevance? How might it still be of interest to black and white readers concerned about racial equality?
2. Reexamine the long sentence in paragraph 14. How does King make such a long sentence coherent?
3. In paragraph 31, what is the effect of King's appeal to famous figures from the Bible and from American history?
4. In paragraphs 16–19, King cites four ways of distinguishing just laws from unjust ones. What are they?
5. King's essay can be roughly divided into eight sections: paragraphs 1–5, 6–11, 12–14, 15–22, 23–32, 33–44, 45–47, and 48–50. Show the unifying ideas of each of these eight sections.
6. In his author's note at the beginning of the essay, King says he is responding to a published statement by eight clergymen. Write an essay in which you work backward from King's letter to infer what the clergymen said.
7. Pick a local or national issue about which you feel strongly, but about which you hold an unpopular position. Compose a letter to your school newspaper in which you state your unpopular views.

✦ Edward I. Koch ✦
Death and Justice

After serving in the United States House of Representatives, Edward I. Koch (b. 1924) was mayor of New York City from 1978 until 1990. He has published two books: Mayor *(1985, with William Rauch) and* Politics *(1986). A staunch advocate of the death penalty, Koch published the following article in* The New Republic *in 1985. In this essay, he advances his opinions about the death penalty by refuting the major positions held by those who oppose it.*

LAST DECEMBER A MAN NAMED ROBERT LEE WILLIE, who had been convicted of raping and murdering an 18-year-old woman, was executed in the Louisiana state prison. In a statement issued several minutes before his death, Mr. Willie said: "Killing people is wrong. . . . It makes no difference whether it's citizens, countries, or governments. Killing is wrong." Two weeks later in South Carolina, an admitted killer named Joseph Carl Shaw was put to death for murdering two teenagers. In an appeal to the governor for clemency, Mr. Shaw wrote: "Killing is wrong when I did it. Killing is wrong when you do it. I hope you have the courage and moral strength to stop the killing."

It is a curiosity of modern life that we find ourselves being lectured on morality by cold-blooded killers. Mr. Willie previously had been convicted of aggravated rape, aggravated kidnapping, and the murders of a Louisiana deputy and a man from Missouri. Mr. Shaw committed another murder a week before the two for which he was executed, and admitted mutilating the body of the 14-year-old girl he killed. I can't help wondering what prompted these murderers to speak out against killing as they entered the death-house door. Did their newfound reverence for life stem from the realization that they were about to lose their own?

Life is indeed precious, and I believe the death penalty helps to affirm this fact. Had the death penalty been a real possibility in the minds of these murderers, they might well have stayed their hand. They might have shown moral awareness before their victims died, and not after. Consider the tragic death of Rosa Velez, who happened to be home when a man named Luis Vera burglarized her apartment in Brooklyn. "Yeah, I shot her," Vera admitted. "She knew me, and I knew I wouldn't go to the chair."

During my 22 years in public service, I have heard the pros and cons of capital punishment expressed with special intensity. As a district leader, councilman, congressman, and mayor, I have represented constituencies generally thought of as liberal. Because I support the death penalty for heinous crimes of murder, I have sometimes been the subject of emotional and outraged attacks by voters who find my position reprehensible or worse. I have listened to their ideas. I have weighed their objections carefully. I still support the death penalty. The reasons I maintain my position can be best understood by examining the arguments most frequently heard in opposition. 4

(1) *The death penalty is "barbaric."* Sometimes opponents of capital punishment horrify with tales of lingering death on the gallows, of faulty electric chairs, or of agony in the gas chamber. Partly in response to such protests, several states such as North Carolina and Texas switched to execution by lethal injection. The condemned person is put to death painlessly, without ropes, voltage, bullets, or gas. Did this answer the objections of death penalty opponents. Of course not. On June 22, 1984, *The New York Times* published an editorial that sarcastically attacked the new "hygienic" method of death by injection, and stated that "execution can never be made humane through science." So it's not the method that really troubles opponents. It's the death itself they consider barbaric. 5

Admittedly, capital punishment is not a pleasant topic. However, one does not have to like the death penalty in order to support it any more than one must like radical surgery, radiation, or chemotherapy in order to find necessary these attempts at curing cancer. Ultimately we may learn how to cure cancer with a simple pill. Unfortunately, that day has not yet arrived. Today we are faced with the choice of letting the cancer spread or trying to cure it with the methods available, methods that one day will almost certainly be considered barbaric. But to give up and do nothing would be far more barbaric and would certainly delay the discovery of an eventual cure. The analogy between cancer and murder is imperfect, because murder is not the "disease" we are trying to cure. The disease is injustice. We may not like the death penalty, but it must 6 be available to punish crimes of cold-blooded murder, cases in which any other form of punishment would be inadequate and, therefore, unjust. If we create a society in which injustice is not tolerated, incidents of murder—the most flagrant form of injustice—will diminish.

(2) *No other major democracy uses the death penalty.* No other major democracy—in fact, few other countries of any description—are plagued by a murder rate such as that in the United States. Fewer and fewer Americans can remember the days when unlocked doors were the norm and murder was a rare and terrible offense. In America the murder rate climbed 122 percent between 1963 and 1980. During that same period, the murder rate in New York City increased by almost 400 percent, and the statistics are even worse in many other cities. A study at M.I.T. showed that based on 1970 homicide rates a person who lived in a large American city ran a greater risk of being murdered than an American soldier in World War II ran of being killed in combat. It is not surprising that the laws of each country differ according to differing conditions and traditions. If other countries had our murder problem, the cry for capital punishment would be just as loud as it is here. And I daresay that any other major democracy where 75 percent of the people supported the death penalty would soon enact it into law.

(3) *An innocent person might be executed by mistake.* Consider the work of Adam Bedau, one of the most implacable foes of capital punishment in this country. According to Mr. Bedau, it is "false sentimentality to argue that the death penalty should be abolished because of the abstract possibility that an innocent person might be executed." He cites a study of the 7,000 executions in this country from 1893 to 1971, and concludes that the record fails to show that such cases occur. The main point, however, is this. If government functioned only when the possibility of error didn't exist, government wouldn't function at all. Human life deserves special protection, and one of the best ways to guarantee that protection is to assure that convicted murderers do not kill again. Only the death penalty can accomplish this end. In a recent case in New Jersey, a man named Richard Biegenwald was freed from prison after serving 18 years for murder; since his release he has been convicted of committing four murders. A prisoner named Lemuel Smith, who,

while serving four life sentences for murder (plus two life sentences for kidnapping and robbery) in New York's Green Haven Prison, lured a woman corrections officer into the chaplain's office and strangled her. He then mutilated and dismembered her body. An additional life sentence for Smith is meaningless. Because New York has no death penalty statute, Smith has effectively been given a license to kill.

But the problem of multiple murder is not confined to the nation's penitentiaries. In 1981, 91 police officers were killed in the line of duty in this country. Seven percent of those arrested in the cases that have been solved had a previous arrest for murder. In New York City in 1976 and 1977, 85 persons arrested for homicide had a previous arrest for murder. Six of these individuals had two previous arrests for murder, and one had four previous murder arrests. During those two years the New York police were arresting for murder persons with a previous arrest for murder on the average of one every 8.5 days. This is not surprising when we learn that in 1975, for example, the median time served in Massachusetts for homicide was less than two-and-a-half years. In 1976 a study sponsored by the Twentieth Century Fund found that the average time served in the United States for first-degree murder is ten years. The median time served may be considerably lower. 9

(4) *Capital punishment cheapens the value of human life.* On the contrary, it can be easily demonstrated that the death penalty strengthens the value of human life. If the penalty for rape were lowered, clearly it would signal a lessened regard for the victims' suffering, humiliation, and personal integrity. It would cheapen their horrible experience, and expose them to an increased danger of recurrence. When we lower the penalty for murder, it signals a lessened regard for the value of the victim's life. Some critics of capital punishment, such as columnist Jimmy Breslin, have suggested that a life sentence is actually a harsher penalty for murder than death. This is sophistic nonsense. A few killers may decide not to appeal a death sentence, but the overwhelming majority make every effort to stay alive. It is by exacting the highest penalty for the taking of human life that we affirm the highest value of human life. 10

(5) *The death penalty is applied in a discriminatory manner.* This factor no longer seems to be the problem it once was. The appeals process for a condemned prisoner is lengthy and painstaking. Every 11

effort is made to see that the verdict and sentence were fairly arrived at. However, assertions of discrimination are not an argument for ending the death penalty but for extending it. It is not justice to exclude everyone from the penalty of the law if a few are found to be so favored. Justice requires that the law be applied equally to all.

(6) *Thou Shalt Not Kill*. The Bible is our greatest source of moral inspiration. Opponents of the death penalty frequently cite the sixth of the Ten Commandments in an attempt to prove that capital punishment is divinely proscribed. In the original Hebrew, however, the Sixth Commandment reads, "Thou shalt Not Commit Murder," and the Torah specifies capital punishment for a variety of offenses. The biblical viewpoint has been upheld by philosophers throughout history. The greatest thinkers of the 19th century—Kant, Locke, Hobbes, Rousseau, Montesquieu, and Mill—agreed that natural law properly authorizes the sovereign to take life in order to vindicate justice. Only Jeremy Bentham was ambivalent. Washington, Jefferson, and Franklin endorsed it. Abraham Lincoln authorized executions for deserters in wartime. Alexis de Tocqueville, who expressed profound respect for American institutions, believed that the death penalty was indispensable to the support of social order. The United States Constitution, widely admired as one of the seminal achievements in the history of humanity, condemns cruel and inhuman punishment, but does not condemn capital punishment.

(7) *The death penalty is state-sanctioned murder*. This is the defense with which Messrs. Willie and Shaw hoped to soften the resolve of those who sentenced them to death. By saying in effect, "You're no better than I am," the murderer seeks to bring his accusers down to his own level. It is also a popular argument among opponents of capital punishment, but a transparently false one. Simply put, the state has rights that the private individual does not. In a democracy, those rights are given to the state by the electorate. The execution of a lawfully condemned killer is no more an act of murder than is legal imprisonment an act of kidnapping. If an individual forces a neighbor to pay him money under threat of punishment, it's called extortion. If the state does it, it's called taxation. Rights and responsibilities surrendered by the individual

are what give the state its power to govern. This contract is the foundation of civilization itself.

Everyone wants his or her rights, and will defend them jealously. Not everyone, however, wants responsibilities, especially the painful responsibilities that come with law enforcement. Twenty-one years ago a woman named Kitty Genovese was assaulted and murdered on a street in New York. Dozens of neighbors heard her cries for help but did nothing to assist her. They didn't even call the police. In such a climate the criminal understandably grows bolder. In the presence of moral cowardice, he lectures us on our supposed failings and tries to equate his crimes with our quest for justice. 14

The death of anyone—even a convicted killer—diminishes us all. But we are diminished even more by a justice system that fails to function. It is an illusion to let ourselves believe that doing away with capital punishment removes the murderer's deed from our conscience. The rights of society are paramount. When we protect guilty lives, we give up innocent lives in exchange. When opponents of capital punishment say to the state: "I will not let you kill in my name," they are also saying to murderers: "You can kill in your *own* name as long as I have an excuse for not getting involved." 15

It is hard to imagine anything worse than being murdered while neighbors do nothing. But something worse exists. When those same neighbors shrink back from justly punishing the murderer, the victim dies twice. 16

QUESTIONS FOR READING AND WRITING

1. For what purposes does Koch quote the words of condemned killers?
2. Evaluate the analogy Koch uses in paragraph 6. How is injustice like cancer?
3. Do you agree with Koch's assertion in paragraph 8 that only the death penalty can ensure that murderers do not murder again? Is this necessarily a convincing argument for instituting the death penalty?
4. Why, in paragraph 12, does Koch cite a long list of literary, philosophical, and political authorities?
5. Write an essay that shows how Koch would attack the views of Clarence Darrow in "The Futility of the Death Penalty."

✦ Lisa Peattie ✦

Normalizing the Unthinkable

Lisa Peattie (b. 1924) is a professor of urban anthropology at the Massachusetts Institute of Technology. Her books include Women's Claims: A Study of Political Economy *(coauthor, 1983) and* Making Work *(1983). In the following essay, which originally appeared in 1984 in* Bulletin of Atomic Scientists, *she describes the human ability (or tendency) to continue "normal" life in the face of outrageous situations or possibilities, including the threat of nuclear war.*

AN ENVIRONMENTAL PROTECTION AGENCY STUDY of "Evacuation Risks" argues energetically against the "panic image" of human behavior in an emergency situation: "People will often stay in a potentially threatening situation rather than move out of it," the report declares. "Human beings have very strong tendencies to continue on-going lines of behavior in preference to initiating new courses of action."

Current planning for the management of a nuclear war in itself constitutes an exemplary confirmation of this principle. The situation which the planners address is the most dreadful conceivable. It involves at the minimum the deaths of a substantial number of the human beings whom we love and with whom we share a common fate, the destruction of the physical places where we live and to which we are attached, the disorganization of our society. It may mean the end of human life on Earth, and thus the very sensibleness of planning. But the tone of the planning studies is entirely normal and normalizing.

One approach is to work from analogies with the familiar. A study of the consequences of "incidents" involving nuclear power plants draws from human actions and reactions in floods, fires, and earthquakes. The data are deaths from motor vehicle accidents; costs for food and housing; salaries and wages for national guardsmen, policemen and firemen; loss of wages per day per evacuee. Such analogies appear also in planning for nuclear war.

Nuclear war, however, even in the world of civil defense research, appears somewhat off the scale of analysis of analogy to the ordinary. Therefore resort is made to rendering the situation playfully, via models and games. One study, for example, declares that "Like war games and business games the post-attack problems for which a single city model might be used are characterized by both rich environments and incomplete sets of decision rules." Such a gaming approach deals in "weapon impacts," "resource availability," "cumulating costs of items or modules damaged beyond repair," and "vulnerability indexes." Dividing reduced resources by a greatly reduced population, it is possible to conclude that "Considering resources alone, a moderate level attack on the nation might reduce consumption to the equivalent of that of the Great Depression."

The principle is correct. There appears to be no situation so abnormal—experientially, socially, morally—that human beings, if not totally stunned out of all reactivity, will not at least strive to assimilate it to normal practice. 5

Even at Hiroshima, there became apparent a certain mad orderliness which we might interpret as the behavioral counterpart of the intellectual processes which would equate the effects of nuclear war with those of the Great Depression: 6

> Those who were able walked silently towards the suburbs and the distant hills. . . . They were so broken and confused that they moved and behaved like automatons. Their reactions had astonished outsiders who reported with amazement the spectacle of long files of people holding stolidly to a narrow, rough path when close by was a smooth, easy road going in the same direction. The outsiders could not grasp the fact that they were witnessing the exodus of a people who walked in the realm of dreams.

Let us consider what we know of human behavior in the concentration camp. Jean François Steiner's account of life in Treblinka describes how, even as the scale and atrociousness of the extermination process advanced, the institutions and social organization of the camp came more and more to parallel those of a normal society. The technology improved; the original clumsy experiments with killing Jews by exhaust fumes in the trucks which brought them from Warsaw were supplanted by the developed technology of the gas chambers. The Germans found it inconvenient to work with a perpetually inexperienced labor force. Thus, from an initial strategy of gassing those who had been forced to strip their fellow victims of 7 clothing, valuables, hair, and gold teeth, they established a set of longer-term workers who would only at extended intervals be sent to the chambers.

Relationships, both bureaucratic and personal, came into being. The longer-term inmates found particular niches in the organization and learned to work the system for their own personal well-being and protection and, when they could, to protect their friends. A prisoners' orchestra was formed, and when the trains unloaded a new set of victims, musicians were pulled out of the ranks to join the music makers. Prizefights became another form of entertainment, and another principle of selection. A park and zoo were built.

Toward the end, when the Germans began to realize that they were likely to lose the war, a goal became that of concealing the evidence. The prisoner-workers were set to digging up, by heavy machinery, bodies which had been piled into deep pits, so that they could be burnt. It took a little time to evolve the techniques for cremating this mountain of bodies, but eventually a regular procedure was developed, and the slow, smoky burning of the old bodies became part of the normal functioning of the camp.

Meanwhile, a new institution came into being: a cabaret, shared by the Germans and some of the more established, and therefore privileged, inmates. Weddings were held and celebrated with festivities.

In the latter period of the camp's operation, the long-term inmates, now able to function on a more extended basis, began to organize an uprising. In Steiner's account of this process—which ended with a bloody battle and the capture and death of almost all of those prisoners who had escaped—the most painful part of the story is the difficulty experienced by the leaders in starting the revolt.

They kept putting it off, although they knew that time was running out for them. They made calculations: the original Jewish population of Warsaw; the thousands who passed through the gas chambers; the numbers that must be left; the weeks it would take to process the remaining Jews into extinction. They knew that at the moment the death factory ran out of raw material they too would go into the gas chambers. But no given day seemed quite right. Steiner wrote that it was as though they were stuck in a dream: the dream of the daily routine, of the normality of ordinary behavior. The camp, with its bureaucracy, its personalities, its roles, its smoking bodies, had become normal.

Steiner's description of Treblinka is particularly rich in recording 13
the normalizing of an atrocious institution, but the theme is in all the personal accounts of concentration camp experience by those who survived for any time in one or the other. There was the daily routine of blows and roll call and soup. There was the barter economy of bread, turnips, scraps of cloth, gold teeth. There were specializations: prison plumbers laid the water pipe in the crematorium and prison electricians wired the fences. The camp managers maintained standards and orderly process. The cobblestones which paved the crematorium yard at Auschwitz had to be perfectly scrubbed.

Germany was not a backward country. On the contrary, it was a 14
world leader in modern music, philosophy, high technology, and the social institutions we call the welfare state. Thus, to normalize the unthinkable, the world of the concentration camp had available to it not only the simple techniques of every human society—the establishment of routine, of social ties and of exchange relationships muting conflict through shared commitment and individual rewards for participation. It also had the sophisticated techniques of technological elaboration and bureaucratic rationality. The inhabitants of Treblinka were able to normalize the atrocious by elaborating around it not only music and art but also technology and management.

Every prisoner had his or her number tattooed on the arm, and 15
this number was carried through in the files and records. The day before Auschwitz was abandoned a new sort of "columns of smoke could be seen rising in all parts of the camp." The SS were burning their card indexes and files.

When we hear of "scientific" experiments performed on inmates 16
in the concentration camp setting we tend to recoil in horror. But is the pretense of science any more horrifying than the rest of it? Indeed, it seems that we must understand these experiments as arising not out of pure sadism, but out of that same human tendency to normalize any setting that generated the concentration camp infirmaries, to which they were often connected. It was quite in keeping with the spirit of it all that these "experimental" tortures

constituted the basis for papers read at scientific meetings where, although the source of the data must have been evident, apparently no protest was made. "Science" in the concentration camp was yet another manifestation of the human normalizing tendency, both noble and horrifying, which came to link victims and torturers in the creation of a shared society based on the production of death.

Are we not today engaged in a similar enterprise?

The SS men watched the crumbling of the German Reich, and the prisoners counted the numbers of Jews in the transports and calculated how many weeks it must be before their turn would come. Yet together, day by day, they scrubbed the cobblestones or ordered the cobblestones scrubbed; went to roll call to count and be counted, maintaining the world of Treblinka. Like them, we collaborate day by day in maintaining the institutions of the warfare state which seems more and more plausibly set to destroy us. We are caught in the human endeavor to create daily life: to normalize the unthinkable.

The devices which we use are roughly similar: the division of labor, which separates, in understanding and potential for collective organization, what it makes interdependent in functioning; the structure of rewards and incentives which makes it to individuals' personal and familiar interest to undermine daily, in countless small steps, the basis of common existence; and the legitimating use of bureaucratic formalism and of scientific and technological elaboration.

The division of labor serves most obviously to normalize the atrocious when it takes the form of institutions specialized for purposes which we must assume that normal people would abhor. We might be somewhat less inclined to out-of-hand rejection of the claims of "good" Germans that they did not know what those crematoria were burning when we consider that Bishop Leroy Matthiesen—now a particularly outspoken opponent of the nuclear arms race—served for nine years as a parish priest, two miles from the Pantex plant at Amarillo, Texas, without realizing that its output is nuclear bombs. Pantex covers 10,000 acres and employs 2,400 people; it does final assembly of the entire nuclear arsenal.

But even within the institutions of death, the division of labor continues in a multitude of ways to normalize operation. At the structural level, it divides participants in the organization into groups with specialized interests, less likely to combine against the higher authorities. So at Treblinka an absolute separation of work, housing, and communication was maintained between the group of workers who received the Jews from the trains and marshaled them into the gas chambers and those at the other side who removed hair and gold teeth and disposed of the bodies.

A more central issue for war planners is the separation of planning from execution. Adolph Eichmann was a thoroughly responsible person, according to his understanding of responsibility. For him it was clear that the heads of state set policy. His role was to implement, and fortunately, he felt, it was never part of his job actually to have to kill anyone. 22

There are gradations of distance from execution which constitute varying levels of protection from responsibility and render the moral problem exceedingly fuzzy. During the debates in the late 1960s at MIT with respect to its role in weapons development, the head of the main military research laboratory argued that their concern was development, not use, of technology. The university administration eventually undertook to sever operational weapons systems research from the Institute, but it still permitted on-campus work, which was funded mainly because of its potential military application. 23

Even while diffusing responsibility by separating planning from execution and one element of execution from another, the division of labor produces complicity through the functional interdependence of the specializations. In Treblinka "the Jews themselves had to become responsible for output as well as for discipline." "Experience with the ghettos had taught [the Germans] that a man who had knowingly compromised himself did not revolt against his masters, no matter what idea had driven him to collaboration: too many mutual skeletons in the closet." 24

The division of labor brings with it an organizational sociology of specialization, hierarchy, and differential rewards. Material rewards are allocated on the basis of active and skillful participation in the system. Defense contractors can bid for the most highly skilled engineers and scientists and pay them handsomely. Weapons research and war planning become the path to material success. In the underworld of the concentration camp, the "low numbers"— 25 those who had survived for relatively long periods—were all specialists. Only they ate enough to keep alive.

The work-Jews at Treblinka ate well and were well-clothed because of the goods which came with the "transports"; there are accounts of storerooms knee-deep in valuables. The transports of persons to the gas chambers were also the camp's lifeline. A survivor of Treblinka described how deep the economic base of complicity came to be:

> Things went from bad to worse that month of March. There were no transports—in February just a few, remnants from here and there, then a few hundred gypsies—they were really poor; they brought nothing. In the storehouses everything had been packed up and shipped. . . . And suddenly everything—clothes, watches, spectacles, shoes, walking-sticks, cooking-pots, linen, not to speak of food—everything went. . . . You can't imagine what we felt when there was nothing there. You see, the things were our justification for being alive. If there were no things to administer, why would they let us stay alive? On top of that we were, for the first time, hungry. We were eating the camp food now, and it was terrible and, of course, totally inadequate. . . . In the six weeks of almost no transports, all of us had lost an incredible amount of weight and energy. . . .
>
> It was just about when we had reached the lowest ebb in our morale that . . . Kurt Franz walked into our barracks, a wide grin in his face. "As of tomorrow," he said, "transports will be rolling in again." And do you know what we did? We shouted, "Hurrah, hurrah." It seems impossible now. Every time I think of it I die a small death; but it's the truth. That is what we did; that is where we had got to. And sure enough, the next morning they arrived.

Along with material success comes prestige. Salaries and positions translate into dinner parties with important people, heads that turn when one enters the conference room. A former research analyst at the Department of Defense recalls:

> When I was "chosen" for a special clearance, my immediate feeling was one of achievement and pleasure. I also remember the earlier feeling when I was not cleared for special intelligence and how important it seemed to me to be one of the

three or four who were cleared among the twenty or so analysts in the Political and Economics Section.

Primo Levi brags at Auschwitz: "In the whole camp there are only a few Greeks who have a [food pot] larger than ours. Besides the material advantages, it carries with it a perceptible improvement in our social standing."

Specialization brings with it the possibility of developing the peculiarly human satisfactions in problem-solving, expertise, and the exercise of skill. High technology is the creative frontier. The development of the atomic bomb is one of the great dramas of creativity of our time, and the subsequent elaboration of the technology has provided, and continues to provide, opportunities for the intellectual excitement of stretching the mind to its limits. 29

In 1947, James Killian, then vice president of MIT and later its president, said of the Institute during wartime: 30

> The concentration of war research on its campus, the presence here of a great assemblage of gifted scientists from hundreds of institutions and the remarkably varied activities of its own staff contributed . . . to the establishment of a fresh and vigorous post-war program. . . . No one at MIT during this period can fail to be impressed by the ferment of ideas.

The concentration camp may seem like an unpropitious environment for skill and discovery, but even there it had its role in the experiments on human subjects. At Treblinka, when they solved the problem of how to burn the bodies, they broke out champagne; it was a technological breakthrough. And in the underworld of the prisoners, Primo Levi boasts again from Auschwitz: "And I would not like to be accused of immodesty if I add that it was our idea, mine and Alberto's, to steal the rolls of graph-paper from the thermographs of the Desiccation Department." 31

Paul Loeb, studying the community developed around plutonium production at Hanford, Washington, shows how organizational process within the enterprise, and family, and community life around it, give the production of bombs the most peaceful of settings. As one informant explained: 32

> We were proud to work for a major company like General Electric. We felt we were part of a well-run industrial enterprise with good management practices, good cost control and a

> good competitive feeling because the AEC [Atomic Energy Commission] would be comparing our cost and productivity figures with those of Savannah River. Some of us even went on recruiting trips, visiting different colleges along with other people from GE divisions around the country—and we explained plutonium as simply our product, just as light bulbs or turbines were someone else's.

In his work on Treblinka, Steiner makes a general point which seems strongly relevant to the movement toward nuclear war: It is not simply the attachment to going concerns which makes it difficult to stop; it is the very seriousness of the situation. An outcome of sufficient dreadfulness becomes, in effect, inconceivable. "One fact played into the hands of the 'technicians'; the monstrosity of the truth. The extermination of a whole people was so unimaginable that the human mind could not accept it." Similarly, nuclear war has been designated "the unthinkable."

This is why the character of civil defense planning is critically important. It is not nuclear war which is unthinkable; it is its consequences. And generally we do not deal with consequences. Policy focuses on purposes; research and development and military planning deal with means. Civil defense has to deal with consequences.

The problems of having, in some way, to confront consequences are increased by the fact that civil defense planning must to some extent be brought before the public. The information most accessible to the public is found in the evacuation plans prepared for each city and town. According to these plans, millions of people will gather their children; arrange to leave their pets with food and water; assemble shovels, clothing, credit cards, and sanitary napkins. Then, affixing the proper Civil Defense stickers to their automobiles, they will move smoothly over bridges, through tunnels and down highways—normally clogged to a standstill by any holiday weekend—to predesignated areas in smaller communities.

Nothing in this picture has any of the characteristics of an emergency situation. Indeed, to remove from the picture any semblance of a real nuclear war situation, all other real-world characteristics have also been removed. There are no traffic jams, no people searching for others, no one demanding to be taken along, or insisting on taking their pets or guns.

Most dreamlike is the absence of any dimension of time. Anyone who has ever tried to pack a picnic, assemble a family, and drive to the country on a Fourth of July weekend is likely to see such a description as lacking verisimilitude. The plans, for this reason, have not been well received. A reading of the Cambridge plan in the City Council chambers stimulated the Council to distribute a pamphlet declaring the concept worthless and urging political activity directed at stopping the arms race. And what happens after the bombs have fallen, when the survivors emerge from the shelters with their credit cards in hand? The plans offer neither description nor instruction. 37

It is as though these planners had fallen into the same solution as the description of the Jewish Holocaust provided by those who designed the Toronto World's Fair Israeli pavilion. Fairgoers learned about Jewish history by passing down a long corridor lined with photographs and objects. At the point in the story where the Holocaust takes place, the fairgoer turned a sharp corner and found himself facing a blank wall—a blank wall, one pair of battered baby shoes and a photograph of a small boy staring up in terror. 38

There are those who argue that preparation for nuclear war is necessary for reasons of national security. I believe, and have tried to show, that the continuation of weapons production and military planning can be explained without recourse to any argument involving national interest. And about the argument as it relates to national purpose, I would say that: 39

- there now exist descriptions of the consequences of nuclear war sufficiently apocalyptic to show that there is no conceivable national purpose for which the triggering of nuclear war would be sufficient justification;
- the continuing institutionalized preparation for nuclear war brings us continually closer to the precipice of its occurrence;
- we ought to move immediately to eliminate preparation for nuclear war from its current place as an instrument of national policy. Even the brutalized and complicitous prisoners of Treblinka eventually rose up against normalization of the unthinkable.

Some of us, confronted with our present situation, are ready to consign the very notion of national purpose to the dustbin of history, along with Hitler's Third Reich. 40

QUESTIONS FOR READING AND WRITING

1. According to Peattie, why do people become so orderly in desperate situations?
2. In what ways are most of us to blame for the continuing peril of nuclear destruction?
3. Peattie relies heavily on comparison in conducting her argument. What points of comparison does she cite between the behavior of Jews at Treblinka and the behavior of citizens or government planners faced with the prospect of nuclear war? Do you find her comparison offensive in any way?
4. Compare what Peattie implies about civil preparedness in the face of nuclear disaster to what Jonathan Schell implies in "Nothing to Report."
5. Write an essay in which you offer suggestions about what the average citizen can do to fend off the nuclear peril.

✦ Adrienne Rich ✦
Claiming an Education

A major American poet and feminist, Adrienne Rich (b. 1929) was educated at Radcliffe College. Her first book of poems, A Change of World *(1951), won the Yale Younger Poet's Prize. Other major works include the books of poems* Diving Into the Wreck *(1973) and* Your Native Land, Your Life *(1986) and a collection of essays entitled* On Lies, Secrets, and Silence *(1979). In the following essay, originally delivered as a convocation speech at Douglass College, she urges her audience of women not to be intimidated by the male dominance of American education, but to fight against that dominance and demand to be taken seriously as students, as scholars, and as workers.*

FOR THIS CONVOCATION, I planned to separate my remarks into two parts: some thoughts about you, the women students here, and some thoughts about us who teach in a women's college. But ultimately, those two parts are indivisible. If university education means anything beyond the processing of human beings into expected roles, through credit hours, tests, and grades (and I believe that in a women's college especially it *might* mean much more), it implies an ethical and intellectual contract between teacher and student. This contract must remain intuitive, dynamic, unwritten; but we must turn to it again and again if learning is to be reclaimed from the depersonalizing and cheapening pressures of the present-day academic scene. 1

The first thing I want to say to you who are students, is that you cannot afford to think of being here to *receive* an education; you will do much better to think of yourselves as being here to *claim* one. One of the dictionary definitions of the verb "to claim" is: *to take as the rightful owner; to assert in the face of possible contradiction.* "To receive" is *to come into possession of; to act as receptacle or container for; to accept as authoritative or true.* The difference is that between acting and being acted-upon, and for women it can literally mean the difference between life and death. 2

One of the devastating weaknesses of university learning, of the store of knowledge and opinion that has been handed down through 3 academic training, has been its almost total erasure of women's experience and thought from the curriculum, and its exclusion of women as members of the academic community. Today, with increasing numbers of women students in nearly every branch of higher learning, we still see very few women in the upper levels of faculty and administration in most institutions. Douglass College itself is a women's college in a university administered overwhelmingly by men, who in turn are answerable to the state legislature, again composed predominantly of men. But the most significant fact for you is that what you learn here, the very texts you read, the lectures you hear, the way your studies are divided into categories and fragmented one from the other—all this reflects, to a very large degree, neither objective reality, nor an accurate picture of the past, nor a group of rigorously tested observations about human behavior. What you can learn here (and I mean not only at Douglass but any college in any university) is how *men* have perceived and organized their experience, their history, their ideas of social relationships, good and evil, sickness and health, etc. When you read or hear about "great issues," "major texts," "the mainstream of Western thought," you are hearing about what men, above all white men, in their male subjectivity, have decided is important.

Black and other minority peoples have for some time recognized that their racial and ethnic experience was not accounted for in the studies broadly labeled human; and that even the sciences can be racist. For many reasons, it has been more difficult for women to comprehend our exclusion, and to realize that even the sciences can be sexist. For one thing, it is only within the last hundred years that higher education has grudgingly been opened up to women at all, even to white, middle-class women. And many of us have found ourselves poring eagerly over books with titles like: *The Descent of Man; Man and His Symbols; Irrational Man; The Phenomenon of Man; The Future of Man; Man and the Machine; From Man to Man; May Man Prevail?; Man, Science and Society;* or *One-Dimensional Man*—books pretending to describe a "human" reality that does not include over one-half the human species.

Less than a decade ago, with the rebirth of a feminist movement in this country, women students and teachers in a number of universities began to demand and set up women's studies courses—to *claim* a woman-directed education. And, despite the inevitable accusations of "unscholarly," " group therapy," "faddism," etc., despite backlash and budget cuts, women's studies are still growing, offering to more and more women a new intellectual grasp on their lives, new understanding of our history, a fresh vision of the human experience, and also a critical basis for evaluating what they hear and read in other courses, and in the society at large.

But my talk is not really about women's studies, much as I believe in their scholarly, scientific, and human necessity. While I think that any Douglass student has everything to gain by investigating and enrolling in women's studies courses, I want to suggest that there is a more essential experience that you owe yourselves, one which courses in women's studies can greatly enrich, but which finally depends on you, in all your interactions with yourself and your world. This is the experience of *taking responsibility toward yourselves*. Our upbringing as women has so often told us that this should come second to our relationships and responsibilities to other people. We have been offered ethical models of the self-denying wife and mother; intellectual models of the brilliant but slapdash dilettante who never commits herself to anything the whole way, or the intelligent woman who denies her intelligence in order to seem more "feminine," or who sits in passive silence even when she disagrees inwardly with everything that is being said around her. 6

Responsibility to yourself means refusing to let others do your thinking, talking, and naming for you; it means learning to respect and use your own brains and instincts; hence, grappling with hard work. It means that you do not treat your body as a commodity with which to purchase superficial intimacy or economic security; for our bodies and minds are inseparable in this life, and when we allow our bodies to be treated as objects, our minds are in mortal danger. It means insisting that those to whom you give your friendship and love are able to respect your mind. It means being able to say, with Charlotte Brontë's *Jane Eyre*: "I have an inward treasure born with me, which can keep me alive if all the extraneous delights should be withheld or offered only at a price I cannot afford to give." 7

Responsibility to yourself means that you don't fall for shallow and easy resolutions—predigested books and ideas, weekend 8 encounters guaranteed to change your life, taking "gut" courses instead of ones you know will challenge you, bluffing at school and life instead of doing solid work, marrying early as an escape from real decisions, getting pregnant as an evasion of already existing problems. It means that you refuse to sell your talents and aspirations short, simply to avoid conflict and confrontation. And this, in turn, means resisting the forces in society which say that women should be nice, play safe, have low professional expectations, drown in love and forget about work, live through others, and stay in the places assigned to us. It means that we insist on a life of meaningful work, insist that work be as meaningful as love and friendship in our lives. It means, therefore, the courage to be "different"; not to be continuously available to others when we need time for ourselves and our work; to be able to demand of others—parents, friends, roommates, teachers, lovers, husbands, children—that they respect our sense of purpose and our integrity as persons. Women everywhere are finding the courage to do this, more and more, and we are finding that courage both in our study of women in the past who possessed it, and in each other as we look to other women for comradeship, community, and challenge. The difference between a life lived actively, and a life of passive drifting and dispersal of energies, is an immense difference. Once we begin to feel committed to our lives, responsible to ourselves, we can never again be satisfied with the old, passive way.

Now comes the second part of the contract. I believe that in a women's college you have the right to expect your faculty to take you seriously. The education of women has been a matter of debate for centuries, and old, negative attitudes about women's role, women's ability to think and take leadership, are still rife both in and outside the university. Many male professors (and I don't mean only at Douglass) still feel that teaching in a women's college is a second-rate career. Many tend to eroticize their women students—to treat them as sexual objects—instead of demanding the best of their minds. (At Yale a legal suit [*Alexander* v. *Yale*] has been brought against the university by a group of women students demanding a stated policy against sexual advances toward female students by male professors.) Many teachers, both men and women, trained in the male-centered tradition, are still handing the ideas and texts of that tradition on to students without teaching them to criticize its antiwoman attitudes, its omission of women as part of the species. Too often, all of us fail to teach the most important thing, which is that clear thinking, active discussion, and excellent writing are all necessary for intellectual freedom, and that these require *hard work*. Sometimes, perhaps in discouragement with a culture which is both antiintellectual and antiwoman, we may resign ourselves to low expectations for our students before we have given them half a chance to become more thoughtful, expressive human beings. We need to take to heart the words of Elizabeth Barrett Browning, a poet, a thinking woman, and a feminist, who wrote in 1845 of her impatience with studies which cultivate a "passive recipiency" in the mind, and asserted that "women want to be made to *think actively*: their apprehension is quicker than that of men, but their defect lies for the most part in the logical faculty and in the higher mental activities." Note that she implies a defect which can be remedied by intellectual training; *not* an inborn lack of ability.

10 I have said that the contract on the student's part involves that you demand to be taken seriously so that you can also go on taking yourself seriously. This means seeking out criticism, recognizing that the most affirming thing anyone can do for you is demand that you push yourself further, show you the range of what you *can* do. It means rejecting attitudes of "take-it-easy," "why-be-so-serious," "why-worry-you'll-probably-get-married-anyway." It means assuming your share of responsibility for what happens in the classroom, because that affects the quality of your daily life here. It means that the student sees herself engaged *with* her teachers in an active, ongoing struggle for a real education. But for her to do this, her teachers must be committed to the belief that women's minds and experience are intrinsically valuable and indispensable to any civilization worthy the name; that there is no more exhilarating and intellectually fertile place in the academic world today than a women's college—*if* both students and teachers in large enough numbers are trying to fulfill this contract. The contract is really a pledge of mutual seriousness about women, about language, ideas, methods, and values. It is our shared commitment toward a world in which the inborn potentialities of so many women's minds will no longer be wasted, raveled-away, paralyzed, or denied.

QUESTIONS AND READING AND WRITING

1. What conventional attitudes toward the education of women is Rich speaking out against?
2. What kinds of behavior does *receiving* an education imply? What kinds of behavior would a woman exhibit, or expect, in *claiming* her education?
3. In paragraph 4, Rich cites the male bias of much contemporary university education. Is this bias present in the curricula of your school, in the make-up of its faculty, and in the books assigned in its classes?
4. Many argumentative essays exhort their readers (or auditors) to some kind of action. What actions does Rich's essay promote?
5. Rewrite all or part of Rich's speech—without altering her essential viewpoint—and address it to an audience of male college graduates.
6. Interview a female faculty member at your school. Focus your questions on the course of her academic career, whatever obstacles she has overcome, and her professional relationships with her male and female colleagues. Write an essay that reports what you discover.

✦ Richard Rodriguez ✦

Bilingualism, Con

Outdated and Unrealistic

Richard Rodriguez was born in 1944 of Mexican-American immigrant parents. He earned a B.A. from Stanford, an M.A. from Columbia, and did doctoral work at the University of California at Berkeley. In The Hunger of Memory *(1982), Rodriguez recounted his struggle to become assimilated into the mainstream of American society. In the following essay, he argues against the wisdom of requiring bilingual education for children of Hispanic origin. This requirement, he claims, serves the needs of adults more than it does those of children.*

HOW SHALL WE TEACH the dark-eyed child *ingles*? The debate continues much as it did two decades ago. 1

Bilingual education belongs to the 1960's, the years of the black civil rights movement. Bilingual education became the official Hispanic demand; as a symbol, the English-only classroom was intended to be analogous to the segregated lunch counter; the locked school door. Bilingual education was endorsed by judges and, of course, by politicians well before anyone knew the answer to the question: Does bilingual education work? 2

Who knows? *Quien sabe*? 3

The official drone over bilingual education is conducted by educationists with numbers and charts. Because bilingual education was never simply a matter of pedagogy, it is too much to expect educators to resolve the matter. Proclamations concerning bilingual education are weighted at bottom with Hispanic political grievances and, too, with middle-class romanticism. 4

No one will say it in public; in private, Hispanics argue with me about bilingual education and every time it comes down to memory. Everyone remembers going to that grammar school where students were slapped for speaking Spanish. Childhood memory is offered as parable; the memory is meant to compress the gringo's long history of offenses against Spanish, Hispanic culture, Hispanics. 5

It is no coincidence that, although all of America's ethnic groups are implicated in the policy of bilingual education, Hispanics, 6 particularly Mexican-Americans, have been its chief advocates. The English words used by Hispanics in support of bilingual education are words such as "dignity," "heritage," "culture." Bilingualism becomes a way of exacting from gringos a grudging admission of contrition—for the 19th-century theft of the Southwest, the relegation of Spanish to a foreign tongue, the injustice of history. At the extreme, Hispanic bilingual enthusiasts demand that public schools "maintain" a student's sense of separateness.

Hispanics may be among the last groups of Americans who still believe in the 1960's. Bilingual-education proposals still serve the romance of that decade, especially of the late 60's, when the heroic black civil rights movement grew paradoxically wedded to its opposite—the ethnic revival movement. Integration and separatism merged into twin, possible goals.

With integration, the black movement inspired middle-class Americans to imitations—the Hispanic movement; the Gray Panthers; feminism; gay rights. Then there was withdrawal, with black glamour leading a romantic retreat from the anonymous crowd.

Americans came to want it both ways. They wanted in and they wanted out. Hispanics took to celebrating their diversity, joined other Americans in dancing rings around the melting pot.

Mythic Metaphors

More intently than most, Hispanics wanted the romance of their dual cultural allegiance backed up by law. Bilingualism became proof that one could have it both ways, could be a full member of public America and yet also separate, private, Hispanic. "Spanish" and "English" became mythic metaphors, like country and city, describing separate islands of private and public life.

Ballots, billboards, and, of course, classrooms in Spanish. For nearly two decades now, middle-class Hispanics have had it their way. They have foisted a neat ideological scheme on working-class children. What they want to believe about themselves, they wait for the child to prove that it is possible to be two, that one can assume the public language (the public life) of America, even while remaining what one was, existentially separate.

Adulthood is not so neatly balanced. The tension between public and private life is intrinsic to adulthood—certainly middle-class adulthood. Usually the city wins because the city pays. We are mass people for more of the day than we are with our intimates. No Congressional mandate or Supreme Court decision can diminish the loss.

I was talking the other day to a carpenter from Riga, in the Soviet Republic of Latvia. He has been here six years. He told me of his having to force himself to relinquish the "luxury" of reading books in Russian or Latvian so he could begin to read books in English. And the books he was able to read in English were not of a complexity to satisfy him. But he was not going back to Riga. 13

Beyond any question of pedagogy there is the simple fact that a language gets learned as it gets used. One fills one's mouth, one's mind, with the new names for things. 14

The civil rights movement of the 1960's taught Americans to deal with forms of discrimination other than economic—racial, sexual. We forget class. We talk about bilingual education as an ethnic issue; we forget to notice that the program mainly touches the lives of working-class immigrant children. Foreign- language acquisition is one thing for the upper-class child in a convent school learning in French to curtsy. Language acquisition can only seem a loss for the ghetto child, for the new language is psychologically awesome, being, as it is, the language of the bus driver and papa's employer. The child's difficulty will turn out to be psychological more than linguistic because what he gives up are symbols of home. 15

Pain and Guilt

I was that child! I faced the stranger's English with pain and guilt and fear. Baptized to English in school, at first I felt myself drowning—the ugly sounds forced down my throat—until slowly, slowly (held in the tender grip of my teachers), suddenly the conviction took: English was my language to use. 16

What I yearn for is some candor from those who speak about bilingual education. Which of its supporters dares speak of the price a child pays—the price of adulthood—to make the journey from a working-class home into a middle-class schoolroom? The real story, the silent story of the immigrant child's journey is one of embarrassments in public; betrayal of all that is private; silence at home; and at school the hand tentatively raised. 17

Bilingual enthusiasts bespeak an easier world. They seek a linguistic solution to a social dilemma. They seem to want to believe that there is an easy way for the child to balance private and public, in order to believe that there is some easy way for themselves.

Ten years ago, I started writing about the ideological implications of bilingual education. Ten years from now some newspaper may well invite me to contribute another Sunday supplement essay on the subject. The debate is going to continue. The bilingual establishment is now inside the door. Jobs are at stake. Politicians can only count heads; growing numbers of Hispanics will insure the compliance of politicians.

Publicly, we will continue the fiction. We will solemnly address this issue as an educational question, a matter of pedagogy. But privately, Hispanics will still seek from bilingual education an admission from the gringo that Spanish has value and presence. Hispanics of middle class will continue to seek the romantic assurance of separateness. Experts will argue. Dark-eyed children will sit in the classroom. Mute.

QUESTIONS FOR READING AND WRITING

1. Cite examples of how Rodriguez uses diction and figurative language to attack his opposition.
2. What argumentative purpose is served by Rodriguez' reference to the Soviet carpenter from Riga (paragraph 13)?
3. In your opinion, should ethnic, national, racial, or religious groups attempt to remain distinct from "general" American culture, or should they, when possible, attempt to assimilate themselves into that culture? What are Rodriguez' views of this matter?
4. Write an essay that compares and evaluates the relative merits of the arguments by Rodriguez and Angelo Gonsalez ("Bilingualism, Pro: The Key to Basic Skills").

✦ Jonathan Swift ✦
A Modest Proposal

Jonathan Swift (1667–1745) is perhaps the foremost satirist in the English language. Born to British parents in Ireland, he studied at Trinity College in Dublin before moving to London. A cleric as well as a writer, he was made Dean of St. Paul's Cathedral (Dublin) in 1713. His most famous work is Gulliver's Travels *(1726), a scathing and sweeping satire on all forms of human pride and folly. In the following classic essay, first published in 1729, Swift describes, through the voice of his narrator, an outrageous scheme for curing the social ills of Ireland.*

IT IS A MELANCHOLY OBJECT to those who walk through this great town or travel in the country, when they see the streets, the roads, and cabin doors, crowded with beggars of the female sex, followed by three, four, or six children, all in rags and importuning every passenger for an alms. These mothers, instead of being able to work for their honest livelihood, are forced to employ all their time in strolling to beg sustenance for their helpless infants: who as they grow up either turn thieves for want of work, or leave their dear native country to fight for the pretender in Spain, or sell themselves to the Barbadoes. 1

I think it is agreed by all parties that this prodigious number of children in the arms, or on the backs, or at the heels of their mothers, and frequently of their fathers, is in the present deplorable state of the kingdom a very great additional grievance; and, therefore, whoever could find out a fair, cheap, and easy method of making these children sound, useful members of the commonwealth, would deserve so well of the public as to have his statue set up for a preserver of the nation. 2

But my intention is very far from being confined to provide only for the children of professed beggars; it is of a much greater extent, and shall take in the whole number of infants at a certain age who are born of parents in effect as little able to support them as those who demand our charity in the streets. 3

As to my own part, having turned my thoughts for many years upon this important subject, and maturely weighed the several schemes of our projectors, I have always found them grossly 4 mistaken in their computation. It is true, a child just dropped from its dam may be supported by her milk for a solar year, with little other nourishment; at most not above the value of two shillings, which the mother may certainly get, or the value in scraps, by her lawful occupation of begging; and it is exactly at one year old that I propose to provide for them in such a manner as instead of being a charge upon their parents or the parish, or wanting food and raiment for the rest of their lives, they shall on the contrary contribute to the feeding, and partly to the clothing, of many thousands.

There is likewise another great advantage in my scheme, that it will prevent those voluntary abortions, and that horrid practice of women murdering their bastard children, alas! too frequent among us! sacrificing the poor innocent babes I doubt more to avoid the expense than the shame, which would move tears and pity in the most savage and inhuman breast.

The number of souls in this kingdom being usually reckoned one million and a half, of these I calculate there may be about two hundred thousand couple whose wives are breeders; from which number I subtract thirty thousand couple who are able to maintain their own children (although I apprehend there cannot be so many, under the present distress of the kingdom); but this being granted, there will remain an hundred and seven thousand breeders. I again subtract fifty thousand for those women who miscarry, or whose children die by accident or disease within the year. There only remain an hundred and twenty thousand children of poor parents annually born. The question therefore is, how this number shall be reared and provided for? which, as I have already said, under the present situation of affairs, is utterly impossible by all the methods hitherto proposed. For we can neither employ them in handicraft or agriculture; we neither build houses (I mean in the country) nor cultivate land; they can very seldom pick up a livelihood by stealing, till they arrive at six years old, except where they are of towardly parts; although I confess they learn the rudiments much earlier; during which time they can, however, be properly looked upon only as probationers; as I have been informed by a principal gentleman in the country of Cavan, who protested to me that he never knew above one or two instances under the age of six, even in a part of the kingdom so renowned for the quickest proficiency in that art.

I am assured by our merchants, that a boy or a girl before twelve years old is no saleable commodity; and even when they come to this age they will not yield above three pounds, or three pounds and half a crown at most on the Exchange; which cannot turn to account either to the parents or kingdom, the charge of nutriment and rags having been at least four times that value. 7

I shall now therefore humbly propose my own thoughts, which I hope will not be liable to the least objection. 8

I have been assured by a very knowing American of my acquaintance in London, that a young healthy child well nursed is at a year old a most delicious, nourishing, and wholesome food, whether stewed, roasted, baked, or broiled; and I make no doubt that it will equally serve in a fricassee or a ragout. 9

I do therefore humbly offer it to public consideration that of the hundred and twenty thousand children already computed, twenty thousand may be reserved for breed, whereof only one-fourth part to be males; which is more than we allow to sheep, black cattle, or swine; and my reason is, that these children are seldom the fruits of marriage, a circumstance not much regarded by our savages; therefore one male will be sufficient to serve four females. That the remaining hundred thousand may, at a year old, be offered in sale to the persons of quality and fortune through the kingdom; always advising the mother to let them suck plentifully in the last month, so as to render them plump and fat for a good table. A child will make two dishes at an entertainment for friends; and when the family dines alone, the fore or hind quarter will make a reasonable dish, and seasoned with a little pepper or salt will be very good boiled on the fourth day, especially in winter. 10

I have reckoned upon a medium that a child just born will weigh twelve pounds, and in a solar year, if tolerably nursed, will increase to twenty-eight pounds. 11

I grant this food will be somewhat dear, and therefore very proper for landlords, who, as they have already devoured most of the parents, seem to have the best title to the children. 12

Infant's flesh will be in season throughout the year, but more plentiful in March, and a little before and after: for we are told by a grave author, an eminent French physician, that fish being a prolific diet, there are more children born in Roman Catholic countries 13 about nine months after Lent than at any other season; therefore, reckoning a year after Lent, the markets will be more glutted than usual, because the number of popish infants is at least three to one in this kingdom: and therefore it will have one other collateral advantage, by lessening the number of papists among us.

I have already computed the charge of nursing a beggar's child (in which list I reckon all cottagers, laborers, and four-fifths of the farmers) to be about two shillings per annum, rags included; and I believe no gentleman would repine to give ten shillings for the carcass of a good fat child, which, as I have said, will make four dishes of excellent nutritive meat, when he has only some particular friend or his own family to dine with him. Thus the squire will learn to be a good landlord, and grow popular among the tenants; the mother will have eight shillings net profit, and be fit for work till she produces another child.

Those who are more thrifty (as I must confess the times require) may flay the carcass; the skin of which artificially dressed will make admirable gloves for ladies, and summer boots for fine gentlemen.

As to our city of Dublin, shambles may be appointed for this purpose in the most convenient parts of it, and butchers we may be assured will not be wanting: although I rather recommend buying the children alive, and dressing them hot from the knife as we do roasting pigs.

A very worthy person, a true lover of his country, and whose virtues I highly esteem, was lately pleased in discoursing on this matter to offer a refinement upon my scheme. He said that many gentlemen of this kingdom, having of late destroyed their deer, he conceived that the want of venison might be well supplied by the bodies of young lads and maidens, not exceeding fourteen years of age nor under twelve; so great a number of both sexes in every country being now ready to starve for want of work and service; and these to be disposed of by their parents, if alive, or otherwise by their nearest relations. But with due deference to so excellent a friend and so deserving a patriot, I cannot be altogether in his sentiments; for as to the males, my American acquaintance assured me from frequent experience that their flesh was generally tough and lean, like that of our schoolboys by continual exercise, and their taste disagreeable; and to fatten them would not answer the charge. Then as to the females, it would, I think, with humble submission be a loss to the public, because they soon would become breeders themselves: and besides, it is not improbable that some scrupulous people might be apt to censure such a practice (although indeed very unjustly), as a little bordering upon cruelty; which, I confess, has always been with me the strongest objection against any project, how well soever intended.

But in order to justify my friend, he confessed that this expedient was put into his head by the famous Psalmanazar, a native of the island Formosa, who came from thence to London about twenty years ago: and in conversation told my friend, that in his country when any young person happened to be put to death, the executioner sold the carcass to persons of quality as a prime dainty; and that in his time the body of a plump girl of fifteen, who was crucified for an attempt to poison the emperor, was sold to his imperial majesty's prime minister of state, and other great mandarins of the court, in joints from the gibbet, at four hundred crowns. Neither indeed can I deny, that if the same use were made of several plump young girls in this town, who without one single groat to their fortunes cannot stir abroad without a chair, and appear at the playhouse and assemblies in foreign fineries which they never will pay for, the kingdom would not be the worse. 18

Some persons of a desponding spirit are in great concern about that vast number of poor people, who are aged, diseased, or maimed, and I have been desired to employ my thoughts what course may be taken to ease the nation of so grievous an encumbrance. But I am not in the least pain upon that matter, because it is very well known that they are every day dying and rotting by cold and famine, and filth and vermin, as fast as can be reasonably expected. And as to the young laborers, they are now in as hopeful a condition: they cannot get work, and consequently pine away for want of nourishment, to a degree that if at any time they are accidentally hired to common labor, they have not strength to perform it; and thus the country and themselves are happily delivered from the evils to come. 19

I have too long digressed, and therefore shall return to my subject. I think the advantages by the proposal which I have made are obvious and many, as well as of the highest importance. 20

For first, as I have already observed, it would greatly lessen the number of papists, with whom we are yearly overrun, being the 21 principal breeders of the nation as well as our most dangerous enemies; and who stay at home on purpose to deliver the kingdom to the Pretender, hoping to take their advantage by the absence of so many good Protestants, who have chosen rather to leave their country than stay at home and pay tithes against their conscience to an Episcopal curate.

Secondly, The poor tenants will have something valuable of their own, which by law may be made liable to distress and help to pay their landlord's rent, their corn and cattle being already seized, and money a thing unknown.

Thirdly, Whereas the maintenance of an hundred thousand children from two years old and upward, cannot be computed at less than ten shillings a piece per annum, the nation's stock will be thereby increased fifty thousand pounds per annum, beside the profit of a new dish introduced to the tables of all gentlemen of fortune in the kingdom who have any refinement in taste. And the money will circulate among ourselves, the goods being entirely of our own growth and manufacture.

Fourthly, The constant breeders beside the gain of eight shillings sterling per annum by the sale of their children, will be rid of the charge of maintaining them after the first year.

Fifthly, This food would likewise bring great custom to taverns, where the vintners will certainly be so prudent as to procure the best receipts for dressing it to perfection, and consequently have their houses frequented by all the fine gentlemen, who justly value themselves upon their knowledge in good eating: and a skillful cook who understands how to oblige his guests, will contrive to make it as expensive as they please.

Sixthly, This would be a great inducement to marriage, which all wise nations have either encouraged by rewards or enforced by laws and penalties. It would increase the care and tenderness of mothers toward their children, when they were sure of a settlement for life to the poor babes, provided in some sort by the public, to their annual profit instead of expense. We should see an honest emulation among the married women, which of them would bring the fattest child to the market. Men would become as fond of their wives during the time of their pregnancy as they are now of their mares in foal, their cows in calf, their sows when they are ready to farrow; nor offer to beat or kick them (as is too frequent a practice) for fear of a miscarriage.

Many other advantages might be enumerated. For instance, the addition of some thousand carcasses in our exportation of barreled beef, the propagation of swine's flesh, and improvement in the art of making good bacon, so much wanted among us by the great destruction of pigs, too frequent at our table; which are no way comparable in taste or magnificence to a well-grown, fat, yearling child, which roasted whole will make a considerable figure at a lord mayor's feast or any other public entertainment. But this and many others I omit, being studious of brevity. 27

Supposing that one thousand families in this city would be constant customers for infants' flesh, besides others who might have it at merry-meetings, particularly at weddings and christenings, I compute that Dublin would take off annually about twenty thousand carcasses; and the rest of the kingdom (where probably they will be sold somewhat cheaper) the remaining eighty thousand. 28

I can think of no one objection that will possibly be raised against this proposal, unless it should be urged that the number of people will be thereby much lessened in the kingdom. This I freely own, and it was indeed one principal design in offering it to the world. I desire the reader will observe, that I calculate my remedy for this one individual kingdom of Ireland and for no other that ever was, is, or I think ever can be upon earth. Therefore let no man talk to me of other expedients; of taxing our absentees at five shillings a pound: of using neither clothes nor household furniture except what is of our own growth and manufacture: of utterly rejecting the materials and instruments that promote foreign luxury: of curing the expensiveness of pride, vanity, idleness, and gaming in our women: of introducing a vein of parsimony, prudence, and temperance: of learning to love our country, in the want of which we differ even from Laplanders and the inhabitants of Topinamboo: of quitting our animosities and factions, nor acting any longer like the Jews, who were murdering one another at the very moment their city was taken: of being a little cautious not to sell our country and conscience for nothing: of teaching landlords to have at least one degree of mercy toward their tenants: lastly, of putting a spirit of honesty, industry, and skill into our shopkeepers; who, if a resolution 29 could now be taken to buy only our native goods, would immediately unite to cheat and exact upon us in the price, the measure, and the goodness, nor could ever yet be brought to make one fair proposal of just dealing, though often and earnestly invited to it.

Therefore I repeat, let no man talk to me of these and the like expedients, till he has at least some glimpse of hope that there will be ever some hearty and sincere attempts to put them in practice.

But as to myself, having been wearied out for many years with offering vain, idle, visionary thoughts, and at length utterly despairing of success, I fortunately fell upon this proposal; which, as it is wholly new, so it has something solid and real, of no expense and little trouble, full in our own power, and whereby we can incur no danger in disobliging England. For this kind of commodity will not bear exportation, the flesh being of too tender a consistence to admit a long continuance in salt, although perhaps I could name a country which would be glad to eat up our whole nation without it.

After all, I am not so violently bent upon my own opinion as to reject any offer proposed by wise men, which shall be found equally innocent, cheap, easy, and effectual. But before something of that kind shall be advanced in contradiction to my scheme, and offering a better, I desire the author or authors will be pleased maturely to consider two points. First, as things now stand, how they will be able to find food and raiment for an hundred thousand useless mouths and backs. And secondly, there being a round million of creatures in human figure throughout this kingdom, whose subsistence put into a common stock would leave them in debt two millions of pounds sterling, adding those who are beggars by profession to the bulk of farmers, cottagers, and laborers, with the wives and children who are beggars in effect; I desire those politicians who dislike my overture, and may perhaps be so bold as to attempt an answer, that they will first ask the parents of these mortals, whether they would not at this day think it a great happiness to have been sold for food at a year old in the manner I prescribe, and thereby have avoided such a perpetual scene of misfortunes as they have since gone through by the oppression of landlords, the impossibility of paying rent without money or trade, the want of common sustenance, with neither house nor clothes to cover them from the inclemencies of the weather, and the most inevitable prospect of entailing the like or greater miseries upon their breed for ever.

I profess, in the sincerity of my heart, that I have not the least personal interest in endeavoring to promote this necessary work, having no other motive than the public good of my country, by advancing our trade, providing for infants, relieving the poor, and giving some pleasure to the rich. I have no children by which I can propose to get a single penny; the youngest being nine years old, and my wife past child-bearing. 33

QUESTIONS FOR READING AND WRITING

1. At what point in Swift's essay do you first notice that he is writing a satire, that he is not literally advocating the eating of children? What "signals" make this clear to you?
2. The tone of "A Modest Proposal" is satiric, but it is also angry. Point out examples of Swift's diction that help to convey his sense of anger and outrage.
3. What specific social ills does Swift bring to the attention of his readers?
4. Point out instances where Swift anticipates objections to his proposal. Why does he do this?
5. Basing your essay on inferences from Swift's text, write a character sketch of the person who makes the modest proposal.
6. Write a persuasive "modest proposal" for one of the following: the care of the elderly, the care of the insane, the eradication of urban poverty. Your intent should be to use outrageous satire, as Swift does, to heighten your readers' awareness of, and concern about, these social problems.

✦ Richard Wright ✦
The Psychological Reactions of Oppressed People

Richard Wright (1908–1960), born near Natchez, Mississippi, became one of America's most important black writers. His works include Uncle Tom's Children *(1938), the novel* Native Son *(1940), and his autobiography,* Black Boy *(1945). In the following excerpt from* White Man, Listen! *(1957), he analyzes the states of mind that lead to white oppression of black peoples.*

BUTTRESSED BY THEIR BELIEF THAT THEIR GOD had entrusted the earth into their keeping, drunk with power and possibility, waxing rich through trade in commodities, human and non-human, with awesome naval and merchant marines at their disposal, their countries filled with human debris anxious for any adventures, psychologically armed with new facts, white Western Christian civilization during the fourteenth, fifteenth, sixteenth, and seventeenth centuries, with a long, slow, and bloody explosion, hurled itself upon the sprawling masses of colored humanity in Asia and Africa.

I say to you white men of the West: Don't be too proud of how easily you conquered and plundered those Asians and Africans. You had unwitting allies in your campaigns; you had Fifth Columns in the form of indigenous cultures to facilitate your military, missionary, and mercenary efforts. Your collaborators in those regions consisted of the mental habits of the people, habits for which they were in no way responsible, no more than you were responsible for yours. Those habits constituted corps of saboteurs, of spies, if you will, that worked in the interests of European aggression. You must realize that it was not your courage or racial superiority that made you win, nor was it the racial inferiority or cowardice of the Asians and Africans that made them lose. This is an important point that you must grasp, or your concern with this problem will be forever wide of the facts. How, then, did the West, numerically the minority, achieve, during the last four centuries, so many dazzling victories over the body of colored mankind? Frankly, it took you centuries to do a job that could have been done in fifty years! You had the motive, the fire power, the will, the religious spur, the superior organization, but you dallied. Why? You were not aware exactly of what you were doing. You didn't suspect your impersonal strength, or the impersonal weakness on the other side. You were as unconscious, at bottom, as were your victims about what was really taking place.

Your world of culture clashed with the culture-worlds of colored mankind, and the ensuing destruction of traditional beliefs among a billion and a half of black, brown, and yellow men has set off a tide of social, cultural, political, and economic revolution that grips the world today. That revolution is assuming many forms, absolutistic, communistic, fascistic, theocratistic, etc.—all marked by unrest, violence, and an astounding emotional thrashing about as men seek new objects about which they can center their loyalties. 3

It is of the reactions, tortured and turbulent, of those Asians and Africans, in the New and Old World, that I wish to speak to you. Naturally I cannot speak for those Asians and Africans who are still locked in their mystical or ancestor-worshiping traditions. They are the voiceless ones, the silent ones. Indeed, I think that they are the doomed ones, men in a tragic trap. Any attempt on their part to wage a battle to protect their outmoded traditions and religions is a battle that is lost before it starts. And I say frankly that I suspect any white man who loves to dote upon those "naked nobles," who wants to leave them as they are, who finds them "primitive and pure," for such mystical hankering is, in my opinion, the last refuge of reactionary racists and psychological cripples tired of their own civilization. My remarks will, of necessity, be confined to those Asians and Africans who, having been partly Westernized, have a quarrel with the West. They are the ones who feel that they are oppressed. In a sense, this is a fight of the West with *itself*, a fight that the West blunderingly began, and the West does not to this day realize that it is the sole responsible agent, the sole instigator. For the West to disclaim responsibility for what it so clearly did is to make every white man alive on earth today a criminal. In history as in law, men must be held strictly responsible for the consequences of their historic actions, whether they intended those consequences or not. For the West to accept its responsibility is to create the means by which white men can liberate themselves from their fears, panic, 4 and terror while they confront the world's colored majority of men who are also striving for liberation from the irrational ties which the West prompted them to disown—ties of which the West has partially robbed them.

Let's imagine a mammoth flying saucer from Mars landing, say, in a peasant Swiss village and debouching swarms of fierce-looking men whose skins are blue and whose red eyes flash lightning bolts that deal instant death. The inhabitants are all the more terrified because the arrival of these men had been predicted. The religious myths of the Western world—the Second Coming of Christ, the Last Judgment, etc., have conditioned Europeans for just such an improbable event. Hence, those Swiss natives will feel that resistance is useless for a while. As long as the blue strangers are casually kind, they are obeyed and served. They become the Fathers of the people. Is this a fragment of paperback science fiction? No. It's more prosaic than that. The image I've sketched above is the manner, by and large, in which white Europe overran Asia and Africa. (Remember the Cortés-Montezuma drama!)

Buy why did Europe do this? Did it only want gold, power, women, raw materials? It was more complicated than that.

The fifteenth-, sixteenth-, and seventeenth-century neurotic European, sick of his thwarted instincts, restless, filled with self-disgust, was looking for not only spices and gold and slaves when he set out; he was looking for an Arcadia, a Land's End, a Shangri-la, a world peopled by shadow men, a world that would permit free play for his repressed instincts. Stripped of tradition, these misfits, adventurers, indentured servants, convicts and freebooters were the most advanced individualists of their time. Rendered socially superfluous by the stifling weight of the Church and nobility, buttressed by the influence of the ideas of Hume and Descartes, they had been brutally molded toward attitudes of emotional independence and could doff the cloying ties of custom, tradition, and family. The Asian-African native, anchored in family-dependence systems of life, could not imagine why or how these men had left their homelands, could not conceive of the cold, arid emotions sustaining them. . . . Emotional independence was a state of mind not only utterly inconceivable, but an attitude toward life downright evil to the Asian-African native—something to be avoided at all costs. Bound by a charged array of humble objects that made up an emotionally satisfying and exciting world, they, trapped by their limited mental horizon, could not help thinking that the white men invading their lands had been driven forcibly from their homes!

Living in a waking dream, generations of emotionally impoverished colonial European whites wallowed in the quick gratification of greed, reveled in the cheap superiority of racial domination, slaked their sensual thirst in illicit sexuality, draining off the dammed-up libido that European morality had condemned, amassing through trade a vast reservoir of economic fat, thereby establishing vast accumulations of capital which spurred the industrialization of the West. Asia and Africa thus became a neurotic habit that Europeans could forgo only at the cost of a powerful psychic wound, for this emotionally crippled Europe had, through the centuries, grown used to leaning upon this black crutch. 8

But what of the impact of those white faces upon the personalities of the native? Steeped in independence systems of family life and anchored in ancestor-worshiping religions, the native was prone to identify those powerful white faces falling athwart his existence with the potency of his dead father who had sustained him in the past. Temporarily accepting the invasion, he transferred his loyalties to those white faces, but, because of the psychological, racial, and economic luxury which those faces derived from their domination, the native was kept at bay. 9

Today, as the tide of white domination of the land mass of Asia and Africa recedes, there lies exposed to view a procession of shattered cultures, disintegrated societies, and a writhing sweep of more aggressive, irrational religion than the world has known for centuries. And, as scientific research, partially freed from the blight of colonial control, advances, we are witnessing the rise of a new genre of academic literature dealing with colonial and post-colonial facts from a wider angle of vision than ever possible before. The personality distortions of hundreds of millions of black, brown, and yellow people that are being revealed by this literature are confounding and will necessitate drastic alteration of our past evaluations of colonial rule. In this new literature one enters a universe of menacing shadows where disparate images coalesce—white turning into black, the dead coming to life, the top becoming the bottom—until you think you are seeing Biblical beasts with seven heads and ten horns rising out of the sea. Imperialism turns out to 10 have been much more morally foul a piece of business than even Marx and Lenin imagined!

An agony was induced into the native heart, rotting and pulverizing it as it tried to live under a white domination with which it could not identify in any real sense, a white domination that mocked it. The more Westernized that native heart became, the more anti-Western it had to be, for that heart was now weighing itself in terms of white Western values that made it feel degraded. Vainly attempting to embrace the world of white faces that rejected it, it recoiled and sought refuge in the ruins of moldering tradition. But it was too late; it was trapped; it found haven in neither. This is the psychological stance of the elite of the populations, free or still in a state of subjection, of present-day Asia and Africa; this is the profound revolution that the white man cast into the world; this is the revolution (a large part of which has been successfully captured by the Communists) that the white man confronts today with fear and paralysis.

QUESTIONS FOR READING AND WRITING

1. Wright's first paragraph is one long sentence. How does the structure of this sentence create a forceful climax?
2. Find examples of what you might consider "charged" language in Wright's essay. How do the connotations of Wright's words help to advance his argument or make his essay more persuasive?
3. Summarize Wright's descriptions of the two opposed historical parties: the European whites and the people of Africa and Asia.
4. What is the significance of Wright's example about the Martians invading Switzerland (paragraph 5)? How does it apply to his essay as a whole?
5. Write an essay that shows the common ground—of tone and theme—that Wright shares with James Baldwin in his essay "If Black English Isn't a Language, Then Tell Me, What Is?"
6. Write an essay that shows how Wright's essay applies to contemporary race relations.

Part 7

STYLE

If you were to ask most people what they meant by prose style, they would probably reply, "the *way* something is written." This isn't a bad definition, but it implies that there is a real distinction between *what* is written (the *contents* of a piece) and *how* it is written (the *manner*, or style of a piece). In fact, when an author has something to say and has taken some care to say it clearly and gracefully, there is little distinction between the words chosen and the ideas they express.

All style is a product of two things: *audience* and *purpose*. How you view these ulterior features of a piece of writing (both of which have to do with content) will determine what combination of the five elements of style you choose. These five elements of style—words (diction), sentence structure, voice, tone, and distance—can be combined in a variety of ways. The possible combinations allow writers to adjust their prose styles to the prospective audience, to the purpose of the writing, and the expression of the writer's personality. Analogous to these choices is the almost automatic way in which each of us talks to different audiences (friends, parents, teachers, acquaintances), varying our vocabulary, our voice, our tone—in short, our appearance—for each different audience. Much the same thing is true of prose style, although there are certain unvarying features of writing style which, like personality, remain constant reminders of our individuality.

If, for example, you read the introductory paragraphs to the five essays in this section, you will easily note that—aside from the obvious differences in subject matter—each of the essayists establishes his or her own voice very quickly. The "voices"—satiric in the case of Amis, authoritative in the case of Eiseley, nostalgic in the case of Hall, inquisitive and mysterious in the case of Kingston, relaxed and engaging in the case of Selzer—are products of the different styles of the writers. These styles are created through diction, sentence structure and length, sensory imagery, and other choices made by the authors.

You need, therefore, to identify your audience at the outset. A professional author is writing for what is in most cases a clearly defined readership: an audience of peers or, at times, a popular audience unfamiliar with the subject matter and special language of the discipline. Student writing is another matter. In most writing classes, your classmates are your audience. In some classes, the instructor is the only audience; in such cases, however, if you write only to satisfy the instructor, you may develop too narrow a range of styles.

Defining your purpose also helps determine your choices among the varying elements of style. For example, you should determine whether your purpose is expressive, recreational, exploratory, explanatory, or persuasive. Looking at examples of each element of style will help clarify how audience and purpose determine the appropriate combination of stylistic elements.

Diction (Word Choice) Because English offers so many synonyms, one of the choices open to you is to select, from among words of approximately the same meaning, the one that is most appropriate. Remember that words differ not only in denotation but also in connotation (see Part 3 on "Description"). Note the significant connotations of the words in the first two paragraphs of "In Hefnerland" by Martin Amis. The satirical or ambiguous connotations of *special*, *scored*, *wanders*, and *ferret-fit*—augmented by the italicized words, the scraps of conversation, and the rhetorical questions—help immediately to create Amis' mocking tone.

Sentence Structure Jonathan Swift defined effective style as "the proper words in the proper place." The first of these elements, diction, we have already considered; the second, sentence structure, has two variables: sentence construction and sentence length.

Sentences can be short, as in most reportorial writing; of moderate length, as in most explanatory writing; or long, as in most exploratory philosophical writing.

Note, for example, how the short sentences beginning Richard Selzer's "In Praise of Senescence" immediately establish a relaxed, informal, colloquial tone. Selzer is not subtly conveying complicated information; he is speculating about thoughts we all might have upon waking. His short sentences help us to apprehend the surprise and the suddenness of the quick impressions we might get of our assorted aches and pains. In paragraphs 12 and 13 of "Man the Firemaker," Loren Eiseley mixes short and longer sentences in describing the effects of fire on a wilderness environment. Generally, the longer sentences are used to offer commentary of a more complicated, scientific, sort. Further still from Selzer's style is that of Allan Bloom, in paragraphs 9 and 10 of "The Poverty of an Open Mind." Here, Bloom uses longer complex sentences as he turns various ideas over in his mind. In the following sentence he begins with a subordinate clause, and then interrupts the main clause with a long parenthetical intrusion, thus withholding the verb of the main clause until the very end. This creates a significantly climactic and emphatic effect that is far removed from the effect created by Selzer's sentences.

> Although many of the persons teaching such courses [in non-Western civilization] are real scholars and lovers of the area they study, in every case I have seen this requirement—when there are so many other things that can and should be learned but are not required, when philosophy and religion are no longer required—has a demagogic intention.*

In contrast to Bloom's *formal* style, an *informal style* uses moderately long sentences mixed with shorter sentences, and uses a mixture of concrete and abstract diction. Consider these two sentences from Edward Hoagland's essay, "Howling Back at the Wolves":

> Wolves have marvellous legs. The first thing one notices about them is how high they are set on their skinny legs, and the instant, blurred gait these can switch into, bicycling away, carrying them as much as forty miles in a day.†

* Allan Bloom, *The Closing of the American Mind* (Simon & Schuster, 1987), 35–6.

† Edward Hoagland, *Red Wolves and Black Bears* (Random House, 1976), 8.

Hoagland's second longer sentence—with its concrete diction and parallel construction—clarifies the first short sentence, especially the abstract adjective "marvellous," and this mixture is characteristic of *informal style*.

Voice, Tone, and Distance The final three elements of style should be considered together because they all have to do with the personality of the writer—that is, how you present yourself to your audience. Just as you form impressions of people from talking to them over the telephone (even before you have met them), you also form impressions about the writer from the *voice* that seems to speak to you from the pages of an essay.

Tone is an aspect of voice. The tone in a speaking voice reveals the intention of the speaker and the attitude of the speaker toward the audience. "You've done it again," could be uttered triumphantly be an excited teammate who is congratulating a place kicker who has just kicked her second field goal of a game or disgustedly by a father who is surveying the second dented fender in the family car. The *tone* of a piece of writing reveals whether it is to be taken seriously, humorously, ironically; whether the essay is exploring ideas, affirming them, or explaining them. Here are two pieces about baseball. In the first, the tone is one of serious reminiscence, recalling a memory from the past to illustrate the vividness of baseball's great moments:

> The presiding memory of that late summer is of Yastrzemski approaching the plate, once again in a situation, where all hope rests on him, and settling himself in the batter's box—touching his helmet, tugging at his belt, and just touching the tip of the bat to the ground, in precisely the same set of features—and then, in a storm of noise and pleading, swinging violently and perfectly.*

Contrast the tone of that paragraph with the following example, where the tone is one of mock seriousness, of humorous imitation of what the writer calls "The Bigs," the players in the major leagues. The slow-pitch softball player is asked to, at least, *look* like a big leaguer:

* Roger Angell, "The Interior Stadium," *The Summer Game* (Viking Press, 1972), 298–99.

> When going up to bat, don't step right into the batter's box as if it were an elevator. The box is your turf, your stage. Take possession of it slowly and deliberately, starting with a lot of back-bending, knee-stretching, and torso-revolving in the on-deck circle. Then, approaching the box, step outside it and tap the dirt off your spikes with your bat. You don't have spikes, you have sneakers, of course, but the significance of the tapping is the same. Then, upon entering the box, spit on the ground. It is a way of saying, "This here is mine. This is where I get my hits." Spit frequently. Spit at all crucial moments. Spit correctly. Spit should be blown, not ptuied weakly with the lips, which often results in a dribble. Spitting should convey forcefulness of purpose, concentration, pride. Spit down, not in the direction of others.*

Finally, *distance* refers to the figurative proximity of the audience to the writer. If, for example, the essay has serious, intimate tone, the distance between the writer and the audience will be small. If, on the other hand, the tone of the essay is impersonal and aloof, then the distance will be great. In most formal writing, the distance between author and audience is greater than in informal or colloquial writing.

In the following two paragraphs, the differences in tone and distance are shaped by the different intentions of each writer. In the first, Edward Abbey is showing that the scarcity of water is the desert's unique characteristic and warning those who believe they can make the arid Southwest bloom that there is a price to pay. The tone is one of serious warning, of irritation with those who fail to see the obvious. There is some distance between the writer and the audience because Abbey assumes the role of a knowing instructor for the audience:

> Water, water, water. . . . There is no shortage of water in the desert but exactly the right amount, a perfect ratio of water to rock, of water to sand, insuring that wide, free, open, generous spacing among plants and animals, homes and towns and cities, which makes the arid West so different from any other part of the nation. There is no lack of water here, unless you try to establish a city where no city should be.†

* Garrison Keillor, "Attitude," *Happy to Be Here* (Atheneum, 1982), 77–78.
† Edward Abbey, "Water," *Desert Solitaire* (McGraw-Hill, 1968), 126.

In contrast, Loren Eiseley's tone of quiet, wondering speculation includes the reader. Consequently, there is little distance separating the inquisitive writer from the equally admiring reader:

> If there is magic on this planet, it is contained in water. Its least stir even, as now in a rain pond on a flat roof opposite my office, is enough to bring me searching to the window. A wind ripple may translate itself into life. I have a constant feeling that some time I may witness that momentous miracle on a city roof, see life veritably and suddenly boiling out of a heap of rusted pipes and old television aerials.*

Style, then, cannot be reduced to a simple formula: words + sentences + voice + tone + distance = style. Effective style is a result of a series of complex interrelationships that, in turn, grow out of the choices a writer has made. It is also, finally, a product of that indefinable element—the personality of the writer. Just as you develop aspects of your personality by imitating people whose traits you admire, you can develop an admirable prose style by imitating those writers whose work you admire.

* Loren Eiseley, "The Flow of the River," *The Immense Journey* (Random House, 1957), 15.

✦ Martin Amis ✦
In Hefnerland

Martin Amis (b. 1949), the son of British novelist Kingsley Amis, received his B.A. from Oxford University in 1971. His novel The Rachel Papers *(1973) won the Somerset Maugham Award. In the following essay from* The Moronic Inferno and Other Visits to America *(1986), Amis takes an insider's look at the world of the now-married Hugh Hefner, founder and publisher of* Playboy. *Behind all the glitter and fantasy, "Hefnerland" looks rather tired and tawdry.*

I. The Playboy Party

AT LAST, THAT VERY SPECIAL MOMENT. Playmate of the Year Barbara Edwards composed herself at the far end of the astroturfed marquee. The stage she stood on recalled the train motif of her 'pictorial' in the current magazine; the blancmange-coloured dress she wore matched the press-kits that lay on every table. With her make-up scored by tears of pride, Barbara thanked the assembly for sharing this very special day. 'And now, the man who makes the dreams come true, ladies and gentlemen, Mr. Hugh M. Hefner!' Barbara faltered, then added, on the brink of crack-up: 'I love him *so much*.' 1

Hef took the stage. For a man who never goes out, who rises at mid-afternoon, who wanders his draped mansion in slippers and robe (whose lifestyle, on paper, resembles nothing so much as a study in terminal depression), Hef looks good—surprisingly, even scandalously so. A little haggard, maybe, a little etiolated, but trim and ferret-fit in blazer and slacks. It was 4.30, so Hef had presumably just rubbed the sleepy dust from his eyes and climbed from the trembling, twirling bed which he so seldom leaves. 'I work in it, play in it, eat and sleep in it' he has said. What *doesn't* he do in it? Well, perhaps this is the look you get, when the day's most onerous chore is your twilight visit to the men's room. 2

'It's a very special day for us,' Hef confirmed—and Barbara was a very special lady. She was also an exception to the recent 'run of blondes': why, the last brunette he'd crowned was Patti McGuire, 3 who went to marry Jimmy Connors'. At this point Barbara seemed suddenly subdued, no doubt by the prospect of going on to marry John McEnroe. 'Without further ado', however, Hef gave Barbara her special gifts, all of them taxable: $100,000, a new car (not a pink Porsche or a crimson Cadillac but a dinky black Jaguar), and the title itself: Playboy Playmate of the Year.

The assembled shower of pressmen, PR operatives, hangers-on and sub-celebrities—Robert Culp and Vince Van Patten were perhaps the most dazzling stars in this pastel galaxy—listened to the speeches, applauded zestlessly, and returned to their lite beers and tea-time vodka-tonics. More animated, in every sense, was the tableful of centrefold also-rans to the left of the podium, who greeted each remark with approving yelps of 'Yeah!' and 'Wha-hoo!' and 'Owl-*right*'. These are the special girls who languish in semi-residence at Playboy Mansion West, sunbathers, jacuzzi-fillers, party-prettifiers. Now what is it with these girls? The look aspired to is one of the expensive innocence of pampered maidenhood, frill and tracery in pink and white, flounced frocks for summer lawns. They also have a racehorse quality, cantilevered, genetically tuned or souped-up, the skin monotonously perfect, the hair sculpted and plumed; the body-tone at its brief optimum. Compared to these girls, the ordinary woman (the wife, the secretary, the non-goddess) looks lived-in or only half-completed, eccentrically and interestingly human.

Now Hef partied—Hef made the scene. Behind him at all times stood his bodyguard, a representative of the balding, gum-chewing, bodyguarding caste. Don't be a bodyguard, if you can possibly help it. You have to stand there all day with your arms folded, frowning watchfully. If you don't look grim and serious, you aren't doing your job. Diversified only by a bit of Pepsi-ferrying to the boss, that's what Hef's bodyguard does all day: look serious, while Hef horses around. A teenage playmate nuzzled Hef's chest and giggled. The bodyguard watched her watchfully.

As the thrash thrashed on, I slipped out of the tent and strolled the grounds. The man-made, bloodheat rockpool, the jacuzzi-infested grotto, the mini-zoos with their hunched, peanut-addict monkeys, smiling parrots, demonic macaws, the tennis court, the vast satellite receiver, curved like a giantess's brassière, which enables Hef to watch even more TV than he does already . . . Hef would later describe an average day in his life. 'Get up in the early afternoon, have a meeting, there's a regular buffet, a couple of movies, go upstairs around 1 a.m. with a girlfriend or whoever, make love then, have a meal, watch a movie or two.' Now that's four movies a day we're looking at. In the early Seventies Hef left the 'controlled environment' of his sealed and gardenless mansion in Chicago and moved out to California—itself a kind of controlled environment. Here the sun's controls are turned up all year long, and the girls are bigger, better, blonder, browner. But Hef isn't much of a fresh-air buff, even now . . . On the edge of the tropical fishpond stands an ornamental barrel, full of feed. Scatter a handful of the smelly pellets, and the fish—gorgeously shell-coloured—will rush to the bank, scores of them, mouths open, like benign but very greedy piranha. 'God, that's so gross,' said a passing partygoer. It is, too. The fish mass so tightly that for a moment, a special moment, there is no water beneath you—only squirming suicide. They look netted, beached, like a fisherman's haul.

2. *The Playboy Salad*

> Keyholder turns Bunny Back cards into Bunny for issuance of desired Certificate. (This offer is not valid in conjunction with any other special promotional offer.)
>
> —Playboy Club Leaflet

To the Playboy Club in Century City, just off the Avenue of the 7
Stars. In the foyer of this desperate establishment you will find a squad of strict-faced, corseted Bunnies, a gift shop featuring various 'celebrity purchases', and a big TV screen showing a big Playmate as she soaps herself in the tub . . . This is hot footage from the Playboy Channel—yes, a whole channel of the stuff, nine or ten hours a day. Playboy Inc. is changing its act: once a paunchy conglomerate kept afloat by gambling profits, it is now a solid publishing company nursing high hopes for cable TV. Hef believes that this is the way forward as the trend of American leisure increasingly shuns the street and huddles up in the home. Hef ought to know. He *is* home-smart, having put in thirty years' experience of never going out. In the submarine sanctum of the club itself you will find a Playboy pinball machine (the artwork depicts Hef flanked by two

playmates in their nighties), a video game with a handwritten Out of Order notice taped to its screen, some backgammon tables, a wall of framed centrefolds, and an oval bar where two or three swarthy loners sit slumped over their drinks, staring at the waitresses with an air of parched and scornful gloom. The wine glasses bear the Playboy logo: the little black rabbit-head does such a good imitation of a drowned insect that the young woman in our party shrieked out loud as she raised the glass to her lips. A 747-load of Japanese tourists in modified beachwear filed cautiously past. The manager or greeter, who looked like the rumba-instructor or tango-tutor of a Miami hotel, showed us to our table with a flourish. The Playboy Club, we knew, was LA's premier talent showcase, and tonight's act, we learned, was straight in from Las Vegas. When questioned, the manager proudly agreed that the club did a lot of package-tour business, as well as 'Greyline Tour bus groups. But the bus groups are very minimal tonight.' We gazed over the shining mops of the Japanese, and over the coiff, frizz, rug and bald-patch of the bus groups, as tonight's act did its thing: three girls in tutus, singing popular hits. At the incitement of the lead singer, the audience clapped its hands to the beat. The sound they made was as random as weak applause.

Over a Playboy Salad (remarkably similar to a non-Playboy salad, though rather heavy on the Thousand Island), I unwrapped my Playboy gift-pack. A dime-store garter belt for the special person in my life, two Playboy bookmatches, a blizzard of promotional offers, and a scrap of paper bearing the tremulous signature of Hugh M. Hefner. According to the new Bunny Pack bonus program, all I had to do was 'enjoy dinner Playboy style' 2,531 times, and I'd win a new VCR. There were other offers: 'Easy-to-take drink prices and complimentary chili every Monday through Friday from four to seven.' Even as I finished my steak, the $1.50 all-you-can-eat brunch was being assembled on the sideboards.

'Playboy Style . . . live it!' say the ads for the club in the parent magazine. But Playboy Style, nowadays, is something you'd have to ask your father about. In this den of innocuousness, you see that the Playboy dream has submitted to the heroic consumerism of everyday America: it has been proletarianised, kitsched, disappearing in the direction it came from, back to Chicago, the Fifties, Korea, the furtive world of *Dude, Gent, Rogue, Flirt, Sir, Male, Cutie, Eyeful,*

Giggles, Titter, Modern Sunbathing and Hygiene. Then, suddenly, there was Kinsey, the bikini, talk of the Pill, penicillin and *Playboy*. In the proud dawn of the Playboy dream, Hef hung out with Ella Fitzgerald, Dizzy Gillespie, Lenny Bruce and Jack Kerouac. Now it's Sammy Davis Jr, Jimmy Caan, John and Bo Derek, and Tom Jones. As it fades, the dream must reach down deeper into lumpen America, searching for the bedroom fevers of someone very like Hef in 1953: the son of stalwart Methodist parents, a fried-chicken and pork-chop kind of guy, miserably married, naïve, ambitious and repressed, someone who connected sex with upward mobility, someone who knew just how expensive the best things in life could be.

3. *The Playboy Playmate*

> My friends all asked me why I wanted to become a Playmate, and I told them I thought the women of Playboy were the epitome of beauty, class, taste and femininity.
>
> —Shannon Tweed, ex-Playmate

Overworked, it seemed, to the point of inanition or actual brain 10
death, Hef's PR man Don was having problems firming up the Hefner interview and Mansion tour. Where, I wondered, was Hef's famous in-depth back-up? But then I remembered what had happened when *Playboy* wanted to interview its own Editor-Publisher, six years ago: 'Hef says call back in a year' was the message from the Mansion. 'We have a problem,' droned Don. And yet problem-solving is his business, as it is with all the corporation Roys and Rays and Phils and Bills. Equally ponderous and evasive, Don is one of many middlemen hired to interpose between Hef and the outside world. Nearly everybody in LA retains one or two of these reality-softeners. What do you get at the end of every line? The smooth interceptions of answering services; the forensic clearances of security people; Hispanic incomprehension.

I drove to Don's office in the Playboy building, up on Sunset, to 11
meet and chat with a 'representative Playmate'. In the sunny, genial, nude-decked PR department I was introduced to Penny Baker and provided with the relevant issue of *Playboy*. Miss Baker was the beneficiary of The Great Thirtieth Anniversary Playmate Search: 250,000 polaroids later, they settled on Penny: 'And now that we've

found her, our greatest reward is in sharing her beauty with you.' What do they look for, exactly? 'Great nipples', 'sincere bush', 'Is there a problem with the breasts?'—these are the sort of concepts (I had read) that are tossed back and forth by Hef's creative consultants. For eight pages plus centrefold, at any rate, Penny's beauty, her charms, were glisteningly revealed. Her turn-ons were 'Mountains and music'. Among her turn-offs were 'big talkers and humidity'. Her ideal man? 'Someone who knows what he wants.' Penny is eighteen.

Monitored by Don's ponderous presence (he lurked there with his little tape recorder—company policy, no doubt), the interview began. Within a minute, I had run out of questions. I would get nothing but company policy from Penny, and we both knew it. Yes, she now worked on the Playboy promo circuit. No, her parents didn't object to the spread: they both thought it was neat. Yes, she belonged to the Shannon Tweed school of Playmate philosophy. 'I have a beautiful baddy,' explained Penny—and why should she be ashamed to share it with *Playboy* subscribers? 'How do you feel about Hugh Hefner?' I asked, and felt Don give a sluggish twitch. Penny's young face went misty. Sweetness, sincerity, sensitivity: like a big family. 'I saw him cry one time,' she confessed. 'It was his birthday. I went up and said Happy Birthday. And he, and he—well . . .' A very special moment, this one, a very special moment, not to be shared.

4. The Playboy Interview

> With another side of the same story comes iconoclast Buck Henry who reveals . . . that those really close to Hef always refer to him as Ner.
>
> —'Playbill', Playboy

What a scoop. I arrived at the Playboy Mansion for my interview to find that a quite extraordinary thing had happened: Ner had gone out! Now as we all know this is something that Ner hardly ever does. He hasn't been in a cab or a shop for twenty years. Only once in that period has he walked a street—back in 1967. At that time Ner still nestled in the sealed and soundproofed Chicago Mansion: he never knew the time of day, or even the season. Playboy Inc. had purchased a new property. Struck by the desire to see the place, Ner decided on a rare sortie: he would walk the eight blocks to North Michigan Avenue. Venturing out of his controlled environment, he found that it was raining. It was also the middle of the night. Legend does not record whether he was still in his pyjamas at the time . . . Today, Ner had *gone out* to the doctor's. But he would shortly return.

You pull up at the gates—Charing Cross Road, Holmby Hills. On 14
my previous visit I'd been unsmilingly cleared by a young man with tweed jacket, guest-list clipboard and turbulent complexion (peanut-butter plus pimple problem). Today the closed gates were unattended. My cab idled. Suddenly a mounted camera jerked its head in my direction—surprised, affronted. 'Let me have your name, sir,' I was asked by an ornamental boulder on my left. After several unfriendly questions and delays, the gates grudgingly parted. WARNING, says a sign on the curved drive: YOUR VISIT MAY BE RECORDED OR TELEVISED.

'An elegant English Tudor home, L-shaped, with slate roof and 15
leaded windows'. Playboy Mansion West teems with car-boys, handimen, minders, butlers, bunnies. Everyone is brisk with corporation *esprit*, with problem-solving know-how. They bear themselves strictly, in accordance with some vague but exacting model of efficiency and calm. Their life's work, you feel, is to ensure that nothing ever gets on Ner's nerves.

The library sports a double backgammon table, a panelled, 16
Pepsi-crammed icebox, various framed mag-covers featuring Ner, and a wall of books: bound editions of *Playboy* and the *Encyclopedia Britannica*, a modest collection of hardbacks—*The Supercrooks, Sex Forever, Luck be a Lady, Winning at the Track with Money Management*. Over the fireplace hangs a jokey, Renaissance-style portrait of Ner, emphasizing his close resemblance to Olivier's Richard III. (I later telephoned Don and asked him if this visual reference was an intentional one. Bemused, Don trudged off to check, and returned with an indignant denial.) As I walked to the window two limousines pulled up self-importantly in the forecourt. Slamming doors, busy car-boys, watchfully craning bodyguards. Having *gone out*, Ner had now *come back*. The interview would soon begin. Normally, I had read, recording equipment is set up to monitor a Hefner interview; also, the drapes are carefully drawn. 'Security request we close the drapes whenever Mr Hefner is in a

room.' But things are laxer now. The sun can shine, and it's still OK if Ner is in a room.

And in he came, wearing scarlet silk pyjamas, with pipe and 1
Pepsi—all as advertised. He apologised for being late and, in answer to my query, gave assurances that all had gone well at the doctor's. We settled down. The interview went through two phases, quite distinct in timbre. For the first hour or so, Ner talked like a politician: he has a hundred well-thumbed paragraphs in his head, each of them swiftly triggered by the normal run of questions. He is comfortable with criticism from the Right (abortion, censorship), rather less so with criticism from the Left (misogyny, philistinism). Actually Ner believes that these orthodoxies go in cycles: now that pornography has become—ironically—a civil-rights issue, he can imagine himself 'returning to the sexual avant garde' and reliving his old crusade. If such a challenge were to arise, the father of sexual liberation won't duck it. Nor shall Ner's sword sleep in his hand—no sir.

During the second part of the interview Ner relaxed: that is to say, 1
he became highly agitated, showing the wounded restlessness of a man who thinks himself persistently misunderstood. His eyes, previously as opaque as limo-glass, now glittered and fizzed. So did his Pepsi: he took such violent swigs that the bottle kept foaming to the brim. His language grew saltier. 'That's all *bullshit*,' he said repeatedly, swiping a finger through the air. You saw the Chicagoan in him then—the tight-jawed, almost ventriloquial delivery, the hard vowels, the human hardness of the windy city, the city that works.

What changed Ner's mood? First, a discussion of Bobbie 1
Arnstein, the private secretary who committed suicide after involving Playboy in a drugs scandal during the mid-Seventies. Ner was able to give himself a quickfire exoneration on this 'very scummy case'. He was far less convincing, though, when talk turned to the case of Dorothy Stratten. There is clearly something central and unshirkable about the Stratten story; it is the other side of the Playboy dream: it is the Playboy-endorsed Hollywood success, Stratten was murdered by her rejected husband in circumstances of hideous squalor. The controversy has been ceaseless (and deeply unwelcome to the corporation), with the TV film *Death of a Centrefold*, Bob Fosse's *Star 80* and now Peter Bogdanovich's

memoir *The Killing of the Unicorn*. Dorothy Stratten was Playmate of the Year for 1980, but she never saw 1981.

'Dorothy', he said, his face briefly wistful, 'was a very special 20
person, very trusting, a very special . . . human being.' People talked about the connections between Dorothy's death and the mores of the Playboy world—'But that's all bullshit. There is not and never has been a casting-couch thing here.' He then went on to slander Bob Fosse (off the record: a private thing between Ner and me). 'Recreational sex can still be moral—and that's what I'm all about. You have responsibilities as a bachelor. Nobody has ever had an abortion because of me. Nobody. It's like a family here. People stay with us for a very long time: my night-time secretary was a Playmate in 1960! I am a warm and caring person and so is the company. That's the kind of guy I am.'

The interview ended with some deliberation about the photo- 21
graphs that would illustrate this article. A recent and idealist portrait of Ner was produced in its frame—the sort of thing a sports or nightclub personality might hang over his bed. Wouldn't this do? 'It's never been used before,' droned Don (who had, of course, been ponderously present throughout). I hesitated. Did they seriously think that any magazine other than *People*—or *Playboy*—would publish such an 'official' study? Was the Editor-Publisher of genius losing his grip? Should I be frank? Was now the time to start calling Hef Ner? I said nothing. We sat there admiring the photograph, all agreeing how very special it looked.

The girls are always saying they feel 'safe' in the Mansion, and yet 22
the Easterner is pretty happy to take his leave—to leave the atmosphere of surveillance, corporation propaganda and PR p's and q's. Ner cruised out of the library and into the hall. An average evening was beginning. In the dining-room two elderly celebrities (Max Lerner and Richard Brook) were ordering complicated meals, with many doctorial vetos and provisos, while in the adjacent room the little squad of playmates and playthings, of honeys and bunnies, sat quietly around a table with their glasses (soft drinks only: Ner doesn't want them sloppy). Momentarily hushed and alert, the girls seemed ornamental and yet not quite passive, on call, expected to disport themselves in a certain way, expected to do whatever is expected.

5. The Playboy Philosophy

> Publishing a sophisticated men's magazine seemed to me the best possible way of fulfilling a dream I'd been nurturing ever since I was a teenager: to get laid a lot.
>
> —Hugh M. Hefner

Hefner has been inviting moral judgments for over thirty years. 2
It shows. It takes it out of a guy. Never altogether cynical, not yet entirely deluded, he is nonetheless committed to a sanitised, an authorised version of his life. The tendency is common enough, especially out here in the land of the innumerate billionaire, where a game of Scrabble is a literary event, where the prevailing values are those of the pocket calculator. 'There are times', Gloria Steinem has said, 'when a woman reading *Playboy* feels like a Jew reading a Nazi manual.' This is a frivolous remark, and blasphemous, too. Say that about *Playboy*, and what's left for *Der Sturmer*? If commercial pornography is imagined as a flophouse, with bestiality in the basement, then *Playboy* is a relatively clean and tidy attic. It is hardly pornography at all, more a kind of mawkish iconography for eternal adolescents. *Playboy* 'objectifies women' all right, in Joyce Wolfe's quaint phrase—but let's be objective here. According to the old Chicago axiom, there are two areas of wrongdoing: ethics and morals. Ethics is money and morals is sex. With Hefner, the line between the two is blurred or wobbly. It is a very American mix.

Three points need to be made about Hefner's oft-repeated con- 2
tention that Playboy is like a family. First, it is a family in which Poppa Bear gets to go to bed with his daughters. Secondly, it is a family in which the turnover in daughters is high. Thirdly, it is a family in which no tensions, resentments or power-struggles are admitted to or tolerated: at Playboy, everyone is happy all the time. Of every conceivable human institution, a family is what Playboy least resembles. True, Hefner's daughter Christie is now the figurehead of the company; true also that he has recently opened his arms, *Dynasty*-style, to a second, putative son (though he admitted to me that there was, of all things, 'a problem' with young Mark). But they're grown up now: they're on the payroll, under the wing, like everybody else. Hefner isn't paternal—he is exclusively paternalistic, wedded only to the daily exercise of power.

At the time of the interview I had not read Bogdanovich's *The* 25
Killing of the Unicorn. More to the point, neither had Hefner. I assume that his tone would have been very different—less spirited and aggrieved, more furtive and beleaguered. The Bogdanovich memoir is a labour of love, verging on a kind of sentimental mysticism, and its central accusation (that Hefner bears a measure of responsibility for Stratten's death, not only metaphorically but directly too) carries more emotion than weight. Some unpleasant facts, however, are now on record; and one is less disturbed by the sexual delinquencies than by the corporation automatism, the commercialised unreality with which Playboy glosses everything it does. Expediency, double-think, self-interest posing as philanthropy—this is the Playboy philosophy, powder-puffed and airbrushed by all the doltish euphemism of conglomerate America.

You are an eighteen-year-old from some dismal ex-prairie state, a 26
receptionist from Wyoming, or a local beauty queen—Miss Nowhere, Nebraska, perhaps. Your boyfriend's salacious Polaroid suddenly transforms itself into a first-class air ticket to Los Angeles. Limoed to the Mansion guest-house, you are schooled by smiling PR girls, aides, secretaries. No outside boyfriends are allowed into the Mansion—and these are, indisputably, 'healthy young girls'. Natural selection will decide whether you will be orgy-fodder, good for one of the gang, or whether you have what is takes to join the élite of Hefner's 'special ladies'. Signed up, set to work in the Playboy Club or on the promo or modelling circuits, you will find the divisions between public and private obligations hard to determine. You will also experience a wildly selective generosity, the also-rans routinely overworked and underpaid, the front-runners smothered in celebrity purchases—jewels, furs, paintings, cars and what Californians call a 'home'. If Hefner wants you to be a special lady then so does everyone else at the ranch. And when the call comes for you to join the boss in the inexorable jacuzzi, it isn't Hef on the line: it's his night-time secretary . . . This process used to be called seigneurism. 'Warm and caring'? Nowadays every business in America says how warm it is and how much it cares—loan companies, supermarkets, hamburger chains.

'Without you', Hefner once joked to a gaggle of Playmates, 'I'd 27
have a literary magazine.' Yes, but what would he have without the

literature? He'd have the Playboy Channel for one thing, and all the footling vapidity of unrelieved soft core. Sexcetera, Melody in Love, Pillow Previews, Alternative Lifestyle Features, 'nudity', 'strong language' and what are laughingly known as 'mature situations'. Christ, a week of this and you'd be like Don the PR man . . . And so we leave him, strolling his games parlour (there are bedrooms in back), his paradise of pinball, Pepsi and pyjama-parties—the remorselessly, the indefinitely gratified self. It is in the very nature of such appetites that they will deride him in time. One wonders what will happen to the girls when they grow up. One wonders what will happen to Hefner, if he ever gives it a try.

Hef at seventy. Ner at ninety. Now wouldn't that be something special?

QUESTIONS FOR READING AND WRITING

1. What aspects of Hefner, the "Playboy Philosophy," and the Playboy "world" is Amis satirizing? Does his emphasis surprise you in any way?
2. What point is Amis making by his reference to Dorothy Stratten, the murdered Playmate?
3. How do the "girls" described in paragraph 4 contrast with real women that we might know? What is Amis' point in making the contrast?
4. What is the effect of the last sentence in paragraph 11?
5. How, according to what Amis says in paragraph 24, is the Playboy "family" not like a family at all? What is Hefner's "family" like in your opinion?
6. Write an essay that criticizes *Playboy* from feminist perspective; that is, what objections against the magazine would be raised by someone who believed in dignity and equality for women?
7. Write an essay that constitutes a kind of "content analysis" of *Playboy*. What is in the magazine? What values are conveyed or implied? What vision of men does the magazine further? Of women? Of morality?

✦ Loren Eiseley ✦
Man the Firemaker

Loren Eiseley (1907–1977) was a poet, an anthropologist, and a historian (and popularizer) of science In the following essay, which originally appeared in Scientific American *in 1954, Eiseley links the development of humankind with our increasingly complicated ways of using fire. The use of fire, that is, helps to define us as a species; it may also, Eiseley warns, prove to be our undoing.*

MAN, IT IS WELL TO REMEMBER, is the discoverer but not the inventor of fire. Long before this meddling little Prometheus took to experimenting with flints, then matches, and finally (we hope not too finally) hydrogen bombs, fires had burned on this planet. Volcanoes had belched molten lava, lightning had struck in dry grass, winds had rubbed dead branches against each other until they burst into flame. There are evidences of fire in ancient fossil beds that lie deep below the time of man. 1

Man did not invent fire but he did make it one of the giant powers on the earth. He began this experiment long ago in the red morning of the human mind. Today he continues it in the midst of coruscating heat that is capable of rending the very fabric of his universe. Man's long adventure with knowledge has, to a very marked degree, been a climb up the heat ladder, for heat alone enables man to mold metals and glassware, to create his great chemical industries, to drive his swift machines. It is my intention here to trace man's manipulation of this force far back into its ice-age beginnings and to observe the part that fire has played in the human journey across the planet. The torch has been carried smoking through the ages of glacial advance. As we follow man on this journey, we shall learn another aspect of his nature: that he is himself a consuming fire. 2

At just what level in his intellectual development man mastered the art of making fire is still unknown. Neanderthal man of 50,000 years ago certainly knew the art. Traces of the use of fire have turned up in a cave of Peking man, the primitive human being of at least 250,000 years ago who had a brain only about two-thirds the 3 size of modern man's. And in 1947 Raymond Dart of Witwatersrand University announced the discovery in South Africa of *Australopithecus prometheus*, a man-ape cranium recovered from deposits which he believed showed traces of burned bone.

This startling announcement of the possible use of fire by a sub-human creature raised a considerable storm in anthropological circles. The chemical identifications purporting to indicate evidence of fire are now considered highly questionable. It has also been intimated that the evidence may represent only traces of a natural brush fire. Certainly, so long as the South African man-apes have not been clearly shown to be tool users, wide doubts about their use of fire will remain. There are later sites of tool-using human beings which do not show traces of fire.

Until there is proof to the contrary, it would seem wise to date the earliest use of fire to Peking man—*Sinanthropus*. Other human sites of the same antiquity have not yielded evidence of ash, but this is not surprising, for as a new discovery the use of fire would have taken time to diffuse from one group to another. Whether it was discovered once or several times we have no way of knowing. The fact that fire was in worldwide use at the beginning of man's civilized history enables us to infer that it is an old human culture trait—doubtless one of the earliest. Furthermore, it is likely that man used fire long before he became sophisticated enough to produce it himself.

In 1865 Sir John Lubbock, a British banker who made a hobby of popular writing on science, observed: "There can be no doubt that man originally crept over the earth's surface, little by little, year by year, just, for instance, as the weeds of Europe are now gradually but surely creeping over the surface of Australia." This remark was, in its time, a very shrewd and sensible observation. We know today, however, that there have been times when man suddenly made great strides across the face of the earth. I want to review one of those startling expansions—a lost episode in which fire played a tremendous part. To make its outlines clear we shall have to review the human drama in three acts.

The earliest humanlike animals we can discern are the man-apes of South Africa. Perhaps walking upright on two feet, this creature seems to have been roaming the East African grasslands about one million years ago. Our ancestor, proto-man, probably emerged from the tropics and diffused over the region of warm climate in Eurasia and North Africa. He must have been dependent upon small game, insects, wild seeds, and fruits. His life was hard, his search for food incessant, his numbers were small.

The second stage in human history is represented by the first true men. Paleoanthropic man is clearly a tool user, a worker in stone and bone, but there is still something of the isolated tinkerer and fumbler about him. His numbers are still sparse, judging from the paucity of skeletal remains. Short, stocky, and powerful, he spread over the most temperate portions of the Afro-Eurasiatic land mass but never attempted the passage through the high Arctic to America. Through scores of millennia he drifted with the seasons, seemingly content with his troglodyte existence, making little serious change in his array of flint tools. It is quite clear that some of these men knew the use of fire, but many may not have. 8

The third act begins some 15,000 or 20,000 years ago. The last great ice sheet still lies across northern Europe and North America. Roving on the open tundra and grasslands below those ice sheets is the best-fed and most varied assemblage of grass-eating animals the world has ever seen. Giant long-horned bison, the huge wild cattle of the Pleistocene, graze on both continents. Mammoth and mastodon wander about in such numbers that their bones are later to astonish the first American colonists. Suddenly, into this late paradise of game, there erupts our own species of man—*Homo sapiens*. Just where he came from we do not know. Tall, lithe, long-limbed, he is destined to overrun the continents in the blink of a geological eye. He has an excellent projectile weapon in the shape of the spear thrower. His flint work is meticulous and sharp. And the most aggressive carnivore the world has ever seen comes at a time made for his success: the grasslands are alive with seemingly inexhaustible herds of game. 9

Yet fire as much as flesh was the magic that opened the way for the supremacy of *Homo sapiens*. We know that he was already the master of fire, for the track of it runs from camp to buried camp: the blackened bones of the animals he killed, mute testimony to the relentless step of man across the continents, lie in hundreds of sites in the Old and the New Worlds. Meat, more precious than the gold for which men later struggled, supplied the energy that carried man across the world. Had it not been for fire, however, all that 10 enormous source of life would have been denied to him: he would have gone on drinking the blood from small kills, chewing wearily at uncooked bone ends or masticating the crackling bodies of grasshoppers.

Fire shortens the digestive process. It breaks down tough masses 1
of flesh into food that the human stomach can easily assimilate. Fire made the difference that enabled man to expand his numbers rapidly and to press on from hunting to more advanced cultures. Yet we take fire so much for granted that this first great upswing in human numbers, this first real gain in the seizure of vast quantities of free energy, has to a remarkable degree eluded our attention.

With fire primitive man did more than cook his meat. He ex- 1
tended the pasture for grazing herds. A considerable school of thought, represented by such men as the geographer Carl Sauer and the anthropologist Omer Stewart, believes that the early use of fire by the aborigines of the New World greatly expanded the grassland area. Stewart says: "The number of tribes reported using fire leads one to the conclusion that burning of vegetation was a universal culture pattern among the Indians of the U.S. Furthermore, the amount of burning leads to the deduction that nearly all vegetation in America at the time of discovery and exploration was what ecologists would call fire vegetation. That is to say, fire was a major factor, along with soil, moisture, temperature, wind, animals, and so forth, in determining the types of plants occurring in any region. It follows then, that the vegetation of the Great Plains was a fire vegetation." In short, the so-called primeval wilderness which awed our forefathers had already felt the fire of the Indian hunter. Here, as in many other regions, man's fire altered the ecology of the earth.

It had its effect not only on the flora but also on the fauna. Of the 1
great herds of grazing animals that flourished in America in the last Ice Age, not a single trace remains—the American elephants, camels, long-horned bison are all gone. Not all of them were struck down by the hunters' weapons. Sauer argues that a major explanation of the extinction of the great American mammals may be fire. He says that the aborigines used fire drives to stampede game, and he contends that this weapon would have worked with peculiar effectiveness to exterminate such lumbering creatures as the mammoth. I have stood in a gully in western Kansas and seen outlined in

the earth the fragmented black bones of scores of bison who had perished in what was probably a man-made conflagration. If, at the end of Pleistocene times, vast ecological changes occurred, if climates shifted, if lakes dried and in other places forests sprang up, and if, in this uncertain and unsteady time, man came with flint and fire upon the animal world about him, he may well have triggered a catastrophic decline and extinction. Five thousand years of man and his smoking weapon rolling down the wind may have finished the story for many a slow-witted animal species. In the great scale of geological time this act of destruction amounts to but one brief hunt.

Man, as I have said, is himself a flame. He has burned through 14
the animal world and appropriated its vast stores of protein for his own. When the great herds failed over many areas, he had to devise new ways to feed his increase or drop back himself into a precarious balance with nature. Here and there on the world's margins there have survived into modern times men who were forced into just such local adjustments. Simple hunters and collectors of small game in impoverished areas, they maintain themselves with difficulty. Their numbers remain the same through generations. Their economy permits no bursts of energy beyond what is necessary for the simple age-old struggle with nature. Perhaps, as we view the looming shadow of atomic disaster, this way of life takes on a certain dignity today.

Nevertheless there is no road back; the primitive way is no longer 15
our way. We are the inheritors of an aggressive culture which, when the great herds disappeared, turned to agriculture. Here again the magic of fire fed the great human wave and built up man's numbers and civilization.

Man's first chemical experiment involving the use of heat was to 16
make foods digestible. He had cooked his meat; now he used fire to crack his grain. In the process of adopting the agricultural way of life he made his second chemical experiment with heat: baking pottery. Ceramics may have sprung in part from the need for storage vessels to protect harvested grain from the incursions of rats and mice and moisture. At any rate, the potter's art spread with the revolutionary shift in food production in early Neolithic times.

People who have only played with mud pies or made little sun- 17
dried vessels of clay are apt to think of ceramics as a simple art.

Actually it is not. The sundried vessels of our childhood experiments would melt in the first rain that struck them. To produce true pottery one must destroy the elasticity of clay through a chemical process which can be induced only by subjecting the clay to an intense baking at a temperature of at least 400 to 500 degrees centigrade. The baking drives out the so-called water of constitution from the aluminum silicate in the clay. Thereafter the clay will no longer dissolve in water; a truly fired vessel will survive in the ground for centuries. This is why pottery is so important to the archaeologist. It is impervious to the decay that overtakes many other substances, and, since it was manufactured in quantity, it may tell tales of the past when other clues fail us.

Pottery can be hardened in an open campfire, but the results can never be so excellent as those achieved in a kiln. At some point the early potter must have learned that he could concentrate and conserve heat by covering his fire—perhaps making it in a hole or trench. From this it was a step to the true closed kiln, in which there was a lower chamber for the fire and an upper one for the pottery. Most of the earthenware of simple cultures was fired at temperatures around 500 degrees centigrade, but really thorough firing demands temperatures in the neighborhood of 900 degrees. 1

After man had learned to change the chemical nature of clay, he began to use fire to transform other raw materials—ores into metals, for instance. One measure of civilization is the number of materials manipulated. The savage contents himself with a few raw materials which can be shaped without the application of high temperatures. Civilized man uses fire to extract, alter, or synthesize a multitude of substances. 1

By the time metals came into extended use, the precious flame no longer burned in the open campfire, radiating its heat away into the dark or flickering on the bronzed faces of the hunters. Instead it roared in confined furnaces and was fed oxygen through crude bellows. One of the by-products of more intensified experiments with heat was glass—the strange, impassive substance which, in the form of the chemist's flask, the astronomer's telescope, the biologist's microscope, and the mirror, has contributed so vastly to our knowledge of ourselves and the universe. 2

We hear a good deal about the Iron Age, or age of metals, as a great jump forward in man's history; actually the metals themselves 2 played a comparatively small part in the rise of the first great civilizations. While men learned to use bronze, which demands little more heat than is necessary to produce good ceramics, and later iron, for tools and ornaments, the use of metal did not make a really massive change in civilization for well over 1,500 years. It was what Leslie White of the University of Michigan calls the "Fuel Revolution" that brought the metals into their own. Coal, oil, and gas, new sources of energy, combined with the invention of the steam and combustion engines, ushered in the new age. It was not metals as tools, but metals combined with heat in new furnaces and power machinery that took human society off its thousand-year plateau and made possible another enormous upswing in human numbers, with all the social repercussions.

Today the flames grow hotter in the furnaces. Man has come far 22
up the heat ladder. The creature that crept furred through the glitter of blue glacial nights lives surrounded by the hiss of steam, the roar of engines, and the bubbling of vats. Like a long-armed crab, he manipulates the tongs in dangerous atomic furnaces. In asbestos suits he plunges into the flaming debris of hideous accidents. With intricate heat-measuring instruments he investigates the secrets of the stars, and he has already found heat-resistant alloys that have enabled him to hurl himself into space.

How far will he go? Three hundred years of the scientific method 23
have built the great sky-touching buildings and nourished the incalculable fertility of the human species. But man is also *Homo duplex*, as they knew in the darker ages. He partakes of evil and of good, of god and or man. Both struggle in him perpetually. And he is himself a flame—a great, roaring, wasteful furnace devouring irreplaceable substances of the earth. Before this century is out, either *Homo duplex* must learn that knowledge without greatness of spirit is not enough for man, or there will remain only his calcined cities and the little charcoal of his bones.

QUESTIONS FOR READING AND WRITING

1. For what audience does Eiseley's essay seem intended? How do you know?

2. In what ways has this essay fostered your sense of respect for the human species?
3. Examine paragraph 9 carefully. By what means does Eiseley achieve variety in his sentences?
4. Eiseley was an anthropologist and biologist; Richard Selzer, author of "In Praise of Senescence," is a physician. What are the principal differences between their prose styles?
5. Write an essay in which you describe the effects that having no fire or fire-related products would have upon a day in your life.
6. Write an essay in which you attempt to explain a difficult scientific concept (evolution, psychoanalysis, the structure of the atom, electricity, and so forth) to an audience of third-graders.

✦ Donald Hall ✦
O Fenway Park

In addition to his highly regarded poetry and nonfiction, Donald Hall (b. 1928) has been a prolific writer and editor of textbooks. Among his collections of poetry are Exiles and Marriages *(1955) and* Kicking the Leaves *(1978). "O Fenway Park" was published in* Fathers Playing Catch with Sons *(1985). In this essay, Hall sings the praises of old-fashioned ballparks like Fenway Park in Boston, still his favorite place to see a ballgame even though it now has a large screen in centerfield to show instant replays.*

On a wall near the grandstand gates there's a bronze plaque: 1

NEW
FENWAY PARK
BUILT 1912
RECONSTRUCTED 1934

It's the oldest, and maybe the best, ballpark in the major leagues.

For most baseball fans, maybe oldest is always best. We love baseball because it seizes and retains the past, like the snowy village inside a glass paperweight. Though baseball goes through continual small changes, we do not acknowledge them. We cherish baseball's 1890s costumes and scarcely notice when the double-knits become as form-fitting as Captain Marvel's work clothes. We accept the designated hitter in the American League and plastic grass in the National, as if these innovations were our heritage. Even conservative Fenway Park has added baseball's newest accessory—the message board—and it seems as if it has been there forever. 2

As you look at the scene outside, you'd never believe that anything was new at Boston's ballpark. Ancient bars, hamburger joints, and souvenir shops jostle each other across from the pitted brick walls. In the streets, vendors of hot dogs, pennants, balloons, peanuts, and illegal tickets cry their wares to the advancing crowd. The streets carry a sweet, heavy, carnival air, like an old-fashioned marketplace. You half expect to run into a juggler or a harlequin. 3

Inside Fenway, late afternoon sun illuminates the grass, making it so bright that I squint to see it. I look around at the old park again, 4 green chairs, iron girders holding the roof up—and young ballplayers taking batting practice. I come to the ballpark early to watch BP, the antique and immemorial rituals of batting and shagging flies while pitchers run in the outfield. Especially I come early to *this* ballpark, tiny and eccentric and warm hearted, because I want to look my fill and to remember.

As I look around, the oldest and smallest ballpark in the major leagues renews itself to my eyes, with its crazy angles jutting into the field. It's like a huge pinball machine designed by a mad sculptor, driving outfielders mad when they try to predict a carom. The box seats everywhere lean into the field, disturbing ballplayers who try to catch foul flies. But the closeness is great for the fans. Even general admission in Fenway Park is nearer the field than the box seats in new ballparks. I sat in the center-field bleachers when Luis Tiant opened the 1975 World Series; as he swiveled toward second base in his rotating windup, Luis and I were eyeball to eyeball.

I remember other games and other years. I went to Fenway first in the early forties, when I was thirteen or fourteen, and watched the young Ted Williams, slim as a trout, arc his flat and certain swing. Returning to Fenway every year, I saw him age. In 1948 I watched the one-game play-off between Boston and Cleveland for the American League pennant, won by Cleveland as Lou Boudreau lifted a fly ball into the left-field screen and a line drive into the right-field bleachers—or was it the bullpen? A year later I came with my grandfather, a New Hampshire farmer who had seen the Red Stockings play once before, late in the last century; he had been hearing about Fenway Park for almost fifty years but had never left his haying long enough to see a game. He decided he liked Fenway Park.

The fifties, the sixties, the seventies . . . All these years, Fenway has gone unchallenged. Back in the forties, there was agitation to remove the short left-field wall and take over Lansdowne Street in order to build more bleachers. The Red Sox listened, but it turned out that three different cadres of politicians had to approve any move they made—city, county, and state; it was unthinkable that three sets of politicians could agree on anything so serious.

In the sixties, agitation came from a football team that rented the stadium from the Red Sox, the Boston Patriots as they were. Understandably, they disliked the seating capacity and the sightlines—the best seats for baseball turned up in one football end zone or the other. In Boston newspapers it was bruited that the two teams would collaborate on a new stadium near South Station, with a movable roof and places to park. But when Boston taxpayers heard the projected cost, the rumors scattered and fled. I suspect this pleased Mr. Yawkey, owner of the Red Sox until his death in 1976, who owned Fenway Park outright—no mortgage—and who would never have taken orders from a commission.

It also pleased nostalgic baseball fans everywhere, who wanted no multimillion-dollar trailer camp to replace this antique jewel, this decadent emerald set in the Boston sea. They showed their appreciation, too. In a park that seats only 33,379 people, the Red Sox have led the American League in attendance seven out of the last ten years. 9

Ten out of ten years, Boston fans have led the league in enthusiasm and madness. They pull me back to Fenway as much as the ballpark does. They're *baseball* fans, knowledgeable and assertive, if a trifle loony. They know their baseball, not from listening to TV commentators but from sitting through hot afternoons in the Fenway bleachers. They make the old green walls palpitate and pulse as their intensity gathers and builds in the pressure of this small cooker. Their numbers include such celebrated eccentrics as the South Boston midget known only as O. O'Sullivan, who hands silver dollars to the fans around him—a dozen each time—when Carl Yastrzemski hits a home run. And there is Lulu from Honolulu, yesteryear's attraction at the Old Howard, who occupies in her dotage a grandstand seat behind the Red Sox dugout. 10

The reconstruction of 1934, commemorated on the bronze plaque, didn't reconstruct a whole lot. As new owner. Mr. Yawkey took down the old wooden bleachers and replaced them with modern ones, which hold up pretty well after these many years. 11

The breakneck urge toward modernization continues apace. 12

In the winter of 1975–1976, after the great World Series of 1975, the Red Sox assembled a vast bank of lights above the centerfield bleachers, an item known as the message board, which can transmit not only messages but pictures—and not only still pictures but moving ones also. Fenway Park becomes an enormous outdoor television set. 13

If baseball fans are nostalgic and Bostonians traditional, then innovation at Fenway Park is doubly cursed. When the newspapers reported the forthcoming message board, Boston's fans were outraged. Quickly the Red Sox assured everyone that at least the message board would not lead cheers; it would never, they swore, tell the fans CHARGE.

By early June of 1976, everyone in the park accepted the message board as *immemorial*. It had become at least as immemorial as hot dogs and possibly more immemorial than Crackerjack. Now in Fenway Park, after a dazzling play, the dazzle repeats itself in the black air over center field, a grainy rotogravure, gross and miraculous, allowing us to savor again, as we learned to savor in the privacy of our living rooms, exact repetition of the glorious act.

For myself, I was in love with it before the first pitch. Warming itself up, the message board showed us the groundskeepers preparing the infield at the same time that they were doing it. Thirty thousand people had the choice: they could observe the reality—a man named Al Forrester watering down the dirt of the infield—or they could watch, one one-thousandth of a millisecond later, the enlarged and fuzzy image of reality.

On the field Al Forrester strolls stoutly, doing his immemorial job. Above him on a screen, a huge sepia Al Forrester patrols the same acreage, his hose blooming with large drops of water, until suddenly the player at the message board console pushes a button, and an enormous Al Forrester *stops*, sharp, like *that*—his hose and its water petals fixed at a permanent moment—while below on the real field the small man, returned to his merely human body, arrives at third base.

Above him, for more than 30,000 people, a moment of our lives stands stock still—like all the moments of all of us here, irrecoverable in fact but secure in our memories: Ted Williams playing a ball in the left-field corner; Lou Boudreau lifting a fly toward the green wall; my grandfather leaning forward in 1949, his eyes electric in his tanned farmer's face. Therefore we cherish a message board—the one outside our heads to rhyme with the one inside.

QUESTIONS FOR READING AND WRITING

1. In what ways do paragraphs 2 and 18 form a kind of envelope that contains the rest of the essay?
2. With what kind of ballpark does Hall implicitly contrast Fenway Park? What features of modern stadiums would Hall be likely to object to?
3. In what ways does Hall establish his authority as a knowledgeable baseball fan capable of making a judgment about Fenway Park that his readers will be inclined to listen to?
4. In paragraphs 15–18, Hall describes the message board at Fenway Park. Of what does the message board become a kind of symbol?
5. Write an essay that describes the peculiarities of your favorite ballpark and tell how they affect any game played there.
6. Write an essay that describes your earliest memory of baseball (or another of your favorite sports). Concentrate upon sensory impressions, feelings, and the way the sport connects with the rest of your life.

✦ Maxine Hong Kingston ✦
No Name Woman

Maxine Hong Kingston (b. 1940) was born in California of Chinese immigrant parents. She graduated from the University of California at Berkeley in 1962. She has published a novel and two books of nonfiction, the best-known being The Woman Warrior: Memories of a Girlhood Among Ghosts *(1975), from which the following selection is taken. In this essay, Kingston writes movingly of a "disgraced" ancestor whose very name should not be mentioned in public. Kingston speculates—as she tries to come to grips with her own ancestral past—upon what her ancestor did and felt.*

"YOU MUST NOT TELL ANYONE," my mother said, "what I am about to tell you. In China your father had a sister who killed herself. She jumped into the family well. We say that your father has all brothers because it is as if she had never been born.

"In 1924 just a few days after our village celebrated seventeen hurry-up weddings—to make sure that every young man who went 'out on the road' would responsibly come home—your father and his brothers and your grandfather and his brothers and your aunt's new husband sailed for America, the Gold Mountain. It was your grandfather's last trip. Those lucky enough to get contracts waved good-bye from the decks. They fed and guarded the stowaways and helped them off in Cuba, New York, Bali, Hawaii. 'We'll meet in California next year,' they said. All of them sent money home.

'I remember looking at your aunt one day when she and I were dressing; I had not noticed before that she had such a protruding melon of a stomach. But I did not think, 'She's pregnant,' until she began to look like other pregnant women, her shirt pulling and the white tops of her black pants showing. She could not have been pregnant, you see, because her husband had been gone for years. No one said any thing. We did not discuss it. In early summer she was ready to have the child, long after the time when it could have been possible.

"The village had also been counting. On the night the baby was to be born the villagers raided our house. Some were crying. Like a great saw, teeth strung with lights, files of people walked zigzag across our land, tearing the rice. Their lanterns doubled in the disturbed black water, which drained away through the broken bunds. As the villagers closed in, we could see that some of them, probably men and women we knew well, wore white masks. The people with long hair hung it over their faces. Women with short hair made it stand up on end. Some had tied white bands around their foreheads, arms, and legs.

"At first they threw mud and rocks at the house. Then they threw 5
eggs and began slaughtering our stock. We could hear the animals scream their deaths—the roosters, the pigs, a last great roar from the ox. Familiar wild heads flared in our night windows; the villagers encircled us. Some of the faces stopped to peer at us, their eyes rushing like searchlights. The hands flattened against the panes, framed heads, and left red prints.

"The villagers broke in the front and the back doors at the same 6
time, even though we had not locked the doors against them. Their knives dripped with the blood of our animals. They smeared blood on the doors and walls. One woman swung a chicken, whose throat she had slit, splattering blood in red arcs about her. We stood together in the middle of our house, in the family hall with the pictures and tables of the ancestors around us, and looked straight ahead.

"At that time the house had only two wings. When the men came 7
back, we would build two more to enclose our courtyard and a third one to begin a second courtyard. The villagers pushed through both wings, even your grandparents' rooms, to find your aunt's which was also mine until the men returned. From this room a new wing for one of the younger families would grow. They ripped up her clothes and shoes and broke her combs, grinding them underfoot. They tore her work from the loom. They scattered the cooking fire and rolled the new weaving in it. We could hear them in the kitchen breaking our bowls and banging the pots. They overturned the great waist-high earthenware jug; duck eggs, pickled fruits, vegetables burst out and mixed in acrid torrents. The old woman from the next field swept a broom through the air and loosed the spirits-of-the-broom over our heads. 'Pig.' 'Ghost.' 'Pig,' they sobbed and scolded while they ruined our house.

"When they left, they took sugar and oranges to bless themselves. They cut pieces from the dead animals. Some of them took bowls that were not broken and clothes that were not torn. Afterward we swept up the rice and sewed it back up into sacks. But the smells from the spilled preserves lasted. Your aunt gave birth in the pigsty that night. The next morning when I went for the water, I found her and the baby plugging up the family well.

"Don't let your father know that I told you. He denies her. Now that you have started to menstruate, what happened to her could happen to you. Don't humiliate us. You wouldn't like to be forgotten as if you had never been born. The villagers are watchful."

Whenever she had to warn us about life, my mother told stories that ran like this one, a story to grow up on. She tested our strength to establish realities. Those in the emigrant generations who could not reassert brute survival died young and far from home. Those of us in the first American generations have had to figure out how the invisible world the emigrants built around our childhoods fit in solid America.

The emigrants confused the gods by diverting their curses, misleading them with cooked streets and false names. They must try to confuse their offspring as well, who, I suppose, threaten them in similar ways—always trying to get things straight, always trying to name the unspeakable. The Chinese I know hide their names; sojourners take new names when their lives change and guard their real names with silence.

Chinese-Americans, when you try to understand what things in you are Chinese, how do you separate what is peculiar to childhood, to poverty, insanities, one family, your mother who marked your growing with stories, from what is Chinese? What is Chinese tradition and what is the movies?

If I want to learn what clothes my aunt wore, whether flashy or ordinary, I would have to begin, "Remember Father's drowned-in-the-well sister?" I cannot ask that. My mother has told me once and for all the useful parts. She will add nothing unless powered by Necessity, a riverbank that guides her life. She plants vegetable gardens rather than lawns; she carries the odd-shaped tomatoes home from the fields and eats food left for the gods.

Whenever we did frivolous things, we used up energy; we flew high kites. We children came up off the ground over the melting cones our parents brought home from work and the American movie on New Year's Day—*Oh, You Beautiful Doll* with Betty Grable one year, and *She Wore a Yellow Ribbon* with John Wayne another year. After the one carnival ride each, we paid in guilt; our tired father counted his change on the dark walk home.

Adultery is extravagance. Could people who hatch their own 15
chicks and eat the embryos and the heads for delicacies and boil the feet in vinegar for party food, leaving only the gravel, eating even the gizzard lining—could such people engender a prodigal aunt? To be a woman, to have a daughter in starvation time was a waste enough. My aunt could not have been the lone romantic who gave up everything for sex. Women in the old China did not choose. Some man had commanded her to lie with him and be his secret evil. I wonder whether he masked himself when he joined the raid on her family.

Perhaps she encountered him in the fields or on the mountain 16
where the daughters-in-law collected fuel. Or perhaps he first noticed her in the marketplace. He was not a stranger because the village housed no strangers. She had to have dealings with him other than sex. Perhaps he worked an adjoining field, or he sold her the cloth for the dress she sewed and wore. His demand must have surprised, then terrified her. She obeyed him; she always did as she was told.

When the family found a young man in the next village to be her 17
husband, she stood tractably beside the best rooster, his proxy, and promised before they met that she would be his forever. She was lucky that he was her age and she would be the first wife, an advantage secure now. The night she first saw him, he had sex with her. Then he left for America. She had almost forgotten what he looked like. When she tried to envision him, she only saw the black and white face in the group photograph the men had had taken before leaving.

The other man was not, after all, much different from her hus- 18
band. They both gave orders: she followed. "If you tell your family, I'll beat you. I'll kill you. Be here again next week." No one talked sex, ever. And she might have separated the rapes from the rest of living if only she did not have to buy her oil from him or gather wood in the same forest. I want her fear to have lasted just as long as rape lasted so that the fear could have been contained. No drawn-out

fear. But women at sex hazarded birth and hence lifetimes. The fear did not stop but permeated everywhere. She told the man, "I think I'm pregnant." He organized the raid against her.

On nights when my mother and father talked about their life back home, sometimes they mentioned an "outcast table" whose business they still seemed to be settling, their voices tight. In a commensal tradition, where food is precious, the powerful older people made wrongdoers eat alone. Instead of letting them start separate new lives like the Japanese, who could become samurais and geishas, the Chinese family, faces averted but eyes glowering sideways, hung on to the offenders and fed them leftovers. My aunt must have lived in the same house as my parents and eaten at an outcast table. My mother spoke about the raid as if she had seen it, when she and my aunt, a daughter-in-law to a different household, should not have been living together at all. Daughters-in-law lived with their husband's parents, not their own; a synonym for marriage in Chinese is "taking a daughter-in-law." Her husband's parents could have sold her, mortgaged her, stoned her. But they had sent her back to her own mother and father, a mysterious act hinting at disgraces not told me. Perhaps they had thrown her out to deflect the avengers.

She was the only daughter; her four brothers went with her father, husband, and uncles "out on the road" and for some years became western men. When the goods were divided among the family, three of the brothers took land, and the youngest, my father, chose an education. After my grandparents gave their daughter away to her husband's family, they had dispensed all the adventure and all the property. They expected her alone to keep the traditional ways, which her brothers, now among the barbarians, could fumble without detection. The heavy, deep-rooted women were to maintain the past against the flood, safe for returning. But the rare urge west had fixed upon our family, and so my aunt crossed boundaries not delineated in space.

The work of preservation demands that the feelings playing about in one's guts not be turned into action. Just watch their passing like cherry blossoms. But perhaps my aunt, my forerunner, caught in a slow life, let dreams grow and fade and after some months or years went toward what persisted. Fear at the enormities of the forbidden kept her desires delicate, wire and bone. She looked at a man because she liked the way the hair was tucked behind his ears, or she liked the question-mark line of a long torso curving at the shoulder and straight at the hip. For warm eyes or a soft voice or a slow walk—that's all—a few hairs, a line, a brightness, a sound, a pace, she gave up family. She offered us up for a charm that vanished with tiredness, a pigtail that didn't toss when the wind died. Why, the wrong lighting could erase the dearest thing about him.

It could very will have been, however, that my aunt did not take subtle enjoyment of her friend, but, a wild woman, kept rollicking company. Imagining her free with sex doesn't fit, though. I don't know any women like that, or men either. Unless I see her life branching into mine, she gives me no ancestral help. 22

To sustain her being in love, she often worked at herself in the mirror, guessing at the colors and shapes that would interest him, changing them frequently in order to hit on the right combination. She wanted him to look back. 23

On a farm near the sea, a woman who tended her appearance reaped a reputation for eccentricity. All the married women bluntcut their hair in flaps about their ears or pulled it back in tight buns. No nonsense. Neither style blew easily into heart-catching tangles. And at their weddings they displayed themselves in their long hair for the last time. "It brushed the backs of my knees," my mother tells me. "It was braided, and even so, it brushed the backs of my knees." 24

At the mirror my aunt combed individuality into her bob. A bun could have been contrived to escape into black streamers blowing in the wind or in quiet wisps about her face, but only the older women in our picture album wear buns. She brushed her hair back from her forehead, tucking the flaps behind her ears. She looped a piece of thread, knotted into a circle between her index fingers and thumbs, and ran the double strand across her forehead. When she closed her fingers as if she were making a pair of shadow geese bite, the string twisted together catching the little hairs. Then she pulled the thread away from her skin, ripping the hairs out neatly, her eyes watering from the needles of pain. Opening her fingers, she cleaned the thread, then rolled it along her hairline and the tops of her eyebrows. My mother did the same to me and my sisters and herself. I used to believe that the expression "caught by the short 25 hairs" meant a captive held with a depilatory string. It especially hurt at the temples, but my mother said we were lucky we didn't have to have our feet bound when we were seven. Sisters used to sit on their beds and cry together, she said, as their mothers or their slave removed the bandages for a few minutes each night and let the blood gush back into their veins. I hope that the man my aunt loved appreciated a smooth brow, that he wasn't just a tits-and-ass man.

Once my aunt found a freckle on her chin, at a spot that the almanac said predestined her for unhappiness. She dug it out with a hot needle and washed the wound with peroxide.

More attention to her looks than these pullings of hairs and pickings at spots would have caused gossip among the villagers. They owned work clothes and good clothes, and they wore good clothes for feasting the new seasons. But since a woman combing her hair hexes beginnings, my aunt rarely found an occasion to look her best. Women looked like great sea snails—the corded wood, babies, and laundry they carried were the whorls on their backs. The Chinese did not admire a bent back; goddesses and warriors stood straight. Still there must have been a marvelous freeing of beauty when a worker laid down her burden and stretched and arched.

Such commonplace loveliness, however, was not enough for my aunt. She dreamed of a lover for the fifteen days of New Year's, the time for families to exchange visits, money, and food. She plied her secret comb. And sure enough she cursed the year, the family, the village, and herself.

Even as her hair lured her imminent lover, many other men looked at her. Uncles, cousins, nephews, brothers would have looked, too, had they been home between journeys. Perhaps they had already been restraining their curiosity, and they left, fearful that their glances, like a field of nesting birds, might be startled and caught. Poverty hurt, and that was their first reason for leaving. But another, final reason for leaving the crowded house was the never-said.

She may have been unusually beloved, the precious only daughter, spoiled and mirror gazing because of the affection the family lavished on her. When her husband left, they welcomed the chance to take her back from the in-laws; she could live like the little daughter for just a while longer. There are stories that my grandfather was different from other people, "crazy ever since the little Jap bayoneted him in the head." He used to put his naked penis on the dinner table, laughing. And one day he brought home a baby girl, wrapped up inside his brown western-style greatcoat. He had traded one of his sons, probably my father, the youngest, for her. My grandmother made him trade back. When he finally got a daughter of his own, he doted on her. They must have all loved her, except perhaps my father, the only brother who never went back to China, having once been traded for a girl.

Brothers and sisters, newly men and women, had to efface their sexual color and present plain miens. Disturbing hair and eyes, a smile like no other, threatened the ideal of five generations living under one roof. To focus blurs, people shouted face to face and yelled from room to room. The immigrants I know have loud voices, unmodulated to American tones even after years away from the village where they called their friendships out across the fields. I have not been able to stop my mother's screams in public libraries or over telephones. Walking erect (knees straight, toes pointed forward, not pigeon-toed, which is Chinese-feminine) and speaking in an inaudible voice, I have tried to turn myself American-feminine. Chinese communication was loud, public. Only sick people had to whisper. But at the dinner table, where the family members came nearest one another, no one could talk, not the outcasts nor any eaters. Every word that falls from the mouth is a coin lost. Silently they gave and accepted food with both hands. A preoccupied child who took his bowl with one hand got a sideways glare. A complete moment of total attention is due everyone alike. Children and lovers have no singularity here, but my aunt used a secret voice, a separate attentiveness. 31

She kept the man's name to herself throughout her labor and dying; she did not accuse him that he be punished with her. To save her inseminator's name she gave silent birth. 32

He may have been somebody in her own household, but intercourse with a man outside the family would have been no less abhorrent. All the village were kinsmen, and the titles shouted in loud country voices never let kinship be forgotten. Any man within visiting distance would have been neutralized as a lover—"brother," "younger brother," "older brother"—one hundred and fifteen 33 relationship titles. Parents researched birth charts probably not so much to assure good fortune as to circumvent incest in a population that has but one hundred surnames. Everybody has eight million relatives. How useless then sexual mannerisms, how dangerous.

As if it came from an atavism deeper than fear, I used to add "brother" silently to boys' names. It hexed the boys, who would or would not ask me to dance, and made them less scary and as familiar and deserving of benevolence as girls.

But, of course, I hexed myself also—no dates. I should have stood up, both arms waving, and shouted out across libraries, "Hey, you! Love me back." I had no idea, though, how to make attraction selective, how to control its direction and magnitude. If I made myself American-pretty so that the five or six Chinese boys in the class fell in love with me, everyone else—the Caucasian, Negro, and Japanese boys—would too. Sisterliness, dignified and honorable, made much more sense.

Attraction eludes control so stubbornly that whole societies designed to organize relationships among people cannot keep order, not even when they bind people to one another from childhood and raise them together. Among the very poor and the wealthy, brothers married their adopted sisters, like doves. Our family allowed some romance, paying adult brides' prices and providing dowries so that their sons and daughters could marry strangers. Marriage promises to turn strangers into friendly relatives—a nation of siblings.

In the village structure, spirits shimmered among the live creatures, balanced and held in equilibrium by time and land. But one human being flaring up into violence could open up a black hole, a maelstrom that pulled in the sky. The frightened villagers, who depended on one another to maintain the real, went to my aunt to show her a personal, physical representation of the break she had made in the "roundness." Misallying couples snapped off the future, which was to be embodied in true offspring. The villagers punished her for acting as if she could have a private life, secret and apart from them.

If my aunt had betrayed the family at a time of large grain yields and peace, when many boys were born, and wings were being built on many houses, perhaps she might have escaped such severe punishment. But the men—hungry, greedy, tired of planting in dry soil, cuckolded—had had to leave the village in order to send food-money home. There were ghost plagues, bandit plagues, wars with the Japanese, floods. My Chinese brother and sister had died of an unknown sickness. Adultery, perhaps only a mistake during good times, became a crime when the village needed food.

The round moon cakes and round doorways, the round tables of graduated size that fit one roundness inside another, round windows and rice bowls—these talismans had lost their power to warn this family of the law: a family must be whole, faithfully keeping the descent line by having sons to feed the old and the dead, who in turn look after the family. The villagers came to show my aunt and her lover-in-hiding a broken house. The villagers were speeding up the circling of events because she was too shortsighted to see that her infidelity had already harmed the village, that waves of consequences would return unpredictably, sometimes in disguise, as now, to hurt her. This roundness had to be made coin-sized so that she would see its circumference: punish her at the birth of her baby. Awaken her to the inexorable. People who refused fatalism because they could invent small resources insisted on culpability. Deny accidents and wrest fault from the stars. 39

After the villagers left, their lanterns now scattering in various directions toward home, the family broke their silence and cursed her. "Aiaa, we're going to die. Death is coming. Death is coming. Look what you've done. You've killed us. Ghost! Dead ghost! Ghost! You've never been born." She ran out into the fields far enough from the house so that she could no longer hear their voices, and pressed herself against the earth, her own land no more. When she felt the birth coming, she thought that she had been hurt. Her body seized together. "They've hurt me too much," she thought. "This is gall, and it will kill me." With forehead and knees against the earth, her body convulsed and then relaxed. She turned on her back, lay on the ground. The black well of sky and stars went out and out and out forever; her body and her complexity seemed to disappear. She was one of the stars, a bright dot in blackness, without home, without a companion, in eternal cold and silence. An agoraphobia rose in her, speeding higher and higher, bigger and bigger; she would not be able to contain it; there would be no end to fear. 40

Flayed, unprotected against space, she felt pain return, focusing her body. This pain chilled her—a cold, steady kind of surface pain. Inside, spasmodically, the other pain, the pain of the child, heated 41 her. For hours she lay on the ground, alternately body and space. Sometimes a vision of normal comfort obliterated reality: she saw the family in the evening gambling at the dinner table, the young people massaging their elders' backs. She saw them congratulating one another, high joy on the mornings the rice shoots came up. When these pictures burst, the stars drew yet further apart. Black space opened.

She got to her feet to fight better and remembered that old-fash- 4
ioned women gave birth in their pigsties to fool the jealous, pain-dealing gods, who do not snatch piglets. Before the next spasms could stop her, she ran to the pigsty, each step a rushing out into emptiness. She climbed over the fence and knelt in the dirt. It was good to have a fence enclosing her, a tribal person alone.

Laboring, this woman who had carried her child as a foreign 4
growth that sickened her every day, expelled it at last. She reached down to touch the hot, wet, moving mass, surely smaller than anything human, and could feel that it was human after all—fingers, toes, nails, nose. She pulled it up on to her belly, and it lay curled there, butt in the air, feet precisely tucked one under the other. She opened her loose shirt and buttoned the child inside. After resting, it squirmed and thrashed and she pushed it up to her breast. It turned its head this way and that until it found her nipple. There, it made little sniffling noises. She clenched her teeth at its preciousness, lovely as a young calf, a piglet, a little dog.

She may have gone to the pigsty as a last act of responsibility: she 4
would protect this child as she had protected its father. It would look after her soul, leaving supplies on her grave. But how would this tiny child without family find her grave when there would be no marker for her anywhere, neither in the earth nor the family hall? No one would give her a family hall name. She had taken the child with her into the wastes. At its birth the two of them had felt the same raw pain of separation, a wound that only the family pressing tight could close. A child with no descent line would not soften her life but only trail after her, ghost-like, begging her to give it purpose. At dawn the villagers on their way to the fields would stand around the fence and look.

Full of milk, the little ghost slept. When it awoke, she hardened 4
her breasts against the milk that crying loosens. Toward morning she picked up the baby and walked to the well.

Carrying the baby to the well shows loving. Otherwise abandon it. Turn its face into the mud. Mothers who love their children take them along. It was probably a girl; there is some hope of forgiveness for boys. 46

"Don't tell anyone you had an aunt. Your father does not want to hear her name. She has never been born." I have believed that sex was unspeakable and words so strong and fathers so frail that "aunt" would do my father mysterious harm. I have thought that my family, having settled among immigrants who had also been their neighbors in the ancestral land, needed to clean their name, and a wrong word would incite the kinspeople even here. But there is more to this silence: they want me to participate in her punishment. And I have. 47

In the twenty years since I heard this story I have not asked for details nor said my aunt's name; I do not know it. People who can comfort the dead can also chase after them to hurt them further—a reverse ancestor worship. The real punishment was not the raid swiftly inflicted by the villagers, but the family's deliberately forgetting her. Her betrayal so maddened them, they saw to it that she would suffer forever, even after death. Always hungry, always needing, she would have to beg food from other ghosts, snatch and steal it from those whose living descendants give them gifts. She would have to fight the ghosts massed at crossroads for the buns a few thoughtful citizens leave to decoy her away from village and home so that the ancestral spirits could feast unharassed. At peace, they could act like gods, not ghosts, their descent lines providing them with paper suits and dresses, spirit money, paper houses, paper automobiles, chicken, meat, and rice into eternity—essences delivered up in smoke and flames, steam and incense rising from each rice bowl. In an attempt to make the Chinese care for people outside the family, Chairman Mao encourages us now to give our paper replicas to the spirits of outstanding soldiers and workers, no matter whose ancestors they may be. My aunt remains forever hungry. Goods are not distributed evenly among the dead. 48

My aunt haunts me—her ghost drawn to me because now, after fifty years of neglect, I alone devote pages of paper to her, though not origamied into houses and clothes. I do not think she always means me well. I am telling on her, and she was a spite suicide, drowning herself in the drinking water. The Chinese are always 49 very frightened of drowned one, whose weeping ghost, wet hair hanging and skin bloated, waits silently by the water to pull down a substitute.

QUESTIONS FOR READING AND WRITING

1. In what respects is Kingston's essay a commentary on the roles and expectations of women in Chinese-American culture?
2. Explain the mixture of love, spite, and desperation Kingston's aunt must have felt when she killed her baby.
3. Examine Kingston's description of the villagers' raid. How might this punishment be considered symbolic?
4. Examine what Kingston means by the following figures of speech: "Necessity, a riverbank that guides her life" (paragraph 13); "After the one carnival ride each, we paid in guilt" (paragraph 14); "Neither style blew easily into heart-catching tangles" (paragraph 24); and "they want me to participate in her punishment" (paragraph 47).
5. Examine the short introductory paragraph. What fears or apprehensions is Kingston's mother trying to invoke in her? How do these affect our reading of the essay?
6. Write an essay about an incident in which you greatly displeased or embarrassed your family. Describe what you did, how and why you were punished, and the long-range effects of your behavior.
7. Write an essay about an eccentric or unusual ancestor. Embroider the facts you may have with intelligent guesswork about the causes and consequences of that ancestor's personality and behavior.

✦ Richard Selzer ✦
In Praise of Senescence

Richard Selzer (b. 1928), an American short-story writer, essayist, surgeon, and teacher of medicine, is an excellent example of a rare species: a person who combines a love for and a proficiency in science with a similar love for, and proficiency in, the creative and compelling use of language. His books include Rituals of Surgery *(1974, stories),* Confessions of a Knife *(1979, essays) and* Taking the World in for Repairs *(1986, essays). In the following essay, Selzer expresses his ambivalent attitude toward aging, that inevitable process that unites us and gives us small, gradual reminders of our growing sense of mortality.*

IT IS TUESDAY, your twenty-fifth birthday. It is your lucky day. 1
Everything good that has ever come your way has befallen you on Tuesday. So that when you awaken from sound sleep to find . . . what's this! . . . your head aching at the temples, your bones and joints stiff, your muscles sore, and a nose that pours and plashes as any freshet at monsoon, you are desolate. How can this be? you think. *It* is Tuesday. If by Tuesday, too, I am forsaken, then am I truly *abandonnato*. So run your miserable thoughts. A sense of impending doom settles over the bed in which you lie, and you arrange your aching body in a sepulchral pose.

Oft and again have I myself awakened to similar indisposition. 2
Let me tell you what is the very best thing to do. Slide down a bit in the bed; take the edge of the sheet in the fingers of both hands and pull it up such that it conceals your face; now smile. You lucky stiff! You are a little bit sick. What, ingrate? Still you languish? Still sniffle? Wake! Enjoy! First, take two aspirin. (The headache is not as bad as you thought it was.) Present your order for breakfast in bed (anorexia is not necessarily a symptom of the disease), and settle in for a day and night of perfect happiness. My Uncle Frank, perhaps arguing contrary to the tenets of veterinary medicine, said, "Never look a sick horse in the mouth." Never mind that the language of this aphorism be quaint; its sense is crystal clear—you've got the day off—make the most of it.

It is not altogether a bad thing to be a little bit sick. La grippe, 3
ague, the vapors and even the common sinking spell offer to

Moslem, Jew and Christian alike the chance to take to bed and to stay there while the rest of the world goes to work.

All at once you have a wave of uneasiness. What if you really are sick? What if you have made a grotesque miscalculation? You feel for your pulse. Why is it so hard to find! *How many heartbeats do I have left*, you think, and the words of Rilke creep into your mind, "Each man bears Death within himself, just as a fruit enfolds a stone." O God! You leap from your bed and run to the mirror. Should you holler for help?

But the sight of yourself in the mirror is somehow reassuring. Twenty-five! Well, well. And you stand there for a kind of quarter-century assessment. Not bad. Not bad at all. Oh there are some minor discrepancies about the face—the nose a bit retroussé, the chin perhaps unobtrusive. But, ungrateful boy, that is to carp. By any standards you are the fulfillment of a fetus's dream.

Satisfied with the externals, you stick out your tongue in the age-old fascination of man for his insides. He would peer further if he could, but it is only the tongue that is willing to be seen, flapping pink and nimble, and on the qui vive. But what is this! As you stare at it, your tongue inexplicably begins to look like something you have never seen before. It has undergone a mythic transformation. Suddenly it is jutting straight out at you, brown and coated and spiteful, like the tongue of a . . . gargoyle. You hesitate to take it back inside for fear it is poisonous. But what else can you do?

Your gaze drops from your face to the rest. Nothing amiss there. It's all the same. You breathe a bit easier. Here and there you test the fullness, the resilience, the hardness. You pinch; you cup; you weigh. But today you are no casual observer. You are intense, a terrier after a rat. That awful tongue has changed you. You search, and what you find are . . . flaws! Two white hairs, one on your chest, and the other . . . O God! Pubic! Twenty minutes more of peering turns up two small flat brown spots, each with a roughened surface. One on your neck, and the other on your tummy. You smile wanly. Is it not, you think aloud, from our very flaws, our kinks and fissures, that springs whatever becomes visible of our souls? But a gray pubic hair! O treason! All at once you hear a belch from deep inside of you. As though you contain a frog. Again, a belch: deep, reverberate and now you know that you do . . . contain a frog, that is. And instantly the whole horrid truth comes clear . . . It was the frog's tongue that you saw a moment ago! You imagine him squatting somewhere near the base of your brain, slowly puffing up his throat and coming out with that belch. You know who *he* is. He is the Frog of Death. Somehow, in your sleep perhaps, he has hopped inside of you. There is no getting rid of him. You have heard the belch of doom! Instinctively you wrap your arms about you, as if to console your flesh, reassure it that it is not so. My body, you think. My beautiful (white, black, yellow) body!

"Don't be silly," says your doctor the next day, and he laughs. A doctor who is a laugher is bad news. 8

"You're in your prime," he says. 9

You whisper a secret to him. About your hair. "It's falling out," you tell him. 10

"You're shedding more than your hair, my friend," he says. "A hundred thousand brain cells per day." 11

"Per day?" 12

"Per day," he says in his deep, reverberant voice. It occurs to you that he is the most repellent man you know—short, fat, bald and with dangerously bulging eyes. 13

"The only prime I'm in," he says, "is the prime of my senility." And he gives that terrible laugh. 14

Caligula, you decide, would be more simpatico than this doctor. Nevertheless, you show him your little brown spots: the one on your neck, and the other on your tummy. He bends to examine them after with a magnifying glass. He rubs his fingertip over them. 15

"Senile hyperkeratoses," he says. "Nothing to worry about. Little excrescences of the skin. Everybody gets them after a while." 16

But you have heard that word that somehow crystallizes the whole clinical picture. Yesterday you were a youth; today . . . senile! 17

"Fit as a fiddle," says the doctor, belching and showing his tongue. 18

You wish for a handful of flies to stuff in his mouth. 19

And bald, fat, bent, senile and mangy you flee from the doctor's office to begin the second quarter-century of your life. 20

Thirty-nine! 21

Once again to the mirror. Already the hair at your crown is scanty. A pale saucer, like some artifact long buried in the forest, 22 emerges there. All too soon, you know, the remainder of your hair will disembed itself to commit suicide in the sink. No saucer then, but a whole platter of scalp is what you'll wear. Your flesh is no longer elastic, but flounce and wattle announce its relentless earthward decurvation. Were you Capital I? Now you are Capital S. You finish shaving and empty from your electric razor a beard dust that is pale as sand, as ash. But your beard is black! You know it is. Your hair is black, and so your beard is black. If there is order in the universe, if physics and chemistry are true . . . And then it comes to you, softly as of a tapping, tapping at your chamber door—your beard is *gray*.

And there are other losses. What was a hitherto unflagging lust 2
has taken on a melancholy periodicity. You have loved; you have lost; you have groped for love again. You pick up a newspaper from your hometown, and you learn that a childhood friend, one of your pals, has died, leaving a grandson of his own! Your own children are large and mighty. They sweat; they swear. At thirty-nine, the days grow shorter, and night kneels like a rapist on the edge of your bed. Here and there, you die. Every hour a hundred red blood cells go to their reward, a hair follicle, another taste bud. From somewhere high above, a brain cell topples.

Forty-nine! You must hurry! Nothing about you has replenished 2
itself. You are balder and mangier than ever, something that has been left out in the sun too long. The whites of your eyes have grown muddy; your teeth are a construct that, unsupported by metal and cement, would splinter on a sunflower seed. Peanut brittle is denied you. You brown away; you yellow off. O profligate body! Where now the streams of tears and sweat? The gallons of blood donated or shed, the white-water rapids of spermatozoa? Spendthrift Skin, how many the generations of perfect cells you have spawned and sloughed! Still, you do not miss that sweat, that blood, those tears. Of these, you have still enough. As for the spermatozoa? Well . . .

There is more. Worse. Somewhere down below, hard india-rub- 2
ber lobes are mounding, mounding. It is the Dreaded Prostate that burgeons, encroaching upon a slender little tube. Live on, and you will learn patience, my friend . . . at the urinal. You too shall stand and wait . . . and wait, and you will know bittersweet mo-

ments when urination, which was once a mere interruption of life, becomes the most exquisite of pleasures, perhaps the very reason itself for living.

26 That which at twenty-five was just a sapling's inkling of the oakhood to come, and at thirty-nine was a brave whistling in the dark, at forty-nine is a certainty to be faced. Of no further use a clever comb or suntan. You know . . . and you yield. That is, if you're smart, you do.

27 The rejuvenation of the flesh is an ancient dream. The cripple who emerged whole and pure from the pool of Bethesda is the object of wonder and envy, for he has won first prize. A loser was Ponce de León, who swilled from every river and spring in Florida and the Islands in search of the Fountain of Youth. Poor Ponce! The zealots of diet and jogging are often blind to the quality of life they would prolong. For some people, a vegetarian diet and the running of three miles a day would be a torture both exquisitely administered and endlessly endured. Physical death, in such cases, would be a technicality, one that might even be thought welcome. Robert Louis Stevenson, frustrated by the restrictions on his life caused by his tuberculosis decided that "death is no bad friend; a few aches and gasps, and we are done; like the truant child, I am beginning to grow weary and timid in this big jostling city, and could run to my nurse, even although she should have to whip me before putting me to bed."

28 It is not always that life is too short; it may go on too long. A visit to any nursing home, or facility for the domiciliary care of the aged, will persuade that shorter is better, what with fecal and urinary incontinence, and an absence of cognition or recognition. To say nothing of pain. Which of us would not forgo five years in such a fix for a sudden, clean and much earlier terminus? Longevity may be a Pyrrhic victory over time. I should far rather keel over at sixty, cut my losses, don't you know? Then firm and vigorous, I'd bound into the next world, ready for the Great Perhaps.

29 Some think to recapture youth through plastic surgery, or by lathering themselves with tinted grease, an even shallower illusion. But pissing in his shoe keeps no man warm for long. Pooh, you say, how sillily you write. And maybe I do.

30 The news of an artificial saliva which, if ingested, will eliminate tooth decay, renders me boggled. Whilst it would be wicked not to

wish well away the ache and cavitation of candied adolescence, the prospect of a full-fanged woman of ninety-two crunching peanut brittle is too, well, ferocious for my taste. I prefer the gummy silence of Cream of Wheat. There is a certain coziness to a bowl of oatmeal that is absent entirely from a wad of taffy. Then too, the persistence of powerful teeth into great age, what with the generally recognized crabbiness that attends senescence, would surely lead to an epidemic of biting in nursing and other homes. Visiting daughters-in-law and attendants in such places would be required to wear leather gauntlets, vests of chain mail and even halberds lest they become the victims of impulsive mastication. One day there would be the inevitable reaction, and the question of defanging the aged would become like abortion, a political football.

One trouble is that you do not all decline at the same rate. Not 3
every part of you vanishes in concert with every other part. It has proved both a delight and an embarrassment that lust remains long after the apparatus for its consummation has rusted. But if lust be the energy that drives the human race onward to new generations, then what is it doing in octogenarians anyway? Many's the brittle hip been fractured in pursuit of the phantasm that if you can fornicate at eighty-five, you are not yet old.

Not everyone acquiesces. There are those who, despite all reason 3
and logic, simply will not go gentle into that good night. William Butler Yeats, for one, raged on. It seems that the poet, while still in his fifties, suffered a precipitous decline in his sexual potency. Which calamity, in a man who claimed that all of his poetry sprang from his rage and his lust, brought on a secondary impotence of the pen. Although Yeats continued to write, the juice and the wit had gone out of him; cool and cerebal grew the art. In the abyss of his despond, the poet moped. A friend, thinking to console Yeats with a hopeful bit of gossip, told him of one Dr. Steinach, a scientist who for ten years had devoted his experiments to the cure of sexual and spiritual impotence. His technique? The transplantation of the testicles of monkeys into the scrota of men. Yeats was more than consoled. He was intrigued. And determined at once to undergo the operation. Lovers of Irish letters everywhere tried to dissuade him from such madness. Yeats would not be put off. He would have the operation. Meanwhile, Steinach had changed his tack, and put it forth that, after all, the testicular replacement was not the essential

part of the surgery. The same revivication, now claimed Steinach, could be achieved by the mere ligation of the spermatic ducts, thereby damming up the precious flow and making its creative spunk available to flesh and spirit alike.

Yeats engaged a surgeon by the name of Haire, and underwent bilateral vasectomy. No sooner had Yeats been discharged from the care of Dr. Haire than he reported to a palpitating world that he had recaptured full use of both pen and penis. The operation had been a complete success. Whilst the matter of Yeats's sexual restitution remains an article of faith, the more easily measurable of the two, his literary prowess, leaves no doubt that the operation was successful. For Yeats wrote some of his finest plays and poems in the postoperative decade. Yeats's case history has encouraged generations of aging poets. Nobody knows the burden of talent, the suffering of old poets. To what indignities, what mutilations will we not subject ourselves to warm up both art and bones grown cold? 33

That no such results have been forthcoming from vasectomy in this day and age is, to say the least, disappointing. I tend to think it is due to the callow indifference of urologists toward matters of poesy. Yeats was convinced that it was the Steinach operation which had saved him. Again and again he paid tribute to his benefactor. Imagine, if you will, the goaty old poet, his vasa deferentia securely tied, grinning and rubbing his buttocks on his bench. And gloating to a youthful seductee: 34

Who can know the year, my dear,
When an old man's blood grows cold?

None of this is to imply that senescence is without its joys. If you can no longer remember the names of your friends and relatives, why, you have also forgotten those of your most devoted bores, your pedants. If the ecstasy of peanut brittle has been long denied you on the grounds of precarious dentition, why, you are even further from the agony of pablum. One of the pleasures ahead of you is giving in to the temptation to mine your own past. Why would a man indulge in self-remembering, retrieving his ancient kinship with rivers and stones and narrow paths? Listen: 35

Forty years ago my father was a general practitioner in Troy, New York. That was before the age of specialization in medicine, and family doctors did just about everything—delivered babies, set 36 broken legs, and removed ruptured appendixes. Despite this last, I do not think of him as a surgeon. I never watched him standing at an operating table, making an incision. But I did see him every Sunday, kneeling in his garden which he treated as though it were a ward full of patients. All day long he spent there, pruning, excavating weeds or splinting a slender stalk and marveling aloud at the exuberant swelling that bloomed at its tip. Now I am the age that he was. Then we are the same age! And now I can see what I must have seen years ago but had forgotten—his hairless white wrists submerged among the carnations, as though gripped by the lips of an incision. I do not see his fingers, hidden as they were in the foliage, busy down below, repairing the works. But I remember the air carved by bees, and the slow respiration of the trees.

Sometimes, even now, in my operating room, as I incise, clamp, 3
ligate, and suture, I know a deeper kinship with my father. Something arcs across the decades, like a rainbow that binds the earth as if it were a gift. Why just today a red flower bloomed at the end of my scalpel: a poppy, I think. It seemed a miracle, like the leafing out of a shepherd's crook. I pinched off the bloom and tied down the stem with thread. My father was right. Surgery is gardening.

I agree with Montaigne that "to learn Philosophy is to learn to 3
die." We start off well—with "Now I lay me down to sleep," that bend of hopefulness and sweet resignation. It ought to be recited by adults. But, not to worry. The intimations of mortality appear so gradually as to be imperceptible, like the first graying in of twilight.

Faced with the inevitable, you can do two things. You can sit in a 3
dark room, hearkening to the thutter of snare drums, or you can adopt a good-natured posture and go about your business. The latter seems better. There is quite enough gloom in the world without your shedding more. And there is a wonderful camaraderie about aging. Come, come, little moper, look around. All the rest of us are doing it too. Except for a few liars and dissemblers. A man can lie about his age, but not about his death. It simply won't work to deny the condition to one's friends.

Think of the fun you can have drawing attention to each other's 4
bunions and dewlaps. The trick is to find someone to get cozy with, someone to whom your warts and knobs and droopery are dear, who will understand about your bronchitic scarf. For, oh, the calmative

power of love! In the profusion and prodigality of the body, who is to say where beauty lies? Some of us are drawn to footprints, which are lovely wounds in the snow.

One adores the old man who retains a touch of youth—as though the boy in him were still visible. The more one gazes on such a fellow, the younger he becomes, until the transformation is complete, and he is again that very boy of his past. Just so does one adore the young man who is early colored by age, who has felt the cool breath upon his cheek, and who has paused, listening in the night for the sound of wings. 41

QUESTIONS FOR READING AND WRITING

1. Why does Selzer begin his essay about senescence with an anecdote about an imaginary twenty-five year old?
2. What is the point of the interchange between the aging person and his doctor (paragraphs 8–20)?
3. What idea about aging—and the changes it brings to the human body—is emphasized in paragraph 30?
4. Reexamine paragraphs 37, 40, and 41. What figures of speech does Selzer use to clarify his meaning? What do these figures of speech "mean"?
5. Write an essay about an old person that emphasizes the elements of youth that he or she retains.
6. Write an "in praise of" essay—modeled after Selzer's, if you wish—about left-handedness, clumsiness, adolescence, illness, or forgetfulness.

COPYRIGHTS AND ACKNOWLEDGMENTS

The Rookers from *Shiloh and Other Stories* by Bobbie Ann Mason. Copyright © 1982 by Bobbie Ann Mason. Reprinted by permission of Harper & Row, Publishers, Inc.

An American Childhood excerpt from *An American Childhood* by Annie Dillard. Copyright © 1987 by Annie Dillard. Reprinted by permission of Harper & Row, Publishers, Inc.

Notes from an Absence and a Return from *A Continuous Harmony*, copyright © 1972, 1970 by Wendell Berry, reprinted by permission of the publisher.

Puerto Vallarta excerpt from *The Diary of Anaïs Nin*, 1966 to 1974 by Anaïs Nin, copyright © 1980 by Rupert Poleas, trustee under the Last Will and Testament of Anaïs Nin, reprinted by permission of Harcourt Brace Jovanovich, Inc.

The Flowers from *In Love & Trouble, Stories of Black Women*, copyright © 1973 by Alice Walker, reprinted by permission of Harcourt Brace Jovanovich, Inc.

A Hanging from *Shooting an Elephant and Other Essays* by George Orwell, copyright © 1950 by Sonia Brownell Orwell, renewed 1978 by Sonia Pitt-Rivers, reprinted by permission of Harcourt Brace Jovanovich, Inc.

Politics and the English Language by George Orwell, copyright © 1946 by Sonia Brownell Orwell, renewed 1974 by Sonia Orwell, reprinted from *Shooting an Elephant and Other Essays* by George Orwell, reprinted by permission of Harcourt Brace Jovanovich, Inc.

Oppressed Hair Puts a Ceiling on the Brain from *Living by the Word: Collected Writing 1973–1987*, copyright © 1987 by Alice Walker, reprinted by permission of Harcourt Brace Jovanovich, Inc.

Mind in the Grip of Language from *Aspects of Language*, Second Edition by Dwight Bolinger, copyright © 1975, 1968 by Harcourt Brace Jovanovich, Inc., reprinted by permission of the publisher.

Matters of Taste (Alexander Theroux) Copyright © 1979 by *Harper's Magazine*. All rights reserved. Reprinted from the August issue by special permission.

Cupcake Land (Richard Rhodes) Copyright © 1987 by *Harper's Magazine*. All rights reserved. Reprinted from the November issue by special permission.

Cinematypes (Susan Allen Toth) Copyright © 1980 by *Harper's Magazine*. All rights reserved. Reprinted from the May issue by special permission.

The Psychological Reactions of Oppressed People Copyright © by Richard Wright. Reprinted by permission of John Hawkins & Associates, Inc.

Erotica and Pornography from *Outrageous Acts and Everyday Rebellions* by Gloria Steinem. Reprinted by permission of Henry Holt and Company, Inc.

Butlin's Holiday Camp from *The Kingdom by the Sea* by Paul Theroux. Copyright © 1983 by Cape Cod Scriveners. Reprinted by permission of Houghton Mifflin Company.

China Still Lifes reprinted by permission of International Creative Management, Inc. Copyright © 1985 by William Gass. First published in *House and Garden*.

A Stranger in Lolitaland reprinted by permission of International Creative Management, Inc. Copyright © 1986 by Gregor Von Rezzori. First published in *Vanity Fair*.

On Rediscovering Evil reprinted by permission of Mark Jacobson. Originally appeared in *Esquire* 1988.

Down to Earth reprinted by permission of William H. Jordan. Originally appeared in *Los Angeles Times Magazine.*

The Future of the Photovoltaic Cell reprinted by permission of Tracy Kidder. As originally published in *The Atlantic Monthly.*

Pornography reprinted by permission of Margaret Atwood, first appeared in *Chatelaine Magazine,* 1983.

In Praise of Senescence from *Confessions of a Knife* by Richard Selzer. Copyright © 1979 by David Goldman and Janet Selzer, Trustee. Reprinted by permission of William Morrow & Co.

Of Accidental Judgements and Casual Slaughters (Kai Erickson) reprinted by permission of The Nation Company, Inc. copyright © 1985. Originally appeared in *The Nation* magazine.

Morocco's Ancient City of Fez (Harvey Arden) reprinted by permission of *National Geographic* magazine.

The Astronomer's Wife from *Life Being the Best & Other Stories,* by Kay Boyle. Copyright © 1936 by Kay Boyle. Reprinted by permission of New Directions Publishing Corporation. U.S. rights only.

Dressed to Thrill (Anne Hollander) reprinted by permission of The New Republic 1985, The New Republic, Inc.

Death and Justice (Edward Koch) reprinted by permission of *The New Republic,* 1985, The New Republic, Inc.

Playing Air Guitar (Adam Liptak) Copyright © 1985 by The New York Times Company. Reprinted by permission.

Emphasis on Stress (William Safire) Copyright © 1985 by The New York Times Company. Reprinted by permission.

A Trader in London (Nancy Bazelon Goldstone) Copyright © 1987 by The New York Times Company. Reprinted by permission.

The Aggressors (Melvin J. Konner) Copyright © 1988 by The New York Times Company. Reprinted by permission.

The Decline of Quality (Barbara Tuchman) Copyright © 1980 by The New York Times Company. Reprinted by permission.

If Black English Isn't A Language, Then Tell Me, What Is It? (James Baldwin) Copyright © 1979 by The New York Times Company. Reprinted by permission .

Bilingualism, Pro: The Key to Basic Skills (Angelo Gonsalez) Copyright © 1985 by The New York Times Company. Reprinted by permission.

Bilingualism, Con: Outdated and Unrealistic (Richard Rodriguez) Copyright © 1985 by The New York Times Company. Reprinted by permission.

The Terrifying Normalcy of AIDS (Stephen Jay Gould) Copyright © 1987 by The New York Times Company. Reprinted by permission.

O Fenway Park excerpted from *Fathers Playing Catch With Sons,* copyright © 1985 by Donald Hall. Reprinted by permission of North Point Press.

Boys and Girls from *Dance of the Happy Shades.* Copyright © 1968, by Alice Munro.

In Hefnerland from *The Moronic Inferno and Other Visits to America* by Martin Amis. Copyright © 1986 by Martin Amis. Used by permission of Viking Penguin, a division of Penguin USA.

Wyoming: The Solace of Open Spaces from *The Solace of Open Spaces* by Gretel Ehrlich. Used by permission of Viking Penguin, a division of Penguin USA.

Playing Cowboy from *Outlaws, Con Men, Whores, Politicians and Other Artists* by Larry L. King. Copyright © 1974 by Larry L. King. Used by permission of Penguin USA.

The Attic of the Brain from *Late Night Thoughts on Listening to Mahler's Ninth Symphony*. Copyright © 1980 by Lewis Thomas. Used by permission of Viking Penguin, a division of Penguin USA.

Television and Reading from *The Plug-in Drug* by Marie Winn. Copyright © 1977 by Marie Winn Miller. Used by permission of Viking Penguin, a division of Penguin USA.

Kiswana Browne from *The Women of Brewster Place* by Gloria Naylor. Copyright © 1980, 1982 by Gloria Naylor. Used by permission of Viking Penguin, a division of Penguin USA.

Rooms Without Walls (Marge Piercy) Copyright © 1988 by Middlemarsh, Inc. Reprinted by permission of Wallace Literary Agency, Inc.

The Maidenform Woman Administers Shock Treatment (Ellen Goodman) Copyright © 1982, Boston Globe Newspaper Company/Washington Post Writers Group. Reprinted with permission.

Posing in Your Undies is Unreal (Ellen Goodman) Copyright © The Boston Globe Newspaper Company/Washington Post Writer's Group, reprinted with permission.

The Futility of the Death Penalty by Clarence Darrow from Arthur and Lila Weinberg *Verdicts Out of Court* (Chicago: Ivan R. Dee 1989). Copyright © 1963, 1969 by Arthur and Lila Weinberg. Reprinted by permission of Lila Weinberg.

AUTHOR-TITLE INDEX

A 0
B 1
C 2
D 3
E 4
F 5
G 6
H 7
I 8
J 9